KEIR HARDIE

KEIR HARDIE

Caroline Benn

Series Editor: Ruth Winstone

RICHARD COHEN BOOKS · London

British Library Cataloguing in Publication Data:
A catalogue record for this book is available from the British Library

Copyright for this edition © 1997 by Caroline Benn

ISBN 1 86066 116 5

First published in 1992 by Hutchinson

This edition published in 1997 by
Richard Cohen Books
7 Manchester Square
London W1M 5RE

Typeset by Palimpsest Book Production Limited,
Polmont, Stirlingshire

Printed in Great Britain by
Mackays of Chatham plc, Chatham, Kent

Contents

Illustrations

Cumnock and Doon Valley Council Archives: Keir Hardie at 16; Inner Circle of Independent Labour Party; Keir Hardie at ILP's 21st birthday party; Emrys Hughes and wife with Hardie's granddaughter and great-granddaughter; Jamie Hardie; May Stoddart; Aggie and Hedley Dennis; Nan and Lillie.

Trustees of National Library of Scotland: Lillie Hardie; the Hardie children; Keir Hardie on steps of Lochnorris; Jamie, Duncan and Nan Hardie; Keir Hardie as leader of Parliamentary Labour Party; Maggie Symons; Hardie and Lillie, 1912; Keir Hardie at work; Keir Hardie with Hughes family; Hardie family at Lochnorris, 1915.

Labour Party Library: Hardie and Lillie; Keir Hardie on Italian Riviera; Keir Hardie and Emmeline Pankhurst; George Bernard Shaw and wife.

Benn Archives: Hardie addressing a crowd; post card to Agnes Hardie; Emrys Hughes.

Glamorgan County Archives: Keir Hardie and his women's election team.

Catherine Hardie: Keir Hardie with original family.

Others: Keir Hardie and Cunninghame Graham; Social Democrats, 1910; Katherine Glasier; Sylvia Pankhurst, Emily Wilding Davison, Christabel Pankhurst and Emmeline Pethick-Lawrence; Sylvia Pankhurst.

Introduction

A hundred and five years after Keir Hardie entered Parliament as the first labour member who was also a socialist, the Labour Party won its largest – ever – majority in a general election. As Hardie never experienced a Labour government himself, it is difficult to imagine what his opinion would have been of the one elected in May 1997. However, it is fair to assume that he would have been surprised that so many of the country's rich and powerful supported Labour, because during his lifetime Keir Hardie was disowned by the British Establishment.

The two main political parties opposed him openly or secretly; and their press denigrated his ideas. So too did many trade union leaders, while he also quarrelled with a whole range of socialists, including the journalist Robert Blatchford, the Fabian, Beatrice Webb, and the self-appointed British exponent of Karl Marx, Henry Hyndman. He was often on bad terms with members of the fledgling Labour Party in Parliament, all of whom agreed he was unsuccessful as leader of the Party. After he died, even his closest political supporter and son-in-law, Emrys Hughes, had to admit that Hardie's life 'was widely regarded as a failure'.[1]

Nor was he compensated by a fulfilling personal life, regularly denying himself the pleasures of living in his determination to concentrate on political agitation. He constantly overworked in order to transform a society he saw to be enslaved by poverty and pulverized by political and economic oppression. He suffered escalating ill health. His family, his friends, his significant relationships were all sacrificed to the cause; and in their own lives many showed their distress.

Most of all, his cause was thought to have failed. The socialism in which he believed and which he spent his mature life working to realize, was shattered by the onward march of capitalism and the events that culminated in the outbreak of the First World War, when, to those involved at the time, socialism seemed to suffer as great a defeat as it did in the Paris Commune nearly fifty years earlier or as it would at the disintegration of communism in Europe seventy-five years later.

Yet throughout his life no other politician drew from such a fund of popular support, or made so much headway in calling society to account for itself. No other activist of the left stamped humanitarian socialism so firmly into the political fabric; or saw the future so clearly, espousing changes in social provision, industrial practice and democratic representation, which came into common being, but at the time were treated as the 'lost causes' his *Times* obituary claimed he wasted his life supporting.

In 1992, one hundred years after he was first elected to Parliament, he was remembered with celebration. Much more of a tribute, people continue to fight for the causes he made his own: class equality, environmental protection, trade union rights, women's equality, popular democratic control of community services, production for need not profit, animal rights, food reform, equality of the world's religions, full employment, and above all, peace and disarmament.

Whether they agree with his commitments or not, today Hardie is claimed by all sections of the labour movement as 'theirs'; Labour's only 'acknowledged folk hero', as a major biographer, Kenneth Morgan, once called him.[2] On a world scale, millions who still live in daily poverty, denied the dignity of useful work to obtain the necessities of life – whether they have heard his name or not – believe in the social justice for which he fought. His socialism is very much alive, and awaits its day.

Interest in Keir Hardie was high from the start of his public life. While he lived there were several interim biographical sketches, most written after 1906 when Labour's appearance as a force in Parliament was first taken seriously. The authors were fellow socialists and journalists, writers who tried to counteract the negative picture of him that socialism's enemies circulated – by stressing his religious and temperance background and his practical suggestions for relieving unemployment.[3]

The next batch were the hagiographies. They include his official biography by a fellow ILP member, William Stewart, and the sketches of James Maxton and Francis Johnson; Hamilton Fyfe's followed in 1935 and Emrys Hughes' in 1956. Written by people who knew Hardie or had the help of members of his family, these accounts contain a great deal of authentic information and anecdote but no critical analysis.

A period of quiescence follows – with the exception of G. D. H. Cole's study in 1941, the first of the critical assessments. With the advent of 'modern' Labour and the pursuit of affluence, Hardie reemerged in a new role – that of the founding father of the Labour Party, a role that watchers of Labour before the First World War, even into the 1920s, did not by any means assign exclusively to him.[4] Men like John Burns, Arthur Henderson, George Lansbury and Ramsay MacDonald were reckoned just as formidable, Hardie only emerging as they dropped out one by one: Burns joining Liberal governments before 1914, Henderson coalitions after, MacDonald defecting to form a 'national' government in 1931; and Lansbury collapsing into ineffectual peacemongering in the late 1930s. By default Hardie was there to claim the title, having died 'young'.

Not only was his slate clean, but he had participated in what turned out to be every important event in Labour's official early life: the strikes of the new unionism in the 1880s, the founding of the Scottish Labour Party in 1888, of the Independent Labour Party in 1893, and of the Labour Representation Committee (LRC) in 1900. He was there during the LRC's transformation in 1906 into the Labour Party in Parliament, when he acted briefly as leader. Just as central, he was present from the first day of the Second International in 1889, the world gathering of socialists; and served assiduously on its International Bureau until he died.

While this historical Hardie was being revived in the 1950s, simultaneously there was an attempt to disown his politics. When Hugh Gaitskell took over as leader of the Labour Party in 1955, for example, *The Economist* urged him to turn his back on the 'age of Keir Hardie',[5] as the Party has been urged to do ever since. The contradiction of claiming Hardie as hero while disowning him as out of date was neatly reconciled in the restless days of the 1960s and 1970s, when socialism and regional nationalisms were in resurgence and dispute, and academics were on the prowl for Labour's early history. To this time belong the biographies of the Scots academic, Iain McLean, and the Welsh historian, Kenneth O. Morgan, author of the fullest and most definitive of all studies of Hardie.

They looked at Hardie the man as well as the politician – but within the politics of a period that gave prominence to the battle for the soul of the Labour Party (which had always gone on, of course) between activists and anti-activists, Marxists and anti-Marxists. The hidden agenda was a re-evaluation of the historical extremist Keir Hardie as a true moderate. Morgan set the pace, concentrating on Hardie in the arena of power politics: Parliament, the unions and the Labour Party.

Unfortunately, an anti-Marxist perspective spawned biographical activity far less worthy – seen, for example, in a play sponsored by a religious movement,[6] where Hardie degenerates into a moral majority hero, crusading against the devil of atheistic socialism, represented on stage as Henry Hyndman. The cloth-cap man, once derided, was now exalted; Hyndman, the wealthy Oxbridge graduate, became villain. Other biographies, no less crude, veiled his personal life by picturing a cloyingly cosy domestic idyll,[7] when even a cursory acquaintance with the facts shows an extremely fraught picture, with emotional as well as social struggle at almost every point.

So far had popular Hardie mythology got from the truth, that had there been a biography in the 1980s it might well have tried to picture Hardie as a self-reliant individualist, rallying the working class to entrepreneurial activity and charity fund-raising in order to relieve social distress. One writer in the ultra-right *Sun* newspaper in 1987 claimed that if Keir Hardie returned he would at once transfer his loyalty from Labour to the now defunct SDP.[8] In the same year even sturdy fellow Scot and longtime Labour politician, Emmanuel Shinwell, reckoned Hardie was 'essentially not a socialist but a temperance reformer'.[9]

Sometimes Hardie's fundamental beliefs were reassigned, one writer alleging that Hardie was opposed to 'the popular myth that you can advance society by changing the system' politically, and believed instead in the need for 'a new type of man of faith'.[10] Yet if there was one thing Hardie believed in from first to last it was that men were as circumstances made them; and that to effect social improvement, it was the political and economic system that had to be changed, not human beings. Hardie called that system capitalism and unremittingly he sought to expose its failures.

That so many are still prepared to claim Hardie as their own – even to believe he argued that which he did not – is testament to his enduring influence. It makes the neglect of him as a man all the more surprising. For in most biographies it is only the political Hardie we see. His family is invisible; his personality is one-sided, and there is total silence on several important relationships. Sylvia Pankhurst, for example, with whom he was particularly close, was not mentioned in any biography until the 1970s. Even then (except for Morgan), there was reluctance to mention her full relationship with Hardie. With a few exceptions, this also extends to those writing about Sylvia herself. Many excellent accounts of Sylvia's life and work still show an 1890s' delicacy preserved intact into the 1990s.[11]

Leaving personal life and the contribution of women out of account was common practice in early Labour and socialist biography. Only in the last three decades has the practice developed of assessing the work of women with equal seriousness. This includes women previously dwarfed by proximity to leading men, Yvonne Kapp's biography of Eleanor Marx providing a model.[12] The women close to Hardie deserve attention not only for a more rounded view of the man Hardie, but also in their own right as components in Labour's early life and the rise of socialism.

So too do Hardie's contemporaries, great and small, with whom he agreed and disagreed, collaborated and refused to work, or even to speak. Perfect harmony never prevailed in the early days of the labour or socialist movements, and the myth that it once did damages present discourse on the left. So too does post-event prejudice when writing of socialists like Ramsay MacDonald during this period, while others, like Robert Blatchford, who deserted the cause much earlier, still retain their place in the firmament. There are many records to set straight, including the fact that Keir Hardie was the first working-class Member of Parliament, the first Labour MP, or even the first socialist at Westminster, when he was none of these. Labour MPs were elected from 1874, all trade unionists and all working class, sheltering under the capacious Liberal wing. The first socialist to sit in Parliament, named as such by Friedrich Engels at the time and still recognized as such fifty years later by Henry Pelling, was also elected by courtesy of the Liberals, Hardie's extraordinary friend and early mentor, Cunninghame Graham.

Important though it is to see Hardie in relation to his colleagues and adversaries, it is also necessary to underline his unique approach. Another area (besides personal life) where many biographers have felt ill at ease has been religion. Yet Hardie was a political crusader who turned his religion into socialism and his socialism into a religion – far beyond the normal connection between church or chapel and political organization. His attack on capitalism was ethical, not theoretical. Intellectuals – whether Fabian or Marxist – were and are uncomfortable with moral politics. Henry Pelling's reaction to Hardie as one of nature's socialists, fuelled by the opinion of Fabians like the Webbs and G. D. H. Cole, survives still in academics of both left and right, who assure us Hardie and his ILP colleagues were 'not socialist theoreticians of even the second rank'.[13]

Kenneth Morgan tried to counter this opinion with a sympathetic defence of Hardie's thought,[14] but the biographer who most challenged the prevailing views of Hardie as political illiterate, and as moderate, was Fred Reid, who studied Hardie's early life in detail,[15] setting his analysis in the context of the industrial changes and trade union agitation in which Hardie participated in the 1870s and 1880s. Reid concluded that Hardie was an experienced political analyst by the age of thirty, who had become a socialist through the experience of attempting to work the route of the advanced Liberal but finding it fruitless in dealing with working-class grievances. Reid found him influenced by Marxist ideas at a period when other biographers saw him still as a radical Liberal. Morgan indeed argued that Hardie always remained in part a Liberal, his socialism only gradually welded. That both 'left' and 'right' views of Hardie can be argued convincingly – as they are by Reid and Morgan – should convince us that Hardie was a highly complex politician.

Hardie was a man full of contradictions; at once stern puritan, but also political libertarian; at once promoter of revolution, while insisting on constitutionality and scrupulous refrain from violence. He was an upright man literally and figuratively, with some large psychological defects, into which he had little insight. The most obvious was the most understandable, a secretiveness and possessiveness over money that led to unseemly altercations throughout his life, and many accusations of bad faith.

His allegiances were profound but so was his ambition for the cause. He was very quick to abandon Scottish Labour in the early 1890s to seek advancement in London's East End, and although his love of the Independent Labour Party stood fairly firm to the end, his attachment to the Labour Party was sorely tested, repeatedly wavered, and, at the very end, all but died, a feature it has been convenient to overlook in a man so often acclaimed as the Father of the Party.

Hardie's commitment to aggressive trade unionism is another feature some biographers have felt compelled to excuse. Yet it was the central spine of his agitation, despite the fact that his life as a worker ended before he was twenty-five, and as a union organizer before he was thirty-five. Again and again through life, whenever he drifted towards political complacency, the spontaneous industrial action of the working class brought him back to his first cause. He never lost his belief in the importance of workers' collective protection and social advance – both within and between nations.

Yet Hardie, as the carrier of a unique and enduring strain of humanitarian socialism, has had less attention, despite the fact that the dilution of labourism and the failure of centralized communism has rendered his socialism more relevant today than at many times in the past.

There has been less interest in these aspects of Hardie's politics than in his proximity to the organization of the Labour Party and its formal evolution in the party-political power structure of Great Britain. This is odd because Hardie had little interest in political power. The advance of Labour in his view did not lie in the acts of a few great men, nor was it tested in how far they got on the ladder of power. It lay in the condition of the people at large and how far that changed. Internationally, it did not lie in the advance of nations but in the cooperation between nations of peoples with common social and political interests.

He spent his life – and earned his living – as an agitator, a word he was proud to be called, understanding it in its seventeenth-century meaning, the soldiers of the Parliamentary army of 1647 who kept the cause before the people. He borrowed the military metaphor while rejecting all forms of military solution, a principle he held from first to last. His agitational work led him from temperance campaigning to evangelical Christianity to 'new union' militancy; from free speech campaigns to women's suffrage and finally to war resistance. The passages were not easy and in negotiating some of them he veered precipitously off the path of his labour and socialist commitment. But he always righted himself, for he had that capacity to retain integrity while also making wider alliances with those who shared a common interest for a common time.

Hardie was always open to argument. Much remains to instruct us from the debates he had with a whole range of colleagues about class and the role of the state, about centralized as against community management of public enterprise, and about constitutional as against direct action. Hardie in action outside Parliament commended himself to the Marxists of his day, particularly on the continent, though many of today's Marxists tend to write him off as a bourgeois parliamentarian who failed to back the working class effectively.[16] Hardie's optimism about Parliament's capacity to assist transformational activity was certainly unrealistic, but no one was more aware of the dangers of Westminster than he. He continually subjected Parliament's vested interests to critical scrutiny. Every complaint any rank-and-filer has ever had about party leaders was voiced by Hardie. He was always ready to listen to ideas about new forms of democratic representation and control. It was democracy he believed to be paramount, not Parliament. He also knew it was only people's own continuing activity that made democracy safe.

Although Hardie's friendships – with both men and women – were all made within his own political group, the range of his contacts in society was wide. So too his political interests. He made use of the Marxians' social science, the Fabians' social research, and the anarchists' social vision. His socialism might have been indigestibly eclectic, if not wayward, had his passion to see the conditions of working-class people changed not forged these influences into a single purpose.

His life was punctuated with misjudgements, false hopes, and, most dangerous of all, negative hostility to individuals and groups which occasionally gained the upper hand. His way of working was individualistic, even Ishmaelite, while yet commending collectivity. He loved the common people *en masse* but often quarrelled with the single individual among them. He had difficulty with figures of authority, but always encouraged the young.

Although he developed throughout life in thought, word and deed, he ended his life standing foursquare for the principles he had unfailingly served from the very beginning. Unlike so many of those who walked with him, said George Bernard Shaw many years later, 'Keir Hardie kept the faith'.[17]

Acknowledgements

Getting at the facts about Hardie's life has involved much patient digging. His personal papers are only fragments, his letters scattered and mostly short; his favourite medium was the postcard. On the other hand he left a large body of writing in the form of articles and pamphlets. He gave endless interviews and his spoken words were relayed in countless local and national newspapers, reports of conferences, commissions and Parliament. By re-examining all this writing and adding significant material not available previously it has been possible to construct a new portrait of Hardie, that seeks to balance the facts of his public life and commitment to well-known and less well-known causes, with an account of his family life and personal relationships. It is as much the story of a whole generation as it is of one man.

Many people kindly contribted material or made archive collections available including: Hardie's only two descendants, Jean Keir Hardie Scott (granddaughter) and Dolores May Arias (great-granddaughter); two eminent Hardie scholars, Kenneth Morgan and Fred Reid; and Fenner Brockway who gave two long interviews in his 99th year, just before he died. Of great importance were the papers saved by Hardie's daughter, Nan, and her husband, Emrys Hughes, MP, deposited in the National Library of Scotland; the unpublished papers of Hardie's friend, Sylvia Pankhurst, in the Institute of Social History, Amsterdam. These are supplemented by information from Richard Pankhurst, her only child; and from Jill Craigie's suffragette collection. Additionally there is valuable correspondence between women in the Hughes and Hardie families which Emrys Hughes's brother-in-law, Hedley Dennis, left to Tony Benn in 1984.'

Among other collections of importance were the ILP papers at the British Library of Political and Economic Science, LSE; the diaries of Bruce Glasier in the Sydney Jones Library, Liverpool University; and the Norman Angell papers at Ball State University, Indiana. Invaluable material came too from the Cumnock and Doon Valley District Council Library; the Baird Museum, Cumnock; the town library, Ardrossan; the South Wales Miners' Library, University College, Swansea; the Aberdare Central Library; and the Glamorgan County Archive.

Further helpful sources were the Marx Memorial Library and TUC Libraries, Nuffield College, the Fawcett Library, the National Museum of Labour History and the Working Class Library in Salford. New matrial about Hardie in Europe has come from the Hungarian scholar, Janos Jemnitz at the Academy of Sciences, Budapest.

Further interesting material or help came from Sean Arnold, the Bond family, Anthony Mor O'Brien, Pat and Trevor Stonelake, John Saville, Jennie Cuthbert, John Forshaw, Gwen Williams, Gwyn Williams, Joe Fleming, William Wood, Barry Winter, Tom Evans, Sylvia Ayling, K Malcolm, Colin Christopher, Bernice Stone and the late Gemma Hunter. Since the book was written helpful corrections have come from Graeme Allan and Colin Waugh. Lastly full thanks to Tony, the family and many friends for their personal support.

Chronology

1856	James Keir Hardie born
1866	James Ramsay MacDonald born
1879	Hardie marries Lillie Wilson
1883	Clement Richard Attlee born
1892	Hardie elected socialist MP for West Ham (South)
1893	Formation of Independent Labour Party
1895	MacDonald ILP candidate for Southampton
	Hardie loses West Ham (South)
1896	MacDonald marries Margaret Gladstone
1897	Aneurin Bevan born
1900	General Election: Conservative Government
	Hardie elected MP for Merthyr Tydfil
	Formation of Labour Representation Committee
1906	General Election: Liberal Government
	29 Labour MPs elected
	Parliamentary Labour Party formed: Hardie elected chairman
	MacDonald elected MP for Leicester
	Hugh Todd Naylor Gaitskell born
1910	MacDonald's son, David, dies
1911	MacDonald elected chairman of Labour Party
	MacDonald's wife, Margaret, dies
1914	Attlee commissioned in infantry regiment
1915	Hardie dies
1918	Special Conference adopts new constitution including Clause Four
1918	General Election: Coalition government MacDonald loses Leicester
1922	MacDonald elected for Aberavon
	MacDonald elected chairman of Labour Party
	Attlee elected for Limehouse
	Attlee appointed PPS to MacDonald
Jan-Nov 1924	First Labour Government
	MacDonald Prime Minister

1928	MacDonald elected for Seaham Harbour
1929	General Election
	Bevan elected MP for Ebbw Vale
June 1929–	
Aug 1931	Second Labour Government
	MacDonald Prime Minister
Oct 1931–	
June 1935	National Government
	MacDonald Prime Minister
1932	Socialist League formed
1934	Bevan marries Jennie Lee, former MP for North Lanark
1935	General Election: National Goverment
	MacDonald elected MP for the Scottish Universities
	MacDonald Lord President of the Council
	Attlee leader of Labour Party
1937	MacDonald dies
	Gaitskell marries Dora Frost (nee Creditor)
1939	Popular Front against fascism advocated
	Expulsion of Stafford Cripps, Bevan and others from
	Labour Party for support of Popular Front
1940–45	Bevan editor of Tribune
May 1940	Formation of Coalition Government
	Attlee Lord Privy Seal
1942	Attlee Deputy Prime Minister
1945	General Election: Labour Government: Attlee PM
	Gaitskell elected for Leeds South
1950	Attlee elected for West Walthamstow
Oct 1950	Gaitskell Chancellor of Exchequer
April 1951	Resignation of Bevan as Minister of Labour, and John
	Freeman and Harold Wilson
Oct 1951	General Election: Conservative Government
Nov 1955	Resignation of Attlee as leader of Labour Party
Dec 1955	Election of Gaitskell as leader of Labour Party
1959	General Election: Conservative Government
	Bevan elected deputy leader of Labour Party
1960	Nye Bevan dies
	LP Conference: unilateral disarmament debate
Jan 1963	Gaitskell dies
	Election of Wilson
Oct 1964	General Election: Labour Government
1967	Attlee dies

PART ONE
LIFE'S WORK
1856–1899

BITTER BEGINNING

Keir Hardie was a Scot. He was born just outside Glasgow, and although he later lived in London for long periods and travelled widely, it was in Scotland that he always chose to make his home and bring up his family.

Keir Hardie was born into the working class, for which he had the same determined attachment. His mother, Mary, was the daughter of a weaver, whose craft was being squeezed out by the machine age of coal and iron ore which was transforming and disfiguring the pleasant countryside around Glasgow. She was born in Airdrie on 20 September 1830, to James Kerr and Agnes Paterson.[1] The Paterson side had been 'country proprietary class' whose affairs had not gone well,[2] with the result that Hardie's grandmother and mother possibly carried the powerful ambition – often cited in relation to the upwardly mobile – that someone in the family would in time reclaim the family's rightful place. If so, it would be a rebellious one, for Mary's side had participated in the Chartist demonstrations – what Marx later called 'the first real proletarian revolutionary movement'[3] – and it was said that even earlier Paterson ancestors had been 'out in the 1745 rising'.[4] Later the Hardie family liked to speculate on their kinship to the folk hero Andrew Hardie who had been hanged in the show trials after the weavers' aborted rising in 1820.[5]

Although Agnes Paterson and James Kerr had Mary baptized in the Church of Scotland nine months after birth,[6] they themselves never married – whether from conviction or circumstance is not known – and James died of cholera in 1836 when Mary was only six. Agnes and her three children – Mary was the oldest – eventually moved to a farm in Lanarkshire, about ten miles out of Glasgow on the Edinburgh road. Twenty years later Agnes was there in a small tied cottage in Laigbrannock village,[7] while Mary worked as a farm servant – at twenty-six rather old to be unattached, which might explain the situation in which she found herself in the spring of 1856.

Whether the following story was what Hardie had been told by his mother, or only what he imagined, is immaterial. It is a remarkable piece of empathetic identification with a 'grey-eyed dark-haired merry-hearted country servant going about her work on the farm . . .

one moment happy, the next . . . near to tears. He would come that
night . . . though he had missed two weeks.' Later, waiting at the gate
for the miners to come off shift, she saw 'the man who had ruined her
life go by with his arms around the neck of a tall rather good-looking
girl . . . a spasm of jealousy swept through her heart . . . the poor
deserted maid threw herself on the ground. I know the very spot.'[8]

She called the baby James Kerr after her father and brother. Gossip
written much later, by a contemporary who claimed to have talked to
those who knew Hardie as a young man, claimed that when labour
began Mary was working in a turnip field and had her boy 'in the open
air . . . before being carried to her home in the village'.[9] Whether true
or not, within a short time she was back at work in the same fields as
the child's sole support.

But she kept a high head and within two months of the birth of 15
August 1856, she brought a paternity action in the Sheriff's Court at
Hamilton against William Aitken, a miner from Holytown.[10] Nothing
is known of Aitken but her claim was accepted and a note added to the
birth certificate. Years later she confided that her affair had been a love
match;[11] but the gossip said that Aitken had been bribed to leave the
area by Mary's mother Agnes and the local doctor, because the doctor
was the real father.[12] Although Reid's research suggests that Hardie
himself may have contributed to notions of a more exalted ancestry
for himself,[13] the gossip, written long after, had several factual errors
and was more likely to be a typical highbirth story concocted by local
hagiographers to give their hero more of a pedigree than just another
working-class illegitimate.

Either way, naming the father was a sign of Mary's defiance, and
it carried over into the boy's upbringing. Several who knew Mary
spoke of her determination from the beginning that her son make
something of his life – to be, possibly, her revenge on fate, or on the
other farm servants who 'gossiped' about her abandonment, in Emrys
Hughes's words, 'a sinner and an outcast' in the small village.[14] She was
a tireless worker, her idea of heaven, Hardie wrote later, being a farm
'whaur ye could get workin' on frae year's end tae year's end withoot
stoppin''.[15]

While she worked, James was left to his grandmother, Agnes,
who still wore the old-fashioned white ruffled cap – and whenever
Hardie saw daisies in later life, they reminded him of her head.[16]
She was a great story-teller, a believer in ghosts, and an inveterate
entertainer who 'sang him waly waly and the raggle taggle gypsies
and a wealth of other songs'.[17] As Reid pointed out, Hardie's early
life had its sweet side too, and Hardie later recalled this early farm
period as 'idyllic'[18] – as well it might be for the child who had his
grandmother's and mother's undivided attention. Despite the ignominy
and poverty, if it be correct that the man who is his mother's favourite

conquers the world, Hardie started with a stunning lead in the great oedipal drama.

This idyll ended after the spring of 1859 when Mary, having spent a time in Glasgow in service, met a time-served ship's carpenter named David Hardie from Falkirk.[19] Mary desired respectability – or perhaps, having been illegitimate herself, did not want the same for any more children she might have. She and David Hardie married in the kirk of the Church of Scotland in Holytown on 21 April 1859 – when Jamie was nearly three. On the register the bride's last name was spelled Kear, her father's name Keer, and her brother, a witness, Kerr.[20] To make it even more complicated, from this time onwards the family decided to use Keir, being the more common variant locally. Whatever the spelling, the word means 'rock'.

The marriage register gave Mary's age as twenty-six rather than her age according to her birth certificate: twenty-nine. In subsequent censuses the three years remained shed[21] – possibly her way of whiting out those three years when she was an unmarried mother. She and David Hardie lived first at Bothwell and within a year a son – David – was registered at Eastfield. Soon after, the Hardies moved to Glasgow where David hoped to find work in the Govan shipyards. The same posthumous gossip claimed that little Jamie was left behind, and spent time as a parish orphan before he joined his parents. Again, this seems unlikely because from the start, David Hardie claimed him as his own – easier in a new place like Glasgow. From then onwards the boy was known – and always registered – as James Keir Hardie.

Those who knew David Hardie recalled him as tall, lean, kindly and hard-working.[22] Luckily he found work at first, as more children were born.[23] But life was hard, and for long periods the growing family teetered on the edge of poverty. Nevertheless Mary was able to indulge her passion of seeing to her children's education, particularly Jamie's.[24] Although later it was often said that James Keir Hardie never had a day of schooling, possibly because he himself even said so, he certainly had some period of tuition in writing as a young child, or at the very least Mary had some help in her own efforts to teach him how to read. A learned gentleman, schooled in religion – possibly a teacher in a voluntary school – was teaching Jamie in Glasgow before the boy was ten.[25] Books were hard to come by, however, and Jamie developed the habit of practising his letters by reading the open pages of books in bookshop windows, or by collecting old newspapers off the street when he was sent out to shop.[26]

Hardie's was the last working-class generation without compulsory education,[27] so when he was old enough to work he was sent out to earn. And glad most families were to have a second wage. A diary he kept in his twenties recorded that he started his first job as a message boy at exactly eight years and nine months.[28]

As an ambitious parent, Mary wanted Jamie to have a trade, the only avenue that offered any hope of betterment. Hardie's diary fragment records he 'wrought for some time . . . in a printing office in Trongate and a brassfinishing shop of Anchor Line Shipping Co.' He had to leave the latter because his parents had not the money for him to work for the first apprentice year unpaid. Besides, he was said to be 'unhandy'.[29] After that there was a shipyard job, working on a cradle in Thompson's shipyards, where young boys heated up the rivets and men hammered them in to secure the plated sides of the great ships. The work was done in cradles hanging suspended from the same towering sides. One day the boy working next to Jamie Hardie slipped from the cradle and plunged to his death. Mary refused to let her son return.

Then bad luck struck. An accident laid David Hardie off work. This was followed by recession and a prolonged shipyard strike in 1866. The family had to sell their furniture and move across the Clyde to even poorer quarters in Partick[30] – one room at the back of a house down a squalid street.[31] David Hardie's embryonic union's benefits were down to 1s.6d. a week. Every day he looked for work while Jamie eventually got a job with a baker delivering bread. His wage of 3s.6d. was essential for the household. For this he had to work twelve hours a day every day of the week. At night there was more work to be done helping at home with three siblings, one of whom, Duncan, was ill with a wasting fever (which meant neighbours refused to visit the family, isolating them still further). A new baby was due any day. It was Christmas-time. Twice Jamie was fifteen minutes late to work, having had to help his mother in the early morning.

Years later Hardie recalled what happened when he was a few moments late to work on the morning of New Year's Eve: 'When I reached the shop I was drenched to the skin, barefooted and hungry. There had not been a crust of bread in the house that morning. But that was pay day and I was filled with hope.' He was told the master wanted to see him upstairs over the bakery where he lived. Hardie waited outside the door while prayers were said, the master being a man 'noted for his piety'.

> At length the girl opened the door and the sight of that room is fresh in my memory even as I write, nearly fifty years after. Round the great mahogany table sat members of the family, with the father at the top. In front of him was the coffee . . . bubbling. The table was loaded with dainties. The master looked at me, 'Boy . . . my customers leave me if they are kept waiting for their hot breadrolls. I therefore dismiss you and to make you more careful in the future, I have decided to fine you a week's wages.'[32]

Jamie Hardie took many hours to face going home and wandered the streets, 'I knew my mother was waiting for my wages.' When he finally returned and told her, 'It seemed to be the last blow . . . that night the baby was born, the sun rose on the first of January 1867 over a home in which there was neither fire nor food.' Duncan never recovered, and died some months later.

These early years, and those that followed, were the wellspring of Hardie's politics and personality. He identified with the poverty and misery of others to a degree that often provoked uncontrollable anger. His hatred for powerful figures who broadcast their Christian piety yet sweated their workers, was never assuaged. Years later he wrote, 'The scars of those days are with me still',[33] and 'Even the memories of boyhood and young manhood are gloomy.'[34] Although he was growing up in a society fed with the morality of the work ethic and self-help – and for a time would adopt it himself – from the first he also had the basic conviction that underlies any socialist orientation – that circumstances condition people's behaviour. In that contest between nature and nurture he had a lifelong understanding, which never left him, of where the balance lay.

After this episode the unbearable life of worklessness and cramped poverty in Glasgow forced David Hardie to sea again, where at least he could come home with wages. It forced Mary back to the country, accepting that the city had defeated them. They settled in Newarthill, a mining village near where Hardie had been born. His grandmother was now living there, and they occupied the room next to hers in the thatched cottage row.[35] For Jamie the only work was down the pits at the Monkland Iron Company.

In one of those twists of fate, David Hardie left for his first voyage on the very same day that Jamie started work. Hardie recalled that his stepfather tried to reassure Mary that 'sailors and colliers are the twa classes that ministers pray maist for'.[36] But Hardie saw his mother turn away to hide her feelings as her husband departed one way, and her son another, to go down No. 2 Pit to earn a shilling a day. He was ten years old.[37]

Mary's and David's opinions and outlook changed after their years in Glasgow. They cast aside their religion and began reading National Secular Society publications.[38] David Hardie became a follower of Charles Bradlaugh,[39] the freethinker and Member of Parliament who fought several by-elections for the right to affirm on his own word rather than take the mandatory religious oath.

Although some have sought to render Mary religious in retrospect,[40] in fact she and her husband shared the same views. The house had no Bible.[41] Jamie was not sent to Sunday School.[42] No ministers were allowed inside[43] and 'books critical of orthodoxy or secular in interest' were bought or borrowed:[44] Paine's *The Age of Reason*, Burns's poems, Wilson's *Tales of the Borders*. Time did not sway them back to orthodoxy, and to Hardie's religious friends his parents were always known as 'lost souls'.[45] Just as important, David Hardie also became a republican, and Keir Hardie's earliest memories of political activism were over this issue.[46] Lastly, David was a Malthusian. The popular motto summed up his views exactly: 'No God, No King, No babies'.[47]

On all three fronts success seemed elusive, particularly the last. When the family left Glasgow there were already six children: Jamie, David, Agnes, Duncan, Alexander, and William. Duncan and David later died, and after the move another child was named David. Two more children, George and Elizabeth, followed.[48] Hardie himself registered the birth of George, always his closest brother,[49] although he thought of himself as responsible for all his siblings, always aware that he had to set an example for them.[50]

Mary continued to care about his continuing education, and shortly after moving, the eleven-year-old Hardie got a birthday letter from Glasgow signed, 'Your Affectionate Teacher'. The writer, in a learned script, enquired first after 'wee David' and added confidently about Hardie's own activity, 'I suppose the copybook will be full.'[51] But Jamie Hardie did not have much time for copybooks now, as his shift was from 6 a.m. to 5.30 p.m. every day and four hours on Sunday,[52] and he had to walk three miles to work on top of that.[53] In winter he did not see the sun at all. 'Strange,' he wrote years later (though it wasn't), 'that nearly all the memories of those days are of evenings.'[54] Not all memories were negative either. He remembered happy days berrying, poaching potatoes and swimming in the Calder with his friends (and spending an hour drying their heads so their parents didn't find out).[55] Hardie recalled with affection 'the single room, the dark thatch showing above, an earthen floor shining black underfoot, the kitchen dresser . . . in the light of the glow from the cannel coal fire. Even a candle was an occasional luxury.'[56] When, later, Hardie went to Fraser's night school in Holytown, he had to bring his own candle.

His first job was operating the trap door that let the air into the mine shaft. A trapper's work was not arduous but it was lonely, as Hardie wrote later, 'day after day . . . sitting all alone . . . no sound except the occasional scamper of a mouse'.[57] Stewart called it 'an eerie job' and Jamie Hardie's imagination was fired by the sighing of the air and the dancing shadows thrown by his miner's lamp.[58] He was frequently frightened. Occasionally he hallucinated, once seeing clearly before him a boy killed on that spot in an underground accident years before.[59] These experiences – along with his grandmother's numerous ghost stories[60] and those of the 'professional tramps' Jamie and his friends would listen to on 'idle days'[61] – were Hardie's self-induced introduction to the world of the supernatural. He was hooked young, and never lost the belief that just beyond what is known lies another world, just as real.

At exactly this time, another boy of the same age was working down the Victoria Colliery in Warwickshire. His job, similarly, was 'to convey the air to the . . . workings in the mine' by clearing the small courses.[62] The boy was Tom Mann, the future trade union leader, working in an area where the pits were soon to close for good, after which his family would move to Birmingham and Tom would become an apprentice tool-maker.

The Hardie family, however, had no alternative but work in the pits and quarries of Lanarkshire, although occasionally at harvest time Jamie Hardie was able to work on a farm. These spells renewed his love affair with the 'all powerful force of Nature'.[63] How hard for city children, he wrote later, to grow up with 'no green fields, no summer birds or music of brooks', just 'hard, cold . . . stone walls'.[64]

When he was about twelve Hardie was promoted to work 'drawing' the pit ponies who hauled the coal underground at the Longrigg works[65] of a local coal-owner. His lonely life was mitigated by an important friendship that every person close to him in life came to know about, with Donald, a shaggy highlander. Hardie first saw the pony when he was refusing to budge and other pit boys had put straw under him and were setting it alight. He rushed up 'and kicked away the straw and . . . stroked him . . . and from that moment he could do with Donald as he would'.[66] Only Hardie could get him to work, so he took full charge of Donald and his stall, even sharing his flask of tea with the animal, which he claimed could open the flask himself and 'sip about' with him.[67]

This friendship tapped a passion for animals that intensified throughout life. When Hardie read Burns's 'On Seeing a Wounded Hare Limp By', it not only persuaded him early not to sanction hunting for sport, but his reaction confirmed his determination to treat animals like sentient beings, 'I have never thrown a stone at bird or beast since.'[68]

Working in the mine was always dangerous, and private coal-owners were notoriously lax in their safety standards. One day Jamie Hardie experienced the terror every miner fears: of distant rumbling, the creaking of wooden supports, the loud noise of the shaft caving in, and the doom-laden sound of the earth slowly shifting downwards. Years later he recalled the panic among the miners as the main lift jammed, 'stuck in the shank'. Men crossed themselves, others wept. The boy Hardie lay down with Donald to wait. Eventually it was discovered there was room for a coal bucket — or 'kettle' — to be lowered; and slowly, one at a time, over several hours, each miner was hauled to the surface, accompanied by the sounds of the straining of the supports always threatening the final collapse.

Hardie wrote of what happened when they had all been brought to the surface and Jamie was not among the rescued:

> . . . no one would have missed him had there not been a mother there waiting for him. And so Rab Mair and two companions had to descend into the depths again . . . For a time their searching was in vain until Rab had bethought him of Donald's crib, and there, sure enough, I was, sound asleep . . . the reception on the top was the most trying part . . . it was the only part where I cried.[69]

When Jamie was about fifteen David Hardie came home to live, having first found work on the Glasgow to Edinburgh railway, and then as carpenter for the Ironmaster at Quarter, south of the Clyde. The family moved again, living in a long colliers' row with no sanitation and no water[70] on Darngaber Row. Yet the Hardies were not among the poorest families where the children had no shoes and the mother but one thin dress worn seven days a week. They all had boots and a second set of clothes for 'best', especially in the years after 1870, at the time of the Franco-Prussian war, when work was plentiful and wages rose. Mary Hardie was thrifty and tireless, with a Calvinistic sense of endurance. She opened a shop in her house in direct competition with the Ironmaster's own stores, and, reminiscent of the days of the company-store 'truck', the master ordered David Hardie to shut it or lose his job. Keir Hardie remembered that David Hardie refused. This was not because he wanted his wife to be a shopkeeper but because 'there was a principle at stake, and he left the wark'.[71] David Hardie's influence was just as important as Mary's.

In time, as Hardie's brothers were working in the pits, and David Hardie was re-employed, there was enough money for small luxuries. The home acquired Cassell's *Popular Educator*. For gifts Hardie's parents gave him books. One of the earliest was *The Races of the World*.[72] He learned young that the planet was shared. Hardie was also fascinated by the physical planet. When he found a fossil in a coal seam, he would carefully 'cut round' it and preserve it for later study.[73]

Tom Mann was already studying at night school, where a Quaker leader of a Bible class – by day a public accountant – was teaching him 'correct pronunciation, clear articulation . . . and proper care in the use of the right words to convey ideas'.[74] Hardie found an equivalent mentor, a young clergyman from Hamilton named Dan Craig,[75] who encouraged Hardie to read and lent him books.

As Hardie left boyhood, he was able to acquire his own books. Like so many nineteenth-century working-class autodidacts whose shelves included the most difficult works of the day,[76] Hardie's reading matter was as ambitious as it was electic. First, the Scots books, Captain Cook's *Tales of the Covenanters* and William Wallace, men who had stood out against all odds for their beliefs. These, Hardie wrote later, made him a 'hater of official tyranny and tolerant of all those who were fighting for conscience's sake even where my conscience doesn't approve of the objects'.[77] Above all, there was Robert Burns, who 'expressed for me as a boy my better self'. Like many Scots, he had Burns by heart. Throughout life he quoted and sang from him, and recommended him to any Scot hoping to enter politics.[78] 'I owe more to Burns than to any other man alive or dead.'[79]

Though Mary was determined to give her children every advantage and see them rise in the world, the family – influenced equally by David Hardie – never assumed it was better than its neighbours. At some point in his life Hardie was offered a place at a college. He later said he turned it down because the village boys who had gone 'seemed to have gained little of real value, and to have lost touch with their own folk.'[80]

There might have been another reason as well. Though Hardie claimed he 'could not go back in memory to a time when he could not read',[81] he was seventeen before he could write fluently, a fact that became increasingly embarrassing.[82] Having internalized Mary's wishes that he continue his education, he not only set off to learn at night, he went on to take a Pitman's shorthand course. Stories abounded later about the way he practised his letters during the day while working underground: in one version he blackened stones with coal dust and picked out the letters in white with sharp metal,[83] in the other he used coal to write on a whitened wall.[84] It was part of the mythology of the simple man who scratched literacy from nothing. But it was a false picture. Philip Snowden was one of those who remembered later both that Hardie was 'unable to sign his name' and yet a few sentences on, that Hardie was 'well-educated . . . his English, both in conversation and public speaking, was perfect'.[85] This is because Hardie was an educated man. That his education was painfully acquired – over a long period of time and in a variety of settings – did not make it any the less an education. The myth that he was intellectually unlettered died hard.

Hardie's education did not just polish his capacities, however; it was inseparable from the shaping of his convictions. Before he could write he began reading Carlyle, the local 'Sage of Ecclefechan'.[86] It was painfully slow work and he had to read *Sartor Resartus* three times before he understood it. When he did, it stuck. He found in Carlyle a concept of 'hero' upon which to pattern a life, a man known by his deeds, needing no election, as easily found in lowly surroundings as high.

One story in particular came with Hardie through life, and repeatedly surfaced in the lives of those around him as the quintessential political parable.[87] It was the simple tale of two villages – one English, one French – from which leaders of these two nations were recruiting thirty men each for war in a disputed territory in Spain. Eventually, says Carlyle:

> thirty stand fronting thirty, each with a gun in his hand. Straight-away the word 'FIRE' is given and they blow the souls out of one another: and in place of sixty brisk useful craftsmen, the world has sixty dead carcases . . . Had these men any quarrel? Busy as the devil is, not the smallest. They were . . . the entirest strangers.

Carlyle asks, 'How then?' and answers, 'Simpleton! Their governors had fallen out and instead of shooting one another, had the cunning to make these poor blockheads shoot.'

Hardie early concluded from passages like these that war was the first and greatest oppression of the common people. 'I mark the reading of *Sartor* . . . as a real turning point in my life . . . the spirit of it . . . entered into me.'[88]

By the time he was sixteen, Hardie was working hard, long hours. But there was social life as well. In addition to steering her children towards education, Mary Hardie steered them away from social pursuits that revolved around drinking.

Everywhere in Britain at this time the devastation caused by drink was evident – today's 'drug epidemic' is mild by comparison. Like drugs today, drink flourished among the very poor, and among immigrants, particularly those fleeing worklessness in Ireland. It was also a strong tradition in certain trades, which included the shipworkers of Glasgow, where David Hardie had worked.[89] Miners too were hard drinkers, and in the polyglot Quarter area near Hamilton, the young Keir Hardie could see the effects not only among men but also among women, one of whom lived nearby and could 'drink, smoke, swear and fight like a man'.[90] Keir Hardie and his mother were equally determined he and his siblings should not go that way – for a reason much nearer to home, the dark shadow of David Hardie's own drinking. Normally mild and kind, Hardie's stepfather became abusive when drunk, and had in the past – when unemployed – cursed Mary for having landed him with 'the bastard'.[91] How fully Hardie understood as a child that he was illegitimate is not known.[92] What is certain is that no one else knew, as everywhere David Hardie was accepted as his father.

David Hardie's drinking was not out of the ordinary. Neither Keir Hardie nor Mary would have believed it was caused by his sinful nature any more than they would have excused his drunkenness because of his stressful life. Their view was that drink was a widespread social evil that had to be countered by social action. Like many others they saw hope in the temperance movement, which had been a growing part of Scotland's society since the 1840s.

Much of the movement had been imported from the United States,

including the Band of Hope, which arrived in 1871 and established
a youth wing for the under-sixteens. In the next decade there was
always a new campaign going on to draw attention. In 1876 women
from Ohio toured Scotland and sang outside bars in most important
towns, 'Sober and Free' being one of the crowd's favourites. The Good
Templars movement had arrived from America even earlier, in 1869,
whereupon it 'spread like wildfire' in Scotland.[93] By the time Hardie
was twenty it had 131 lodges and 83,000 members.[94] Although Mary
Hardie herself did not join – possibly because she was unsympathetic
to its religious aspects – she did not object to her son's decision to take
the pledge at the age of seventeen.

Modern readers tend to regard temperance as quaint or puritanical,
and underrate its importance politically. Yet it was where many
learned their first political lessons. It was strongly associated with
radical liberalism and with several political families. Early socialists
were also drawn to it, including A.J. Cook and George Lansbury. In
Scotland, the editor of the *Good Templar Journal* was Dr G.B. Clark,
a Paisley industrialist, who had been active in Marx's Working Men's
Association, and was one of the first Scots to call himself a socialist.
Later came other Scottish socialists,[95] including John Maclean, Willie
Gallagher and Tom Johnston.

Strongly allied to the working-class self-help ethic, the pledge
brought many advantages. A great deal of the social organization and
widespread appeal of later movements – including the Co-operative
Society, trade unions and *Clarion* clubs, even the ILP and Labour Party –
were based on early temperance organizations. For temperance societies
were not merely campaigning bodies organizing parades and marches
(which later political parties and trade unions adopted as well), but –
like the Rechabites, for example – friendly societies organizing sick
clubs and funeral funds. Temperance activity was also socially advanced.
For example, most groups gave equal status to children and women,
speaking especially to their own powerless condition, very like the late
twentieth-century organizations for the families of alcoholics and drug
dependents.

Abstinence was Keir Hardie's first political cause. He threw himself
into it fully, campaigning for strict enforcement of existing laws and
for legal prohibition. It is easy to make fun of some of the campaigns
Hardie later endorsed, such as boarding up the back entrances of pubs,
and refusing them licences for dancing because he thought that where
there was both dancing and drinking, 'immorality was apt to be great'.[96]
But campaigners against drugs would do no less today; indeed, Hardie
might have argued that until those from communities worst affected by
drug dealers organize themselves politically, the problem will remain –
as it did in the nineteenth century until the liquor trade was met head
on. To many Liberals, the idea of the state legislating to restrict drinking

freedom was repugnant; to Hardie, it was axiomatic. When he later read of a proposal in the Queen's Speech in 1884 to enact legislation to grant a 'local option' to control the trade, he wrote that it brought 'tears of joy' and would be Gladstone's 'crowning deed of a glorious record'.[97] Hardie's instincts sided early with state control and overrode his Liberalism, a harbinger of his own future socialism.

Nor was temperance a renunciatory or negative experience. Quite the contrary, it was often highly celebratory and provided a strong social network for people of all ages. There were temperance tea rooms and temperance hotels – which Hardie always tried to use in later years whenever he travelled. There were choirs and outings and parades and a host of social events. More important, for a young man in a mining village, temperance events were where young men met young women. They were often held at church halls, themselves almost the only alternative to public houses, for Hardie did not merely disapprove of pubs, he had a fear of them, and wrote with distress of girls who 'seemed to consider it quite the proper thing to go into public houses with their sweethearts. Poor things, they know not what they do.'[98] Thus miners' social life was divided between those who went to pubs and races – girls as well as men – and those who socialized in the temperance world, around which Hardie's social life revolved from then onwards. It was at temperance dances and outings that he met his early girlfriends. Girls came to all temperance events on their own, without the tedious shackle of a male escort required so scrupulously in more refined circles, or at the universities, where women attending lectures had to have older women chaperones.

Although below medium height, Hardie always stood tall and well. His chest was broad, his brow broader. A photograph at sixteen shows him with a round face and pert nose and clean shaven – but by his twenties the face was finer, and he had grown a full, dark red beard to match his dark, curly hair. He enjoyed female company. All through his life he was sympathetic to women and interested in their views. In his mother's affections he had no peer, and in his own, neither had she – one factor contributing to some later unsatisfactory relationships with women. But as a young man, this gave him the conviction he could not be stopped. In this assurance lay the ground of his success as well as the egotism that offended not a few. It attracted young women, and he was well known for having had several close relationships. His official biographer, William Stewart, refers to 'love affairs, more than one' as a young man.[99] One was with a girl named Maggie with whom he spoke of having spent 'many a happy evening . . . in . . . company . . . when she was young, pure and innocent as a dewdrop. But a time came when our roads diverged.'[100]

Some years later as a young married man he went to look her up at Leith, where she was living. He walked from Edinburgh, and on the way saw for the first time sea water and fresh water mixing, adding darkly, and appropriately for the occasion, 'It reminded me of good and evil trying to unite.'[101] He found Maggie married, with two children. He also found she was ill and not likely to live long. Privately, in his Diary, he recoiled at the thought that he and she might have been married. How much 'better for one of us at least' that they had broken up earlier.[102] He didn't want a wife who would die on him, an early indication of what he expected, a wife who was strong and enduring, someone, say, like Mary.

Another girl he met was Lillias Balfour Wilson, daughter of a publican living near Hamilton. We can only guess what experiences in this family trade convinced her of the need for temperance, but joining the Movement showed she had an independence of spirit that matched Hardie's own, since temperance could hardly have been good for the family business. Lillias – always known as Lillie – met Hardie when she was very young, possibly only seventeen. She was still wearing her hair 'hanging down her back'[103] and not yet piled upon her head, the sign of entering adult life. Unusually for a girl, she had enjoyed a measure of education, for she liked to read and knew how to write. She had also trained for a trade and was a dressmaker.[104] Tall for a girl – nearly Hardie's own height – she was also handsome. It is very likely she stood out among the temperance girls as more successful and ambitious than the rest. At twenty-three Hardie was courting.

At work Hardie brooded often on why miners' work was so arduous, with 'so much poverty in the midst of abundance?'[105] It was important personally because he was destined to be a miner, and so were his brothers and everyone else he knew. Families could move from one pit to another but they still had the same living conditions, long hours, restricted lives and precarious incomes. Hardie was luckier than many, for in winter he could choose to work in the pits – because it was warmer – while in summer, he could work outdoors in the quarry.[106] Moreover, he had progressed up the mining ranks as a drawer or haulage worker and was now a fully fledged hewer or coal-cutter. But in an industry where the iron- and coal-masters could bring in other labour to do any man's job at any time, even earning the best wage was no safeguard. Nor were there many literal safeguards in this dangerous trade. When Hardie was twenty-one over 100 men died in a neighbouring pit in Blantyre in one gigantic explosion, caused by the mine-owners' failure to enforce safety measures. Such disasters consolidated mining society in a way that those outside could never appreciate.

Inevitably, improving matters began to absorb Hardie and he became interested in the collective associations which miners in Scotland had been attempting to organize since the early 1870s – the trade unions.

Though a National Miners' Association was started in 1863 by Thomas Burt,[107] it was not until the 1870s that unions generally began meeting in a yearly Congress, or had a Parliamentary Committee for all trades to press the claims of workers collectively. In the late 1870s miners in Lanarkshire were being organized by a legendary local leader, Alexander MacDonald, who had started a miners' association in Fife in 1871. MacDonald continued to organize even while simultaneously winning a degree from Glasgow University, becoming a school-teacher, and eventually, along with Burt, entering Parliament in 1874. They were the first working-class men to be elected and MacDonald was still being cited in Labour Party writing of the 1920s as Britain's 'first Labour member'.[108]

When Hardie was thirteen he had gone to hear MacDonald speak. With two other young miners he played truant from the pits and walked six miles at dawn to a quarry near Hamilton – they ate berries from hedgerows to keep themselves going – just to hear MacDonald on the need for strong union organization.[109] In time he would come to realize that such union leaders, like any other Liberal, deprecated state help to improve mine safety or miners' conditions as 'interference' and opposed it as much as the Liberal mine-owners themselves. In the late 1870s this 'ambiguity', as Reid so often calls it, was not yet a conscious cause of friction; workers and owners were all part of the same political family, and at election times stood under the same Liberal banner against the landowning Tories. MacDonald was Hardie's first political role model.

As a result of his education and temperance work, Hardie stood out among his fellow miners. It was only a matter of time, as Stewart said, before 'brother miners pushed him in to the chair at meetings . . . and appointed him on deputations to the colliery managers'.[110]

In the late 1870s, however, employers were back in the driver's seat. It was a time of depression and wages eventually went down to two shillings a day. The tactic of the unions, under MacDonald's guidance, was to try to negotiate a sliding scale of wages and to limit output so that the price of coal – and their wages – stayed high. This did not impress the masters, who merely reduced wages still further. Inevitably, there was pressure to organize in even the most backward pits. One result was the formation of a Hamilton District Branch of the Lanarkshire Miners' Union. When its convening members looked around for someone to act as secretary – to build up recruitment for an organization still regarded with suspicion by many miners – Keir Hardie was the obvious choice. He took on the task in July 1878 when he was still twenty-one.

Now a labour organizer within the Liberal fold and a temperance

worker within the self-help tradition, Hardie lacked only one dimension of the fully established labour aristocrat: membership of a religious
congregation.

Religion was an issue difficult to avoid. Temperance was closely
related and religious experience often central to it. Inevitably this
raised for Hardie the question of his own beliefs. Here he faced a
dilemma. The life of the spirit was very real to him, but he had been
raised in a free-thinking household. He was not knowledgeable about
religion. In fact, he could be embarrassingly ignorant. When he was
addressing a crowd of miners – and anxious to extol the virtues of
Alexander MacDonald as a reformer – he compared him to Martin
Luther.[111] Immediately the meeting came to a rowdy end, as Hardie
was booed off the platform. The miners in this particular pit, as Hardie
would have known, were Irish. What he should also have known was
that they were Roman Catholics, to whom the name of Luther was
as unwelcome as low wages. It was Hardie's first introduction to the
religious divisions in and around Glasgow – as well as to the dangers of
sectarianism, which he always detested, believing it 'of greatest service
to the employing class'.[112]

Neither was Hardie particularly grounded in the Scriptures. Having
had no Bible at home, it is entirely possible he had never read the
Old Testament in the way most nonconformist contemporaries had,
and that his knowledge of the New Testament was limited to the
passages preachers used most often. In later years he mentions the New
Testament as having been influential in his life[113] but in all his writing
and speaking there is little evidence of the widespread familiarity with it
that thoroughly religious churchgoers in the nineteenth century would
have had.

What Hardie had in abundance was a reverence for the concept
of a Christ who came to earth to fight for humanity's conditions.
Industrialization and the rise of concern for social issues had lead to
a reworking of the life of Christ as a social activist. Highly popular
and influential new versions of Christ's life were widely read, including
Strauss's *Life of Jesus*.[114] A more popular version, a translation of Christ's
life by Ernest Renan, which had so scandalized French clerics in the
1860s (by placing the origins of Christianity among the socially active
poor), had wide circulation in Britain, and it was Renan's *Life*, not the
Bible, that Hardie later counted among the books most influential in
his own life,[115] saying he had been unable to 'appreciate' the New
Testament 'until he had read Renan's "Life of Jesus"'.[116] Unlike many
who were brought up in a religious way and later moved to social
action, Hardie, brought up politically, became attracted to religion as
an extension of an already formed social conscience.

He also identified with Christ personally and saw himself – and was
clearly seen by many later in life – as a man with a messianic mission.

His earliest teacher had written to him when Hardie was eleven years old to say he hoped it could be said of Hardie, 'as was said of one greater', that he increased 'in stature but also in favour with God'.[117] The comparison was not idle. In later life Hardie often used Christ's words himself. When his comrades turned on him he said, 'I understand what Christ suffered in Gethsemane as well as any man living';[118] when soldiers fired on strikers, 'Poor lads, they know not what they do';[119] and he scourged industrialists who sweated their men and befouled the environment as Christ dealt with the money changers.[120] It is hard to resist the suggestion that Hardie saw himself not just as a campaigner socializing the Christian message, but as one with an even more onerous task.

Both Reid and Morgan comment on this self-identification with Christ.[121] Dozens are the references to his religious aura during his life, although many saw Hardie as an Old Testament figure. Hardie's own words often underwrote this identification: 'I come from a race of seers and I see clearly in prophetic vision',[122] quoted by Snowden, who refers to Hardie's 'fine, rugged appearance . . . powerful voice [like] the old Hebrew prophets thundering forth'.[123] Even casual journalists saw him as 'spiritual . . . a high minded moral type' whose hair was as 'the glory round the head of a saint'.[124]

Neither can Hardie's personal circumstances be altogether over-looked – even if the influence was unconscious – that he was born without a father to a mother called Mary, living with her own mother, who afterwards married a carpenter and had many more children. There is even the distorted attempt to give Hardie, when he turned out to be an extraordinary man, a mysterious and unusual pedigree, to complete the picture.[125]

Hardie's religious trek is confused in terms of dates[126] because it was not one step. First he took the pledge, and only later became converted to what he called 'orthodox' religion. He wrote tersely in his CV attached to his Diary, 'Brought up an atheist – converted to Christianity in 1878.'[127] As he later wrote, this meant that he 'insisted on personal responsibility in his life, the life to come, and to a Supreme Being'.[128] None of this sounds particularly 'orthodox' save in relation to a family that did not acknowledge such a Being.

The last stage of Hardie's trek was choice of a specific church. Had he truly been orthodox he would have chosen the Church of Scotland (which had a church in Quarter). Had he been the dour Calvinist he was often characterized as being – for example, by Robert Blatchford[129] – he would have chosen the Covenanter tradition. But his spiritual instinct reacted strongly against the established bourgeois Kirk and equally strongly against 'Holy Willie', the prurient Calvinist hypocrite of Burns's poem.[130]

Scotland during this period was full of sects competing for attention.

As with temperance, many of the most popular movements originated in the United States. Evangelists such as Moody and Sankey enjoyed huge audiences as they toured Britain during this period – in much the same way that Billy Graham would do in the 1960s and 1970s. They inspired Scottish hearers to consider other forms of religious activity and worship than those that prevailed in the 'established' Churches, and to this extent they were regarded in Scotland as being quite revolutionary.[131]

Hardie chose a Scottish sect, established in 1841 by the Reverend James Morison: the Evangelical Union. The Reverend Morison had been expelled for heresy by the Presbyterians for defying the doctrine of election. Predestination was inconsistent with human freedom for people to remake themselves. Morison's view was that such élitism also prevented the working classes from being drawn in to an equal place with other classes in Christian worship. The Evangelical Union's doctrine and programme were spare, not to say naïve: the universal atonement of Christ for the world's redemption, Christians and non-Christians alike. Its tenets were total abstinence, use of lay preachers, and autonomy of local branches. Most crucially, it was almost completely working class, and not 'respectable' in either Established or Free Church circles

It was the religious equivalent of the Good Templars, a movement similarly looked down upon by the Temperance Committee of the Church of Scotland for being 'embarked on by working men almost exclusively'.[132]

The class-conscious Hardie would have found this an attraction. He would not have been bothered that its theological pedigree was flimsy, since his own commitment to ideology was low. To him, the Evangelical Union was humanistic, international, working-class based, and democratic in its organization – altogether lighter and brighter than the Kirk. Hardie felt right about it, and he was happy he had found it.

The heretical implications might even have attracted him, for one of the Union's heresies – defying predestination – was a very old one, with echoes as far back as Britain's only Roman Catholic heretic: Morgan, the pious fifth-century Welsh monk, who lived in Rome for years as Pelagius, and whose followers founded a tradition based on free will and judgement by works. Holding that man's redemption lay in his own hands was seen as a denial of God's grace and an enormous threat to Rome, and rightly so, since Pelagius's followers in Britain resisted Roman rule in an attempt to set up their own church. It took several popes over centuries of repeated military expeditions, as Bede records, to stamp out the Pelagian tradition, which amounted to a long revolutionary movement, a crucial early source of social consciousness in Britain.[133] Pelagius has been wiped from history but the impulse to prove your religion in action, rather than by observances, was impossible to kill, and repeatedly returned. Hardie might have put it thus, parodying Karl Max's epithet: many theologians have interpreted the Word; the point, however, is to use it to improve the human condition.

Hardie's problem was not his religion's theological pedigree but rather how to reconcile his religion with the family tradition of atheism. His own early views, he acknowledged, had been 'very negative'.[134] It was outsiders who changed him. While working on a farm during haymaking, for example, Hardie had been moved by a devout farmer's prayer sessions which he had attended, where the kindly 'patriarch . . . knelt by his old armchair, a man in whom all that was best of the old Covenanters still lived'.[135] Later, the humanist minister, Dan Craig, pastor of the Evangelical Church in Hamilton, himself once a working-class joiner, not only befriended Hardie and loaned him books, but 'completely changed the course of my religious thought'.[136] Hardie did not join Craig's church until four years after the minister's early death.[137] Reid suggests the delay may have been fear of David Hardie's reaction, but it is just as likely Hardie delayed because of his own doubts. What probably pushed him over finally was his desire to belong, his ambition to rise in the community, his commitment to temperance, and perhaps the faith of Lillie Wilson, who was already a member.

Hardie and Lillie were by now very close. It was later said that Mary objected because the Wilsons ran a pub[138] but Lillie's own commitment to temperance would have overcome this, as Hardie's commitment to their mutual church finally overcame any objections his stepfather could have had to his religion. Hardie and he finally argued out his commitment one day[139] and the subject was closed. Years later Hardie had cause to remark that his stepfather, though an atheist, was far more Christian in his behaviour and principles than most who 'sailed under Gospel colours'.[140] In all other matters parents and son remained close in outlook, and throughout his life Hardie was in touch with them both, as well as with his siblings. He never sought to impose his religion on any of them.

All the same, as Hughes reported, they thought his move to religion 'a little strange'.[141] Neither is there any doubt that in making it – possibly also in his choice of Lillie – Hardie was going against his parents for the first time (perhaps also expressing indirect defiance of the free-thinking stepfather with whom his mother so clearly sided on these matters). Hardie put it in perspective when recalling that his conversion had been a product of that time when he began 'to think on his own account'.[142]

2

CLIMBING THE LIBERAL LADDER

Hardie at twenty-two was active in both temperance and union work, although they did not sit easily together. He regularly addressed meetings at the Old Quarry at Hamilton from on top of a large boulder, urging miners years older then he was, and bluelined with coal dust, to organize. At the same time his church colleagues were warning him not to get mixed up in union work,[1] it was much too risky. Far from taking their advice, Hardie only got further involved. By May 1879 there were meetings almost weekly about low wages. Hardie took the 'wee darg' line from Alexander MacDonald: restrict output to keep the price of coal high and enable the coal-masters to pay better wages. But where miners were paid by what they produced, the incentive was always to produce more and earn more – exactly what the coal-owners wanted, as they could always regulate matters by reducing wages. Hardie saw this clearly in retrospect some ten years later[2] but in 1879 he deferred to the respected MacDonald.

By the summer pressure to strike was growing in the Hamilton pits. Hardie opposed such action, as he knew the union had no funds to provide for the men if they came out. Striking would not be effective until he had organized all the miners. On 3 July he was elected Corresponding Secretary, which meant he was now able to get in touch with neighbouring coalfields. One of the first he contacted was Ayrshire, immediately to the south. Although it only had an embryonic organization, he was appointed as its agent. He began taking up miners' grievances with management.[3] On 24 July the Hamilton men chose Hardie as the local delegate to go to a meeting in Glasgow.[4]

All too soon the warnings of Hardie's temperance colleagues came true. His activities came to the ears of the coal-owners. At some point – it is not clear exactly when, except that it was the morning after a union meeting at which Hardie had been elected to yet another post[5] – the colliery manager at No. 4 Pit in Quarter, where he and his brothers Alexander and Willie were working, stopped the cage taking them down to their shift and had it brought back to the surface. He dismissed Hardie on the spot and for good measure, his brothers as well, saying, 'We'll hae nae damned Hardies in this

pit.'[6] Hardie was blacklisted in all Lanarkshire pits. From that day —
in his twenty-third year — the champion of the working class never
held another working-class job.

If ever mine-owners could have been given the gift of clairvoyance,
Hardie was one miner they would never have sacked. With no
labouring underground any more, he had all his time to devote to
organizing the men, living on what they could pay him. Loss of job
— even at a time of unemployment — was not the personal catastrophe
it had been for the errand boy. Along the way he had taken care
never to be in that powerless position again. One of Hardie's favourite
quotations was from Browning: 'We fall to rise'.[7] Adversity exhilarated
him. By now, the family had moved to Low Waters, virtually in
Hamilton, where the Cadzow collieries were located. Hardie and his
mother opened another shop and his brothers found work. This was
closer to Lillie's home and it was now that she and Hardie decided
to get married.

Whether they lived with either of their families or in a room of
their own is not known. Lillie was very close to her mother, Sarah
Wilson, a woman as determined in her own way as Mary Hardie in
hers, especially for the welfare of her daughter. Moreover, unusually,
Hardie liked his mother-in-law.[8] Far from its being a case of Hardie
marrying beneath him, it was, if anything, the other way round.
In working-class communities publicans were tradespeople. One of
Hardie's colleagues wrote later that their sons and daughters were 'the
leaders of fashion . . . How we poor boys and girls envied them, as,
nicely dressed, they walked through the street on a Sunday morning
on the way to Church.'[9]

Hardie was as yet only at the start of his career but Lillie and her
family might have expected him to take MacDonald's path as a union
leader: respected and well-to-do.[10] In every way it seemed a likely
match for both in that time and place, and they were married on
3 August 1879. There was no honeymoon, and the day after the
wedding Hardie attended a miners' meeting.[11] The cause came first;
it was the shape of a whole married lifetime to come.

In September there was a huge rally of 15,000 at the Old Quarry,
where MacDonald, as well as Hardie, addressed the miners. The men
were angry over low pay and wanted to take action, but MacDonald, as
always, urged conciliation. The next day the coal-owners announced a
6d. a day rise, and the crisis abated.[12] Unaccountably, they reversed this
a month later, with a further 6d. reduction the following month. Again
MacDonald appeared at a delegate meeting and advised accepting the
first reduction and offering the masters a sliding scale to avoid the
second.[13] Reluctantly this was accepted by the delegates but when
Hardie brought this decision back to the Hamilton branch, it was
rejected. Hardie's branch decided to strike.

This was Hardie's first test as a working-class leader. As Reid commented, he had 'to make a choice between MacDonald and the men',[14] between the favour of the union establishment and the action his men wanted to take. He knew that the union was not strong enough yet to strike, but 'Hardie did not abandon his men . . . when they did not listen'.[15] He seems to have been aware early on that his strength was only as great as his capacity to command the loyalty of what came to be known as 'the coming class', and he began work to raise funds to make it possible for them to stay out as long as possible (and incidentally, to pay himself).

Other pits disowned the strike, which led the Hamilton branch to withdraw its subscription to the parent body, and go it alone.[16] They asked Hardie to draw them up their own separate rules.[17] Hardie was not anxious to break with Lanarkshire but he was determined to clarify the real cause of the strike and at a meeting in January 1880 told fellow delegates that 'what the employers aim at is the break-up of our organization'.[18] Although he was careful to make it clear he opposed the strike and sought only to preserve the union, it is also possible that he was glad the men were taking action. He continued his appeal for funds and told everyone 'the men had a fair claim'.[19] By now the men were desperate, as all they were living on was the credit that Hardie had been able to arrange with certain local merchants, mainly for the supply of potatoes. For this reason the series of strikes became known as the Tattie Strike.

Suddenly, in early January, the coal-masters restored the last 6d. (though not the first) and the strikers returned to work. The result had been a draw. But nothing was really settled, for in the summer of 1880 matters were just as bad again owing to a new depression. The strike call was renewed and Hardie was sent to canvass neighbouring Ayrshire to encourage support for the claim of a shilling a day increase. He organized a 'big meeting' on a hillside outside Irvine and brass bands were sent to march through the surrounding pit villages long before daybreak. Miners rose from their beds and followed. In the morning sun marching columns advanced on the meeting, some carrying old Chartist banners. It looked as though the stoppage was complete. Hardie gave them a spirited address which was greeted by prolonged cheering (according to the local paper), especially when he criticized MacDonald's sliding-scale policy obliquely, 'There's a sliding scale that was always sliding down and there was a fair one' that offered a minimum wage. He said, 'They must tell their employers, "we will work no longer for the wage you offer us because it cannot keep us" . . . show him the power on earth that could stop them!'[20]

The Ayrshire men voted to back the Lanarkshire men in a strike action. At first miners treated it as a holiday. At least they saw the summer sun, and could be with their families. The strike attracted attention throughout the Scottish coalfields and enthusiastic supporters who came along were offered a cricket match. Hardie loved cricket and soon met other young miners' leaders from Scotland,[21] such as Chisholm Robertson, with whom he was later to quarrel, and Robert Smillie, who was to be his lifelong friend – alternative outcomes that were to characterize most of his later personal relationships. Few were ever neutral about Keir Hardie.

'As a boy practically, Hardie was leading the strike,' Smillie recalled admiringly,[22] and there followed days of feverish activity to keep it going. He organized miners' wives in pickets of the coal supplies, which blacklegs had been brought in to shift.[23] He ran a soup kitchen.[24] Union funds ran out almost at once and he worked all the hours of the day and night collecting more money. But it ended abruptly within a month, when the employers declared a lockout, and prosecutions were enforced against pickets, including miners' wives.[25]

For Hardie it had a dramatic personal aftermath, the wrath of Alexander MacDonald, who in a ferocious letter accused him of trying to undermine MacDonald's authority and deceiving 'the miners by making them believe you could get enough to support them' for however long they stayed out.[26] The men 'loathe you,' MacDonald wrote. 'They do not,' Hardie replied, reminding MacDonald that the men had voted for him and not MacDonald. Hardie made it clear he had opposed the strike but that the men would not listen, including the men from MacDonald's own district, who 'turned . . . out in such . . . large numbers as to carry everything before them'. Hardie's decision was to stick by the men, for which he offered no apology. He told MacDonald, 'Your chief fault with me appears to be that I would not follow the lines you laid down.'

The letter shows Hardie far from cowed by his mentor's anger, and characteristically returning shot for shot: 'I have tried to be plain without being abusive.' As Hughes scribbled in an unpublished note, 'It was Hardie's first clash with the leaders of the old school'.[27] And in subsequent years (even after MacDonald had died) Hardie continued to snipe at him.[28] At the same time, Hardie was able to see beyond and grasp the political meaning of the men's struggle, for two weeks later he wrote to the *National Labor Tribune* in the United States (with whom he corresponded for many years) describing what he called 'the battles that have lately been fought here between capital and labour'.[29]

But the personal dispute would not go away. Its core was money, as it was in most of the serious quarrels Hardie had in life. In this case, the honour of the Lanarkshire union was at stake, as debts had been run up with 'certain merchants', as Hardie put it to MacDonald, from whom he was requesting help in payment. All local union funds were gone, and for this Hardie blamed the miners themselves for believing they could pay their debts when they could not. He was also having a running battle with one of his collectors whom he claimed was 'falsifying' his accounts and keeping back subscriptions.[30]

Not unreasonably, MacDonald held Hardie responsible for the debts, and eventually found a rich Liberal businessman from Glasgow willing to pay them. But MacDonald set one condition, which Bob Smillie conveyed to Hardie, who relayed to a colleague: MacDonald 'refused to render any assistance . . . so long as I am taking anything to do with the miners' affairs of the district'.[31] For the union's sake, Hardie agreed to go. He was forced to leave the area, reaffirming his grievance against the Tory mine-owners and adding a new one against the Liberal union leadership.

Thus it was that at the start of 1881 Hardie travelled south to Ayrshire into the Cumnock valley, where the Ayrshire miners were more than willing to have him as their permanent paid organizer. Cumnock was not a company town, although it was in the middle of coalfields. It was divided into Old and New, the old a substantial village around a martyrs' memorial, boasting banks and shops; the new, some miles away, clustered around the pits. Hardie chose to stay in Old Cumnock. His first task was to draw up some rules for the Ayrshire Miners' Association, which he presented in March 1881.[32] They showed a typical class-collaborationist spirit, and also his fascination for other peoples, American Indians in this case: 'the war hatchet will be buried for ever, and . . . capital and labour shall meet together under one roof tree, to smoke the pipe of peace,' as they were 'twin brothers whose best interests are inseparable'.[33]

The work was arduous, trudging from pit to pit, trying to build up enthusiasm for the union and getting men to join, overcoming the considerable fear that taking part would mean loss of job and loss of the cottage which went with the job. The mine-owners of Ayrshire were no happier to have Hardie than those in Lanarkshire and in several villages miners were told they would lose their jobs if they invited Hardie into their cottages.[34] One night he was in just such a cottage when a knock at the door came from the local manager to warn the miner that his job would be gone in the morning if Hardie stayed the night. Accordingly, Hardie insisted on leaving and walked the whole twelve miles home during the night.[35]

Lillie was still in Hamilton because she was expecting their first baby. It was a boy, and they named him James after his father and grandfather. In practice they called him Jamie and from this time onwards he was the 'Jamie' of the family, his father increasingly using the surname Keir as his first name.

The three of them left their extended families in bleak Lanarkshire and travelled southwards on a descending road that gradually wound down to the milder, wooded Cumnock valley through which flowed three streams associated with Burns: the Afton, Lugar and Nith. Home turned out to be 'a room and a kitchen' in Waterside Place.[36]

At first it looked like a move for no purpose, for by the end of the year the Ayrshire Miners' Association had disintegrated. Hardie had called for a partial strike in December but got no more response from the men than he had in previous months when asking for restricted output or for an eight-hour day, the first time his support for this latter remedy is recorded.[37] There was no more money left to pay Hardie, though he continued to attend meetings and act for the Association when he could, and kept his membership. But he had to look for other paid work – and it could not be in the pits. For no mine-owner would hire him.

For a while he became a local agent for a London insurance company but it did not produce a regular income.[38] Lillie and he were living on savings, and these were all but gone when by happy chance work came his way through his association with the local Congregational Church, the church the Hardies had decided to join when arriving in Cumnock (there was no Evangelical Union Church). It was the main church in Old Cumnock and in 1884 was rebuilt as a handsome brick building by the river Lugar (where it still stands). Congregationalists, like Presbyterians, had been hit earlier in the century by arguments and expulsions over the issue of evangelism, but these breaches were now largely healed. They were like the Evangelical Union in their support for abstinence and encouragement for lay preaching, but they were much less democratically organized and working-class orientated. Nevertheless, the minister was a kind soul under stress in his job, for reasons Hardie would discover later. He had been advised to take a long holiday by his doctor and was looking for someone to continue the job he had undertaken as weekly correspondent for the Cumnock News section of the region's main Liberal paper, the *Ardrossan and Saltcoats Herald*. Hardie's facility with shorthand and his own previous experience of sending in the occasional reports to US and Glasgow newspapers[39] induced the minister to suggest him as a likely temporary correspondent. He was given a trial with the job of sending in local information, canvassing for advertisements, and selling the paper. The pay was good, one pound a week. Hardie sent his copy in regularly; it was topical, readable and lively. The editor liked it. At one bound in 1882 he became a young professional, or as he called himself, 'a newspaper correspondent'.[40]

In the General Election of 1880 the Labour contingent in Parliament had been much increased, and now stood at eleven. It included Henry Broadhurst, a stonemason, who soon became chair of the TUC. The year 1880 marked the start of what came to be called 'Liberal-labourism' – Lib-Lab for short – the decade in which the

Liberal Party sought to stake its claim to the political allegiance of the emerging labour movement, which was slowly being enfranchised. It was very important to court. A Liberal paper was glad to have a link with mining men in the Cumnock area, and Hardie's job was soon secure. The ailing pastor never returned.

Hardie signed his columns 'Trapper' at first, then 'Black Diamond', and used them as a platform to engage in homely advice and cracker-barrel reminiscence, at that time the fashion in journalism both in the USA and Britain. He preached both in the real pulpit and in the editorial one, often the quintessential classical Liberal spreading the gospel of self-improvement; he even mentioned Samuel Smiles.[41] He had sermons to give on the necessity to save and the need to keep out of debt. He stressed family entertainments rather than going out. He cautioned against all forms of gambling. He chided the poor for untidy homes and lack of cleanliness[42] and for mismanagement of household funding when all wages were spent on 'cash night' and five days later everyone was starving again.[43] He urged 'lessons . . . on thrift at school'[44] and when asked what advice he would give young men who wanted to get on in life, replied, 'Drink less, read . . . and think more'.[45]

Drink was still the greatest evil and he pounded this theme in print and pulpit and in private. Meeting a nice young man, he recorded in his Diary, 'Very sorry to learn he drinks'.[46] In a few years the Good Templar membership in Cumnock had quadrupled and it was acknowledged in the local press that this was entirely Hardie's doing.[47] By 1883 he was promoted to Grand Worthy Chief of the local Templars' Lodge. Politically, he supported the Liberal cause and attacked Conservatives.[48] He explored profit sharing and pay according to productive capacity.[49] He continued to stress that 'employers and employed will recognize their interests are identical'.[50] He and Lillie moved to a slightly larger two-roomed tenement on Barrhill Road.[51]

Yet parallel to this self-righteous and self-improving current was one going in the opposite direction. Hardie was running free classes in shorthand at night for workers[52] and in his columns producing investigative journalism of a very high order. He exposed neglect of safety in the pits and offered a running Good Pits Guide, praising a few owners who had introduced safety measures, condemning those who still refused. He laid bare the racketeering of the company stores. He took up grievances against mine-owners and encouraged readers to bring these to the paper's office in Cumnock.[53] He urged the Ayrshire miners to organize and enforce concerted action for better wages and conditions.[54] He excoriated an Education Act that was supposed to have brought free education but in reality was charging 3d. a week per child.[55] He welcomed calls for disestablishment, land law reform, votes

for women and the further extension of the franchise. He deplored
the 'Jingo element' in foreign affairs, as if Britain 'depended on the
slaughter of so many thousands . . . of Arabs fighting for home and
liberty'.[56] He suggested the old solution of limited output give way
in future to restricting hours of work, and suggested a five-day week
and an eight-hour day as a goal.[57] At the same time he took the local
Liberals to task for their attitude to the working class. At first he warned
them they were not doing enough to get 'the horny-handed sons of toil
. . . added to our rolls of voters',[58] but by 1884 he had realized that
Liberals 'thought it *infra dig* to have anything to do with a gathering
of colliers'.[59] Thus was Hardie's working-class pride doing battle with
his middle-class aspirations, the latter symbolized at this time by his
purchase of a tall black silk hat and a frock coat, the uniform of those
who had crossed over.[60]

Tom Mann had no such conflict, although he had gone through
a similar religious conversion and done his time as a temperance
worker and religious pulpiteer for moral self-improvement. But he
had also travelled, to the USA and France, and finally, settling in
London as a fully skilled engineer, grew increasingly angry to find
himself repeatedly unemployed. By 1880 he realized that the 'evils of
the community . . . were not to be . . . cured by urging individuals
of every class . . . to live Godly, righteous and sober lives'.[61] People
were unemployed 'quite irrespective of personal habits'.[62]

Although the 1880s was a decade in which the Lib-Labs grew in
strength, reinforcing the all-powerful Liberal Party commanded by
the ever-enduring Gladstone, Mann found Liberalism increasingly
unable to show a remedy. It was not until 1884, however, that
Mann was able to say at last, 'Something is buzzing'.[63] It was the
first anniversary of the death of Karl Marx and the police had to
be called to Highgate Cemetery to control the unexpectedly large
crowds rallying at his grave. For the 1880s was also the decade when
socialism showed itself.

Karl Marx's works were not generally available in Britain, but
people who knew French and German could read them. One such
was Henry Hyndman, old Etonian, barrister and Oxford graduate,
from a family with extensive mining interests. Hyndman was a Tory
who detested the Liberals, sympathized with the Irish, and had stood
as an Independent Conservative in the 1880 election. He had already
decided to revive the Chartist campaign[64] in order to forestall a
revolution he believed inevitable otherwise. He was very impressed
by the scale of Marx's economic analysis and Marx's opinion that, in
a rapidly enfranchising Britain, revolution might not be necessary if
socialism could be established.[65] His first call was thus on Disraeli,
to try to get Marx adopted by the Conservatives. Disraeli, near the

end of his life, was tactful in rejecting the plan, 'Private property . . . and vested interests which you openly threaten, have a great many to speak up for them still. I do not wish to discourage you . . . but it is a very difficult country to move.'[66]

Hyndman was not discouraged. He promptly formed his own group, the Democratic Federation, giving each person who attended its inaugural meeting on 8 June 1881 a booklet he had written called *England for All*. The booklet was based entirely on Marx's writing yet failed to mention Marx's name. Marx himself, then living out his last years in London, was incensed. He and his great friend, Frederick Engels, ridiculed Hyndman's 'sect' as one of those 'little societies which for at least 20 years under various names (but continually the same members) have . . . with lack of success tried to get themselves taken seriously'.[67] But they were wrong. Interest in Marx's ideas, however imperfectly relayed, began to grow, and Hyndman continued to attract those who wanted to know what this new socialism was all about. Tom Mann by then was one of them.

Hyndman's approach to audiences was to speak in the tall silk hat and frock coat of the upper-class gentleman he was, thanking his working-class audience for supporting him and his kind, and belittling them for their gullibility in accepting the yoke of capitalism. Even Hyndman's most loyal supporters always had 'a chill sinking of heart' at his stockbroker appearance and continual harping on his upper-class origins;[68] yet he was well informed, indefatigable in debate, and ready to regale listeners with the latest scandals of inequality, while spelling out the iron law of wages.

Marx believed Hyndman falsified his teaching and made it superficial; Engels, that he had developed a version of Marxism as hidebound by 'dogma' as 'Catholic prayer'.[69] Even more unacceptable was Hyndman's negative view of the working class's own organizations. He couldn't conceive of working with workers 'at every possible stage of their development', as Engels wrote was essential,[70] for he regarded unions as groups that 'stand in the way' of proletarian organization.[71] Hyndman's plan was that he himself would lead the workers. It is one of the ironies of socialism in Britain that the political party created to put Marxist theory into practice was for so long tied to a single individual with a proprietorial mania and such hostility to labour. Yet for all these faults, Hyndman was dedicated to the work of spreading what he believed to be Marx's socialism. In 1883, just before Marx died, Hyndman wrote *Socialism Made Plain*. Marx and Engels thought it an improvement; at least this time it mentioned Marx's name.[72]

Skilled workers and members of the middle class flocked to hear Hyndman and by 1884 he had upgraded his sect to a party, the Social Democratic Federation, with a journal called *Justice*. William Morris was its star convert, soon followed by Marx's daughter, Eleanor, and her charismatic common-law husband, Edward Aveling. In fact, there was hardly a socialist in the decade that followed who did not join the SDF – and leave it soon after. As Engels calculated in 1894, one million people had passed through it, but only 4,500 had stayed.[73] The first to leave – after one year – was William Morris, taking with him the majority of members, all either unable to stomach Hyndman's autocracy or unwilling to centre activity around parliamentary elections rather than propaganda work. In addition, Morris was quite put off by all the 'insane talk of immediate forcible revolution' designed to frighten the upper classes.[74] He at once formed the Socialist League but within a short time that too fell to fighting when 'anarchist communism' (as Tom Mann called it)[75] fell out with William Morris's communism, and Morris seceded from his own organization to form the Hammersmith Socialist Society. Despite these disagreements at the top, branches of the Federation and the League continued to be formed, as well as to co-operate together locally with no difficulty. This included a few branches in Scotland. The SDF even had a Cumnock convert, who was one of Hardie's fellow miners, James Neil. He had returned from a visit to London in 1885 bringing copies of *Justice* and tales of listening to socialist speakers in London parks.[76]

It was in Battersea Park that Tom Mann heard early SDF speakers and soon joined them on the hustings. Political meetings at the time were arduous affairs, for the expected minimum length of speech was two hours, even for the novice.[77] Every query and heckle had to be answered, every interruption tolerated – even by the most exalted orator. Today's politicians who speak only to handpicked audiences or are interrogated only by deferential journalists, lack the discipline of continuous living encounter with the random mass of humanity, of hearing every conceivable objection to their position and having to answer it intelligibly on the spot – so different an exercise from preparing the packaged brief for passive consumption.

By 1884, when Eleanor Marx was saying, 'If only we had better leaders than Hyndman',[78] a group of social activists in London, willing to do without leaders, was announcing itself as the Fabian Society. It had been spurred into existence by an American movement called the Fellowship of the New Life and its members hoped to 'permeate' other parties, particularly the Liberals. Supported by middle-class reformers with a conscience, with George Bernard Shaw, Sydney Webb and Mrs Annie Besant among its early stars, it came to specialize in well-researched documentation designed to influence the influential. Unlike the SDF which believed 'the party' was central, Fabians professed not to care about parties or principles, but only about actions which 'make for socialism and democracy'.[79] Their formation did not disturb the byways of Cumnock.

Much more influential in Scotland than any brand of socialism was a single American, Henry George, whose book, *Progress and Poverty*, had taken the English-speaking world by storm in the late 1870s. It was followed by George himself, making a series of lecture tours in the early 1880s. He concentrated heavily on Scotland where his ideas on land restoration won not only a rural audience which still remembered the clearances and was now experiencing the crofters' agitation, but also won among the urban poor. A single land-tax to eliminate poverty and redistribute wealth was inviting, if simplistic. However, it was not so much George's tax scheme that compelled people like Tom Mann, who credited his own 1881 conversion to socialism not to Marx or Hyndman or the Fabians but to George. It was George's optimism. After all the pessimism of Liberalism, George gave him 'a firm conviction that the social problem could and would be solved'.[80]

George spoke in Ayr in 1884 and Hardie very likely heard him and, later in life, spent two days with him. Many years later still he credited George with having 'led me to communism'[81] (the word communism, as Hughes explains, in 'the William Morris meaning').[82] But this did not happen in 1884. Hardie in that year was still committed to upward progress through 'pulpit, press and platform',[83] as he termed the activities in which his interest centred. Yet every one of those activities bristled with contradictions he was still trying to reconcile. We learn this from a large 'Scribbling Diary' he bought at the end of 1883 with the intention at last to make 1884 the year he kept a daily account of his life.

Unfortunately he did not start regular entries until February, which he noted dispiritedly was quite in keeping with his greatest fault, 'procrastination', a habit 'I would like to break off . . . which I have had ever since I can remember.'[84] In addition, 'I must confess that I WASTE . . . a good deal of time in desultory reading.'[85] Hardie was a voracious reader, but it was not structured work such as an academic course would have required. He still had before him the example of such men as Alexander MacDonald, with his classics degree from Glasgow University, and Chisholm Robertson, who had qualified through extension classes at Durham University.[86] His aim in 1884 was therefore to spend two hours before breakfast every day in serious 'study', a move he realized would not please Lillie, as a wife who kept a strict domestic routine. All the same 'I must endeavour . . . even at the risk of a little unpleasantness.' Both Hardie and Lillie had short fuses and strong characters. Hardie records that on one occasion he lost his temper at a meeting before he was five minutes in the chair.[87] The study Hardie had in mind and believed he had missed in life 'was with Latin & French . . . [and] arithmetic of which I know absolutely nothing . . . grammer & logic of neither of which do I know anything'. It was hard going, he confessed to the Diary, amidst so much 'temperance and evangelistic work'.

He started by recording retrospectively that he saw in the New Year 'with silent prayer at a watch meeting in church vestry' and afterwards first-footed the minister, the young Reverend Andrew Scott. In the morning he attended a free breakfast for old people given by the Templars, where local notables also assembled and he 'heard a lot of twaddle talked about the benefits of temperance by men who enjoy their wine every day'.[88] Hardie had already seen through the temperance establishment he was so busy joining. Another testing time was a lodge meeting where he had to read an essay on 'Was Burns a drunkard?' He records the group concluded 'he was not', but adds privately that this was 'open to question even in my own mind'.[89]

His days were full of organizing meetings, attending committees, and seeing people who had problems. His advice was blinkered by temperance concerns, at the expense of genuine social assistance. Thus he congratulated a young sales clerk who had lost his job because he refused to move to a section of his employer's general store where liquor was sold, but did not advise him where he could find work; and to a young miner of nineteen who showed him poetry he had written and wanted published, Hardie's only suggestion was: '. . . advised him to become a total abstainer'.[90] Almost every day involved a train journey to meetings in Muirkirk, Auchinleck, Kilmarnock, Mauchline or Kirkconnell. Hardie loved travel; and both his editor and Templars' organizers were getting a man who covered his beat.

Hardie spoke often and regularly assessed his own performance on the platform. At a 'Cooperative soiree' (sic), for example, he concluded his speech was far 'too full of figures';[91] but on another occasion he 'made what has been described as a very impressive address'.[92] Inevitably he was courted by the Liberal Association locally, for his influence over the working-class community, and in March formed a Junior Liberal Association, with his own speech 'considered THE speech of the evening' – to which he added that this seems 'egoism but is simply opinion'.[93] At the same time he sensed that all this activity would still not be enough to get him up the Liberal ladder. For that, you had to go around gladhanding and 'making friends' and this he found he could not 'bend to do . . . unfortunately, I belong to that class of men who do not . . . push themselves forward, nor seek for favour by currying'.[94]

Hardie made notes about his domestic life, showing a conventional and ordered home. Before he went to bed every night he recalled the day's weather, on one occasion a storm which blew down his plants. Hardie was a dedicated gardener wherever he lived. Every day he recorded exactly what time he and Lillie put out the lights and when they awoke. Even on workdays the Hardies slept a full nine hours, usually ten. He always ended each day with how much he had earned during the day, the entry usually reading, 'Income: nil.'

Victorian prudery and gender-divisions were evident too. In his entry for 5 February he records naïvely or discreetly (it is hard to tell which) that Lillie appears to be 'unwell & so will sit up with her for a short time to see if she gets better'. The next sentence, written only six hours later, announces, 'Our 2nd child born this morning. Lillie was ill all night but after the birth got wonderfully well and continued so.' For a second child Hardie seemed very ill-acquainted with the process of labour.

During the night he had by-passed his studies yet again to read a biography of James Garfield, one of several Ohio-born American presidents to have started with few advantages. Hardie noted, 'He refused to believe himself incapable of doing what others had done', and adds, 'shouldn't wonder if our little son is another of the same' (or, more likely, himself). Little Jamie was then three and the new baby, a girl, was named Sarah Wilson Hardie after Lillie's mother. The elder Sarah arrived later that day to help out. When she left a week later she suggested that Hardie should think about moving back up to Hamilton. He told his Diary he would not consider it. He thought a great deal of his mother-in-law, precisely because she lived where 'distant fields look greenest'.[95] If she were too near, the relationship might be jeopardized.

The most significant event in the Diary, however, was one that all biographers have underestimated in terms of its importance in Hardie's break with the prevailing Liberal and nonconformist establishment. It relates to Hardie's role as a member of the local Congregational Church and his defence of Andrew Scott, its evangelical minister. Scott was not getting on well with the powerful local deacons – such as the Liberal ironmonger Adam Drummond, who controlled the church – for he was thought to be too lenient in hell-fire dispensation. Matters came to a head over one of the congregation, Mr Elliot, who, Hardie wrote, had 'got drunk about new year time',[96] not altogether unheard of in Scotland. Scott, the deacons insisted, should have visited him to remonstrate. Despite his own strong temperance views, Hardie thought this a very 'unscriptural' attitude and privately backed Scott, who was refusing to upbraid Elliot.

However, publicly, Hardie was very anxious about opposing the elders, so on the following Sunday he records he stayed at home out of fear that he was going to be called upon to declare himself in the dispute.[97] Unfortunately, in his absence the congregation voted that he should visit Elliot himself. During the following week Hardie gave a lay reading in which he inadvertently used the same text and made the same points about it that Scott had made on the Sunday Hardie had missed: the Epistle to St James dealing with the need to give equal place to a man in rags as to a man in fine clothes in terms of where they sit in God's presence, an issue charged with meaning in a society that accorded special pews up front to the well-to-do. As he preached, Hardie noticed the deacons glaring and stopped abruptly. Scott was not there, as he was now 'ill . . . from abuse'[98] just like the previous incumbent. A few days later the deacons decided to dismiss Scott.

This was the crossroads. Hardie hesitated no more. He came out for Scott openly and went with him to Glasgow to appeal to senior deacons. There he learned a further lesson about the fallibility of the establishments which he was courting, for the deacons told them that of course they were in the right, but Scott must resign because 'those who are opposed to him, were the pillars of the church (financially) and therefore should be given in to'.[99] This pushed Hardie even further, as he noted indignantly: 'Principle to be overthrown to please mamon [sic]. This may be Christianity but I will have none of it.'

He had already shown his determination, for when Sarah was baptized, only the Reverend Mr Scott and the sinner Elliots were invited back to their 'very merry' tea party.[100] Mrs Scott in particular took Hardie's attention; she was incensed over the treatment of her husband and was standing firm at his side. Hardie liked forthright women and records he talked with her at length about her belief in reincarnation. In her anger she declared she would come back to Cumnock as a lion and eat everyone up. Hardie replied he would come back as a whale, just to tax her powers. Although he treated it as a joke, Mrs Scott may well have been the first to steer him towards a belief he afterwards came to hold very seriously.

When the Reverend Andrew Scott was finally ejected from his living, with further vindictive acts by the deacons, including an attempt to deny him his salary for the year he had served and – the final straw – sending in the sheriff to evict him from the manse three months before the agreement to quit which Hardie had personally negotiated with the deacons, Hardie took another vital decision. He wrote with finality, 'I resigned my membership of the church.'[101] This was a big step, for it meant cutting himself off from an important part of the local establishment that he had obviously targeted for his advancement. When faced with an issue of principle, however, the decision had been easy.

What was important about the break, however, was that Hardie did not merely resign. He at once undertook a project that prefigured his course in later life. He decided to organize a new church in Cumnock, independent of those already established, based on his own original choice, the Evangelical Union. Every Sunday thereafter he hired a hall, and wrote to evangelical ministers in the area to come to preach. He organized everything for the services from the after-church pastries to the harmonium. By the end of the month he had even assembled a choir of fifty and was holding social events, including 'A do in the Hall til 11', after which he and Mrs Elliot swept up and 'consecrated the work with a word of prayer'.[102] He wrote in his Diary of how successful his new church was and how relieved he was to be released from the kirk-like grip of the deacons. He wrote with pleasure how his own activity had reduced the Congregational numbers and, more important, their Sunday collections.[103] He also had his first taste of public abuse, for the same local newspapers which had praised his evangelical skills a year earlier now had 'no fewer than 3 scurrillous [sic] paras . . . directed against me' – all planted by the Congregational Church.[104] But instead of being cast down, he was exhilarated, for reasons he had already analysed, 'How I do like to be busy. How Happy I always feel. Oh that I could apply myself in the same way to self improvement that could compare with the real pleasure derived from seeking the happiness of others.'[105]

He had articulated one of the truths of his own life, to which he would return again and again, as depression weighed him down in later years. What drew him out of the slough was activity on behalf of others rather than activity turned to his own advancement. Perhaps he had already accepted it, since the self-advancement Diary stopped abruptly in mid-April and he never attempted to keep another.

Hardie's break with the Church was an important step in his conversion to socialism. As Henry Pelling observed, nonconformist congregations Methodist, Presbyterian or Congregational. 'bore an unfortunate resemblance to the Liberal Associations with which they were closely connected'.[106] They may have started as democratic organizations open to the poor, but in time they became 'oligarchies of local wealth'.[107] This was so in Cumnock.

Hardie's experience showed that the nonconformist churches, so often assumed to be the bedrock of labour and socialist support, were just as likely to be reactionary as the established one, and were themselves split apart by the rise of the working class and the increasing importance of social issues. Although Hardie made his break by substituting a new church, in time this would prove inadequate to carry his projects. For one effect of political development towards socialism was to reduce church-going among working-class people, in nonconformist and established churches alike. Ultimately it resulted in what Beatrice Webb later called the flight of emotion away from the service of God to the service of Man.[108]

3

CONVERSION

Hardie's conversion to socialism, though he often talked of it later as a sudden and dramatic event,[1] was a slow process. Perhaps because of this there has been much disagreement not only about how socialist Hardie really was, but also about when he became a socialist.

Morgan makes the case for Hardie's radical Liberal heritage never having been eclipsed, and his socialism gradually evolving over decades,[2] with particular emphasis (along with McLean and Fyfe) on his distance from Marx;[3] while Reid demonstrates the change to socialism, including aspects of a Marxist perspective, as early as 1887, as a result of renewed trade union conflict in that year.[4] Emrys Hughes believed Hardie had become a socialist in 1877 when he first became a trade unionist,[5] McLean in the late 1880s or early 1890s as a result of his first parliamentary contests.[6] G. D. H. Cole believed he made the turn through his connection with G. B. Clark and James Neil in 1885 and so did Hardie's contemporary David Lowe,[7] while Francis Johnson, another contemporary, dates it to the day Hardie read Carlyle's *Past and Present* and accepted his statement that 'What they call the organizing of Labour is the problem of the whole future'.[8] It is a question to which the answer depends very much on whether socialism is defined as an economic doctrine, a set of ethical principles or an issue of labour organization. If its definition is problematic today, it was more so in Hardie's day. So too the term 'Marxist', which even Eleanor Marx and Engels sometimes put in quotation marks, not being quite sure what it was themselves.[9]

However much writers disagree on his attitude to Marx, which will be discussed later, looking at Hardie's early life in more detail, especially comparing it to that of some of his contemporaries, it is hard to avoid concluding that his conversion was not only gradual, but it had several distinct phases. Breaking with Alexander MacDonald and the orthodox nonconformist church were only the first two steps.

Politically, during the years 1884–6, it is more than likely that he would have heard socialism increasingly discussed, not just by James Neil and Alexander Barrowman, whom Hughes calls Cumnock 'rebels like himself',[10] so 'advanced' they were almost socialists, but also by William Small, a Lanarkshire draper, who had been converted in

1884.[11] Hardie and his colleagues used to meet in Small's house and in 'the dynamite room' in Cumnock.[12] Through James Patrick, a converted miner Hardie might possibly have had access to socialist journals such as *Justice*, and almost certainly he read William Morris, who was much admired.[13] Yet it is the Liberal Party he campaigned for in the elections of 1885 and 1886.[14] True, he was becoming increasingly radical, later recalling that he and his friends in 1884 'marched and sang, "down with the Lords!"'[15] and in the same year organized a political demonstration in favour of mining reforms that the local Liberal establishment cold-shouldered.[16] But in the 1885 election he campaigned for the Liberals as those who 'desire the greatest good for the greatest number'.[17]

In that election Liberals captured South Ayrshire from the Conservatives on an electoral register four times the size of the previous roll in 1880, owing to the extension of the franchise in 1884. That many miners were now voters fuelled Hardie's political ambitions for himself, and in the next year at the School Board election in Auchinleck, he put himself up for a vacancy. Auchinleck was a few miles from Cumnock, and he was known there for his temperance work. It was his first bid for elected office, and he succeeded.[18]

His success was in marked contrast to the fate of the first three socialist candidates standing under the banner of the SDF in the general election of 1885. Hyndman, wealthy though he was, could not afford to bankroll the entire campaign when he was already spending so much on *Justice* and the SDF. They needed £400 and Hyndman accepted money that was channelled through a friend, Henry Champion, an ex-artillery officer who later ran the Labour Electoral Association. The money was actually raised by Maltman Barry, formerly a member of the First International but now a paid Tory agent, as he later freely admitted.[19] Barry and his backers had a good motive: if the Liberal Party could be split by socialist votes, Tories would gain. However, not only did the socialist candidates all lose disastrously (the Hampstead candidate got only twenty-seven votes) but the news that 'Tory gold' had financed the socialists was leaked in the *Pall Mall Gazette*.[20] It caused widespread dismay among socialists, Fabians in particular. Accepting this money was a serious mistake on Hyndman's part, for the charge that socialists were in the pay of 'Tory gold' dogged Hardie and every other socialist candidate for office for the next thirty years. It also led to more splits in the new movement. One new group was called the Socialist Union,[21] dedicating itself to a constitutional approach to socialism. Its supporters in 1885 included a young clerk working in Bristol called James Ramsay MacDonald. Like Hardie, MacDonald was a Scot, from Lossiemouth, and like him as well, had been brought up by his mother and grandmother, his natural father, a ploughman, having either disappeared or been sent away without marrying his mother.[22] Unlike Hardie's mother, MacDonald's mother, Annie, never found another partner in life. She and her mother made MacDonald the whole object of their lives, and toiled relentlessly – at domestic work and dressmaking – to forward his prospects. Like Hardie he was taught at home with Cassell's *Popular Educator*, but later the local schoolmaster took over as his mentor. Scholastic success – in biology – brought him to London, where he enrolled at Birkbeck College. But he dropped out, more drawn to socialism than to study. In Bristol, which had a flourishing group of socialists at this time, he was known as an assiduous political worker.[23]

Keir Hardie was well behind MacDonald in coming to support socialism. One reason was almost certainly because of his family responsibilities. During 1885 he and Lillie had a third child, another girl, called Agnes Paterson after Hardie's sister and the grandmother who had brought him up in his early years. To avoid confusion in the family, the child was always called Nan. Lillie, with three young children under five, was by now heavily homebound. Hardie was helpful and sometimes took over the children for an afternoon,[24] but all evidence points to a firm division of labour, if only because Hardie already had that restless compulsion to be out and about on a daily basis, garnering obligations of service. It did not grow less.

For working people 1886 was a year of continuing economic downturn and rising misery. The dynamo of free trade and market forces was creaking, as Britain's manufacturing monopoly continued to be broken up by foreign competition. Parliament was occupied with the issue of Irish Home Rule, Gladstone's support for it having leaked out during the course of the 1885 election. Turmoil followed and the Liberal Whigs departed to join with Conservatives in opposing Home Rule. This cheered Hardie, who assumed that with a more progressive Liberal Party, 'we are left with a free hand' to get on with reforms.'[25]

Certainly reforms were needed. In London the unemployment problem was reaching crisis point, and a series of meetings had been held to campaign for relief through limited public works or tariffs on foreign imports. One such meeting was held on 8 February in Trafalgar Square, but it was hijacked by Hyndman, who addressed the crowd forcibly on socialism as the only cure for unemployment. With him were Champion, and John Burns, a flamboyant, bowler-hatted journeyman engineer, who later that day led the crowd along Pall Mall. When they were jeered, the unemployed threw stones in return. Then they smashed shop windows as they proceeded through St James's and Piccadilly, all reported luridly in the press the next day, including the fact that Burns had been carrying a small red flag which he waved throughout. To many readers, it was the French mob of 1789 or a new Commune uprising. Queen Victoria was alarmed at what came to be called the Black Monday Riot. She wrote to Gladstone to say this 'triumph of socialism' was 'a disgrace to the capital'.[26]

The result was that Hyndman, Burns and Champion were charged with sedition and tried at the Old Bailey in April. In fact it was socialism on trial, and those who followed the proceedings, undoubtedly including Hardie, followed also the defendants' spirited cross-examination of witnesses about what had really been said. The defendants, acting for themselves, insisted on speaking at length to explain socialism. When they did, the jury and judge heard nothing about riot or revolution, but only Hyndman explaining that socialism was 'all a matter of pure economics', after which he delivered them his sermon on surplus value. After two hours both judge and jury were convinced of socialism's non-inflammatory nature. All three defendants were acquitted.

The trial restored the SDF's credibility among socialists but it was a financial disaster for Hyndman and his wife, Matilda. She was the daughter of a farmer and there is virtually nothing about her in any account of his life – other than the usual mention of her presence on the platform. However, when Marx and Hyndman had been on speaking terms, Marx had written of her, 'I quite like the wife for her blunt, unconventional and decided manner of thinking and speaking', however annoyed he was to see 'the admiring way she hangs on the lips of her self-satisfied garrulous husband'.[27] Hyndman could not have had much satisfaction in the debts incurred by the trial or in legal fees for a libel suit pending over remarks he had made in *Justice* about a quarry-owner. Nor, the last straw for the loyal Matilda, the enforced sale of their large house on Devonshire Street and a move into rooms.[28] Almost certainly, she never complained.

In the summer of 1886 there was another general election. Hardie campaigned once more for the Liberals – on the cheap loaf, statutory mining regulations, control of the liquor trade, abolition of the Lords, and now Home Rule – all standard radical fare. But Gladstone was defeated and in Ayrshire the Liberal seat was lost. In London, in response to the TUC's regular calls for more electoral representation, a Labour Electoral Association was set up calling itself the 'National Labour Party'. Henry Champion was put in to run it and T. R. Threlfall of the TUC claimed it was to be 'A hearty advocate . . . of a genuine and distinct labour party . . . whatever its politics'.[29] Threlfall hoped its politics would be Liberal; others began to hope the politics might be more independent.

There are a few signs that Hardie was beginning to see how there could be conflict about Labour 'politics' within the Liberal fold. In 1886 he put himself forward for election to the Cumnock Town Council, but was not successful,[30] and it was not unlikely that Hardie and his supporters were already considering the possibility that he would put himself up for one of the Ayrshire parliamentary seats. There was tension too on the School Board, where none of Hardie's recorded initiatives found backers. They showed Hardie's basic instincts to be moving in a democratic direction, for one of his resolutions was to let the press in to Board meetings (closed to the public) in order to report the debates. The other was to get school fees – still being charged for all pupils and soon to be charged to Hardie for his own son's school attendance in Cumnock – reduced. Among his fellow Liberals, he did not find a seconder for either.[31]

But the most important factor in swinging Hardie's politics to socialism at this time was the decision he took at the end of 1886, to go back to his work as a miners' union agent. Ayrshire miners, not having been on strike for several years, now had the funds to employ him again and they sent a deputation to ask him to help get the union on its feet. He did more than agree. He threw himself into their cause with redoubled intensity. The salary they offered was £75 a year, later augmented to £80 for taking on the work of the Scottish Miners' Federation as well. This was formed later in the year, and Hardie was elected its Secretary.

He was back in the trade union world, the world of the working class, no longer just writing about legal regulation of mine safety, employers' liability legislation, action on mineral royalties, arbitration machinery, and the eight-hour day – but working for them again. But his approach to the work was far wider after six years away; indeed his ideas had evolved even more in the last two years. Whereas he had written in 1884 that campaigns to get land nationalization, even nationalization of the mines, were diversionary ideas likely to put miners 'off the scent' of building up the union – without which 'there is no hope'[32], in 1886, when James Neil, the SDF convert, arranged a debate on socialism,[33] Hardie said that 'legislation . . . must advance on the lines of socialism until the people are in possession of the land'. His slow slide towards socialist ideas was also reflected in the new preamble he wrote for the reborn union, significantly subtitled 'The Guild of Comrade Colliers'.[34] Gone was the cosy metaphor of the Indian powwow. Instead there was a potted version of *Capital*, which declared that:

> All wealth is created by labour. Capital is part of this . . . stored up and used for assisting labour to produce more wealth . . . Profit is . . . wealth which remains after wages, interest and rent have been paid. If all land and capital was [*sic*] owned by those who produce wealth, the wages of labour would be the same as the wealth produced by labour . . . Capital which ought to be the servant . . . has become the master of its creator.[35]

He may not have read a word of Marx, but socialism's basic perspective was intervening in his Liberalism – like that mix of fresh and salt water that had so fascinated him when he was walking to Leith.

Ten years later Hardie saw this decision as a sea change. He looked back on his life between the two spells of union work and saw himself as a smug man who had respectable work on a newspaper and 'a good, comfortable situation, such as Labour leaders dearly loved ... becoming sleek and fat ... and a member of the School board',[36] until he broke away from it all and rededicated himself to serving fellow workers. As Hughes wrote many more years on, being back with the working class was 'something more than a mere job'.[37] It was a life commitment.

During 1887 Hardie stopped writing regularly for the *Cumnock News*, and in saying goodbye to readers said he had always tried to practice what he preached: 'manhood was preferable to money'.[38] Just as well, as he was losing the income the paper paid him. At the same time he was gaining access to their presses. For with funds from the new Scottish Miners' Federation, on which he could call as Secretary, and his own savings, he began his own paper for Scotland's miners, which he called *The Miner, A Journal for Underground Workers*. His first editorial said he intended to use the journal to 'advocate reform in EVERY DIRECTION ... to bring relief to the toiling millions'.[39] 'The whole system under which wages are paid is rotten to the core', and he urged the miners to 'make war' against it. Although the Federation adopted *The Miner* officially and distributed it to miners,[40] Hardie was careful to keep the paper his own property. This was a sign of his obsessive interest in money matters as well as political ambition: he knew the importance of controlling the funds and he wanted his own journal that could link organization with propaganda. Like many editors, Hardie wrote much of his paper himself – over a third of the copy.[41] The contributors he chose reflected the ferment of ideas crossing his field of vision at this time: land leaguers, socialists, anarchists, trade unionists. A year later he added *Advanced Political Journal* to the title,[42] showing which way he was moving.

He was moving in other ways as well. From the end of 1886 Cumnock was no longer where he spent the most time. He now made Glasgow, where the journal was printed, the centre of his work.[43] He also paid his first visit to England – to a miners' conference in Manchester,[44] where he met miners' leaders such as Thomas Burt and William Abraham (always known as 'Mabon') and, initially, wrote about how impressed he was.[45] Burt even contributed cautionary Lib-Lab home truths to *The Miner's* first issue in an article called 'Self Help'. It warned that 'newly formed unions everywhere have ... a tendency to travel at too quick a pace ... Learn to Labour and to wait.'

But waiting was impossible to enforce. Times were too hard, the men too impatient. Another national miners' meeting in Birmingham on 11 January 1887 taught Hardie how hard it was going to be to get a co-ordinated national approach to wages policy. Scots miners would have to fight their own battles for some time to come,[46] even though Hardie knew a full strike was not yet possible. His favourite weapon had been one-pit strikes, 'idle days', and one-week stoppages, to keep the price of coal high. Inevitably, however, some pits went further.

The Lanarkshire men, led by Bob Smillie, decided to extend a week's stoppage to a full strike in December. It was the dead of winter. By the start of February they had been out for nearly two months and their families were desperate. Although Hardie thought their strike precipitate, events soon compelled him to give 100 per cent support, and revealed to him his own naïvety about any 'labour and wait' philosophy. For as the unions had federated, the coal-owners had done some combining of their own to deal with any action the strengthened union might sanction to improve the miners' lot. By February 1887, mine-owners were ready with their new plans. These included by-passing the usual negotiations and refusing to meet the union's representatives, dealing only with their own handpicked men in each pit. This was immediately followed by blacklegs rushed in to the coalfields from Glasgow – protected by large numbers of police – which provoked rioting, as miners saw other men given their jobs. At Blantyre a few men reacted by looting a food van for their starving families, and the next step – obviously planned – was the despatch of army Hussars, again sent from Glasgow. The Hussars raided miners' cottages and arrested men indiscriminately on several nights running. In his column Hardie wrote of 'mounted policemen riding down inoffensive children nearly to death, and felling quiet old men with a blow from a baton', while wives and children were 'in the very throes of starvation'.[47] Hardie had never experienced anything like this before.

In the great Liberal press there was no condemnation.[48] Only in the socialist press – in *Commonweal* for example – was there any outrage, any support.[49] Only socialist groups supported the strikers. Hardie shared their outrage and noted their support. The brutality with which the strikers were put down, the unholy collusion of owners, police and military, the humiliating terms of defeat enforced on the miners in the end, combined with the Liberal silence, abruptly changed the key of Hardie's activity. Until this time his policy had been gradual amelioration that went hand in hand with progressive improvements in organization. He had assumed that when miners were totally organized mine-owners would see the wisdom of conceding improvements. Now he saw he was mistaken. Mine-owners were not only not going to accept improvements, they were not going to accept unions. This conclusion was reinforced when police in Ayrshire were sent to stop Hardie from going to miners' cottages to encourage them to stop work in support of the Lanarkshire men.[50] The second edition of *The Miner* was thus quite different from the first. It bristled with the realization that this was the gravest crisis 'in the history of coal mining' and urged miners to 'violent activity' to 'make their power felt'.[51]

It was the state's violence that hit Hardie hardest and brought to the surface one of his most basic beliefs, the necessity for non-violence in all human struggle. Violent agitation, yes; but physical aggression, no. He resisted to the full any thought of 'armed' counter-organization by the men. Perhaps it was this aspect of Hardie's belief that influenced his contemporaries more than any other, including another Scotsman he met at this time, John Bruce Glasier.

Three years younger than Hardie, Glasier had been brought up in Ayr by atheist parents who had been unable to marry because his father, a prosperous farmer, had left his marriage to live with Glasier's mother, the daughter of a Gaelic poet.[52] When his father died (and the money went to his legitimate family) she moved to Glasgow, where she endured much poverty. Nevertheless, she saw her son educated and he grew up determined to be a poet. More practically, he had trained as an architect and now designed wrought-iron railings and gates in Glasgow. But he was often unemployed and spent his time reading and going to political meetings. He heard Michael Davitt, the one-armed Irish patriot and socialist, after which he joined the Irish Land League. When he heard Hyndman debating with Henry George and read Hyndman's exposition of elementary Marxism in *England for All*, he joined the SDF. But most of all he admired William Morris, the great giant who was both artist and political activist. When Morris split with Hyndman in 1885 Glasier left too, and ever after viewed Hyndman and the SDF with pathological distaste. A contemporary later recalled Glasier at this time as 'the communist spirit incarnate',[53] speaking on public pitches and working arduously on street corners to sell *Commonweal*, Morris's stylish journal, just then in the middle of publishing 'The Dream of John Ball'.

In 1885 William Small had asked Glasier to speak in Hamilton, where his name might have come to Hardie's attention. But the first time Glasier recalled meeting Hardie was in Edinburgh a year or so later, where both had been invited to the home of Dr John Glasse, a socialist cleric and minister of Greyfriars church. Glasse taught at Edinburgh University and had made his living-room a centre of socialist debate. On this occasion people were invited to listen to Leo Mélliet, one of the survivors of the French Commune. In Britain Commune survivors enjoyed unlimited respect in socialist circles, and each year's Commune commemorations were one occasion when warring factions met together without acrimony.[54] Hardie was invited as a miners' leader making his mark, Glasier as secretary of the Socialist League's Glasgow branch, where he was known as a young 'hothead', one of the 'barricades men' who wore red ties and identified with the French tricolour.[55]

Mélliet did not disappoint Glasier, for he was still advocating a 'slay and spare not' policy for socialists,[56] something that could be characterized as armed struggle. At the time socialists, including Morris, were undecided about the role of armed rebellion. During the course of his talk, Mélliet, who also taught French at Edinburgh University, suggested that when the revolution came, the first victim should be the university's rector. At this point Hardie rose to his feet, and said, 'If, sir, I believed that was socialism, I should never be a socialist . . . it is pure madness'.[57]

This impressed Glasier enough to invite Hardie shortly after to speak at an SDF meeting in Glasgow, where despite hospility at the top, local League and Federation co-operated fully. Hardie chose to talk about the mundane problems of organizing workers. Glasier thought Hardie a 'socialist in all but name', but that the 'practical domain of trade union organization left him little heart . . . for abstract theories of democracy or revolution'[58] which all present wanted to discuss. Hardie may already have been labelled an extremist agitator by mine-owners and the press (because unions had the power to disturb profits), but young men in favour of transformational action (who are always allowed to discuss, so long as they do not act) found Hardie far too tame and unideological.[59] They were on him in a flash, or as Glasier put it, 'pounded him . . . with texts of Adam Smith, Mill and Marx',[60] the list itself a sign of the mixed messages socialists were sending. 'We felt we had confounded him,' but 'To our surprise, Hardie did not flare up,' but dealt 'with our points in a quiet argumentative way.' Hardie always answered serious criticism seriously. This trait persisted throughout his life. The more agitated his opposition became, the more doggedly calm he often stayed.

Glasier correctly spotted that Hardie did not care for economic theory. It was not lack of intellect, but his own turn of mind. In this he was like Morris who, when asked by a Hyndman heckler, 'Does Comrade Morris accept Marx's theory of value?', replied:

> To speak frankly, I do not know what Marx's theory of value is . . . I have tried to understand . . . but political economy is not my line and much of it appears to me to be dreary rubbish. But I am, I hope, a socialist none the less. It is enough political economy for me to know that the idle rich class is rich and the working class is poor, and the rich are rich because they rob the poor.[61]

It was easy for Hardie to define himself in relation to Glasier and the old Communards; what was more difficult was dealing with his own

Liberal leaders, particularly those union leaders who were MPs and believed — as old individualist Liberals — that any collective action weakened personal responsibility: their support was required for a Mines Bill, backed by a coalition of Liberal and Irish interests, which was due to be introduced in a Conservative Parliament, to make sure that important demands, such as the eight-hour day, were included in it. The Blantyre strike had convinced Hardie that for miners to stand up to mine-owners, the union was not enough. Parliament's protection through legislation was now required. 'It would be better', Hardie wrote, if the miners could 'carry out an eight-hour movement without the aid of Parliament', but it would not be possible, as it had not been possible to stop female pit labour without legislation.[62]

By now Hardie was well known in Scotland, where he regularly toured mining communities to lecture on safety and the need for a united miners' organization. What he lacked was a mentor to help him make the transition from regional to national stage, and from a parochial mining perspective to a larger political outlook. At just this time — and from a most unlikely quarter — such a one appeared outside Hardie's Cumnock home one day, dazzlingly well dressed and riding a beautiful black horse. While visiting an estate he owned in the area, he had decided to ride over specifically to meet Hardie. Well beyond the reach of puny mine-owners, who could still warn local people away from consorting with Hardie, he accepted Hardie's invitation to come inside. Later they met at the *Herald*'s editorial offices for a long talk, and Hardie took him down a mine, a privilege he had never had, though he had just been elected MP for North West Lanarkshire. Not only did he and Hardie become immediate friends, but according to Emrys Hughes, they became inseparable. Or, as Glasier later put it, for virtually the next six years, they 'went about in harness'.[63]

His name was Don Roberto Bontine Cunninghame Graham, thought by some to be the 'uncrowned king' of Scotland[64] owing to his descent, as heir of the Earls of Menteith, from Robert II. In addition to his Ayr estates, he owned an even larger tract of land called Gartmore, set in the hills below Stirling and crowned with a Robert Adam house.[65]

As a boy he had run away from Harrow, which he hated, and divided his time between Scotland and the home of his maternal grandmother in Spain. She was from a family of Spanish hidalgos, one of whom had commanded ships in Venezuela as a friend of Simon Bolivar. Cunninghame Graham had spend his twenties horse ranching in the South American pampas and the American West, and in exploring Spain and North Africa. When he settled in Britain again he was a fluent linguist, explorer, naturalist, and author, and undoubtedly the most accomplished equestrian ever to enter Parliament. Pampa was his legendary mount, an Argentinian mustang he had found pulling a tram in Glasgow and bought on the spot, unhitching the animal and riding it straight home to Gartmore. Pampa went with him everywhere, travelling by railway horsebox to the London station from where Cunninghame Graham rode him to the stables in Parliament. He never used a mounting block, but sprang straight into the saddle from a standing position. Everything about his life was encased in tall tales, all of which were true. He had married a young French girl when she was still in a convent and to whom he was devoted. Gabrielle too was remarkable. She was a first-class botanist and expert in Scottish mosses, as well as a student of religion, possibly the first woman to write a life of a saint (Theresa of Avila) from a social perspective – for which she had to obtain Vatican approval.[66] Both were thought by Cunninghame Graham's biographers to be unrecognized manic-depressives,[67] as indeed Keir Hardie probably was himself.

Neglected in Scottish history for a century, Cunninghame Graham has recently enjoyed a revival of interest[68] as an early advocate of devolution, having campaigned in the 1885 election[69] for separate parliaments for Scotland, Wales, Ireland and England. Hardie's biographers differ in the importance they give to him. Morgan considered him a 'maverick'[70] and marginal to the exercise of political power. McLean dismisses him as an 'upper class' adventurer who quit politics for travel and had 'nothing in common' with Hardie.[71] To Emrys Hughes, however, Hardie 'had more in common [with Cunninghame Graham] than with the Miners' MPs'[72] and was 'far nearer' to him in his opinions than to any of the Lib-Labs.[73] Reid considered he offered Hardie a 'model for Parliamentary agitation'[74] and was a significant influence on his thinking.

For Cunninghame Graham was a socialist, the first ever to be elected to Parliament. Eleanor Marx called him 'the only socialist in the House of Commons'[75] and Pelling still saw him as such[76] seventy years later. From his maiden speech onwards he single-handedly espoused the cause of the common man, and unleashed a running denunciation of capitalism, condemning it for 'giving 30,000 heaven while condemning 30 million to hell'.[77] He asked:

> What does the British Empire . . . mean to the Lanarkshire miner or the outcasts of our great cities? . . . Simply permission to toil all his life for . . . thirteen hours daily for insufficient remuneration.[78]

Engels wrote to a continental friend at this time that Cunninghame Graham was 'an enlightened Marxist'.[79] But he was much more. He was a notable humanitarian and early environmentalist, espousing causes decades, if not a century, ahead of their time. These included many of the causes Hardie came to support in later life.

High on the list was animal welfare, including rescue and care of pit-ponies, which Cunninghame Graham believed was a political issue. Later he protested at the overloading of cattle ships; and urged a rescue operation worldwide for vanishing species of animals. He opposed the construction of a railway in the Lake District; opposed both capital and corporal punishment (and interceded for two Zulu tribesmen convicted of murder). He favoured prison reform, the right of the public to meet at all times; a free press (which he did not believe Britain had) as well as free Sunday opening of all museums. He campaigned for the removal of illegitimacy as a legal status; and protection for American Indians, whose treatment he regarded as a world scandal. At home, at the time Hardie met him, he was in favour of a mix of radical and socialist causes: disestablishment of the Church of England, direct veto of liquor, an eight-hour day, abolition of mineral royalties, the nationalization of the mines and land, a graduated income tax, triennial parliaments, universal suffrage for men and women, home rule for Ireland, national parliaments, abolition of the House of Lords, free secular education, and an end to all sweated trades and piece-working. He also believed war was an unnatural state in society and 'can be subdued by reason'.[80] What characterized his outlook was the vast range of concerns he considered properly 'political', an approach that Hardie was also to find irresistible, and one he possibly learned from Cunninghame Graham. He also learned from him that the present system can only be changed by workers themselves. Early on Graham told Hardie, 'It would be absurd to expect the capitalists to do it'.[81]

The English establishment dealt with Cunninghame Graham by deriding him. *The Times* called him a 'cowboy dandy',[82] while a more kindly contemporary merely said he was fond of 'lost causes'.[83] But to Hardie he was not only an ally but an important spur to Hardie's growth of outlook. During 1887 Hardie's comments on political life widened out and his judgements became bolder as well as more socially directed. He did not see why, 'under a system of democratic government, the State should not be the possessor of at least all natural means of production such as the land, minerals, together with the means of transport'.[84]

He was ready to drop drink as the cause of all evils, explaining that even if working men stopped drinking entirely and the money was divided between them, 'it would not remove poverty from our midst'.[85] He began to express anger: 'Why should a man be kept with his nose continually at the grindstone, while the man who employs him has, perhaps, £10,000 a year?' This had clear echoes of the Levellers' question, why should one man earn £100 in a year while another earned only £1?

Hardie's steps towards socialism quickened in 1887. 'Capital,' he concluded in May, 'is necessary, but not the capitalist';[86] while by July he had concluded that no programme will succeed 'which does not poach on the preserves of the privileged class', and spelled out some of its provisions: triennial parliaments, adult suffrage, abolition of all non-elected institutions, graduated income tax, free education, an eight-hour day in industry as a whole, state ownership of mines and land, and 'compulsory provision of healthy dwellings for working people'.[87] These were old radical demands combined with giving the state new responsibilities. More significantly, Hardie did not just see it as a programme for miners alone. It 'has an interest for every working man'.[88] In the same way he widened the demand for an eight-hour day from a proposal to replace output restriction, into a proposal which had implications for the quality of life of every worker.[89] To Reid this programme represented a 'volte-face . . . so sudden . . . that it seems to justify the term conversion'.[90]

But it was one thing to come to collectivist and humanitarian views; it was another to see the Liberal Party as incapable of enacting them. Here too Cunninghame Graham's influence may have been significant, for he disliked the Liberal Party and believed it was little different from the Tories. Parliament was a sham, just 'the rotation of rascals in office'[91] making a show of opposition to each other. He called it a 'huge ostrich nest' because if you stood in the gallery of the House, whichever side of the Commons you threw your hat down on, it would land on the bald head of a millionaire.[92] He did not like the Lib-Lab trade union MPs, nor they him.[93] He saw them seduced by upper-class blandishments until they had forgotten why they were there, a view Hardie came to hold strongly, although at the time it might have come as a shock. So too Cunninghame Graham's opinions on the much vaunted Liberal ethic, 'an amorphous crowd of non-conformists, temperance reformers, deceased wife's sisters . . . the dried fruit of outworn . . . politics'.[94] Cunninghame Graham hated Gladstone, for whom Hardie had always retained respect. Lastly, of course, Cunninghame Graham was one of those who wanted a distinct Labour Party to be formed. At the end of the year *Commonweal* was already predicting that he would be starting one in Scotland.[95]

Hardie may not have gone along with every opinion voiced by Cunninghame Graham, but by April 1887, there are distinct echoes in *The Miner*: 'while working men are quarrelling as to whether Whig or Tory shall rule them, both are fleecing him and sharing the plunder. We want a Labour Party . . . and the trades unions have the power to create this.'[96]

Hardie's and Cunninghame Graham's friendship was not unusual in politics, as each possessed what the other lacked: for Cunninghame Graham it was a knowledge of working-class needs and what would meet them, and for Hardie, an inside knowledge of how the governing classes really worked, and the courage to stand up to them.

Cunninghame Graham and Hardie did not only meet in Scotland. Early in 1887 Hardie came to London for the first time[97] to visit Parliament. He and Bob Smillie and several other miners made a number of visits that year to lobby in respect of the Mines Bill. On a February visit they met the Home Secretary as well as Lib-Lab MPs Burt and 'Mabon', to lay out the reforms they expected the Bill to contain.[98] But when the Mines Bill was finally introduced in March, these MPs were absent. It was Scottish MPs such as Cunninghame Graham and G.B. Clark (the crofters' MP), who put on the pressure, not miners' MPs. Just as it had been Cunninghame Graham, said Hardie, 'setting an example other MPs would do well to follow,' who had stood by the miners in Scotland, attending their strike meetings throughout the two months that led up to the Blantyre repression in February 1887.[99]

Throughout 1887 Hardie watched as Lib-Lab MPs continued to waver in their support for the clauses required. Burt and Mabon prevaricated so much that the eight-hour clause was eventually lost.[100] In July Hardie paid another visit and clashed with Burt about putting the clause back in, but when the Bill was presented again in Parliament on 17 August, only Cunninghame Graham supported this proposal – with fierce opposition from R. B. Haldane, a leading Liberal, and virtually no support from the trade union Lib-Lab MPs. Henry Broadhurst even tried to claim there was no real support for it among miners.[101] In the end the Bill was passed with none of the reforms required, merely new regulations mine-owners favoured.

This was another important stage of Hardie's conversion: loss of faith in Liberal politics. For on these occasions Hardie watched Lib–Lab MPs from the Strangers' Gallery. During the first debate in February he confessed a 'feeling . . . akin to anger' about the way 'those men were doing everything possible to keep up an appearance of wanting to do something, while all the time they were glad of any excuse which prevented them from doing it.'[102] By the last debate he was appalled by the servility of Burt, Fenwick, Broadhurst and Mabon, all of whom refused to support the measures which the miners advocated.[103] In July's *Miner* Hardie coined a phrase for Lib-Lab MPs, 'dumb dogs who dare not bark'. By September they were 'snakes in the grass'.[104]

Something had snapped in Hardie, as was evident when he went to Wales for the first time in the following month to attend his first TUC Congress as the Ayrshire Miners' delegate. Everything he said there suggested he had accepted Cunninghame Graham's view that Liberal trade union leaders co-operated fully with Liberal mine-owners in preventing any legislation to regulate mining in the workers' interest, both locked into their old-fashioned Liberal opposition to state activity in any sphere of living. Hardie intended to make this plain by attacking Broadhurst in particular, not just because Broadhurst had opposed the eight-hour day, was a junior minister, and was in the chair as president of the TUC, but because the MP epitomized Liberal double standards. Hardie had already criticized him as a hypocrite on temperance[105] and now he attacked him for having given by-election support to Sir John Brunner, a rich Liberal industrialist notorious for sweating his workforce. Broadhurst also had shares in Brunner's chemical company. Hardie accused Broadhurst of betraying labour and of failing to represent the miners' best interests in Parliament. He moved an amendment for an agreed programme that 'every candidate for Parliament should know that unless he could support it he must look elsewhere for a seat'.[106] He also heckled continually from the floor during other speeches. On neither vote he forced did he get more than 10 per cent of the delegates' support. But the whole congress knew who Keir Hardie was by the end and so did the general public. Next day Glasier said he got his 'baptism of political abuse from the press',[107] where he was excoriated for attacking the respected Broadhurst. He got it too at the end of the conference when Charles Fenwick, a miners' leader, dressed him down imperiously from the chair, telling him that both Congress and the working class 'had . . . a policy of reform not revolution . . . and . . . he refused to take his instructions from one who, like Jonah's gourd, sprang up in a night, only to collapse as soon'.[108] It was a major public humiliation, one of many his family had to live with, for he was denounced in Glasgow's papers as well;[109] and long after he had died his daughter Nan recalled that hostility to him, and to the family, for this single speech 'lasted until the day of his death'.[110]

Hardie must have known he was taking a terrible chance. The war he had declared was one that could never end in truce. Eighter he had to go; or the union leaders did. During the year he kept up the pressure, calling trade union leaders 'holders of a fat, snug office, concerned only with maintaining the respectability of the cause'.[111] He wrote to his friend James Young that Congress discussions were 'trivial' and that 'trade unionism today is one of the conservative forces which have to be . . . reckoned with'.[112] The next year he and Cunninghame Graham were back at the TUC Congress in Bradford, where they stationed themselves outside the Methodist church on the Sunday and 'to the disgust of brother delegates', handed out leaflets to the men for a meeting at which Gabrielle Cunninghame Graham was speaking to visiting French delegates.[113] Two years later, when the congress was held in Dundee, a delegate supporting the platform called Hardie one of nature's 'stinking foxes'.[114]

Reaction was so strong because there was an unacknowledged truth in what Hardie said. Many big industrialists – and most entrepreneurs –

were supporters of the Liberal Party. Yet so were many, if not most, of their own workers. This was the dilemma of the Liberal Party and its labour wing. How could the Party represent the interests of both employers and workers at the same time? The answer, as Hardie had discovered, was only by commandeering the union leaders, to whom the men in turn were loyal. To cut this cosy connection was the task Cunninghame Graham and Hardie seem to have set themselves. Unknown to them as yet were other forces working in the same direction, namely, pressure for representation at the TUC – and in unions – by the vast army of unskilled and semi-skilled workers, women as well as men, who had no organizations as yet to fight for them. The venerable labour leaders represented the highly skilled only, a fraction of Britain's workers. This élite resented the unskilled majority, as was evident when they jeered a group of firewood-cutters who invaded the 1890 TUC Congress and demanded to be admitted officially.[115] This was the Achilles heel of the Lib-Lab establishment, its refusal to see itself as the representative of all workers. As Pelling observed of Hardie's attack at his first Congress, its significance was that it was 'the prelude to the New Unionism' that was to come.[116]

Hardie's London visits were not confined to union business. He was also an enthusiastic tourist. On their first visit Bob Smillie and other miners trusted Hardie to show them the city, only to find that he got completely lost.[117] There were further disappointments in store. For even before Hardie was branded as a revolutionary by Broadhurst for his attack at the TUC (and hailed as a socialist in *Commonweal* for the same act)[118] he had decided to try to make contact in London with socialist forces. His intention, according to James Neil, was to look out the SDF and join it.[119] On his visits in 1887, therefore, Hardie listened to speakers and visited working men's clubs. What he found were speeches that were inflammatory (possibly hinting at violence). Others were crude. On the eve of the Queen's jubilee, for example, he heard her being attacked as 'that old woman' who has never spent 'ten minutes washing a shirt' in her life.[120]

He also found that beer seemed to be the 'dominant influence' in most clubs;[121] and at one meeting he asked the audience why they 'robbed themselves of their manhood by swilling in a public house', for before 'we could have socialism we have to have a fit and prepared people'.[122] Unfortunately his temperance antipathy got in the way of appreciating the working men's clubs in London, where a great deal of serious discussion was going on.

There was a further factor, where Hardie's objections had more substance. SDF clubs, as he soon found, featured speeches 'full of denunciation of . . . trade unionism' and it was this that he said 'repelled me'.[123] This was Hyndman's influence at work, a feature of the SDF

which Tom Mann, though he had now joined the Federation and was
actively working for it, found equally dismaying. Because the SDF was
so unsympathetic towards encouraging workers to improve their own
conditions, Mann had formed his own campaigning group which he
called the Eight Hours League.[124] Cunninghame Graham helped him
to organize and it was probably he who introduced Hardie to Tom
Mann on one of the London visits.

Mann gave Hardie a copy of his eight-hours pamphlet.[125] Hardie
found Tom Mann, with his religious and temperance background and
his strong union beliefs, much more to his taste. When he got back to
Cumnock, having decided not to join the SDF, he praised Mann for
being a 'moderate' and 'constitutional' socialist.[126] Mann later wrote
that had Hyndman not been so dogmatic about unions and had he
been prepared to work alongside working people's own organized
efforts, as his supposed mentor, Marx, had always urged, there would
have been no need for a Labour Party in Britain.[127]

The SDF may not have influenced Hardie but his London visits
reinforced his socialism, not least because he also met the legendary
Frederick Engels.[128] He was introduced by Eleanor Marx, who was
already a friend of Tom Mann's and of Cunninghame Graham's.[129]
She took Hardie to the house in Regent's Park Road where Engels
lived, receiving and corresponding with socialists the world over, and
exercising paternal care for Eleanor, as she laboured to continue her
father's work. His disagreement with Hyndman had continued and
when he met Hardie he roundly denounced the SDF,[130] confirming
(possibly even causing) Hardie's decision not to join it.

Later Eleanor wrote to Wilhelm Liebknecht, the German socialist
leader, that Hardie 'would interest you ... he gets £80 a year as a
secretary of his union – not much for a wife and four children ...
and is quite self-educated',[131] adding that both she and Engels thought
him 'a splendid fellow'.

Sharp though the rivalries were between radicals and socialists, and
between the various socialist groups – with the SDF fighting the
Socialist League, the League split over the issue of anarchism, Irish
socialists pitted against Parnellites, and the Fabians in turmoil over their
own political line – radical and socialist groups were always ready to
sink their differences on specific issues in most localities. In 1887 one
of the big issues continued to be unemployment, still a plague on
the capital. The misery of the poor was everywhere evident and all
during the year socialist and labour groups continued to parade the
unemployed through the West End, with petitions asking for public
works to give them employment. The object was to call the attention
of the influential to the suffering, but its effect was to alarm the affluent.
By the autumn of 1887 there were almost daily demonstrations, usually
in Trafalgar Square, followed by marches around the area. As the

Illustrated London News reported, shops and hotels were complaining bitterly of 'such occurrences frightening away' customers.[132]

Eventually a ban was declared on using Trafalgar Square for demonstrations.[133] The authorities were anxious to stop the demonstration planned for Sunday 13 November, where both Cunninghame Graham and John Burns, the trade union leader, were due to speak. Immediately the issue became instead the suppression of free speech, which galvanized all radical and socialist and labour forces. For nothing bonded disparate opinion like a threat to stop people meeting. On the 13th, from early morning contingents assembled all over London with wagons and banners and marching columns. They trooped separately in their thousands from every part of the compass, to converge on the square.

But the authorities were ready. The marchers from Battersea, Notting Hill and Rotherhithe were ambushed by the police as they came down the Haymarket. William Morris was with a group that was attacked just as it passed Clerkenwell Green, where police pursued demonstrators with clubs and cracked their banners in two. The police were soon backed by the army, who blocked all entrances to Trafalgar Square. Those at the head of the columns coming up Northumberland Avenue or Whitehall who finally got through, decided to turn and run rather than proceed.

It was a total rout and a terrible disappointment to many who watched. 'Entre nous,' wrote Eleanor Marx to her sister in Paris, 'the people behaved in a most cowardly fashion . . . It was sickening to see the men run.'[134] George Bernard Shaw, who was also there, called the flight 'abjectly disgraceful'[135] and everyone noted that only the Irish had stood their ground.[136] William Morris, according to a contemporary, found 'the rout of the thousands on whose resolution he had counted' brought him to recognize 'it would be far longer than a lifetime before social equality would be realized'.[137]

But not everyone ran. Cunninghame Graham, followed by John Burns, pushed his way through the police and military to gain the plinth, where he climbed up to speak. The military cut down both men with savage blows to the head. Both were arrested, removed to Rochester Row police station, and charged with infringing the Riot Act. The young barrister who came to defend them, Herbert Asquith, was little help. The courts were determined on an exemplary punishment and gave Cunninghame Graham six weeks, which he spent recovering from his head wounds, far more comfortable in a British prison, he claimed, than in most of the places he had been held captive on his travels. Cunninghame Graham was hailed as a hero by *The Miner*, as well as by every radical and socialist group. The day soon became known as Bloody Sunday, and prompted the formation of Britain's first national civil liberties association.[138]

*　　*　　*

Hardie's first yearly report as the secretary of the Scottish Miners'
Federation was submitted during the same month of November 1887.
The report showed evidence of the steady shift towards socialism
which Reid noted taking place during this same year.[139] 'Ours is
no old-fashioned sixpence a day agitation,' Hardie wrote, 'We aim at
the complete emancipation of work from the thraldom of wagedom'
with co-operative production 'under state management'.[140] Hardie
also set out his previous year's gruelling schedule on behalf of the
Federation, 77 meetings with 6,000 railway miles travelled.[141] During
the year he spoke with passion about the inevitable mining disaster[142]
that had occurred, once again due to owners' negligence. All owners
cared about was profit, he had written; only miners cared about other
miners.[143]

Hardie was unable to deliver the report personally.[144] In July
Sarah, then three-and-a-half, had become ill with fever, probably
scarlet fever,[145] for which nothing could be done but tend and wait.
Whenever there was serious illness in the family, Hardie dropped
everything and took a full hand in the nursing and bedside-sitting.
He and Lillie kept their vigil, but on 29 July he wrote to a friend that
although 'the doctor gave her up yesterday,' today she was 'livelier'. He
added, 'What a feeling it gives a parent to see his wee favourite writhing
in pain . . . and be forced to stand by helpless.' Sarah was very special
to him, 'She is not yet five but has intelligence far beyond her years'
and occupies the central place in 'my affections'.[146] Suddenly without
warning, Sarah worsened, her temperature shot up, convulsions came
on, and she died.[147] It was a death from which neither Hardie nor
Lillie ever recovered. As Stewart recalled over twenty-five years later,
it 'affected him very keenly and made it impossible for him at the time
to be interested in anything else'.[148] For both Lillie and Hardie 'the
one that was taken had no peer'[149] and her remains went with them
into their own communal grave.[150]

Only two of Hardie's biographers mention Sarah's existence, let
alone her death. Personal events often get elbowed out of male
political biography, which tends to centre on the pursuit of power.
No biography of a woman would omit the death of one of her
children. Although child death was more common at this time,
and few families escaped, living on with 'the sad blank in our
nursery', as Hardie's contemporary, W. H. Smith, referred to it,[151]
took the same courage whatever the income level. It was an event
that was also bound to have reinforced Hardie's social bitterness,
taking him back to the nightmare death of the small Duncan after
the excruciating poverty of the Glasgow slums. For this reason,
possibly, the Hardies had called their fourth child, born earlier that
year, Duncan.

Three years before, when a young Cumnock child had been found dead in the Lugar – strangled as it turned out – Hardie had written that 'my heart bleeds for the poor parents but trust they can look with the eye of faith and see their little one safe in the arms of Jesus'.[152] Since then Hardie the evangelical preacher had turned more to politics. We cannot know whether religion comforted him in his own child's death, but what the death did inaugurate in Hardie, however, was a committed interest in hydrotherapy, the science of cure by water. In this case it was not entirely without foundation, for it may have come to his knowledge – too late – that anyone with a sudden rise in fever, if immediately plunged into a cold bath, might have been saved. That it would have been the temperature drop rather than the water made no difference to Hardie, or to those who ran the many hydropathic institutes that were springing up all over Britain at this time. Water bathing was the therapy for every kind of ailment, succeeding the taking of waters internally, so popular earlier (and preceding fresh air and sunbathing, so popular later). Whenever Hardie felt unwell in later years (which was often) his immediate response was to sign into a hydro and spend as much time as possible being plunged in and out of baths. According to later testimony, Hardie became adept at this time at giving hydrotherapy treatment himself, and was so much in demand by neighbours in Cumnock for his 'cures' that he was even approached by the owner of a spa to see if he would work for him.[153]

But Hardie was not destined to stay in Cumnock and eventually returned to his political activity. Cunninghame Graham left a graphic description of him. Although only just over thirty Hardie looked 'old for his age . . . his face showed the kind of appearance of one who had worked hard and suffered, possibly from inadequate nourishment in his youth.' He was 'an almost ceaseless smoker'. He was not the ill-educated provincial which tradition has sometimes painted him, for 'Nothing in his address or speech showed his want of education . . . his accent was of Ayrshire . . . he took pride in it. He could, however . . . throw it aside.' His voice was 'high pitched but sonorous . . . and very far-carrying. He never used notes and never prepared a speech, leaving it all to . . . inspiration.' This meant wonderful moments, wrote Cunninghame Graham, but also 'very flat passages when he was not inspired'.[154]

Hardie always began his speeches with the straightforward words, 'Men' or 'Now Men'. Cunninghame Graham by contrast was fluent and witty, and completely disdainful of those who did not want to hear the social criticism he unleashed in the House of Commons, where he would begin his own speeches with phrases like, 'Gentlemen, I shall be brief but tedious'.[155] George Bernard Shaw admired him inordinately and wrote later that 'of all that silly Parliament there remains only one single dam', and it 'survived the front bench . . .

as the word of Cervantes survives the Dons . . . who put him, too, in prison'.[156]

Cunninghame Graham maintained he was only 'standing up for socialism in the House', and Shaw, hearing him once asked to withdraw a remark and answering, 'I never withdraw', said he 'promptly stole the potent phrase . . . and used it . . . for the Bulgarian hero of *Arms and the Man*'.[157]

Cervantes is an apt comparison, for Don Roberto behaved, and looked, like Don Quixote: tall, lean, trimly bearded, for ever on horseback seeking adventures, serving all in distress. But Hardie was no Sancho Panza, however much it might have seemed so to others. When Cunninghame Graham first welcomed him to the House of Commons at the start of 1887, Hardie wrote that the scene reminded him of when Carlyle had brought Emerson to see his first debate in Parliament.[158] Hardie saw himself as anyone's equal. He was ready for the national stage.

4
NATIONAL AND INTERNATIONAL STAGE

The steady growth of support for socialism in the 1880s involved some crucial decisions for its converts, whether they came to it through Owenite co-operation, Georgeite land reform, Christian brotherhood, secular progressivism, industrial organization or Marxist economics. A key question then, and still, was whether bourgeois democracy was worth bothering about, or whether, as William Morris thought, it was better to accept 'the futility of sending . . . Socialists or anyone else to Parliament'[1] when what was needed was agitation, education and organization throughout society. It was not merely a matter of revolutionary versus constitutional activity, but of what new forms of government could be developed out of the old. Marx had regarded this as an open question, particularly in Britain and the USA, where suffrage was so advanced. Others believed it would always be necessary to bypass bourgeois institutions; while the largest group, including Hardie, was prepared from the start to try to capture Parliament for the people.

The question arose directly for Hardie when the MP for Mid-Lanark retired in early 1888 and a by-election was declared. Mid-Lanark was a large area with 9,000 voters, including many newly enfranchised miners, taking in the district where Hardie grew up and had since become known as a miners' representative. Among other issues, it again raised the question of how far the Liberal Party was in any way suitable to carry the new forces for change.

It was on the cards that Hardie would want to stand. Not only was he already putting himself forward as a miners' nominee for several parliamentary seats,[2] but, as Reid suggests, he already had a 'strategy' and programme worked out by 1888 for a new Labour Party programme in Scotland,[3] which included specific demands on behalf of miners that needed parliamentary legislation. Hardie had no reason to believe they did not support him. For example, he and Cunninghame Graham, still continuing to move around together, had been given a standing ovation when they appeared at a miners' conference in the autumn of 1887.[4]

Cunninghame Graham was also speaking of the need for 'a labour party in the House', and assuming it would be socialist in perspective.[5] By January 1888, Hardie was saying there were 'two schools of politicians' to choose from: 'the one individualist . . . the other Socialistic', the first decrying the state's help in relieving distress or regulating the conditions of work, the other 'recognizing Parliament as the servant of the people and the protector of the weak against the strong'.[6] There is no doubt that Hardie's romantic vision of parliamentary renewal had been disturbed by having seen the real thing in action, where he had looked down not only on havering Lib-Lab MPs, but had seen his father's hero, Charles Bradlaugh, now an elderly anti-socialist and full of wealthy display, lolling about and point-scoring with the best.[7]

Hardie had seen at first-hand that existing Lib-Lab MPs were unlikely to advocate the range of changes required, since only proposals that had the approval of the Liberal Party leadership could be advocated. Thus Hardie's intervention in Mid-Lanark was not just to get a working-class candidate accepted as an alternative to the standard middle-class Liberal but also to get Labour candidates to present – and press independently in Parliament – a programme dealing with labour grievances. For ultimately Mid-Lanark was also about the capacity of Parliament to deal with the problems presented by the 'condition of the people', as Hardie called it.

Who better to try than one who knew these conditions? Hardie's intentions had already been made public by Cunninghame Graham at a meeting in September 1887 in Kirkintilloch – with Hardie sitting on the platform next to him. He said Hardie 'was not going to stand as a Liberal, a Conservative or a Unionist . . . [but] as a . . . working man . . . who had starved and sweated'.[8]

Hardie announced he was seeking the Liberal nomination, and in a note to the chair of the local Liberals asked 'respectfully' to offer himself in the hope 'that the desire of the labourers to be represented by a man of themselves will not be overlooked'.[9] In Hardie's case, however, neither the national nor local Liberal party was prepared to accept him, not least because they doubted that he would always support the Liberal Whip or define 'labour questions' as they did. In the event the issue was settled by local middle-class Liberals who wanted a respectable radical rather than a working-class hothead. They duly nominated what Nan later called 'a careerist lawyer from London'.[10]

To the dismay of the 'wire pullers' (Hardie always called the Liberal leadership by this popular epithet), Hardie did not quit the contest but campaigned on, activating the Liberal leaders to press him to step down. Hardie himself wrote out an account of two attempts, for which he said Bob Smillie would vouch.[11] The first involved a visit from T. R. Threlfall of the TUC Parliamentary Committee, who had come to support Hardie, since his committee had now set up the Labour Electoral Association to get more working-class candidates. But Threlfall failed to show up for the meeting and arrived only later that night, having been waylaid by Liberals at their headquarters in the George Hotel. He was very excited.

'I've settled it,' he told Hardie. 'I've been in conference with them all evening and it is all fixed up.'

'Conference with whom? Settled what?' Hardie asked.

'In conference with the Liberals,' he replied, '. . . and you're to retire.'

Hardie wrote that he rose to his feet with such a look that Threlfall 'ceased speaking' abruptly; and promptly left for London.

A few days later, according to Hardie, another emissary arrived, a radical Liberal who had been helping Hardie up to that point.[12] He persuaded Hardie to come to the George Hotel, where the Liberal Party's Treasurer, who had come from London, was waiting to assure him that a seat at the next general election would be his, his election expenses would be paid, along with a guaranteed salary of £300 a year — if he stood down now. He gave Hardie names of other Labour men who had already accepted this offer. Again, Hardie drew himself up: 'I explained why this proposal was offensive.' The treasurer 'was surprised but courteous'.[13]

Even though it is likely that Hardie had already decided to continue, even then he claimed he was prepared to stand down if Liberals would agree to balloting all Liberal voters before the next election (in effect, he proposed an American form of primary) on the issue of whether they wanted a labour man to represent the Liberals.[14] Frederick Schnadhorst, secretary of the National Liberal Federation, who also journeyed up to Glasgow, declined to concede this, no doubt believing Liberals had offered Hardie enough. Only when this was refused was the matter at an end. Hardie's representatives in these negotiations informed the press that Hardie supporters now 'pledged Mr Hardie to go to the poll'.[15]

Hardie was now left with an impossible task, to convince the electorate that he would be different from other Liberals and yet would be the same. He would 'press . . . the claims of the people' and 'agitate for every reform likely to promote their welfare', while at the same time he would always vote Liberal in the House, as he was a lifelong supporter of the Liberal Party.[16] His programme included standard Liberal fare like Home Rule (with which he hoped to impress the large numbers of Irish voters) as well as 'advanced' proposals for land nationalization and the eight-hour day. If anything, Hardie erred on the side of conservatism, as he always did during election campaigns, since a candidate bent on winning will often lean to the middle.

But it was to no avail. Although Hardie's Election Address was 'by no means a revolutionary document', as Emrys Hughes pointed out later,[17] it was treated as so extreme that no local printer would put it out.[18] Hardie was already branded. *The Times* had commented on the startling fact that only local working miners had signed his nomination papers,[19] as if this was an affront to society. Soon, however, the complaint was that outsiders were running him because a number of radicals, socialists and trade unionists, attracted by his stand, had come to help: Cunninghame Graham, G. B. Clark, Bob Smillie, John Mahon, Michael Davitt and, last but not least, on his way north to take up a new job organizing for the SDF in Newcastle, Tom Mann. By now Tom Mann was fully converted to socialism and believed that however caring employers were in private and however much they gave to the poor, it was all 'nullified . . . every hour of the day by the profit making system they were identified with as businessmen'.[20]

Mann wanted to change that system, others merely to achieve specific reforms. From one such organization in London, the newly formed Scottish Home Rule Association – because of Hardie's proposals for a Scottish assembly – came support from its secretary, James Ramsay MacDonald.[21] Although most of Hardie's supporters were local, the opposition (whose own candidates were both outsiders) used these additional Hardie supporters as propaganda about reds and outsiders taking over. Posters were put around the constituency (reminiscent of some campaigns a hundred years later) warning voters that if they voted for Hardie they would be controlled by 'Londoner loons'.[22]

There was also anxiety and mystery over funding. Henry Champion, now running his own 'Labour Party' section of the Labour Electoral Association, was soon on hand with offers of cash. In the space of three weeks he wrote to Hardie fourteen times, assuring him he would find any money needed, including Mann's expenses[23] and that he knew several 'wealthy men' ready to give it,[24] meanwhile asking Hardie not to consort with Cunninghame Graham.[25] Hardie ignored this and asked Cunninghame Graham to speak for him.[26] Polling day was 27 April and it was not until 13 April that £300 was sent by Edward Harford on behalf of Champion.[27] Hardie publicly announced it had come from the Labour Electoral Association, but six days later Threlfall and the Association had to deny it was from them.[28] Hardie supporters became alarmed. One wrote privately to Cunninghame Graham, 'Where do they get the money from? We have a clear right to know.'[29] But there was no clear answer. To add to the mystery, a large sum was sent by a John Law, whom no one could trace. Law was really Margaret Harkness, a friend of Eleanor Marx and Olive Shreiner, who wrote socialist novels (which both Hardie and Engels had reviewed).[30] When she did come forward to reveal her identity,[31] it was long after the election. In any case, even if she had sent the money, it was only £100. Where had the rest come from? All too many assumed it was the Tories who were paying, and this could have been possible. Hardie was remiss in not concerning himself on this issue, but behaved, as he always did, as if the Lord would provide and what he called a 'gullible public' not question too closely.[32]

With the splits and wrangles and charges and counter-charges of the campaign, many voters, not knowing which way to turn, and hearing Hardie one minute stressing his Liberal allegiance, the next claiming the Liberal Party would one day 'be dead and buried' and only a Labour Party would survive,[33] decided in the main to stick to previous electoral loyalties.

Hardie lost badly, gaining only 617 votes. (Although 8 per cent of the vote could be enough to make Liberals cautious in marginal seats in future.) At the time the victory was treated very much as a great Liberal event, where it was generally concluded that a potential danger had been overcome. Hardie, however, treated it as a great Labour event. His tactic was to greet the result exactly as if he had won. He immediately toured the district praising the 'gallant 600' who had voted for him and 'raised the condition of the peoples to first place'.[34] He told them that 'in days to come the great Liberal victory in Mid-Lanark will be remembered only in connection with the stand you made'. Little would he know how even that was to be exceeded, as in subsequent years the numbers who claimed to have been among the 617 rose to thousands.

At the time, however, to Hardie's family – Lillie, Mary, his brothers, even Jamie, now seven – it must have been a gigantic anxiety. First, the humiliating defeat, and next the funding problems and the prospects of debt (even if he had been elected, MPs received no salaries). There was also the denigration in papers like the *North British Daily Mail* and the *Scottish Leader* and the additional money worries of a libel suit that Hardie had begun against the latter, with attendant lawyers' fees to pay.[35] Almost certainly, the episode seemed like a nightmare; but not for Hardie. Looking back later, he claimed he had had 'more fun than he had ever enjoyed before or since'.[36]

If Lillie and the family thought they were in for a quieter period politically, they were mistaken. Hardie quickly became addicted to political struggle. Smillie records Hardie took only one day off and that 'two days after', he and Hardie and Cunninghame Graham met 'to mingle our tears' and 'call a conference of trade unionists and socialists to lay the foundation of a society independent of all other political parties'.[37] By now Hardie had developed a sufficiently clear understanding that the Liberals would never be able to represent working people, even if every representative they chose was a union leader or common labourer. After a busy spring spent meeting and working to set it up, on 25 August at a public meeting in Glasgow the Scottish Labour Party (SLP) went public.[38]

Cunninghame Graham was president, Dr G. B. Clark vice-president, John Ferguson treasurer, and Hardie secretary. The first was a land-owner, the second a cotton manufacturer (as well as an MP and land reformer), and the third a Liberal Glasgow councillor (as well as chair of Davitt's Irish National League in Scotland). Only Hardie could possibly be called a worker (and he was a miners' agent and part-time journalist). Nowhere, press representatives commented pointedly, was there to be seen a 'horny handed . . . son of toil'.[39] Behind this flippant comment was a serious question, destined to come up repeatedly in labour politics: whether membership of organizations set up to promote the working-class interest should be limited to that class.

Luckily Hardie had sufficient ideological wit to understand that mere promotion of working-class candidates was not a socialist position. It is the programme that is central, and while this must be addressed to improving workers' lives, and needed working-class people to formulate it (as he insisted to the Labour Electoral Association at this same time),[40] anyone could advocate it. He thus poured scorn on the suggestion that a Labour Party 'should consist of the begrimed ones only',[41] writing that the Labour Party in Scotland 'exists for the purpose of educating people politically and securing the return to Parliament and all local bodies of Members pledged to its programme. If, therefore, anyone, peasant or peer, is found willing to accept the programme and work with the party, his help will be gladly accepted.'[42]

At the launch of the SLP Hardie formally set out the Party's programme: disestablishment of the Church; reform of the Civil

Service; graduated income tax; free education at all stages; control of the liquor trade; eight-hour-day legislation; national insurance for working people; wage arbitration courts; legislation providing homes; land reform with a tax on large landholdings; nationalization of the railways, banks and mineral rights; and abolition of the Monarchy. Morgan comments that there is 'little that was specifically socialist' in it,[43] but it is hard to envisage such a programme without the movement towards socialism in the 1880s.

Although the Scottish Labour Party lacked a defined following (even more so once the Scottish Miners' Federation began to disintegrate), it promoted Hardie's conviction that parties should have programmes and only those who support the programmes should stand in their name. It also forwarded the idea of independence from other parties, though those who assembled on that launching day differed a great deal in the extent to which they were prepared to be independent rather than to continue negotiating with the Liberals around individual seats. Everything depended on how many real 'sons of toil' the SLP would attract.

The workers who were destined to show the way forward at this time were not in Scotland, however, but in London. In 1888 trade was still improving and those most impoverished were finding the courage to organize. One of the first groups to rebel were London's matchgirls, whose success in carrying off a strike for higher wages and safer working conditions against their employers, Bryant and May, electrified the labour and socialist movements, as well as the general public – not just because this was an unskilled trade paying appalling wages but because the workers were all young women. The match-girls' leader was one of those present in November at the TUC Parliamentary Committee's week-long International Workers Congress in London,[44] the first such congress it had ever organized. In the chair was George Shipton, a Lib-Lab trade unionist MP noted for his hostility to socialism[45] who wanted this to be a gathering of 'possibilists', the nickname given to French right-wing labourists who opposed the 'impossibilist' socialist wing led by Jules Guesde.[46] Although it was an international gathering, with trade unionists from most European countries, German and Austrian trade unionists (the most socialist) did not get to this occasion owing to the anti-socialist laws still in force in these countries. One who protested about this was Keir Hardie, who came as the Ayrshire Miners' delegate, along with Cunninghame Graham, sponsored by the Labour Electoral Association. Hardie also spotted the glad-handing John Burns, a 'thick-set, black-haired tyke ... with a voice of ... modulated thunder' who 'keeps running about and appears to know everybody'.[47]

This was Hardie's first international conference and he made some important discoveries. The first was that he was an internationalist at all. Previously he had occupied a position of hostility to foreign workers because he saw them only in the context of imported blackleg or cheap labour. Understandable in itself, his campaigning had been unedifyingly xenophobic against 'beastly, filthy foreigners' who ate garlic and for whom 'decent men are turned adrift'.[48] These opinions were virtually stopped in their tracks by this week of fraternizing with fellow trade unionists, comparing notes on their respective struggles. Thus Hardie, the trade unionist whose only earlier international dealings had been to get agreement between unions to stop foreign labour coming in,[49] proposed at this conference that there should be an international organization of all trades.[50] He made further interesting discoveries. One was that in contrast to the TUC establishment present, 'all the continental trade unionists were socialists to a man!'[51] What's more, all their delegates knew what they wanted, while British ones did not. Back in Scotland his message was new, 'henceforth there can be no more alienation between British and continental workers' — to which he added, 'the Broadhurst School has now . . . [to] . . . accept the new gospel or go down', for 'socialism is in the ascendant and everyone knows it!'[52]

Another new experience was that a substantial percentage of those attending were women. He noted 'the tall, good-looking lassie with . . . clear-cut features who leads the match girls' union' and Annie Besant (who along with Cunninghame Graham had helped their efforts) wearing a red tam-o'-shanter on her grey hair.[53]

Hardie's political life to date had been in organizations dominated by men, centring around mining, the Liberal caucus and radical clubs, with no women involved. The new Scottish Labour Party had no women. Indeed, in mining, the absence of women was a sign of progress, since one of the few pieces of progressive legislation earlier had been laws forbidding their employment underground. Suddenly, Hardie saw women who wanted to take part in labour and socialist work just as men did, another change fostered by the rise of social consciousness during the 1880s.

So many women delegates in their own right, as well as in the galleries, would have been unlikely even ten years earlier. In London a play from the pen of a social democrat opened that year, the portrait of women's dark position in a society which did not recognize their aspirations. Ibsen's *A Doll's House*, followed by *Hedda Gabler* a few years later (with Shaw and John Burns at its first night), later became favourites with Hardie.[54] The 1888 Congress, however, was one of the first events where he would have experienced women with equal status since the days of his Evangelical Union work. He rediscovered his commitment to female company.

He also met Eleanor Marx again, for she was translating the proceedings of the Congress, a job for which she was constantly in demand, being fluent in English German and French, knowledgeable about labour and socialist issues. After every speech at international conferences, there was a break, while delegates congregated around the translator speaking in their language. The task was very demanding, to which Eleanor added the work of translating political tracts, including her father's work. She lived with Edward Aveling, a lecturer on scientific subjects, equally active in socialist and trade union circles. They were unable to marry as his first wife was still alive, but were accepted as husband and wife within the socialist world. Despite Eleanor's non-stop translating work (she had only just completed a translation of Ibsen's *An Enemy Of Society*),[55] she and Aveling were constantly insolvent and had to rely, as her parents had done, on Engels's generosity.

It is quite possible that Eleanor Marx once again took Hardie to see Engels during this week in London. Certainly Hyndman, when he later delivered his vitriolic attacks on the circle around Engels, which he called the 'Marx family' (as if it had been the mafia) chose to include along with the John Burns, Tom Mann, Cunninghame Graham, and the Marx-Avelings, the name of Keir Hardie.[56]

The Marx-Avelings were not the only couple Hardie met at the 1888 conference. Also there were a couple typical of the middle-class radicals who were converting to socialism. The Pankhursts were from Manchester. Richard, a barrister, had been an evangelical Baptist[57] who had encountered the poor as a Sunday School teacher. It changed his life. He deserted religion and joined both the SDF and the Fabians almost as soon as they were formed. In 1885 he stood for Parliament as an advanced radical, who went about campaigning, literally, with a soapbox to put down on street corners. He was made to pay for deserting his class by the press, who denounced him as an atheist, republican and revolutionary, the *Spectator* claiming, 'Dr Pankhurst is substantially a French Red, not an English Radical at all'.[58] He was defeated.

Pankhurst was at the congress with his wife Emmeline, who was twenty years younger, the wilful, beautiful daughter of an industrialist. When she found her father would not be leaving her the money she expected, she never spoke to him again. She was unsentimental but charming, whereas her husband was kindly but difficult; and both were impractical.

Like the Hardies, the Pankhursts had had all their children in the 1880s. Just a year after the Hardies had lost their small Sarah, the Pankhursts lost Frank, who died from diphtheria at the age of four.[59] The remaining children, Christabel, Sylvia, Adela and Harry, were brought up as socialists and strict atheists. Dr Pankhurst taught them they were on earth only to serve others. Emmeline taught them to keep up with events in the political world. Sylvia, their second daughter, was taken to her first meeting at the age of eight, to hear Henry Hyndman speaking on socialism in unsalubrious rooms over a London stable.

Emmeline loved attention and her real interest was public life. She was well dressed, regal, and well mannered, with a voice that commanded attention; while her husband was small and dark, with a voice like a woman's.[60] Emmeline persuaded him to move to London where life would be more interesting, and at this time they were living in Russell Square, where Emmeline maintained a salon. The Marx-Avelings, Tom Mann, John Burns, Annie Besant, Wilhelm Liebknecht and William Morris had all been visitors.

Dr Pankhurst had one further passion. He was committed to women's suffrage and had drafted a Bill to promote it as far back as 1870, which Jacob Bright tried unsuccessfully to introduce in the Commons.[61] The women's issue continued to gain support. In 1884 even Gladstone's daughter, Mary, had said, 'I am come round to it',[62] though her father had yet to offer tacit support to the 'Appeal Against Women's Suffrage',[63] where the signatories would include Beatrice Potter, later Mrs Sydney Webb.[64] Not all were in their final positions by 1888.

It is more than probable that the assured and resplendent Emmeline dazzled Keir Hardie, though on this occasion he appears not to have found extra time to visit her home. The congress kept him busy. As often happens, the smallest item gave rise to the most prolonged argument, in this case the date of the next convening, which the organizing committee wanted to hold the July following in Paris on the 100th anniversary of the French Revolution. Unfortunately, this was the day that the continental social democratic parties – in their own International Socialist Labour Congress – had decided to make the first meeting of the new Second International. Not only at the London conference but for the next nine months the rivalry between the two conferences flared. It led to 'splits and divisions . . . libels and intrigues . . . lies, denunciations, muddles and manoeuvres . . . beyond all reason', according to Eleanor Marx's biographer.[65] On the one side were the British trade unions, on the other British socialists, a political fault-line that runs still through the landscape. It was complicated then as now by the fact that many of the trade unionists were also socialists, and socialists themselves divided between the constitutional side, including the Fabians, and the extra-parliamentary. 'Continental' Marxists were further divided into non-insurrectionists and revolutionaries. Hyndman managed to muddy the waters completely, for while he ran the British equivalent of a continental Marxist party, he chose – because of his running feud with the 'Marx family' – to side with the possibilist Fabians and TUC in the matter of the conferences. Eleanor Marx, chief organizer of the continental side in London, found it a choice entirely in character for a Tory Socialist (as she always called him) who did not like foreigners, particularly Germans.

While this tug-of-war was going on for ideological allegiance, with delegates like Hardie being wooed by both sides, British workers were breaking out of some old bonds. In London's East End, now attracting an ever larger influx of unskilled labour, conditions were forcing workers to act and were throwing up new leaders. In Canning Town the Beckton Gas works employed Will Thorne, a man who had gone to work as a child at the age of six in Birmingham, but later came to London looking for work. Life was little better for him and the SDF seemed to speak to his condition. He joined it in 1884 and was befriended by Eleanor Marx, who was still helping him to learn to read in 1889.[66] Thorne had a wife and five children, one named after Karl Marx.

In 1889 conditions in the Beckton Gas Works were now oppressive to a degree. New technology had brought in compressed air machines that required unbroken tending – twenty-four hours a day, 365 days a year – like a site with blast furnaces that could never be allowed to go cold. All shifts were twelve hours each, continuous round the clock seven days a week. Thorne and his colleagues, influenced by arguments Tom Mann was making on the eight-hour day, became convinced that this would be the single biggest improvement they could get. Since eight-hour shifts would mean the private gas companies increasing the labour force by a third, none would agree to any change when approached individually.

Thorne decided to organize workers across all the gas companies and on 31 March 1889 called the first meeting at Beckton in Canning Town. A band played and 'a big enthusiastic crowd' gathered, with anticipation that was 'electric', Thorne later recalled.[67] Almost every man present paid a shilling and 'joined' the non-existent union on the spot. With the money Thorne set up headquarters in a temperance bar in Barking Road[68] and went in turn to recruit members at every other gas company in London. National attention followed when John Burns and Tom Mann came to help out in this work.

Later came Ben Tillett, a wharf worker who had earlier been 'starved out of the city' of Bristol by worklessness.[69] Two years earlier he had started a small union of his own in London for dock workers. He called it the Tea Coopers and General Labourers' Association. Gas workers, like dock workers, had no ancient craft traditions, medieval pedigrees, apprenticeships or associations. Thorne and his colleagues recognized this in the name they chose for their new union, the National Union of Gas Workers and General Labourers of Great Britain and Ireland.

So relentless was their organizing – and so appalling the conditions men had to face – that within a few months over 90 per cent of gas workers had thrown their shilling into the hat. Thorne and his colleagues were able to send a petition to the main gas companies north of the Thames. The workers asked for eight-hour shifts and no Sunday work except where paid double rates. The companies, which had a long record of sweating and victimization of workers, knew the union was in a position to stop production, and they had to agree to the changes, having been completely caught out by the successful organization among supposedly 'unorganizable' workers; and, possibly, they were aware that electricity was coming in to compete for their market. The first area of Britain to have electric lighting, Kensington, had switched on in 1887. The first eight-hour shift at a gasworks started on 31 May 1889. Those who might have thought the matchgirls' action the year before a fluke were now aware that 'the new unionism' had arrived. Soon it was spreading. Eric Hobsbawm later called it labour's historical 'turning point'.[70]

These events were going on while Tom Mann, Eleanor Marx, John Burns and Cunninghame Graham were meeting in London at Eleanor Marx's house at 65 Chancery Lane to plan their campaign to get as many trade unionists as possible to the Second International. Eleanor wrote to her sister in Paris, 'I'm very glad we have Keir Hardy [sic].'[71]

Engels and Hardie had been corresponding during the winter, possibly to ensure that very attendance. Engels sent Hardie money and pamphlets to distribute to Scottish workers; the pamphlets were almost certainly Edouard Bernstein's *The International Working Men's Congress of 1889 – A Reply to Justice*,[72] for Hyndman's propaganda for the possibilists had continued. According to Eleanor, Hardie 'helped us immensely in Scotland'.[73] He and Engels continued to share their distrust of the SDF and Hardie reported that Hyndman's 'social democracy as an organized force in Scotland is nowhere'.[74] Although Scotland was not having the same upsurge of union activity that occurred in England, agitation levels were rising. By mid-June Hardie reported to Engels that Ayrshire miners were on the verge of a new strike.[75]

The correspondence was very much at arm's length, however, Engels addressing Hardie at first as 'Dear Sir', while he wrote 'Cher Citoyen Guesde' to the French socialist leader.[76] In subsequent letters there was less formality and Engels told Hardie about the ruses and wiles of capitalists in Europe, to which Hardie replied that the 'deductions for improperly filled tubs and apparent as distinguished from real earnings . . . might have been written of Ayrshire'.[77] But Hardie was a lax correspondent – by contrast to the fluent Engels, who seemed to reply by return of post. He apologized to Engels for his old failing, 'procrastination'.[78]

Engels was unconcerned; he had what he wanted, both Hardie and

Cunninghame Graham had added their names to the impossibilists' list, and Hardie had denounced Hyndman for printing his name under his possibilists' column in *Justice*. At the same time Hardie told Engels that he hoped that when the two conferences assembled 'it will be possible to bring about a reconciliation'.[79]

Long before anyone left for Paris, Eleanor Marx had reported that Hyndman 'was staggered when he heard that all Socialist Europe is practically with us'.[80] Eleanor's only fear at this point was that Hardie might not 'get money to be at the congress'.[81] Eleanor didn't know Keir Hardie. He never let shortage of funds stop him going anywhere.

Hardie sailed for his first trip abroad on a hot July day. Cunninghame Graham and Burns were both delayed a day celebrating at a Gas Workers' picnic, so Hardie, representing the Ayrshire miners, went with Bruce Glasier, representing Scotland's Socialist League. On the way over they decided they would try to go to both congresses.[82] So too the Pankhursts, who were also attending as observers. The Second International was the main attraction, however, the congress everyone wanted to see, where all the important leaders had assembled: Wilhelm Liebknecht, Edouard Bernstein (editor of *Sozialdemokrat*), Auguste Bebel, Jules Guesde, as well as Marx's son-in-law, Paul Lafargue, one of the leaders of the French Workers Party.

At the first session the crowd was so great it could not squeeze into the small assembly hall hired. Hurriedly the venue was changed. The British contingent that Hardie and Glasier joined included William Morris from the Socialist League and Edward Aveling from the East Finsbury Club, one of the radical clubs which had gone over to socialism (as a result of the diligent lecturing of Aveling and Eleanor). Also present were Clara Zetkin, the widow of a German socialist, and Edward Carpenter, a Cambridge cleric (one of the first gay socialists to declare himself) who had renounced academic life to adopt a socialist lifestyle, sent by the Sheffield Socialist Society. Sponsoring organizations were essential, for they decided entrance and entitlement to vote. Numbers were strictly limited and every occasion, including the Second International, began with disputes about accreditation.

Joining the possibilists' meeting at a much smaller hall were delegates from some of Britain's radical clubs, the Fabians, and representatives of the TUC's Parliamentary Committee, plus, of course, Hyndman's SDF, continuing their feud with continental socialists. Most possibilists wanted to federate the two congresses but Hyndman refused to consider it,[83] backed by supporters of Paul Brousse of the anti-socialist Federation of French Workers. Back at the Second International there were also arguments for and against merging with the possibilists, which took up most of the first two days and were inconclusive.[84] When delegates got down to work, they debated child and female labour and the abolition of standing armies. But the main resolution was support for an eight-hour day for all workers. Cunninghame Graham spoke on the last day (in French, Spanish and English), Hardie on several days. Hardie also presented a report on the British trade union movement, which he had no hesitation in speaking for in the absence of the TUC.

The impossibilists' most protracted debate was once again over the smallest matter, and arose while they were airing the idea of a general international strike. It was the date workers should adopt for their own demonstrations each year. In the United States a congress of the American Federation of Labour had met in St Louis in December 1888 and chosen 1 May 1889 as the date of the first general strike of America's new unionism. Some in Paris thus proposed 1 May be taken over as a yearly workers' day in Europe as well. Others argued for the day to be the Sunday nearest to 1 May[85] in order to avoid a conflict for religious workers. Reminiscent of passions generated by the early Christians' debate over the date of Easter, recorded so graphically by Bede, the debate over the date of 'May Day' was protracted. Indeed, it still goes on. A temporary solution was reached in Paris for an international strike to take place on 1 May 1890.

The Second International ended on an upbeat note with a 500-strong march through Paris to lay a wreath on the Communards' graves at Père Lachaise cemetery. The ribbon read, 'The Commune is dead. Long live the Commune'. Hardie was one of the marchers, and so was Glasier, at long last able to pay his respects to his youthful heroes. Later there was a banquet and dancing and the customary singing of the 'Marseillaise', still the hymn of most revolutionary and radical movements, whatever the nationality.

Much mythology attaches to this conference as far as Keir Hardie goes, many writers since stressing that this is when he made it clear he was not a Marxist. The quotation taken is from his speech on the eight-hour day[86] that 'progress must come . . . of something more tangible than talking of a bloody revolution in which nobody here believes and which would do no good there if inaugurated tomorrow'. By tangible he meant the eight-hour day, a cause everyone supported. Thus his Paris intervention was no different from the views he had sent only a few weeks earlier to Engels: 'Mr Graham's eight hours agitation has made more progress here (in Scotland) in six months than the SDF has made in six years or could make in sixty.'[87]

All the negative references are clearly to the SDF and not to Marxism, and to the SDF revolution-around-the-corner, upon which Hyndman – and many gurus of the left since – sought to hook hearers. Hardie deplored this, and so did the 'Marx family'. Nor can Hardie's words be interpreted to mean he deplored ideology, when he had written to Engels specifically that, 'We are not opposed to ideals and recognizing . . . their power in inspiring men, but we are more concerned in the realization of an ideal than in dreaming of it.'[88] It was in this vein that Hardie addressed the Second International, on the importance of achieving practical results, as the gas workers had just done, and with which Engels concurred. It had little to do with Marxism, in which Hardie as yet had little interest.

His intervention had much more to do with pacifism. The word 'bloody' is to be taken literally, not as an expletive. His view that armed conflict was madness was not new. He might even have held still to his earlier view that he would rather live under the 'autocratic rule of the Russian emperor' than the 'democratic rule of an unprincipled, ignorant mob'.[89] Although he might now be writing, as he did earlier that year[90] that 'We don't believe it is possible to reconcile the antagonistic interest of the capitalist and the worker', this did not mean he advocated armed conflict to reconcile these interests. Some in Paris might well have done so. At the Second International was an enormous range of opinion on the issue of armed struggle and its relation to social purpose. Hardie was luckier than most. As a war resister his views were clear, he was opposed to such means. Pacifism was not a socialist belief any more than it was a constitutionalist belief. It was Hardie's personal belief, easier to win support for in Britain than on the continent. Britain had not had armed conflict internally on a grand scale for 200 years. On the continent experience of civil conflict was recent. States were less liberal and the hope that peaceful progress was possible was less widespread. Britain at this time was considered a liberal state where outcasts from less liberal states that still outlawed socialists, like Marx himself, found a home. But anti-socialism was taking hold and Hardie's intervention was important on this account.

Hardie's attendance at the Second International was important to his development, not only because it widened his outlook but also because it brought him into contact with socialist leaders throughout Europe, with whom he would collaborate until the end of his days. He always got on better with continental colleagues than with many of those with whom he worked in Britain, perhaps because they did not have to work closely. The occasion also increased his stature in his own eyes. From this time onwards he was to be a prophet honoured in many other places even if not in his own country. That the International had not quite understood what country that really was, annoyed him. Most speakers adopted the common practice then (still common in the United States) of using the word 'England' to stand for Britain. Hardie was thus determined to enlighten continental comrades on this point. Every time someone in the International's proceedings said 'English', Hardie resolutely rose to his feet and shouted, 'And Scots!'[91]

After Hardie had returned to Scotland from the International's meeting in 1889 London once more became the focus of events in the labour world. On 14 August dock workers were unloading a ship called *Lady Armstrong*. Poorly paid at 5d. an hour, the job was taking many hours over a day's work. When the men heard that the customary overtime payment was no longer to be given, they walked off. The next day they refused to return, reporting instead to Ben Tillett, who sent a telegram to Tom Mann.[92] Along with Mann came John Burns and Will Thorne; and it was agreed the men should stay out and some way be found to keep them going. Within three days 10,000 further dock workers had joined in the action. The long-smouldering grievances of a degraded work system – the despised 'call-on' that permitted employers to pick and choose workers on a daily basis and send the rest home workless, with a sixpence wage only possible if many extra hours were worked (and now being stopped) – suddenly flared to life. A strike committee was set up at the Wades' Arms, run by Mrs Hickey and her family. Since many of the dockers were Irish, and so was Mrs Hickey, she said she would keep 'a shillelah handy' just in case.[93] It was never needed. The committee was a disciplined group, each with an allotted task. Tillett and Burns organized to keep the strike going. Cunninghame Graham and many others filled the speaking slots, to keep up enthusiasm. Mann was put in charge of the food tickets which strikers could redeem to keep their families alive. For workers it was a case of nothing to lose. The motto during the strike was, 'It's better to go idle and starve than to work and starve'.[94]

All the same, most of the effort went in raising money to keep the strikers from starvation. It was raised from collections, benefits, street boxes and newspaper funds. The new international labour networks were tapped, and donations came from France, Belgium, Germany, the USA, and included over £30,000 from the flourishing Australian trade unions. Some money went on propaganda and there was even a little kept back to pay off the blacklegs brought in from Liverpool and Glasgow, who were met at railway stations as they arrived and sent straight back on the same trains.[95] The strike organizers missed very few tricks.

Soon the dockers were joined by those working in associated trades and women poured in to help as well. Eleanor Marx was not just a casual visitor. Together with John Burns's wife, Patricia, she acted throughout as correspondent and minute-taker for the strike committee. The two kept the books and undertook the vital task of liaising with supporters the world over. Thorne, Tillett and Mann all paid tribute to Eleanor, who worked 'unceasingly, literally day and night', every day, Sundays included.[96] Thorne recalled that both Eleanor and Patricia Burns had to stay beyond the hours of public transport and every evening 'walked bravely late at night . . . to their distant homes'.[97]

On 1 September, a Sunday, there was a meeting in Hyde Park to which 100,000 came, many dockers walking all the way from East London. Mann, Burns, Tillett and Cunninghame Graham all spoke, but according to Cunninghame Graham it was upon 'Mrs Aveling [that the] eyes of the women fixed . . . as she spoke of the miseries of the dockers' homes'.[98] Hardie in Scotland followed events closely, as did Engels, who was away for his health on the south coast.

Engels wrote to Eleanor's sister in Paris, explaining that the dockers were 'the broken down ones . . . the lowest stratum' of British workers. To see these 'poor famished . . . creatures who bodily fight amongst each other every morning for admission to work' not only 'organize for resistance' but 'draw after them into the strike all and every trade of the East End in any way connected with shipping', and even more incredibly, 'hold out above a week and terrify the wealthy and the dock companies – that is a revival I am proud to have lived to see'.[99]

The wealthy and the owners of shipping companies were rightly terrified of the new unionism, so different from the old deferential skilled workforce whose leaders Parliament had learned to tame so well. The new unionists were not few, but many; unskilled, not time-served; they included women as well as men, and most important, they were not rioting, they were organizing. Alarmingly, they were also enjoying wide support from the middle classes. A decade of socialist propaganda about workers' intolerable living conditions was getting through. Pawnbrokers refused to charge interest for articles the strikers had to pledge[100] and hostel keepers remitted dockers' rents.[101] Large numbers of professional people, particularly clergy, supported the strike or were anxious to inform themselves further on what was called 'the social question'. Some had supported Will Thorne's earlier action out of dismay that workers were being forced to work every Sunday and never got to church. The Lord Mayor of London held conciliation conferences at the Mansion House, where both the Bishop of London and Cardinal Manning were tireless in attendance.

Very shortly London was standing still; 'the paralysis of trade . . . could hardly have been much greater . . . if a hostile fleet had held . . . possession of the mouth of the Thames,' wrote an official of the Chamber of Commerce.[102]

In the end the pressure succeeded. Since so many of the dockers were Irish and Roman Catholic, it was Cardinal Manning who went to the Kirby Street Catholic School in Poplar to meet the strike committee and convey the terms which the dock directors were at last forced to offer:[103] a sixpence standard wage and an end to the call-out.

Hardie was thoroughly heartened by the events in London, though he did not meet the protagonists until the TUC Congress in Dundee a week later. On 5 September he moved the motion for the eight-hour day which the Second International had passed. This time he had much more support than in earlier years, including a speaker from the floor requesting that Henry Broadhurst resign if he could not support the resolution. Broadhurst answered loftily, but with a tinge of panic: 'I insist on political freedom, and that politics have nothing to do with trade-unionism.'[104] Hardie's motion was defeated – but he now had 42 per cent of the vote.[105] He also had support from workers' groups in London for his 'manly and straightforward exposure of Mr Broadhurst'.[106] A net was closing in on the old Liberal union leadership.

Although there was an increase in organized activity among the dockers and transport workers in Scotland, the new unionism did not set Scotland alight with the same wildfire as it did England, where strike upon strike continued to take place in the months that followed in trades as disparate as merchant seamen, shipmakers, bricklayers, boot and shoe makers, firemen and bookbinders. Many strikes were lost, but there were political gains. In Bradford, for example, cotton workers at the Manningham Mill found wages reduced by 30 per cent, followed by a strike, followed by a lockout which eventually forced them back without any ostensible gains. But in the course of these events they formed a strong local political union, a labour 'party' in all but name. Pete Curran, an Irish socialist active in Glasgow, who came down to help Will Thorne, concluded that strikes were 'not only . . . a means of raising the general standard of living of men and women . . . but also . . . a means of good organization and discipline'.[107]

Tillett agreed that 'the real victory' was not the money or even the decasualization. It was the new spirit between workers with the end of competitive relations. Soon there were 'attempts at courtesy' and 'people grew in self respect . . . the docker became a man'.[108] The men became organized.

But so too did employers. Within a year the dockers had lost many of their gains. The gas workers' first strike as a union was a failure. Eleanor Marx wrote what many already realized: no strike was 'pure gain' even if won. The important lesson was that a union was not 'enough'.[109] There had to be a political movement.

Hardie knew this and he noticed too that it was also being canvassed by Tories. In the late autumn of 1889 Lord Randolph Churchill made a speech in which, hardly naively, he said it was only natural that as the landed interests had the Tories and the industrialists the Liberals, the labouring classes would want their own party. Churchill was using labour to serve his party's cause and Hardie sought to use Churchill to support his. He wrote to Churchill in December, as secretary of the Ayrshire miners, to ask him to speak to a miners' meeting. He claimed that 'we are not party politicians . . . [but] working men prepared to support . . . any candidate . . . who will support shortening of the hours of labour and the general social elevation of the masses'.[110] Luckily for Hardie, Churchill refused. Had he accepted, every rumour about Tory support for labour would have been revived. This exchange showed that Hardie's political judgement still left a lot to be desired. Perhaps the local electorate thought so too. During this same autumn he was defeated in an attempt to win a local seat on the new County Council.[111]

To add to his frustrations about this time, he lost *The Miner* as his personal megaphone. 'I regret to say,' he told James Young, 'the *Miner* is a one man affair' and 'I have spent £110 in hard cash on it' over two years.[112] Although he renamed it the *Labour Leader* and attempted to keep it going by widening its politics and turning it to serve the Scottish Labour Party, it did not thrive in a situation where the Scottish Miners' Federation was continuing to disintegrate (consequent on the formation of a National Miners' Federation) and where petty jealousies flared. Hardie fell to serious quarrelling with Stirling miners' leader, Chisholm Robertson, who later implied that Hardie was backed by Tories in his politics, and also accused him of using non-union labour on his journal.[113] Nor did the new Scottish Labour Party provide the satisfaction expected.[114] Its greatest achievement was probably to further consciousness about Scotland, a goal that was never sufficient for Hardie, Scot though he was. His political heart had already emigrated. It was London upon which he had set his sights.

Cunninghame Graham, Scot though he also was, continued to assist Hardie in his quest for a parliamentary seat – in England, if need be. In 1890 he took him to see the Liberal Whips[115] but the wire pullers were hardly likely to give the trouble-making Hardie priority for a safe seat, much less do any favour for Cunninghame Graham, who was calling for an independent Labour Party in Parliament as well as harrying Liberal organizers in Scotland.[116]

Much more likely to help Hardie, as they both soon realized, were Cunninghame Graham's contacts with radical Liberals and the forces of the new unionism. For during this period Cunninghame Graham was in constant demand by working-class organizations. In 1889 he had addressed over 100 miners' meetings.[117] On 4 May he spoke at the first British May Day in Hyde Park (the British Labour Movement had decided on the nearest Sunday rather than 1 May) along with Davitt, Shaw, Burns, Lansbury and Pete Curran. A week later he was back in Hyde Park leading a demonstration for a railway union organized by railway workers, and a few weeks later led the march to Hyde Park to protest against the inevitable ban on union meetings that was swiftly enacted.[118] He chaired a branch of the shop assistants' union[119] and was the guest speaker at the fifth anniversary of the Berner Street Club, a well-established international workingmen's club that had been started by Jewish Marxists in 1885.[120] At the start of the year he had risen to defend Parnell in the House when Parnell was hounded from public life for his love affair with the wife of a fellow MP, Mrs O'Shea. Had Parnell cheated or lied, said Cunninghame Graham, he might deserve it, but 'when the offence is one that the vast majority of men take pleasure in committing [and] . . . which two thirds of the House of Commons are in the habit of committing, let him who is innocent cast the first stone'.[121]

As Cunninghame Graham's stock shot up in radical, Irish, and trade union circles (as well as among socialists – he was a guest at Engels's seventieth birthday party that year),[122] it declined among the genteel. Shaw spoke of walking with his mother in London one day when Cunninghame Graham passed by and politely raised his hat to them.

'Who was that?' Shaw's mother asked.

When he told her, she was incredulous: 'But that man was a gentleman!'[123]

Hardie joined with Cunninghame Graham on several London occasions during 1890, one being the Gas Workers' and General Labourers' Union yearly concert and picnic on 15 July,[124] the high point of which was Hardie's and Cunninghame Graham's unfurling of the new banner that had just been made for the Union. Hardie spoke about the importance of solidarity. He addressed his remarks (in retrospect rather sexist) to the women present: men not likely to be true to each other are unlikely to be true to them.[125]

Will Thorne, still leading the gas workers, had already decided he would be standing for West Ham Council as a socialist. West Ham, with Canning Town, was the cradle of the new unionism and was an area of London where the SDF, always strongest in London, was organizing politically. Cunninghame Graham also knew the leader of West Ham's radicals, Dr John Moir, who believed a challenge to the local Liberal Party was necessary. It was undoubtedly on the strength of these contacts that Hardie was invited to come to West Ham several times during 1890 when he was in London on business for the Ayrshire Miners. The first occasion was in February.[126]

From the first Hardie made it clear he was talking to them as electors and that his intention was to secure the Liberal Party nomination for the parliamentary seat (then held by a Tory). During the year he even joined the Fabian Society,[127] a group for which he had never felt any affinity. Hardie was not an intellectual and he would have been against the Fabians' current opposition to forming a labour party. Whether the move increased his respectability among Liberals is doubtful. The local West Ham Liberal ruling caucus had already chosen a candidate, who was widely expected to win the nomination. The most Hardie could hope for was another Mid-Lanark challenge.

As well as coming to London whenever he could, Hardie also travelled to Europe for his first international miners' conference in

1890. It was held in Jolinot in Belgium, and at it he proposed an international strike of miners for the eight-hour day.[128] When he returned, he wrote that 'nearly all British delegates were Socialists while in Belgium' whereas 'at home many of them have no word too hard for the Socialists'.[129]

Possibly this filtered through to the unions' activity at home, for when Hardie went to the 1890 TUC Congress in Liverpool, he was respectfully heard for the first time, despite the fact that the leadership was busy manipulating entry rules in order to screen out agitators. Eleanor Marx, for example, was refused credentials (although elected by the gas workers as one of their nine delegates) on the grounds that she was not 'a working woman'. She replied forcefully that she was, 'I work a typewriter.'[130]

When Hardie had first spoken at the TUC only three years earlier, laissez-faire and individualism had dominated ideology. By 1890 the TUC was on its way to the collectivist thinking that would soon permeate it entirely. The tangible issue of the eight-hour day was the catalyst. It was popular and relevant to wages, conditions and quality of life. It was common to the Hardie of both the early 1880s and the early 1890s, and to others making the same transition. It was common to the trade unionists and the socialists. It united across national boundaries and was the centrepiece of the Second International.

But its backers argued that it involved legislation. Both the older craft leaders and some of the new unionists (for different reasons) were wary of having the state take a hand in union business, the former out of traditional Liberal opposition to state interference in the affairs of free men, the latter suspicious that Parliament would be used against workers in time. In these and subsequent debates Hardie's position was positively pitched on the essential need for the state to act to protect the worker.

He had come to this view during the 1880s in his move from liberalism to socialism. It was experience as a miner that brought him there, for he was neither a barricades man nor a serious student of scientific socialism. He had always admired the 'Great . . . Gladstone' for enlarging the franchise for workers – which he continued to believe had made socialism possible[131] – but, little by little, Hardie had compiled an ever longer list of legislation Parliament must enact if progress was to be made in the area he knew best. If it was so with mining, so must it be elsewhere. Belated concessions wrested from employers or owners who might be pressed into making changes that they could later retreat from, were not enough.

But legislation was not enough either; structures had to change. In 1889 he was writing to Engels asking him for some details of state industries in Germany.[132] In particular, he wanted news of the publicly run mines in the Saarbrücken area because he wanted to counter the argument that public control could mean 'red tape and jobbery'.[133] From Engels he hoped to get proof that public control 'is being done'. Hardie had thought about the way public ownership might work, as he showed when he gave evidence in 1892 to the Royal Commission on Labour.[134] He did not favour contralized control or a national bureaucracy. He wanted mines to be run by their present management but under democratically controlled local authorities' oversight in the interests of the community. Miners' state insurance would be managed by miners themselves.[135] The state's role was only to set broad policy outlines.

In 1890 the TUC voted for an eight-hour day for the first time and Broadhurst retired as TUC chair. Hardie had won the day. But was it remotely possible that the changes he wanted would ever be conceded by a legislature completely dominated by two largely conservative political parties? Or even if they were, that they would be more than palliatives? To prove otherwise was the immense task he seems to have set himself for the immediate future.

★　★　★　★　★

Despite his ambitious agenda, Hardie had not yet come to see himself as the leader of a new national labour cause. During 1890 and 1891 it was to John Burns that both Hardie and Cunninghame Graham looked for a lead. He seemed best placed, with radical credentials from Bloody Sunday, a trade union background, socialist training in the SDF, electoral experience as a member of the London County Council, and the best chance of any of them of being elected an MP – since he had already negotiated with Liberals not to put up against him in Battersea at the next general election. How independent any MP could be with this arrangement was the real question, and both Hardie and Cunninghame Graham made every effort to spur John Burns in the direction of independent labour representation. In May 1891 Hardie wrote to tell him he planned to come to London, bringing other Scots socialists, and wanted to join any group Burns was forming to try to 'detach' Liberal 'rank and file' voters from allegiance to the Liberal leadership. He wanted Burns to set up a conference to discuss such a project and he indicated he was free to stay the month if need be.[136]

Cunninghame Graham was equally willing to follow Burns, already well aware that his own background as an upper-class man of letters prevented him from taking the lead himself. It had to come from labour, and soon, for without such a movement he represented no one. 'Anyone but those idiots in Parliament would have seen this long ago,' he wrote to Burns at the end of 1891.[137] But Burns did not respond. He continued with inflammatory speeches but in deeds he sat on his hands. His excuse was always that it only served the

Tories if anyone rocked the Liberal leadership's boat. Eleanor Marx
wrote to her sister at this time that despite his red profile John Burns
was really a very 'uncertain quantity'.[138]

At the end of 1890, at the age of thirty-four, Hardie made a
decision. Slim though his chances were of a career in national politics,
he nevertheless decided to pack his carpet bag in earnest. The decision
must certainly have seemed precipitate to Lillie and his colleagues, but
to himself possibly long overdue: to give up his job as paid secretary to
the Ayrshire Miners' Association, leaving himself free for the national
stage. 'I am not especially anxious to go to Parliament,' he had written
earlier, 'but I am anxious that the wants and wishes of the working
class should be made known and attended to there.'[139]

Though he would still go to congresses and conferences as the
Association's delegate, the move effectively ended his trade union
connection for good. In December 1890 the Association had given
him and Lillie a dinner at the Ossington Coffee House in Cumnock,
and Hardie was given 'a pile of sovereigns', some of which had come
from the mill girls of Newmilns whom he had supported in their
struggles to organize a union. Hardie gave the money to Lillie as their
nest-egg and opened an account in the Ayrshire Building Society.[140]

The union gave Lillie a 'handsome gold broach' to honour her role
as essential support, one of the 'tokens' any consort gets, saying 'Thank
you for not complaining'. Such trophies only made it harder for Lillie
to speak out against the life she was living, with Hardie away for
increasingly long periods and the whole of the domestic burden falling
on her shoulders. Lillie was a wife hoping to play a traditional political
role, which depended upon having standing in the community, with
a husband on hand to share it with her. Instead, his work brought
notoriety. At the miners' dinner Hardie, well aware that 'I say the
right thing in the wrong place', was asked why he never answered
the scurrilous press abuse. He said he settled any action of his with
his own conscience and once that was done his action 'must supply
its own defence'.[141] At least he could use it to attract a hearing, as he
was now beginning to realize. The family had no positive use for the
negative aura, yet they were identified with his career, since all those
they encountered treated them as extensions of it.

By far the biggest domestic issue for the Hardies, however, was
money. Lillie desired to keep an establishment that was a credit to
a husband who seemed determined to make his mark. She probably
thought still of Alexander MacDonald, the union leader and respected
MP with a private income from part ownership of a mine, who
lived in a large house with its own stables. Even if she did not,
she must already have been angry – whether she knew it or not
– that there was enough for Hardie to attend an increasing number
of conferences and congresses, to travel the country and abroad,

and, until recently, to finance a journal, but so little for the household.

For much of the 1890s Hardie allowed Lillie only £1 a week for feeding and clothing the family and running the house.[142] This was only twice the average wage of the highest-paid London matchgirls in 1888.[143] Lillie managed because she was industrious, as Hardie's mother had been. She was houseproud and hardworking, and followed a strict routine the year round. May was devoted to spring cleaning, December to extra seasonal baking to send as gifts. She made the family's clothes. She bottled and preserved and pickled, and organized the seeding, planting, hoeing and harvesting of a small garden in which Hardie also took the keenest interest and worked on regularly when he was at home. They grew a great deal of their own produce, as it helped to reduce expenditure. But the small tenement and garden were being outgrown. Hardie was well aware of the unsatisfactory home situation, particularly as he was now looking south and intending to travel continually. He did not want Lillie and the children to come with him, or to have to provide for them in London. They had to be settled well in Scotland, where he also needed his own retreat. But Hardie now had no income, as he was giving up the Miners' job. He admitted blithely later, 'it was a risky thing to do'.[144]

However, matters were not hopeless. By now Keir Hardie was beginning to attract wealthy backers. One of the murkiest and most mysterious aspects of the period was the funding that sprang up for the socialist and labour movement. Some of it came from the penny subs of organized labour or dues from political groups, and some of it undoubtedly came from wealthy Tories who wanted to split the Liberal Party. But it came from other sources as well, and offers of money to Hardie were to be a feature for the rest of his life. Most came with strings attached and Hardie recognized this. Some givers may have hoped to head off extremism by making likely labour leaders dependents (a role corporate foundations and government agencies still seek to play); others were industrialists who had made it big and were into philanthropy, believing the world would be safer if the working class was tied to benefactors rather than led astray by revolutionaries. Others, like the Cadburys, had political ties, and were only prepared to support labour independence that did not harm the Liberal Party. Still others, like Andrew Carnegie and Thomas Lipton, were spurred by sentiment for those struggling where they had once been. Hardie had offers from all of them in time.

In 1891, however, Hardie decided to accept the offer of a well-to-do local businessman dedicated to the socialist cause and busy extending his influence in the Glasgow area. Adam Birkmyre had already bought Robert Owen's New Lanark mills, and offered Hardie money to build himself and his family a proper house.[145] Hardie refused the gift but agreed to take the money as an interest-free loan, which he would pay back in instalments. Hardie knew he had to steer completely clear of anything like a charge of bribery. Thus he paid off the loan at set periods each year, always accompanied by a letter showing the current balance. In effect, it became a mortgage – except that Birkmyre would never have repossessed had Hardie defaulted.

In 1891 building began on a site Lillie and Hardie selected on the River Lugar, one of Robert Burns's favoured streams, a wide and shallow river that rushes down over boulders through old Cumnock. The site selected was up one of its steep wooded banks, on a hill by the road winding up out of town to Auchinleck. The house, still standing, is directly on the road, as if to insist we notice its substantial three storeys and sturdy plain stone. Inside it was surprisingly 'modern', perhaps an Arts and Crafts reaction against Victorian excess, in its clean geometric lines and tiles. For a family of republican sentiments, the Hardies chose an unexpected name for it, Lochnorris, the name of a ruined castle on the estate of the most eminent local aristocrat, Lord Bute.[146]

Lochnorris was undoubtedly Lillie's pride and joy, and from about this time Morgan dismisses Lillie from Hardie's life and claims she took no further interest in his career. He also claims Hardie centred himself in London and that Scotland had little further hold on him.[147] Certainly it is true that Hardie had been forced to look beyond Scotland. But Lochnorris was as dear to him as to Lillie, even if for quite different reasons. It was his ground base, where his parents and siblings could always visit (as they regularly did, along with Lillie's), and where his children could have the life of security he never had. Jamie and Nan were already in the village school, another luxury he had never enjoyed. In Lochnorris Hardie now had a place where he could go when exhausted, which was often, and be thoroughly coddled. He could tend to his much larger garden and keep in touch with his Scots friends. He needed all this badly and he needed Lillie there to run it. While Morgan claims the marital relationship all but ceased to be from this point, Emrys Hughes goes to the opposite extreme and claims that from the start of their relationship in Cumnock 'the bonds of sympathy and understanding between them grew'.[148] Hardie's and Lillie's relationship has been caught between two stereotypical characterizations, and in reality conformed to neither.

Between them was unspoken agreement, but also outstanding disagreements. Hardie had regular deep depressions which made him hard to live with. Although Lillie never complained directly, she certainly felt her isolated position and, as we learn later, had ways of letting Hardie know. Her sullen silences caused Hardie pain.[149] But Hardie also acknowledged her fortitude: 'she has a brave heart,' he told David Lowe a few years later, 'and does not show her sorrows on the surface.'[150] On both sides was unacknowledged disappointment, which would grow. But there was now a solid stone foundation which gave Lillie domestic standing, if not social respectability, and Hardie an important peace of mind. The bonds Emrys Hughes spoke of were there, but they were linking both to the foundations of Lochnorris rather than to each other.

Lillie, Jamie, Nan and Duncan were taken care of – or so Hardie assumed. Now he was free to go prospecting for his life's work. But even if by chance he were elected to Parliament, how would they live? MPs had no salary, one reason why it was thought so laughable that a working-class man without private means (or a respectable union to fund him) should seek to enter Parliament. Perhaps Hardie counted on the parliamentary fund that the TUC had agreed to set up one day, or was influenced by Cunninghame Graham and G. B. Clark to think money would be found, as someone had certainly found it to finance him at Mid-Lanark. Henry Champion's Electoral Association was still offering to fund labour MPs, though it had lately become much less interested in the Scottish Labour Party owing to the Party's insistence on negotiating with Liberals,[151] a factor that could well also have influenced Hardie to go south, where the focus was on the new unionists. Tom Mann, for example, received an offer from an 'anonymous donor' to support him with £2 a week indefinitely should he wish to stand for Parliament.[152] In 1892 also, Edward Aveling was offered all the money he needed if he wanted to stand. The offer came from Champion.[153] Very probably Champion had made the same promise to Hardie.

To earn his daily bread Hardie capitalized on what he realized by now was his real asset, the growing demand to hear him speak. He began a habit that was to last a lifetime, saying yes to all invitations. His working life was thus built around itineraries from venue to venue,[154] sometimes visiting two or three major towns in a single day, or spending a week on the road criss-crossing the country several times. All biographers give examples of these marathon treks, which Hardie loved to record. Ostensibly to cover his costs, he carefully added up how much such engagements cost in a typical month and took an average,[155] which turned out to be three guineas. This he charged as a flat rate to all who asked him to speak (except for meetings for which he did not have to travel).

Anything he saved by cutting costs on food and lodging, he pocketed. Whenever he could, he stayed with comrades. On the road he did not live high on his own account. Hardie was careful not to risk bad publicity. From this point onwards he took a great deal of care of his public image.

According to Cunninghame Graham, Hardie was an 'abstemious' eater and, as he went about, it was enough for him to munch on 'an oatcake, a scone, a bit of cheese'.[156] But a lifestyle viewed by the wealthy Cunninghame Graham might look different when seen by a poor Scot like David Lowe, who came to Glasgow in 1892 to join the Scottish Labour Party. Lowe recalls going to meet Hardie at St Enoch's Hotel and finding him dining with George Carson, a Scottish Liberal, in a private dining room, being served a multi-course dinner, while supposedly 'working' on Scottish Labour Party affairs. The provincial idealist commented sarcastically that this was a very odd 'modern form of martyrdom'.[157] Yet it was this same Lowe who wrote about the later Hardie who lived notoriously frugally on his lone trips round the country, staying at temperance hotels, eating in temperance tea rooms, 'sitting alone in a bedroom of some cheap hotel writing through the early hours of the morning wet to the skin in view of a fireless grate'.[158]

It was Reid's view that from now on Hardie would adopt an increasingly middle-class lifestyle, devoted to culture and refinement, which would come between him and the very poor whose plight he sought to espouse,[159] while to others Hardie represented the campaigner for working-class justice determined to endure the privations of the class for which he fought. No wonder the word so often used about Hardie was 'enigma'.

As well as a lecturer, Hardie also believed himself a journalist. He sorely missed his own regular publication. In 1890 he had merged his *Labour Leader* with Champion's *Labour Elector*, but the venture failed. Hardie's great ambition was to start it again. This was an era when labour and socialist publications were growing. The Fabians' essay series of 1889 had enjoyed great popularity, presenting the case for socialism as evolutionary and gradual, through public ownership rather than class struggle. *Justice* and *Commonweal*, published by Hyndman and Morris respectively, were influential and widely quoted. Belfort Bax edited *Today*. Local areas and towns had their own papers; in the East End of London there was the Yiddish *Workers' Friend*, in Leeds, *The Weekly Citizen*, in Huddersfield, *The Worker*.

What was badly needed was a national paper. In Germany at this time there were already thirty-two daily socialist newspapers.[160] In Britain the Conservative and Liberal press dominated. Some concentrated on building up resistance to the new worker militancy, enflaming fears of a bloody revolution (as they have ever since); others wanted to inform readers on social issues. One such paper was the Liberal *Manchester Sunday Chronicle*, owned by Edward Hulton.[161] Its editor was curious about the poor and the real conditions in which they lived, a subject little discussed. During 1889 he had sent a bright young reporter out to write a series about it.

Robert Blatchford was the son of a brush-maker who had run away to join the army and afterwards chose to climb the ladder of professional journalism. At a time when most reporters were doing stories on Jack the Ripper, then in the midst of his murders, Robert Blatchford went into the Manchester slums, many of them only 200 feet from streets the well-to-do travelled every day. His series was a systematic presentation of the poverty, ill-health, and rat-ridden housing he found, and when he had finished he was a changed man. What pushed him to the next step was a chance reading of Hyndman's *A Summary of The Principles of Socialism*,[162] which seemed to explain it all.

Hyndman was so politically obtuse that it is easy to overlook his immense influence. His interpretation of Marx changed Blatchford's whole direction. At the time the reporter was earning nearly £1,000 a year and was married and had children. But he gave up his job to go to Joseph Burgess's small *Workman's Times*. By the end of 1891 he realized this worthy journal was nowhere near ambitious enough and he left to found his own. If Hyndman could popularize Marx, he could popularize socialism. Blatchford founded the *Clarion*.

Blatchford was intensely professional and hated cliché writing. Almost alone among socialist papers the *Clarion* paid for its articles, ten shillings a column.[163] He also believed that the social spirit had to be fed. In connection with his paper he started Cinderella Clubs, which brought street parties to the slums he had visited. For those who objected to socialist contributions going on dancing and drinking, his answer was that fun was as sacred as water and food. His paper not only sold on the street corner, it was taken out into the country. Within a year he had organized a fleet of horse-drawn vans, reminiscent of the red vans of the Land League that had toured the countryside in the 1880s.

Soon the *Clarion* vans became well known as travelling information units. A horn sounded as one came into a village and people gathered for political discussion. *Clarion* clubs were formed, built on an extensive existing network of ramblers' and hikers' clubs. But most important of all, Blatchford's increasingly popular individual articles were made into a book that soon circulated nationwide. It was called *Merrie England* and it outsold any other socialist publication during the whole decade. It was said to have made more converts to socialism than any publication before or since and certainly more than *The Communist Manifesto*, which was generally available in English after 1887. Everyone could understand the parables of *Merrie England*; they dealt with situations and arguments people heard every day. The same was true of the *Clarion*, which socialists, no matter where they stood, looked back on later – as did Edmund Stonelake, a colleague of Hardie's – as 'the best socialist publication the country has ever seen'.[164]

Blatchford was dark and quick and small, 'like an Italian organ-grinder',[165] and he was unashamedly a hedonist, posing a challenge to the long-dominant puritanical temperance wing of the Left. Although he claimed he was simply carrying out Morris's dictum that 'fellowship is life',[166] to some his advocacy of new social mores appeared a threat. Soon after Blatchford had started the *Clarion*, Keir Hardie came to Manchester to speak. Blatchford was eager to meet this fiery spirit and sent a note over to the lecture hall inviting Hardie to the club which Blatchford and other journalists frequented after a working day. It was a bar attached to a theatre, where actors and actresses mingled with customers drinking and smoking, and it was said some of the actresses would agree to accompany gentlemen upstairs.[167] When Hardie pushed open the door he faced a dilemma. For if a village pub caused him to recoil, and working men's clubs had repelled him, a theatre bar stopped him cold. It is said his eyes were riveted at once on a woman sitting upon a man's lap, as Blatchford came forward with out-stretched hand. Later Blatchford said, 'I offered him the warmest welcome that I ever gave another man and he held out a hand that was like a cold toad and ran away.'[168] What Hardie did was immediately pull out his watch, make his excuses, and leave.

The music hall and evangelical traditions had clashed, and even socialism could not bridge that gulf in a hurry. Yet the *Clarion* clubs and choirs and the Co-op and SDF clubs were not on the whole so very different from the temperance groups and evangelical choirs Hardie knew well. They all included fun and merriment and country outings. They all encompassed the whole family, although there were probably more events for young people to meet and mix in the *Clarion* network, where undoubtedly some had more interest in mixing than in listening to socialist discussion. Yet there grew up a distinction between socialist hedonists and puritans, which later extended to disagreement between traditional moralists and those who entertained 'advanced' views about human relationships.

Hardie's religious background automatically classed him with the puritans. So did his demeanour. Hardie was always a dignified man in public. 'He carries himself seriously,' G. K. Chesterson commented later.[169] He was not one of the lads. As Tom Johnston, a socialist colleague, wrote, 'a smutty story made him leave a railway carriage'.[170] John Burns called him a 'dour, dogged fellow'.[171] Journalists were particularly put off by this side of Hardie. A. G. Gardiner, famed editor of the *Daily News*, put it simply: there 'was no fun . . . about Keir Hardie'.[172] As for Blatchford, fatefully, he took against Hardie from this first meeting, calling him later a 'sanctimonious prig' and 'the only man I have ever tried to like and failed'.[173]

The caricature of Hardie was one-sided, just as any strict distinction between puritan and hedonist socialist is artificial. For although Hardie observed decorum in public, and inevitably stuck to activity that did not centre around drinking, he was fond of social occasions, smoked a good pipe, and when occasion offered, loved the chance to sing and to dance a reel. He probably yearned more for Blatchford's world than he knew. But it was hard to take to Blatchford, who, as the classic journalist, said with such hearty feeling, 'I dislike politics and politicians'.[174] Blatchford, however, probably yearned for platform power more than he knew. On the strength of his paper's influence, Cunninghame Graham wrote to him in 1892 to suggest he stand for Parliament.[175] Blatchford scorned the offer, but later allowed himself to be tempted on to a platform in Bradford to make a public speech. He found himself unable to communicate with the public face to face and he had to sit down in confusion and disgrace, from where he retreated to the editorial office for ever.[176] What each man disliked in the other was a part of himself he did not wish to face.

On 22 January 1892 a man's body was discovered in some woods in Croydon, south of London. He had been shot. He was Hume Webster, a small-time Liberal politician who had tried to mediate in the 1889 strike of cable makers in Silvertown in London's East End. His efforts had met with little success and the strikers had refused to go back to work. He was the typical self-made businessman whom the West Ham Liberal Establishment had nominated as their candidate for the imminent general election to fight the sitting Tory, a remote and inactive member called Major Banes.

As it turned out, Webster had killed himself over a failed business venture involving a South American racehorse.[177] It was an odd reason for a suicide and although there appears to have been no connection with Cunninghame Graham, the country's leading expert on South American horses, it is a coincidence that Cunninghame Graham had been helping Hardie make political connections in West Ham. But so too had G. B. Clark, who knew John Moir, head of the local branch of the Land Restoration League and a leading radical. Another interested go-between was Joseph Burgess, who edited the *Workman's Times*,[178] a paper which expressed the anger many radicals and socialists felt about working men who lost 'all backbone' when 'brought into the presence of the aristocrats of the [Liberal] Party', and always agreed to the 'suggestions of the wire pullers', ending up with candidates 'in whom they have no confidence'.[179] Hume Webster had been one such candidate, which is why a vociferous group of radicals and socialists in West Ham wanted to put up a working-class candidate who would not be compromised by business interests when arguing the cause of labour. Thus did representatives from the Land League, local socialists and radical Liberals form a committee to get their 'own' candidate.[180] Hardie's supporters were growing in numbers but they were not enough to win an official Liberal nomination. Until, suddenly, by one of those massive strokes of fortune that were to favour Hardie several times in his life, there was no rival. What would the wire pullers do now?

Hardie was very confident that after three years of campaigning for the Scottish Labour Party and lecturing the country over, he could take on even an alien urban constituency in the heart of London, the epicentre of the new unions' struggles. By now he had extrapolated the lesson that strikes built unions, not unions strikes – and unions in turn could build political alliances. Hardie was assuming such an alliance in east London. After Webster's death, official West Ham Liberals sought for a new candidate[181] but Hardie's headstart was too great. National Liberal bosses such as Schnadhorst knew that Hardie would not withdraw, and that forcing their own candidate into the field would mean the Tory retained the seat. Reluctantly, at the last minute, they left the field to Hardie.

Privately, he spurned official Liberals. When Schnadhorst sent a message asking if there was anything he needed – a friendly gesture in the circumstances – Hardie replied in a most unfriendly manner, 'Nothing – only leave us alone to fight the battle.'[182] Publicly Hardie was more emollient and stressed his orthodoxy. He agreed with Gladstone's newly minted Newcastle Programme (though a few years later he would call it a 'miscellaneous compendium of odds and ends'),[183] stressed Home Rule, and pulled out the old evangelical and temperance stops.

The latter were probably his greatest asset. Several local Nonconformist clergy stood up to tell the crowds, or wrote to local newspapers, what a sober and God-fearing candidate Keir Hardie was. In London this counted for even more than in rural Scotland since drunkenness was a huge problem in the East End. West Ham, still classed as a county borough,[184] was a constituency changing fast, with the well-to-do and middle class fleeing to the suburbs beyond,[185] as poor workers and industry moved in and the River Lea filled up with foul smells. The respectable who had stayed wanted to make sure they had a traditional representative.

On money matters Hardie was at his least convincing. Early on in the West Ham campaign he was asked whether he had ever received money from Champion or Barry and denied it.[186] He also assured his audience he belonged to no socialist society.[187] Who then was really paying for him? The local Plaistow paper said it was the Carlton Club. Hardie said it was the Ayrshire Miners,[188] who were certainly paying something but not the whole bill. The *Daily Mail* raked up Mid-Lanark again and asked who had paid then? Hardie said he had told the *Mail* at the time it was Margaret Harkness, but again not the whole bill.[189] In fact, much of Hardie's funding was probably coming still from Champion, who in turn was still receiving money from Barry. But this time it appeared to have been laundered through the *Workman's*

Times,[190] whose radical standing was impeccable and whose editor, Burgess (who may not have known the source) could plausibly have collected for Hardie. Hardie also had a cheque for £100 that came from Andrew Carnegie, the Scots emigrant who had made it in the United States and was at that time actively repressing his own striking workforce at his Homestead Steel Works in Pennsylvania. Initially, it appears, Hardie accepted his money too, put it in his campaign fund and said nothing.

Hardie's campaign was very well organized in all West Ham's twelve wards, thanks to a vigorous registration drive Hume Webster had already carried out. Several of the wards were also successfully organized by socialists, as the Canning Town branch of the SDF had succeeded in getting six councillors, including Will Thorne, elected to the West Ham Council the year before. This showed that a lot had happened since Engels had written in 1885 that 'socialists are nowhere' in the East End of London.[191] Many who were Liberals were socialists in all but name, including George Lansbury.

Lansbury and his wife and six children lived in St Stephen's Street in neighbouring Bow, where his father-in-law ran a small sawmill. Like Hardie, Lansbury had been brought up first on 'religious agitation' and then joined the Liberal Party,[192] where, like Hardie at the TUC Congress, he had fought the eight-hour-day issue against Liberal leaders at Liberal conferences, and on one occasion found himself strong-armed off the conference platform to keep him quiet.[193] Like Hardie he had published a small radical journal[194] and been successful in a local election in 1892 – to the Board of Guardians in Poplar, where he was engaged in a running battle with the Lib-Lab right wing, or what was known as 'sound' labour men, who simply wanted to manage, while he wanted to use every statute or loophole to improve the poor's lives, and claimed he 'stamped and shouted' until he got changes made.[195] Although Lansbury in 1892 remembers he was already 'tramping around' London to hear 'Morris and Hyndman' and had taken part in Bloody Sunday, he was working during the 1892 parliamentary campaign (helped by Hardie) in a neighbouring constituency as agent for the Liberal candidate, J. A. Murray MacDonald.[196] It was not until the night of the general election itself, having seen his man become an MP, that he walked out and joined the SDF.

Another London socialist, moved by Hardie's speaking and high moral purpose, was Frank Smith, a man of independent means and strong religious views, who was standing in Hammersmith as a Labour candidate. Hardie had met him four years earlier and 'took to' him at once.[197] He began turning up at Hardie's election meetings rather than holding his own.

Cunninghame Graham was also helping, as neither he nor the rest of the Scottish Labour Party had drawn Hardie's luck of being unopposed by Liberals, although that was the original intention of Liberal Whips in London in respect of Cunninghame Graham's constituency in Calmachie, Glasgow. It was local Liberals who opposed Cunninghame Graham's commitment to stand on the ballot as 'Labour'. They put up against him and against all six other Scottish Labour Party candidates. Henry Champion was also standing in Scotland as 'independent Labour' (and so was Maltman Barry as 'independent Tory'). The SDF was putting up two candidates; while the Fabians were supporting Ben Tillett in Bradford. Joseph Arch, a farm workers' leader, who had been elected once before, was being put up in East Anglia by agricultural workers. Even Broadhurst was standing again. In fact, under a 'Labour' banner positions ranged across the whole political spectrum.

Placing Hardie on that continuum was difficult for electors at this time. His party position was ambiguous, since his election address stated he was an 'independent' supporter of the Liberal Party who would place the 'claims of Labour above Party' if it ever came to the choice. Privately, at a local conference during the campaign, he was already saying that he intended to form an independent Labour Party as soon as possible,[198] and his Election Address said he was standing at the 'unanimous invitation of the United Liberal, Radical and Labour Party of South West Ham' − a party that did not exist.[199]

When he had left the Ayrshire union he had written, 'I was saying goodbye' to trade unionism. He saw his life's work now as to wean the working class away 'from blind adhesion to party politics'.[200] He probably had no clear idea what independence for labour meant, but he was perfectly clear that the issue which mattered was 'the moral and material well-being of the working classes'.[201] Employment was central. Why were there not enough jobs for honest men and women to earn enough to keep themselves and their families? It was an issue which had been before society since the riots of the 1880s, and Hardie had long realized that a 'far more drastic cure' for unemployment than the eight-hour day was necessary.[202] Capitalism had a built-in need for unemployment; a new social order was required which provided work for all.

Hardie set himself up as an expert on the issue during the campaign, since unemployment was, if anything, even more important to London's East End than in Scotland's mining areas. Both Liberals and Conservatives believed it was a concern for individuals, or at the most a local government matter, and there had been few initiatives for dealing with the workless (as distinct from the destitute). Hardie's argument throughout was that this lack of initiatives was a national scandal, not a local matter. Unemployment was government's responsibility. Instead of urging individuals to act, governments should provide a framework in which work could be provided. He claimed five million were out of work, a statistically uncertain figure,[203] but no one, including government, had any better one.

He tentatively suggested 'Government and local councils . . . own and manage all Mines, Banks, Railways, Docks, Waterways and Treasuries'[204] and he introduced the idea of direct labour, which local councils could use to build houses, for example – both to employ people and to provide for social need. He firmly suggested municipalized workshops and the common ownership of land. But the remedy that most interested him, and had done for some years, possibly since H. V. Mills's *Poverty and the State*[205] had stimulated rural nostalgia, was the idea of 'home colonies', where the unemployed could be usefully set to raising their own food on publicly financed farms. Originally a demand of the Chartists, Hardie saw such farm colonies being run on co-operative lines by workers themselves. Hardie had given evidence on land as well as on labour to the Royal Commission on Labour a few months earlier:[206]

> 'You say that land, not having been created by labour, cannot belong to any individual, but . . . to the community. What community?'
> Hardie: 'The people as a whole.'
> 'Mankind?'
> Hardie: 'No; the workers.'
> 'I see. The present owner of the land is not entitled to any share of it at all?'
> Hardie: 'If he becomes a worker he is entitled; if he is an idler he is not entitled to anything and should not be entitled to anything.'

The Royal Commission on Labour never amounted to anything and was widely regarded as a cynical parliamentary manoeuvre to deal with matters like the eight-hour legislation that Cunninghame Graham kept insisting on introducing (and which the Miners' Federation had now adopted officially). According to one coal-owner, the Commission's real purpose 'was meant to shelve the questions affecting the working classes'.[207]

Hardie did not intend to shelve these questions, though his proposals at this stage were limited, as Reid has shown.[208] Hardie was not asking for the socialist solution of public enterprise the SDF was advocating; and his thoughts on poor relief and work for the willing worker may well have rested uneasily on widely held views about the distinction between deserving and undeserving poor. But these gaps and inadequacies were subsumed in his clear moral purpose to make society recognize the needs of the 'toiling millions', for 'the labour movement is the outcome of a quickening of the public conscience towards the extremes of wealth and poverty which at present exist'.[209] So said his election address.

During the campaign itself he was tireless, addressing mass meetings throughout the area, not only at factory gates but also in local fields and streets. These meetings were where he aimed to contact his newly enfranchised poor electorate. The largest meetings, running to thousands, were at the dock gates, as workers waited for the revived version of the 'call on'. Cunninghame Graham was with him regularly early on, and wrote later of West Ham itself:

> Street upon street of half crooked brick abominations falsely called houses; here and there a 'little Bethel' chapel . . . row upon row of stalls at night when the stale vegetables are sold . . . on one side, lines of endless docks, and on the other, lines of endless misery.[210]

Hardie was the new model social politician, no longer the preacher exhorting working people to be less feckless. He outlined his vision of how society could be to men who came from this misery, and told them not to fight for a party victory but for 'thousands of starving children . . . the man out of work . . . the poor and the aged', for 'their share of liberty . . . justice to everyone and privilege to none'.[211] Cunninghame Graham observed the effect of 'this northern miner, shaggy of head, earnest in manner . . . like the Scots of old'. His hearers listened intently, it was 'so strange to see a man in earnest . . . so unusual to be addressed as "men" and not "gentlemen", so beyond experience to see the speaker so moved by the strange inward something.'[212]

Although local Liberals never opposed him, officially they did not recognize him either.[213] He had told audiences anxious to know his party political position that, 'If Liberals are prepared to accept our principles, we are prepared to work with them. If . . . not, they are no more our friends than the Tories.'[214] To the massed and miserable who jammed the workplace gates, to whom he returned again and again, party politics were far away. He told them unemployment was a denial of the means of life, and that it 'went to his heart to see men standing on the stones as if they were so many head of cattle'.[215] The issue always brought out anger in Hardie. As he had written earlier, it 'makes me frantic with a desire to do something to remove the causes which produce the misery'.[216] The sights he saw returned him to his childhood and the experiences that 'scarred the very springs of my being'.[217] He could not offer any cast-iron solutions, but he could offer himself. He told them simply, 'It is not my fight, men, it is yours. If you return me to the House of Commons, I will fight for you.'[218]

When the votes were counted at West Ham Town Hall on 4 July 1892, Hardie had beaten Major Banes by 5,268 to 4,036. When this was announced to the excited crowds waiting outside, they broke through the cordons of police and surged up the town hall steps, 'waving hats, handkerchiefs, and umbrellas'.[219] and carried Hardie off on their shoulders.

The *Daily Chronicle* called his win the 'first curl of the wave which is issuing from the dim depths of popular life'; while Engels wrote, 'the spell which the great Liberal Party cast over the English workers for almost 40 years is broken!'[220]

5

DOMESTIC DIVISIONS

Observers said Hardie responded without excitment to his election.[1] Next morning at dawn he was down at the docks where supporters hoisted him high again, but within hours he was off around the country (general elections in those days being held over a number of weeks). Although the Liberals were to regain government and had already announced Hardie as one of their own gains, he appears to have been as anxious to defeat the Liberal TUC members standing – at any cost – as to support independent and SLP colleagues. Possibly he recalled the repeated humiliations these men had inflicted on him in successive TUC congresses, ridiculing his knowledge of history, even making fun of him for going bald. Hardie campaigned in their constituencies against them, even urging voters to vote for the candidates opposing them which inevitably meant for the Tories. Morgan called it very mistaken[2] as he would have to work with these same Lib-Labs in Parliament. But Hardie had no intention of working with Lib-Labs anywhere. More serious for Hardie, however, was loss of support from principled political groups like the Fabians who expressed disillusionment. It was from such tactics as this that Hardie would soon seem to Engels to be an opportunist.[3]

To Burns and Joseph Burgess, editor of the *Workman's Times*, his conduct seemed both wayward and too ready to assume leadership no one had given him.[4] Carping began shortly after the election when Burns let it be known that both he and Hardie had had £100 from Champion during the election (originating from a Tory soap baron named Hudson), an allegation soon overshadowed by the revelation (when election expenses were published) that Hardie had also accepted Andrew Carnegie's £100.[5] Hardie wrote at once to the press that he had not used any of the money personally, and had given no pledges to Carnegie.[6] But the storm was not stemmed until Hardie announced that he was sending £100 of his own money to the strikers then holding out against Carnegie at his Homestead Steel Works. It was announced in the *Workman's Times* that the money represented all of Lillie Hardie's savings (the 'nest-egg' Ayrshire miners had given two years earlier)[7] and that Hardie challenged supporters to make good the loss to Lillie. The paper opened a fund but the money never came in. Lillie's reactions to this can be imagined.

Accusations over the funding of the West Ham election followed Hardie for years, but in time he and those who supported him learned how to soften the story. In Hardie's own words at the end of his life, Maltman Barry had become a friend of Karl Marx, Hudson a socialist supporting only labour candidates; and as soon as Hardie had received Carnegie's £100, he had 'promptly forwarded' it to the secretary of the strike fund resisting the company's 'atrocities'.[8]

Despite these exchanges, labour's flag was flying high after the 1892 election. Besides Burns and Hardie, Havelock Wilson, secretary of the Sailors' and Firemen's Union, in Middlesbrough, and Joseph Arch in Norfolk were elected as independent Labour candidates – like Hardie, without official support from any party. Among those who lost were Champion and Broadhurst. Ben Tillett almost won at Bradford but the two SDF candidates received only 695 votes between them. All members of the Scottish Labour Party were defeated, including Cunninghame Graham, who had put so much effort into getting Hardie into Parliament. To the Establishment, the news of even a few Labour men victorious was an affront, and it was said that when the High Sheriff of Norfolk had to announce Arch as the victorious candidate[9] he 'wiped his hand ostentatiously with his handkerchief' after Arch had shaken it, so great was his disgust that a man who had once been a common agricultural labourer was going to Westminster.

Socialists counted the elections as part of a larger advance. On Good Friday in 1893 Frederick Engels was entertaining three guests in his Regent's Park home when he suddenly realized their special significance. The first was John Burns, the second Auguste Bebel, the German socialist leader, and the third, Paul Lafargue, married to Marx's second daughter, Laura, and leader of the Workers' Party in France. All three had recently been elected to their respective legislatures as workers' representatives, and now they were all in one room. Engels saluted them and said, 'If only Marx were here to see this.'[10]

The general public were well aware that workers had reason to celebrate – if only because they had read about Keir Hardie's arrival at the House of Commons the previous summer.

He took his seat on 3 August, his thirteenth wedding anniversary, driven to Parliament Square in a hired wagonette by his constituents. On board was a lone trumpeter, who played the 'Marseillaise', a traditional practice. The wagon stopped in the square and Hardie got down and walked in alone. The high-coloured press version was of a rabble marching from the East End, accompanied by brass bands playing the 'Red Flag', wildly and rudely forcing its way into Parliament's precincts.[11] The intention was clearly to spread alarm about Keir Hardie as a representative of a potential revolution that would need to be curbed.

There are as many accounts of what Hardie chose to wear as there were those to pass them on. A contemporary described him in a plain rough tweed suit but Burns later claimed he was in 'knickers of check . . . you could have played draughts on'.[12] Around his neck one contemporary said he wore a 'home made purple comforter'[13] while a later biographer claimed it was a red tie[14] and others a red kerchief. As for what was on his head, the *Clarion* called it 'a tweed travelling cap'[15] and Bruce Glasier 'a workman's peaked cap'.[16] Press descriptions in later years referred to it as both 'a blue scotch cap'[17] and a 'soft cap'.[18] Emrys Hughes pronounced it a 'deer stalker', and this is probably the right description for today's reader.[19] Hardie can be seen wearing it, flaps tied back on top of his head, dressed in a tweed suit, in all his West Ham election posters. Today his dress looks like the clothes a country gentleman would wear to hunt in Scotland.

Hardie arrived about the same time as Gladstone,[20] who was seen to notice at once that Hardie was not dressed in the parliamentarians' uniform of black frock coat, black silk top hat, and starched wing collar. Few MPs – including no Lib-Lab working man – had ever arrived in anything else.[21] John Burns, as a new MP, had already decided to conform and was boasting of the tailor's fittings he was having for it,[22] the funds, he claimed, being raised from public subscription by his constituents. There was widespread criticism in the press that Hardie had not conformed. The *Telegraph* said he had left 'a painful impression'.[23] Liberals in particular were quick to contrast Hardie with Burns, who had 'dressed like a gentleman'[24] while Hardie had dressed like 'a bugger'. There was a false press report that the Speaker had rebuked him for his clothes and the next day the Speaker had to write Hardie a personal note to disown this newspaper account and to apologize for it – a fact never made public.

The criticism of his attire stung his family, especially Lillie, who, as a dressmaker, made a lot of his clothes and was proud of her skill. His scarf had been woven by his mother. Decades later Nan was still concerned to make it clear that Hardie had tried to dress for the occasion, was not wearing workclothes but 'his every day suit', and retelling yet again the story that Lillie – still burdened with childcare and thus not able to be there for his arrival – had made a soft felt hat for the occasion, and had posted it to him by express mail. Perhaps it did not arrive in time, or perhaps Hardie decided against it.[25]

For far from being the bumpkin who stumbled unawares into high politics by wearing his campaigning clothes, Hardie was the consummate image-maker, determined to give notice of the new route he intended to pioneer. The clothes he chose were not those he had worn as a representative of the Ayrshire miners in the 1880s, when, as Cunninghame Graham noted, 'he always wore a blue serge suit and a hard bowler hat'[26] (the same dress that John Burns is described as wearing at the same period). His dress for West Ham, said Cunninghame Graham, was 'an entirely different style of dressing, entirely foreign to his custom when a little known man'.[27] The larger meaning of the sartorial statement can be found in words Cunninghame Graham himself had written five years earlier:

> a working man in Parliament . . . should go to the House of Commons in his workaday clothes . . . He should address the Speaker on labour questions and give utterance to the same sentiments in the same language and in the same manner that he is accustomed to utter his sentiments to . . . the local Radical Club . . . Above all, he should remember that all the Conservatives and the greater portion of Liberals are joined together in the interest of Capital versus Labour.[28]

It was among socialists that revolution in dress, signifying overthrow of the older order, had established itself as common practice in the 1880s. A friend had written to Hardie in early 1892 to urge him to give his evidence to the Royal Commission on Labour wearing his work-clothes.[29] A fellow ILP member, Raymond Unwin, later writing of being a young man in the SDF in the 1880s,[30] said that 'when the coming revolution loomed large in our imaginations' we were also rejecting the top hat and frock coat and 'stockbroker respectability . . . we all stripped off starch and put on red ties.'

As one of Hardie's later biographers put it, Hardie's clothes were his 'oriflamme',[31] a national rallying standard which challenged the mystique of representative government which had developed in the nineteenth century: that of the two-party gentleman's club. Widening the franchise merely meant giving more people a chance to choose which well-to-do man they wanted. If a working-class man was exceptionally admitted, it was understood he would transform himself into a respectable fascimile. With sartorial transformation went political.

What so alarmed the governing class, wrote Glasier many years later, was not Hardie himself, but 'the omen they beheld in him . . . the dread apparition of the great common people divested of their servility . . . awakened . . . to their power . . . that vast unseen power of which Shelley speaks'.[32]

Hardie won an instant reputation for refusing transformation and retaining the right to choose ever after the kind of clothes he preferred. Whatever press and parliamentary colleagues assumed, Hardie was not dressed like a typical worker in 1892 or at any time later. Snowden called him 'something of a dandy' in his younger days.[33] As early as 1888 a colleague had noted he was 'very fastidious about his dress', already adopting the 'light brown finely woven materials which the Jagerites affected later'.[34] Hardie had his suits made from cloth woven specially for him by comrades who were weavers.[35] He loved coat, waistcoat and trousers 'of different patterns'.[36] He preferred flannel shirts, and was only once seen in starch, 'apologizing, He had been to his brother's wedding'.[37] Photographs taken throughout his life show Hardie by turns looking like a banker in a double-breasted three-piece suit or a bohemian with floppy foulard tie. He wore a constant succession of hats: felt, straw, wide brim and narrow. At the end of Hardie's life Fenner Brockway[38] remembered him best with a romantic Inverness cape swirling around his shoulders. Bruce Glasier said that if you had seen Hardie without knowing who he was, you would have said from his dress that he was a biology professor from some provincial university.[39]

His manners were not those of a working-class man either. Long before he arrived in Parliament colleagues were able to say he was 'the only really cultivated man in the ranks of any of the labour parties',[40] and Cunninghame Graham had commented on the fact that Hardie's 'want of education' was not visible at all in the way he spoke.[41] He had a highly inquiring mind and had kept up his habit of reading voraciously, even if he had had to give up ideas of qualifying academically. One who had qualified and become a lecturer, Frederick Rogers, the bookbinders' leader, told of walking through Edinburgh with Hardie while they quoted William Dunbar to each other. Rogers said that he knew the poet well 'but Hardie knew him better'.[42] Hardie was far from both the dangerous ruffian pictured or the simple rustic which has come down in labour movement myth, an impression reinforced at once in August 1892, when he tried to secure a debate on the 'condition of the people' but failed to rise at the appropriate moment owing to lack of knowledge about the formal procedures of the House.[43] He had to wait another six months to make his maiden speech.

What most concerned Hardie, however, at the time was how he could afford to go to Parliament at all. Every day he attended – unpaid and running up expenses – was a day he could not lecture and earn 3 guineas. Of particular importance was where he would stay in London and how he would keep himself.

Necessity breeds friendship and in this case it was Frank Smith
(defeated in Hammersmith) who came to the rescue. Frank Smith was
a middle-class man of means and like all Hardie's enduring friends, both
a committed socialist and a Christian, as well as teetotal. Like them all,
and Hardie himself, he had accepted an entirely self-imposed obligation
to improve life for others. His early life had been aimless before a
Thames bargeman he met by chance converted him to religion. Later
he joined General Booth's new Salvation Army and was put in charge
of its 'social wing', organizing the Army's first poor relief shelters in
the East End of London. It was work he undertook so well that Booth
eventually became alarmed about secular activity over-shadowing the
Army's religious work. Booth reorganized operations so that social
action was brought back under his own control, and Smith left.
Through a family friend (William Saunders, founder of the Press
Association) he then became a journalist, imitating Booth by starting
a paper called *Workers' Cry* and hoping to form a 'Socialist Army'.[44]
This did not succeed and Smith's writing never got very far either,
possibly because he was not highly literate. He made up for it by
enthusiasm for a 'brighter, cleaner, happier and more prosperous
London' with 'the workers' life ... a pleasure'[45] and he saw in
Hardie a man who would make this possible. He solved Hardie's
living problem by offering him permanent room and keep in his
large Chelsea house during the parliamentary term.

It was not only a place to eat and sleep that Smith offered. With
Cunninghame Graham no longer regularly in London – and perhaps
for Hardie's own independence it was as well that Don Quixote was
not in Parliament – Hardie had found a real Sancho Panza, someone
ready to devote himself singlemindedly to Hardie's welfare and work.
Smith had begun this new job on the day Hardie took his seat in
Parliament, by joining him in the wagonette ride from West Ham.

In the early 1890s both major political parties must have been congratulating themselves that the parliamentary system was weathering labour
unrest and making the transition to an increasingly enfranchised state
relatively smoothly. But they were largely unaware of how quickly
matters were moving where they could not see: in the working-class
communities of Britain and in certain middle-class groups. By 1892 the
Scottish Labour Party already had thirty branches; and in England there
were hundreds of independent labour groups and socialist societies,
particularly in the north. Despite its poor showing in the election, SDF
branches were increasingly active, co-operating readily with others.
Hyndman's influence in the organization was waning, as working
men continued to join. More influential now were such men as
Harry Quelch, a printer, who had played a key part in organizing
dock workers south of the Thames during the 1889 dock strike. Social

democrats like Eleanor Marx and Aveling, who rejoined the SDF when Morris's League collapsed, and who also saw the importance of organized labour, contrived to ignore Hyndman on this issue.

As these groups proliferated, interest rose again in forming a national Labour Party. In 1888, during the TUC Congress, Mann and Champion[46] had met with a few others, possibly including Hardie, at the Central Coffee Tavern in Bradford, to try to get such a venture off the ground. But there was not enough support at that time. Another attempt was made just before the 1892 election – on 13 June – when Joseph Burgess, editor of the *Workman's Times*, organized a meeting in London of the District Provisional Council of the Labour Party (whose meetings Hardie attended when he was in London).[47] It proposed to base a national party on 'all hand-and-brain workers' who would stand as Independent Labour, but to refuse admission to any 'labour exploiters, landowners, lawyers or usurers',[48] posing the issue in terms of the nature of the membership.[49]

At the 1892 Trades Union Congress Cunninghame Graham and Hardie appeared together as usual and a motion calling for independent labour representation was debated. This time not only was it carried, it was followed up by an informal decision by some of those present to set up an organizing committee. It began canvassing members attending the TUC to take part, among them a pretty young socialist, dancing the night away at the SDF social, Katharine St John Conway.[50] Katharine was a middle-class, university-educated teacher from Bristol, where she had been converted to socialism after her work had taken her into poor homes and sweated shops employing young girls.[51] She left teaching and took to the Fabian lecture circuit, where she had been an instant sensation in her Medici collar, with her mix of enthusiasm and erudition. During the summer's general election she had electioneered in Bradford for Ben Tillett, and it was then she had met Hardie.

Katharine Conway was living at this time in a strange triangular relationship in Bristol with a socialist working-class couple. The husband was a merchant seaman who had lost a leg in an accident, the wife an invalid with a 'uterine disorder'.[52] Katherine knew that the husband, Dan Irving, who was also an SDF organizer, was 'violently in love with her', though she maintained that, even though she was living in his home, there was no impropriety. She was his 'spirit wife'.[53]

Personal relationships caused socialists a great deal of heart-searching at this time because they highlighted the conflicts between the diverse moral and religious traditions which fed the new movement. Integrating sexual relations with an evolving political belief system was proving difficult for many. At one end of the new spectrum was friendship or an emotional relationship with no physical side, exploring new ways of being but keeping to the rules of Christian ethics upon which so many socialists had been raised, while at the other was a growing interest in a new code which sought to overthrow conventions and acknowledged no rule other than agreement between the partners concerned. Those socialists who had removed themselves from religion found fewer difficulties, but only so long as they remained in the movement.

Every socialist organization had its protagonists of what were known as 'advanced' relationships. At this time Fabian lecturers were being organized by a Fabian called W. S. DeMattos, who had taken a proprietorial (and apparently prurient) interest in Katharine, and was particularly anxious to release her from her relationship with Irving. DeMattos had elevated promiscuity to high theory, according to Katharine's friend and fellow Fabian lecturer, Enid Stacey, who wrote at the time:

> DeMattos stayed with us here for two or three days, and during the whole of that time he tried his utmost to fill mother and my sisters and father with the idea that to be a socialist and a 'free lover' was one and the same thing. At all times and in all places the talk would be brought round by him to the same subject.

Enid Stacey was less than convinced:

> Though I am by no means a believer in conventional morality, I feel such views . . . could not possibly do anything else than bring destruction on any . . . society.[54]

Bernard Shaw, another Fabian, saw through the theorizing, and wrote characteristically to Sidney Webb, 'I hear . . . DeMattos is ravishing every maiden in the country'.[55] But Shaw had his motive. According to Katharine, he proposed marriage to her several times. She turned him down, saying marriage would interfere with the career she was planning as a campaigner and writer for socialism. Eventually the tension in the Irving household became unbearable and Katharine moved out.

At the TUC Conference in Glasgow, where Katharine was elected the only woman on the new committee to form a labour party, she was asked by Cunninghame Graham if she knew the fiery young Scots socialist, Bruce Glasier, whom Hardie had known for nearly eight years by then. Since she did not, Hardie and Cunninghame Graham took her along to meet him[56] after the committee had decided to convene the conference on 13 January in Bradford.

Like West Ham, Bradford already had independent labour councillors and probably more thriving local labour clubs and parties – twenty-three by then[57] – than any other town in the country. It had a Labour Church (a non-sectarian religious society) and a strong Trades Council. The group that assembled in a Wesleyan Chapel that, symbolically, had been revamped as a labour hall, included all shades of opinion from Fabian through to SDF[58] as well as several old trade union friends of Hardie's such as Bob Smillie. Katharine Conway attended in company with Bruce Glasier. Eleanor Marx came as an observer. The majority came from outside London, mainly from the north of England, and a third were from Yorkshire.[59] The meeting started with the usual challenging of credentials – Shaw's and Aveling's this time – but both were finally allowed to stay.

The most important argument was whether this new party was to be a socialist party or a labour party. Again, this was put in terms of who could join. SDF representatives proposed it should be for socialists. Ben Tillett argued it should be for trade unionists, since they were 'socialists in their work every day and not merely on the platform'; and he went on to rail against 'hare-brained . . . Continental revolutionaries'.[60] Hardie took a more conservative and populist view, harking back to his earlier concept of a labour party that both Whigs and Tories would join.[61] Had he known it (maybe he did), the *Bradford Observer* had just studied local voting in the 1892 general election, where Ben Tillett had polled so well. To their surprise they found that half of Tillett's votes had come from Conservatives.[62]

Hardie's lifelong animosity to Tillett might have begun at this meeting, since he might have taken Tillett's scornful reference to 'platform socialists' to apply to himself. Hardie did not want membership restricted to trade unionists or those already committed to socialism. Nor would Hardie have liked Tillett's negative view of continental socialists, for whom he had a high regard, including Edouard Bernstein, London editor of *Vorwärts*, also present as an observer. Hardie wanted a broad membership. It was vital to him that the new group attract the working man who was dissatisfied with orthodox Lib-Lab representation. Blatchford, who arrived late, fuelled the issue further by trying to force an electoral policy on the new group: that it should abstain from all voting unless there was a socialist on the ballot. The 120 delegates rejected this by a large majority. They wanted to decide voting according to circumstances. They also wanted the same wide membership as Hardie.

Creating an umbrella organization, encouraging a variety of clubs, unions, trades councils, and campaigning groups to affiliate, and making itself open to trade unionists, socialists and radicals alike, to agree to campaign for specific policies that supported the working class, was not an ideological exercise but a practical alliance – and typical of Hardie's way of working. It was made to serve a purpose, open to any who wanted to further that purpose. This included women, for unlike the other political parties, who had their separate women's committees, this one aimed to include women on the same basis as men.

Significantly, Burns did not attend (though he was asked repeatedly). Until then he had been assumed to be the joint leader with Hardie. Now Hardie stood alone. For all his rhetoric, Burns accepted the argument that Henry Broadhurst went on making for the next decade: that the Liberal Party could represent both the labour interest and the employer interest at one and the same time.[63]

Hardie's view was that the labour interest had 'to take precedence' over an idea of one nation.[64] This was an implicit rather than an explicit class position, acknowledging tacitly William Morris's claim that 'radicalism . . . was made for and by the middle class'.[65] Hardie and those present in 1893 did not oppose self-help, they simply disagreed with the view that the state could and should do nothing, even when all around were starving, homeless, workless and suffering growing industrial pollution, because action might sap the independence of a few people. This was the dogma of Bentham maintained by a hierarchy of MPs, councillors, clergy, nouveau-riche industrialists and the bulk of the trade union leaders.[66]

The group adopted a programme that was largely the same one that the Scottish Labour Party had adopted four years earlier (see pp. 61–2) with the addition of public provision for the sick and old, collective ownership of land and production, free unsectarian education from school to university, and full employment.[67] Although Morgan characterized it as merely 'standard advanced radicalism',[68] it was seen by the later Labour Party as 'a socialist programme but without a socialist title'.[69] There may not have been any formal ideology, but as Pelling observed, the new group showed where it stood by placing economic objectives before constitutional ones.[70]

Most of those who organized and participated, though not impossibilists, operated within an intellectual climate profoundly altered by Marx. A contemporary, asked to explain the difference between the old 'Lib-Labs' and the new 'Independent Labour', answered unequivocally that the new group 'recognized the theory of the class war'.[71] Immediately after the group's first meeting Engels had written to Sorge that 'the programme in its main points is ours';[72] and a few weeks later he told a meeting commemorating the Commune that he recommended the new organization as 'the very party which the old members of the International desired to see'.[73] Five years later Hardie himself was anxious to make sure everyone knew that Engels had joined the ILP, and that had Karl Marx lived, he too would have found its membership congenial.[74]

Yet the new group had no worked-out theoretical position, merely members who wanted to argue for practical working-class advances in a pragmatic way. Hardie put the point of the movement in a way everyone could understand:

> the first serious attempt to teach the democracy how to use the power of which it is possessed, and use it in its own way, free from either patronage or dictation from privileged classes of society. 'Til this has been accomplished, common people will remain enslaved and unrepresented however much the franchise may be extended.[75]

The new movement was the product of many minds[76] but it had Hardie's stamp. It was to be evangelizing, with mass national membership, inclusive rather than exclusive, and only loosely organized by a National Administrative Council, with minimal rules, autonomous local sections, maximum democratic organization and minimal executive dictation − a difficult prescription for effective organization in the highly controlled party political world that has developed since, but at the time entirely effective in unifying the atomized organizations responding to its call.

But it was not just a party. To many who joined, it was a 'great social fellowship . . . a communion comparable to that of some religious fraternity whose members have taken vows of devotion to a common cause'.[77] Hardie specifically disavowed any parliamentary exclusiveness, 'Instead of seeking to convert legislators to its programme . . . it is endeavouring to convert the community itself' to the idea of working 'not for self but for the general good'.[78] It aroused visions of a society that would not be taken seriously for a hundred years. As Katharine Conway put it, it was 'in league with life . . . every living thing is sacred', it opposed 'the smoke that robbed the spring' and the 'foul pollutions that made our rivers a danger'. It cared for all, even the 'poor, over-driven . . . cab-horse, the joke of modern society'.[79] It was called the Independent Labour Party (ILP).

In helping set up the ILP for others, Hardie also fashioned it for himself. He was elected to chair the first session and given the order-bell to keep as a souvenir. A year later he agreed to become president. It was closer to him than the Labour Party that came after or the Scottish Labour Party that went before. As Margaret Cole wrote many years later, the ILP was 'his creation and his darling',[80] and some of its distant descendants gather yearly at Labour Party conferences. When its first meeting ended, Hardie insisted that 'Auld Lang Syne' be sung. In his rich baritone voice he struck up the tune and sang it through twice, for the English and non-trade unionists who did not know the words. The Labour Party sings it still.

To the general public the ILP was just another new organization cooked up by cranks, attracting attention because of the 'novel idea . . . that working men should be capable of running a political organization of their own'.[81] Hyndman, who believed men like himself were required to lead the workers, found the idea of a rival party to the SDF chilling. *Justice*, the SDF's journal, immediately intoned a premature epitaph,[82] 'We know the attempt will fail . . .'

Gladstone was present on the government front bench when Hardie made his first speech to the House and was said to have been roused from the book he was reading, to listen.[83] Hardie did not disappoint. Armed with figures he had gathered from around the country, he pitched right in to 'widespread misery due to large numbers of the working class being unable to find employment' in cities[84] and claimed that 'Any government that can ignore . . . the unemployed and yet claims to represent . . . the interests of every class . . . is unworthy of the confidence of this House and of the Nation.'

He said Parliament speaks only 'for a section of the nation' and he introduced his remarks by moving an amendment to the Queen's Speech, a move that usually only the official opposition makes. 'I am told my amendment . . . will be a vote of censure . . . It is meant for a vote of censure.'

John Burns was asked to second the amendment, for without a seconder there could be no vote. But John Burns, for all his 'barricades' talk outside, was proving less courageous inside. In the previous August he had balked at the idea of sitting with Hardie on the benches opposite the Liberal government (since Hardie regarded himself as much in opposition to Liberals as Conservatives). Burns owed his seat to a pact with the Liberals and did not wish to upset this. Now, only six months later, he was finding equal difficulty in seconding Hardie's amendment. When it went for the vote, therefore, Hardie had his first taste of the new Burns as well as of the parliamentary manoeuvres which had so alienated Cunninghame Graham. A Tory seconded it and Hardie was supported by 109 members, almost all Tories, whose main motive was to embarrass a Liberal government. Most of the Liberals voted against him, including all the trade union members. John Burns solved the problem by staying away that day.

The winter of 1893 was so bitter that the Thames froze over. Hardie asked questions about what local authorities were doing to help the poor and the destitute. The answer was that this was not the House's business. When members heard Hardie argue that 'the worker in his workshop is fettered by the thought that outside . . . are thousands . . . willing to step into his shoes should he be dismissed in consequence of any attempt to improve his position',[85] they were bemused to hear such views in a chamber devoted to the great affairs of state. In any case, Hardie himself had earlier supplied the answer, capitalism needed unemployment to discipline those who are already at work.[86] When he made practical suggestions for improving matters he had been advocating in West Ham, including a sixpence-an-hour minimum wage for labourers in the government's dockyards and arsenals, combined with the enactment of a forty-eight-hour week for all government employees, this was thought to be proposing unwarranted interference by government.

Yet Hardie's postbag brought request after request from individual workers or unions to urge such interference.[87] His work in Parliament was being watched closely. One shop assistants' union official wrote to say he was disappointed to read that Hardie was consorting with the Trades Parliamentary Alliance,[88] the shopkeepers' group. But Hardie did little such consorting. Much more likely were complaints like that from Charles Dilke that Hardie was misusing the House's adjournment procedures to raise matters relating to workers' grievances.[89] During the first session Hardie also made tenacious use of question time to take up one individual case after another, each with an important principle at stake: a twelve-hour day in one factory with only one thirty-minutes break allowed;[90] workmen dismissed in another case ostensibly for poor work, in fact for signing a petition complaining about working conditions;[91] dismissal of mail carriers for having attended a meeting called by a union.[92] When a minister said that even though the government ran the postal service the latter case was nothing to do with the government because it had happened with sub-contractors, Hardie pursued him to withdraw their government contract. The minister was forced to say he would look into it. On several occasions Hardie asked Gladstone himself why government workshops permitted abuses, with always the same reply, 'It is not open to me to disturb the general course of business of the House for discussion of a matter lying outside the business of the House.'[93]

Getting such matters recognized as House 'business' became Hardie's objective; and his tenacity was noticed. Very shortly after his election two unmarried middle-aged women from Edinburgh, daughters of an East India trader who had made 'judicious investments' in the USA,[94] took themselves across to Hamilton to pay a visit to Sarah Wilson, Hardie's mother-in-law. They were the sole inheritors of their late father's money and were determined it should go to further the causes he supported, Scottish land restoration and the Parnellite wing of Irish independence. Hardie was the agent they had chosen, since the Scottish Labour Party was supported by Land Leaguers and the Crofters' Movement and Hardie had admired Parnell. But the sisters were cautious. They had to determine if Hardie's character was sound and his family well treated by him.[95] When the Misses Elizabeth and Jean Kippen had finished with Sarah Wilson and her daughter, Lillie, who had joined her, and had asked questions in Cumnock, which they also visited, they summoned Hardie to their Edinburgh home and offered him £300 a year so long as he remained an MP and loyal to the cause of land nationalization and Irish independence.[96]

Hardie went home and talked it over with Lillie. Perhaps she put the case for taking it, as, after all, he supposedly had accepted Margaret Harkness's money in 1888 – and Lillie was still owed the £100 that had gone to Carnegie. But it was precisely these experiences that had made Hardie wary of bad publicity (he was still locked in an unpleasant argument with Champion over funding of both previous elections). In the end he decided against it, saying he would 'gang his ain gait',[97] one of his favourite expressions, and one he had also used when the ILP was founded,[98] he would go his own way.

It is not hard to imagine Lillie's anger at this refusal. Certainly the Kippen sisters were angry and promptly withdrew the offer. But not before Hardie had suggested to them that although he would not accept their financial support personally, he would be glad to accept money donated to his causes – like the Scottish Labour Party (or the ILP into which it was soon incorporated) or the *Labour Leader*, which he was trying to revive. This decision to make a distinction between personal money and cause money was designed to set his conscience at rest and keep scandal at bay, but drawing the line in practice was quite another matter. For Hardie came increasingly to assume a proprietorial attitude to money he had helped to raise or had himself solicited. His charisma had brought the money in and he did not willingly submit to democratic decisions about its use. This led to an unending series of unseemly arguments about funding throughout his life. The Kippen money was to be no different.

Luckily, in London he had Frank Smith to count on for support, both personal and financial. Smith was enthusiastic about the ILP and made himself available to stand at any by-election, paying the costs himself. Hardie believed that contesting all possible elections, however hopeless, was an essential form of propaganda, and urged it as an ILP tactic throughout his life. But it would be wrong to assume Hardie's friendship was won with largesse. From the first he valued Smith personally; 'somehow we took to each other,' Hardie wrote.[99] Frank Smith was a man who never asserted his ego and was always willing to be part of the collective fellowship.

Frank Smith also shared Hardie's sentimental streak. He still worked on his own among London's 60,000 homeless who were sleeping rough on the streets. Hardie called him 'St Francis'. Like Hardie he was full of schemes, including support for unused land upon which the unemployed could grow food for themselves and others who were poor. While Hardie argued for government-backed farm colonies, and Lansbury for farm colonies overseen by the local Board of Guardians, it was Frank Smith who put land use into effective action. Not on the lines of elaborate colonies nor yet the starry-eyed rural enterprises tried by several middle-class socialists at this time – such as Katharine Conway and Enid Stacey, who had joined a Yorkshire farming commune which came to a disastrous and costly end.[100] Or the legendary model rural community the socialist Edward Carpenter had started outside Sheffield, backed by his own considerable funds.[101] Smith's plans were modest and sustainable and involved the concept of individual accessible plots in cities. He started the allotment movement, serviced by a journal he published himself called *Vacant Lots*.[102] Frank Smith's useful and far-seeing social activity was unknown to most of Hardie's political colleagues and fellow socialists like Blatchford or Ramsay MacDonald, who disliked him because they saw him only as a Hardie henchman and an extension of Hardie's ego. MacDonald called him disdainfully 'a secretary paid to arrange cheers',[103] while Blatchford repeatedly savaged him in the *Clarion*.

The root of much of the antagonism lay in religion. For the socialist movement was then – as it remains – caught between secular and religious wings. Not only were Hardie and Smith on the latter, but they were also alive to the mystic and irrational. Smith was a firm believer in the reality of spirits, and Hardie became a convert to the idea that minds could communicate even when apart. He frequently arranged with Lillie or the children – and later, with the women in his life – to think of them, and they of him, at precise predetermined moments, believing they could be in touch in some real way.[104] At the time spiritualism was not as déclassé as it might seem today. In some circles it was rather fashionable. Conan Doyle, for example, was a keen advocate of extra-sensory perception and a campaigner on the subject.

Almost as soon as Hardie had entered the Commons, opponents were on to what they imagined were his weaknesses, relating to both superstition and poverty. On one occasion Liberal colleagues invited him to visit a well-known spirit medium.[105] Hardie was curious, but as a precaution took Frank Smith. Robbie Burns was promised from the beyond. He duly spoke – followed by Parnell and Bradlaugh, both recently dead and thought likely to influence Hardie. Their messages were identical: oppose the Irish Home Rule Bill. It must have amused Hardie to outwit these men so easily, who mistakenly thought his informal dress bespoke a simple mind. The next occasion, which followed shortly, was an invitation to a club by a Unionist MP who posed as a radical, and made progressive noises during the meal, but ended by saying that if Hardie would vote against the Home Rule Bill and immediately leave the chamber and go to the terrace by the river, 'there would be a bag containing 500 sovereigns on a certain part of the ledging' waiting for him. That such incentives should have been offered in order to win Labour to the Unionist cause tells us about the way politics operated (possibly also about what had worked with other 'Labour' members in the past). No doubt the word soon spread that Hardie was not for sale.

Such events – and many more that followed – confirmed in Hardie a lifelong misgiving about the seductions surrounding the life of an MP. He saw life for the reformer as a 'thicket of thorns'[106] and Parliament as a highly 'dangerous' place.[107] As he put it later, elected labour men 'lose their heads and lose sight of the work they had been sent to do.'[108] This was not because of this kind of crude bribery, but because of what he called 'the unlimited opportunities for meeting wealthy people and being patronized by "society"'.[109] Hardie's stern attitude might have been influenced subconsciously by his own susceptibility, 'I don't fear the women. It's the wealth that kills.'[110]

Some in the socialist movement saw an equal danger in the super-natural views of men like Hardie and Smith – in their allegiance to the unreason of religion, the 'cant' of the second verse of the 'Red Flag'. Many rationalists and secular socialists never understood, and therefore distrusted, the Christian and temperance tradition in which so many working people had been raised. This was a split at least as great – and certainly as enduring – as that between Marxist and non-Marxists, which Labour historians make so much of retrospectively. Many Marxists were secularists, but so also were hard-headed journalists like Blatchford, and many Fabians. And within the SDF there were still those with religious views – like Mann. Hyndman wrote scornfully of Mann's and Hardie's 'queer jumble of asiatic mysticism and supernatural juggling . . . called Christianity'.[111] During the dock strike Hyndman had scorned Tom Mann's repeated visits to Cardinal Manning,[112] alternating with visits the next day to preach in Congregational pulpits, or to visit the drawing room of the inquiring Lady Aberdeen, who assembled the well-to-do anxious to inform themselves on the 'social question'. Although Mann was vigorous in denouncing the churches for failing to deal with social issues, as well as the Lib-Lab trade union leaders for being 'utterly callous . . . to poverty',[113] his pious reputation grew. Eventually *The Times* claimed he was about to quit trade unionism and take holy orders.[114] In fact, Mann was about to leave behind his religious phase for a new libertarian life.

Although Hardie was firmly rooted in the religious tradition, his own commitment to religion – in the organized form of its earlier days – was declining. He particularly disliked the nonconformist churches, dominated, as he had experienced, by professional and trades people. The popular myth may have grown since that Methodism and not Marxism fuelled British socialism, but Wesley's tradition, peopled by wealthy industrialists, had grown respectable by the middle of the nineteenth century. As Pelling wrote, the local nonconformist establishments 'thus bore an unfortunate resemblance to the Liberal Associations with which they were closely connected . . . nominally democratic, they became oligarchies of local wealth'.[115] It was this establishment that became Hardie's main political target.

To combat it he used its own weapons against it. During the early

1890s Hardie renewed his religious quest but in wholly political form. He did not abandon Christianity. He used it to express his new class-consciousness that had been developing from the late 1880s onwards, reinforced by his election and the formation of the ILP – not consciously, as Marx and Christ were joined in so much twentieth-century 'liberation' activism, but implicitly, in the way he worked and the arguments he used. Hardie began a crusade against 'churchianity', claiming that 'the rich and comfortable classes have annexed Jesus' and made him a 'symbol of respectability rather than a force to combat social evils'.[116]

His development was paralleled in the Labour Church move-ment, where various clergy began establishing religious centres to link working-class politics and religion. One of the first was John Trevor's Labour Church in Bradford, established in 1891.[117] Inside Labour Churches class-conscious arguments from preachers like Ben Tillett were heard, criticizing existing nonconformity for excluding working people. Services were indistinguishable from political meetings; when Christ's name was introduced into one of Tillett's addresses, there was prolonged applause.[118] The doctrine was simple, God had a 'divine plan' which people had to implement in society, like a political manifesto. Carlyle, Ruskin, Walt Whitman and Morris were 'teachers and prophets' along with Isaiah and Christ.

Hardie was at home in this new tradition, as he was with other groups beign formed like the Christian Socialist League in Scotland, a group he described as involved in 'theo-social' agitation.[119] There he met another wealthy supporter whose funds he soon canvassed, C. W. Bream Pearce, the son of a Chartist. Not for himself, of course, but for the cause. A year later Pearce put up £200 to revive the Labour Leader.[120] Thus did all Hardie's projects reinforce each other.

Gradually Hardie's religious convictions, already limited in their theological grounding, became wholly fused with his social conviction. This armed him well against those who attacked socialism as godless, as increasingly began to happen. On one occasion in 1894 he clashed with Edinburgh's Divinity Professor Robert Flint, an avid anti-socialist.[121] Flint attacked Hardie for a creed that attached so much importance to 'social life on earth', to the 'condition of men rather than their characters'. Hardie's reply was head on, socialism teaches that character depends on circumstance and can only be developed 'when fear has been taken away', when hunger and want of work and dread of the poorhouse are gone. Neatly, he turned Flint's own argument back on him: 'Yet Professor Flint tells divinity students that to alter this is anti-Christian'. He rounded off his contribution by saying 'that the more a man knows about theology the less he is likely to know about Christianity'.

Hardie did not reject orthodox Christianity any more than he rejected orthodox Marxism. He ignored them both and concentrated on the socialism that he perceived to be common to both. What gave his emerging views coherence was his passion to preach the gospel of socialism, not as ideology but as religion: 'Socialism is the modern word for Christianity', he claimed.[122] Morgan sees Hardie's earlier religious conversion preceding the later socialism.[123] In fact, they were one and the same, the first now absorbed into the second until they were virtually indistinguishable.

Hardie's own class background in temperance and union activity – as well as his evangelical preference – may not have given him the edge as theologian or ideologue, but it had wide resonance in the radical wing of the Liberal Party and with the generality of the working class. He had an appeal denied to socialists in the secular societies like the Fabians or the Social Democratic Federation. Yet Hardie did not think of himself as less practical than the former or less revolutionary than the latter. Revolution in the name of Christ on earth was sanctioned in the market place in a way that revolution in the name of an atheist German philosopher or an industrious group of middle-class intellectuals never would be.

In a growing commitment to socialism Hardie also rediscovered the faith he had found in religion as a young man. 'Socialism, I say again, is not a system of economics. It is life to the dying people.'[124] Hardie regarded his conversion to socialism as a religious event. Sylvia Pankhurst claimed that looking back, he would often say that

> Socialism came to him as a revelation . . . filling him with joy and eagerness to tell the great hope to everyone he would see.[125]

Hardie knew his long absences from home were a trial for his family and he adopted the practice of writing to Lochnorris every day when he had to be away. Sometimes it was a postcard, often a picture of himself. Political postcards showing well-known figures were common and those featuring Hardie popular, as were cards showing Lochnorris. In 1905 Hardie sent a postcard photograph of himself to Nan: 'I am told this is having a big sale . . . It was taken almost exactly a dozen years ago.'[126]

That would have been at the beginning of June 1893 when he was thirty-six. It showed a handsome and dapper Hardie with well-trimmed beard and a red-striped tie. His clothes were more dashing and fashionable than those he had worn for campaigning in West Ham. His demeanour was alert, not at all like the description he had given of himself five years earlier as 'a prematurely old man in spirit and body'.[127] He was more like the description David Lowe had given when the Scottish Labour Party was formed, 'with dark brown hair long and plentiful; a beard brown-red and bushy, flowing over a broad chest; a brow . . . spacious like a philosopher, eyes hazel and a watchful mouth, hinting at a weakness for sensuous good things.'[128]

The photograph was taken in the month he was completely absorbed by a young woman named Annie Hines. In one of his letters asking Annie to London, he says, 'I want your photo. Perhaps you could have it taken while here.'[129] Perhaps he had his own taken at the same time – to exchange?

It was eleven months after he was elected to Parliament, and he was enjoying the flush of national celebrity status – unabated until his death. On May Day that year, he had attended three demonstrations,[130] one of which was broken up by the police. He was at the Commons the next day, and in Scotland the day after, speaking in Dundee. From there he went to Leeds, then on to Keighley and the day after to Halifax, Bradford and Bolton before returning to London. These speaking marathons had to continue even while Parliament met, for this is how he was earning his living. On the trains between stops he would answer his mail: every post brought a hundred new letters asking him to speak.[131] Hardie had rules he asked hosts to observe: 'Meet my train, have a cup of tea ready, and do not introduce me to every local person we pass on the way to the meeting.'[132]

One of these engagements was at the Old Schoolhouse in Botolph Claydon, Buckinghamshire, where a day-school had been arranged some time in early 1893. The schoolhouse still stands (part of a bijou row of homes in commuter country). When Hardie visited it was a remote village where agricultural labourers were organizing, assisted by socialists from Oxford. One was Annie Hines, the daughter of Alfred Hines, a well-known autodidact, atheist, Socialist League member, and organizer of the Fabian Society in Oxford, where he worked as a chimney sweep in several colleges.[133] Annie and her three sisters were as politically minded as their father. Lansbury knew the family and reported that once when he was in Oxford and trying to speak at the Martyrs Memorial, which noisy undergraduates were protecting from rabble like himself, it was the Hines girls who forced their way imperiously through the 'young gentlemen', and made a path for the working-class speakers.[134]

One letter from Hardie is addressed to 'Dear Miss Hines' at 92 St Clements, and gives notice of his arrival for a Fabian Society meeting her father has arranged for Sunday 11 June in Oxford. Hardie enclosed *Labour Leaders* and hoped a further meeting with local students could be arranged after the one for the Fabians. He also enclosed a copy of *Woman Free*, knowing Miss Hines was what would later be called a feminist. By almost the same post he was writing another letter to the same girl, addressing her by his pet name for her of 'Sparks'. It showed he already knew her very well. The formal letter was for the outside world.

The correspondence shows they had met several more times at the
Old Schoolhouse, and later near Oxford, where there had been time
for long walks in the fields and by the water. Many of the letters are
bantering. He teases her when she is unwell; 'emancipated women'
are not supposed to be ill (feminism at the time insisted on girls' equal
capacity for health). She sent him poems through an intermediary. He
enclosed a poem upon which he will be glad to have her opinion so
that he can submit it to the judgement of 'some much abused married
woman', as Annie had put it, and 'learn what she thinks'. Annie had
given her decided views against marriage.

He wrote to her from Lochnorris to tell her that his children had
acquired a kitten which he insisted be called Sparks. He told her it
'is as full of mischief as its prototype'. In a further letter he noted,
suggestively, that Sparks slept 'inside my waistcoat somewhere near
. . . the heart'.

Her father wrote back to Hardie to finalize arrangements for his
visit to Oxford and Hardie wrote to tell Annie separately that 'I will
be early, though I have told your father different'. Throughout the
correspondence is the collusion of a couple of children at play, in
league against elders. One letter encloses a yellow flower and with
it a children's story Hardie has written about a knight in a far-off land,
'NODYALCHPLOTOB' – Botolph Claydon backwards. He says the knight
was going about his task of slaying monsters and was 'silent and gloomy'
because he had few 'with whom his heart could hold communion' until
he met an 'angel in woman's guise. She was full of sympathy and her
wondrous eyes spoke with a power which thrilled him through and
through.'

Hardie described the knight as 'unversed . . . in the artifices practised
by the insincere' but with 'a whole-hearted devotion'; and the 'damsel
seemed not unresponsive'. They walked together by the brook hand-
in-hand, 'heart throbbing against heart' and 'love was ever the tale he
told'. The maiden plucked a yellow flower and gave it to him. During
all his wanderings 'one idea . . . had steeled his heart. The thought of
again seeing the woman'.

What looks like being a love declaration ends abruptly when the
knight dies and explorers dig up the flower. Hardie asked, 'Did he find
her true or had she merely been amusing herself with him?' Perhaps
Annie wondered the same thing. Hardie insists, 'write every day', while
his letters (on House of Commons paper) continually apologize for not
being able to write because of too much work. And then more jokes:
'You only spelt my name wrong three times in your letter.'

Eventually the letters got more intense. He kept asking her to get
permission from her father to come to London, and set out an itinerary
there. It included staying in Wimbledon (with a chaperoning family).
He adds that 'a week here will do you a lot of good and you need it

... Try to arrange to come on Tuesday.' She wrote with questions and he replied that he only wanted to answer 'viva voce'. Earlier he had said, 'I did not forget my pipe at BC but a pipe is a poor substitute for——. But, as you say, I will whisper the rest.' Just as we think she is the eager one, we find her putting him off because she has to make a dress, and he is writing that he will meet her at Oxford at 6.30. 'Your dress should be finished by then.'

Soon there were references to the pain of parting, 'Your face on the platform haunts me.' He compared it to the portrait of Lady Russell parting from her husband before his execution, hanging in the House of Lords. He told her he often looked at it. 'Today the likeness was complete.' After another meeting, 'You must think me very cold ... not to have noticed the quiver of the lip and the drooping of the eye at the station. I hate partings. Its shadow ... was over the morning walk.'

By now the meetings are no longer jolly and Annie is withdrawing. By late June he is asking, 'Why are you so sad? Write me freely and unreservedly. If it is a matter of confidence you know that I will guard it well.' He speaks again of repeating 'the pure delight of the Claydon days, 'Make what arrangements you please, sweetheart, and I will prove a willing slave. Then you are coming to London with me when I return. Does your sister know and has your father agreed? No lonely hours.' One letter ends, 'Nine whole days yet before I see you. They will resemble nine ... centuries.'

Annie remained 'depressed in spirits'. He replies consolingly, 'I have been in the dumps myself and know what it means to be there. For one thing it doesn't pay. But like the wind of which we know not when it cometh or whether it goeth, so too it is with fits of depression.' He adds hopefully, 'like other troubles' these 'have their day and cease to be'.

Some of the letters refer to Annie as being 'angry' and having many 'troubles'. One appears to be that she wants to leave home and find work. Hardie encourages this, 'I wish I saw you in a situation. It would be so much better for yourself and all concerned.'

The most revealing of the letters is when he again tries to deal with the subject of depression:

there is no balm for weariness of heart like being able to place your head on a sympathetic breast and there hear sweet true strong words of encouragement. Life without such sympathy – some will call it love – is barren indeed. After all our progress and learning and advancement and emancipation, we find old fashioned human nature will assert itself. Philosophy theories are delightful as theories, but they invariably break down when applied to the cares of everyday life. In reality pure affection alone is worth anything as a sweetener of the bitter cup ... the firm grasp of a ... hand with never a word spoken is worth all the philosophy of life ever written.

To which he adds (in the longest letter he ever wrote her), 'It is the knowledge of this which makes me somewhat conservative on the marriage relationship.' Here Hardie touched gingerly on the issue of free and married love: 'Sympathy is . . . communion of spirit and if the marriage tie . . . degenerates into a business partnership . . . finer . . . feeling may be checked . . . and no freedom will ever compensate for its loss . . . this question resolves itself into one of . . . character . . . Given men and women of the right stamp', all is well, but with the wrong people 'the relations can never be right'. Whether this was his way of saying he was unhappily married is hard to say. Morgan thought it was.[135] Equally, it could be Hardie regretting that early love gets replaced by a 'business' relationship. Money loomed large to Lillie and Hardie, and there are many indications it soured family life. Or perhaps he had found that the real Lillie was not of 'the right stamp'. Over the passage looms the word 'sympathy'; Hardie uses it dozens of times in his letters to Annie. But he only once says, 'some call it love'. It was clearly more than physical attraction.

He ends this particular letter by saying 'there is nothing I would not do to make you [happy]'. He adds if he were a 'spooney young man he would send kisses on the page' but 'probably you will respond by saying "shut up"'.

It seems she did. On one occasion she did not arrive as arranged and he had to walk alone in 'the old haunts'. The skies were 'draped in funeral gloom'. He quoted the Burns poem about a country scene delightless because 'My Annie's awa'. He said it hit off his present mood to perfection.

Twice more he asked was she playing with him? 'That was more then he could endure.' He told her he even composed some 'rough verses' to send back but never sent them. His suspicions get some reinforcement in a report from the go-between that her illness 'was not so bad as it was represented'. Was it the best excuse she could invent to stave him off?

We get a picture of the thirty-six-year-old family man and a young girl stringing him along. Just as clearly we see an older, powerful male pressurizing a much younger woman. A third possible view is of two playful innocents, caught in a net.

Soon there are the expected brick walls. He cannot come as arranged, as 'It might lead to further complications and unfounded suspicion . . .'

The relationship flared up and died within a few months. The fact that Annie saved the letters and passed them to his heirs is a clue that Annie, at least, retained some positive feelings. Reading between their lines we find a twenty-one-year-old working-class girl with no little ambition, striving for emancipation, writing poetry, receiving increasingly intimate letters, and in the end refusing to go on – either because she broke down under the strain, or someone (like her father) stepped in to end it, or she feared Hardie was getting too serious.

It was unlikely Hardie did the signing off, since his insight was so lacking. 'Will you, Annie, tell me what stands in the way?' he asks, when it is all too obvious what stands in the way. That Hardie does not himself see it suggests he had not fully realized the implications of what he was doing. His attempts to revive the relationship with a new ending for the 'Knight Story' were thus to no effect. There is no new ending to this story.

One barrier in our own way is Hardie's reputation as a moral paragon. Could it be he was like many men identified with great moral crusades – exceptionally drawn to moral danger personally? Or like Gladstone, who made repeated forays into the streets to contact prostitutes, and was only saved from scandal because of his personal stature and his inability to see any other motive within himself save that of honest rescuer?

Hardie plainly found in Annie someone he needed. There is much in the correspondence to suggest he wanted her to regard him as a father or older brother, equally much to show, whether he realized it or not, that he put himself forward as a lover, or at the very least 'a spirit husband'. The relationship and correspondence, like all those he was to have with young women, were extraordinarily ambiguous.

Just as Annie and Hardie were breaking up, on 21 June 1893, on the shores of the sea off Scotland, Bruce Glasier and Katharine St John Conway were marrying in the simple Scottish manner – outdoors, with only two witnesses. After Hardie had introduced them, their love affair had blossomed quickly. Katharine had even consented to give up her scruples and marry. George Bernard Shaw sent his usual wicked respects in the form of a single-line telegram, 'Invite me to the christening.'[136]

Elsewhere in Scotland, Lillie, then thirty-three, was in Cumnock struggling to keep the new house and bringing up Jamie, twelve, Nan, eight, and Duncan, six. In later life Nan recalled the vital weekly payment Hardie would send. 'I well remember the envelope; it used to arrive on a Saturday.'[137] In good weeks it could be as high as twenty-five shillings, but 'mostly a pound'.[138] When Hardie was at home he handed the money over personally. But increasingly he was away. Lillie would not have been helped to cope with physical absence by Hardie's signing off emotionally, and withdrawing from her that 'sympathy' he clearly thought so important for himself. Yet for all this, it is unlikely he would have applied Annie's phrase of 'a much abused married woman' to Lillie. But perhaps Annie did.

These constant desertions, together with the growing notoriety attached to the Hardie name, and having to manage on so little, took their toll. The family began to react to the pressure. They started what was to become a marked pattern, particularly for Nan and Lillie, they became ill. Health became as important as money. As a bonus, it sometimes brought the absent father back. In January 1894, Hardie had to cancel a meeting with David Lowe, 'My little girl was suddenly taken ill yesterday . . . and I write this at her bedside getting on for cockcrow. I think the danger is past.'[139] What the illness was is not said. The Hardie family had a way, like many Victorians, of talking elliptically about 'turns' and 'bad spells'. But like most Victorians Hardie had also experienced enough sudden illness in children (and in his own home, death) to take no chances. Serious health crises always took priority and kept him at home for their duration. The strain on Lillie would have been no less, especially as she would have had to do all the nursing during convalescence, when Hardie had departed again.

Had the Hardies the money, Lillie would have wanted them to be an orthodox political couple in the mould of William and Catherine Gladstone or Harry and Matilda Hyndman, where the husband was politically active, while the wife supported by appearing at his side. For this is the style she adopted later. But this pattern was changing in socialist circles, where more and more wives wanted to be as politically active as their husbands, and couples became teams: Sidney and Beatrice Webb, Gabrielle and Robert Cunninghame Graham, Katharine and Bruce Glasier, Emmeline and Richard Pankhurst, Eleanor Marx and Edward Aveling.

Soon a new political couple – cast in the modern mould – joined the circle of socialist agitators, Ramsay and Margaret MacDonald. MacDonald by the early 1890s was back in London working as a paid secretary to a Liberal MP and hoping to rise on the political ladder as a Liberal-backed Labour MP. He had resisted joining the ILP when it began. He thought it 'an idealist communist society' with an 'atrociously bad' leadership.[140] But he could see that the ILP was making converts and gaining influence, and he had become increasingly angry about his own failure to be selected by the Liberals to fight a constituency.[141] Suddenly he saw he never would be. What finally made him snap was a by-election at Attercliffe in 1894 when, instead of the trade unionist Liberals had virtually promised would have the seat, they chose – yet again – another middle-class manufacturer. The obliging Frank Smith put up at once against the Liberals as the ILP candidate and MacDonald went to help him. He also wrote to

Hardie on 15 July 1894, that it was 'impossible for me to maintain my position any longer'. He was making a formal application to join the ILP because men of working-class origin would never be given Liberal seats. He claimed he had always supported the ILP's goals even if not its methods and he used prophetic words to describe what had happened to him, 'I have changed my mind.'[142]

Shortly afterwards MacDonald was sought out by Margaret Gladstone, the daughter of a Liberal professor of chemistry and niece of another scientist, Lord Kelvin. She was an altruistic and independent-minded young woman who had willingly educated herself at the ladies' classes at King's College, London. She then started work for a charity in London's Hoxton area, where she saw working-class conditions and formed a great desire to change them. She was distressed to hear people opposing Ben Tillett.[143] She read the famous Fabian essays. In time, she was a socialist, a school manager in London's Portobello Road and able to write that she found it hard to spend £3 'on a new evening dress when I wd rather give it to Tom Mann's election fund'.[144]

Earlier she had confided in her diary that she hoped one day to find 'my knight'.[145] From afar she cast MacDonald in the role and in 1895, when he stood as a candidate, she sent a cheque to support him. He dressed smartly and had been quick to lose his provincial ways, unlike Hardie who often cultivated them. MacDonald had not entered a working-class trade but had skipped directly into the middle class, as an intending student of biology. His separation from home and kirk had been through allegiance to Darwin. Nevertheless, when he and Margaret met he was very diffident about the social gap between them. But Margaret encouraged him to think of her as a suitable partner and eventually, her charm prevailed. Although she jokingly wrote to him that 'no-one believes that you marry me for the filthy lucre',[146] it must have made a considerable difference that her allowance was £450 a year from her mother's estate, with more added by her father upon the marriage.

Margaret gave MacDonald emotional and financial security, and what MacDonald afterwards called 'her cheery faith and steady conviction'.[147] From the first she wished to be active in political life on her own account. Luckily her middle-class background gave her the wherewithal to do so.

The socialist world gradually developed a distinction between wives, which Stewart expressed in relation to Lillie. On the one hand there were the 'fighting wives' and on the other, the 'home keeping women . . . whose devotion made it possible for others to do the work of socialism.'[148] Lillie was the latter, typecast retrospectively as a 'hame-loving Scots guidwife'.[149] Although settled in her large house, she still thought of Cumnock as off the beaten track and continued to read Glasgow newspapers. She caused some local difficulty by failing

to patronize the Cumnock Co-operative shop.[150] She was aspiring
but she was not aiming to be a politically active 'fighting' wife like
Emmeline Pankhurst or Beatrice Webb. One reason is obvious: in
these new pairs, though the husband was usually working class, the
wife was middle class. She had had time and money to pursue her
own education, and if she was a married woman or a mother, someone
else could be hired to take care of the home and the children while
she was out campaigning. Biographers who assume non-participation
was Lillie's choice fail to see she had no choice. Thus in the world
at large Hardie was usually without Lillie by his side, and seen as the
lone warrior. Lillie got left further and further behind.

She was not too far away to escape the backlash against Hardie,
however. In his first Parliament Hardie made a point not only of
pursuing ministers with questions, but of lifting the lid on parliamentary
life itself. He relayed back to radical and socialist supporters what life
was really like inside the House of Commons: its absurd customs, the
wining and dining, the wasted time. For the benefit of those who could
hardly afford a single meal a day, he printed MPs' menus. In turn the
press and his enemies stepped up their denigration by tarnishing him
with the high-life brush too. There began a spate of stories – going
on for years – that he was a 'sabyrite and a glutton', that he smoked
cigars costing 2s. 6d. each.[151] Later came 'stories freely repeated in
the press'[152] that Hardie and colleagues were 'living in hotels and
having dinners with ten courses and asking the rank and file to pay
for them'. One orator stated 'he had stayed in the same hotel with
Hardie and had seen him enjoying champagne'. The reality, as his
friend Lowe readily attests, is that Hardie was trudging from town
to town[153] living with extreme frugality, still teetotal and virtually
vegetarian, spurred increasingly by that 'implacable determination to
win well-being for the working class'.[154]

It is no accident that with the rise of socialism there was a rise of
'gutter' reporting about socialists from what Hardie called 'the highly
imaginative penny-a-liners who hang about the purlieus of Parliament
picking up such garbage as they can transform into cash'.[155] Not the
real stories of public figures' lives, all of which would have made
better reading, but politically motivated stories. As Lowe confirmed,
they emanated from the Liberal press as often as the Conservative.[156]
Hardie was well aware that journalists 'invented these things' about
him and that the intended message was to disillusion supporters by
portraying him as one who had betrayed them by joining the upper
classes. If the socialist was already in the upper classes, as Cunninghame
Graham was, he was laughed at for slumming, a view some modern
writers still echo.[157] If he was middle class, like Frank Smith, he had
to face posters which held up socialists as 'lunatic . . . atheists and
sensualists',[158] or tales that they were robbing their gullible followers.

Ben Tillett and Tom Mann, for example, were both branded as swindlers, to discredit them with union members.[159] Every one of these campaigns has its modern parallel.

The Hardie family read newspapers avidly and felt the comments keenly. Knowing of their sensitivity, Hardie did his best to shield them from the worst. When Jamie was old enough to read, Hardie stopped the 'prurient' press coming into his own home.[160] Mistakenly he assumed this would protect the family.

On the plus side, all the attacks made Hardie into a figure of national prominence. More people than might otherwise have done so came to hear him. His meetings were often broken up. Sometimes he was chased, and often heckled. Someone from the back of a meeting taunted him once for taking three guineas for each speech and yet calling himself a working-class man.[161] University students pelted him with eggs; 'roughs' broke up a meeting where he and other speakers were standing on a cart in a field by pushing the cart into the river.[162] Hardie never became angered by any attack and always ploughed doggedly on to finish what he had come to say – often to the admiration of those who watched.

An American journalist came to see Hardie the year he was elected. He expected him to be a crude and violent atheist, since, as he wrote, Hardie was regularly 'used by nurses to frighten children: "Keir Hardie is coming in his cap!"' they would say. When he saw Hardie, 'a single look . . . was sufficient to outweigh . . . the testimony of the whole press'. Here, said the reporter, was someone of common sense, with spiritual understanding and the 'head of a saint . . . deep, straight and steady . . . resolute, kindly and reliable'.[163]

Thousands of supporters saw this side of Hardie too. They organized his meetings like religious festivals. On one occasion he spent two days making a single progress[164] between Hebden Bridge, Bradford, Halifax and Keighley, with meetings preceded by massed bands, choirs and floats. Hardie communicated well and was rarely abstract. His particular way of explaining socialism was always to talk about events going on at the time which illustrated people's discontents, and then to show how socialism would help.[165]

But he was anxious to write as well as speak. When, in 1894, the *Workman's Times* ceased publication and transformed itself into the *Labour Leader*, to be the ILP's paper, Hardie regarded the revived *Leader* as 'his' and set himself up as editor with offices at 53 Fleet Street and in 66 Brunswick Street, Glasgow.[166] He attached as much importance to his comments in the *Leader* as to anything he said in the House. It was acknowledged that what funding it drew was mostly due to Hardie's pulling power. Yet it was never enough. Hardie spent lavishly on the paper as, according to Lowe, he 'had a burning desire to be the editor of a national newspaper'.[167] Hardie admitted much

later, 'I was having a terrific struggle to keep the *Labour Leader* alive
. . . there were not trade unions prepared to finance the paper'.[168]
He claimed the money came from those who bought it, but a lot
of it came from the 'generosity' of better-off ILP members such as
T. D. Benson and Bream Pearce, and any others he could persuade
to donate.

At the *Leader* office Hardie was called 'The Chief'.[169] He wrote a
large part of the copy himself. For example, he was 'Daddy Time', the
children's columnist. There was always a slot for young people. He had
founded a Children's Crusader movement, based on the temperance
model, where children in Glasgow of socialist sympathizers marched
in red sashes in street parades. Glasier's sister, Elizabeth, helped him
organize these events. Hardie thought it important for children to be
familiar with a socialist view of life, an idea mostly abandoned now.
Later, he took a great interest in the Socialist Sunday Schools, often
presiding at their events and writing for their own magazines.

Hardie's running feud with Blatchford continued – made no easier
by Blatchford's new closeness with Hyndman. In the war of words,
Blatchford was the winner. His *Clarion* was overwhelmingly the most
influential of the papers and with its vast associated culture of vans,
clubs, outings, choirs, banks and funeral clubs, it was an alternative
society for vast numbers of working people.

The *Leader* took its place in the rack of left publications not
because it was great journalism but because it was Hardie's own –
and because it was the voice of the ILP, now growing at a much
faster rate than the SDF. The *Leader*'s offices, especially the one in
Glasgow, became a hive of work, and Hardie looked in often (and
after 1895 every day when he was not travelling). Many came in to
help during these years, including Caroline Martyn, a young governess
from a Conservative family (from whom she was estranged over her
conversion to socialism). Everyone was very fond of Caroline Martyn,
who also trudged the rural lanes with the *Clarion* van. At local level
the rivalries at the top mattered little.

Also helping was Lily Pearce (wife of the Socialist Christian, Bream
Pearce), who had her own column, and Mary McPherson, wife of
Fenton McPherson, a Paris-based journalist who sent the *Leader*
international items. Mary was a university graduate, and, according
to Lowe, a woman of 'singular discretion'. She soon became Hardie's
'amanuensis' during these years in the middle 1890s, running the
Leader office, acting as his personal secretary and travelling with him
to ILP conferences.[170] Most important for the *Leader*'s development,
however, was David Lowe himself, a Scottish journalist and critic, an
expert on Zola and Scottish literature, who later published the poems
of Robert Burn's contemporary, Mrs Grant.[171] Not before time, he
took over the *Leader*'s finances.

Last but not least in the office (probably part-time, probably unpaid, like most of the others) were Hardie's most political younger brothers, George and David. Hardie's original family was still living close to Glasgow and he was regularly in touch with all of them. His parents supported him politically and followed his every move. The only known portrait of the entire family was taken about this time, either just before Hardie entered Parliament or when Hardie was standing in Mid-Lanark. Hardie family members regularly visited Lochnorris, and Mary Hardie had the habit of coming to stay unannounced and uninvited.[172] Lillie made them all welcome.

Life at the *Leader* during the 1890s was close-knit and typical of Hardie's way of working, closely surrounded by personal supporters whose commitment to the cause was through him. The staff instituted the practice of regular office parties, inviting families as well. Mary Hardie attended, as did Lillie and the children. The supposedly dour Hardie would enter into the activity as enthusiastically as anyone else. He danced reels, he played the melodeon and the flute.[173] He was naturally musical and he loved to sing. Said Sylvia Pankhurst later, 'He never lost touch with the old village world of folk song and story and the fancies of the child'.[174] He would sing the songs his mother and grandmother had taught him, 'Mary of Argyle', 'Robin Tamson's Smiddy', and 'Annie Laurie'. When Mary Hardie was asked to sing at one *Labour Leader* party, she chose 'Robin's Rural Cot'.[175]

Absent from this scene now was Cunninghame Graham. He and Hardie had had a quarrel during a by-election at Leicester in 1894[176] at just about the same time as the Scottish Labour Party was wound up[177] and submerged within the ILP. It might have been about this, or, possibly, about unpaid bills for SLP literature which remained at the Labour Literature Society, a printing firm that took over printing Hardie's *Leader* and with whom Hardie also eventually fell out. Lowe called the latter a 'financial entanglement'[178] and the printer took the matter to court. Glasier listened to the whole story from Hardie some while later but confided to his Diary on 12 August 1896 that Hardie was probably to blame. One result of the argument was the final break with Henry Champion, who departed Britain to live permanently in Australia[179], his political projects having failed.

As a result of such skirmishes the *Labour Leader*'s coffers were empty. In January 1895, at Cumnock during the parliamentary recess, Hardie decided to hold an auction of his own beloved books – in this case, his set of Carlyle – to try to raise money to keep the *Leader* going.[180] The loss of goods, with no gain to the household, was no doubt another blow to Lillie. So too was the loss of gifts which Hardie always appropriated for his own purposes. At this time a Quaker couple who had inherited £200 from a relative who had prospered at 'the turf', found themselves unwilling to use money from such a source, and offered it all to Hardie and his family.[181] He refused it for his family but accepted it for his projects, presumably the *Leader*. Lillie was left to struggle on with £1 a week.

Inevitably the strain showed. In March 1895 Hardie returned from addressing a miners' meeting to find Lillie ill, her condition 'depressing'.[182] Hardie expressed annoyance and called the doctors 'born alarmists and mostly charlatans', but the Hardie household colluded with the idea that women were expected to be ill. Lillie did not aspire to being a 'new woman' – who was proud to enjoy good health – any more than Hardie tried to become 'a new man'. According to Lowe, all the 'increased labours and anxieties sapped his vitality' too.[183]

Hardie returned to London once he had seen Lillie, but said he intended to 'return to pull her through'.[184] In April she was still ill. What was wrong was never said. Nor was any name found for Richard Pankhurst's continuing bouts of indigestion. When they caught up with him, he and Emmeline would visit Smedley's Hydro in Matlock[185] to take water cures. The Hardies could not afford such treatment. In any case, during Lillie's illness, Hardie's main concern, as relayed to Lowe, was that word of it should not get out at the *Labour Leader*'s office, as it 'might upset my mother'.[186]

In 1894 the TUC changed its rules in a last-ditch attempt to screen out Trades Council agitators and other promoters of change. In future delegates would not be allowed to attend unless they were practising the trade they represented. This meant it would be Hardie's last year to represent the Ayrshire Miners, and the end of the trade union chapter in his life. He made the most of it by proposing that the TUC commit itself 'to nationalize the land and the whole of the means of production, distribution and exchange'.[187] Although the TUC was unlikely to promote this, the fact that Hardie got a majority for it showed that in the mere seven years he had been going to the yearly congresses, there had been a complete change from a majority for Liberal individualism to one endorsing collectivity. The new rule change, trying to stem the tide, was unlikely to make much difference, although it indicated the continuing fears of the old Lib-Lab union leadership concerning the spread of working-class organization and socialist ideas.

The congress was held in Norwich. After the debates were over, Hardie and several colleagues went walking in the cathedral close. They stood under an old Norman arch to watch the sun go down. As the lights started to shine over Norwich, all was intensely quiet. One of those present recollected that 'suddenly the voice of old Hardie rose through the stillness, giving vocal expression to the twenty-third psalm, and we all joined, Christians and agnostics alike'.[188] Hardie believed socialism had a mission to feed the soul as well as the body

and that 'of all forms of poverty . . . poverty of the spirit is altogether
the most appalling'.[189]

During the next year, however, the man already thought of as 'old
Hardie' at only thirty-eight, stepped up his fight against poverty of
the body. His journalism reinforced his hustings and parliamentary
sermons, telling of November winds 'howling angrily . . . tonight and
every night' while 'millions of British subjects will crouch together for
warmth in their wretched, fireless hovels or wander homeless in the
streets of our great cities'.[190] At that time Hardie heard the House
of Commons lamenting the fate of those caught in the Armenian
massacres, while close at hand were 'the poor children who gasp at the
grating of a cellar for air. It makes the cynic scoff . . . when they find
all this zeal for humanity abroad, and a devilish callousness to suffering
at home'.[191] He challenged Joseph Chamberlain in a debate in the
press,[192] 'We can organize an army for purposes of destruction . . .
is an industrial army to ply the arts of peace beyond our powers?'

In the House of Commons he kept up his steady pressure. A. J. P.
Taylor claimed that Hardie had made a decision not to squander his
efforts on any matter other than social reform.[193] Certainly he stuck
to working-class issues. But although Hardie is most noted for having
raised the issue of unemployment, the majority of his interventions in
the Parliament of 1892–5 were on behalf of those already employed.
particularly those of men and women in poorly paid work. The workers
he concentrated on most were those employed directly or indirectly by
government itself: in the Woolwich Arsenal, the prisons, the Admiralty
works at Deptford, or the Post Office. He even asked about workers
in the House of Commons – messengers and waiters – the first MP
to look at Parliament as a government workplace. His interventions
were designed to force government to improve conditions, hours
and wages and to set a standard that would force private employers
to follow.

A related concern was industrial action. Wherever there was a strike
in Britain, Hardie found something to query in the conduct of the
government's paid agents, the police or the military. It might be the
use of soldiers to put down a strike, as in the Hull Dock Strike of
1893; or of the police in arresting three striking cotton workers who
were singing in the streets to raise money to feed their families. He
regularly asked about charges for books and schools in the so-called
'free' state system. He introduced a Bill to nationalize the mines.[194]

Another subject that interested him was privilege. He opposed a
£400 pension for Lord Peel on the grounds that the House had not
yet been able to 'provide a system of pensions for the aged workers of
the country'.[195] Attempts to compare the two situations were shocking
to his listeners, but Hardie had learned the value of the shock approach.
It got a hearing and it let supporters outside know that he was fulfilling

his mandate. He was aggressive but never gratuitous. There was always just cause. In the summer of 1893 he objected to giving up a whole day to congratulating the Duke of York on his marriage instead of attending to the 'cancer of unemployment eating into the national life'.[196] A year later, on 28 June 1894, the royal couple had a baby. On the same day 251 men were killed in a mining disaster at the Albion colliery, Cilfynydd, South Wales. Again Hardie was dismayed to find the time of the House of Commons taken up for the whole day by a torrent of congratulations, as MPs vied with each other to make flowery tributes, while there was no mention at all of the disaster.

This drove him to table an amendment that offered condolences to the miners' families. The House was scandalized at this attempt to hijack the loyal debate by a topic which all members considered to be completely out of place. They were to be outraged further when Hardie began speaking, for his anger on behalf of the grieving miners' families came out in comments on a subject little acknowledged in public, popular sentiment against the monarchy. A reporter present wrote, 'I've been at a football match when a referee gave a wrong decision . . . but I've never witnessed a scene like this.'[197] The House 'howled and yelled and screamed'. Hardie held his ground, telling MPs that if they 'mixed as freely with the common people as I do' they would know what they thought about royalty, or, as he put it later, most workers had only one view, 'contempt for thrones and for all who bolster them up'.[198]

He went one better, asking 'what particular blessing the Royal Family has conferred upon the nation that we should be asked' to spend a whole day on this issue? 'I know nothing in the career of the Prince of Wales which commends him especially to me' and much that does not. He spends his time 'at the gaming tables . . . [and] on the race course' and 'He draws £60,000 a year from . . . property in London . . . made up of the vilest slums'. His son will go on doing the same, for he 'will be surrounded by sycophants and flatterers by the score' and 'will be taught to believe himself as a superior creation'. Prophetically, Hardie claimed that the baby, the future Edward VIII, would also face 'rumours of a morganatic marriage' with 'the country . . . called upon to pay the bill'.[199]

Hardie's words caused a minor scandal. Even while he was speaking, Liberals were conferring hurriedly about whether it was wise to let him continue.[200] Gladstone's secretary called it 'a most ill-conditioned speech'[201] and the press played it up hard. Yet Hardie then and after had no regrets and kept up his harassment of royalty throughout his life. In 1901 when Queen Victoria died,[202] he mentioned the 'sickening' lies of the press, talking about London's tears. There were few tears in London, Hardie said. The tears were in the valleys after mining disasters. A few days after what he always referred to in later life as 'My Royal Baby Speech',[203] he analysed the national press[204] to show that many papers never even mentioned the mining disaster, among them the *Sun*, the *Star*, the *Echo*, and the *Evening News*, all 'lickspittles . . . who have no ear for the cry of the poor window and orphan' but only for the royal story.

The editor of the *Daily News*, A. G. Gardiner,[205] said at the time that Hardie 'hates the palace because he remembers the pit', and there was truth in this. He did not advocate a republic. When pressed later on this point, he said that 'until the system of wealth production be changed, it is not worth while exchanging a Queen for a President'.[206] He thus failed to strike the last link of the revolutionary chain he always appeared to be forging. Nor was the motivation inverted snobbery, class hatred or even constitutional reform. It was rather straight Old Testament rage against kings, taken out on a House that could talk for a day about a prince but could not find an opportunity 'for a vote of condolence with the relatives of those who are lying stiff and stark in a Welsh valley'.[207]

The incident struck a humanitarian chord outside. He was inundated with letters of support[208] and had to hire two people just to open them. But it alienated an equally large section of public opinion, and this did not endear him to his more traditional parliamentary Labour colleagues.

Before the three-year term was out it was particularly clear that the 'Labour' contingent of fifteen in the House had lost any coherence. Hardie did not expect anything from the twelve Lib-Labs, but he did from the two elected as Independents, John Burns and J. Havelock Wilson.[209] Wilson was still pursuing trade union causes outside Parliament[210] and Burns still considered himself a leader of Labour inside. Yet there was increasingly less co-operation with Hardie, and Hardie made little attempt to co-ordinate any of his own activity with theirs. The advocate of co-operation and collectivism was somewhat prone to acting individually.

The result was total ineffectiveness. During the dock strike in Hull, for example, in which all Labour members took some interest, Hardie bombarded the government with questions and criticism and kept insisting a day be allotted to debate this national issue. Eventually, it was granted, the first time a whole debate had ever been allotted on a labour issue. But it was given to Havelock Wilson rather than to Hardie. To Hardie's great disappointment, Havelock Wilson, after speaking mildly, withdrew his motion and refused to divide the House; and again Burns was absent from the debate.

Election to Parliament by means of an unwritten agreement with the Liberal wire pullers was turning Burns. By the end of the Parliament he was arguing the old individualist line that governments did not need to do anything about poverty because it was a local matter, and that in any case, 'state' action might encourage 'vagrants'.[211] Personally a highly arrogant man,[212] he was already conforming to the black frock coat he had decided to wear, a victim of a common form of political vanity, he believed that Labour's cause had arrived because he had arrived.

One by one all fell away, until Hardie was left 'a Party of One', as Stewart christened it.[213] Increasingly this was recognized outside the House, and spurred support for the ILP, which began to grow. By now Tom Mann had joined and had become its secretary at the 1894 February conference, after which he set about trying to unite socialist and trade union forces, as well as to bring the SDF and ILP together. During 1893 the prospects for labour and socialist unity had seemed bright. The International, held that year in Zürich, had a huge delegation from Britain, ranging from the ILP, Fabians and SDF, to the Parliamentary Committee of the TUC. There were even five women, including May Morris and Eleanor Marx (who translated proceedings as usual). The aged Engels made what he decided would be his last public appearance, to incredible scenes of welcome. He complimented 'the English' especially, for it is they who 'have been our teachers in organizing workers'.[214] He also concluded that a return to the tactics of the Commune would lead to 'martyrdoms out of all proportion to their effect'. It was wiser that the proletariat of each country 'organize in its own way'. Hardie was not present that year, but these were sentiments he would have endorsed, as no doubt he endorsed Mann's pamphlet, written shortly after, *What The ILP is Driving At*, saying workers were to blame as much as politicians for the 'social difficulties they experienced' because they had failed to take the only step possible to protect themselves by joining a union.[215] He stressed the commonality in aims between the ILP and SDF.

But Mann had taken on a heavy task. In the end he concluded that it was a 'difference of temperament'[216] in the leaders that stood in the way of unity. But it was more than that. Although Hardie and Hyndman appeared to illustrate Engels's complaint about 'bickering, squabbles and . . . sects' jeopardizing socialism's advance in Britain, as opposed to the 'unity of purpose' among German socialists,[217] their disagreements represented real differences[218] that had to be worked through. In any case, German unity was always too good to be true and also had its squabbles too. In 1893, for example, Rosa Luxemburg had been excluded as a delegate to the International. Hardie had to bear his share of the blame. As well as quarrels with Hyndman, he also quarrelled with the Fabians. He was particularly critical of the policy of 'permeating' the Liberals rather than fighting independently, and was heckled by Shaw[219] for his opposition. Hardie argued that taking over Liberals was a recipe for dividing workers, and he continued to insist that 'some plan must be adopted which would induce the working classes, backed by those of other classes who . . . were willing to support them, to leave their respective political associations and unite on a common basis'.[220] It could not be left to the middle classes. Hardie mentioned on one occasion that he had just been to Oxford and found that the young men may be sincere but 'most . . . know as little of real life and the feelings of the common people as if they did not exist'.[221] The working class had to lead itself.

Hardie also kept up the sparring with Blatchford, who believed Hardie had been wasting his time in Parliament, where his proposals to help the unemployed or the poor were just drops in the bucket. The only concession Hardie had really won was the setting up of a Parliamentary Select Committee on unemployment in 1894. Although this would never have been agreed had Hardie not been in the House, it produced nothing tangible. Like the Royal Commission on Labour before it, it was just talk; possibly only serving to arm employers and government better in the struggle against labour. Outside, therefore, there was growing disillusionment among socialists and radical trade unionists. Unrealistically, they had counted on too much from one man. Equally, Hardie had counted on too much from one institution. Towards the end of the lifetime of that Parliament, Hardie said, 'We will cram another Blue Book, and next winter the unemployed agitation will begin again'.[222] According to Lowe, Hardie became increasingly more sympathetic to those who had always said Parliament was a waste of time.[223]

Nevertheless he did not give up his hope that the place could one day be converted into a 'socialists' assembly' with 'the state . . . used to help . . . realize' socialist ideals.[224] He firmly believed in collective action and in social change enacted by governments. Not governments as they had existed in the past, but transformed by new ways of working and by an influx of new representatives. Hardie had the inflated hope of the time, that extended suffrage was the key, along with much more extra-parliamentary pressure. Once the vote was available to the poor and to women (he was just beginning to talk about female suffrage) he believed their combined pressure would refuse to re-elect any who failed to introduce revolutionary social change.

Although it is easy to see that Hardie's vision of a truly representative Parliament developing revolutionary potential was flawed, it struck fear among holders of wealth and property and passed on hope to millions of workers who were struggling.

Right up to the last days of the Parliament he kept putting down his amendments as a Party of One, designed to embarrass the government. Liberals crowded round him at the time of the debate on the Queen's Speech in 1895, once again trying to get him to withdraw, this time a motion requiring an immediate report from the Unemployment Select Committee.[225] Such MPs as John Gorst, Sir William Harcourt and

John Benn were sent to reason with him. But Hardie stood firm. Said a northern paper (incidentally showing the way he was patronized as well as vilified), 'representatives of rank and title tried to bend the shaggy pitman to their will', but to no avail. He forced the vote and all the Labour side voted against him, including Cremer, Hardie noted, who had been one of the founders of the First International.[226] Once again John Burns solved his dilemma by staying away.

Hardie might well have preferred desertion to the constant attention of Liberals, 'I was . . . sick . . . of the attempts . . . to rope me in.'[227] When he and a friend passed Gladstone in a corridor one day and the friend tried to get Gladstone to speak with Hardie – and Gladstone refused – Hardie interpreted this as Gladstone having the dignity to respect Hardie's independence. 'I honoured him for it.'[228] Hardie thus remained the odd one out – in manner as well as matter. For he was not fluent. When he spoke, he gave the impression of being in torture and with 'difficulty he quarried from his memory words to express his meaning'.[229] His voice was harsh, having to be thrown long distances outside, even though it was mitigated by 'an earnestness' and a 'considerable vein of pathos'[230] that compelled attention among the general public, according to Cunninghame Graham. Not so inside the House, where Hardie's whole style offended, particularly his way of addressing fellow MPs as 'Men'. No one understood that it was a point of principle to him to address the House just as he addressed constituents. According to the radical Liberal, Arthur Ponsonby, however, MPs thought it insulting that Hardie did not observe the niceties. Cunninghame Graham too, agreed that his 'homeliness, directness and sincerity'[231] all 'gave great offence to paternal capitalists, baillies, councillors and other worthy men . . . who failed to detect Hardie's sincerity . . . and felt him far too "familiar."'[232] He may have been respected for his natural dignity but once curiosity wore off, to many he was merely tedious.

Nor did many think his career in the House had been successful. The press criticized him for being an extremist; and so occasionally did acquaintances,[233] while twentieth-century critics often find he was too timid. Reid, for example, criticizes him for haring after farm colonies rather than proposing major social transformation by public ownership on the lines the SDF was already arguing.[234] But Hardie was restricted in what he could propose because Parliament was restricted in what it had the power to do, a fact that did not escape those who said it was a waste of time working for change through Parliament.

But his three years of slow chipping away were not without effect. Again and again he raised subjects that had not been raised before, such as the plight of the destitute, unemployed and the waged artisan earning mere subsistence pay. Hardie's achievement was not that he got much done for any of these groups, but that he had made questions concerning them questions which the House had to hear and in the long run could not ignore. Hardie's contribution to Parliament was not in oratory or outrageousness. It was to insist that Parliament honour all citizens equally and hear the innumerable small questions of working people's lives that mattered more to them than trade or treaties: degrading Poor Laws, low wages, unsafe working practices, long hours, ill health, charges for schools, denial of rights to assemble, and the wanton use of police powers to 'discipline' citizens with grievances into silence. Hardie had insisted such issues, which he constantly raised outside the House, were proper subjects to raise inside it – by raising them agian and again and again. A popular cartoon of him during this time showed him carrying an unemployed man on his back into the House of Commons. As a symbol of his insistence that Parliament recognize what he called 'the condition of the people' as its main business, it was an accurate summary of his achievement.

6

DEFEAT AND DEPRESSION

The general election in July 1895 found Hardie truculent and confident of victory. Not just for himself in West Ham but for the twenty-seven other ILP candidates standing, including Tom Mann, Ramsay MacDonald and Richard Pankhurst, as well as four from the SDF.[1] Only a few years earlier, when the ILP was doing remarkably well in by-elections, he had boasted that soon 25 per cent of the electorate nationally would be ILP.[2]

Several seats were offered to Cunninghame Graham too, including one in Edinburgh, but he declined.[3] Cunninghame Graham seemed to lose his zest for politics after the loss of the Scottish Labour Party, a transformation he probably regretted as a supporter of a more independent Scotland. Although he wished the ILP well, he had doubts about how far it could stay independent. He was also grievously in debt. He had failed to keep up his estates, generously allowing them to be treated as common land for hunting and fishing and woodcutting and building homes. Now there was no income to pay taxes and keep up his own house. He decided to increase time spent exploring and writing and he and Gabrielle began spending ever longer periods in Spain, Africa and the Americas.

In West Ham Hardie too had grown careless, not financially but politically. To the many Irish he said his support for Home Rule had been with a 'bad conscience', since it was proposed to set up a House of Lords there. Remarks like this offended two local priests, who asked Roman Catholic parishioners not to vote for Hardie, believing he made Ireland the 'tail of a socialist programme'.[4] In addition to the controversial speeches he had made in Parliament, which offended some constituents, especially if they read highly coloured accounts, he pressed his luck on temperance. He supported 'local option' proposals to shut down the local liquor trade. 'Those who can take a glass or let it alone,' he said, are 'under moral obligation for the sake of the weaker brethren who cannot do so, to let it alone.'[5]

Most of all, Hardie continued to berate the Liberal Party. Liberals nationally were determined to defeat him. In the previous general election these forces had been neutral. Now they were his main enemy. Their press boycotted all his campaign activities and speeches, and on the day of the election their influential *Daily Chronicle* denounced him. Mistakenly, Hardie perceived his only opponent to be the candidate standing against him, the same tired old Tory as before. Of him Hardie said squarely, 'This is not a fight between me and Major Banes. It is between the worker and the capitalist . . . between righteousness and the powers of darkness.'[6] Banes increased his vote slightly, while Hardie lost a quarter of his own. The result was defeat by 775 votes.[7] It was an unexpected blow, not just for Hardie but for the whole ILP, every one of whose candidates lost, as did all four socialists. Hardie put it down to everyone working against him, 'Teetotallers [with] publicans . . . Trade Unionists [with] Free Labourers, Liberals [with] Tories . . . professed Home Rulers with coercionists . . . all to secure the defeat of the representative of Labour.'[8] But as Pelling wrote, 'The socialist boom was over.'[9]

This crushing defeat was a great relief to the two-party establishment, for it signified that the anticipated surge to labour militancy was not, after all, going to disturb the workings of Parliament. Socialists outside the ILP were not surprised. The SDF, which took the 'attitude of pioneers whose claims had been jumped by new-comers' when it came to the ILP,[10] believed it was the political pandering of the ILP to the conservative union leadership that was the root of the trouble. Engels (now dying of cancer) made it clear he knew the Tories would win[11] and a letter during the campaign to Eleanor[12] made a sarcastic reference to 'the noble nature of KH', whom he no longer admired, having written him off earlier as that 'super-cunning Scot'.[13]

Although colleagues remembered that there was 'great rejoicing by the Liberal press' when Hardie lost personally,[14] Liberals were angry that so many ILP voters appeared not to have obeyed the ILP directive to vote Liberal where there was no ILP candidate. As a result, Tories won unexpected seats. But it was the moderates who turned on Hardie hardest. Fabians were delighted. Beatrice Webb crowed that 'Hardie has probably lost for good any chance of posturing as an MP and will sink into the old place of a discredited Labour Leader'.[15] Beatrice Webb disliked both the ILP[16] and the emotional Hardie.[17] Hardie in turn disliked Fabian influences in places like the London County Council, which kept Labour tied to Liberalism. Hardie resented the Fabian view that it was middle-class progressives who could best represent the working class. According to Hughes, Hardie also disliked Beatrice Webb personally as 'a middle class intellectual who had tried to be patronizing' to him.[18] If there was one thing Hardie hated, it was being patronized. Once when a northern industrialist met him in the Central Lobby and hailed him over-familiarly, Hardie cut him dead, causing much offence.[19]

Even inside the ILP and the Labour Movement itself, moderates sought to pin the blame on Hardie. Ramsay MacDonald wrote to Herbert Samuels that it was Hardie who had lost MacDonald's seat for him.[20] MacDonald made his complaint privately, but other Lib-Labs were very public. Champion's Labour Electoral Association[21] spoke of the 'labour barque . . . treacherously piloted upon rocks by frothy, ecstatic dreamers . . . who seek to ruin . . . unity', while John Burns (who had only just retained his seat despite his tacit support for Liberals and refusal to stand as ILP) was the most scathing of all,[22] citing Hardie's 'unscrupulous demagogy . . . trying to bribe voters by promising the gov't would build an "ironclad" in West Ham Docks.' Burns had failed to support Hardie's unemployment agitation in Parliament (which had included asking for government orders for West Ham's shipyards) and now took the opportunity to justify himself by claiming that Hardie's three parliamentary years had been 'senseless, sentimental, anti-socialist and futile'.

Hardie was not the least downcast by his defeat, and reacted with the same stoicism as he had greeted victory three years earlier.[23] 'Despondency?' he wrote in the Leader just afterwards,[24] 'No, no . . . half the battle won . . . the most difficult half. We must learn how to fight elections.' (His own campaign had been very badly organized.) As always, Steward noted, 'defeat . . . only made Hardie more stubborn and stimulated him to greater effort';[25] as well as to stepping up his criticism of the Liberals. Hardie wrote that 'Liberalism . . . is no longer a modern movement'; it was dying. As always, Hardie drew the moral against a political philosophy that presupposes that selfishness is the golden rule of life, 'as wealth grows, it brings in its train an ever increasing weight of rent and interest . . . an ever lengthening tale of men out of work'.[26] Hardie urged socialists to organize demonstrations to recruit new members and to 'fight every by-election and . . . the municipal elections . . . [and] prepare for the next election'.[27] This is just what thousands of socialists and radicals wanted to hear, 'prepare for the grand struggle!' The years that followed seemed to see socialism in the doldrums, but underneath great shifts were taking place, because so many acted in this spirit.

If Lillie or the family thought ousting from Parliament meant Hardie would now come home, they were mistaken. His impulse was always to fresh fields, and he decided to take a trip he had long been planning, to see the United States. Although 'neither he nor the good wife at home ever made mention' of their financial struggle, according to Stewart,[28] we can be certain Lillie, and many others, asked themselves, where has the money come from for the trip? Not that it was unusual to go to America. On the contrary, relationships between American and European socialists and labour movements were far closer than they are today. Tours of each other's countries were standard practice. Eleanor Marx and Edward Aveling had gone in 1886 as guests of the Socialist Labor Party of North America,[29] and Engels toured with them again in 1882; Wilhelm Liebknecht in 1886.[30] Tom Mann had already worked there for a year. Hardie was being paid for in part by the American Labor Day Committee based in Chicago, who asked him to address a meeting there on 2 September. (Americans had adopted the first Monday in September as its industrial holiday in preference to their original May Day.) Hardie's only problem was Lillie's continuing ill health, which made him put off deciding until the last moment. Finally, Hardie said his wife's 'devotion to the cause' had made her agree he could go, and in doing so, said Stewart, 'she sank herself once more'.[31]

Hardie celebrated his thirty-ninth birthday at Cumnock, and was gone the next day. He was seen off at Liverpool on the *Campania* on 17 August[32] by a large crowd of well-wishers singing the 'Red Flag', in small boats following the liner out to sea. Hardie may have been defeated in the polls but he was still the working-class politician who could draw bigger crowds than any other in the UK. Frank Smith accompanied Hardie, and possibly paid towards expenses. On shipboard they were stars, Hardie agreeing to lead a debate on 'competition' in society,[33] which he cunningly illustrated by using the way British ships divided their passengers into steerage and upper classes. He refused to put his watch ahead to accommodate the time in the USA but kept it always on Cumnock time – to know what Jamie and Nan and Duncan were doing. He called it 'Daddy Time'.[34] As was his lifelong habit, he sent a postcard or letter every day. By the end of his much-travelled life the Hardie collection of postcards for the period[35] is one of the finest in existence.

After his Labor Day speech Hardie visited the American socialist Eugene Debs, a colourful folk hero like himself, who was a 'political prisoner' in jail near Chicago, where he had been confined following his successful campaign in the Pullman strike of 1894. 'I spent a whole day with him in Woodstock Gaol . . . discussing this whole question of socialism and Labour.'[36] By now addicted to travel, Hardie found a labour network that passed him from town to town westwards, through Wisconsin, Missouri, Kansas, Colorado, Utah, and finally to California – everywhere banqueted by 'little groups of earnest men', mostly Germans, who were trying to teach the US worker that he was a wage slave.[37] Interest was high in Hardie because the USA was undergoing its own severe labour troubles. In his speeches and interviews he said he was sorry that organized labour was not campaigning politically 'by going straight for the socialist ticket'.[38] (Debs did not yet see the need for a distinct socialist and labour party.) Hardie also dealt with race, union rights, and the extremes of American wealth and poverty. But always his message was that change could only come about by peaceful means and labour organization. The press reported him everywhere he went, as usual impressed with him once they had had a chance to talk at close quarters. In New York they said:

> He is intensely earnest . . . He dresses simply . . . He is temperate . . . He does not expect to raise society ninety feet into the air in his lifetime. Those who argue with Mr Hardie will always find one difficulty about him. He knows pretty well what he is talking about.[39]

In San Francisco he and Frank Smith went sightseeing to the local land-marks, and having made contact with the municipal Socialist Society, led by a Presbyterian pastor, found themselves invited unexpectedly to meet the mayor.[40] Not only that, they found themselves put up in his Nob Hill mansion for two days. The mayor, who swore he was a socialist, had made a fortune in silver mining and Hardie was offered $100,000 (£20,000) 'if I declared the ILP to be probimetallism'[41] when I got back to London. Hardie refused the bribe, to the amazement (so he claimed) of all present.

By this time Hardie and Frank Smith were very low financially, down to $1.40 between them. They got only as far as Montana on the way back to New York for their return boat. The Knights of Labor hosted them for a tour around Butte City, and while going along the street, Hardie suddenly heard bagpipes.[42] Despite the fact that the pipes were coming from a saloon, Hardie went inside. There he discovered a homesick Scot named MacDonald, who was overjoyed to meet someone who appreciated his strange music. When he heard of Hardie's plight, he immediately organized the bar's regulars to call a meeting that night at the local 'opry' house to hear Hardie speak on socialism, for which he was given half the house takings, $75.00, enough to get him back to his boat.

But not before one last tourist event which Hardie no doubt insisted on, a visit to an Indian encampment.[43] For this the Knights provided him with an armed escort because the Indian men were in warlike mood, as Hardie recorded, 'blanketed, befeathered and painted'. The women were absent gathering firewood. As the white and red men talked uneasily, and Hardie no doubt adjusted his romantic vision of Indian life, a baby began to cry from a teepee. Hardie automatically went in and picked it up.

The braves were astonished at this gesture. No doubt they wondered at the white man's world where men were doing women's work, not knowing that many in the white man's world would also have been just as surprised at Hardie's interaction with children. Cunninghame Graham had spoken of visiting miners' cottages in Ayrshire with Hardie: 'I have seen him take the baby from the miner's wife and dandle it on his knee.'[44] Graham added, 'One felt he was a "family man".'

Hardie was, but increasingly with everyone else's family but his own. It is certain his own children, growing up largely without him, felt his absence.

Hardie arrived back in Britain in early December in time for a dinner in London's Albion Hotel, where the *Labour Leader* was honouring some of its special contributors, including a forty-four-year-old Russian exile, Sergius Stepniak.[45] Russia was the great dictatorship, the sign and symbol of feudal cruelty and imperial oppression in Hardie's political world, and British socialists were working closely with Russian exiles at this time. Some were wealthy dissidents editing *Free Russia*; others were Jews escaping persecution. During Hardie's absence in America, Russian and British Jewish socialists had picketed the TUC Congress over its new anti-immigration policy.[46]

Stepniak was a nihilist, whose writing was alerting British socialists to the revolutionary movements building up in his native country, little remarked by Europeans outside socialist circles. Stepniak had been a well-to-do member of the Russian upper class, like his anarchist compatriot, Prince Kropotkin, another member of this exiled group and present at the dinner. Hardie particularly liked Kropotkin, and visited him several times. The two would smoke their pipes and talk for hours, drinking tea from Kropotkin's samovar. Through these meetings Hardie came to a kindlier view of anarchism, 'Were we all Kropotkins, anarchism would be the only possible system, since government . . . would be unnecessary'.[47] In giving his thanks at the dinner, Stepniak specially singled out Hardie for praise for his political activism.

In 1896 Lillie was ill again;[48] nor would her health have been improved when she learned that Hardie had decided to contest a by-election for Parliament, when a vacancy arose at East Bradford. The faithful Frank Smith went with him and acted as his agent. Perhaps Hardie had been assured of the money to fight it by T.D. Benson, a middle-class accountant, who had just become the ILP's treasurer. During the campaign Hardie arranged for a convalescing Lillie and the children to visit Clitheroe, where Benson had a large house, which would certainly have pleased Lillie. During the course of the visit, Benson, who had been approached as an intermediary, tried to persuade Hardie to get the ILP to do a deal with the Liberals over future parliamentary seats. Hardie told him that this was impossible.[49]

The Bradford campaign had seemed to go well in terms of enthusiastic meetings, and Hardie had much support, particularly from women. Emmeline Pankhurst came to speak. They went out into the constituency, preceded by cyclist outriders who blew a bugle to gather a crowd. It was Bruce Glasier's first glimpse of Emmeline Pankhurst and he recorded that she was 'as lively as a cricket, full of clever comment, criticism and scandal. I sit quite diverted.'[50] Margaret MacMillan, a local teacher, who was politically active in Bradford with her sister, Rachel, also helped out, and put Hardie up for some of the time. At one meeting she played Mozart on the piano. At another she spoke, but since she refused to remove her veil, no one could hear her.[51] In the end, the same combination of forces that had defeated Hardie at West Ham did so again, even though he was careful this time to woo moderates and greatly modify his remarks about the Liberal party.[52]

Hardie's overtures to Liberalism made no difference and his unpopularity with Labour moderates continued. They thought he was prey to revolutionism and systematically tried to freeze him out during these years. Trade union leaders at a Durham miners' demonstration in 1897 refused to speak on the same platform with him, and miners' leaders refused to have him as a speaker at a meeting in Fyfe.[53] At Durham a second platform was put up for him, a tradition that afterwards long persisted. When Pete Curran stood for the ILP at another by-election in Barnsley in 1897, Henry Broadhurst made a point of coming to speak for the Liberal candidate, and miners stoned Curran.[54] Hardie came to help Curran, but another miners' MP, William Harvey, pilloried Hardie and Curran as 'wreckers and snatchers who have never done anything for the masses'.[55] Despite a good vote, Curran lost. Hardie wrote David Lowe, 'I am wearied, worried and a bit disgusted';[56] the old unionism and the Liberals seemed harder than ever for Independent Labour to dislodge.

The new unionism seemed to do best when it was avowedly socialist. Earlier in the year, Tom Mann had stood in a Scottish by-election on a platform of socialist unity, with SDF support, and though he had not won, he did much better than Hardie.[57] Pressure among socialists to unite in a single political organization began to grow. Hardie was ambivalent. He knew that progress required trade unions and socialists to unite, but he hoped it meant avoiding formal links with the SDF. He did not wish to share honours with Hyndman; he did not wish the *Leader* to be joined with *Justice*. Hyndman felt precisely the same about Hardie and the ILP. While they each held these views, a merger was impossible, no matter how thoroughly their respective parties canvassed for it. However, the acrimony did not mean that in his round of meetings and events Hardie had no contact with the full range of labour and socialist opinion. On the contrary, all the 'enemies' – just as today – met frequently for meetings and campaigns on specific issues, because comrades on the ground who did not take part in the disagreements at the top usually forgot about them. In 1897 Hardie, Burns, Quelch, Eleanor Marx and Thorne all spoke together in Battersea.[58] On another occasion it was Hardie and Blatchford, together with Tom Mann and Carrie Martyn, speaking together at an ILP bazaar.[59] Occasionally the comrades would even apologize to each other, as Blatchford did for his 'humphs' one night;[60] while Hardie was regularly making it up with Burns and Hyndman, and Burns even claimed he was ready to join the ILP.[61] And, of course, Cunninghame Graham eventually returned. To Hardie's amazement, during the Bradford by-election in autumn 1896, at a meeting held in Huddersfield, and 'without an invitation',[62] Cunninghame Graham suddenly appeared and leapt up on the hustings to take his place among the speakers, urging voters to support Keir Hardie. Cunninghame Graham had far too big a soul to nurse a petty grudge. Whatever Hardie's failings, they could not override the admiration Cunninghame Graham had for his tireless advocacy of socialism and labour independence.

Not so the 'Marx family', who had lost their faith in Hardie. In particular, Hardie had disappointed Eleanor, who felt his power 'growing less and less' in society.[63] She wrote to a Dutch socialist[64] to say Hardie's trip to the USA had been 'a fiasco' and 'no one knows who paid his very heavy expenses', although Hardie's trip was a model beside hers and Aveling's, where Aveling had fiddled expenses and been sued by the American labour movement.[65] Politically, Eleanor was on firmer ground in saying Hardie was trying to make common cause with both reformists and anarchists and 'any other stragglers he can pick up' to try to 'rehabilitate himself'.[66] Eleanor represented the view of many socialists in viewing Hardie as ideologically unstable – in too many places at once.

After Engels died Eleanor and Aveling began speaking at SDF meetings and writing for *Justice*. Eleanor remained as cynical about

Hyndman as ever[67] and so did other international Marxists. Karl Kautsky, for example, said at the time that he almost preferred the Fabians to Hyndman's 'utopianism concealed behind Marxian phraseology'.[68] Eleanor Marx's commitment to the SDF was to a body of political activists who consciously supported Marx's ideas, were in her opinion more 'socialist' than members of the ILP,[69] and were gradually taking the organization over from Hyndman.

Much of this suspicion of Hardie was fuelled by anger over the division which had occurred at the International Socialist Congress in July of 1896. The congress was held in London at the Queen's Hall in Langham Place and spent three days of the week debating the old issue of whether the anarchists present should be allowed to stay. Delegates divided once more along the same lines that Marx and Bakunin had fought out in the very first International, with the arguments made more acrimonious now by the election in the interval of socialists to national parliaments. Removing anarchists from socialist decision-making was what Engels had identified as still one of two key goals at the previous International.[70] Wilhelm Liebknecht tried several times to see Hardie before the 1896 congress to make sure there would be no new split,[71] but Hardie avoided him and went out of his way to campaign for anarchists' admittance as did Mann and libertarian delegates such as Domela Nieuwenhuis from the Netherlands. Hardie's motive was fear 'of doing an unfair thing towards a body of socialists with whom he did not see eye to eye'.[72] Marxists, opposing anarchists, were joined by Fabians. They included Ramsay MacDonald, who hated anarchists, linking them in a curious piece of writing with Ibsen (whom Hardie so admired) and opponents of marriage.[73] Though the congress voted to exclude anarchists, Hardie was undeterred and contributed often during the week, once on the need for a free, comprehensive education system without academic selection at any point[74] and, later, on the need to fix a date four years hence for a world general strike on wages and hours. Over the proceedings, wrote Tom Mann, watched Rosa Luxemburg, 'alert and keen . . . tactfully exercising great influence'.[75]

But the International did not succeed in bringing the ILP and SDF together, nor did this happen even when delegates to both parties' conferences in 1897 – and 85 per cent of the ILP membership at large in 1898 – voted for such unification themselves. Their leaderships were still against it. Glasier managed to persuade ILP delegates in 1898 to vote in favour of 'many pleasant rivers and brooks' of socialism rather than 'one straight, flat . . . central canal'.[76] His political development had moved imperceptibly from youthful revolutionism to what E. P. Thompson called a 'sentimental afflatus'[77] that threatened ILP development, defining socialism on this occasion as 'a very marvellously pervading and encompassing power'. This was hard for a daughter of Karl Marx to relate to.

Labour and socialism had run aground temporarily, while Liberals were reviving. When a cause appears to have been set back, everyone casts around for somewhere to lay the blame. *Justice* readers slugged it out with 'the lying venom of Mr Hardie's organ',[78] while the *Clarion* and *Labour Leader* had an exchange of 'vulgar smears', according to Glasier,[79] and ILP supporters complained that Blatchford was unfair to Hardie and that the *Clarion* refused to print any pro-Hardie letters.[80] Anger was vented widely in private. Glasier wrote in his Diary, 'I have lost all faith in . . . Blatchford'.[81] Blatchford said of Hardie, 'He makes my flesh creep.'[82] Glasier criticized MacDonald for being a politician who 'has nothing to say and says it loudly'.[83] Hardie called Ben Tillett 'a dirty little hypocrite'.[84] At one point the Glasiers were threatening to sever relations with the *Labour Leader* because it had printed a scathing review of Katharine's latest book.[85] Glasier, now on the NAC committee of the ILP, told his Diary he had to hear others' complaints about Hardie's 'less principled actions . . . [and] petty purposes',[86] and wrote he even caught Hardie out in an untruth himself at a NAC meeting.[87] Mann's supporters called Hardie 'weak' for advocating socialism in a form so generalized that no one could fear it and for abandoning the fight in the workplace.[88] In public Hardie denounced Broadhurst for exactly the same sins, and for wasting his time on his 'Sandringham junketings' to meet royalty.[89]

The rosy notion of the Labour movement built on foundations of consistent brotherhood is chimeric; likewise the picture of Hardie as a dear old gentleman everyone loved. Hardie had few friends and was widely distrusted. It was not just a case of those who knew him least. Those who knew him best often disliked him most. Nor was the working-class public, where he was so revered, always behind him. The press saw to that. Tom Johnston, a socialist comrade, said Hardie was hated in thousands of working-class homes, 'shunned . . . mocked . . . [and] misrepresented' by the press,[90] in particular by the Liberal press. David Lowe wrote a long passage about the way reformers of the left in the nineteenth century were destroyed by 'the revilement of the press'.[91] All of which Hardie understood. 'I am the best hated man in the movement . . . I know. But the cause for this dislike is not one for which my children will ever have occasion to blush. That is my only . . . reward.'[92]

Although he made light of these severe tensions, and still retained the support of millions of ordinary people, the odium was a burden when it was combined with the ever-present need to keep afloat financially, and to see to his own inward spirits. It is no wonder that Hardie was already spoken about as (and considered himself to be) 'a shattered and aged man',[93] even though he was only just forty.

*   *   *

During the last few years of the nineteenth century Hardie kept up his gruelling speaking rounds, but he also spent much more time in Scotland, working and writing for the *Labour Leader*.

The *Leader* could not compete with the *Clarion* and its vans, camera clubs, and the newly popular cycling clubs with their staging houses prefiguring later youth hostels.[94] Nor did Hardie's style have the combined daring and professionalism of Blatchford, who kept socialist sentiment fuelled with such stories as the ostentatious and costly ball held at Warwick Castle in 1895 for Frances the beautiful young Countess of Warwick Her personal income was £30,000 a year. Blatchford did not blame capitalism or the family; he denounced her personally for cruel behaviour as millions starved. To his surprise the next day an angry Frances appeared in person in the *Clarion* office to protest.[95] Blatchford (father of loved daughters of his own) was taken aback but nevertheless argued his case. After Frances returned home, she sent for £10 worth of pamphlets on socialism. She later said that when she had read them, she became a socialist. The conversion of a countess was eventually to be big news.

The *Leader* became bolder too in these years. One journalistic coup arose out of a police raid on a brothel in Glasgow, and the trial of the girls found working there. In each case the girl's name and address was printed in the press, resulting in her loss of job in service or factory, or at the very least, an attack by a co-worker. By contrast, names of the men who patronized the brothel were not allowed to be revealed. When the brothel reopened, the *Leader* decided to follow patrons home. The next day it printed their addresses. The series was entitled, 'Following the Salacious Serpent'. The addresses were the homes of philanthropic, business, industrial, professional and titled Glaswegians. Sales of the *Leader* climbed, as customers queued for them on street corners on publication days. Eventually the Glasgow Establishment appealed to the Home Office, who sent in the police to the *Leader* offices. Hardie was told to stop the series or be shut down. The articles stopped, Hardie being satisfied the *Leader* had made its point. Lowe in particular was delighted, 'It would have satisfied Zola.'[96]

The 'Salacious Serpent' was followed by the 'White Slave Series' – attacks on bad employers. Its centerpiece was a pamphlet which set out to destroy the reputation of a pious Scottish industrialist and Liberal notable, Lord Overtoun.[97] Few who have written about Hardie have failed to mention the fact that part of his passion against Overtoun must have been fuelled by a chance to expose a man so very like the one who had fired him from the bakery all those years ago. Overtoun too was a self-satisfied entrepreneur who made much of his Christian philanthropy. Hardie looked behind this model citizen and found that he compelled the workforce in his chemical works to work a twelve-hour day, seven days a week, and gave no meal breaks. Workers received only 3d. or 4d. an hour. Overtoun's life 'is such a living lie', Hardie wrote.

But Hardie's case was wider. Like Marx before him, who had traced pollution through factory inspectors' reports and the medical reports of public health officers,[98] Hardie was conscious of what unmitigated greed did to the environment. Socialists and trade unionists were the first modern environmentalists, pointing out the deadly consequences of new productive processes which manufacturers had every reason to hide, and which they never experienced, since they lived far away from the factories. Overtoun's factory made chrome. Its fumes were poisoning the surrounding air and the lungs of workers. The workers experienced 'chrome holes' in their hands; none had any protection. The pamphlet's cover shows a worker in a crude air-filtering device he had made himself, much like today's workers or residents make themselves when they live near polluting factories.[99]

Hardie had been alerted to the scandal of Overtoun's factory conditions when men working there had come to him for help when the chemicals brought them out in rashes, or affected their lungs. Overtoun's representatives, as their counterparts do now, claimed their factory was 'as innocuous as if they were in an open field',[100] but Hardie showed its pipes 'tipped revolting looking . . . greenish . . . yellow liquid into the River'.[101] Some years earlier Hardie had taken an interest in water purity and received evidence that companies sent false water samples to the public analyst.[102] What was Overtoun doing about any of this?

The Overtoun pamphlet was a huge success, and Hardie ran two sequels[103] before moving on to attack Thomas Lipton for dismissing workers who joined unions, and for good measure exposed the putrid fruit then used in Lipton products and their deceptive labels – as well as counting the money Lipton squandered on yachts. Next came an exposé of the *Daily Chronicle*'s treatment of its compositors, working conditions at the Army and Navy Stores, followed by those after the Prudential Insurance.[104] Ever since Tom Mann had taken a job in 1889 using the name of Joe Miller, to expose the alkali poisoning and long hours in Mond's Chemical Works (now ICI), labour publications had pioneered the kind of investigative journalism which today's media sometimes behave as if they had invented themselves. Although such journalism is more commonplace today (indeed, so commonplace that once a grievance has been aired, some people assume it has been rectified) it is seldom more effective now than it was when it was raised directly by those affected in order to organize for industrial and political action. Only relatively recently, with heightened environmental understanding, particularly in the developing world, is the link between exposure and action being reforged.

Hardie's writing and speaking on behalf of improving working conditions was a long, rough ride; success came only gradually. Not so activity championing free speech, which succeeded or failed more quickly. Hardie had regularly opposed attempts to ban people meeting during his years in Parliament.[105] In Manchester in 1896 another free-speech issue arose when magistrates tried to ban public meetings at a place where radicals and socialists and anarchists were accustomed to reach the public. It was a natural amphitheatre in a public park, known locally as Boggart Hole Clough. The origin of the ban was one particularly officious councillor who was anxious to silence another councillor, Richard Pankhurst, because Pankhurst was attacking the council's policies regularly at this site. When Fred Brocklehurst, ILP member and secretary of the Labour Church Union, tested the ban by preaching, he was arrested and confined in Strangeways prison. Hardie was soon in Manchester. So was Bruce Glasier. They hit upon the clever device of having Emmeline Pankhurst chair the next meeting, which she gladly did, being one who enjoyed the limelight. Although she was summoned for 'causing an annoyance', and Hardie went to court with her,[106] she was fined rather than imprisoned. The ILP did not leave the matter there, however. To publicize the issue and provoke the authorities further, Hardie was invited as the next speaker, ensuring that an enormous and defiant crowd gathered from miles around. While he spoke, ILP members gathered the names and addresses of those listening. When Hardie was charged with breaking the bylaw, he handed the magistrates a list of over 400 people he wished to call as witnesses. The court adjourned and Hardie was never recalled. The ILP counted it a momentous victory.

Battles of this kind were what Hardie enjoyed, where middle- and working-class agitators worked together. During these events Hardie had a chance to catch up with the Pankhurst family, where Emmeline reigned as 'queen' to the serious Dr Pankhurst.[107] A contemporary recalled her as 'a living flame . . . she was very beautiful and like the model of Burne-Jones' pictures, slender, willowing'.[108] She was also fashionable and healthy and charming, while Dr Pankhurst was awkward, earnest and frequently ill with stomach pains. Sylvia was fourteen and it was already clear she had none of the beauty and intellectual capacity of her older sister, Christabel. Emmeline left Sylvia and siblings to nurses, but Christabel she increasingly tended herself.[109] Others later confirmed her preference for 'this first darling', one contemporary saying she was a woman 'who would walk over the dead bodies of all her children' to get what she wanted – save Christabel's.[110] For this reason Sylvia favoured her father and during the 1895 election, when he had been an ILP candidate, she had

accompanied him every day while he campaigned. Impressed with
the enthusiasm of the crowds, she was quite unprepared for his defeat.
When the results were declared she stood on the platform beside him,
tears running down her face.[111]

Hardie had called at the house once during the campaign and Sylvia
had run home from school and rushed up the stairs to see who was
sitting in the visitors' chair by the fireside. Years later she recalled
finding a man with 'the strength of a rock, the sheltering kindness
of an oak, and the gentleness of a St Bernard dog'.[112]

Hardie came to stay once too (during the Bradford by-election),
always glad of free lodging on his travels. On the road he would
sometimes share a bed with comrades. Once it was Bruce Glasier;
on another occasion, Robert Smillie, who said later, 'No one could
sleep with Hardie because the whole night through he put forth his
dreams of a regenerated working class movement.'[113]

Hardie knew that the lull in national electoral advance was deceptive.
In the German Parliament by 1895 there were already fifty socialists.
Locally, in Britain, by 1895 there were 600 Labour members on
borough councils and the red flag flew over several town halls. In
West Ham, though Hardie had failed to be re-elected, within three
years trade union, SDF and ILP candidates won 29 out of 48 seats on
the local council, the victory attributed by the *Labour Leader* to the fact
that 'socialism and labour joined hands'.[114] Though Richard Pankhurst
failed to be elected in Gorton, in Manchester, in 1895, Emmeline,
standing as an ILP candidate, was elected to the Board of Poor Law
Guardians in Chorlton in Manchester the same year; Lansbury was
re-elected to the same Board at Poplar; and Margaret MacMillan to the
Bradford School Board in 1894. Even Frank Smith finally got elected
– to the London County Council in 1898, where he chose to align
himself with a new socialist group that included R. C. K. Ensor and
Lansbury rather than joining the progressive coalition with Liberals
and such LCC Labour members as John Burns and Will Crooks. One
of the great disputes between the *Clarion* and the *Leader* was over this
LCC split.[115] Hardie was abnormally upset by the argument[116] but
it was part of the process of town councils becoming the training
ground for socialists and labour activists, including the disagreements
between them. Local government was a key, as Annie Besant, another
LCC member, had already recognized in her Fabian essay of 1888.
It was the Tories' own Local Government Act of 1888 that 'has
established the Commune ... [and] created the machinery without
which socialism was impracticable',[117] one reason local government
became such a target for Conservatives a hundred years later.

By 1897 Labour was able to claim 38 per cent of the vote in certain
municipal elections.[118] In the same year Hardie was claiming that a

third of Britain's teachers in the new state schools were socialists[119] and that it was impossible to find a trade union leader now 'to a avow himself anything else'.

The years after 1892 had seen an economic downturn, but towards the end of the century trade improved. This spurred labour militancy. In 1897 there were strikes in the cotton industry and on the railways. There was a prolonged strike in the Penrhyn Slate Quarry. Then came the great lockout of engineers, fought by the Amalgamated Society of Engineers to get the eight-hour day agreed by every employer. Throughout it Eleanor Marx worked at the head office of the Engineers' Union,[120] concentrating on obtaining financial support from abroad. Half of the £28,000 raised came from her letters to Germany.[121] Eleanor thought it 'a GRAND struggle. The men are simply admirable, though the suffering is very great. How some of the families live is a mystery.'[122] Hardie, who was campaigning equally hard, also managed to raise funds. The elderly Kippen sisters had not forgotten about him and tried again, sending £100. This time he did not refuse it.

The *Labour Leader* wrote that the lockout was an attempt by 'federated capital – Liberal and Tory – to dictate terms to the trade unions throughout Britain',[123] and Hardie toured the country speaking of the 'outrage' that the eight-hour day had not been conceded to the engineers. What was even more outrageous was that the Lib-Lab MPs in Parliament were 'standing aloof and taking no part in that struggle'. Not one had 'opened his lips' on the issue, or had protested at 'a quarter of a million for the Prince of Wales' new toy' another yacht.[124] This last speech was made in Plaistow, for Hardie still entertained hopes of standing again for West Ham.

One area of the country he did not know well was Wales, but when a miners' strike in South Wales began – with miners asking for a 20 per cent wage increase and the right to a minimum wage – Hardie threw himself and the *Labour Leader* into their action. Miners, like engineers, belonged to unions with conservative leaderships. That they were becoming militant in normally unmilitant Wales was a sign of how bad living standards had become. The strike dragged on and on. Hardie and the *Leader* set up a special strike fund. Donations came from the socialist faithful, such as Walter Crane, but Hardie also wrote unashamedly to wealthy men, laying before them the plight of miners' families, who were slowly approaching starvation. Thomas Lipton (despite Hardie's attacks on him) sent tea and George Cadbury tins of cocoa.

Hardie felt driven to tour the South Wales area's coalfields from one end to the other during June 1898. A colleague later described how he first came across Hardie in Aberdare, 'I was just sauntering in to town one afternoon, when I was attracted by a small crowd of people standing round a man.' He was standing on a soapbox, 'a short man with a magnificent head, a gingery beard, a good body and very short legs'.[125]

Hardie identified instantly with the Welsh and wrote at the time that 'all Celts . . . are socialist by instinct'.[126] His meetings were well attended, and several flew the red flag as well as the Union Jack.[127] As his standing in the area grew, that of the old labourist union leadership was being discredited with its own supporters, for Hardie did not neglect to attack Lib-Lab miners' MPs for failing to support the strike adequately, and in particular for not complaining in Parliament about the heavy military presence being sent in to 'police' miners' lives and homes. Hardie saw this as pure intimidation in a dispute where there had been no violence of any kind, just prolonged withdrawal of labour. He urged people to carry on regardless, as he did himself, even where soldiers stood by. Although he saw them as the arm of imperialist power, he also saw them as human beings, young men 'for whom the labour market offers no useful opening', sent 'to shoot . . . other working men who are struggling to make the condition of their toil a little easier'.[128] Hardie noted in his letters back to the *Leader*'s office that it rained every day of his tour,[129] later seen as an omen of the eventual outcome: enforced return to work after a ruinous six months, without gaining a single concession. The engineers' strike also ended in total defeat.

Sometimes, the more spectacular the loss, the sharper the political outcome. This was so in Wales, where the experience jolted Welsh labouring communities out of a passivity which had prevailed for years. The strike had brought a new political consciousness, where the bitterness of loss was channelled into productive planning for future political activity. During the strike some miners took to meeting locally in a barber's shop in Penydarren. After the defeat, they resolved to put up labour candidates against the Liberals at the first opportunity. Proof of how quickly support grew can be seen in the figures for ILP branches in South Wales: only eleven before the strike, but very shortly after it, thirty-one.[130] The strike brought South Wales abruptly into the national labour family. It also brought middle-class Welsh people into the struggle for the Welsh working class. Hardie's friend, Robert Williams the architect, threw himself into organizing Welsh choirs to perform in London to raise funds for strikers. Hardie wrote back to the *Leader* office, 'You ought to hear these people sing!'[131]

Labour troubles at home increased contact with socialists and labour movements abroad, and during these years Hardie extended his international ties. A. J. P Taylor's criticism that Hardie took no interest in foreign affairs[132] is only sustainable if foreign affairs is limited to what is raised in Parliament about great international affairs of state. Outside this arena Hardie kept a wide watch on the world, particularly through the *Labour Leader* and the ILP. In the year 1898 alone, the *Leader* took up the cause of the Italian massacres in Milan,[133] specially commissioned articles on the Dreyfus affair in France,[134] and made a point of commandeering the young American black, D. E. Tobias, who had written *Freed But Not Free*, to write an account of the black American's struggle in capitalist and racist America.[135] His views produced denials from trade unionists that white working men were racist.[136] In addition, most issues of the *Leader*, as, earlier, Hardie's *Herald* columns, had regular round-ups of foreign news.[137] Hardie was responsible for managing all of this.

Through the ILP and the International, socialists and leaders of labour movements kept in close touch with each other. In fact, they were moving closer together, even while national parliaments were showing increased hostility to one another. A mere ten years before, Hardie had barely left Scotland, but by the end of the century he had met Friedrich Engels, Rosa Luxemburg, Wilhelm Liebknecht, Auguste Bebel, Eugene Debs and Daniel DeLeon. In March 1898 at a get-together at Hyndman's new house in Queen Anne's Gate, after the International had held a London meeting for European socialist leaders, Hardie met Jean Jaurès for the first time. A friend of Hardie's later commented that Jaurès, although a philosophy lecturer, was like 'a shrewd farmer from Ayr' and about as far removed 'from the typical Frenchman as depicted in our comic papers as it would be possible to find'.[138] From this first meeting Hardie and Jaurès became firm friends.[139]

While Hardie was thoroughly international in outlook, he was not a man of the world. The domestic disputes of the ILP, which, as chairman, he was called upon to settle, undoubtedly taxed him beyond his powers. During the spring of 1899, for example, he was bombarded with letters about a married ILP organizer in Hull named George Belt, who became entangled with Dora Montefiore, an ILP member who lived in London. Montefiore, the widow of a rich businessman, was known to have 'advanced' sexual views. Belt left his pregnant wife to go to Montefiore but was removed by friends and placed in a padded cell in a mental institution. Hull ILP then sacked him. He protested. Their behaviour amounted to a public scandal, which worried Margaret MacDonald, who was promptly sued for slander by Montefiore for discussing the matter in an ILP meeting. Each of the protagonists bombarded Hardie with their version of events,[140] calling for his decision.

Hardie would have taken a stern moral line. In 1895 it had come to his attention that John Trevor, the respected founder of Bradford's Labour Church, had married for a second time. Hardie wrote at once to say this conduct had 'given the movement . . . a blow . . . it will not recover from in a hurry', and asking Trevor to resign, saying, 'I value most, as you know, the moral side of our agitation.'[141] Trevor replied magnanimously to say he had no intention of resigning but had enough confidence in Hardie to believe 'you will discover your error presently'.[142]

An even bigger test came for Hardie with Tom Mann, who had been conducting highly successful campaigns for the Party as its general secretary, which Glasier thought had done 'enormous good'.[143] Mann was still pursuing his campaign to have the SDF join the ILP and the ILP declared a socialist party. He said he 'does not wish always to have to explain that he is a socialist not merely a labour advocate'.[144] One day Hardie, as chair, received a report from ILP member Russell Smart, to whom Mann's wife had gone, that questioned Mann's suitability on the grounds that the one-time temperance man was now drinking heavily and neglecting his wife for other women. At first Hardie let things drift.[145] Two weeks later, however, he was about to share a platform with Mann when he found him so drunk and saying such 'stupid things' that he had to abandon the meeting.[146] Within a month Mann was attending meetings with women other than his wife. One of them, a sister of an ILP member, Glasier primly records was 'regarded as a prostitute'[147] and another Mann placed in a gallery during a meeting 'as if to flaunt his profligacy'. Ben Tillett was also the subject of similar rumours about 'misconduct', to which Glasier commented, 'Ugh!'[148] In Glasier's moralistic view Mann had 'ceased to be a serious propagandist'[149] but he was still an ILP official. Hardie was at last prevailed on to speak to him and ask him to 'step down from the ILP Secretaryship'.[150] After a wrangle, Mann agreed to go and the matter was smoothed over and presented as Mann's wish to get more involved again in industrial organization.[151]

Mann's autobiography makes no mention of the event other than to say that 'at this period I became the tenant of The Enterprise'.[152] This was a public house in Long Acre, central London, which Mann put to excellent use, making it available for every kind of radical, anarchist and socialist body. Mann's special favourite, Morrison Davidson, the Scots Home Ruler, lectured regularly on the Diggers and Levellers of the Cromwell period, introducing socialists to these men, and to Scottish heroes from his book, *Scotland for the Scots*, which had a preface by Cunninghame Graham. Mann continued with his political work in London and for a time became secretary of the National Democratic League. But Britain was not comfortable for him while domestic difficulties continued. In 1901 he left for New Zealand to start a new life. Thus passed both the moment – and the man – that might have helped to weld all socialists, radicals and trade unionists into a more unified democratic political movement.

★   ★   ★

The lost strikes, which Hardie felt deeply, affected his spirits. He seemed in some way to be having his faith tested. Some of his positive fire went to chasing money changers like Overtoun, but in the middle of the engineers' increasingly disastrous lockout he wrote a particularly tragic Christmas message which biographers always cite.

'My heart is bitter tonight,' he wrote, summing up his anger with the Christian establishment and the 'white-livered poltroons' of the churches:

> [who] take the Christ's name in vain and fail to see His image being crucified . . . in every hungry child . . . I have known as a child what hunger means, and the scars of those days are with me still . . . and unfit me . . . for the work . . . to be done. A holocaust of every Church building in Christendom tonight would be as an act of sweet savour.[153]

The loss of the strikes, on top of his own loss of a parliamentary career, was certainly good reason for gloom. But it was also the case that Hardie had wild mood swings as well. At the end of the engineers' lockout he was on a high, 'I feel this week as if great events are going on all around us, the old tumbling down, the new beginning to be upreared';[154] but a week later, 'We have no right to be merry this Christmas' and then, most uncharacteristically, 'I cannot think of peace . . . Christ came not to send peace but with a sword against wrongdoing'. His friend Lowe commented at the time on the depth of Hardie's 'spiritual bitterness'.[155] Behind it all was rather a large personal depression, which he could not shake off. It showed in all kinds of ways, but none more so than in his reaction to the experience of loss in a long series of deaths, which convinced him the old order was passing away and nothing new could be expected. Beginning with Parnell, 'the one man in politics of whom, as a politician, I was ever able to feel genuine respect', adding 'there is nothing in history more tragic than his death', he dwelled on each one as it occurred. And found only diminishment.[156]

Next came Stepniak, who had been killed on a level crossing in Bedford Park, West London, apparently too absorbed in his book to notice a train was coming; followed by Caroline Martyn, the quiet young Christian governess who had converted to socialism and had helped Hardie form the Young Crusader movement. In the summer of 1896 she went to Dundee to campaign for Tom Mann in his by-election, wearing herself down with incessant work and refusing all rest.[157] She contracted pneumonia and died during the campaign, at the age of twenty-nine. Hardie was affected also by the suicide of another young socialist, a student in Nottingham, who threw himself into a canal, followed closely by the death of his friend, the architect Larner Sugden. Later, there was a middle-class socialist whose family had disowned her for her politics. Not a single relative turned up at the graveside and there were only three mourners besides Hardie.[158] He wrote to Lowe, 'I detest funerals . . . I have no black clothes . . .'[159]

Deaths of public figures upset him as well. In October 1896 William Morris died. Morris had always been attacked because he was a well-to-do socialist and Hardie had always defended him as 'the living embodiment of a genuine, hearty, human, socialism'[160] as well as for his great 'honesty of purpose' and contribution to socialism and art. When Ruskin died in 1900 Hardie said, 'Thus disappeared from earthly view the last of the giants who make the modern British socialist movement possible.'[161] He had said the same about Gladstone when he died in May 1898, for Hardie never lost his youthful admiration for the great Liberal leader and wrote fulsomely about his 'native grandeur' and total absence of pomposity.[162] He admired Gladstone for not accepting a peerage, for bringing up his family to eschew honours and to give service, and for his hard-working ways. He called him 'the great commoner' and claimed his love of freedom and toleration made him an 'indispensable pioneer of the socialist movement'.

Nevertheless Hardie had earlier correctly caught Gladstone's failings after a deputation to his home in St James's Square about the eight-hour day.[163] Gladstone had refused to support it on the grounds of liberty, and was completely incapable of understanding that 'fully grown men' could be 'compelled to work long hours against their will'. Magnanimously, Hardie claimed Gladstone was not a worker and simply never understood 'the modern labour movement'. Significantly, reading about the tributes to Gladstone just after his death, Hardie singled out as 'the only touch of real eloquence in the eulogiums pronounced in Parliament' those that were given 'to the solitary and pathetic figure who for sixty years . . . shared his triumphs . . . and cheered him under his defeats . . . by her tender vigilance', Mrs Catherine Gladstone.[164]

Lillie in the same late spring of 1898 was keeping her own vigil by the bedside of her dying mother, Sarah Wilson, now aged sixty-five. She had been brought to Lochnorris, where one of her last acts was to make a donation of £25 to the miners' strike fund in Wales, where she had grown up.[165] When she died Hardie came back to Cumnock at once and did something he rarely did, cancelled several political meetings. A few days later Richard Pankhurst suddenly experienced excruciating pain and took to his bed in Manchester. Emmeline was away speaking and Sylvia, now aged sixteen, was the only family member at home. She stayed by his bed for several days, as his condition worsened, but was no more able to help him than the doctors, for no one really knew what the problem was, except that his long-standing indigestion was a great deal worse. Slowly he slipped away and died, and Sylvia ran screaming from the house.[166] It was discovered that he had had a long-standing stomach ulcer, which had perforated. Hardie desperately wanted to go to Richard Pankhurst's funeral but had to say no, explaining to David Lowe that 'Mrs H requires consideration just at present'.[167]

Perhaps the most tragic of the deaths was that of Eleanor Marx at forty-three. She was working in the labour movement right up to the end, and when Hardie heard of it his reaction was the same as that of every other socialist: 'the brute . . . killed her'.[168] This was a reference to Edward Aveling, her common-law husband for fourteen years. What quickly came out was that unknown to anyone, his wife had died some years earlier, but instead of marrying Eleanor, who had risked so much for their relationship, and whose 'family' had given him such a lot, including so much money, Aveling had secretly, using a false name, married a young woman called Eva Frye whom he had met doing amateur dramatics – presumably, says Eleanor's biographer, Yvonne Kapp, 'because she would not sleep with him unless he did'.[169] Hardie was later taken to task by Kapp for repeating the myth that an anonymous letter had reached Eleanor and that she had killed herself when she received it, that Aveling thereafter lived high with his woman (who became 'an actress') and was spending all Engels's money.[170]

The truth about Eleanor's 'pathetic end',[171] as Hardie called it, was not so simple, although Hardie never made any effort to discover it. He preferred to 'kill' Aveling and wipe him from history with invective like everyone else. Yet for all his faults, Aveling had been a dedicated socialist who was almost as unsparing of himself as Hardie or Eleanor Marx in addressing meetings and supporting workers. Eleanor had freely chosen Aveling as her partner, who, like her father, became a man she constantly had to defend. With Marx, however, it was his ideology, with Aveling his character – largely matters relating to other women and money. She hid the truth from herself for a long time. But she learned of his marriage some while before her death and spent her last months in frantic bargaining to get him to stay with her. Her only confidant, ironically, was Marx's natural son by the family domestic, Lenchen.[172] Freddy Demuth, whom Engels had long before agreed to pass off as his own son to keep the truth from Marx's wife, had been sent away to London's East End to be brought up. Eleanor had only learned about her father's paternity at Engels's deathbed when Engels insisted on telling her the truth. Possibly the loss of her faith in her father at some subconscious level started her down the spiral of depression, and she chose Freddy as the only one in whom she could confide her own terrible truth, that Aveling was asking for money to stay, and she was paying him.

But Aveling was also gravely ill with serious kidney disease, contracted in 1897. Eleanor cared for him with almost maniacal intensity and on the day of her death had brought him back from the hospital to convalesce in their comfortable home in Sydenham, knowing that somewhere he had another home with a wife waiting. That morning he insisted on leaving the house (in fact, he went to the SDF offices for a few hours). But Eleanor's demented mind assumed he was leaving for good. Outwardly calm, she sent her maid to the chemist to sign the poison book for chloroform and prussic acid, saying they were for the dog. She wrote a short line to her nephew, Johnny, 'Try to be worthy of your grandfather',[173] and drank the acid. Death came in two minutes.

Far from living it up after she died, Aveling died four months later, thus adding a pitiful coda to the tragedies of Karl Marx, whose only legitimate son had died as a child and whose older daughter had died as a young mother. Later, Eleanor's last sibling, Laura, followed with her own suicide. A life of financial harassment, exile, social excommunication, constant denunciation, ideological argument and fear – combined with the need to sustain the struggle for social change for which Marx laboured all his life through his writings, and to preserve and spread the ideas that were to accomplish his mission – all took their toll. Not only on the man, but on all around him. Far more lives than one were required as sacrifice. The Hardie family had yet to learn the cost of one member's political mission.

Hardie's reaction to all these deaths betrayed his own depressed spirit, 'one by one the props are being removed upon which the movement has rested'.[174] He wrote Glasier that 'there are times when I have seriously and sanely' considered 'taking a plunge into the void'.[175] At other times depression gave way, if not to mania, to lightheartedness. He managed to make merry at a Burns night and to go on 'the sick list as a result',[176] but most of all it was his children who pulled him out of himself. He wrote that he had been intending to work 'but the Hallowe'en tatties are waiting', so he was taking the day off.[177] On another occasion it was a 'brambling expedition' that pulled him away. He loved being with what he called 'our two young folks' (Jamie was now an apprentice in Glasgow). Hardie once told his brother, 'I am bringing our two young folks in to see the Big Show – Barnum and Bailey's.'[178] However, he had to ask if there were any free tickets, 'a melancholy sign', Lowe commented, 'of the state of Hardie's purse'. It was a purse that continued to bear strain. When his brother George was ill, Hardie knew this would affect the £1 a week that the brothers sent to Mary Hardie. Hardie paid George's share as well to make sure his parents did not go without.[179]

In the autumn of 1898 Hardie asked his brother David to get him tickets to see Henry Irving and Ellen Terry playing *The Merchant of Venice* in Glasgow. 'I have never seen either of them.'[180] And earlier, in April, 'in company with Ramsay MacDonald . . . he saw his first and only big game of football'.[181] It was during the ILP's annual conference in Birmingham and England was playing Scotland. Hardie wrote that he and MacDonald sneaked out to attend the game; 'in the midst of twenty thousand Englishmen ... taking our lives in our hands, Mac and I cheered until the zinc roofing vibrated' as Scotland beat England 2–0.

While Hardie experienced feelings he could not explain – and did not talk about – so too did Lillie. After her illness in March of 1896 Hardie wrote that the 'reports about improvements' are just 'fudge',[182] because 'she has a brave heart, and does not show her sorrows on the surface'; nor would he. They both suffered on, and neither communicated on these matters, leaving their feelings to show in other ways.

By 1897, however, Lillie was freer to travel with Hardie, and this she made a point of doing. She was at the Scottish Trades Union Congress that year where she sat on the platform. Afterwards, the Hardies and Glasiers lunched together. Katharine was expecting her first child and yet was full of her own political plans to carry on campaigning after it was born. Lillie found the continuing arguments within the left upsetting, and Katharine reported that Lillie was 'temperamentally unfitted for the storms and vicissitudes of her husband's public life'.[183] Nevertheless, Hardie reported with evident pleasure in January 1898 that Mrs Hardie 'is nearly herself again'[184] and for the next two years Lillie accompanied Hardie to ILP conferences. Before the 1899 conference the Hardies visited Oxford where they stayed with a Scots landlady called Sarah Tytler who ran the settlement house for Ruskin Hall. 'Mrs Hardie is delighted with her,' Hardie confided to Lowe.[185] Later, they were surprised to discover that her real name was Henriette Keddie and that she had passed much of her life 'in the education of girls' and was the author of a book entitled *Miss Nanse*, written after she had retired. The state of social enlightenment as far as women went can be judged by the fact that all these facts were judged matters to hide.

At Bradford on the same tour they called on another educationalist, their friend, Margaret MacMillan, who lived with Louise Michel ('heroic, passionate and slightly mad', Eleanor Marx called her[186]). Hardie liked Margaret MacMillan, whom Lowe called 'a big woman in every respect'.[187] She had been born in New York and worked as a governess before becoming a Christian socialist in 1888. She made her political debut in Britain in 1892, speaking on one of the platforms at the May Day rally in Hyde Park. Margaret MacMillan was in constant demand for lectures, and when the Hardies called she was full of the new book on education she had just written entirely for ordinary parents, dedicating it, therefore, to 'Mrs John Smith' (a century ahead of its time). Lillie could identify with Margaret MacMillan, who knew what it was like to be invisible in society, as Lillie was. Margaret MacMillan once wrote to Sally Blatchford to complain about having no status as a woman[188] and she told Lillie about attending a civic reception when not a single person spoke to her.

The last summer of the century Hardie spent at home in Cumnock with his dog, his garden and his family. Lillie's father was visiting and far from well;[189] 'we were up most of the night with him . . . his mind wandered', Hardie reported to Lowe. Nor was Hardie taking care of himself. 'I sat on a lorry for ninety minutes with a keen west wind blowing, and then had to talk. Result . . . washed out.'[190] His friends worried increasingly, and Lowe said, 'Hardie was careless about his health and seemed to think his iron constitution could stand any strain'.[191] He never wore an overcoat, no matter how cold it was. Just a scarf and an old pair of gloves.

During this period Hardie was more aware of tragedy and of death because they reinforced feelings he was experiencing inside himself, 'I am terribly out of sorts . . . without any apparent cause';[192] while on another occasion it was 'a strange succession of moods . . . sometimes . . . cheered . . . sometimes cast down and depressed'. He could not find out why. But he was anxious to keep track, sensing that somehow the pattern had a meaning. After the end of the decade, he said,

> I now feel worn out in body and very very sad in spirit, not sad because of failure but because I feel that my work has cut me off from communion with my fellows. I have few friends and cannot, somehow, enter into the healthy and legitimate light side of life.[193]

He added with resignation, 'However, I have been true and faithful to the interests of my class. That is all I claim.'

Hardie was a better analyst of his own problem than any onlooker, for later in life he wrote that 'I am of the unfortunate class who never knew what it was to be a child – in spirit, I mean.'[194] Like many working-class children, he had missed childhood, as the boy who had to go to work, the breadwinner by the age of eight, saddled with so much responsibility for his mother and younger siblings. The gloom stayed with him for ever.

The only time it seemed to lift was when he was with his own children, briefly, or with young women. When we look again at Hardie's correspondence with Annie Hines, as well as at his later relationships with women, we see they might be interpreted as attempts to reconstruct the lost play of childhood, the 'light and legitimate side of life', as much as passionate affairs of the heart. There were the teasing, the games, the secrets and nonsense, the time doing nothing – too little of which he had ever had – and which, with Lillie, in the hard grind of poverty repeated and the struggle to survive (and the anger surrounding his constant absences and conflict over money) he could not have.

For Lillie, who had had a girlhood, the need to play was not so great. What she lacked was support, but instead she was called upon to support everyone else. Her outlet came in being ill, seeking oblivion in sleep or its substitutes – a path no one could share with her, as, indeed, no one could share with Hardie the path he had chosen.

Fortunately, Hardie looked at it the other way round; he believed his path had chosen him. And that this is what would save him.

Through trial and error and unsparing effort, Hardie found the answer to his problem. Indeed, a few years earlier, when fighting depression, he had told an ILP meeting that working for a socially transformed society was the only thing that ever brought him cheer. Working to bring that society about was his life's work, and it had given him 'more joy' than 'I have ever experienced in any other part of my life'.[195] Later, looking back on the first half of his life, he added, 'Not until my life's work found me, stripped me bare of the past and absorbed me into itself, did life take on any real meaning for me.'[196]

PART TWO
DIVINE DISCONTENT
1900–1914

POLITICAL RETURN,
BODILY RETREAT

Keir Hardie had found his life's work, agitating for a new social order that would transform the life of the working class. Although he believed he had been chosen to preach the gospel of socialism, the causes into which he would throw himself – to bring this change about – were his own to choose. One that loomed ever larger in his mind, as both the twentieth century and a new general election approached, was securing effective labour representation in Parliament.

As labour had become better organized in the 1890s, so too had employers. They formed their own federations in shipping and engineering. By 1895 they had their own parliamentary committee. Blackleg labour was being made available through the Free Labour Association. Legal moves against picketing had had limited success,[1] and everywhere there were attempts to remove gains in wages and conditions won earlier by individual unions. Then, in July 1899, a leader of the conservative cotton spinners union stood as a Tory in a by-election.[2] He didn't win, but it was a sign that labour was not well enough organized. Slowly the bulk of the unions came to see that concerted political action was going to be necessary sooner rather than later.

At the end of 1899 Hardie began to speed matters up. He realized that the ILP had now stopped growing. Possibly even more alarming, the SDF had not.[3] He began his push in Scotland because his old friend Smillie was now head of the Scottish TUC's parliamentary committee and willing to call special conferences to let Hardie put the case for 'a long term association' between trade unions and socialists.[4] He made such a nuisance of himself in 1899 during the Scots TUC[5] that a woman secretary present was forced to complain to Ramsay MacDonald that 'Congress is being nobbled' by a visiting Keir Hardie who 'was never off the platform the whole time'.[6] Hardie got what he wanted at every Scottish conference, however: commitment to action that would further labour representation, or as the STUC's motion put it, 'united working class action at the next General Election'.[7]

Action in Scotland's TUC was designed to sway the national TUC at its 1899 conference in Plymouth. This time Hardie kept out of it. Instead, ILP leaders oversaw a resolution which was moved by James Holmes of the Amalgamated Society of Railway Servants. Much argument has gone on about who actually drafted this resolution, MacDonald, Hardie, both, or neither.[8] Whoever did, it wasn't very complex, merely asking approval to 'devise ways and means for securing the return of an increased number of labour members at the next Parliament'.

Dozens of such resolutions had been passed at dozens of meetings in a whole range of organizations in the previous forty years. But this one had some important riders, to hold a special conference to organize for this objective and to invite a wide range of 'politics . . . co-operative, socialistic, trade unions, and other working organizations'.[9] In other words, it was to be a new alliance, and it was to have a political dimension that included socialists. The resolution was debated heatedly with the usual opposition from the conservative 'battalions of Coal and Cotton'[10] who were still in favour of unions acting individually rather than collectively. It was so close that a card vote had to be taken, followed by 'pandemonium'[11] when the result showed the motion carried by 546,000 to 434,000. But the margin of victory was small. Negotiations for the conference to come needed careful handling. They got this from Ramsay MacDonald who drew up proposals (which Hardie approved) that were hard for trade unions to oppose: unions were to run and pay for their own candidates, as could other groups like the SDF, ILP and Fabians (it was left in the air how far money would be pooled). All any one of them had to agree in return was that candidates from this new Labour Representation Committee (LRC) would stand independently of all other parties and that the combined forces, as MacDonald phrased it, would have an overall 'political' committee.[12]

Invitations to the conference brought only 129 delegates. Those from the TUC did not represent even half the total TUC membership.[13] Other delegates came from the ILP, SDF and the Fabians.[14] They met just over a month after the start of the twentieth century on 27 and 28 February in the Memorial Hall, Farringdon Street, London. W. C. Steadman of the Bargebuilders was in the chair. Experience at the Scottish conference had led Hardie to expect that there would be an argument between those who wanted the broadest possible alliance – to get all the unions in (including those still allied to the Liberals) and those wanting a specific commitment to a socialist policy or party.[15]

The argument duly repeated itself at the Memorial Hall meeting, where socialism's main advocates were SDF delegates who moved bull-at-a-gate to commit the new alliance to the class war, the central tenet of social democracy. This was promptly opposed by trade unionists with their own proposals, including one that only working-class men could be chosen to stand. This provoked John Burns to weigh in crudely against any class dimension, 'he was getting tired of working class boots, working class trains, working class houses, and working class margarine' and wanted the LRC to 'break away from class prejudice'.[16] The Fabians took practically no part at all in the proceedings, only having come 'on the principle that any organization was worth while permeating',[17] while Hyndman stayed away on the mistaken assumption that it was a gathering for working-class people only.[18] Blatchford also stayed away. His elitist view from his editorial office, according to Hardie, was that society must look 'for its salvation' to the 'educated' rather than the working class.[19]

In view of the standoff – which Hughes says Hardie had expected after Scotland[20] – Hardie drew up a compromise motion. He knew from Scotland that any explicit commitment to socialism would fail to secure a majority vote, especially among the unions (who were needed for the funding). His motion was awkwardly worded, since it took some phrases from the SDF's 'class war' motion, and some from that of the upholsterers' representative who had proposed working-class MPs. Only Hardie could have drafted it because it resolved the conflict by framing agreement entirely in terms of parliamentary procedure, proposing a 'distinct labour group in parliament, who shall have their own whips and agree upon their policy'.[21] Electoralism had claimed its first victory, for it was left wide open what that policy was to be – contrary to Hardie's earlier proclamations of principle that in any political alliance it is the programme that should come first. The motion also kept a lifeline open to the Liberals by adding that the group should be ready to 'co-operate with any party . . . for the time being . . . engaged in promoting legislation in the direct interests of labour' and equally ready not to co-operate with any party promoting measures 'having an opposite tendency', leaving wide open also how labour 'interests' were to be defined. But if anyone saw these difficulties, no one raised them. The majority wanted to agree. They voted for Hardie's lowest common denominator.

In retrospect the conference was hailed as an ILP success not because of the motion but because of the surprise 'tour de force', as Pelling called it,[22] which changed the composition of the new Committee's ruling executive. As Shaw noted later with his usual mischievous eye, 'if the LRC had been democratically established', the trade unions 'would have swept out all the Socialists and replaced them with . . . Conservative or Lib-Lab members'.[23] But it was not. Warring trade union and socialist interests were resolved by reducing both TUC and Fabian representation, leaving the ILP with more places than before. Even so, according to Pelling, it was only going to be possible to get a socialist majority 'if two out of the trade union seven turned out to be socialists'.[24] The odds were by no means foolproof.

The SDF was not impressed and was quick to condemn the ILP for 'treachery' to socialism.[25] Hardie's view was that it was as good a working arrangement as could have been devised. Hardie did not see the Labour Representation Committee aspiring to be a political party like those that existed.[26] Ever since he and Cunninghame Graham had campaigned to free labour representation from the political party system,[27] he had hated the idea of a poor-relation labour 'bedraggled in the mire of party politics . . . begging ministers to grant . . . boons'.[28] His expectation was a greatly enlarged labour pressure group that would act – somewhat as the large body of Irish MPs acted – to force the two main parties to legislate in the labour interest, or risk their governments being brought down.

Despite the fact that the new Committee had rejected restricting membership to one class, Hardie was seen by contemporaries as championing the idea of the 'working classes being represented in the House of Commons by members of the working classes'[29] because he had refused the idea of political parties 'acting' for them. But during the 1890s Hardie had also committed himself against a tight party organization with insistence on 'pledges' and 'expulsions'.[30] He believed 'room must be kept for the individual . . . the rule of democracy cannot possibly mean conformity to iron clad regulations'. Nor did he care much for constitutions, believing that once 'paper' is in force, the 'cordial spirit of sympathetic trustfulness . . . the only tie that can bind has been broken'.

The essence of the new group, as far as Hardie was concerned, was its independence. This meant no political pacts with parties. 'I would rather fight on independent lines and lose in every case, my own included, than win ten seats . . . as a result of compact or compromise'.[31] But compromise was in the nature of electoral politics, which Hardie had just sanctioned by his proposal to define the new group by common whips in the legislature. This being so, it was going to be difficult to remain outside the party system. In effect, Hardie chose his own form of compromise, to sideline socialism to win trade union support. MacDonald chose his, to accept labour independence to avoid any revolutionary commitment that would mean a final break with the Liberals, with whom he was already in touch and with whom he would remain in touch. Nor was Hardie in the dark about this connection, since MacDonald had just stood in 1899 for the LCC as a 'Labour and Progressive' candidate,[32] making common cause with London radicals. In short, the divisions and attachments destined to characterize the politics of labour and the Left for decades to come, were already in place.

G. D. H. Cole later characterized the new labour alliance as having the ILP as its soul, the trade unions as its muscle, and the Fabians as its brain.[33] What Cole neglected to include was the heart, for which

Hardie assumed responsibility. He wanted nothing to do with the mechanics. Thus MacDonald (who was elected secretary) took on the necessary 'arrangements' between members (and other parties) as well as the task of drafting a constitution. He designated a corner of his and Margaret's Lincoln's Inn flat as the new LRC headquarters. The flat, a few streets away from Hardie's, was shared with their first baby, Alister, and a second expected imminently. Margaret was already active in the National Union of Women Workers and other causes[34] and for this reason had insisted on living in the middle of London and not in the suburbs, where MacDonald had wanted to live.[35] The flat was lively and chaotic, and the housekeeping minimal. A friend commented, 'he wanted to be tidy, but she never'.[36]

MacDonald wanted to be tidy in political life as well. He was temperamentally suited to rules and regulations. Hardie was not. Hardie was an old hedgerow preacher without a pulpit – like John Ball. 'Agitators we have been and agitators we must remain,' he told Lowe in 1898,[37] adding significantly, 'not party men'.

But Party there was to be. MacDonald from the start seems to have understood this. In 1899 he had said he looked forward to 'a genuine Labour Party in the House of Commons'.[38] Twelve years later he looked back on the Memorial Hall meeting and called it momentous.[39] At the time, however, few among the public or the press that served it singled this meeting out from dozens like it in the previous twenty years. Like so many events that later turned out to be significant, when it happened it was barely noticed.

One reason was the war into which the country had been plunged on 12 October 1899, when Britain attacked small, Dutch settler farmers in South Africa. The Liberal Party was split over it, with its radical wing passionately opposed to the adventure but its old guard in favour. Conservatives approved the military venture half the globe distant to enhance the imperial interest.

Hardie called the Boer War a 'foul crime' and blamed the press and its proprietors for whipping up enthusiasm while failing to say what this 'capitalist war' was really about. This he set out himself in *L'Humanité Nouvelle*:[40] 'We are told it is to spread freedom and extend the rights of the common people' but it is really about getting 'markets for goods, investors an outlay for capital, and . . . companies cheaper labour'. Hardie found further rose-tinted reasons: 'As socialists, our sympathies are bound to be with the Boers.' They have a republican form of government and they produce 'for use' rather than for 'exploitation for profit'.

Luckily the LRC was so new that it did not have to agree a policy. For although Hardie claimed 'the socialist Movement in England . . . is solid against the war and for peace',[41] the war was popular and many working-class people supported it, including men like the seamen's leader, J. Havelock Wilson. Glasier also recalled meeting an old friend, 'a man who has read ... Carlyle', only to find he was also now a jingoist. 'I return home a pessimist,' said Glasier.[42] Blatchford, the ex-soldier, eventually supported the war as well, marking the start of his slide away from socialism. Shaw belittled the war as a situation where one of those 'stray little states' cause the big powers big trouble.[43] ILP members who were also Fabians, including MacDonald, resigned from the Fabians in protest at such equivocation.[44] As usual, it was Cunninghame Graham who made the calmest and most farseeing comment, as wittily as Shaw might have written the line for the stage. The Boer War, he said, 'is a struggle between two burglars', since South Africa belonged to neither Boer nor Briton.[45] Although Hyndman picked up the point that 'the future of South Africa is, I believe, to the black man',[46] he came round in the end to supporting the British military; his socialism, as one Labour commentator wryly noted later, 'is the kind that flies readily to the rifle'.[47]

Once more the kaleidoscope shook, and Hardie found himself (as he often did on issues of war and peace) with those he would otherwise have opposed. John Burns was back in favour overnight as an opponent of the war; and Hardie acted for the Liberals at Glasgow City Hall where he 'generalled' the stewards for a meeting at which Lloyd George delivered a fiery speech against the Boer venture. Lowe reported it was 'an oratorical triumph'. Even so, Lloyd George had to be escorted away from the meeting by the police. The same police were less attentive to the *Labour Leader*'s offices, which had their windows smashed that night.[48] As Glasier wrote,[49] 'The *Daily Mail* ... excited madness among ... workmen, poor girls, and ladies and gentlemen parading the streets' and shrieking against anti-war people. Hardie's own meetings were regularly broken up by 'war toughs', who have 'taken possession of the public', and at one of Frank Smith's peace meetings 'blood flowed freely'.[50] For the next two years those who spoke for peace were liable to invasion by 'organized' mobs with Union Jacks who would break into 'jeers, boos and catcalls' as soon as the chair rose to start proceedings. Even Quakers reading the Bible were howled down.[51] Hardie toured the country week after week meeting the same reception, although occasionally there was a pleasant surprise (at the Oxford Union – where he was given leave to appear without evening dress – he carried the debate by five votes).[52] In the *Leader* he attacked Cecil Rhodes as a 'dipsomaniac' who had to be watched constantly by his friends in order to perform his duties[53] and from the back of wagons he denounced a government that had committed the nation to war without consulting the people. He and his colleagues remembered their Carlyle, as 'hungry British workmen, who had become soldiers were sent across the seas to kill Boers, with whom they had no quarrel'.[54] Hardie told audiences the dead lying on the far-off veldt ran to 10,000, almost all working men, while vast profits were being made on the Stock Exchange. Neither 'the business patriots, to whom the war means money', nor the politicians, 'give the working man a single thought'.[55]

Hardie's generation barely comprehended him, yet the coming century already had a quintessential spokesperson. When the new century had been rung in, inevitably journalists asked politicians about their hopes for the next hundred years. A *New York Tribune* reporter came to interview Hardie and asked him two questions: what the twentieth century's main political issue would be, and what would be its main danger? Hardie answered both questions quickly with a single word: 'militarism'.[56]

Hardie was still earning his living by lecturing. He was known by people all over the country as a man who 'dwelt in their houses and chatted by their firesides' because every comrade that put him up for the night saved him a temperance hotel bill as, 'weary and often wet . . . he trudged from town to city in every corner of the land bearing witness to the cause of socialism'. Staying with local people also kept him in touch with the grass roots and earned him a reputation as one who had not 'stood aloof from his comrades'.[57]

So began the tribute to Hardie at the ILP Conference in 1900, when Hardie finally succeeded in standing down as chair, a post he had wanted to resign in 1896[58] after only one year in office – and again in 1899. He hated the burden of committees and decisions, and the ILP's finances were often as chaotic and debt-ridden as his own. David Lowe spoke wistfully in 1899 of the sound finances of the Fabians under the stockbroker, Edward Pease.[59]

The tribute was spoken by Glasier:

> a man rises from the people, who unattracted by the enticement of wealth or pleasure or unbent either by praise or abuse, has remained faithful to the class to which he belongs . . . he is a man of the people and a leader of the people.[60]

But not a leader of a party. As Morgan noted, Hardie had 'an aversion to the operation of power'.[61] Or more particularly, he thought the power that mattered was what people exercised for themselves, not what 'leaders' wielded. Hardie's speech in reply, which, uncharacteristically, he read from longhand, was 'wordy and bad', according to Glasier, who took over as chair.[62] Even though Hardie had chosen to give up the post, perversely he felt bereft after he had quit. Writing to Lowe on 2 May from Cumnock, he said, 'For the past ten days I have been in a sulking mind and the garden has been the gainer.'[63]

Hardie was planning to spend the summer at home in Cumnock,

relatively free from burdens,[64] but the Conservative government
decided to strike while the 'Khaki War' was hot and called a general
election in September. An election in the middle of war fever seemed
just about the least favourable time for Hardie personally. Yet he was
determined to stand, and immediately set out from Cumnock. Once
again Lillie was to hear that 'insistent call which kept her man so
much away from his ain fireside',[65] as Stewart put it; and she was
not happy.

Hardie was having trouble finding a constituency with any hope of
success. West Ham was out because Will Thorne wanted to be the
Labour candidate there and Hardie had already had to conceded to
him.[66] The ILP in Preston wanted Hardie, yet Preston was a hard
seat to win. It had returned Conservatives for years. Although it had
a large Liberal contingent, many of its voters were Roman Catholics,
a denomination Hardie had always found hard to handle. It also had
a large military barracks which attracted child prostitutes clattering
over its cobbles in their clogs.[67] What brought him there finally
was probably the offer of £150 from Cadburys (Hardie called them
'the chocolate folks').[68] George Cadbury as a Quaker was anxious to
support anti-war candidates but his money was only available for those
not intending to oppose Liberals; if they did, he said, 'they will get
no more from me'.[69] Liberals were not standing in Preston, no doubt
because they believed they were unlikely to win (or Hardie either –
which probably pleased them).

Although Hardie had said he was 'not the least bit drawn' to
Preston,[70] he threw himself into the campaign, automatically stressing
his Liberal roots and allegiance. He also made plain his opposition
to the war, in contrast to MacDonald, fighting in Leicester, who
decided not to mention the war at all in his own campaign.[71] Both
men stressed poverty heavily. The LRC's first pamphlet, *Labour and
Politics*, was available for them to use:

> one of every two of the working class . . . has to live by charity
> . . . Every year it is becoming more difficult for the working man
> to find a decent house at a reasonable rate . . . Industry is crippled
> . . . and the life of the worker rendered precarious by extortionate
> railway charges . . . and rents.[72]

At the same time as Hardie was fighting Preston he was also in touch
with miners in South Wales, who wanted to nominate an independent
Labour candidate (the law allowed candidates to stand in more than
one constituency). They had decided this at a meeting in June at
Bethel Chapel vestry, Abernant. Their spokesperson was the barber
Llewelyn Francis (later known to Hardie's friends as St Francis).[73]
Glasier negotiated with him in early August about who would pay
should Hardie win their nomination.[74] They concluded that between

the ILP and local Trades Councils (just being formed), they could meet expenses for the election. Glasier assured them that Hardie, if returned, would support himself by his pen and lecturing as he did when last in Parliament. He also had to assure Francis that arrangements would be 'entirely above-board', meaning the ILP money did not come from Tories but from such men as Cadbury and journalists like W. T. Stead or Alexander Thompson ('Dangle'). The rumours had begun again that ILP candidates were obtaining Tory money.[75] They were so strong that the *Labour Leader* had begun the practice, still carried on by the Left press, of printing the names and addresses of all donors to the cause, together with the amounts sent, to show where their money came from. All this turned out to be very necessary. The election campaign in Merthyr had to spend over £300.[76]

On the face of it, Merthyr was even less hopeful than Preston, for not only had Hardie little chance of visiting it, but there would be two Liberals and a Tory against him. Moreover, the local miners' leaders were all moderate Lib-Labs, so powerful nationally that their MPs organized separately in Parliament and the union had not yet felt the need to join the TUC. Merthyr miners' leaders were supporting a Mining Federation official, a conservative Lib-Lab called Brace, for the Merthyr seat. Hardie's reputation was also a problem. A son of one local supporter recalled years later, 'everybody was throwing stones . . . and threatening him for supporting Hardie'.[77] But Hardie's backers were the more determined – mostly miners who had been supported so stoutly by Hardie during the long and disastrous mining strike of 1898. When the miners' leaders got to the September meeting called to decide the Labour nomination, they found that Hardie's men had already put up Hardie's name.[78] After a bitter argument about the rules of nomination, the miners' leaders and their supporters suddenly walked out. This left a highly motivated political minority of only thirty-two. They nominated Hardie.

Hardie accepted, even though he was an absentee candidate and had already said that a 'Welsh-speaking Welshman' should contest the seat.[79] Yet Hardie had the advantage of being known and having a congenial religious background. Welsh chapel-goers warmed to his stand on secular education. Hardie's opposition to the Boer War, and general pacifist opinions, also favoured his cause, since one of Merthyr's earlier MPs, Henry Richard, who had died only twelve years earlier, had been a notable pacifist, known locally as 'the apostle of peace'.[80] There was also, long before that, the near-mythical 'Dic Penderyn', an early striking miner and Chartist leader, who had been executed as an example to frighten workers into submission.[81] Those who believed old wrongs live on and await their time to be righted – even when most of those living have all but forgotten the original events – had reason to hope.

What gave most hope had been the events of 1898 in which Hardie had so fully participated. 'It was the six months' miners' strike which caused the great awakening in the minds of miners and other classes of labour, and which spurred them on to organize industrially and politically,' wrote a Welsh colleague of Hardie's years later.[82] The new Trades Councils were not limited to men working in iron and steel and coal but included tailors, carpenters, masons, bakers, compositors and railway men. In 1896 Hardie had targeted South Wales as ripe for socialism and distributed leaflets he'd had translated into Welsh.[83] A socialist society had started in 1897 with a secretary, Edmund Stonelake, at that moment away studying at Ruskin College. Stonelake later recalled Hardie's earlier visit, together with Bob Smillie, in 1898, and Hardie's pledge 'to kill Liberalism' because it stood in the way of socialism. Hardie had urged working people to have independent representatives not just in Parliament but your 'own men on Boards of Guardians and on the . . . borough councils'.[84] He had made a great impression as 'he stood alone in the open air, suffering the taunts, jibes and jeers of a crowd of enthusiastic Liberals'.[85]

The most important piece of luck, however, was that the two Liberals standing detested each other more than either disliked Hardie. They exemplified the Liberals' two wings, for D. A. Thomas was a radical who opposed the war, while Pritchard Morgan was a jingoist who supported it, as well as a freebooter and gold prospector, constantly absent from Wales. This meant that Thomas, the more popular Liberal, did not send his own machine out to campaign against Hardie but remained neutral about the possibility of Hardie's being the second member in this two-member constituency.

A final gift of fortune was the monumentally ill-fated Tory candidate. A journalist by trade, he first went to Newcastle upon Tyne under the impression that Merthyr was in that vicinity. On contacting the Carlton Club and being told to head for Cardiff, he began canvassing there under the second mistaken impression that this at last was Merthyr. By the time he finally got to the real Merthyr he had missed his own nomination and retired. Shortly after, *The Times* sent him to Singapore to cover Far Eastern trade, where, sadly, he became the legendary Englishman who went out in the midday sun – dying of sunstroke after only a few weeks.[86]

All this was going on in Wales while Hardie was still dithering about whether to stand in Preston – as late as the end of September, according to Glasier.[87] Eventually he agreed to stand in both at once which sent Tories after him in Preston with the charge of 'political bigamist'.[88] This helped to further undermine an already doomed campaign. Despite solid minority support in Preston, the two Unionist Conservatives defeated him by a massive margin of nearly 4,000 votes.[89]

As soon as he realized he had lost, he headed for Wales and Merthyr. In all, he spent only eleven waking hours there before polling day. Yet when the Merthyr poll was announced, to everyone's amazement Hardie had squeezed into second place, some 1,700 votes ahead of the second Liberal, to win one of the two seats. As usual, Hardie greeted the result without emotion, only saying he was glad that 'a man with opinions can still win'.[90] The Glasiers, with their baby daughter, read the news on their way back from campaigning in Lancashire. Glasier recorded he 'could hardly speak for joy'. At once 'I kissed my dear wife and Jeanniebell and we danced in the train'.[91] In Merthyr, Hardie was hoisted on the miners' shoulders and carried back to his hotel, where he was due for an even bigger surprise. In his own words:

> that night from the hotel window in response to cries loud and long continued, I witnessed a sight I have never hoped to see this side of the pearly gates. My wife was making a speech to the delighted crowd![92]

Lillie had joined him during the campaign and had become, for a brief moment, a fighting woman. Quite possibly she looked forward to more such work. The previous day she had experienced another first: someone had got hold of that latest invention, an automobile,[93] and taken the Hardies through the Merthyr and Aberdare valleys. It was her first ride in what he always called 'a motor'. A new era, indeed.

Back in Cumnock supporters pulled Hardie and Lillie home to Lochnorris in a horse-drawn cab, as they always did when he won an election. This time he also had a welcome in Glasgow Town Hall. But he did not stay at home long, being off within a week for a victory tour of Britain, including a quick return to Wales, where he made a point of visiting an eisteddfod in progress to show he had already learned to sing the Welsh national anthem in Welsh.[94] After that it was to a 'big meeting' in Manchester's Free Trade Hall, where he, Emmeline Pankhurst and Glasier had tea together.[95] Afterwards Glasier's Diary glowed with an account of Hardie's 'wonderful power' as a speaker; 'We have none like him'.[96] At Bradford even Blatchford was on the platform to welcome him (Hardie whispered to Glasier that he hoped Blatchford had got 'through his sulks').[97] Blatchford used the occasion for backhanded praise by calling attention to the fact that Hardie was 'prematurely ageing' because the Labour movement was 'overworking and underpaying' him. Certainly Hardie had not been feeling well, and spoke of being almost 'comatose' after the election.[98] A few weeks later he wrote to Lowe that he had 'not been in good sorts' and had a bad cold.[99] While in Bradford, he had consulted Margaret MacMillan about his health and reported that 'Miss MacMillan explained that [it was] waste matter in the blood . . . the scavengers whose work it is to get rid of it . . . have been shirking their work'.[100] To a Scot, reared in constipation theory, this homily had a ring of credibility. 'At least that explanation will serve as well as any other,' he reported. Hardie disliked illness, was not well informed on bodily matters and believed his best defence was to remain so.

When Hardie finally returned to Cumnock for his first long stay after the election he found another elderly lady had been visiting the town and inquiring about him.[101] She invited him to see her at the local hotel, explaining that she was from Ulster and offering to leave Hardie £20,000 – her entire fortune – on condition he 'undertake a campaign against popery', since Rome was 'the embodiment of Satan'. Hardie explained he did not agree with her. She left in anger.

At home the hidden anger at Hardie's perpetual absences was also building up. The gladness with which his returns had once been greeted, when the children crowded round to hear tales of the wider world, was ever harder to recapture.[102] All three children posed for the usual seasonal photograph that would accompany the Hardie family greeting card sent out in December. It showed James at nineteen, handsome and stiff, Duncan, a small thirteen, still chubby of face and dressed in a man's suit with a watch-chain, and Nan at fifteen, her thick curly hair still down her back, and sitting in her best dress with leg of mutton sleeves, a tomboy with booted feet straddling the leg of the photographer's table.

The Hardies had long since decided to apprentice both Jamie and Duncan to engineering firms in Glasgow as soon as they left school, and Jamie had already started work. Like most working-class parents, they regarded a skilled trade as a first-rate start in life. A secondary education required payment – even a scholarship would have entailed some cost. Their finances were far too precarious to finance this route for any of their children.[103]

For Nan their plans were very conservative. She would not be sent out to service but neither would she be educated. Whenever anyone asked about her, she was 'helping her mother at home'. Nan, as we learn later, regarded it as her duty to accept this decision without demur, and saw it as her fate. Since the age of fourteen she had been helping her father as well. When he was at home Hardie would empty his large, worn leather case, which he carried everywhere as his travelling desk, and Nan would sort his letters for him. At one point she was collecting stamps for some local cause and Hardie was amused when she complained that he had 'only received 42 letters that day'.[104] Hardie was starting to use Nan as Gladstone had used his daughter, Mary, as 'a supernumary private secretary'.[105]

Although the boys' engineering apprenticeships were a luxury that Mary and David Hardie had not been able to afford for their sons, nevertheless for Jamie and Duncan they meant years of dependence

on the family, while they served their time. To be out and about in
the world, living in Glasgow, as Jamie now was, but still dependent on
home, where money was so short and everyone lived so 'thriftily and
frugally', as Hughes put it later,[106] and with his father often absent,
and always on the verge of bankruptcy (or saying he was) while yet
travelling widely, was to prove a trial. That James and his siblings
missed their father, and possibly unknowingly resented his lack of
attention and support, and Lillie's small allowance to them, is possible.
If so, they certainly found dramatic means of getting such attention.

In January 1902, Nan, now seventeen was again 'taken dangerously
ill'. Hardie came straight home. Lowe said she 'hovered between life
and death' for weeks on end.[107] Hardie was 'absent from Parliament
and from the public platform' the whole time – missing the opening
of Parliament – waiting, so Stewart reported, 'by the bed of sickness,
nursing the girl, comforting the mother and hiding his own fears'.

The nature of the illness was never stated. It was simply called 'the
trouble'[108] and Stewart reports that it 'left effects from which she could
never entirely shake herself free' for the rest of her life. In Stewart's
opinion, this health weakness of Nan's made Hardie more 'tenderly
solicitous' to her than to the two boys who 'had inherited his own
sturdy constitution'. In fact, the boys were regularly ill as well. Duncan
was kept at home and indoors often during this same year suffering
from erysipelas.[109] Earlier, both Jamie and Lillie had had 'la grippe'.[110]
Nor was Hardie's own health all that good, as anyone looking at him
could see. In July 1901 he had already had what Stewart called 'his first
touch of illness' and had had to spend a week in bed.[111] Again, no
name was put to it. Lowe said it was 'a breakdown, accompanied by a
good deal of suffering'.[112] Stewart said there were stomach pains; Lowe
that 'morphia' was given. No one was surprised. Hardie had been doing
the work of several men: 'committees, deputations, interviews, visitors,
parliamentary duties, editorial duties and interminable speechmaking
. . . the fever of wartime and incessant financial worry'.[113]

Hardie was 'in great distress' about Nan's illness until, 'with relief',
he was able to say she was 'out of danger' – news that he announced
in the Labour Leader.[114] When Nan was recuperating, Hardie felt free
to leave again and Lillie took over the care. Hardie had already
remarked on Lillie's 'powers of endurance' with 'love . . . [as] the
driving force'.[115] Wives were expected to have the knowledge of
physicians, and Lillie more than most. Hardie never liked doctors
and appeared to resent depending on them, no doubt because they
were so costly. Lillie became health obsessed and regularly consulted
a number of popular books on medical matters, which were kept on
the Hardie shelves.

Health was not the reason Hardie favoured his daughter over his
sons. Nor was it, as Emrys Hughes claimed, that she was 'so very like

him in appearance',[116] though both were short and slim and had pert faces. It seems more likely that it was because Nan identified with all he did, and never sought to have a separate, or rival, life. Jamie did. It preserved him intact in the end, while the others, including Lillie, identifying wholly with Hardie's struggles, found themselves submerged in the same way that Eleanor Marx was submerged in doing her father's work. Marx, whose pet name for his daughter was Tussy, had also identified with a daughter so like himself: 'Tussy is me', he was fond of saying.[117] The more the parent incorporated the child, the greater the possibility of tragedy if the child was unable to break free.

Jamie, first out in the world, and clearly not the favourite, was already showing signs of resentment. If he had set out to gain his parents' attention, he too could not have chosen a better way: he began to run up bad debts in Glasgow. These, it turned out, were from gambling, and those whom he owed – or Jamie himself – applied to Hardie to settle up.[118] The sums were not small – one bad debt was £45 – almost half the household income for a year. It caused Hardie great distress, but he paid up. Perhaps Lillie thought Hardie was soft or resented this money not coming to herself and Nan and Duncan. Whatever the reason, Hardie reported to Glasier that Lillie's 'sullen temper greatly hurts him' and possibly it hurt Jamie as well.[119] She and Jamie got on bad terms with each other and it is doubtful if they were ever on really good terms again. Jamie's debts can be interpreted as attempts to get the attention 'paid' that was owed, and Lillie's temper as resentment arising from her allocated role of policing and managing children and household without real assistance, and living on next to nothing. In 1903 Jamie, at twenty-two, 'went to sea', a standard route of escape from a situation which no one could resolve. He took work as an engineer on a merchant ship.

Hardie not only had his immediate family to remember, he also had his parents and brothers and sisters. The youngest brothers, George and David, identified closely with him politically and in their passion for self-education; all his siblings had followed him in total abstinence.[120] Glasier describes an ILP dinner in June 1901 at which Hardie 'comes late – with him was his old mother and a sister and brother – all making their first visit to London'.[121] Three days later he had the whole of the ILP National Administrative Committee (NAC) to tea on the terrace of the House of Commons, after which they all adjourned to Ramsay and Margaret MacDonald's flat at Lincoln's Inn Fields.[122] On another occasion it was Adam Birkmyre who arrived unexpectedly in London and had to be given a whole day in which to discuss Port Glasgow's mussel-beds.[123] The government was seeking to lease these beds – previously a marine 'common' – to private owners, and Hardie was protesting against this 'enclosure' in Parliament. Hardie was still paying Birkmyre £25 each January and June, repayment on the Lochnorris loan. Tom Johnston wrote later about Hardie, 'How he lived in London and kept up his home in Scotland . . . is a mystery'.[124] At this time the answer was that he didn't. In the summer of 1901 Hardie confessed to Glasier that he was 'financially broke'.[125] Everyone comes to see me, he said, and 'I have to give them tea on the terrace and that takes £2 a week.' Glasier noted feelingly, 'It's pathetic, I feel sure he is frugal.'

After the election campaign Hardie had put in a claim to the ILP for expenses and for fees for speeches he had made to ILP branches. The ILP had agreed that it would fund ILP MPs in future, starting with Hardie, and had voted to levy itself enough to raise £150 a year for the purpose; ILP members referred to this as the 'Keir Hardie Wages Fund'.[126] But £150 was not a large sum for an MP to do his constituency and parliamentary work and keep up two homes. Most agreed the job took £350 as a minimum, the sum the Miners' Federation was paying its MPs at this time.[127]

Hardie enjoyed showing his mother and siblings the sights of London. His mother, at seventy-two, was still his favourite human being, and he hers. After she had returned to Scotland, he wrote long and lovingly in the *Labour Leader* of seeing London anew through her eyes.[128] She was then living with David Hardie in retirement in Cambuslang near Glasgow, supported by regular contributions from Hardie and his brothers. Having had such hard lives, the senior Hardies must have counted it a great fortune to have survived into their seventies.

In September Hardie and Lillie went on a holiday to the western highlands, where one of Hardie's brothers lived, a period of time away together that was to become their yearly habit. Equally a habit was its disruption. In 1901 it was a by-election at North East Lanark. Hardie's old friend, Bob Smillie, was chosen by the ILP and the LRC as the Labour candidate. Both Hardie and MacDonald went to campaign for him in a seat they had hoped the Liberals would not contest, on the understanding Labour did not contest certain Liberal seats, an understanding MacDonald was coming to see as essential. But at the last minute local Liberals decided to put up their own candidate, the London tycoon and imperialist, Cecil Harmsworth. Smillie, the local working-class candidate, lost badly, and matters seemed no further advanced in Scotland than when Hardie had fought Mid-Lanark.

Queen Victoria when died a year after the old century ended the new Parliament was about to convene in January 1901. Hardie was in Cumnock, where he reported 'our little town quite undisturbed by the event'.[129] Of Victoria the woman he wrote, a 'respected

... middle class matron ... whose manner of dressing was plain, almost to dowdiness' and who preferred Balmoral to the 'intrigue of fashionable society'.[130] On Victoria the Queen, however, his views had not changed. He particularly objected to 'the barbarous display of the bloodthirsty implements of war' accompanying her to the grave. Monarchy always made 'militarism ... the very spirit of the nation',[131] glorifying a country at war, with soldiers and cannon and cavalry sweeping aside the representatives of culture and commerce. He particularly objected to the downgrading of elected representatives, and the fact that LCC members like Frank Smith had not been allocated any place to stand.

'Parliament, not the Monarch, is the real seat of authority,'[132] he proclaimed, and 'the soldier is the servant of the state', not of the monarch. Hardie's democratic commitment increased with time: 'I owe no allegiance to any hereditary rule.'[133] As he grew older, he grew bolder, and regularly refused to stand for the national anthem, bearing with equanimity the outrage of monarchists – on one occasion, for example, a group of well-heeled golfers at their annual dinner in a hotel dining room.[134]

To show his strong feeling when Parliament reconvened, he tabled a motion regretting that Queen Victoria had not seen fit to 'recommend the office of hereditary ruler be abolished'.[135] As this was ruled out of order, he had to settle for opposing the civil list expenditure for the new king on the grounds that 'when taxes were being increased ... when wages were going down', huge increases for the royal family were 'indefensible'.[136] Only four of the eleven working-class MPs supported him. The rest of his fifty-eight votes came from the Irish.

Hardie drew comfort from the Irish. When he opposed a £4,000 yearly pension in July 1901 for a Boer War commander in the field because 'thousands of poor men had come home wounded' and nothing had been done for them (and Tory MPs were shouting, 'workhouse!'), Swift MacNeill led the Irish into the lobby to back him up.[137] On another occasion the police were called when certain Irish members refused to leave the Chamber, as ordered by the Speaker, the first time police had ever been summoned to a debate. Hardie wrote glowingly of the Irish being carried out (in the manner that came to be associated later in the century with demonstrators' passive resistance in the streets).[138] 'The Irishmen are an inspiration and dominate the assembly', Hardie wrote to Lowe in February.[139] Earlier, he had even been toying with the idea of widening the Labour Party in Parliament to include them.[140]

If nothing else, the House was well aware that Keir Hardie – or 'Queer Hardie' to his enemies – was back again as a thorn in their side. He continued to question the government in the House about the drain on Britain's resources caused by the Boer War. When taxes on sugar were raised to pay it, Hardie gave up having sugar in his tea as a personal protest.[141]

He also returned to his defence of working-class living standards. In 1901 he wrote a pamphlet, *Can a Man be a Christian on a Pound a Week?* The answer, he concluded, was no. Trying to get governments to accept responsibility for maintaining people at some kind of agreed level was one of Hardie's objectives for the new Parliament. By now, thanks in part to Hardie's earlier agitation, society had a better idea of the indices of poverty. Social activists such as Seebohm Rowntree – in a major study of poverty in York – had set down criteria for basic living.[142] Hardie told the House that '30 per cent . . . of our working class population . . . live below the poverty line'. He also conducted his own 'research' by sending out requests for information to Trades Councils and trade unions in towns like Hull, Middlesbrough and Leeds, to show the House how arbitrary provision for the poor really was, and what huge differences there were in terms of benefits for those out of work. He regularly sparred with MPs to defend workers, who were not 'drunkards or incapables . . . [or] lazy' but just plain workless because 'trade is depressed' and there were no jobs.[143]

He added new fields in which he was prepared to do parliamentary battle. He opposed stag hunting in Maidenhead; he interceded for a woman condemned to the gallows. He opposed the exploitative trade in child minding known as 'baby farming', and he kept up the pressure for free meals for schoolchildren, painting stark portraits of the suffering of the underfed.[144] Other socialists argued in the same month for exactly the same improvements but on different grounds. Hyndman, for example, said that 'lack of good food, good clothes and good air in children' means 50 per cent 'of our urban working class population is unfit to bear arms'.[145] Nationalist and humanitarian socialism were already characterized by identical arguments – but for different ends.

Clarifying his own socialism was an urgent task. As independent Labour's most prominent person in the House, he awaited the chance. Unexpectedly, in the first session, he drew a place in the ballot for a private members' Bill and put down the first motion for socialism ever tabled in the British Parliament. He chose St George's Day for a short, classic statement asking for a Socialist Commonwealth whose aim would be 'The common ownership of land and capital, production for use and not for profit, and equality of opportunity for every citizen.'[146] This was simple, and in some ways, surprisingly modern, but to the Tory and Liberal establishments, revolutionary extremism. Not that Hardie spoke in an extreme manner. Though he was direct and lacking in fluency, said one parliamentary journalist from a northern paper,[147] he was still 'one of the most cultured speakers the . . . House of Commons can boast'. In his 'faultlessly fashioned phraseology', Hardie made his prediction that, as surely as radicalism had democratized 'the system of government in the 19th Century, so will Socialism democratize . . . industrialism in the coming century'.[148]

Hardie's Socialist Commonwealth Bill provided an early chance in the new Parliament to see how socialism stood. Most Lib-Lab MPs refused to support it. When the self-proclaimed socialist, John Burns, also refused, and Glasier read about this, he sent Hardie a telegram, 'Burns is a Humbug!'[149] Hardie had suspected this since 1896 when he had predicted[150] that Burns would end up in a Liberal or Tory 'individualist cabinet'. In the 1900 election Burns had refused LRC sponsorship, taking yet another step in this direction. Fellow trade unionists like the weaver David Holmes, called him 'the greatest bundle of conceit' ever to hit British politics.[151] Hardie too had noted his 'fatal egotism'. Yet still Hardie deferred to him, one of those men who exuded leadership potential but always stepped back at the critical moment. Richard Bell, who took over the chair of the LRC in 1902, was the only other successful LRC candidate besides Hardie. Yet it was only with the greatest reluctance that Bell would second Hardie's socialist motion. It did not augur well.

In reality, despite the LRC, Hardie was for all practical purposes still a Party of One. By the end of the first session he had realized it. Writing to Glasier,[152] he said he felt beleaguered. He urged Glasier to get more socialists to stand for Parliament. Over the next few years he himself tried to get men to stand in by-elections and in 1903 he was still appealing to Burns himself to break loose from the Liberals and lead an independent Labour group.[153] Hardie even toyed with the idea of Lloyd George accompanying him.[154] What stands out is Hardie's own continuing reluctance to see himself as a leader – despite the fact that outside Parliament he was the one man most identified with socialism and the independent Labour cause.

What gradually drew more trade unionists into the political camp was not Hardie's leadership, nor yet his evangelizing socialism, but the law lords' judgment in the Taff Vale case, delivered at the end of 1901. It concerned the case of a railway that ran along the Taff River in Hardie's constituency, carrying coal to Cardiff. The railway owners sued the unions for loss of profits after a strike and the Lords ruled for the owners. This judgment threatened all trade unions with legal liability for damage to employers' interests as a result of industrial action. Labour unions realized at once that only new legislation could reverse this judgment. Support for the LRC thus began to grow.

This judgment also had the effect of bringing Labour members together in the Commons, and of inducing radicals and Lib-Lab MPs to seek out independent Labour members for common action. Hardie was defensive and suspicious about all such moves. He cold-shouldered 'that gang working in the interests of Dilke' when Charles Dilke tried to get labour and radicals together to deal with Taff Vale, and he told the TUC parliamentary committee chairman, the MP Sam Wood, that he refused 'to have Labour dragged at the tail' of the Liberal Party.[155] But it was difficult drawing a strict line between groups, made all the harder when some Labour people called themselves Liberals, some Liberals called themselves Labour, and when most Labour members in the House had not yet agreed to independence. In May 1902, Hardie sent a postcard to MacDonald to say he had little idea when Labour MPs 'may be . . . transformed into the Labour group' and 'as much as can be said with safety at this stage is that the Labour Party in Parliament is coming into being'. It did not yet exist.[156]

There were also troubles on the socialist side. At the LRC Conference in February 1902, Harry Quelch, the SDF's spokesperson, had tried once more to get the LRC to adopt the class struggle as an objective. It was voted down. In a by-election later that year in Dewsbury, Quelch put up as the SDF candidate, defying the LRC agreement about prior approval. Many ILP branches supported him. By then it was of little account, as the SDF had decided to secede from the LRC – 'quite incorrectly', wrote the Communist historian James Klugman years later[157] – leaving the Labour Party's socialist wing even further diminished. This withdrawal was partly because of Hyndman's continued failure to understand the important role of trade unions in social transformation, but also because dissident socialists inside the SDF began to go their own way. One group formed a connection with Daniel DeLeon in New York and began using his newspaper to attack Hyndman, who had lost their support by siding with the French socialist, Millerand. Millerand had joined the Liberal Waldeck-Rousseau government in 1899, fuelling a controversy that split the Socialist International in 1900 (a congress Hardie did not attend). Another SDF group, mainly printing workers in Scotland, started their own paper in 1902, called *The Socialist*, with help from James Connolly. When they were finally expelled from the SDF, they formed the Socialist Labour Party in 1903. Hardie had met DeLeon earlier and admired him, but later came to regard him as doctrinaire. Hardie had also formed a fast friendship with Connolly in the 1890s – when each sent the other financial support – but after Hardie formed a tie to Irish Liberals opposing the Boer War, Connolly lost faith in him.

A last group of SDF dissenters, led by internationalists like Theodore Rothstein, objected, as Eleanor Marx had done, to Hyndman's everlasting jingoism, allied to what she had long before called his 'Tory democratic party'.[158] This group also began meeting on its own and was eventually expelled in April 1904, setting up the Socialist Party of Great Britain. They called their paper the *Socialist*

Standard, because they felt that Hyndman had 'lowered the flag' on real socialism.[159]

These events brought Hyndman himself to the verge of collapse, a state his wife, Matilda, had already reached. In early 1902 he had bought a house in Kent for her to recover in and within a year had exiled himself there as well, writing to a friend of 'no sleep & great depression, complete breakdown of nerves'.[160] Hyndman had been losing his dream of a spontaneous revolution for some while and a year earlier had stood down from the SDF's executive. Unsure what to do after his ultimate descent, he plunged himself back into business, investing in gold mining companies in North America and becoming a director of a new gun company making Colt pistols (after he had formed a runaway passion for this particular gun).[161]

Rank and file members of both the SDF and ILP were never happy at the separation. They continued to defy leaders and worked together in every local area. Hardie had his quarrels with Hyndman, but he worked with Quelch on national unemployment committees; he worked with George Lansbury on farm colony matters. It was Glasier and MacDonald who were the ones most virulently opposed to any collaboration with the SDF.

Yet in January 1903 MacDonald began secret talks with the Liberals' Chief Whip, Herbert Gladstone, youngest son of the late leader. Hardie took no part in the negotiations, although he certainly knew about them. What concerned him much more was the fact that when independent Labour men began being returned to Parliament in by-elections, the last thing any of them wanted was to have Keir Hardie around. First in March 1903 it was Will Crooks, a popular cockney cooper, later the subject of one of the upwardly mobile books so fashionable at the time, *From Workhouse to Westminster* (much like the one written later about Hardie, *From Pit to Parliament*).[162] Crooks had the support of the *Daily News, Sun, Star* and *Chronicle*, the mainstream Liberal press. He was, of course, along with Tillett, one of the progressive group on the LCC, opposed by the Independent Labour group there of Frank Smith and R.C.K. Ensor. Behind Hardie's running fight with Tillett was the fact that Labour in the LCC had no rule about independence whereas the LRC in Parliament did. When Crooks moved to Westminster, therefore, Hardie was annoyed to see him carry on openly collaborating with Liberals.[163]

Other Labour men soon joined him. In Yorkshire, the Taff Vale ruling had forced the élite textile workers into the LRC almost at a stroke, and when a seat became vacant in Clitheroe, a local weaver, the immensely tall David Shackleton (it was unusual for a worker to be very tall at that time) was returned unopposed. At a by-election in Preston, where Hardie had lost so badly (and was not invited to help), the seat was almost won for the LRC by John Hodge of the steel smelters, confirming the wisdom of not letting Hardie take part and alienate voters. He was kept away too from the by-election in County Durham in July 1903, where the iron-foundry worker, Arthur Henderson – with much tacit Liberal support – just scraped home at Barnard Castle; and where, even at subsequent elections, opponents went around trying to scare voters with the slogan, 'A vote for Henderson is a vote for Hardie'.[164] Whether these victories were due to the unions' fright at Taff Vale, MacDonald's success behind the scenes, or because Hardie was kept away – or even because despite his absence he had pulling power – cannot be known. What is ironic is that nationally these gains for the LRC were often ascribed to Hardie. The *Glasgow Herald*, for example, called the Barnard Castle win 'a triumph for Keir Hardie'![165]

Thus although LRC moderates and Lib-Labs thought of Hardie as an 'extremist'[166] and the SDF continued to say he had sold out, the public at large saw him still as the main embodiment of working-class advance. Hardie took his view of himself from Henrik Ibsen: 'The strongest man . . . is he who can stand alone.'[167] He kept on plugging his line that the Liberal Party was dying and that the independent Labour interest was rising in its place. Had all socialists and labour interests believed in Hardie's long-term vision, they might have sunk their differences. But most see only today, and all they saw was a Liberal Party raising social issues in the wake of the end of the Boer War in 1902, forced into a more collectivist and reforming posture, and stealing the thunder of the new 'representation' movement of Labour. Hardie, who had already told Glasier he wished Liberals were in office again so Labour 'could make things hum' once more in opposition,[168] now had to watch the Liberal opposition under Campbell-Bannerman, bending to acknowledge the need to deal with slum housing and gross undernourishment, issues Hardie had battered away at for so long, and which a Liberal press were now taking up. In opposing the new Education Act that put church schools on the rates, it was Liberals under Lloyd George who were making the running for nonconformity, not Labour.

It was no wonder Hardie preferred the ILP where socialism was secure, trade unionists were not hostile, and Labour independence was understood. In April 1903 the ILP Conference was at York and everyone was high-spirited. After Lillie and Emmeline Pankhurst had gone to bed, MacDonald wrote that at 1 a.m. they were still up singing 'We're all Brothers',[169] while Fred Jowett, a Bradford socialist councillor, was marching round the room shouldering the fire-irons. The ILP was a much more congenial political medium for Hardie than the LRC in the House of Commons. Not only did he find the 'proceedings of the House a mockery',[170] he also complained that as 'the guardians of labour' we are treated as '. . . of absolutely no account'.[171] Contemporaries noticed that whenever Hardie got up to speak, an 'ill bred murmur'[172] would invariably start. He did not abandon his hope that 'a labour group in Parliament should be militant' and command power,[173] but he could not afford to give up his life's work outside. The key to victory was there. Hardie had been in Parliament long enough now to know the truth, 'Parliament responds to pressure, not to argument.'[174]

The first thing Hardie had done when he had won his Merthyr seat was to send his mother a telegram. In April 1902 he got a telegram during a Commons debate to say his mother was desperately ill. He immediately took the train to Glasgow, but very shortly after he arrived at the modest house in Cambuslang, she died. Hardie comforted his father. The old man, customarily 'full of the vocabulary of the vigorous Saxon', as Hardie tactfully put it, was refusing his medicine and asked Hardie to 'tak that damned stuff awa'.[175] Within a few hours David Hardie too was dead. Either the same acute condition carried them both off or David had given up once Mary had gone. Either way, Hardie thought it was 'meet' that since 'as socialists they had . . . fought life's battle together . . . they should enter the void together' on the same day.

Hardie noted that their attitude to the void was one of absolute confidence, with none of the agitation of believers about their fate in any afterlife. They 'talked about death as if it were an everyday incident in their lives . . . without emotion or excitement or interest of any kind', as if it had 'been a visit to Glasgow . . . they were planning'. Their end reinforced Hardie's positive views of death, which he always called The White Herald. He had never yet seen a deathbed – 'and I have seen many' – where the Herald has not been 'welcomed as deliverance'.

In the *Labour Leader* Hardie wrote a short tribute to his mother – significantly, not about his love for her, but about hers for him, 'Closed forever the grey eyes which blazed resentment . . . when untrue things were spoken . . . about me' and 'stopped the warm . . . heart which throbbed with joy unspeakable when any little success came her laddie's gait'. His own life was now the one with the void, without the one person who had loved him unconditionally. Where was he to replace this support?

More immediately, where was he to stay in London now that Frank Smith's commitments to relatives meant he could no longer offer Hardie his London bed? After an extended search for cheap lodgings, in May 1902 he found a room to rent for 6s.6d. a week, tucked behind Fleet Street in Fetter Lane.[176] It was around the corner from the *Labour Leader*'s offices and within walking distance of Parliament along the river. The room was in a late-medieval half-timbered five-storey tenement building called Neville's Court, one of the oldest buildings still standing in London.[177] He moved in to No.14, a single room on the ground floor with a curtained alcove for the bed, an open coal fire, a hob, and a tiny courtyard outside. Stewart called it 'slumland'[178] and Fenner Brockway, a young journalist Hardie would shortly meet, a 'rabbit warren',[179] and it was certainly modest. But Hardie loved its simplicity. His taste in art and architecture was very much for the starker form of Arts and Crafts work and for 'dark polished wood and old silver'. He always appreciated good 'workmanship', especially in wood.[180] This spare setting – such a contrast to the cluttered late-Victorian homes of the day – suited the odd assortment of 'modern' furniture he eventually collected, including a university chair, a 'bentwood' table and an oak chair carved and shaped like a church pew.

In the same month he had a second stroke of good fortune[181] with the arrival in his life of the daughter of his old friend, Robert Williams, the Welsh architect. Maggie (as she was always called) asked if she could help him in his work and he accepted at once. At that time an MP's secretary was usually a man, who received a clerk's pay. Margaret Symons was then a woman of about thirty, small, shy and intense. She had married a New Zealand landowner, Travers Symons, of somewhat cavalier character, and they were living in Willow Road in Hampstead. Maggie began visiting Neville's Court as soon as Hardie moved in, to see to his mail, arrange his appointments and run his errands. As well as being an educated woman and a first-class linguist, she also turned out to be efficient, conscientious and industrious. Soon she had Hardie's parliamentary work organized. However, as one who aspired to being a 'new woman' (and who had had a spell as treasurer of the WSPU), she did not wish to remain a mere helper to her father's friend any more than she wanted to remain a mere wife. She wanted to earn her own way with her own work. Her ambition was to be a writer, possibly a journalist – one of the few professions open to women where, in some cases, equal pay was offered.[182] By Christmas 1902 Hardie was sufficiently guilty about the time she spent with him to send her three guineas, which he called 'a small honorarium . . . in recognition of the excellent work you have done for me'.[183] Three pounds and three shillings was all she got for two-and-a-half days a week for six months. Hardie was slow in picking up the principle of equal pay or a fair wage.

Morgan claims that having moved into Neville's Court, Hardie was 'leaving Cumnock behind' for good, the room in London becoming 'the nearest he came to having a home for the remainder of his . . . tortured life'.[184] Possibly this reflects Morgan's own understandable interest in the power of Westminster-based politics, but the truth was probably more complex. Neville's Court became a much-loved *pied-à-terre*, but it was not home. Hardie continued to spend all his holiday time in Scotland and to visit during his travelling. In homes, as in life, Hardie was divided, as he had been divided for years between speaking and editing, national and international politics, industrial struggles and the promotion of socialism. The latest election merely gave Hardie the classic three-cornered political life: a home in one place, a constituency in another, and parliamentary duties in London.

McLean claims that Lillie – left behind in Scotland – did not join him because like Mrs Lloyd George later, she preferred to stay away.[185] We know, however, that Lillie wanted to be in London and that it was Hardie who did not wish it, almost certainly because of the expense. She remained in Cumnock but serviced Neville's Court by sending down bannocks, produce from the garden, and receiving back laundry.[186] Far from Scotland fading in Hardie's desires, on the contrary, Lochnorris became a potent symbol of retreat. A year earlier, as Parliament had dragged on into the summer, he wrote to Lowe, 'I can think of little else save Saturday and home.'[187]

In later years Hardie referred to Cumnock as his 'proper home' and to Neville's Court as somewhere where 'there is not much time spent . . . unless you count sleeping'.[188] Assuredly, this did not reflect the great attachment he came to have for Neville's Court or the many uses he put it to, but it reflected his need for Lochnorris. Home may not have been the saccharine temple biographers like Fyfe have made it, with phrases like 'happy in his home – devoted and proud of wife and bairns',[189] but Morgan's assurances that his visits there were increasingly infrequent from 1892[190] or that he 'found a calm release' at Neville's Court 'that he seldom found at home', do not take account of the fact that he was more at home from 1894 to 1900 than in many an earlier year, and that Cumnock continued to be where he found peace, especially after 1900. Everyone who visited the Hardie home commented on his love of it. James Maxton[191] found 'a man who was a natural homelover' and Hardie confirms this over and over, as he did that summer of 1901 when he finally got to Lochnorris:[192]

> . . . what a blessed thing is the holy calm of this home retreat. Not a sound to be heard save the slow tick of the old grandfather clock on the stair and the soothing murmur of the Lugar water at the foot of the garden. London is a place which I remember with a haunting horror, as if I had been confined there . . . in a former existence, the weary feet on the pavement . . . the jungle of cabhorse heels, the babble of St Stephen's. Were they real? God knows. Enough for the moment that they are not here. Here there are warm hearts and – peace. Where these are, heaven is.

Hardie wanted that 'heaven' in Ayrshire to remain – and Lillie in it – for his regular regeneration.

But it was not merely the house. He loved the land as well. In the country, 'Life begins to reassert itself . . . moonbeams can be seen and silence felt is a luxury . . . Then . . . to drive the good steel spade . . .

into the brown earth is to get in touch with nature and reality.'[193] He wrote elsewhere of the 'exquisite green of the beech, the birch and the elm', he sang the praise of the 'stately kingfisher [and] . . . the valiant otter'.[194] Contact with nature was important to Hardie, even though it became ever more fleeting. A picture of Hardie and Lillie that summer taken in the rustic cave half-way down their back hill that overlooked the Lugar shows him to the faithful as he wanted to be seen: a rural soul in straw hat and boots with collie dog at his feet. Lillie, by contrast, is in the formal black dress of full mourning for Hardie's mother (a custom Hardie never adopted), with a black apron and even black knitting resting on her lap. What strikes us at once is that if Hardie was said to look older than his age, Lillie looked even older. This grave and white-haired matron is only forty-two. Morgan is probably right to speak of 'little joy' for Hardie in the marriage; or for Lillie either.[195] Hardie had little joy in any of his relationships, except, briefly, those with young girls, and those with children, including his own; although days with the latter were drawing to a close, as they became adults and showed the wounds of neglect.

Hardie compensated by finding joy and sympathy elsewhere, as he moved about the world at large garnering what Morgan calls his 'towering national . . . reputation'.[196] For there was another division in his life, between those who knew him well and with whom relations were always difficult, and those who knew him little. This contradiction was observed by David Lowe, who called Hardie 'a difficult man . . . trusting few, but friendly to the mass'.[197] Here was the key; Hardie invested the 'mass' with his sympathy, elevating it by a collective love he was rarely to feel for any individual among it. The mass in turn sent back their collective feeling.

The 'desire to make socialism understood is growing into a passion', Hardie said.[198] This passion went out to his audiences. No tramping in driving rain or travelling in roaring wind was too much to keep in touch with them. Although there were many women who were prepared to give their time and attention, and he formed some close relationships, few ever aroused the passion that his 'life's work' continued to offer.

It was not mere visionary messianism, nor was it love of the crowd's flattering attention (which MacDonald and Glasier so often assumed), but emotional identification with those he sought to reach. He was constantly drawn to the masses – literally, to their presence in large numbers. Crowds sometimes numbered up to 300,000 at political meetings from the 1880s onwards,[199] and regularly 5,000. To Hardie, they were aphrodisiacs and he sought them again and again. At some meetings speeches had to be given more than once, as speakers visited the platforms in turn. The speaking could go on from 3 p.m. to 8 p.m. To many politicians this would be a hard grind, but not to Hardie. It is clear such hours were his reward, and he describes the communication in terms that others would use for the act of love: 'I absorb and am absorbed by my audience . . . we seem to melt and to fuse into one, and I am not speaking to them, but through them, and my thoughts are not my thoughts but their thoughts.'[200]

This transcendental relationship with a mass he did not know but was drawn to and believed he had a mission to serve was in striking contrast to the relationships with individuals he did know and was unable to feel for as he might have wished, where relations were often fraught and difficult. His friends treated his addiction exactly as if it were a sin of the flesh. Glasier, for example, called such a craving for audiences 'a great weakness'. But he adds, 'He is forgiven, he is so great an agitator.'[201]

Hardie found it hard to relax. His now usual September holiday with Lillie in 1902 to the west highlands was deserted midway to attend a political meeting at Ballachulish, then in the middle of a quarrymen's strike.[202] Yet he needed the time off, for his health was under real strain. When he met Glasier again in October Glasier noted that he was walking as if in pain.[203] By November doctors advised more rest, but this time he decided to go to the continent on his own, fortified with his morphia.

His journey was not restful. First there was a duel which a French socialist deputy insisted he witness (but which luckily came to nought).[204] Then there was an invitation to the opera, for which he borrowed evening dress from a waiter, assuming it to be needed, only to find when he arrived that he was the only one wearing it.[205] At his next stop, Belgium, the farce was even more intense. For during his visit an attempt was made on the life of the king by an anarchist, and Hardie was at once arrested as he tried to contact local socialist deputies, no doubt themselves under government surveillance. When he was back in Parliament he asked for an apology from the Belgians through the Foreign Office, but its arrogant minister, Lord Cranborne, tried to blame Hardie for not letting the Belgian police know he was an MP. Hardie said he had told them but had not been believed.[206]

Despite doctors' warnings, Hardie continued his maniacal pace, 'toiling like a galley-slave on the propaganda platform', according to Stewart,[207] who, like every other biographer, cannot resist giving a real-life example of how many engagements in widely scattered venues he could cram into a small space of time – as it happens, a single weekend in March 1903: to Manchester, then Bolton, then Blackburn, with huge meetings in London on both the Friday and Monday nights, plus a full day at the House of Commons. The point about all these 'examples', which sound exceptional, is that they were not. This was his 'life's work'. At every stop there were the masses he craved. When asked why he kept on, he replied simply, 'I love doing it.'[208]

In May 1903 Joseph Chamberlain exploded his bombshell on the country by coming out for a policy of colonial preference in trade, and abandoning the Liberals' long-standing support for free trade. The House and the country were torn apart by the ensuing argument. Hardie did not take much part. His instinct favoured free trade in a perfect world, but his view was that it did not make much difference which kind of trade you had in a capitalist world. For either way, the poor suffered. His speeches, therefore, in the Commons told of 'still thousands of hungry people [who] . . . walk the streets of London without a copper in their pocket, with little clothing and with no place of shelter wherein to lay their heads'.[209] He began skipping Parliament altogether or leaving early and joining the Salvation Army in its nightly rounds, feeding London's growing numbers of homeless. Hardie greatly admired General Booth (despite quarrels over socialism, which Booth later denounced). He believed that Booth made 'Christianity a reality. Whilst others have been praying to God to do something, Booth has been doing it.'[210] Hardie once visited a Booth home for abandoned babies, but after a moment looking down on the cots, his own tears overwhelmed him and he had to leave the room.[211]

Hardie's health continued to decline. After a holiday with Lillie in September, this time in Ireland, he returned none the better for it. Glasier's view was that the bad feelings in the Hardie home, lingering after Jamie's gambling, 'had everything to do with this . . . misery'.[212] He and Hardie met in London at the end of September and Hardie confided his troubles, both the gambling and Lillie's 'strange behaviour to him'. It upset him greatly, for 'he feels . . . Mrs Hardie's ways keenly', Glasier confided to his sister.[213] In reality, Lillie trouble and money trouble were one, for Hardie asked Glasier if money might be raised by public subscription for his medical bills; and, if it was, that 'some little token also be given to Mrs Hardie'. Hardie confessed that after paying off Jamie's debts, 'There's not a sovereign between me and destitution.'[214] Yet he still insisted on going with Glasier to Regent Street to buy Lillie a keepsake (while Glasier bought one for Katharine) in hopes of placating Lillie's feelings.[215] Lillie was assumed to be fond of jewellery and as the years went on, the attention she got came parcelled up in innumerable brooches and beads. Unfortunately Lillie was no better than Hardie at expressing her feelings, so they remained a mystery which the keepsakes symbolized.

Yet Hardie was generally sensitive to women's predicaments and appreciated their inner lives. He spent a whole editorial praising a Mrs Edwards of Liverpool, wife of an obscure Liverpool comrade, for her 'great soul . . . noble enough to forgive . . . and search out the kernel of goodness . . . hidden by the hard covering of one's defects'.[216] In the previous July he had been at a meeting for French delegates when he noticed a 'yank . . . the handsomest girl I have ever seen . . . displaying a very full bust'.[217] She was also noticed by Dr Stanton Coit, Secretary of the South Place Ethical Society and the ILP candidate in Wakefield. His face, Hardie wrote to Glasier confidentially, 'was literally ablaze with passion' as he made for the girl. Hardie also saw that Mrs Coit had noticed and 'was miserable and wandered about disconsolate looking what she felt. Then she disappeared . . . whether gone home or not I cannot say.' Hardie would never have subjected Lillie to such a public humiliation. Even Glasier had to admit, 'he is very loyal to her, and, I believe very attached to her'.[218]

In October Hardie collapsed with renewed pains.[219] Lillie hurried down to London and found him once more dosed with morphia. Over-work, everyone said; Lillie, Glasier probably thought; but a specialist diagnosed appendicitis. In those days this was an exotic illness, and operations to 'cure' it had only just been introduced. They were considered a real risk to life, as the public was well aware, since the King had just had one himself, with much fanfare. A public subscription was launched to pay for Hardie to have the same costly operation. Glasier wrote privately, 'It will be a failure . . . he has too many enemies'.[220] But he forgot that to many people, Hardie was already a 'national possession', as Stewart later wrote.[221] Hardie thought that Lillie too did not appear to know 'what a terribly important body her man is in other folk's opinion'.[222]

Glasier should have been worrying about whether the expensive diagnosis was even correct. Hardie was sceptical about his pain, which 'I doubt . . . is due to the inflamed appendix . . . time will tell'.[223] He believed his illness was fated, recalling for readers of the *Leader*[224] that ten years earlier (during the Annie Hines period) a fortune teller predicted illness ten years hence. Perhaps he thought it was deserved.

He got through the operation, and received an avalanche of goodwill messages, including some from those he had made his special targets, King Edward VII, and Major Banes, his West Ham opponent. John Burns urged 'speedy recovery . . . the forcible expropriation of your pipe . . . and immunity from "Marxian" for three months'.[225] ('Marxian' was the name under which Hardie sometimes wrote in the *Leader*.) Lillie kept everyone informed by telegram of his condition and stayed close by, probably at Neville's Court, until he was ready to leave the hospital. 'She has proved a wife indeed all through this business . . . it is the hour of trial which reveals qualities', Hardie wrote to Glasier,[226] aware that she suffered as much as he did when he was attacked, whether by the Liberal press or bacteria.

Lillie was surprised – pleasantly, we assume – that the public appeal was oversubscribed and brought enough money to pay something towards her own expenses, and to enable Hardie to convalesce in Falmouth. There is a photograph of Lillie on Falmouth beach, showing her under the visor of a jaunty sailor hat.[227] It is one of the few photographs ever taken of Lillie where she is even near to smiling.

The Hardies were back at Lochnorris for the New Year, since Hardie never missed spending this particularly Scots festival in Scotland. Christmas he always considered inferior, writing on 29 December to Maggie Symons that it was only the 'petit bourgeoisie' locally who paid attention to Christmas, what Hardie termed the 'apeing set'.[228] Everyone else celebrated Hogmanay. He did not rush back to the new session of Parliament either but spent most of the early winter in Cumnock, idling in bookshops, walking out towards Glenbuck with his dog, and visiting old friends like John Glasse in Edinburgh and William Haddow in Glasgow. Nan helped him in Cumnock. Maggie kept up the office in London and sent him what he needed to see.

It was more than an operation Hardie had to recover from. He had also been locked in a bitter battle over the *Labour Leader*, the paper whose masthead proclaimed it to be the ILP paper, but which he ran as his own. It was his line of communication with the masses whose emotional support was so necessary to him. He used it too to answer the jabs from *Justice* and the *Clarion* and to continue assaulting the Liberals.

Glasier and MacDonald tried to stay out of Hardie's quarrels. Glasier particularly kept up good relations with Blatchford, though he had to concede that of the two, 'Hardie . . . is the greater man'.[229] But not the greater journalist. Glasier thought Hardie an indifferent editor,[230] and so did many other ILP members. The *Leader's* management was 'pottering' and its ideas old-fashioned; something new was needed to keep pace with the racier *Clarion*.

When Hardie's friend and colleague, David Lowe, left the paper in 1903, critics made their move. Their plan − backed by Glasier − was to buy the paper from Hardie and take over the editorship, but offer Hardie a weekly column. With all the other claims on his life, and his illness, they thought he would welcome the chance to be free of the drudgery of filling every column inch himself. But they were wrong. He was stunned by the criticism, and he (and his brother) haggled protractedly over the financial compensation − as he always tussled over money. They asked for £1,500 with £250 at once, well above what the proposers had in mind. Eventually a settlement was reached where Hardie was bought out for £250 at once with £500 later (and his debts cleared into the bargain) − not a bad deal. Yet he wrote to Glasier that nothing in his life had ever caused him so much 'heart-breaking resentment' as the way the *Labour Leader* was taken away from him and 'nothing that I can recall has ever depressed me so much'. He stressed all the hours of 'unpaid drudging on the paper' he had put in over ten years.[231]

Glasier was tactful enough to thank him warmly, while taking over editorship himself at a welcome salary of £2 a week, just enough to keep his growing family, since he and Katharine now had another child, Malcolm. In public Hardie gave no hint of this bitter battle and his own anguish. He said farewell to *Leader* readers on grounds of ill-health alone.

Not only was endless convalescence the vogue for those who hired the 'best' doctors (because such patients had the time and money to take the advice) but there was still a primitive fear about appendicitis as a special killer – even after the offending organ had been removed. Rather than return to Parliament for the new session in February, Hardie chose to go to Bordighera, on the Italian Riviera near the French border. A month later Ramsay MacDonald, who had himself been ill and had also been prescribed a long rest, chose (or was sent by mutual colleagues) to take it with Hardie. By the time MacDonald arrived at the Villa Viale, Hardie was feeling fine and we get the impression he only 'rested' intermittently, otherwise enjoying himself seeking out local artists and artisans, reading and writing, and taking a lively interest in the political life around him, as was his way when abroad. Photographs show him swimming by the sea with young men and young boys, presumably a school and its teachers. He kept up a running correspondence with Maggie at the office, ordering books that he wanted to read:[232] Caroline Martyn's *Life of the City Beautiful* for the spirit; and for other cultures, *Abdullah, or the Poor Farm Hand, My Life among the Indians* and Jack London's *Hunting of the Stag*. Jack London, the American socialist writer, was a Hardie family favourite.

Hardie was not socially ambitious but his international life had made him by now into a very cosmopolitan figure. He knew his way around. He particularly knew his way around the world's labour movements, and his acceptance there was something Ramsay MacDonald coveted. Despite the fact that with his marriage to Lord Kelvin's niece, he had 'vaulted in to the middle class',[233] MacDonald was, as was later remarked, 'the outsider who longed to be inside'.[234] He saw himself outside the labour movement as well as outside the world of the prominent. His social insecurity was deeply ingrained, and contrasted with Hardie's conviction of his own social worth. Hardie reported that the two soon quarrelled about what they would do. MacDonald, Hardie said, 'wanted to see everything not so much . . . from an interest as to be able afterwards to talk at dinner tables about what he had seen'.[235]

Long before he had ever entered Parliament, Hardie, spurred by the observations of such men as Cunninghame Graham, had been wary of the way the parliamentary life sets a trap for the people's representatives. Over and over they become weakened by social flattery or financial inducement, or, most deadly of all, office. On 7 March 1903 Hardie had written an open letter to Lloyd George about Liberals

> inveigling the leaders of the people into their net and always with the same result. The earnest reformer, once he has tasted the cloying sweets of office, loses the taste for strenuousness; finds a thousand good reasons why he should cling to office, even after he knows he has been fooled and the people betrayed for whom he at one time fought.[236]

Long before MacDonald went the same route, and while they were still comrades, if not exactly the closest of friends, Hardie had instinctively caught this weakness in him.

But what of Hardie's own weaknesses? One was certainly a love of lingering in foreign places. On this occasion he was only brought back by another of Lillie's illnesses. Reluctantly, he wrote to Maggie sometime in May, 'Mrs Hardie is out of sorts and at this distance that does not make for comfort.'[237] Besides, he himself was running a fever of 104°. He had been recuperating for six months and yet still illness plagued him. He had to face it, he was never again going to enjoy good health. Nor was he going to let a failing body keep him any longer from the great work that had to be done.

8

THE WOMAN QUESTION

When he had first moved in to Neville's Court, Hardie wrote, 'My mansion is perfect'.[1] By 1904 it was even better, as if Robert Williams 'had drawn the plans to my orders'. Hardie was eating leeks and arranging gowans in jugs, both brought from Cumnock and growing in the tiny courtyard garden. Ox-eye daisies were Hardie's favourite flowers, common and beautiful, the flower he wanted as the world-wide socialist emblem. His one room was decorated with busts of Whitman, Emerson and Burns, and with photographs of two dead ILP women, Florence Grove and Caroline Martyn, as well as Karl Marx. He did his own cooking, cleaning and bootblacking. He did not stand on domestic patriarchy in Cumnock either, and once laughed at the idea of what his 'respectable' constituents would say if they 'knew that their junior MP had been washing dishes, lighting fires, carrying up coals and playing the part of the scullery maid'.[2] In ILP circles, however, such choring was not unusual. Even the middle class Margaret MacDonald had chided Ramsay MacDonald for imagining she had never darned socks,[3] and their informal home life suggests he too made attempts to be as much a 'new man' as other socialists. Isabella Ford, daughter of a Quaker businessman, who organized Leeds tailoresses in the 1890s, said one of the reasons she joined the ILP was because on her first visit to one of their labour clubs (in the Colne Valley) she saw that men had 'poured out the tea, cut the bread and butter, and washed everything up without any feminine help'.[4]

Hardie's own 'club' was important to him. In Neville's Court he could entertain his friends from Scotland, constituents from Wales, and comrades from all over the world: Russian exiles, Indian political leaders, and travellers from Australia. But not the press. 'Never was any . . . newspaper gossip monger able to break into this sanctuary', said Stewart. Sometimes even friends found the door shut: 'Companionship is good, but solitude is best.'[5] In an increasingly pressured life, Hardie liked time to be alone.

Only Maggie Symons was a regular. Hardie continued to give her small money gifts with notes; 'what I should have done without you I cannot imagine'.[6] He also offered to introduce her to editors at the *Daily News* and the *Echo*, to further her writing career, for Hardie gradually began to realize that many women wanted economic independence. His basic thesis was very much along the lines argued by Auguste Bebel in *Women and Socialism* in 1879. As he became more conscious of these arguments, the causes of the unemployed and the poor gained a serious rival, the cause of women. Since the ILP and the Labour Party in Parliament were both in favour of women's voting equality, it should have posed no problem as regards Hardie's relationships with his own colleagues. But more than any other issue, it drove a wedge between him and almost all of them.

By contrast to the LRC, which had practically no women, the ILP's ruling committee was building up a formidable collection on its NAC: Katharine Glasier, Margaret MacDonald and Margaret Bondfield. While he and MacDonald were away in Italy they missed the ILP annual conference at Cardiff, where Mrs Pankhurst was successful for the first time. After Richard's death Emmeline Pankhurst had had to sell her house and possessions to pay his debts. She was elected to the Manchester School Board in 1900 and took a job as a minor civil servant to augment her income.

Unlike the working-class Hardie children, the four middle-class Pankhursts were continuing their education. Sylvia was at the Manchester School of Art, painting and drawing, fields in which she had shown talent from childhood. At Manchester she found a temporary 'father'-cum-mentor in the socialist artist, Walter Crane, one of her teachers.[7] He helped her to keep up her commitment not just to art but to her father's causes; and at the college she had campaigned vigorously against the monarchy. She and her mother and siblings had also opposed the Boer War and experienced considerable local hostility. Harry was attacked at his school and Emmeline resigned from the local Fabians because of their support for the war.

Outwardly united, internally the family dynamics were anything but harmonious. Emmeline's preference for her eldest daughter, and 'first darling', became obsessive after Richard's death.[8] Christabel's career became the focus for her ambition. Emmeline persuaded Christabel to follow in her father's footsteps and read law. She had a good memory and began to make progress. She was beautiful, tall and fashionable, while Sylvia was plainer and shorter, completely uninterested in clothes or beauty, her hair always flying away from its clasp.

In Manchester she and her mother and sisters found employment decorating a meeting hall which was to be dedicated to Richard Pankhurst, and was being built with money donated by radical Liberal and trade union supporters in the area. The hall would be used as a club and meeting house. In 1903, as it was nearing completion, Emmeline and her daughters discovered that women were to be barred from ever using it, in the normal tradition of labour clubs. It was this discovery – and learning that they could not change the rules – that prompted Emmeline to call an immediate meeting in her own small house in Nelson Street. Women who wanted to work seriously for women's suffrage were invited, even though most already belonged to one of several existing organizations, including the National Union of Women's Suffrage Societies (NUWSS) run by Millicent Fawcett. Emmeline was suddenly impatient with their slow progress. She wanted her own organization. So she formed the Women's Social and Political Union (WSPU). Suddenly Christabel's law course had a purpose, and so did Christabel.

In 1904 Sylvia won a scholarship to the Royal College of Art in London and arrived to take it up with £50 a year to live on. She found a small flat at 45 Park Walk, Chelsea, and spent her time with her brother, Harry, newly transferred to a school in Hampstead. She had had no involvement with men, other than a few casual encounters, to which she had reacted vigorously. In Venice an old count, a friend of the woman with whom she had stayed, had tried to seduce her.[9] The incident upset her. On the train home from Venice to London a ticket inspector had tried to kiss her and at the next stop she reported him indignantly to Thomas Cook. One of her biographers remarks archly that at twenty-two she arrived in London a psychological as well as a physical virgin.[10] A more sympathetic view might be that she was a determined young woman who did not find sexual harassment flattering.

One of her first acts, accompanied by Harry, was to call on her parents' old friend, Keir Hardie. He was now forty-eight and they had not met, except possibly in passing, since she was a young girl. Since then she had lost her most important champion in life, her father; and Hardie had lost his, his mother. In time each seemed to recognize what was missing in the other but in these early days it was very much a guardian with his two wards: 'Keir gathered us both under his . . . wing', Sylvia wrote.[11] After a while, Harry stopped coming and Sylvia continued to visit on her own.

Hardie felt comfortable with a young woman for whom he had no responsibility, and with whom he could be playfully paternal. She found Neville's Court a haven, and in her reminiscences spends a long time describing it. Having spent a life where neither she nor any of her family would have had to perform domestic chores, she was intrigued with Hardie's skill at lighting the fire and preparing tea and scones.[12] After they got used to each other, Hardie would work, answering letters or writing articles, pointedly giving her a book to read. 'As a rule he spoke little,' she recalled.[13] Nor did he gossip. 'In intimate conversation he seldom said harsh things of people . . . even of those by whom he had been most bitterly attacked.' He got on with his work surrounded by endless piles of paper. Hardie was not tidy. Lowe recalled, 'I have seen him snowed up with letters, manuscripts, books, journals, magazines, photos . . . tables, chairs and floor covered . . . in hopeless confusion.'[14]

During the first autumn in which Sylvia was in London, Hardie was also introducing his daughter, Nan, to the city. She came to stay for several weeks. Her brief was to help her father, as Maggie Symons was having some time off, presumably trying to write. Hardie wrote to Maggie to say that Nan was opening the letters and filing the press cuttings (Hardie always kept everything said about him).[15] Hardie and Nan did not appear to have met Sylvia, but on several occasions they tried to contact Maggie, asking her to join them for evenings out.[16] She had gone to ground. Soon Hardie began to wonder if something was wrong. If there was, he would be diffident about talking it over with her. He had already confessed to her his own 'inherent dislike, almost . . . a constitutional weakness, for saying what I feel'.[17]

The reticent Hardie, who had been used to intimacy with an equally reticent Lillie, was entertained by the unreticent Sylvia. The relationship was congenial from the start. It lightened his soul. In December, back in Cumnock for the holiday season, Hardie was able to declare to Maggie that 1904 was the 'healthiest and happiest Christmas for years at Lochnorris'.[18]

*   *   *

When Hardie's protracted convalescence finally ended and he returned to the House, a parliamentary correspondent wrote that 'we are sorry to hear he is not as well as he looks'.[19] Perhaps that was because he had stopped on the way back to attend the 1904 Congress of the International, held that year in Amsterdam, where he led the British delegation. The Russo-Japanese war had just broken out and socialists were once more fearful of mass conflict on a world scale. Delegates from both Russia and Japan attended.[20] Dramatically, as soon as they saw each other on the platform, they 'rushed into each others' arms', according to Glasier, embracing before thousands. To Hardie, this spectacle was 'worth having lived to see'.[21] At the same congress the Indians sent a delegate for the first time to alert world socialism to the evils of the Raj.[22] These events reinforced Hardie's growing conviction that the collective action of the working class worldwide would be strong enough to stop wars and ensure colonial emancipation. After all, no country could wage war if its working class refused to take up arms or make armaments – or bow to the yoke of imperialism. Hardie was also cheered by the racial harmony, calling the embraces of 'white and . . . yellow race . . . worth all our . . . resolutions put together'.[23]

There were plenty of those. Socialists from countries at war might have been able to agree, but not those making up the British delegation of representatives from the LRC, ILP, SDF, and Fabians. There was a proposal to remove credentials from the LRC because it still had not committed itself formally to the class war. The SDF was behind the move, just as in 1900 Hyndman had tried to stop the International admitting Connolly's Irish Socialist Republican Party.[24] Again, as with the Millerand controversy, the ingenuity of Kautsky was required to unpick the knot; he took the problem away to report back. Meanwhile, the British rank and file expressed their views on factionalism by electing both Hardie and Hyndman as their two representatives on the new International Bureau, a permanent body set up to meet between Congresses.

The Congress moved on to the running argument over Bernstein's recent criticism – revision – of Marx's theory of revolution, an argument which had already split French and German socialists. Hardie contributed to this discussion (siding with Bernstein) as well as to the continuing Millerand controversy (siding with Jaurès). Generally, Hardie disliked political disputation in the same way he disliked religious disputation, which he once called 'talking theology at midnight with the silent stars overhead'.[25] Ideology made few converts. After this International, however, he relaxed his rules because of the challenge to the LRC by the 'heresy hunters'.[26]

When he returned he wrote three long essays in the *Labour Leader*, declaring in the first that the Labour Party, working within the LRC,

is 'as true an application of Marxian teaching as the socialism of the
SDF is an exposition thereof'.[27] But he believed times had changed
since Marx had written. Society was no longer in terrible turmoil.
Hardie the pacifist believed socialism was 'revolutionary' but 'that
it can only be won by violent outbreak is in no sense true'.[28]
Hardie the parliamentarian, who had not yet experienced legislative
disappointment, imagined revolution could translate into 'one reform
after another' being won in Parliament.[29] Hardie the democrat, who
had not yet felt the full blast of capitalist propaganda against socialism,
declared that 'no revolution can succeed which has not public opinion
behind it'.[30]

All this being so, he wrote 'An Indictment of the Class War',
and in it coined the phrase that 'socialism declares war upon a
system, not upon a class', an argument Cunninghame Graham had
used when explaining his own socialism.[31] Hardie wanted people to
be conscious of socialism, not of social class. On the face of it, the
distinction seemed rather semantic, particularly as he goes on to say
that 'it is not disputed' that workers and employers have differing
interests that 'lead to an inevitable conflict and antagonism'; and that
'class' and 'war' are 'terms which may be fittingly used in connection
with trade unionism'. They should not be used in connection with
socialism, however, because socialism's objective is the 'blending of
the classes into one human family' by removing the causes of dispute
between the classes. We see a split between Hardie the class-conscious
trade union activist and Hardie the preacher of a classless new world
order, reconciling these differences by ignoring the dialectical process.
All social transformation in his analysis is shrouded in mist. We become
like children waiting for Christmas, for 'the world may wake up some
morning to find that socialism has come'.[32] Alternatively, socialism
will come he said, quoting from the bible, '"like a thief in the
night", without observation, by constant uplifting of the mass of
people'.

Such glossing of elementary socialist argument stirred up incredible
controversy, and many socialists Hardie would not have wished to
alienate began writing to him or to the *Labour Leader*.[33] Some agreed
('"War" is a horrid word'); others merely pointed out that every
word Hardie wrote 'proves there is a class war!' Eventually Max
Beer, the new editor of *Vorwärts*, wrote a succinct and scholarly
summary of Marx's main arguments[34] in an attempt to reconcile
them with Hardie's. Where Hardie had said 'materialist theory makes
no allowance for ... development', Beer writes tactfully that 'the
struggle of a new social class is always a struggle for a higher stage
of evolution so that the interests of class coincide with the interests
of humanity'.

Beer's clever contribution almost managed to reconcile Marx with

MacDonald as well, for MacDonald, who had entered the Millerand debate on the side of pacts with radicals whenever labour parties wanted them,[35] had also stirred his pen on socialism. He had written a year earlier[36] and he wrote again a year later.[37] His contribution, as an erstwhile biology student and admirer of Darwin, was a home-made theory of socialism as a higher form of life emerging from liberalism, a lower form of life, by evolution, not conflict.[38]

His arguments were more fluently expressed than Hardie's but just as unable to engage with the central issues posed by Marx. Nor was it much of a trumpet in the land to read in MacDonald that socialism 'cannot create for itself a political party . . . it can only hope to become the spirit of a party which may or may not profess . . . socialist ideas . . . in practical legislation'. MacDonald's efforts brought a knee-jerk response from *Justice*[39] to condemn him for clinging to Liberalism, but Britain's Marxists failed to subject his 'may or may not' socialism to any real critical scrutiny.

The combined ILP and LRC aversion to ideology gave British Labour practical strength and helped it avoid what Tawney called the 'dogmatic petrification of the pre-1914 German Social democracy',[40] but it left it floundering intellectually. Anyone could define socialism as he or she pleased. Frances, Countess of Warwick, who also attended the Amsterdam congress, sent her own definition back to her friend, Lady Dorothy Neville,[41] 'the ONE religion that unites the human race all over the world in the Common Cause of Humanity' – to which she added, 'it is growing as mushrooms grow'. Although this was much nearer Glasier's than Hyndman's definition, it was to Hyndman that she looked for guidance.

Hyndman had returned to politics again in 1904 after his brief fling as a company director, arranging with great flair a series of meetings around the country in the wake of Joseph Chamberlain, then touring Britain to advocate trade protection. Everywhere Chamberlain went Hyndman went a few days later, to debunk him. At one such meeting he met Frances Warwick and they were soon having long discussions. A few months later they were in Paris, where he introduced her to his old friend, the radical deputy, Clemenceau, as well as to Jaurès. Hyndman reported that 'they were both quite swept off their legs by her beauty', adding artlessly, 'tho 42 . . . she looks 26'.[42] It was really Hyndman who was swept off his legs. Frances as well. She duly joined the SDF, where she was a great draw, and became a Blatchford favourite.

Later that year she attended an ILP meeting held at St Andrew's Hall in Glasgow, where Hardie, accompanied by Nan, was also a speaker, his first major speech after his long convalescence. According to Glasier, he turned up in an incredible costume of 'rough tweed knickers – very much out of taste',[43] failed to acknowledge the countess with the usual courtesies, and made a bellicose speech denouncing the hereditary principle. A reporter present thought it 'the finest speech he had ever delivered'[44] but Glasier thought it uncharacteristically rude. It was Hardie's old fear of being patronized – by Beatrice Webb in a tiara. He refused to meet Frances Warwick, though she wrote several times to ask to see him both before and after the meeting.[45] In one reply Hardie accused her of having come to the International in Amsterdam as a spy for the King (later her lover).[46] Hardie had some unacknowledged class feeling of his own.

The result of this flurry of discussion around class was inconclusive. While Britain's main Marxist party stood aloof from industrial issues, while ethical socialism failed to engage in continuing ideological debate, and while the trade unions remained uninterested in extra-parliamentary struggle, the necessary dialogue for the founding of genuine democratic socialism marked time in Britain. This stand-off was characterized by regular refusals by Labour and socialist leaders to contemplate co-operation, matched by continual liaising at local level between all groups, including close collaboration between socialists and Fabians in local government.[47] During this period and the years that followed, the single question that speakers on all platforms most often faced was, when were all socialists and trade unionists going to agree to have a single party? Year after year the ordinary activist – like eternal children of divorce – kept on about reconciliation.

Both the ILP and the LRC took no notice, and relied heavily on Hardie's continuing agitation, particularly on the issue of unemployment, a subject he still regarded as his own. Unemployment had become acute again after the Boer War, which had 'employed' over 200,000 in military activity. Now society had them on its hands, nearly 6 per cent of the workforce by 1904.[48] Hardship was widespread and could be seen everywhere. Many blamed Chamberlain's tariff reforms, which restricted trade outside the Empire, for restricting jobs at its heart. But Hardie saw it as capitalism's consequences and his objective was still to get the government to recognize a responsibility for dealing with it. He proposed that central and local government should jointly undertake responsibility for getting the unemployed work.

Unemployment programmes were an idea Hardie had been pushing for ten years. One of his first set of questions in the House in 1893 had been about West Ham's poorhouses and why the poor had to break stones in a yard to prove fitness instead of being set to work on unused land?[49] The question seemed even more reasonable ten years later when he raised it again.[50] Within a year he had come up with a string of further positive suggestions in an ILP pamphlet, *The Unemployment Problem and Some Suggestions for Solving It*, 1904, including local authorities building houses and roads. Ingenuously, he argued that old statues of 1601 and 1694, compelling overseers of the poor to provide work, were still operative. (Hardie harboured a genuine belief in an earlier golden age.)[51] He wanted work programmes to switch on automatically whenever employment levels fell. On 1 February 1904, during his supposed convalescence, he had placed before Parliament a plan for a Ministry of Labour to organize a whole range of useful public works not unlike the American New Deal thirty years later.

In 1905 he organized marches on unemployment, elaborating the public works that would be useful, such as afforestation and sewer improvements, that the workless could undertake while still enjoying all civil rights and full trade union rates of pay.[52] He set out a blueprint for legislation, including elected local authority committees to provide work-schemes. It never occurred to him that a Conservative government might steal the shadow but ditch the substance of his plan, or that he himself might show them how to do it.

His most favoured public works were still farm colonies and in this he was joined by George Lansbury, by then a borough councillor in London's East End for over a decade. Like Hardie, Lansbury had been married young, to his working-class schoolmate, Bessie. They had joined the Band of Hope and all their children attended Church of England Sunday Schools. Then he joined the SDF and abandoned religion. Unconventionally, daughters and wife were treated equally with sons and husband. Despite being burdened 'with a large family and small income', Bessie attended the same classes as Lansbury on Marx's and Engels's works.[53] The large Lansbury family were brought up to campaign independently on their own and to sell *Merrie England* in Victoria Park. They lived in a close-knit community where life and politics were integrated, for though Lansbury travelled the country speaking, his main political work was in nearby Poplar and Forest Gate, where he dedicated himself to poor law administration and the improvement of local schools and workhouses. He had already been personally surcharged for authorising a pathway through a muddy school playground. By 1904 he had given evidence to the Aged Poor Commission and in 1905 was appointed a member of the National Commission looking at the poor law. As with most such exercises, the Poor Law Commission drew fire by taking all the complaints, then recommending no change. But this time there was an outcome. Along with Sidney Webb, another member, Lansbury signed a landmark minority report proposing the abolition of the poor laws and their replacement by modern social legislation.[54]

Lansbury had been pushing farm colonies since the early 1890s as a way to ease unemployment in London's East End. The idea would have come to nothing had a millionaire whom Hardie had met in 1895 in Philadelphia, not arrived in London to finance them. Joseph Fels was a tiny, wiry humanitarian Jew who had cornered the US market in laundry soap, using a process based on naphtha. In 1900 he came to Britain, bought a mansion in Kent, and established a UK branch of his works. He and his wife had lost their only child and had turned to social action. He had been converted early by Henry George to the single land tax to end poverty. He did not believe in charity, since it made workers passive. He believed in empowering working-class leaders. Together he and Lansbury (with Hardie providing support in Parliament) proposed an imaginative but ideologically precarious project to 'cure' British unemployment – precarious because the demand came not from workers themselves or local government but from Fels, who wanted to try out his schemes in England, buying up land in the countryside and renting it at a peppercorn rent to local Boards of Guardians in cities, to enable their unemployed to become self-sufficient.[55] The tracts of land he bought were in East Anglia.[56] The borough he persuaded to co-operate was Poplar. On the land he built accommodation for the homeless poor; he furnished it, provided farming instruction, and even a piano for recreation.[57] 'He spent his money like water,' according to Lansbury,[58] in order to force government approval. This was finally attained for Poplar, with the ultimate aim to get government to take over the funding and spread the schemes to every local area.

The Fels projects eventually foundered for reasons Fels himself shrewdly diagnosed later: a new community has to have a common social or spiritual purpose to succeed (which is why the kibbutz movement in Palestine, the last such 'farm colony' venture he funded, finally did). Without this it becomes exploitation of the poor. Before this became apparent, the friendship between Hardie and Lansbury flourished, their separate SDF/ILP allegiances no hindrance. For a while it even looked as though they had pulled off a real coup, when the government began consulting on an Unemployed Workmen's Bill. But when the small print was read in April 1905, it showed that the government had seized on the connection with private money that Hardie and Lansbury had inadvertently fostered through their association with Fels, making 'partnership' with voluntary funds the key rather than state support, or municipal or co-operative funding of public works. This allowed the government to escape from any serious commitment to fund unemployment relief measures, and when the very smallest print was produced in July it was plain to all that charitable organizations and local public donations were to be the mainstay of relief work, with the government's contribution limited to help with organization. It was also clear that workmen on the schemes were going to be little short of slaves – with no rights and only token pay. Hardie turned on the punitive and bureaucratic Act, as did the SDF and other socialists. Even Burns disowned it. The ILP condemned the measures as half-baked and a mere drop in the ocean, and Hardie set out his views in *John Bull and His Unemployed*. 'I hope the new authorities will point blank refuse to administer them.'[59] He harangued the government clause by clause in the House, as the Bill was debated from June through to August. He organized angry protest marches (for which Fels paid). But Hardie was stuck. Although he refused to vote for the Bill, he could not oppose it either because of pressure from Labour members to support its meagre improvements, the very members whose support was required to turn the LRC into a Labour Party in the House.

The whole episode set back the chance of Labour in Parliament working out any coherent political or economic policy on the vast issue of work, if it did not destroy it completely. Right to Work Bills to amend the Act in later years, realigning it in a socialist direction, did not have the necessary Liberal backing to win, and every year they fell. Hardie had organized the agitation without the political campaign to carry it through, and without understanding the way his own much publicized proposals and campaigns of 'joint action' with a millionaire's private money had undermined any chance of a socialist solution. As was to happen often in the coming century, a Conservative Act, purporting to meet the need for 'reform', merely entrenched bad practice under new state apparatus.

But Hardie was not put off. In late 1905 a national Right to Work Committee was set up, with Frank Smith as secretary, and Hardie and Cunninghame Graham, Lansbury, and Harry Quelch as members. This made the LRC wary, for MacDonald and Glasier did not like Frank Smith, much less Lansbury and Harry Quelch, both SDF members. But the LRC finally came round to support Hardie's policy of forcing the state to take responsibility for unemployment. That any progress was being made at all on this important socialist issue, however adulterated, was due in large measure to the kind of agitation at which Hardie excelled. He correctly noted the real gain that had been made, that however poor the funding, something important and 'entirely new' had been conceded on unemployment in this Parliament, 'It was no longer said the matter should be left to private charity.'[60] The state had assumed a new responsibility.

At the LRC's yearly conferences, there were almost no reports back about this parliamentary activity, however. Discussion was taken up with its rules for itself. In 1903 it agreed a rule telling all members 'to abstain' from identifying with Liberals or Conservatives in elections, and they must 'resign' if they broke it.[61] It was broken at once in December 1903 when Richard Bell failed to support the young compositor nominated by the Trades Council for a by-election in Norwich. Bell sent a telegram to congratulate his Liberal opponent instead. The 1904 LRC Conference at Bradford was fully occupied with Bell's sin. By 1905, thanks to MacDonald's assiduous work with the TUC Parliamentary Committee and the Management Committee of the General Federation of Trade Unions, a concordat was presented, the key point of which was that no Labour person 'shall . . . be considered disloyal' for refusing to support a labour candidate who runs under Tory or Liberal banners.[62] On the other hand, if there is no LRC candidate, labour voters are free to vote for whomsoever they wish. It was not much of a rallying cry, but at least it secured agreement.

During this same Conference delegates heard about the Czar's massacre of Russian workers in front of the Winter Palace in St Petersburg. They raised nearly £1,000 to send to Russian exile organizations,[63] receiving warm thanks from Prince Kropotkin as well as from Vladimir Oulianoff, editor of *Vperiod* in Geneva, who was organizing exiled socialist opposition. He later called himself Lenin. His letter of thanks for the money pointed out that the money itself had not actually arrived.[64]

Behind the scenes MacDonald (still concerned with electoral pacts) continued talking to Liberals. When the inevitable news leaked out, and MacDonald was confronted by a comrade in Leeds demanding to know if the LRC was really in league with the Liberals,[65] he denied the allegation roundly. A few weeks later Hardie's old friend, John Lister, the ILP's first treasurer, wrote a poem about MacDonald's activity, enshrining a perennial rank and file complaint about Labour's leadership:

> Anything! Anything! just to get in
> Any tale! Any tale! so you may win
> All the false lying spirits unchain,
> Barter your soul, man, your voter to claim.[66]

Hardie let MacDonald alone in this area just as MacDonald let him alone in making unilateral proclamations of Labour policy. Each was doing what each did best. Whenever Labour has fared badly, it is because one or other activity – electoralism or popular agitation – takes over and rules the other out. As 1906 approached at least the two were in some sort of balance. In an arena increasingly circumscribed by 'parliamentary' politics, where the issue of socialism had been left as an optional extra, perhaps this was the most that could have been expected.

In Hardie's case, any political vacuum was fully filled, however, for from 1905 onwards he put himself at the disposal of the women's movement – that is to say, of the Pankhurst family. Sylvia's visits to Neville's Court had by now become a regular feature of his life. In Parliament he even asked a question about scholarships for women to the Royal College of Art. She was worried that hers would not be renewed for 1906.[67]

At the best of times Hardie consulted little with colleagues, or tried to get an agreed line. The suffrage issue was no different. He never discussed the choice that was to be made between a policy that asked for women's voting parity with men, aware that many working-class men were still excluded from voting, and a policy that held out for unviersal suffrage for both sexes, as full democracy required, but which was likely to take much longer. The decision was made no easier by the way anti-suffragists in the Tory and Liberal establishments hypocritically pretended to support the latter option as a way of opposing women's suffrage without seeming to do so. On the other hand, there were many, particularly socialists in the ILP and SDF, who believed universal suffrage was the only principled position to take.

The Pankhurst line was the more conservative, to go for a limited franchise rather than universal suffrage. It was the principle behind Richard Pankhurst's 1870 Bill,[68] adding 'woman' or 'women' to the election laws whenever the words 'man' or 'men' appeared. This approach was absorbed into the radical establishment in 1893 when it was adopted by the Liberal Women's Federation, with Catharine Gladstone presiding.[69] It was part of wider nineteenth-century pressure to give middle-class women greater responsibility for effecting social improvements in an industrializing society that was producing too many unwanted ill-effects. This 'domestic feminism', as one of Lansbury's biographers called it,[70] presupposed qualified suffrage. The Liberal Party never adopted it, and almost all Conservatives openly opposed women's suffrage on principle. John Stuart Mill's argument that a middle-class woman can have a profession like a man was opposed by both tradition and the newer sciences. Freud, for example, wrote to his wife before they married, 'Am I to think of my delicate sweet girl as a competitor?', later adding that 'housekeeping and the care of children rule out [any] education . . . any profession' for the married woman.[71] It was a standard view in all social classes.

In backing the limited Bill, Hardie also came into conflict not only with this traditional view but with much Labour and socialist opinion that interpreted it as ignoring the rights of poorer women and working-class men. To have a parliamentary leader who appeared more attentive to middle-class women's rights than working-class suffrage was potentially destructive of relations. No one had any doubt why Hardie had taken this side: the hold that Emmeline Pankhurst had on him.

The Pankhursts were not popular with Hardie's political colleagues and friends in the socialist and labour movements. Bruce Glasier particularly disliked Emmeline and Christabel and believed Hardie was being flattered by them, so that they could use him and his connections. Glasier's attitude to the Pankhursts at this period, betraying a lingering sexism, was typical of Labour's complex political reaction to the suffrage issue. Hardie took the woman question much more seriously. He never trivialized women's campaigns, while Glasier, when visited by Emmeline and Christabel in 1904 to press for action from the ILP, recorded,[72] 'A weary ordeal of chatter about women's suffrage from 10 p.m. to 1.30 . . . belabouring me as chairman . . . for neglect of the question. At last get roused and speak . . . with . . . scorn of their miserable individualist sexism.' It was true that the WSPU had never cared for collectivism, apart from that of enlightened women. It was Glasier's view, and that of many others, particularly in the Labour Party and the ILP, that mother and daughter were not 'seeking democratic freedom but self-importance'.[73]

Nevertheless, Glasier's comments reveal a pettiness of spirit and some little personal prejudice, 'Christabel paints her eyebrows grossly and looks selfish, lazy and wilful.' Glasier, like many socialists, disliked high social fashion. Katharine Glasier – his ideal of woman – had made a distinct point of renouncing modish dress. She was known for her scrubbed appearance and increasingly eccentric and old-fashioned costumes. One visitor to the Glasier's 'little cottage in the Peak Hills' (Katharine's description of where the Glasiers were now living in Chapel-en-le-Frith) found her wearing an amazing 'home-made one piece gown'.[74] Never as eccentric as Katharine Glasier, Margaret MacDonald was also immune to high fashion and an equally serious supporter of women's suffrage as part of a commitment to equality generally.[75] That the exquisitely high-fashion Christabel, who had no obvious commitment to any other form of equality, should be posing as women's one and only champion annoyed Labour women exceedingly.

Ramsay MacDonald's commitment to women's suffrage was different again. It was based on the 'family as the foundation of the State'.[76] Women have a place in the world because they have a place in the family. It was because 'women's experience is different . . . [that] women should be enfranchised'. As his biographer, David Marquand, comments, this was a view essentially no different from that 'of many die-hard opponents of women's suffrage'.[77] It was a late-Victorian extension of women's natural domain.[78] MacDonald also disliked the WSPU, and later called them 'pettifogging middle-class damsels' hiding hammers in their muffs.[79] Margaret MacDonald's commitment was deeper, possibly because she did daily battle to make her own independent contribution despite domestic burdens in 3 Lincoln's Inn Fields. There, a growing family, now four in number, tested her resolve. In addition to their own work, the MacDonalds also held 'at home' evenings every three weeks. According to Sylvia,

Hardie never attended these or any of the other 'banquets' of the parliamentary season,[80] but Sylvia went to the MacDonalds' on several occasions. Later, describing how difficult it was to combine home and work, she wrote of seeing Margaret MacDonald 'with her blouse put on back to front, several of its buttons undone',[81] an anecdote suspiciously like the one told by Ramsay MacDonald in his own *Memoir* of Margaret,[82] from which Sylvia probably got it. A more reliable witness to the conflict of duties, MacDonald's daughter, Ishbel, speaks more graphically of her parents' committee meetings in the family flat, while children were 'crawling around under their feet'; 'We'd be crying in the corner. And my mother just went on with the business.'[83]

The most modern of the protagonists for women's suffrage was George Lansbury, who had been campaigning on women's issues since the end of the 1880s, when he had acted as Jane Cobden's agent to test the right of women to be elected to the new LCC. In 1890 he wrote to her that it was vital to 'train daughters to look on life as something besides being married'.[84] Later, he wrote 'how hard the working woman's life was'. As for the working-class girl:

> I saw ... that if the boy went out to work he could have his evenings to himself for play or study, but the girls, however hard their work, must always work in the house and wait on the men and boys. This ... seemed ... grossly unfair.[85]

Sitting between MacDonald's 'family feminism' and Lansbury's socialist feminism, were the views of large numbers of working-class men, including trade unionists sympathetic to Labour politics, who opposed gender equality as a mark of masculinity. John Burns, who lived in London with a quiet wife and an only child, a timid boy, was typical of this view. He bragged that his wife always sent suffragettes packing whenever they had the gall to call at his house.[86] Even within the ILP, committed union activists, including women like Margaret Bondfield, the shop workers' organizer, could be impatient on the issue. Bondfield told one rally that 'what women required was not votes, but industrial organization'.[87] Sylvia Pankhurst claims Bondfield went even further in debating with the ILP member, Isabella Ford, a 'plain, middle-aged woman with a red face', who argued for women's suffrage, only to be told by Bondfield that the suffrage movement was merely 'the hobby of disappointed old maids whom no one had wanted to marry',[88] a very common response, but usually coming from men. There is no doubt that through the ranks of labour, even within the ILP, hidden sexism and opposition to equality ran as rampantly as it did through the Carlton Club or Mr Asquith's bedroom.

Hardie was not in this mould but neither was he advanced in his views. He prized the 'old fashioned woman' who was 'willing to bear a large family' of eight or ten (his mother had had nine) and get through her work in 'bright, clean, bien, couthie cottage homes . . . patching, darning, knitting' and crooning 'some old ballad'.[89] He believed 'Capitalism has much to answer for' in her replacement by the 'modern woman' who had 'freedom of factory or shop or office' and 'considers herself disgraced if her family exceeds two or three'. Hardie never appreciated the full dimension of the 'woman question' in the way Lansbury did (who tried to practise equality within his own home) but he nevertheless had a firm political commitment to suffrage equality for women.

Despite his rumoured status as the Pankhursts' poodle, he was not a late convert to a pretty face, though Morgan argues that sexual interest 'added fire' to his advocacy.[90] He defended his choice of the limited franchise because it posed suffrage equality directly – on the single issue of gender. He also believed it had more agitational potential because it was more immediately achievable than universal suffrage. It would draw more women into the cause and this in turn would put more pressure on Parliament to act. When it did, universal suffrage would come sooner rather than later. All the same he was sensitive to the argument that it was mostly middle-class women who were doing the work and likely to benefit. In his preface to a collection of essays on the suffrage issue during this period (to which Christabel also contributed)[91] he made much of its being a campaign 'for women of all classes', naming the WSPU's token working-class women. He also talked of progress in other countries, including Finland and (less convincingly) Persia. Hardie overlooked (or failed to realize) ideological difficulties and continued to believe his arguments were valid whether the tactic chosen was limited or universal suffrage. It was the principle of gender equality which mattered.

Other socialists, particularly in the SDF, believed that the principle of class equality was what mattered. Most SDF men believed the suffragette movement was a middle-class phenomenon that had little to do with the struggle of the working class. To them, the Pankhurst policy of limited suffrage, inevitably linked to existing property rights, heralded the 'reign of the female capitalist'.[92] Blatchford believed the women's suffrage issue was 'a small thing', not a real issue;[93] and Hyndman's private view was downright contemptuous, writing that women who advocated emancipation 'ought to be sent to an island by themselves'.[94] However, Marxist men and women had differences that were if anything more marked than those between men and women in the ILP. One objector to the prevailing male SDF view was Dora Montefiore, now an SDF member and a socialist suffragist from the start, very much on the lines Eleanor Marx had been, seeing working-class women's inequality as the main issue. Montefiore later wrote, 'The working woman is the . . . more downtrodden in the last resort than is the working man, because, though under capitalism the working man is a wage-slave, yet his wife is the slave of a slave.'[95]

Montefiore tried to set up a women's group inside the SDF in 1906 but it failed to gel.[96] Later she refused to pay her income tax on the grounds that women as voters were not represented in Parliament, after which she was besieged for weeks by bailiffs in her Chiswick Mall home, christened Fort Montefiore by the press.[97] Earlier, in 1904, she had worked with the Pankhurst family and the WSPU. Sylvia made her first suffrage speech in Ravenscourt Park, West London, when accompanying Dora Montefiore, carrying the box on which Montefiore intended to stand. The second speaker failed to arrive and Sylvia was called on instead. She made an important discovery that changed her life; she found she loved public speaking.[98]

On 21 February 1905, Sylvia accompanied Emmeline to the Central Lobby of the House of Commons to canvass MPs during the balloting for Private Members' Bills. When the 'welcome figure' of Hardie appeared, according to Sylvia, Emmeline immediately berated him for all the effort he was putting into unemployment legislation. Did he not know that women's suffrage was more important, for 'when women had won the vote such matters would be dealt with as a matter of course?'[99] Like most campaigners, Emmeline (and Hardie too) ascribed far more benefits to women's suffrage than could ever be justified.

Finally, a Liberal MP, Bamford Slack, was found who was prepared to introduce the Pankhursts' Bill. It was set down for May. At the Easter ILP Conference in Manchester Sylvia helped her mother successfully lobby for an ILP commitment to this limited Bill. Hardie was in the House (and the Pankhursts in the gallery) on 12 May, when it was introduced to 'roars of laughter from the opponents'.[100] It was talked out by agreement, which meant no vote was taken. At the end a man in the gallery shouted out objections and the women surrounded him to thank him for his support. He turned out to be an SDF member who had come all the way from the north to protest at Parliament wasting time on 'votes for ladies' when they should be discussing employment for working men. Rowdy scenes followed and the women were pushed out of Parliament by the police. Keir Hardie accompanied them across the street to the gates of Westminster Abbey, where they held an impromptu meeting. All the while, Hardie held hands with the veteran suffrage campaigner, Mrs Wolstenholme Elmy.[101]

By this time Mrs Pankhurst and Christabel were making more and more forays to London for suffrage activity, when they always stayed with Sylvia in her tiny flat. During the Pankhursts' visits to London and Hardie's stop-overs in Manchester, both Sylvia and Emmeline took it upon themselves to persuade Hardie to enjoy life a little more than his strict lifestyle permitted. Sylvia took him out to restaurants, where she persuaded him to drink coffee, which he had never tasted before.[102] She was suffering from neuralgia and on one occasion fainted.[103] Fainting enjoyed a vogue among middle-class girls in the nineteenth century, but Hardie had never seen it happen, and was very alarmed. Sylvia also managed to get Hardie out for walks in St James's Park and in the years that followed, Richmond Park, even occasionally farther into the country. There he discovered to his amazement that she could not juggle with little stones, exclaiming, 'All the little girls do it!'[104] Sylvia answered, 'I never played games,' whereupon Hardie told her playfully that she had had far too serious an upbringing.

Emmeline also sought him out. On one occasion she took him to a vaudeville performance, which he approached very unsurely. Once inside, however, he was amused by its crude melodrama and reassured by finding himself sitting next to a small boy, with whom he made instant friends.[105] Hardie always made friends with children. The MacDonald's son, Malcolm, remembered Hardie's occasional visits to the flat where he would take the MacDonald children aside and tell them 'Little Red Riding Hood', or tales of Donald the pit pony or Roy, 'the wise collie waiting to welcome him home far away in Cumnock'.[106]

In London, Frank Smith, who continued to look after Hardie's welfare, was the friend most likely to get him out of his den. He would arrange (and no doubt pay for) theatre excursions. Hardie had no aversion to serious theatre, and Sylvia, who got on well with Frank Smith, was included on several visits during this time. After a performance of *Romeo and Juliet*, she was surprised to hear Smith ask who had written the play,[107] testimony to Smith's erratic education. He would not have had to ask who wrote *John Bull's Other Island*, an early performance of which the three of them also attended. At one point, perhaps on this occasion, Hardie introduced Sylvia to Shaw, after which she wrote regularly to the playwright. Sylvia wrote to almost everyone she met.

But Hardie was the one with whom she felt most at ease; he was also the one her mother had chosen to further the women's cause. Mary Stocks, another WSPU member, called Emmeline 'a spell binder'.[108] During 1905 letters and cards flew from Hardie to 62 Nelson Street. Hardie was also attentive to Christabel. When she and Annie Kenney were arrested for disturbances at a Liberal political meeting in Manchester's Free Trade Hall in the autumn of 1905, she received an immediate telegram from Hardie in London, 'Can I do anything?'[109]

*   *   *

By the end of 1905 the Conservatives could no longer carry on as a government and resigned. A Liberal government was formed in December. John Burns completed the last stage of his move from revolutionary agitator to establishment hero by accepting ministerial office as head of the Local Government Board, exactly as Hardie had predicted. One of his first acts later was to clamp down on work schemes for the unemployed, Hardie shrewdly concluding that the basic problem with Burns was his 'lack of faith . . . in democracy' and 'distrust of the people'.[110]

An election was called for January 1906. Hardie had been prepared for it for a year. The journalist W. T. Stead had interviewed him in January 1905 in a series called 'Coming Men on Coming Questions',[111] where Hardie set out his idiosyncratic programme: (1) organize society not for profit but for all; (2) set up work-schemes for the unemployed, including home colonies; (3) ensure everyone had a minimum wage, covering all 'necessaries' (elsewhere Hardie suggested this should be thirty shillings a week);[112] (4) legislate for an eight-hour day for all workers; (5) reform the land laws, to keep workers on the land; (5) transfer all home-working to municipal workshops; (6) start creches at work for women; (7) make state provision for the old and ill; (8) provide houses locally for the homeless and working class, with all the 'appliances' of 'middle-class dwellings'; (9) open reading rooms, recreation rooms, and play spaces for children; (10) reforest Lancashire, Wales and Yorkshire; and (11) give Boards of Guardians the power to give the unemployed work on useful local projects. Stead commented that you might not like Hardie's programme but at least he had one, which, Stead implied, was more than most other politicians had. That included MacDonald, who had made it clear a few months earlier that as far as the LRC went, 'the time for a programme is not yet'.[113]

In 1903 Hardie had forecast a Labour Party of fifty with a rallying cry of 'People vs Privilege'.[114] In 1906, the LRC were putting up fifty candidates,[115] thanks in part of MacDonald's assiduous work behind the scenes. The majority were trade union men, funded by their unions. Ten had ILP nominations. The SDF were putting up ten, including Hyndman who had been nursing Burnley since 1903. Hyndman had drawn much closer to the ILP since his return from 'exile' in 1904. He had even given a cautious welcome to a motion to reaffiliate the SDF to the LRC.[116] But the SDF was no longer his to control and the resolution was defeated. Privately he was becoming more conciliatory to ILP members at International Bureau meetings, and Glasier in particular commented favourably on the change. Hyndman particularly wanted to make his peace with Hardie on the class war issue and wrote to him several times in 1905 to say he doubted if there 'is any material difference between us';[117] it was only that he was 'churned' to know that if 'the workers don't recognize the class war the capitalists do'. Hyndman's election campaign in Burnley, however, made no mention of class war and there was only one small reference to his socialism.

Like Hardie during previous elections, hardly a postcard could be got between Hyndman and the Liberals, as he proclaimed his support for Home Rule and Free Trade. Although not endorsed by the LRC (he stood as a 'Socialist, Labour and Democratic' candidate), Hardie sent him a message of good wishes.[118] George Bernard Shaw came to speak, and the Countess of Warwick sold jewellery to raise £500 for his campaign.[119] She also sent three motor cars to West Ham to help Will Thorne carry voters to the poll. Thorne, however, finally agreed under pressure from MacDonald to stand as a LRC candidate rather than a socialist under the SDF. With so respectable a label and no Liberal against him, Thorne felt free to fill his election literature with class war references.[120]

His East End neighbour, George Lansbury, stood as 'Independent Labour' in Middlesbrough against the trade unionist, Havelock Wilson (and was paid for by Fels[121] who had earlier poured money into Philip Snowden's successful by-election campaign at Wakefield.)[122] Although Lansbury was not sponsored by the LRC, Hardie went to speak for him anyway, the only national speaker who did. To the right of the LRC fold was Richard Bell, the first deselected Labour MP. He stood as one of the large contingent of trade union men still under the Liberal banner.

Absent from the hustings were Tom Mann, who was still in Australia, and Cunninghame Graham, even though James Connolly offered to back him for an Edinburgh seat as a socialist candidate. Cunninghame Graham declined, 'I have no money.'[123] This was despite the fact that every year between 1900 and 1906 he had written a new book: poetry, travel guides, histories, and social studies of some of the world's most remote societies, as well as over one hundred short stories. His explorations were legendary and he had many fans, including Theodore Roosevelt. Shaw continued to adulate him, and had sent him a copy of his *Three Plays for Puritans*, dedicating the flyleaf to 'the only begetter of Captain Brassbound'.[124]

In between his writing and travelling Cunninghame Graham rode around his Scottish estates on Pampa, trying to find some way to rescue them from debts, while the beautiful Gabrielle kept accounts and wrote her own books of poetry and travel. Every year the doctors warned her about her excessive smoking, to which she was now enslaved, smoking 'more than . . . a hundred in twenty four hours . . . and there were days when [she reached] the two hundred mark'.[125] Eventually, these candles burning at both ends delivered their pain. Cunninghame Graham saw Gartmore put under the hammer, while 'he stood and wept in public'.[126] Gabrielle declined and, at forty-five, died. Cunninghame Graham dug her grave himself and buried her in the grounds of a ruined Augustinian priory on an island in Lake Menteith, one of several pieces of property he still owned. He had not been completely ruined. When his lawyer protested that he should stop the rumours saying he was, he always answered, 'Let people believe it; it gives them such pleasure.'[127]

During the 1906 campaign Hardie made his usual grand parade around the country, drawing enormous crowds. When he stopped at Merthyr midway, he told electors that in only three days he had travelled '1120 miles in railway trains' and addressed seven meetings, but added ominously, 'It is very significant that not a single reference to these meetings has appeared in any of the London Liberal daily papers.'[128]

Morgan believed that Hardie had neglected Merthyr since he had been elected.[129] No doubt this was one of the factors that sent Frank Smith, who was running his campaign from hired rooms in the High Street in Merthyr, into a state of panic, particularly as a second (and very hostile) Liberal called Radcliffe had unexpectedly entered the field to challenge Hardie. Frank Smith sent telegrams in all directions, claiming the seat was in imminent danger. In response came Emmeline Pankhurst and Annie Kenney of the WSPU, Michael Davitt, the Irish MP, and Ramsay MacDonald, fresh from fighting Leicester.

Smith need not have worried. Hardie's support in Merthyr had consolidated considerably during the previous five years, aided and abetted by newly formed and very active local Trades Councils as well as by a new wave of evangelical activity that called itself the 'new theology'. In the 1880s and 1890s the Church of England's Christian Social Union (as well as the socialist Guild of St Matthew) had been dedicated to 'overthrow the Nonconformist capitalist',[130] but not until after 1900 did nonconformist ministers themselves in areas like South Wales begin rebelling against their identification with great and small Liberal industrialists, and taking an interest in larger social issues. When they did, on the whole their influence came Hardie's way. During the campaign several spoke out in the local press for him.[131] The 'new theology' was essentially what Hardie had come to support on his own in the 1880s; he found its chief exponent, the Revd R. J. Campbell, editor of the *Christian Commonwealth*, pastor of the City Temple in London and a friend of his friend Robert Williams, often in tune with his own thinking.

Hardie's election campaign played up the fact that both he and the senior Liberal MP, D. A. Thomas, had been endorsed by the local Dowlais Free Church Council for having stood out against the Conservatives' 1902 Education Act that forced ratepayers to finance Church of England schools. Nonconformist areas throughout Britain were enraged; and Parliament had seen several severe storms on the subject. In the election Hardie made education a major issue, 'Every school which is maintained by public moneys must be put under public control.' Like the Liberals, he was opposed to a law that gave 'religious sectarians' the chance 'to have their special form of religious belief taught . . . at the public expense', as he did not see how you could avoid giving 'preference to one sect over another'; adding that in any case, 'I altogether question the wisdom of having children taught religion as a task':

> Religion should be voluntary . . . Let every denomination have whatever facilities can be given outside of school hours for imparting religious instruction . . . place all denominations on an equality and lift our whole system of education beyond the reach of sectarian disputes.[132]

Many other endorsements were received as well.[133] One handbill printed dozens of respectable trade union leaders saying what a fine fellow Hardie was; plus a special scroll attesting to the support of national notables like George Bernard Shaw, H. G. Wells, George Meredith, George Cadbury, Cunninghame Graham, Robert Blatchford, Joseph Fels and Sidney Webb. On 11 January a telegram arrived too from the United Irish League in Liverpool, always essential to obtain the Catholic vote. Those who failed to get their Irish telegram (as Hyndman did in Burnley) had reason to fear.

Hardie probably worried less than Frank Smith, as except for the year of his illness, he had a solid parliamentary record upon which to base his appeal. He had continued to insist that every workplace disaster, including continuing mining accidents, be recognized as national events. He had continued his stringent cross-examinations on strikes and the treatment of those taking part, and pressed his plans for unemployment relief. But most of all he pressed questions about employment itself. It was 'his work on behalf of the workers in Government' that Morgan Thomas singled out for first mention and special praise in moving Hardie's selection as candidate on 6 January,[134] for it was well understood that by continually forcing the government to be a better employer, Hardie was forcing private employers to follow suit. He had put question after question on the army, the naval dockyards, the telephone service, the war office, the West India docks, the Woolwich Arsenal, the Gibraltar docks – and any firm contracted to deal with them. He queried the lot of workers of every colour in every part of the world, where Britain was responsible, from women typists in Whitehall to 'coolie' labour in China. He asked about wages, safety, pensions and hours, even down to the exact time off that postal workers could expect for the coronation of Edward VII (an occasion he attended and called a 'meaningless ceremony' viewed by 'whole rows of fantastic nobodies').[135]

In accepting his nomination, Hardie recalled that they had taken him in five years earlier in Merthyr as a pro-Boer, a 'wild socialist' and an advocate of an independent Labour Party. He had stuck to his guns and everyone knew the 'calumny and abuse which has ranged around me . . . greater than that which has been directed against any other man in public life', as you would expect for one 'who takes a stand by the working class'. Again, as in West Ham, he was called on to answer the question, 'Why do you not reply to the charges made against you?' His reply was now well practised, 'The traveller who stops to cast a stone at every cur which barks at his heels will be a long time reaching the end of his journey.'[136] Unlike colleagues and his family, it is probable that had Hardie to choose between press boycott and press attacks, he would have chosen the latter.

His programme mixed grand and small commitments willy nilly: support for graduated income tax (to deal with the 'parasites whose incomes are the product of other people's labour'), through the 'co-operative organization of industry', to the abolition of customs duty on tea and coffee. For the first time he included women in his section on the right to work.[137] His speeches were laced with implicit class war references, skilfully adjusted on one occasion to include in the 'useful classes', not only the whole of the 'working class,' but also 'professional men . . . shopkeepers and . . . [the] struggling', ranging these against 'owners of land and capital . . . and gamblers on the Stock Exchange'.[138] Earlier he had even included 'business men' as part of the working class, for he profoundly believed the entrepreneur was as ill-served by giant cartels and monopolies as were working men. (Much later in life, however, he denounced 'landlords, employers, brewers, financiers' – and the, always mandatory, 'lawyers'[139] when all business and professional people were lined up with capitalists against the working class.)[140]

If his class line wobbled, his moral one did not. He made a virtue out of the criticism that had come to him from standing aloof from 'the well-to-do classes' – 'maybe too aloof', he conceded. He was not prepared to spend the £150 a year on 'gifts and donations' that he had been told he would have to make to keep a parliamentary seat, a practice 'more corrupting than the open purchase of votes . . . by . . . beer'.[141] This was greeted by a volley of cheers. His electors knew by now that Hardie was the last man in the world who would give away money, much less buy anyone a beer.

When the results were declared, Hardie was shown to have improved his vote as well as his standing against the second Liberal.[142] After only a day's rest, he set off for Ireland, along with George Barnes, another newly elected MP. It was supposed to be a holiday but turned out to be another triumphal political progress, meeting Irish counterparts. He took more than a polite interest in the new Sinn Fein movement, which he noted encouraged the Irish to 'set about doing things for themselves'.[143]

While Emmeline was campaigning with Hardie and Lillie (who accompanied him throughout), Sylvia stayed in London. On election night she went to Fleet Street and stood with the crowds looking up at the board outside the *Daily News*, where results were chalked up. No one was surprised that the Liberals won, but the size of the majority exceeded expectation. So too did Independent Labour's successes. She saw Will Thorne had won in West Ham. There were wins too for Jowett, Snowden and, at last, Ramsay MacDonald in Leicester. Among those who lost were Lansbury and Glasier, by many thousands of votes; and Hyndman, by only 400.

In addition to the twenty-nine LRC MPs (soon to be thirty, exactly matching the prediction Hardie made during the election itself),[144] there were also twenty-two trade unionists, backed by the Liberals, including many of the old familiar Hardie enemies such as Bell, Mabon, Fenwick and Broadhurst. A contemporary account tries to sort this out for readers:[145] 'The Independent Labour Party [*sic*] in the House of Commons numbered thirty, of whom nineteen belong to socialist organizations. Of the Liberal-labour group, at least five were socialists. We may reckon the labour members at fifty-four, of whom about half were socialists.'

Josiah Wedgwood, looking back as a radical Liberal,[146] saw an LRC group only 'nominally socialist and collectivist . . . [the] thoughtful ones . . . divided between Fabian right and rebel left, and the more numerous only asked to be left . . . in peace from the ILP'.

Thus the contingent which gathered was much more a confused church than a broad one. The TUC now had about a million affiliated members[147] but socialists within the LRC numbered only 20,000, or 2 per cent of this total, even assuming most affiliated trade unionists would have voted Labour. Locally, the organization of the Labour vote did not so much depend on the activity of individual unions as on their activist members who had organized themselves into Trades Councils. Trades Councils grew rapidly in response to the LRC's local needs, from a mere seven in 1901 to 155 by 1910.[148] Their joint organization with local labour and socialist groups – of which the ILP was the most important – formed the real basis of the LRC electoral success.

Puffed up by having gained 37 per cent of the vote in seats they contested,[149] the new LRC contingent met when Parliament reconvened in February 1906. A contemporary commentator characterized the grouping as the 'oil and water of socialism and radical trade unions' and claimed it would never mix.[150] This was demonstrated immediately when LRC members met to elect a leader. Hardie was the obvious choice but trade union members of the LRC believed their organizations paid the piper and the extremist Hardie did not play a tune they wanted. They were determined to oppose him, and he found himself up against David Shackleton of the weavers. One thing that was certain, with twenty-nine members at that time, it could not be a tied vote. But it was. Only when MacDonald, having refused to vote twice, reluctantly voted for Hardie,[151] did Hardie scrape home as the leader of the LRC's parliamentary group – which from that meeting onwards became known as the Labour Party.

This close call discouraged Hyndman, looking on from outside. He and Hardie had had their quarrels but in his view Hardie 'had just the qualities needed for the present juncture',[152] while Shackleton was 'not a socialist at all'. As for 'J.R.M.', Hyndman added, he was 'an outrage upon the Movement'. Those holding out for a Socialist Labour Party (like George Lansbury) thought that if the new party had a problem, it was that 'Social reform and socialist reform are not always convertible terms'.[153] The truth of this would soon be seen.

This time there had been no dramatic entry to Parliament at the start of the session, although people noticed that Hardie had given up his tweed cap. He felt guilty about not wearing it but he had formed a liking for a soft felt trilby-style after visiting America.[154] By 1900 this trilby too had acquired a political reputation. 'Only socialists, nihilists and atheists wore it,' one of his Merthyr constituents claimed.[155] In dress Hardie stuck to his simply tailored suits; he hated all padding and starch.[156] In the summer he began wearing sandals rather than shoes. His collars were always flat, MacDonald's often winged, but only trade unionists in the new Labour Party – John Hodge, for example – still wore the frock coat and tall silk hat. As Snowden said later, it was a standing parliamentary joke that trade unionists (especially those still clinging to the Liberal Party) dressed more like the boss than the boss did.[157]

These assorted styles can be seen in the official group photographs taken of the newly elected Labour Party under various parliamentary arches in early 1906. Hardie was always centre front, the obvious leader. But it was a different story out of range of the camera. From the first he disliked the job. He had been reluctant to take it on and had written to Cunninghame Graham only a few weeks earlier to say he wasn't cut out to be a leader, he was a pioneer.[158] His parliamentary colleagues had little confidence in him either – particularly MacDonald, as he would soon make clear. Other colleagues, such as Glasier, did not want Hardie to take on the job for a different reason: he would be wasting himself on committee work in London when he was needed to 'lead the socialist policy . . . outside of the movement'.[159]

This conflict of interests for Hardie sounded from the moment he took up the reins and had to reconcile the rival claims of the Labour Party inside Parliament and the ILP outside. He now had two political allegiances to try to treat equally – as he now had two personal lives to treat equally. Increasingly he came to prefer the social life of suffragette women to any other company, just as he preferred the socialist ILP to the equivocal Labour group in Parliament, and extra-parliamentary life to the life of party manager. But he also felt a deep obligation to keep up the parliamentary pressure.

1906 was a crucial year, when socialist and trade union causes could have been fused, and related movements, such as the Co-operative Society which already had three million members, drawn in, along with the growing body of opinion – religious and voluntary – sympathetic to socialism.[160] Hardie was in a key position to assist a living amalgamation – at a time when hopes were high. The *Labour Leader* had printed a triumphant heroic couplet that expressed the feeling of the time:

> Our hope is in heroic men
> Star-led to build the world again.[161]

The same flurry of excitement invaded Neville's Court. Years later Maggie Symons wrote to Hardie to remind him of:

> what a lot there was to do and how exciting and interesting it was when the Labour Party got returned to Parliament in January, 1906. All that time I was fearfully unhappy and wanted to give it all up but I kept telling myself it would be selfish to do so and so with a breaking heart day after day I went on.[162]

It was during 1906 that Maggie's problem, long suspected by Hardie, came to a head: her husband had formed an attachment to another woman and had, it appeared, expressed the view that having more than one relationship at one and the same time was part of the modern political code. Hardie wrote to his old friend Robert Williams (now in Cairo designing government buildings) to say how unhappy he was about the 'domestic trouble' in his daughter's life. Hardie also gave his own views on the subject of 'open marriage', as it might be called today:

> The more I see of 'practical idealists' the more I distrust them and their methods. The customs and habits which are ours from generations of slow growth are not to be lightly cast aside. Newer and freer conditions will come in time but their coming must be gradual.[163]

Unfortunately, at the end of the year he himself had an even bigger blow for Maggie;[164] he told her the ILP had withdrawn the £50 secretarial allowance he was getting and that he could not pay her any more. He was having Frank Smith come in to do his ILP work and office mail. Although it was hardly likely that in the year when Hardie was leader of the Party he would be left without assistance, it was certainly possible that Frank Smith had offered to do for nothing what Hardie was now paying Maggie 6d. an hour to do, and that reluctantly he let her go to save money. She left London defeated in spirit, to go out to 'Egypt to help' her father. 'I regret this exceedingly,' Hardie wrote before she left, 'You have of late known so intuitively what to do and how to anticipate my wants that I shall feel for a time as though a part of myself has been taken away.' Hardie had grown very fond of Maggie. His letter ended, 'Brave Heart, good bye. There is sunshine for you somewhere.'[165]

Despite Frank Smith's assistance, Hardie was even more inundated with paperwork than in the previous Parliament. Even if he had not been elected leader, he would have been overwhelmed with the public's sudden interest in the thirty new Labour men. Journalists from every quarter wanted to interview them. In 1906 sales of all socialist and radical journals soared. New ones were started, including *Forward* in Scotland, with Tom Johnston as editor. The *Labour Leader* had doubled its circulation since Hardie had stepped down as editor, and the *Clarion* reached a circulation of 74,000.[166] Robert Blatchford was just as much in demand, as 'editors sought him to explain this mysterious Socialism to their benighted readers'.[167] He did, and socialism brought prosperity to Blatchford and Yorkshire Sallie, the wife he had married many years earlier and to whom he still continued to address affectionate letters signed with rows of crosses and postscripts like, 'I wish you were here now. I don't think a good long squeeze would hurt either of us.'[168] That Hardie could ever express himself so affectionately to Lillie is hard to imagine, though Sallie was, like Lillie home-body, polishing everything every day, even the stair-rods, and always available to drop everything when Blatchford wanted a break.

Inside the Palace of Westminster there was also a stir. Snowden reported that the police were 'particularly friendly to the new Labour members' despite not being sure who they were.[169] The *Labour Leader* told of Hardie coming in one day and being stopped by a policeman and asked, 'Are you working here, mate?' 'Yes,' said Hardie. The police asked, 'On the roof?' (which was being repaired). Hardie replied, 'No, on the floor.'[170] The movement loved these standing stories of turned tables, and followed closely the activity of the small band that sat in the corner below the gangway. It now had an office on an inner courtyard (still used by MPs), official Whips, and Hardie had two parliamentary private secretaries. One of the first rules he made was that no MPs who took the Labour Whip were to be seen drinking in any House of Commons bar.[171] 'Labour and Liquor don't mix' was the motto. This was not so much temperance commitment as determination that the new members not be prey to social temptations – what Cobden once called the 'allurements of the season' and what William Morris saw as the worker 'tending to rise out of his class before he has begun to think of class politics, got at by the governing classes, not formally but by circumstances'.[172] A contemporary observer reported that working men in Parliament were still subject to the same temptations[173] and Sylvia Pankhurst later confirmed that the drinking ban was to retain the connection with 'our own folk'.[174] Most Labour MPs probably followed it, however, because of the cost. Prices put a simple meal in the Commons dining room beyond their reach, let alone drinks in the bar. In time a cheaper dinner was offered in the dining rooms,[175] confirming many Conservatives in their view that there had indeed been a social revolution.

The first Parliamentary Report to the first Labour Party Conference after the election in February 1906 hardly confirmed this view. Hardie had no political plans to announce and was only able to say that Labour 'is already a menace to the easy-going gentlemen of the old school'.[176] In a way, it was true, for their presence had sent a shock wave through Liberal Party managers. Within a few weeks of the election a frantic letter was sent out to all trade union members in the House to say it was time to start a 'Labour Party within the Liberal Party', and promising 'considerable financial support' for the venture.[177] But there was no one to respond. Independent Labour MPs had their own party and Lib-Lab MPs were content to remain sheltering under the Liberal tree as the easiest way to keep getting elected. They did not need any 'separate organization'. Nevertheless, the letter showed that Liberal leaders were alive at last to the fact that they had missed the boat with labour.

They would have been less alarmed had they known that inside the Labour Party, as Snowden recalled later, trade union MPs were already calling for strict discipline against any who opposed majority opinion, in the hope of getting rid of 'extreme socialist' views.[178] Labour offered no amendment to the King's speech, another sign of the tame tactics it would adopt, to try to win concessions rather than go straight into opposition, as Hardie would have preferred. To redeem their electoral pledges, they decided to rely on Private Members' Bills, pooling success in the ballots to take their most urgent measures: reversing the Taff Vale ruling, providing meals for needy schoolchildren, organizing pensions, dealing with unemployment and the sweated trades, and, important to trade unionists, a measure to regulate checkweighing. Missing from the list was any Bill for suffrage, women's or otherwise. This brought an enraged Emmeline Pankhurst to Parliament to seek Hardie out in the Party's new room. She expected a limited suffrage Bill at once, indeed had expected an amendment to the King's speech. Why was nothing yet done? Sylvia was with her and later wrote that 'in the muffled voice with which he always cloaked distress', Hardie told Emmeline of 'the decision already taken by the Party'. He added, however, 'that . . . should he . . . win a place . . . for [a] Resolution, he would use it for Votes for Women, the . . . Party notwithstanding'.[179] This was a commitment Hardie had no authority to make. Not appreciating this gesture, a furious Emmeline 'swept it aside . . . She would take no denial . . . She would not go back to Christabel in Manchester and tell her this had been refused.' After that she wept; and then implored, asking, 'was it for this she had joined the ILP?' Through this hectoring Sylvia reported that Hardie 'sat dark-browed and silent. I was between them.'[180]

A few weeks later Hardie won a chance to introduce a simple resolution. It could not change the law but it could force the House to vote – for the first time ever – on the principle that 'sex should cease to be a bar to the exercise of the Parliamentary Franchise'.[181] Without consulting colleagues he put it down for debate. On the day, Emmeline Pankhurst and WSPU supporters crowded into the gallery. However, they had not listened to Hardie's explanation of the difference between this resolution and the 'talked-out' Bill of a year before. This time there was a good chance a vote would be accepted at the closure. However, as the clock ticked towards the end of debating time, forgetting what he had said and thinking it was being talked out, Emmeline and Sylvia suddenly leapt up and protested with much shouting. Hardie's motion fell without a vote and he went off without speaking to them.

But he was now too embroiled to stay away long and was soon back in harness. He introduced Emmeline to Emmeline and Frederick Pethick-Lawrence, well-to-do socialists and supporters of the suffrage cause. Before the end of the year the Pethick-Lawrences had hired rooms for the WSPU below their own flat in Clement's Inn and had helped launch a WSPU paper, *Votes For Women*. During this time Hardie too raised money for the women's cause. Sylvia Pankhurst said he presented the WSPU with £300.[182] Where this came from is hard to tell, except that at the end of the year the Kippen sisters, watching from their Edinburgh mansion, had sent him £2,000. He promised it to the ILP provided they could raise a matching sum.[183] Perhaps during the negotiations he kept some back for the WSPU; or asked Joseph Fels. Hardie was shameless about writing to ask for money. A few years earlier, in 1902, Glasier had been much taken aback to find out that without telling him Hardie had written to Glasier's own brother-in-law (a businessman) asking for funds to keep the *Leader* going.[184]

Hardie was also helpful to the WSPU in organizing meetings.

When Emmeline wanted to launch the WSPU in London with a large meeting and had sent Sylvia to set it up, Sylvia appealed to Hardie, who hired the Caxton Hall. When Emmeline saw how large it was she was angry, they could never fill it. Sylvia – again with Hardie's help – called on George Lansbury, who brought in a large contingent of East End women and filled it to the full. George Lansbury's daughters had been militant supporters of women's votes long before the *Daily Mail* gave the name 'suffragette' to militant campaigners during 1906. Originally coined to denigrate, along with the later 'martyrette', used when women began to be jailed, it is a tribute to the cause that the word left its source so far behind.

Hardie's main effort for WSPU women in 1906 was to organize a deputation to see the prime minister Campbell-Bannerman in May which he attended. No assurances were given that votes for women would be introduced in the foreseeable future, and afterwards a big demonstration was held in Trafalgar Square where both Hardie and Emmeline Pankhurst spoke. By the summer Emmeline and Christabel began to argue that no other political issue should be discussed – or campaigned for – by any who supported women's suffrage, until women had been given the vote. In August matters came to a political head at a by-election in Cockermouth, Cumberland, where Bob Smillie was the Labour candidate. Emmeline and Christabel and their forces swept into the small port, turning their ferocity on the Liberals but making no appeal to vote for Smillie who supported women's suffrage. Worse, several times Christabel said, 'We don't care who you vote for', implying Tory was as good as Labour. Smillie retaliated against Christabel in the *Leader* on behalf of 'our poor women workers'. He had seen 'tears start to their eyes to hear such an answer'.[185] This much publicized intervention was widely credited with helping to lose Smillie this election. Hardie realized it had been damaging,[186] and knew he too was being widely blamed. Even before the by-election Snowden had complained, 'Hardie never speaks to me. He seems completely absorbed with the suffragettes'.[187] That autumn too the progressives lost control of the LCC, and John Burns had Christabel campaigning against him in Battersea during the whole election period. Christabel had lately received her law degree with first-class honours, as well as a college prize for international law.[188] Yet, as a woman, she was not allowed to practise law. She was more admired than ever, her academic accomplishment only adding to her lustre. Her meetings drew vast crowds and endless attention; her 'flawless colouring . . . easy grace' and modish dress were extolled; in time plays and novels were written about her by women who 'fell in love with her' on all sides.[189]

Sylvia, by contrast, was dowdy, 'her clothing', according to Fenner Brockway, 'just flung about her'.[190] She was not without charm, but Emmeline Pethick-Lawrence, herself extremely elegant as well as hardworking, saw in Sylvia at this time a disconcerting contrast between a 'childish face' and a 'hardness of character'.[191] What she was seeing was Sylvia, unconcerned with fashion, but determined to be a principal person herself.

But she faced problems. Christabel and her mother, by now clearly the leaders of the WSPU, had completely commandeered her flat for WSPU activity. Christabel also told her that she did not want any more of George Lansbury's East End women coming to WSPU meetings because Parliament preferred a 'feminine bourgeoisie' to a 'feminine proletariat'.[192] Sylvia sensed that her mother and sister were abandoning her father's cause, while her own instinctive wish was to combine equality of women with class equality. Of Christabel at this time she wrote, 'I detested her incipient toryism'. Yet she also said, 'her speaking . . . delighted me . . . I admired her, and avoided crossing swords with her.' In the end, 'There came a time when I could efface my desire for another policy no longer; but this was not yet.'[193] For Hardie it was not yet either. He and Sylvia both continued to allow Emmeline and Christabel to answer 'the woman question' for them.

Sylvia finally decided to move to a place of her own and chose two unfurnished rooms by the river in Cheyne Walk, Chelsea. The move induced a great depression in her; she was racked with rheumatism and neuralgia, physical pain reflecting the emotional pain of losing her old base, and her slipping place in the suffrage panoply. Her scholarship had not been renewed and she had no income. Egyptian lentils were all she could afford to buy. Later she wrote that alone in the new flat,

> I sat among my boxes, ill and lonely, when all unexpected, Keir Hardie came knocking at my door. He took command . . . He lifted heavy things into position and when all was in order, took me out for a meal at a little Italian Restaurant.[194]

From this point their relationship began to intensify.

9
HIGH TIDE

In 1906 Hardie was fifty. Snowden remembered, 'he looked sixty . . . old and grey, almost white'.[1] Yet writing from Cumnock at midnight on his birthday, Hardie said, 'I am younger in spirit at fifty than I ever remember to have been.'[2]

Not only had it been a euphoric year politically but he was also gradually falling into a relationship where there was a chance of the personal sympathy he sought. Most of all, he was uplifted by the messianic mission to convert the vast unseen to socialism. On the hustings, according to Glasier,[3] Hardie spoke without 'gesticulation' and with a voice 'high rather than deep, always completing his sentences . . . grammatically'. He had no 'brilliancy' or fluency, none of MacDonald's gifts. Yet his words were invariably moving. Their 'force and substance' and the 'elevation of appeal' made a 'deep impression on hearers'. For they retained the old religious ring, 'Now I know the main secret. He who would find his life must lose it in others.'[4] His contemporaries called him a prophet rather than a politician.[5] Hardie always preferred to call himself by the old seventeenth-century name of agitator. In this same passage, he wrote, 'The agitator who has the touch of the seer in him is a far more valuable asset than the politician. Both are necessary, but if one must be sacrificed let it not be the agitator.'

It was the politician that Hardie began to sacrifice, spending much of early 1906 touring the country taking advantage of the last rays of the election sun, and making several trips abroad to congresses and the International Bureau, travelling with Hyndman, who continued to bridge-build. Hardie said of him, 'a more charming and agreeable companion no wayfarer ever had'.[6]

The House of Commons, by contrast, he did not find agreeable. In the sophisticated exchanges his direct speaking style was not a success. Glasier acknowledged, 'He was not a good debater.'[7] As leader of the Party, the committees he had to attend were irksome and the daily meetings that were required – especially with the government and Tories, the type of liaising MacDonald loved – were distasteful. Chairing the by turns fractious and over-cautious Labour group was unrewarding. He was absent frequently; he delegated continually, which infuriated those left with decisions to make but no authority. As MacDonald later remarked, 'We never know where to find him'.[8] By Hardie's birthday in August, Snowden was writing to Glasier what most already felt but had not said, 'Hardie's leadership of the party [is] a hopeless failure.'[9]

All the same the 1906 session saw the passage of at least one measure which the Party regarded as central, the Trades Disputes Bill, reversing the worst effects of the Taff Vale decision. Although Hardie told the House that it passed because Labour had acted as 'a corrective to the blighting . . . of the two party system',[10] the truth was that the government eased its passage to placate Labour; and it did not by any means restore every trade union right that had been removed.

In the same way, the Education Bill introduced that year did not reverse the Tories' 1902 Act (since it fell victim to the Lords' amendments on behalf of the Church of England). Hardie did not like the compromise that resulted. His view was that state education was 'an essentially working-class question' and that working-class opinion had already expressed itself in favour of a fully secular system.[11] An Education Bill had been proposed by the TUC (Will Thorne introduced it), providing for free secondary education for all,[12] but it had been ignored by both main parties. They had permitted the issue of church schools to sweep all other 'reforms' aside.

The other major legislation, also a great disappointment, was the Workmen's Compensation Act. There was criticism from the ranks that Labour had spent its time in collaboration with the powers that be rather than fighting its own way. Hardie, sounding very much the leader, wrote in answer at the end of the year that it was not a wise tactic to 'run amok at the Treasury Bench'.[13] With only thirty MPs, what had been achieved was 'the most that can be expected'.

Two months earlier Hardie's ILP supporters had organized a 50th birthday party on 24 October in the Memorial Hall, London, where the LRC had been formed. He received 447 telegrams, including best wishes from the SDF, who praised 'his work with the people', and Cunninghame Graham, who wished he could 'live a thousand years'. He was presented by the Fabians with a gold watch and chain. 'I've aye wanted to have a gold watch,'[14] he told Stewart, who called it the ultimate ambition of 'douce Scots working men'. Hardie wore it incessantly. Fatefully, as if to punish his one innocent avarice, two years later in the Bermondsey by-election, it was stolen.[15] He went back to the old metal watch that bore the teeth marks of Donald, the pit pony.

Lillie got her glittering prize too, a gold-topped umbrella. It was added to her long list of consolation awards. Hardie thanked them particularly for honouring his wife because it was she who 'had borne so well the toil of his home and so often his long separation from her and their children'. Lillie's real claim to fame, however, was that she had lived for years on practically no income.[16] Hughes says Hardie was 'lucky in his wife' because 'she kept the house going on the very small weekly sum' he sent, at this time still possibly no more than £2 a week. Discussing this, Hardie admitted, 'I earned much more but save for the pittance named, every penny went into keeping the *Labour Leader* going and helping the cause.'[17] Lillie had been forced to live on a 'pittance' for years, in order to pay for the cause, yet had never been encouraged to play her own part in it; or, alternatively, to develop in a direction of her own.

This was the irony of Hardie's and Sylvia's position as socialists and suffrage supporters; Lillie was the typical working woman they were seeking to free and provide with economic independence. Yet it was Sylvia's prison which claimed Hardie's attention during this time, not Lillie's. For Sylvia had continued to throw herself into the WSPU, showing intense eagerness to respond to Emmeline's and Christabel's increasingly strident campaigns – even to compete personally for public martyrdom. The day before the birthday party several women, including Emmeline Pethick-Lawrence, Dora Montefiore and Adela Pankhurst, were arrested for holding a suffragette rally in the central lobby of the House of Commons. At Cannon Row Police Court after they had chosen prison rather than fines (a point of honour with suffragettes), Sylvia burst into the courtroom to remonstrate with the magistrate, now hearing another case. For this she was summarily sentenced not to division 1, reserved for higher-grade prisoners, but to division 3, reserved for common criminals and prostitutes. On the way in the van she said women were 'shrieking words I had never heard before'[18] and inside Holloway she was forced to bathe in water 'clouded with the scum of previous occupants'. She shivered awake all night in her tiny cell and in the morning gagged on the breakfast gruel. The experience was a tremendous shock but it also intrigued her. Pressure from Hardie and other MPs soon secured her Division 1 status and she sent for her drawing materials – to set to work drawing scenes of prison life.

In contrast to his handling of Labour Party affairs, where he was defensive about what it was possible to do with only thirty MPs, Hardie responded to the 'woman question' by taking the initiative. From the day after Sylvia's arrest there was a stream of questions in Parliament and two weeks later he introduced a Ten-Minute Rule Bill on women's suffrage.[19] Although it was signed by Henderson and Snowden, privately both these colleagues were growing increasingly impatient with his continuing absorption with the women's issue at the expense of holding the Labour alliance together in Parliament. Glasier confided to his Diary that Hardie was too soft on the 'Pankhursts etc' who were now turning away from Labour's cause,[20] while Benson concluded that the Pankhursts had already abandoned Labour and were 'now under rich Tory control'.[21] Glasier responded tartly in his Diary when Hardie relayed Emmeline Pankhurst's opinion on the best tactics for Labour, 'why should we care what Mrs P wishes us to do?'[22] By January 1907 Jowett put it even more bluntly, the 'suffragists have run away with him'.[23]

Hardie's colleagues were making Hardie the problem rather than looking closer to home in their own contradictory responses to the 'woman question'. Neither the ILP nor Labour Party gave it priority, which could be forgiven with so much else at stake, but even had they wished to do so, neither had agreed on a policy, some taking the Pankhurst line for a limited Bill, others sticking to universal suffrage as the goal (with a third group who opposed women's equality altogether, particularly in the trade unions).

Within the women's movement at large there were also divisions, particularly between the WSPU and the much larger group of suffragists led by Millicent Fawcett of the National Union of Women's Suffrage Societies (NUWSS), who later came to believe the tactics of the Pankhursts were extreme and damaging, though there was always grudging admiration for Emmeline Pankhurst personally. The WSPU viewed the NUWSS as spineless and unimaginative. It had never considered a parliamentary Bill until the Pankhursts lobbied to get one, according to Sylvia. When they had joined in that earlier initiative,[24] Sylvia wrote that it was a case of fifty MPs 'all in evening dress . . . on the platform' who testified approval in a few 'trite words' each, after which 'trim, prim . . . Millicent Fawcett . . . and other ladies . . . followed . . . in nervous, high pitched voices' with tame argument. This is just the kind of sexist comment SDF socialists or right-wing trade unionists would have made against the Pankhursts themselves.

Meanwhile, the WSPU was not only turning against Labour, Emmeline was even talking about the need for 'a new party of goodwill'.[25] This alienated yet more socialists. Hardie spoke privately of the 'wickedness of the WSPU' which has 'just about succeeded in souring even me'.[26]

On the face of it Hardie might have been expected to support the NUWSS, for it did not ask for a boycott of all other political activity, did not support violence, was willing to accept either Bill, and alone supported the Labour Party (as the only party committed to women's suffrage). That he chose a position so at variance with what might have been expected, one of Sylvia's biographers, Romero, puts down to his love for Sylvia, but almost everyone else at the time to Emmeline's hold upon him. Even Fenner Brockway at the age of ninety-nine, looking back eighty-two years, said firmly that it was Emmeline who persuaded Hardie.[27] The more likely answer, however, is that Hardie was so emotionally committed to the issue of women's equality, which had got itself so embodied in his relations with the Pankhursts, and particularly with Sylvia, that he failed to see the political problems WSPU proposals presented to the labour movement and socialists. At heart it was a failure to see the way gender and class politics could clash at a certain point. For Hardie and Sylvia still accepted Richard Pankhurst's claim that the women's cause was the workers' cause.

On no other issue did Hardie compromise the primacy of the working-class interest, or the need to avoid violence (as he was forced to do after suffragettes began to practise it). The suffrage issue called from him an almost mystical commitment. In time he would proclaim that 'woman, even more than the working class, is the great unknown.'[28] This was not surprising for a man whose life was built on the support of women. Yet most Hardie biographers have given little attention to either the women's issue or the Pankhursts. To McLean the Pankhursts were merely 'middle class women with time on their hands . . . more concerned with gestures than achievements'. None mentions Sylvia except Morgan, who is the only biographer to recognize Hardie's 'absorption . . . to the point of obsession' with the woman question in 1906 and 1907.[29]

When Sylvia was released from jail, Hardie arranged for her account and sketches to be published in *Pall Mall* magazine, for which she was paid 'a most needed windfall' of £10.[30] It was gratifying to her to have something published after years of rejected articles and sketches. She realized at once that she had found her own cottage industry: writing about herself and her own adventures, rather than trying to report what others were doing.

After another imprisonment in February 1907 resulting from demonstrations at the first 'women's Parliament',[31] Sylvia took more of her sketches to Fleet Street with introductions from Hardie, this time to W. T. Stead, the radical journalist Hardie had known for years, who had himself gone to prison for his principles over a story about child prostitution. He was said to be a firm supporter of the women's movement. There Sylvia had another sharp lesson in sexual politics. Instead of discussing her work, Stead suddenly forced himself upon her in the stranglehold of an embrace, implying that this was what any woman approaching an editor on her own for a favour should expect. She was exceedingly angry[32] and fled without a word. When Stead later pursued her, she brushed him aside, 'wondering why a man . . . so zealous a friend of women's movements should behave like an uncouth bear'.[33] This was one more illustration of the unexplored issues involved in the 'woman question' which so many, Hardie included, confined to the single issue of suffrage.

Suffrage matters came to a head at the 1907 conferences of the Labour Party and the ILP (and relations between conference and the Labour

Party did as well). Lillie accompanied Hardie to Belfast for Labour Party proceedings in January, which began with seventeen resolutions asking the Party to do 'this and that' in Parliament, as Hardie phrased it when introducing the issue.[34] Henderson said the seventeen requests were from 'affiliated organizations' rather than conference resolutions proper. But they were so numerous and varied, Hardie told delegates, that the NEC had decided to substitute its own resolution, saying that such 'instructions "would henceforth be taken" as the opinions of the conference, on the understanding that the time and method of giving effect to them' be 'left up to the Party in the House acting in conjunction with the National Executive'. They could not be regarded as commands, if for no other reason, Hardie explained, than that the PLP was made up of both socialists and trade unionists and some 'free play between' the two should be allowed Party leaders.

When Quelch of the SDF objected, Hardie assured delegates it did not mean the Party 'wanting . . . to play . . . dictator', for 'The Party in Parliament desired to be nothing but the servant of the movement as a whole'. Tillett, always Hardie's fiercest foe on the conference floor, then rose to say Hardie's speech was patronizing, an 'insult to the intelligence' of delegates. A Workers' Union delegate, giving his view that 'Conference . . . not the Parliamentary Party' should decide parliamentary business, then brought out the conference's grievance against Hardie over the suffrage issue, which lay behind the objections. He 'had never known Hardie lower the colours of unemployment until he was taken in, seemingly, by petticoats,' a clear reference to Hardie doing less for the unemployed than for the suffragettes. He said Hardie knew full well that the Labour Conference had voted '3 to 4 times for adult suffrage,' so who gave Hardie any right to recommend otherwise? Hardie did not rise to the bait, for the issue being debated was about letting Parliament decide 'the time and method' of carrying out conference votes. To Hardie's satisfaction, the Executive's resolution proposing this easily carried the day.

There followed two critical constitutional debates on (yet again) whether the Labour Party should declare itself for socialism (on which Hardie advised abstention, since socialists could not force their views on others), followed by whether all Labour Party members should not be fully practising trade unionists. Moving this last, Tillett pointedly claimed that the man who 'did something . . . to put more food upon the table of the worker was doing a greater work than sentimental men talking about theories' (which Hardie could well have assumed was a reference to himself), with a few good swipes at 'those literary, clever well educated men' who tell the working man how to think, whom Tillett identified as the ILP's 'middle class friends'. Whereupon a delegate got up to oppose him and asked, what about Hyndman, what about Cunninghame Graham? This seemed to answer the point, and once again Hardie was rewarded by seeing his advice on both issues accepted by conference.

Trouble only arrived with the overt proposal on suffrage, in the form of a tactful resolution from H. S. Wishart that could be supported by both universal and limited suffragists alike. It would have been the end of the matter had not Harry Quelch, spurred by the knowledge that a Liberal was putting down a limited bill in the new Parliament (which Labour had to decide whether to support or not), got up to put an amendment, 'any measure to extend the franchise on a property qualification to a section only . . . should be opposed'. Hardie gave a passionate defence of the limited Bill (which everyone knew would mean property qualification) and the 'injustices . . . inflicted on women by present political laws'. But he met a wide array of opposition, including a woman postal clerk, Miss Hope, who said that much as she admired the suffragettes, she had to point out 'they had created a sex antagonism instead of a class antagonism and it was contrary to the spirit of socialism'. The Labour Party could only support the principle of universal suffrage, which would include all men and all women without imposing qualifications. When it came to this vote, Hardie lost as heavily as he had won all the earlier votes.[35]

He said nothing immediately and it was only at the end of the conference in bidding farewell, that he dropped his bombshell: 'if the motion they had carried was intended to limit the action of the Party in the House of Commons, he should have seriously to consider whether he could remain a Member of the Parliamentary Party'. He did it in the full knowledge that the Party was 'largely his own child [and] his life's work'.[36] Everyone was dumbfounded. Glasier said the announcement that Hardie might resign over the women's issue left them all 'sprawling' and caused men like the emotional Pete Curran to wipe away tears.[37] In effect, he had said, choose the issue or choose me. It is ironic that Hardie, the least compromising of leaders and the one who always argued so strongly for MPs to be bound by ties to those who sent them to Parliament, should have set in motion the tradition so often used to weaken that tie.

From afar Sylvia dispatched an anxious note to plead with him to reconsider. She was waiting in the lobby of the House a few weeks later when he came out from the Parliamentary Party meeting which resolved the matter,[38] on Henderson's suggestion, by giving MPs a free vote on the women's issue – in effect, instituting the tradition of the conscience vote. Hardie told Sylvia the decision with relief, and as an aside, added that he had been re-elected leader. Thus to the parliamentary prerogative was added the conscience clause, consistent with Hardie's individualistic approach even while he extolled collectivity. The 1907 Labour Conference had provided two important ways for the new Labour Party to survive and prosper in a bourgeois Parliament.

During Sylvia's second prison spell in February, Hardie wrote her two letters. Both survive and both are brief. In one he told her he was sorry to have missed her when she called at Neville's Court recently, but that he was having her manuscript typed. In a second he sent her *Noctes Ambrosianae*, a book he said was having a vogue in Scotland. He hoped she would not take risks with her health, though 'the cause I know has just claims'. The letters are signed, 'Yours aye, J. Keir Hardie'.[39] No letters survive from Sylvia that can be dated to this period. Her prison writings to Hardie, upon which one biographer rests claims for a sexual love affair already begun,[40] are all undated. Sylvia went to prison many more times and these could date from later occasions. They are largely love poetry. In the first poem she writes:

Dear face so fond to me
Dear sturdy neck that my arms love to twine
Curls that are white before their time . . .
Dear breast on which my head lies when I'm tired
To which I cling and sob my sorrows out[41]

The context is ambiguous. It could be the small child to a parent; or a mistress to her lover. If this and the other poems were written at this time (rather than later), Hardie's two replies are quite unlike the highly personal letters he later wrote. Although friendly, they acknowledge no intimacy. They are either the letters of a man who has not yet acknowledged love, or a man, showered with a young woman's emotional attention, careful in what he writes.

During Sylvia's second spell in prison in early 1907, Hardie went to speak to the Fabian Society at Cambridge University. This visit revealed the first hint of the backlash against socialism that was building up. First, undergraduates tried to kidnap him on the way to the meeting (foiled by a decoy), and then used 'stink bombs and catcalls' to kidnap the meeting itself, according to one undergraduate present, Hugh Dalton, a future Cabinet Minister.[42] Hardie was 'hooted and mobbed'[43] until the meeting had to be abandoned. Much the same occurred when Hardie visited Oxford a few years later, where the 'young gentlemen' pelted him with rotten fruit.[44] On that occasion Hardie expressed no 'anger', only 'pity'; as earlier at Cambridge, he had assumed that those yelling were not typical of Cambridge students. Hugh Dalton was so overwhelmed by Hardie's 'total lack of fear or anger', as he continued trying to say what he had come to say, that he became a socialist 'that night'. As if this was not action enough for a day, that same evening Hardie returned to London and at midnight took up his usual position among the destitute on the Embankment, helping in the Salvation Army's feeding campaign. He was used to opposition and knew it did not only come from wealthy young fanatics. As Glasier wrote later, 'large sections of radical and trade union working men raged against him' as well – because, said the sensitive Glasier, he was their 'own spirit within them'.[45]

In March relations with Sylvia became clouded because Hardie began at last to have doubts about the limited Bill, no doubt occasioned by the strong vote against it at the Labour Party Conference. Accordingly, just before a big suffrage rally at Exeter Hall in London, where Hardie and Emmeline Pankhurst were both to speak, he told Sylvia that he had come round to adult suffrage as a proper long-term goal for women's suffrage. She told him that the very words 'adult suffrage' were a 'red rag to a bull' inside the WSPU, and this was confirmed when he mentioned them on the platform later. Sylvia noted that Emmeline was hardly able to treat Hardie 'with civility'.[46] The news also put Sylvia on the spot, still committed as she was to her mother's stand, and striving to hold her place in the WSPU ranks.

There was more trouble at the ILP Conference at Derby at Easter, although the ILP was officially committed to the WSPU line. At the conference once again WSPU members of the ILP were ready to do battle to see it stayed that way. Emmeline spoke at a fringe meeting along with the personable and lively Ethel Snowden, who had married Philip Snowden two years earlier and was already showing an appetite (disapproved of by Glasier)[47] for the kind of social round in London Hardie hoped Labour MPs would avoid. The WSPU line was opposed by trade unionists in the form of Mary MacArthur's and Margaret Bondfield's Adult Suffrage League, which objected to the limited suffrage Bill,[48] as it would mean setting back the chance of full suffrage indefinitely. There was also Margaret MacDonald's Women's Labour League, formed to bring together Labour women who supported suffrage. The WSPU regarded these other organizations, particularly the Adult Suffrage League, as phantom groups invented solely to oppose the WSPU. According to Sylvia, Hardie was against organizing women separately from men inside the Labour Party.[49] If these reports had any truth, such views would hardly have decreased the tension within the ILP or on the ruling NAC, which had both Emmeline and Margaret Bondfield as members. Tension was already at fever pitch before the conference in any case, because MacDonald had seen the NAC Report,[50] and was fuming that it 'is just a huge puff for the WSPU', adding, 'I shall not allow such a thing!' He made it clear that one cause of his anger was the failure of the report even to acknowledge Margaret MacDonald's Women's Labour League.[51]

At first all went well because the conference again confirmed its commitment to a limited Bill. Hardie then decided to push his luck. He moved that a telegram be sent to congratulate those suffragette women coming out of jail the next day, among whom was Christabel Pankhurst. This led to an explosion of anger, according to Stewart, particularly from Margaret MacDonald and Bruce Glasier, who declared that it was a slap in the face to 'our own women who had stuck faithfully to the Party'.[52] Ramsay MacDonald summed it up years later, still remembering the slight to Margaret MacDonald, by saying Hardie 'sorely tried the loyalty of our own women' by going out of his way to greet 'opposing ranks'.[53] Stewart said it was because many ILP rank and filers were not 'inclined to subordinate every other social question' to suffrage, nor to support tactics about which they were never consulted.

To the radical women campaigners in the ILP, however, there was no other issue but suffrage; to them, like the Pankhursts, it was the duty of all political groups to drop all political activity until equal rights were granted, even though this would still leave many working-class women and men without the vote. Just as quickly, those on the other side asked themselves, would the Pankhursts in turn fight for working-class men's rights to vote? Many socialists doubted it, but to the militants this was not the point; it was the principle of equal rights for women they sought to estab-lish in Parliament by legislation that would force the hand of all those who claimed to be in favour. A vote to cancel Hardie's suggestion was defeated by only eight votes.[54] Had Hardie not laid himself on the line, it would certainly have been carried. The ILP was left split in half, exactly as the Labour Party was. As Stewart understand it, the 'woman question' had 'disintegrating potentialities'.

The most immediate casualty was Hardie himself. The first sign was a 'strange numbness all down the left side' which he noticed just after the conference.[55] It is likely that Hardie had had a small stroke, but either he did not recognize it or did not wish to, and he carried on without seeking attention. But others noticed Hardie was unwell, including Sylvia;[56] and in early May MacDonald wrote to Glasier, 'I am very unhappy about his condition.' In the same letter MacDonald told Glasier that he and Margaret had been going through Euston Station when they saw Hardie going off to the train 'with Mrs Pankhurst on one arm and Mrs Cobden Sanderson on the other. We could not help laughing.'[57] MacDonald thought nothing more about it, or if he did, might privately have surmised that Hardie and Emmeline were unwisely close. Years later Glasier wrote in his Diary that Emmeline was 'the Delilah who had cut our Sampson's locks',[58] giving some idea of opinion held in the inner circle. Hardie was worried enough that MacDonald had seen him thus in 1907 to

ask Frank Smith to write to MacDonald and say that he had not made
a 'tryst' with Emmeline, their meeting was absolute coincidence.
Smith wrote faithfully that Hardie 'had not the remotest idea she
was anywhere near. For various reasons he would like you to know
this.'[59] What were these reasons? That Hardie did not wish his name
to be sullied with any sort of sexual scandal? After all, it was only a
few months before that he had said solemnly that he had kept to the
'steep straight path of duty' and had 'never yielded to the temptation
to try the . . . easier way without having cause to rue it'.[60] Was it
to protect himself and Sylvia? More probably it was because he
now realized the political danger of the Pankhurst position and did
not want it thought he was deserting Labour. Pethick-Lawrence
wrote that the party conferences in 1907 had marked 'the final
severance of the women's movement from the labour movement'[61]
and a few months later Emmeline Pankhurst quietly broke her ties
with the ILP for good. Hardie saw the danger in hanging on to
these women, literally and figuratively, and he wanted MacDonald
to know.

But the letter did not alleviate the stress arising from his clinging to
an ideological position that could no longer be sustained. Women's
suffrage and the interests of the working class were not identical.
This realization came to Hardie not through any theoretical argument
but in his ordinary experience, and particularly in his relations with
Sylvia. One night just before the ILP Conference, she records
that she and Hardie had 'paced the Embankment' discussing the
issue – an issue made all the more complex by their growing
emotional involvement with each other. Sylvia had virtually given
up her art and her own independent self and was firmly back under
Emmeline's spell, enjoying being a WSPU official. She could not
accept Hardie's shift towards universal suffrage and told him plainly
that their own 'friendship . . . might become a competitor . . . with
her loyalty to the suffrage cause'. Hardie understood the conflict at
last because he pointed to the ragged men lined up on the pavement,
whom he nightly helped to feed, and whom he had described in
Parliament only a few weeks before as 'men of all ages . . . standing
shivery with cold and hunger waiting for a basin of soup from the
Salvation Army'.[62] Hardie asked Sylvia, 'Do you expect me to desert
these?'[63]

Hardie knew he was still expected to turn up every day at the House
of Commons as leader of the Labour Party. The work was no more
to his liking in 1907 than it had been in 1906, and he was no more
capable of managing the diversity of opinion – particularly when he
held strong views himself on almost every issue. A Bill to set up a
Territorial Army was being introduced by Haldane, which Hardie

strongly opposed as the thin end of a wedge, 'turning Britain into an armed camp'.[64] It would introduce militarism to children and 'create an army of workers officered by rich men'. He was determined Labour MPs, most of whom were not pacifists and some of whom were jingoists, should oppose it.

On the issue of the liquor trade, one year the Labour Conference had voted for state control, the next for local option.[65] Hardie favoured state action to ban the sale of drink; but many Labour MPs were not temperance men; others were temperance in theory but drank in practice.

On education policy, the ILP, Labour Party and TUC all continued to support a secular system, but a few new Catholic members like James O'Grady were considering claiming the same 'conscience' rights to vote for church schools as Hardie had obtained for himself over suffrage.[66] In time they won their way, perpetuating a disagreement within the Labour Party that continues to the present.

The strains and tensions piling up for Hardie, together with the fear that the Parliamentary Labour Party was about to disappear under the shadow of the Liberals, finally cornered him. He did what he always did when things got bad. First he fell ill. Then he travelled.

After the stroke which no one had diagnosed, Hardie was assailed anew with intestinal troubles. Frank Smith tried to tend him at Neville's Court but eventually he was moved to St Thomas's Hospital. Lillie was sent for. Before she arrived Sylvia visited him there, where his bed had been moved for the day into the garden overlooking the river and the Houses of Parliament.[67] Three doctors, speaking 'in their human rather than their professional capacity', according to Stewart, warned him that 'another attack ... would be serious, necessitating an operation'.[68] An attack of what is not said, since no proper diagnosis was given, nor, characteristically, asked for. This new trouble in the gut – Hardie later reported he 'could keep nothing down' – renewed fears of another operation. So Hardie asked that 'nature and more gentle ... measures ... have their chance first'.[69] Rest was prescribed for at least a month and Hardie went back to Cumnock, handing over all his work to Frank Smith. 'Frank Smith keeps my faith alive,' he wrote to Robert Williams in Cairo.[70]

At last Hardie and Lillie were able to go for the treatment Hardie had always believed in. They spent what was required (or were financed by friends) to go to a hydro – one at Wemyss Bay. Whether the treatment was appropriate for a stroke plus intestinal disorders ('six and seven times a day I have dressed and undressed to undergo treatment', plunging into coldwater baths)[71] is another matter. He stayed for several weeks, enjoying the luxury of the resort, which he wrote

was set high above 'gleaming waters . . . and glorious sunsets'. He
felt guilty to be there while

> thousands of pain-stricken poor . . . moaning in the midst of dirt
> . . . in cheerless homes, are harassed by . . . debt and hurried off to
> work ere they are half well . . . Surely the day will come when such
> places as this will be open to all the stricken . . . and no longer a
> preserve . . . of the rich.[72]

After a few weeks Lillie wrote to Glasier that 'as far as looks go,'
Hardie is better, 'but that does not always count'.[73] He is still in
pain and 'Our doctor in Cumnock thinks the trouble is gallstones'.
The hydro doctor suggested he see a surgeon but Lillie said firmly,
'there must be no more cutting'.

At the end of June Nan came to replace Lillie as his companion at
the hydro. Her own health was not good and she wanted to take the
treatment too. Unfortunately, Hardie reported to Robert Williams,
Nan 'does not improve any'.[74] Again, nothing is said about what is
wrong. Duncan too was off work, this time with an accident to his
hand, which 'owing to carelessness on the part of doctors, developed
blood poisoning'. Hardie had a last bit of news for his old friend,
he was thinking of taking a long trip around the world. 'As far as
possible,' he told Williams, 'I want to make it a British Empire tour'.
He was concerned that while some parts of the Empire were free to
run themselves, others were still run from Britain.

When Hardie returned to Cumnock, he did not race off again. He
was reading Wilhelm Liebknecht's notes on Marx, telling of Marx's
decline in health due to overwork.[75] He therefore resolved to be
'docile and tractable'[76] and devote himself to fighting the illness 'as
I would to fighting a by-election'. In fact, he spent his time finishing
a report on Haldane's Army Act, and starting his tract, *From Serfdom
to Socialism*. He was ill enough to say, 'I pray that the end may be
sudden when it comes. A lingering illness must be dreadful.'[77]

On the wider political front, Hardie was worried that Labour's cause
was ebbing away, even 'the cartoonists seem to be forgetting us'.[78] He
must have been cheered by the return to Parliament of Pete Curran
in June at a by-election in Jarrow (where he stood foursquare against
the Liberals as a representative of 'unskilled and poorly paid toilers'),[79]
and by the miraculous revival of socialist hopes in Colne Valley a few
weeks later, where a twenty-five-year-old with a wonderful speaking
voice, who had until only a few months earlier been a Unitarian
divinity student in Manchester, suddenly appeared, preaching 'plain,
strong and richly defined socialism', according to one of the *Labour
Leader* editors.[80] The young man was Victor Grayson and he got the
enthusiastic support of the local ILP, who were backing him in a
by-election there.

He did not have the support of the Labour Party whose right wing
wanted him disowned for standing as a socialist rather than a Labour
candidate; Party officers were inclined to say nothing, even though
his candidature was not being promoted in line with the Party's
constitution. Hardie took advantage of the 'conscience' decision and
declared that each MP should decide for himself.[81] His choice was
to support indigenous agitation and to send Grayson a message of
best wishes. Perhaps because of this, certainly against all the odds,
this unknown young man, arguing for the socialist millennium in
a wild and charismatic way, won a spectacular victory at the polls,
defeating Liberal and Tory candidates in a seat Labour had agreed not
even to contest, its hopes of winning there were so remote. Snowden
recalled later that the effect of Grayson's election (possibly assisted by
public anger at the much delayed pension provisions promised by the
government) was electric. To many it meant that the 'social revolution
was coming'.[82]

When Grayson arrived in Parliament, however, instead of joining
the Labour Party, he chose to remain aloof, an unfortunate omen,
and another set of troubles which Hardie, had he remained leader,
would have had to tackle. According to Glasier, the Party leadership
had proved 'a . . . misery to him'.[83] Snowden's view, looking back,
was that 'Hardie had not the accommodating spirit which is essential
in a successful parliamentary leader. The humdrum everyday work of
the House of Commons was never to Hardie's taste.'[84]

During this time 'he left the arrangement of business . . . to
Henderson', the Chief Whip. MacDonald, as Secretary, took over
negotiations for the Party. Hardie could never have managed the
compromises that were required in a group that was slowly becoming
a party like any other. Said Snowden, 'Compromise was not in the
man's nature'. He pursued his own goals 'regardless of the hostility of
his enemies and the advice of his friends'. Hardie was 'not a success'
as chairman. Nobody recognized this more than he himself.

Morgan excuses him on the ground that 'imposing a coherent
policy on the Party in Parliament, let alone the rank and file in
the constituencies . . . [was a difficulty] almost insuperable'.[85] Yet
agreeing a policy was precisely what Hardie had claimed was essential
to do, when he proposed the compromise measure that brought it into
being in 1900, and why a socialist commitment had been relinquished.
Morgan puts much of this down to the clash of individuals, but the
failure to develop any ideology was also a large factor. Without
MacDonald and Snowden and Henderson in the House at this time –
compromising daily to cover this over – the new Party might well have
fallen to pieces. MacDonald particularly was able to keep a wide watch
on opinion, and liaise with everyone. He performed essential public
relations tasks, and made speeches, according to Snowden, that 'were

open to any interpretation a person chose to place upon [them]'.[86] In short, he had the gifts Hardie lacked.

During this crucial year Hardie failed to make the Party in Parliament a working political force in partnership with social forces outside. The great apostle of independence left the Party prey to continuing dependence, of which he was going to be the first to complain.

Hardie's escape came in July 1907 when, with the help of friends overseas, and money said to have been donated by the Salvation Army but more likely to have come from his industrialist friend, Joseph Fels,[87] who travelled with him on the first leg of the journey, he set off for his planned trip around the Empire. He called it a fact-finding and speaking tour. Once again Lillie had had to drop her life to play nurse, only to be rewarded by being deserted. The trip served the purpose of disentangling him from his political and personal problems, to shelve responsibility temporarily for both, but opening up an opportunity to see the globe from the perspective he had always had: the world as one common humanity. Local socialists, singing the 'Red Flag', which by now had replaced the Marseillaise for special occasions, saw Hardie off from Liverpool on the SS *Empress of Britain*.[88] Travel always raised his spirits, and his health improved dramatically, a fact which he later put down to having stuck to Scots porridge for breakfast for six days a week throughout all the months he was away.[89]

His first stop was in Canada, where the president of the Canadian TUC presented him with a new walking stick.[90] Then on to Japan, Malaysia and India, where he was warmly received by the Indians, and collected several more walking sticks. It was here the trouble began, when Hardie expressed himself forcibly on the iniquities of the Raj. Official reports grew increasingly more hysterical about his outspoken opinions, although in the House of Commons he had regularly denounced Indian poverty and low wages and the failure of the British to give Indians any say in their own government.[91] He had complained that 'the ordinary affairs of India' could not be discussed when Indians were 'excluded from the higher offices of government in their own country' because the educated English classes wanted to keep India as a preserve for their own sons. 'The sooner the people of India controlled their own affairs the better.'

In India Hardie said India should be as free as Canada to determine its national life. For good measure he also identified corruption in the Raj and spoke out about the racism he observed. Pointedly, whenever any Indian with whom he was travelling was denied entry to any gathering or precinct because of his race, Hardie would also refuse to enter. To put matters right, he advised 'agitation though not violence', and he promised he would relay Indian demands to MPs in Britain 'outside the Labour Party'.[92]

No mercy was to be shown to the leader of the Parliamentary

Labour Party as he made his discerning observations. Intelligence reports relayed that he was consorting with revolutionaries, most of them modern India's founding fathers (including B. G. Tilak, to be jailed a few months later by the British, and S. K. Gokhale) a pacifist colleague of Mahatma Gandhi, also later jailed. His visit was causing immense alarm to the British authorities, whose main concern was to protect British commercial interests. They knew many Indians shared Hardie's view and feared Hardie would give the impression that the Liberal government as well as the Labour Party shared these ideas, which might encourage real rebellion.

As an MP Hardie could not be jailed, so the tactic was to whip up so much hostility to him that he would be asked to leave. The British press co-operated fully, particularly the *Daily Mail*, and Reuters, which Emrys Hughes later suggested played a special intelligence role.[93] Years later, Nan recalled the incredible misrepresentation, particularly the false portrait of him as inciting armed rebellion,[94] a tactic anyone who knew Hardie would know he would never have urged. Indeed, he went out of his way, according to the official report, to insist Indians 'conduct their movements on strictly constitutional principles and with dignity'.[95] But Hardie was an uncompromising speaker and it was not difficult to 'colour' and 'rearrange' his words; or, in the case of the *Daily Mail*, to falsify them. Hardie wrote direct to the *Daily Mail* to say your 'statements are fabrications',[96] but on the same day Reuters cabled falsely that Hardie admitted the statements. 'Thus lie followed lie,' wrote Stewart.

Back in Britain Cunninghame Graham complained about the reporting; even the *Clarion* asked the press to give Hardie a fair hearing.[97] But the charge of sedition had already been made. A *Punch* cartoon showed Britannia gripping the agitator by the scruff of his neck to throw him out. Soon the desired calls for his deportation were being made. And Hardie was called in for redress by British officials and told 'that the literate classes could no more govern India now than the clerkly classes could govern Europe in the middle ages'.[98]

Hardie enjoyed it all, including a love affair with a new mass audience, as Indians in their hundreds of thousands turned out to hear him. They pressed to touch him when he spoke. 'I honestly believe . . . I am being worshipped,' he wrote to Glasier.[99] Even Lenin (whom Joseph Fels had paid for to come to Britain this same year to attend a social democratic congress) was following Hardie's progress with grudging admiration. All this was too much for King Edward VII. It 'makes one's blood boil' to read about that 'scoundrel' Hardie, he wrote later to the Indian viceroy, the Earl of Minto.[100] These reports did Hardie great damage in some parts of British public opinion. As might be expected, however, it cheered his own supporters immensely, and educated them not a little about India. When Hardie returned to the UK he redoubled his attack on conditions under British rule, and kept up the pressure in Parliament for the rest of his life. In a pamphlet he sold for a shilling, called *India: Impressions and Suggestions*, he virtually outlined what was to be the Left's position on India for the next fifty years.

After India came Australia where he provided nothing more controversial than scoring eight runs at cricket against a journalists' team. This proved his health was restored, as did an incident later, when he was thrown from a runaway horse-drawn carriage in New Zealand but got up and walked away.[101] He looked up his old miner colleague, Andrew Fisher, who against all the odds had become the world's first Labour prime minister in Australia, and met Tom Mann and Henry Champion. Mann, never one to stay in the same place long, had returned to trade union activity and was revolutionizing Australian trade union organization.

Hardie's next visit was to South Africa, where he conferred with the suffrage campaigner and pacifist, Olive Schreiner, before proceeding to a tour that was even more controversial than the one of India. Hardie was so immersed in issues of social justice and had so wide an experience and so synthetizing a cast of mind, that, like an experienced doctor who can diagnose simply upon the first sight of a patient, he felt able to speak freely of South Africa's problems from almost the moment he arrived. He immediately raised the issues of poverty and low wages, matters he raised everywhere he went, arguing, as he always did, that the basic problems of Indian workers or black South African miners were the same as the poor of Lanarkshire and South Wales. They were suffering appalling living conditions, while those who oversaw them or who owned the land or the means of employment exploited them and lived well.

But more than this, he looked far over the head of current economic or diplomatic problems, and raised the issue of race, setting an agenda for the Left which has even yet to be completed. The language then in common use may grate badly, but the goal Hardie identified when he said he saw no reason why 'South Africa should be made a white man's country and the nigger kept in his proper place' remains.[102] He suggested trade unions open themselves to blacks; he suggested whites find a way to share the farmland with blacks. Inevitably, Conservative activists, right-wing racists and jingoists dogged his trail, breaking up meetings and smashing windows at the hotels where he stayed. From one meeting he addressed in Johannesburg he was only just rescued in time. While fighting his way out, Hardie grabbed his assailants' Union Jack. Forever after it was displayed on the wall at Neville's Court, his version of a distinguished service medal for his part in the long war against imperialism.

*   *   *

Lochnorris received Hardie's daily communications, as Lillie and Nan continued their life in Scotland. Occasionally, comrades whom Hardie met sent messages, no doubt prompted by Hardie. A gift of a desk to Lillie was accompanied by the usual note to say that the 'women who wait' were just as heroic as those out working for the cause.[103] It hardly felt heroic.

In the autumn of 1907 Christabel and Emmeline changed the rules of the WSPU without consulting anyone, to take more power for themselves. Several key women left in protest over this assault on democracy and the continuing failure to identify with working-class women. Tessa Billington and other democratic socialists joined the Woman's Freedom League, formed to include all social classes. There was a similar split among Scottish women campaigners, where the WSPU was known as the 'direct political daughter of the ILP Keir Hardie'.[104] One of its leaders was Flora Drummond from the Isle of Arran, who had been rejected as a postmistress because she was too short. She remained with the Pankhursts while other Scottish women formed a Scottish version of the Women's Freedom League that based itself on working women's interests. (A Men's League was founded at the same time, backed by Cunninghame Graham.)[105]

In London several WSPU women left to work for wider changes than just the vote. They later called themselves 'feminists'. Dora Montefiore left the WSPU to join the Adult Suffrage League. As its delegate, she attended the International Socialist Women's Conference at Stuttgart in 1907. This was a group of social democratic women who adopted a policy of 'universal womanhood suffrage' and rejected limited measures as an 'adulteration . . . of the principle of political equality of the female sex'.[106] This line, the work of Clara Zetkin of the German Social Democratic Party, and secretary of the newly established International Socialist Women's Bureau,[107] represented social democratic women's response to the potential conflict of gender and class that the WSPU refused to face. Not many ILP women joined, remaining divided between the Pankhursts and the Women's Labour League led by Margaret MacDonald. Thus did the differences between socialist women campaigning for the vote mirror the differences between socialists generally.

During these months of 1907 Sylvia was spared the new autocracy in the WSPU, for she was sent north by the Pethick-Lawrences, commissioned to do drawings of working women, which were printed later in *Votes for Women*. There is every likelihood that she and Hardie had agreed not to communicate during his absence. There is no record of any correspondence, with one exception, and we cannot be sure this was from Hardie. It was a letter that was waiting on Sylvia's hall table when she arrived back in London at Christmas. She wrote years later that it caused her great heartbreak but made no mention of its contents or sender. Romero suggests Hardie wanted to break off their relationship.[108]

There is certainly a very odd letter from Hardie – undated and without signature or heading – that Sylvia kept in her personal archives.'[109] Romero assumes it was written from St Thomas's Hospital in May 1907, but its contents are more appropriate to a situation where they were apart rather than seeing each other on a daily basis. Hardie began by saying, 'I feel as though I had passed through fire and water and a long valley of bitterness.' He is unable, he writes, to 'feel keenly . . . things that I would wish to feel'. And he cries out, 'I prayed. I longed. I cried in agony to be more stollid [sic] and self-contained – I feel I AM now.' Yet, he did not wish to 'lose the power to pour myself out for others and to forget myself in enthusiasm' or lose that 'ability to be . . . all but consumed with grief even for slight things . . . so too I shall lose the power to love without reserve'. At this point the letter ends with a sad extra line, 'I wonder – when will you write to me again.'

It is the letter of a man who has renounced, and at terrible cost. Whether this was the letter which so disturbed Sylvia and which she described as 'killing my inner life, transforming . . . a pleasant garden . . . to a waste and barren place',[110] we cannot know. Only that she reports that her sorrow over it was 'dispelled as suddenly as it came'. If it was Hardie who had caused it, he soon put it right. Whether the Hardie letter was written while he was struggling against illness – or against his feelings for Sylvia – it was characteristic of Hardie's depressive side when facing the common human dilemma of how to lead a life of self-control but at the same time continue to feel deeply.

While he was travelling, Hardie wrote to Snowden[111] to give advance notice that he would not be standing for leader of the Parliamentary Labour Party in 1908. 'My strongest reason for desiring to get out of the Chair is that I may be free to speak out.' Hardie was worried that Labour in Parliament was losing its identity. He suggested a new group in Parliament, 'those of us . . . who are socialists and who believe in fighting will have to get together occasionally on our own account, and if we cannot drag the party with us, we will "gan oor ain gait".'

Hardie had reason to worry. Looking back on this time from the 1920s, a Labour commentator said Labour parliamentary activity was 'indistinguishable from that of the radical wing of the Liberal Party'.[112] During the winter of Hardie's absence only Grayson had seemed to challenge the drift. He put down a resolution at the Labour Party Conference (opposed by Shackleton in the chair) calling on the Party to adopt 'socialisation of the means of production, distribution and exchange to be controlled by the democratic state in the interests of the entire community', to free labour from capitalism and 'establish economic equality between the sexes'. Unexpectedly, enough trade union delegates voted for it to pass it. Had Grayson been bending his efforts to effect socialist and trade union unity, it might have been significant. But he still held aloof from Labour. No one knew where he stood. Max Beer of *Vorwärts* wrote that he still had a lot to learn about socialism.[113]

So too did the Labour Party. Snowden, looking back, confirmed that after 1906 the Labour Party had indeed 'abandoned' much of its social propaganda in society at large and had made a 'shift' to parliamentary activity.[114] Frank Smith's worry was different again, the new parliamentary leadership 'is likely to lack the determined note'.[115] Though Hardie had stood down as leader, Smith wrote Glasier, 'He always will be' – which is possibly what annoyed MacDonald. Glasier compared the two men at this time. MacDonald was 'always given . . . to modifications which irritate'. He preferred Hardie's 'great intuition in keeping in touch with democratic emotion and his rocklike attitude in Parliament'. Hardie was unique, 'none of the other men have any "religious power"'.[116]

To welcome Hardie back to Britain in the spring of 1908, Frank Smith organized a 'big meeting' on 8 April. For the first time in the history of either the ILP or the Labour Party the largest venue in London, the Albert Hall, was being hired. MacDonald was asked to chair the event, but he was not happy. His feelings for Hardie had not improved during Hardie's absence. On the political side, he had to contend with all Hardie was saying, and its effects on the Party in Parliament. On the personal side, he was nursing a grievance regarding his own foreign trips which had not received the same attention. During the previous year Hardie had also continued making policy on his own, MacDonald being particularly infuriated that Hardie had proposed a Right to Work Bill without consulting anyone and had made an 'unauthorized and inaccurate' statement not approved by the Labour Party. This was on top of Hardie's 'utter neglect of parliamentary business' while he was leader.[117] Parliament was much more central to MacDonald's political life than Hardie's. Hardie's life's work among the people MacDonald downgraded as 'tub-thumping' and mere 'platform idealism', while criticizing those who saw 'policy' issues as 'marks of the beast'.[118] MacDonald, labouring with Jim Middleton at pedestrian tasks, approved those 'who care for administration and do not put their trust in fireworks and windbags'.

His resentment of Hardie had some justification. Hardie had ducked his leadership responsibilities. He did care less for the Labour Party in Parliament than he did for the ILP; and he did believe that

agitation was more important than administration. But he did not
neglect policy; he just had different views about what it should
be. He was more popular with the rank and file than MacDonald,
which MacDonald, and to a certain extent Glasier, put down to his
uncontrollable lust for attention; 'the showman business is one of my
most deep seated antipathies' to him, MacDonald wrote to Glasier
later.[119] MacDonald tried to present Hardie as a cheap entertainer
and he hated Frank Smith for being a mere 'agent' for the 'circus',
and Fels for paying for it.[120] But when the time came he chaired the
Albert Hall meeting.

Fears that the hall might not be full were swept aside, as every seat
was taken and standing room filled. When Hardie got up to speak
it was fully ten minutes before he could be heard. Red flags and
white handkerchiefs were waved; 'For He's A Jolly Good Fellow'
was repeatedly sung. When at last the cheers ended, and Hardie had
given his report on his tour – continually interrupted by applause –
he was in a mischievous mood. He had read the press, he said, and
realized he 'was not a success as a political leader'. But then he had
never posed as a leader. He had not even tried to please the Labour
Party. His whole work had been one long attempt to make peace
with his own conscience. To renewed cheering, he added resolutely,
'I am an agitator. My work has consisted of trying to stir up a divine
discontent with wrong. With what remains of my life I intend to
follow the same course.'[121]

10

ACTION VERSUS IDEOLOGY

'We are in for a big Hardie boom,' wrote Glasier just after Hardie
had returned from his Empire trip.[1] But other events soon overshadowed it. Asquith took over from the dying Campbell-Bannerman as
Prime Minister, Lloyd George became the Chancellor, and Winston
Churchill, a rising Liberal, was defeated in a by-election in Manchester.
Emmeline and the WSPU suffragettes campaigned vigorously against
him, and were widely credited with having influenced the result.

Whether or not Hardie had tried to use the world trip to break
it off with Sylvia, he could not ignore the WSPU campaigns. He
wrote to Glasier shortly after his return that Emmeline Pankhurst's
acts were 'folly' and 'will in time drive all the better spirits out of

the WSPU which is destined to become to the women's movement what the SDF has been to socialism'.[2]

He cautioned, however, that 'we don't want it to look like the ILP drove them out' because women 'look to the ILP to fight their battle'.[3] He decided the battle on behalf of women – against both main political parties – had to take precedence over WSPU folly. In short, he found a way to fall right back in with Sylvia and WSPU work. His colleagues continued to search for the reason why he chose to limit his support for women to an organization that was increasingly separating itself from both Labour and socialist politics. Glasier could only conclude, 'I fancy I can detect a conscious desire on his part to figure in history as the women's champion.'[4] That was hardly generous. Hardie was wholly committed to the cause, and at a time when the Labour Party offered little else to commit him. Besides, the demonstrations women were now beginning to organize were irresistible and overrode all his misgivings.

He took his full part in the mammoth women's day event in June in Hyde Park (paid for by the Pethick-Lawrences, who also paid for the women's fair a year later). Sylvia helped in the making of the white/green/purple banners being sold in London in special WSPU shops, and led the Chelsea contingent of 7,000 women. Hardie carried a banner in the procession that said, 'The World for the Worker'.[5] He was also among the twenty-one speakers on several platforms, sitting with the George Bernard Shaws and the H. G. Wellses.

Speaking too was Mrs Thomas Hardy, whose husband was one of the few writers who had tried his hand at what he called that 'delicate task' of making an intimate relationship between working-class and upper-class characters central to a novel.[6] So forbidden was sexual liaison across the class line at the time it was written, 1895, that he asked the reader's 'pardon' for presenting the working-class heroine and her family as 'beings who come within the scope of congenial regard'. In a preface to the same work seventeen years later, however,[7] Hardy was able to say that 'the subject of this book was growing more welcome', for nowadays 'servants were as important as . . . masters'. The labour movement had made them so, while the suffrage movement had underlined women's freedom of will, and socialism had provided a social context in which liaisons across class lines were supported.

This made it easier for Hardie to be with Sylvia, although most of his colleagues had little awareness of their growing intimacy. When they saw them together, on the terrace at the House of Commons, for example, they assumed it was just another suffrage tête-à-tête.

But there could be complications. On one occasion Hardie had to call off a plan to visit Sylvia because it meant going through Hyde Park, where a public meeting was taking place at which he had refused to speak on grounds of a previous engagement. His letter[8] asked Sylvia to come to Neville's Court instead and prescribed the route carefully. Romero is not sure whether this was to avoid her being seen arriving or to protect a woman alone.[9] It is much more likely to ensure that Sylvia did not run across the meeting either. In general, they did not hide themselves. They would often go for walks in the park, and later,[10] when Hardie was convalescing from illness and stayed at the Roebuck Hotel on Richmond Hill, Sylvia would journey down and spend the day, sitting on the terrace or walking with him in Richmond Park, while he enthused about the nightingales. On these occasions he told her about his childhood and she poured out whatever was on her mind; and, as she reported, they were often 'merry' together.

Sylvia wanted to keep up her commitment to socialism and working-class politics – as well as to shine in the WSPU. Unlike her sister and mother, who grew more fashionable every year, she began dressing increasingly 'like a young working-class woman', according to Fenner Brockway.[11] Although inexperienced with men until she met Hardie, Sylvia nevertheless held 'advanced' views on sexual matters which were shortly to be proclaimed. She admitted no barriers of class or age. She had no religious guilt, having been brought up an atheist – possibly likely to increase her appeal to Hardie, since the only other close relationship he had ever had with a non-believer was with his mother. Sylvia in return identified Hardie with her father and his causes, and saw him as a protector. But she never subordinated herself to him. She always insisted that her own concerns should have equal prominence in all they said and did together. This is what saved her in the end.

Frank Smith was well aware of Sylvia's many visits to Neville's Court, where she brought work to do alongside Hardie, or sat and listened to his readings from Burns or Whitman, sharing tea from the hob. It was there she did her two portraits of him, an early one, showing a kindly Hardie, and a later one in chalk, older and more care-lined.[12]

Other visitors who came to see Hardie would often find Sylvia there. Fenner Brockway, the young journalist whom Hardie had personally converted to socialism during an interview,[13] remembered, 'I used to go to . . . his rooms. Sylvia would be there . . . they did not hide their attraction . . . I remember her sitting on his knee with her arms around his neck.'[14] Hardie gave no indication to close friends that he regarded his behaviour with Sylvia as dishonourable in any way. Brockway was very surprised to learn later in his life that many people thought Hardie and Sylvia had had an affair.[15] Then again, he could remember nothing being said about Lillie or Hardie's home. Looking back, he admitted, 'There really was a deep silence about it.'[16]

Yet Hardie constantly had Lillie on his mind – and the need to

(*Above*) Keir Hardie (front left) with his original family (circa 1890): his mother, Mary, and stepfather, David Hardie, with sisters Elizabeth and Agnes, and brothers David, George, William and Alexander

(*Right*) Keir Hardie at 16: taken in a Glasgow studio. Almost the only known photograph without a beard

(*Below*) Lillie Hardie aged about 30 with the Hardie family dog; and the Hardie children Nan, Jamie, and Duncan (Cumnock, circa 1890)

(*Above*) R. G. Cunninghame Graham (left, painted by Lavery) and Keir Hardie (in the 1892 election) pictured together by Henry Pelling in *The Origins of the Labour Party*, 1965, and captioned 'First Socialist MPs'

(*Left*) Keir Hardie standing on the steps of Lochnorris, the home the Hardies built in old Cumnock, Ayrshire, in 189[...]

(*Below*) Keir Hardie and Lillie in 1902, with Roy, the family dog. They are in the 'summer house' behind Lochnorris

(*Above*) Keir Hardie addressing an open air meeting

(*Right*) Keir Hardie (centre) with local friends on the Italian Riviera near Bordighera, 1904, when Hardie was recovering from his appendectomy; and (*far right*) Jamie, Duncan and Nan Hardie (circa 1900), posing for the usual family greeting card sent at the end of each year

The inner circle of the Independent Labour Party, 1905. From left: T. D. Benson, Keir Hardie, James Parker, Philip Snowden, Bruce Glasier, Ramsay MacDonald

Keir Hardie and Emmeline Pankhurst (right) speaking at a suffragette rally in Trafalgar Square, May 19, 1906

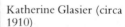

Katherine Glasier (circa 1910)

Keir Hardie as leader of the Parliamentary Labour Party, 1906, newly assembled at the House of Commons. Front from left: Arthur Henderson, Ramsay MacDonald, Keir Hardie, David Shackleton. Back from left, George Barnes, Philip Snowden, John Hodge, Will Crooks, James O'Grady

(*Above*) The Social Democrats in 1910, A. Purcell, Dan Irving, Harry Quelch, Henry Hyndman

Maggie Symons at work in Hardie's political office (circa 1910)

Postcard to Agnes Hughes from the last Conference Hardie ever attended of the ILP, 1915.

Independent Labour Party
ST. BRIDE'S HOUSE, SALISBURY SQUARE, FLEET STREET, LONDON, E.C.

14496

Dear A - The spirit animating the Congress is splendid, and hitherto not a discordant word has been spoken. E. told me of his intentions. I regret them for the sake of the movement, but it will be best for him. Regards all round J.K.H.

(*Left*) George Bernard Shaw (*at right*) and his wife Charlotte arrive in Merthyr to campaign for Hardie, January 1910. With them is Revd. Geoffrey Ramsay

(*Below left*) Sylvia Pankhurst (second left) with Emily Wilding Davison, Christabel Pankhurst and Emmeline Pethick Lawrence in a suffffragette demonstration, 1911

(*Below*) Keir Hardie and Lillie posing in a studio (circa 1912)

(*Foot*) Keir Hardie with his women's election team, Merthyr, 1910. Rose Davies is on the right

(*Left*) Keir Hardie presented with a daisy by a young member of the audience (circa 1914)

(*Below*) Keir Hardie working in Neville's Court (circa 1910)

(*Foot*) Emrys Hughes (left) and his second wife, Mattie (right), entertain Jean Stoddart Keir Hardie Scott, Keir Hardie's granddaughter, and Dolores May Arias, his great-granddaughter, on a visit to Lochnorris in 1964

(*Above*) Keir Hardie visiting the Hughes family in Abercynon, 1913. The Reverend John Hughes sits beside him; Rowlie and Aggie Hughes are behind them

(*Right*) Emrys Hughes just before his imprisonment as a conscientious objector in World War I

(*Right*) The Hardie family in the garden at Lochnorris after the outbreak of World War I. Duncan stands beside his father, Nan sits beside her mother. Lillie's sister is on the right
(*Below*) Wedding photographs of Jamie Hardie and May Stoddart, New York, August 1912

(*Above*) Aggie and Hedley Dennis with their dog, Turk, visiting Lochnorris, 1927

(*Above right*) Sylvia Pankhurst (left) leads a deputation of old age pensioners from London's East End to see the Prime Minister, 1915

(*Right*) Nan and Lillie at Lochnorris in the early 1920s

(*Left*) A bust commissioned from Benno Schot 1939, Cumnock High Street, Ayrshire

(*Below*) A popular Hardie postcard made from photograph taken in June 1893, possibly to exchange with Annie Hines

(*Above*) Hardie depicte by 'Spy' in *Vanity Fair*

(*Left*) A portrait in charcoal and crayon by Sylvia Pankhurst (circa 1911). It is now in the possession of the National Portrait Galle and (*far left*) Another popular postcard commissioned from Cosm Rowe (circa 1906)

assuage his neglect of her, all the more so since, although she may not have been mentioned, it was not class that was the barrier between Sylvia and Hardie, or even differences in religion and age. It was Lillie.

Hardie told women to agitate, because the more they 'agitate . . . the more clearly will the root cause of all their trouble' be seen, economic dependence on men.[17] Lillie seemed to confirm this constantly.

Immediately upon his return from America Lillie had joined him in London, and they travelled to the ILP Easter Conference in Huddersfield. The issue of Grayson was coming up: should he be endorsed by the ILP or not? Hardie was still willing to give him the benefit of the doubt, but had written to Glasier that 'Grayson . . . needs careful handling'.[18] So too did Lillie. In the same letter Hardie said, 'She has had a lot to try her during my absence and her nerves have given way under the strain. If she doesn't mend we shall flit to London.'

Lillie managed to last out the conference and later travelled with Hardie to Bradford, where, he reported, 'Jowett presented her with a very handsome dressing case. It was nice of them.'[19] Hardie appreciated whatever comrades could do for Lillie and expressed the hope to Glasier that the next time Lillie came to London, she could 'break the journey at Chapel-en-le-Frith' and visit the Glasiers. We get the impression he wanted comrades to give her the attention he could not.

The main business of that ILP Conference was to declare once again its opposition to the Russian government and its 'infamous tyranny' which 'condemned great numbers of our Russian comrades to imprisonment, torture and death' – so ran the resolution.[20] The Russian cause still loomed large in the life of the labour and socialist movements in Europe. Thus Hardie was dismayed when King Edward VII announced shortly after that he was going on an official visit to Czar Nicholas II. Hardie protested in Parliament, accusing the King of going in order to render Russia safe for European capitalists to exploit; he was condoning Russian 'atrocities'. There was a momentary parliamentary crisis over Hardie's use of the word 'atrocities',[21] which he was repeatedly asked by the Speaker to withdraw, and repeatedly refused (until forced by colleagues in order that the House's business could continue).

When the Czar was invited to return the visit and sailed in to Cowes, Hardie was one of the first to speak out against this visit as well. Speaking in Arthur Henderson's constituency, he predicted that the Czar 'would not dare to set foot on British soil'.[22] In Parliament he made it even plainer: the Czar 'did not represent the people of Russia and King Edward did not represent the people of Great Britain'.[23] Though Labour's motion to denounce the visit was defeated in the

House, in fact the Czar did exactly as Hardie predicted. He never left his ship at Cowes.

Although Hardie's attacks against the Czar were part of his long-standing campaign against tyrannical governments, many, including Edward VII, saw the criticism as just another round in his equally long-standing campaign against royalty. On his return from Russia in 1908, therefore, the King ordered the names of Hardie, along with Grayson, a third MP with bad debts, and Arthur Ponsonby, a newly elected Liberal who had supported Hardie in condemning his visit, to be struck off the summer's garden party list. According to Hardie it was the Prince of Wales who was really behind it, using almost exactly the same words as had been used by the colliery manager nearly thirty years earlier when Hardie was dismissed from his job as a miner: 'We don't want that bloody agitator among us.'[24]

The ban had the same long-term result. Garden parties, held each summer at Windsor (today, at Buckingham Palace) were mammoth affairs to which MPs, among countless others, received invitations. It was their official seal of acceptability; and the press played up Hardie's 'exclusion' for all it was worth. Living in a tight political world, the King was no doubt assured that after Hardie's exploits in India, ostracizing him would be approved by the mass of conservative trade union MPs. He was mistaken. At a public meeting in Stockport Hardie replied that 'the incident shall not be allowed to pass'. He said that he would always be a republican and would never attend a garden party, but 'I don't receive these invitations because I am Keir Hardie but because . . . I . . . represent the working classes of Merthyr Tydfil'.[25] Labour MPs reacted as to a social insult to their class – an injury to one is an injury to all. The Party sent word that none would attend any future royal event unless Hardie was also invited. The King had to climb down. Since then monarchs have taken more care to keep their views to themselves. The event was also significant for the Labour Party, for as A. J. P. Taylor said years later, it was 'the first occasion when the Labour Party claimed its share in the establishment'.[26] Hardie would not have liked that interpretation at all.

Hardie was glad when the August recess came in 1908. Instead of the usual summer sojourn in Cumnock, he decided on yet another Atlantic crossing, this time taking Lillie and Nan, their big reward for waiting patiently: a trip to Nova Scotia for a Dominion Trade Union Congress in Halifax. Before leaving he claimed he was going to further the plans he had discussed on his earlier Empire world trip, to organize 'a Federation of all Labour Parties within the Empire'.[27] They sailed from Glasgow and it was almost certainly Lillie's and Nan's first visit outside the British Isles – undoubtedly paid for by the ever-present Joseph Fels, who accompanied them.

Fels was an extremely likeable character with a genuine desire to assist working-class leaders like Hardie and Lansbury, who he believed embodied the entrepreneurial spirit in its best form. Hardie in turn tried to persuade him about socialism and they corresponded for years, but Fels was not persuaded.[28] Nor would he ever contribute to the ILP.[29] Hardie's colleagues did not like this personal patronage approach. Glasier particularly felt Hardie was wasting his time. Glasier had met Fels only a few months earlier in Manchester where Fels tried to persuade him that millionaires like himself could help Labour. Glasier replied, 'I declared they could not. Their money only ... corrupts it.'[30] It was exactly at this time that Snowden wrote mysteriously to MacDonald[31] that he knew 'of things' which Hardie had done 'of which I have been ashamed for the sake of the movement'.

Hardie was treated respectfully, particularly in Canada, where he was the darling of all the political parties. Stewart comments that the presence of Lillie and Nan meant Hardie did not fall into 'propaganda traps lying in wait for him everywhere',[32] which the press, always following, loved to spring. He managed to get away briefly for a visit to the USA, where he took the salute at the Labor Day parade in New York City, watching thousands of teamsters and 'housesmiths' marching past in 'red blouses, white trousers and grey hats'.[33] Debs was running for president, living aboard his Campaign Train, 'The Red Special'. According to Hughes, Hardie firmly believed that the United States would 'see the first socialist government in the modern world'.[34] Hardie loved the USA, and he was back yet again a few months later for another brief visit.[35]

In the autumn the British section of the Socialist International Bureau held a meeting in London to welcome the respected German socialist, Karl Kautsky. The main business, held in St James's Hall, Piccadilly, was to denounce the idea of war between Germany and Britain. Unfortunately, there was a sharp disagreement among socialists about what was to be done. Hyndman, who chaired the meeting, supported a citizens' army – in line with the Second International's earlier endorsement of the abolition of standing armies, a call one hundred years old;[36] Hardie, who also spoke, opposed all armies, 'whether citizen or by whatever name'.[37]

Owing to the formalized split between socialists in the UK, as well as to the doctrinaire nature of the European parties, discussion on the risk of war had not taken place among European socialists and trade unionists in any real depth. Now in the Socialist International there were severe differences between German and French socialists (as well as within the German ranks). On this occasion the Germans were particularly hostile to anti-militarist opinion. These general differences were being covered up by the International's leaders[38] in the interests of harmony. Even those as close as Hardie and Sylvia were not communicating on this subject. Years later Sylvia remembered Hardie's own passionate agitation about conscription in relation to Haldane's Bill. She admitted she had failed entirely to understand its significance at the time.[39] Once again, the spectre of war was banished by Europe's socialists on this occasion – as on others – by passing a strong resolution against it.

Such meetings underlined the poverty of ideology within the British labour movement and among socialists who supported an alliance with it. In 1908 the ILP, at last aware of the gap, started a theoretical journal, the *Socialist Review*. Its first edition, of March 1908, featured the correspondence between Marx and Engels and Victor Sorge, the last secretary of the First International.

At about this same time Hardie's long essay, *From Serfdom to Socialism*, was also published. Although Hardie found 'theoretical disputation among socialists . . . distasteful'[40] and had singed his wings over the class-war issue, where he had confused the concepts of class-hatred and class-consciousness, he wanted to try again. His earlier views had caused much puzzlement among continental socialists, for whom the struggle between economic interests was a central belief. The general opinion was that here was a man who disowned the class war in theory, yet in reality fought it harder than anyone else.[41] This was certainly the verdict of the Second International's International Bureau on the Labour Party; for, finally, that autumn the Party was admitted formally to the International, the vote supported by both Kautsky and Lenin (with Hyndman against) on the grounds that 'although it does not avowedly recognize the class struggle, it actually carries it on . . . because the Labour Party, being independent of bourgeois parties, is based upon class struggle'.[42]

It was largely on Hardie's own record that this was based, for it was his uncompromising defence of working-class interests by which he and the parties with which he was associated were best known. As Glasier commented, neither Henderson nor MacDonald had that 'instinct of agitation'[43] which Hardie continued to display, as good as his word, stirring up divine discontent, using 'discontent' as William Morris had used it, to criticize modern civilization for being in a position to give everyone a good life but failing to do so.[44]

In writing *From Serfdom to Socialism*, Hardie said his aim was not a learned treatise, as 'these things have been done by other . . . hands',[45] but to continue with his thesis that it was not class-consciousness among the working class he wanted, but rather that the working class become conscious of socialism. This appears to be a tautology until he goes on to say that the object is not to pit human against human but for socialism to 'blend . . . the classes into one human family'. Hardie started, rather than ended, with Marx's classless society. *From Serfdom to Socialism* reflects on the human family's pilgrimage towards this goal. 'Socialism is not . . . recently invented [but] woven from the same loom as the vision of Isaiah and the Kingdom of God the early Christians believed to be at hand.'

Hardie saw the struggle for social justice as one long historic movement carried on by men as different as Plato and Spartacus, the Levellers and Huss, Morris and Marx. But it also came through events and movements like the Peasants' Revolt, the French Revolution and the Chartists. Each event, like each person, added something unique. In *From Serfdom to Socialism* class overrides gender. In considering the 'woman question', Hardie says that neither changes in 'franchise laws' nor even in the marriage laws 'will . . . materially alter her condition'. Only socialism will bring women, as men, freedom to 'live and the means of life in exchange for performance of some duty to the community'.[46]

It is a piece of writing that can easily be faulted. Hardie as ideologue has never commanded respect from intellectuals; he does not, for example, appreciate the Marxist meaning of materialism. He evades all economic theory. He is naïve in assuming 'the enlightened capitalist will be as anxious to bring . . . the human interest . . . about as the enlightened workman'; but the essay is entirely consistent with Hardie's humanitarian values.

Although his socialism incorporated religious movements, there is no hint that human beings need to change. What is required is 'a new form . . . of social organization'. Communism is the name Hardie gives to this society. Its base is both ethical and economic, 'Communism . . . is a form of social economy very closely akin to the principles set forth in the Sermon on the Mount.' Hardie believed 'communism' in goods was practised by Christians for at least 300 years after the death of Christ and that St James in his Epistle 'rivals the old prophets in his treatment of those who grow rich at the expense of the poor'.[47] Christianity's communist phase ended with Constantine and the consolidation of a 'state' church in Rome. Hardie did not believe the Reformation provided the antidote, for he saw it as having unleashed into society a destructive and selfish individualism. The injustices that existed thousands of years ago, existed still. So did the remedies. Socialism was the first step. Putting his own period's events in the context of the past, Hardie saw that state socialism would be followed by communism, just as Early Christianity had followed from the Old Testament prophets.

Thus Hardie's socialism was not defined historically or economically but culturally – a 'political force' akin to the 'life force' of Shaw's *Man and Superman*. He perceived human society as being in a steady state of ever-recurring build-up to communism, followed by break-down and renewed rebuilding. Although it is written as prose, the essay is a long, Whitmanesque prose poem, and might be read as such. Morgan appreciated this analogy.[48]

From Serfdom to Socialism was Hardie's attempt to synthetize his moral, spiritual, political and economic beliefs into a single document. What holds it together is not his intellectual argument or ideological insight, nor yet his religious conviction, but his humanitarian passion for all who are exploited, oppressed, cheated and enslaved by a social and economic system that exalts those who own and invest rather than those who create and labour. It was not (as no theory ever was with Hardie) a substitute for face-to-face agitation that impelled people to think about taking action themselves. It was meant to help in the educating of public opinion; for Hardie's view was that 'public opinion is a manufactured article, and represents that amount of agitation and education which any given cause has been able to exert upon the community'.[49]

Achieving socialism was thus a matter of education. This had been Robert Owen's view, and one that the elder Liebknecht had come to as well, moving away from advocating overthrow by revolution to overthrow by education. Hardie had already written, 'No revolution can succeed without the force of public opinion behind it'.[50] What he seriously underestimated were the forces building up against socialism, against himself, and even against the moderate trade unions.

The Prince of Wales had written to his father after the 1906 election that the return of so many Labour MPs was 'rather a dangerous sign' – to which he added, 'I hope they are not all Socialists'.[51] He was expressing the fears then invading the top ranks of society. After 1906 anti-socialism became serious business for the makers of opinion representing the interests of capital. Socialism had become a cause which now had a widespread following, if only because a feature of political reporting during this and earlier periods – absent today – was the willingness of newspapers to print political speeches in full, those made in Parliament, on the hustings and at foreign congresses – including socialist speeches. It was not only *Merrie England* that increasingly literate working people could read; it was socialist speakers almost every day, their arguments presented in their own words, not mediated by 'commentators'. Editorials may have denounced the arguments, but the arguments themselves – for unemployment relief, or votes for women, or tax on unearned incomes – were widely relayed to a new mass readership in the words of those who argued for them. During the years when socialism was an exotic curiosity, this practice posed no threat to established opinion. Years later, once Labour became a government – indeed, once the Russian Revolution had succeeded – the practice changed dramatically and in most papers political issues were automatically reported from an anti-socialist perspective.[52]

It was in 1906, when a shadow no larger than thirty men appeared in Parliament, that the anti-socialist lobby began to form. It spawned bodies such as the Anti-Socialist League (which harassed Hardie particularly) and 'The Enemies of the Red Flag'. A.J. Balfour sounded the alarm in the preface to *The Case Against Socialism*, brought out at the same time and by the same publisher as Hardie's *From Serfdom to Socialism*, to warn that socialism 'has now come down from the study of the nineteenth century theorist to the marketplace adn the street corner'.[53]

The Conservative press had been particularly alarmed by Grayson. Thus the *Daily Express* after his election, 'Social revolution [is] no less disastrous . . . accomplished without bloodshed at the polls.'[54] But it was clear that the target was the Labour Party, which, said Balfour, receives 'far too little attention from the opponents of Socialism'.[55] Just when Hardie had almost begun to give up on the Labour Party for its failure to pose any threat to the system, it began to be attacked for posing too great a one. Ironically, such hostile propaganda probably helped to consolidate support for it. So too support for closer links with Liberals, for just as Hardie was in despair about a Labour Party dominated by Liberals, anti-socialists proclaimed Liberals had been taken over by socialism. Proposals for income tax in 1906 were 'regarded as confiscation' by the Right, and the Liberals were said to have introduced a 'Red Flag Budget'.[56] Reporting became more aggressive – the treatment of Hardie in India being one example. It became more personal. Snowden, who had a leg deformity, was described as a near-ghoul, a man who 'gives us the creeps'.[57] Conservatives commissioned popular music hall artists to adapt popular songs to denigrate socialism, some mentioning Hardie,[58] and new tracts proliferated,[59] calling up spectres of the French Revolution and the Commune, implying that socialists aimed to see these upheavals repeated. It was not hard to find a few who did, particularly in the SDF. But anti-socialists quoted with equal alarm the tactics of the Fabians with their 'infiltration' policy – Shaw's boasts particularly. Like more recent anti-Left argument, no attempt was made to distinguish between constitutional and anti-constitutional opinion. Christian socialists were attacked equally with secular, and Roman Catholics were reminded of the Pope's encyclical of 1891 condemning socialism,[60] as Catholic Socialist Societies began to appear. Willie Gallagher, a young dock worker, formed one on the Clyde in 1906 and socialist newspapers like *Forward* started separate Catholic Socialist columns. Hardie was always liberally quoted and so too were many women, for anti-socialist argument was hostile to female suffrage and linked it to 'free thinking' and immorality, all claimed as the products of socialism. Socialism meant the end of marriage, for example, the forcible introduction of free love, and the removal of children who would henceforth belong to the state, which would see that all relationships were 'regulated'. There was no attempt to distinguish[61] between the tame arguments of Ethel Snowden who merely advanced the case for easier divorce and civil marriage, and those of Harry Quelch who had said, 'I do want to abolish marriage. I do want to see the whole system . . . swept away . . . We do want free love . . . no sexual bonds except those based on no other foundation than mutual affection'[62] – a view which Sylvia Pankhurst was soon to express as well. As we know, it was not the view Hardie and most people in the labour movement held.

Communism, Hardie's goal in *From Serfdom to Socialism*, was not a problem to anti-socialists or to anyone else in pre-1917 Europe. 'Communism . . . is now generally regarded as an effete . . . form of socialism,' said one anti-socialist tract, more to do with Thomas More's *Utopia* and early nineteenth-century poets.[63] It was 'collectivism' they feared. Collectivism is socialism that 'can only be realized through the state and which must have a whole nation as a subject on which to operate'. In particular, collective ownership of land and the means of production. This last, said a think-tank of right-wing authors, was 'the GREAT test'.[64]

What worried the Right was that collectivism was actually taking root in the UK. They blamed themselves in part for the fact that trade unionists, hitherto a malleable quantity of respectable workers who knew their place, had been lured into alliance with socialists through the LRC, which would have failed had it not been for the Taff Vale decision in the Lords. Looking back, Tories after 1906 were scathing about this ill-judged decision on the part of the legal system, which put an end to strikes and thus to 'the safety valve to industrial and artisan discontent' which strikes had afforded.[65]

There had been alarm in 1906 when the Labour Party had decided that no trade union candidates would be supported by Labour where they wee not in the Labour Party itself. There was even more alarm when, finally, in 1909, the last of the large unions, the miners, joined the Labour Party – making a contingent in Parliament of forty-five supporting the Labour Party. The *Daily Express* tolled the bell, 'The Labour Party has won trade unionism from Liberalism.'[66]

The task of routing Labour now assumed a new importance and there were attempts to woo the unions back into the Liberal fold by frightening them with socialism. The mild-mannered Labour Party, Liberal trade unionists were informed, 'is little else than the Independent Labour Party' but kept hidden so unions do not find out.[67] Hardie would have had a wry smile at that; and at this: some socialists were given the special job of keeping 'the full socialist fare' constantly watered down to assist this deception, none more 'skilful beyond the ordinary' in this than J. Ramsay MacDonald. More convincing was the argument that the Labour Party's leaders always voted against changing its constitution (in a more socialist direction) because they fear 'a rupture with trade unions' who support it with their funds. For Conservatives and Liberals anxious to prove that within the working class 'many . . . are bitterly opposed to socialism', what better advocate than John Burns? Burns, now a government minister, was a great favourite with anti-socialists. In 1907 he reminded the Labour Party that it had been 'elected by Radical enthusiasm, Liberal votes and trade union funds'.[68]

It was not long before right-wing union men like Burns, who were still in the Liberal fold, realized that breaking the union connection was the key. Richard Bell, who had originally been elected with Hardie, had by 1908 turned against what he called 'The Socialist Labour Party', and saw himself as campaigning on behalf of 'thousands of trade unionists' who objected to their money, paid for improving their own conditions, being put to wider social objectives.[69] Bell was a member of the Society of Railway Servants and opposed to the constitutional changes his union had been making since 1900 in order to levy members for political action. Perhaps not by coincidence, it was another Railway Servant, a station porter at Clapham Junction named W. V. Osborne, who began a challenge in the courts to test the legality of the levy in relation to union law. The lower court decided it was legal, but the House of Lords reversed the decision at the end of 1908, which made the basis of Labour Party funding illegal. This was the first big victory for the anti-socialists; but, like the Taff Vale judgment, it did not necessarily drive trade unionists away from the Labour Party. If anything, struggling to get the law reversed gave the Labour Party a new fighting cause of its own in Parliament at a time when it had few others.

In the autumn of 1908 Hardie planned to return to the issue of unemployment, which was rising menacingly with another deepening recession. Now that he had secured from government the important principle that charity could no longer provide for society's basic needs, he was adding to his list of public works which would meet needs as well as provide employment: road repairs, coastal protection, sewer construction, hospital building and renewing forests. 'This government has not planted a single tree!'[70] he proclaimed, a cry that had to wait for over sixty years to be appreciated. The *Labour Leader* had also campaigned against 'the rabid destruction of the American forests . . . to the utter disregard for the common welfare and the rights of posterity'. This was another cry no one in 1906 heard.[71]

Hardie was looking forward to new effectiveness in Parliament because, out of the blue, Maggie Symons had returned from Egypt. He telegraphed her with joy to 'fire up as from October 14th'.[72] This was followed by a letter to say that 'under your changed circumstances the old happy go lucky financial arrangements ... [are] no longer to be thought of'. That such an advanced egalitarian was only now considering paying Maggie (and only because her husband had left her) what he called a 'full-time living wage', so strongly insisted on for men, is an indication less of Hardie's caution with money than of the undeveloped state of the women's movement. Suffrage had usurped every issue relating to women's lives, and demands in other directions were still struggling for recognition. Without waiting for her reply, Hardie suggested twenty-five shillings a week,[73] not a full wage. He remembered her ambition to be a writer, and added that he hoped she could get another ten or fifteen shillings by 'literary work', though he must have known how unlikely this was. She had even less confidence now after two years with her father, and though Travers was now back in New Zealand, she had taken no steps to end the marriage.

On 13 October, the day before she was due to start work with Hardie once more, she came to the Commons to meet Frank Smith. There was a demonstration going on outside the House by the suffragettes, with Sylvia among them. Maggie had already been named by the *Daily Express* as one of the 'fooligans' who supported the suffragette cause,[74] but she had taken little part in any militant activity. Under her arm she held a copy of that days' *Star* with a report of Hardie's question in the House the previous day, criticizing the continued prosecution of suffragettes. Herbert Gladstone for the government had told him that the police action against them was 'not instigated by the government but the government will certainly support the police'[75] – a reply still given by governments seeking to evade political responsibility for matters on which they are free to act.

While waiting, Maggie exploited a facility offered to women who worked for MPs, which she would have known about: a small glass panel in a side door giving on to the floor of the House of Commons. Invisible, women could watch, symbolizing their political status. The debate was a government Bill to outlaw the sale of cigarettes to anyone under sixteen. Tories were opposing it as another manifestation, said one, of 'true socialism' out to destroy individual choice.[76] The City of London's MP[77] said he had smoked as a boy and it never did him any harm; why should it hurt his sons? As the talk went on, the mild and accommodating Maggie was unaccountably overcome with anger that women were not allowed to enter the discussion, much less vote on any measures proposed. No doubt it was mixed with unrecognized anger at her own stymied position in life, perpetual helpmeet, her writing career not yet begun and the prospect next day of slipping back into

the harness of servitude once more. Suddenly she flung open the door
to the Chamber and ran into the middle of the floor between the two
front benches. 'Why are you discussing children without hearing what
women have to say?' she called out. She got little further, as attendants
bundled her out. She remembered later that she was still clutching her
newspaper.[78]

'Triumph! Woman Raids the House' was the headline the next
day in the *Chronicle*,[79] with columns about the suffrage demonstration
and about Maggie personally, 'a woman between 30 and 40 ...
[in] a large mushroom hat'; 'a most cultured woman, has travelled
considerably and is a linguist'. There was comment on her father,
the distinguished architect, formerly a member of the LCC, and on
Travers in New Zealand (he should come home and take her in hand,
one critic ventured); and, of course, the fact that she worked for Keir
Hardie. The next day MPs were complaining about 'some members ...
[having] more regard for feminine approval than for the dignity of this
Chamber'.[80] Immediately after the interruption Hardie was summoned
to collect Maggie. He managed to keep her from being charged. It was
a matter for the Speaker, who promptly closed the 'peephole' facility
to women (it was never reopened) and barred Maggie from entering
the House indefinitely, a prohibition which meant she now had to
set up office in Neville's Court and could not use the Party's room
at the House.

Suffrage items were the press's favourite copy and coverage of the
event went on for days, with a great deal of attention being given
to the modest Maggie. But there was also coverage of 'the shrieking
sisterhood' and disgust that Maggie should be treated like a 'heroine'.[81]
Reports were sent worldwide. Within a few days came a telegram from
her father in Cairo: 'Bravo Maggie.' Maggie was henceforth a militant
suffragette, whether she had intended it or not.

Once Maggie was back at work, Hardie got down to agitation on
unemployment, introducing legislation to beef up the Unemployed
Workmen's Act of 1905. He wanted to give Local Authorities the
right to deal with unemployment by hiring men for useful work and
paying their wages from the rates at trade union rates of pay.[82] He found
Labour colleagues uninterested and, of course, no government action.
Hardie wrote with dread to Glasier of 'another year of Henderson's
chairmanship, which means ... reaction and timidity'.[83] He was
equally depressed by the miners' decision to affiliate to the PLP.

As he had written to Glasier, 'I am quite certain ... I could be
of more real service to the cause were I not in Parliament.'[84] He
had decided to revive the old tactic of making the unemployed
visible. In Glasgow workless men were led by the ILP into the City
Council chamber, demanding work. When Parliament reconvened in

February 1909, Hardie organized a huge demonstration of unemployed to march past outside. MacDonald derided such extra-parliamentary efforts, particularly the tactic of making 'the suffering of . . . poor men and women the raw material for mere party coin'.[85] But Hardie continued to believe that nothing happened inside the House without pushing outside. He himself found the march past 'heartbreaking',[86] and he was shocked at its treatment by the police. In the House, he said, we cheer the Territorial Army when it marches by but 'when the unemployed army in their rags . . . helpless women . . . and . . . helpless children tried to parade their misery' they were hounded by the police. He rounded on John Burns who said there were plenty of hostels for the poor who were sleeping rough, 'Oh, the mockery of man!' to imagine these wretches are on the pavements 'by their own choice'.[87]

These moments aside, Hardie's speeches in the House were lower key than in earlier days. He told the House he had no quarrel with what was in the Liberal government's King's speech – only with what was left out.[88] Within the ranks of the ILP, however, were many who did have a quarrel, particularly with Labour for failing to put up candidates in by-elections against the Liberals. Many ILP members in 1908, therefore, had voted for the SDF candidates who were put up.[89] As a result, Hardie began himself to preach socialist unity in the Leader. 'There is room inside the Labour Party for every section and phase of socialist thought and activity. We are out to capture power, not to create sects.'[90]

But more sects threatened. Ben Tillett brought out a pamphlet entitled, Is the Parliamentary Labour Party a Failure?,[91] calling the Party a lion with 'no teeth or claws . . . and losing its growl too'. He was especially sharp with those who spent all their time on temperance platforms – shared with Liberals – or campaigning to end the House of Lords or to get Welsh disestablishment, men like Shackleton, Henderson, Crooks and Snowden, 'who takes the chair for Winston Churchill while textile workers are starving'. He condemned the Commons, the Boards of Guardians, the relief committees who spend '80 per cent of their income in expenses', and 'the army of central and local government officials [who] will not get off the backs of the poor'. The Parliamentary Labour Party should put its energy into the condition of the poor, he wrote, 'and make the rich think over the . . . the system which gives them plenty and the wealth-maker nothing at all'.[92] Much as he disliked Ben Tillett, Hardie almost certainly half agreed with him.

The Labour leadership's view, however, was that there was little to be done in a year when the mantle of reform passed to Lloyd George's budget, battling its way through Parliament. Many working people supported its insurance provisions, and Labour politicians, instead of suggesting how much further the principle needed to be carried, simply kept quiet. Liberal policy became indistinguishable from Labour policy. On 24 July Hardie joined Liberal speakers, including John Benn, in a Hyde Park rally to support Lloyd George's budget (and found himself captured on motion picture film for the first time[93].) Hardie even agreed to have a meal with Lloyd George[94] and might have discussed the idea of some kind of electoral pact, should it be required to protect the budget and defeat the Conservative majority in the Lords. Although Hardie soon disowned the idea, the fact that such a lifelong advocate of Labour's independence had even considered it was a sign that things were bad. In July the first miner, J. A. Hancock, stood for Labour in a Derbyshire by-election, where his agent told voters, 'the LRC is not socialist . . . and Hancock is a Liberal'.[95] Yet Hardie went to campaign for him anyway. He had to stick it out – even though, as he wrote to Glasier a few months earlier, 'there are times when I confess to feeling sore at seeing the fruits of our years of toil being garnered by men who were never of us, and who even now would trick us' out of our own movement.[96]

How quickly had the high hopes of 1906 evaporated. Even social reform was to prove pitifully inadequate, despite the fact that this was a reforming Liberal government which passed measure after measure on many of the issues, such as the right to work, child nutrition, or old age pensions, which Labour had clamoured for. When the legislation finally appeared, however, it was the palest version of what Hardie and his colleagues had advocated originally. As with the earlier Tories' Unemployed Act of 1905, the heart of each reform had often disappeared. Provision of school meals was not made compulsory, merely an option for local authorities. A universal old age pension, introduced in 1908 after much delay, did not start at sixty but at seventy and was by no means universal, or even adequate. Most particularly, maintenance for the workless was entirely inadequate and highly selective. In Hardie's view the relief he had pressed for merely 'mocked' the poor.[97] The new Labour Exchanges did not provide work, they just made it easier for employers to 'select hands'; he hoped no Local Authority would agree to work the system. Even the eight-hour-day legislation, when it finally came, was diluted with endless concessions to employers.

As for Labour's Unemployed Workmen's Bill of 1907, it was never passed. Nor was right-to-work legislation or a minimum wage. The only real legislative successes of those years were concessions to the trade union wing such as the reversal of the TaffVale decision in the Trades Disputes Act, 1906 – effectively Labour's Act – and much later, the reversal of the Osborne judgement.[98] As far as trade unions went, this justified the formation of the Labour Party, but it did not suffice for socialists whose goal was deeper change. What came over clearly in these years was an establishment prepared to concede to organized labour but not to class-conscious socialism. Socialism as such had no parliamentary representation. 'If you want socialist law, you must find socialist legislators', said a leaflet in 1906 supporting the candidatures of independent socialists like Lansbury,[99] or alternatively you can take extra-parliamentary action.

As 1909 advanced, the Labour Party was weighed under with problems arising from the Osborne judgment, threatening to limit trade union affiliations and funding. This meant that already falling ILP and Labour membership was about to fall further. Everyone looked for scapegoats. During the winter of 1909 Hardie complained privately about Henderson's leadership, while MacDonald and Snowden complained about the *Leader*[100] still being edited by Glasier. Out on the circuits Grayson's seeds of dissension were also bearing fruit. Even faithful ILP speakers, like Katharine Glasier, were being heckled. At one of her meetings someone shouted, 'Dare to be a Grayson'.[101] Her husband commented gloomily, 'Are we feeding wolves?'

By the time the ILP Conference came round in April – it was held at Edinburgh – Glasier surprised everyone by resigning from the editorship of the *Leader*. He was angry at the criticism and had only retained the post so long because he needed the weekly wage. Now he no longer did, as he and Katharine had just met a rich American philanthropist who thought their social work so akin to the 'early Christians' that she wanted to support them financially.[102] MacDonald and Snowden were also in a resigning mood. The rank and file of the ILP interested them far less than the House of Commons, which had imprinted itself on both. Hardie, however, had come to the conference having told Glasier, 'we must save the ILP'.[103] There he had an unpleasant surprise.

It was the culmination of a series of incidents that had begun the previous autumn when there had been riots about unemployment in most cities. In Parliament Victor Grayson suddenly tried to move the adjournment on unemployment – without notice to the Speaker. The next day he tried again. When told he was out of order, he said, 'I . . . refuse to be bound by such rules,' and went on speaking. He was ordered out, but not before turning on the Labour benches with insults to 'you well-fed men', saying he felt 'degraded in a company that will not consider the unemployed . . . you will not stand up for your class. You traitors!'[104] Since he was clearly drunk, no one rose to back him and he was ejected from the House. Grayson had already been called to account by supporters in Manchester for wearing evening dress and drinking champagne – too much of it at that.[105] In the ranks in the country, however, many ILP members, reading what he said, supported him. Hardie reacted touchily by saying that if 'protest is to be made, it must be done unitedly',[106] a reasonable view, except that he himself had often protested without notifying anyone – and would again.

Imperceptibly, and probably without noticing, Hardie was becoming 'old guard'. Grayson was counting on younger socialists having all the impatience Hardie once had. Soon there were reports that Grayson was aiming to set up a Socialist Representation Committee and split the ILP.[107] The climax came in November 1908 when Hardie received a note withdrawing an invitation to speak at the demonstrations for the London unemployed to be held at Holborn and Finsbury Town Hall. The reason given was that Grayson, due to speak too, would not consent to stand on the same platform with him.

In taking on Hardie Grayson had gone just that one step too far – as he would find out; but in doing so he was able to force Hardie into a corner he would not have chosen. At the ILP Conference in Edinburgh Grayson was severely criticized by a large majority for his failure to join the Parliamentary Labour Party, which had withdrawn his salary. He got round this by promising at last to join. A second report criticized him over the withdrawal of the invitation to Hardie, but surprisingly, the conference relented, and referred the whole report back (including the criticism). Hardie, who had let much heavier 'insults' go by without reacting, suddenly overreacted. A hurried consultation with MacDonald, Snowden and Glasier, each with his own reasons to want to storm off the platform, produced a hurried decision by all four to resign from the ILP Executive. MacDonald told the conference that the 'impossibilists' had to be curbed; Hardie that the cry for socialist unity was a 'chimera',[108] not so much because he really believed it as because those who had adopted this cry – including the *Clarion* and *Justice* – were spreading it about that he had betrayed the movement and were calling him a limpet clinging to his position. This had hit home. But so did the mass resignations, which dismayed the majority and enfeebled the ILP at an important time. Glasier stood again a year later, but Hardie, MacDonald and Snowden, though they retained their local memberships and status as delegates to international conferences, did not offer themselves again until 1911 or later. The action merely served a short-term purpose of killing off Grayson, who got the blame. Within a year he had been defeated in a general election and so became the Jonah's gourd which Hardie had once been called, growing and withering all in a 'day'.

After his defeat Grayson worked with Blatchford and Hyndman, the three of them increasingly involved in campaigns to push for military preparedness against Germany. Snowden later wrote that Grayson 'came under malign influences ... [which] used him as an instrument to sow dissension in the Labour movement'.[109] It is certainly true he sowed dissension, but it is also possible that he was the user, not the used. It would not have been the last time, though it could have been the first, when a Party member worked secretly as a government informer.

In July 1909 Hardie himself told an international socialist congress in Geneva on Egyptian independence that the socialist movement was 'honey-combed' by spies,[110] which made it important for true socialists not to do anything clandestinely themselves.

During 1909 government and police had their work cut out tracking the suffragettes and their activity. In most cases the resourceful women outmanoeuvred them. They managed to get at Asquith as he was playing golf. They disrupted a Liberal meeting by occupying the front row seats and then at a given signal jumping up and throwing off their coats to reveal prison uniforms – tactics to keep the issue before the public.[111] Like animals mesmerized by lights, however, the public was wholly caught up by the political excitement generated by the government's clash with the House of Lords, who were refusing to pass the Commons' budget. Hardie had the same problem as the women: how to keep labour issues in front of his own audience, most of whom were equally absorbed by the parliamentary drama.

Hardie went on trying to encourage the movement to leave disputes over doctrine behind and concentrate on converting the people to socialism and winning elections. He would rather have one Labour mayor in Merthyr safely in office than face a host of 'slaughtered socialist candidates, however valiantly they had waved the red flag and shouted their class war dogmas'.[112] This was some way from the Hardie of sixteen years earlier who said he 'would rather fight on independent lines and lose in every case . . . than win ten . . . seats . . . as a result of compact or compromise'.[113] Hardie knew compact and compromise were taking place but he chose to overlook them. Glasier told his Diary in 1909 that 'Hardie like all of us realizes that the road to Socialism is going to be a slow . . . one'.[114] What mattered to Hardie was to go on with the hedgerow preaching, the socialist mission. People had to believe in the possibility that society could be different, 'Where there is no vision the people perish.'[115]

In January 1910, George Bernard Shaw sent Hardie a telegram, 'What is best hotel (with motor garage) in Merthyr?'[116] There was none, but he drove down anyway, to help Hardie in the general election that took place that month. The Liberals had decided to go to the country over the deadlock with the House of Lords. Shaw and Hardie were photographed together many times during the visit, two white-haired and white-bearded men in old-gentleman tweeds. They looked so much alike that one newspaper photo carried the caption, 'Shaw is the one holding the pen'.[117] In his speech Shaw predicted that one day a king would send for the Keir Hardie of his day to form a government. 'Would to god it were the Keir Hardie of today.'[118]

There was special concern over this election because Hardie – as Labour's leading edge – had been the chief target of the anti-socialist campaigners in Britain. As well as his Liberal and Tory opponents, Hardie had to face the Anti-Socialist Union, which set up shop in Merthyr with the explicit objective, so said its representative, of 'campaigning against Mr Hardie'.[119] It flooded the constituency with anti-Hardie material, helped by the *Merthyr Express*, the *Western Mail*, and Pritchard Morgan, Hardie's old right-wing Liberal opponent, who was standing again. The fly-posters and leaflets concentrated on lies about Hardie as a wealthy man, a libertine and an atheist. Hardie later said the campaign had come to his attention when a local minister's wife 'reproached me . . . for . . . being "a very wealthy man" . . . Someone had told her that I had sold the *Labour Leader* to the Labour Party for £20,000.'[120]

In addition, it was said, Hardie owned a 'great estate' from which he derived 'a large income' – apparently a 'castle in Scotland'.[121] In order to counter this he published his current yearly income of £210 (the largest, he said, he had ever earned) and broke it down: £120 a year for his job – at which he never spent less than fifteen hours a day. And £90 a year for his 'food and raiment', from which also 'my wife and daughter have to maintain themselves'.[122] From this we can guess that both Jamie and Duncan were supporting themselves; and that even allowing for the hyperbole of electioneering, Nan and Lillie were still required to practise great economy.

It was now the custom for Labour wives to work alongside their husbands during elections. Ethel Snowden spoke at three meetings a night in this campaign,[123] and in Merthyr Nan and Lillie accompanied Hardie during the whole election. Even Jamie had joined them. The smears affected them all deeply. Nan wrote later that the worst was 'an indecent picture of him reprinted from some dirty racing paper calculated to make people think him an advocate of free love . . . distributed by Liberals'. Hardie was also constantly questioned about 'his country mansion and the retinue of servants', to which Nan adds in a plaintive parentheses, '(my mother and myself)'.[124]

Years later Glasier also recalled this time: 'No political leader of his day, not even Charles Stuart Parnell, experienced' what Hardie did.[125] MacDonald remembered that Hardie had told him, 'No one can know what suffering a man has to endure by misrepresentation'.[126] MacDonald and Hardie used to go over their anonymous letters together,[127] MacDonald commenting naïvely, 'written mostly by educated middle class people'.[128] Only the active politicians who wrote about Hardie – like Hughes, Stewart, Glasier or Maxton – ever understood what other biographers either ignored or treated as

a 'weakness',[129] that the 'suffering ... calumny and insult heaped
upon him day by day in the press for over a quarter of a century,
had left their mark'. When begged by a minister to answer the
press in this campaign, Hardie merely said, 'Let conduct be its own
reward'. In the face of it a person either retires or fights his ground
the harder. Either way, systematic misrepresentation distorts all social
relationships, including those one has with oneself. A large part of
Hardie's apparent intransigence and Ishmaelitism was the essential
reflex action of self-preservation in the face of calumny.

This reflex had induced Hardie to consolidate himself in Merthyr
since 1906. He was particularly conscious of Welsh nationalism, and
had written to Glasier just before the election to share his fears about
'the undercurrent of Welsh national feeling to be reckoned with' in
Wales.[130] It was probably more 'in out of the way places' where no
English was spoken, said Hardie, but all the same he couldn't 'leave
the election to chance'.

Nor had he left the constituency to chance in recent years, including
its Welsh dimension. The ILP had organised political meetings and
held cultural events, including an Eistedfodd at Mountain Ash, where
bards competed to praise Hardie in Welsh.[131] He and Lillie had spent
time in the constituency, usually staying with a local schoolmaster, W.
W. Price, with whom Lillie kept in touch from Lochnorris, enquiring
with tactful regularity after the Price family's yearly new baby.[132]

Yet while he wooed the Welsh in Merthyr itself, Hardie did not
pander to nationalist sentiment more generally – at least, not in
between election times. Speaking later to an audience in Dowlais,
he said that as a

> 'Scotsman, he believed in nationality. But they should beware that
> nationalism was the genuine article, not some spurious imitation.
> They had members of the Nationalist party going about in Wales
> making speeches ... talking about Welsh Nationalism; had they
> heard one of them offer one single word of sympathy or compassion
> to the old mother and father who were crying their hearts out in
> the lonely home in Llanelly for the Welsh lads who were shot
> through the heart (for going on strike)? Not one. They talked of
> Welsh Nationalism when they wanted votes, but when it came to
> doing anything for the workers they were not nationalists, they were
> not even Welshmen, they were simply party politicians intent upon
> keeping the workers in their rightful place'.[133]

Hardie then told them that

> 'The Nationalist Party I have in mind is this: the people of Wales
> fighting to recover possession of the land of Wales, the working
> class of Wales acquiring possession of the mines, of the furnaces,

and the railways, of the great public works generally, and working these as comrades, not for the benefit of shareholders, but for the good of every man, woman and child within your borders. That is the kind of Nationalism that I want to see ... and when that comes the red dragon will be emblazoned on the red flag of Socialism, the international emblem of the working class movement of the world'.

Another step Hardie had taken was to start his own political paper in the constituency, the *Merthyr Pioneer*, financing it by selling shares among the faithful. One of those who bought shares in 1908 was a keen young woman named Rose, newly married to Edward Davies, a local ILP member and schoolmaster then living in Abernant. Rose Davies had trained as a teacher and was bright and energetic – short, sharp and pretty. She became a valued political lieutenant, corresponding regularly with Hardie, and visiting him both in Merthyr and London. When the election was announced Hardie asked for her advice on the education section of his election address.[134] He also asked her to form a women's committee to help him get re-elected, instructing her to canvass and sell buttons showing his photograph, as well as to make rosettes in his colours of green, white and red. Rose and her husband were also asked to put up young Jamie Hardie, who came to stay for the whole campaign.[135] The Labour Party was better organised now and sent the women's committee leaflets to distribute. These listed all the issues that the Party had raised[136] or promoted in Parliament, including unemployment legislation, introduced twenty-two times since 1906 (but as yet unpromoted by the Liberal government).

During this election Hardie stuck much closer to Merthyr than in previous campaigns. As always, he made plain his support for Liberal policy and the Lloyd George budget, but this time he put his socialism more up front. Balfour had decided to play up socialism as the election bogey, which Hardie met head on, 'I accept Mr Balfour's challenge and put my socialism against his Tariff Reform. He wants to use the State for the benefit of the rich. I want to use it for the benefit of all'.[137] The *Labour Leader* reported from the election that 'the old warrior was in magnificent form – morning, noon and night and often far into the night, he kept at it with infectious enthusiasm. It was not so much an election campaign as a crusade'.[138]

Crusade is apt, for Hardie had the support of a local religious network, possibly his most important electoral bulwark. One of Hardie's greatest assets had grown even greater in the ten years of Labour representation: his capacity to unite political and religious agitation. The Christian argument for social change still had wide resonance among radicals, socialists, trade unionists and the working class population generally. It gave Hardie an appeal denied to ethical secular socialists, to the intelligentsia in the Fabians or to Marxist parties like the SDF.

Gratifyingly, clerics of every kind sprang to Hardie's defence in 1910. Canon Adderley, writing in *Christian Commonwealth*, denounced attempts to smear as an unbeliever and an advocate of free love a man like Hardie, who was campaigning 'surrounded by his wife and family pleading for the kingdom of God'; and a petition circulated throughout the constituency by the Rev R.J. Campbell, together with ministers of many denominations, explained that the 'implications' of their religion required them to 'advocate socialism'.[139] Its language, far from pious, was tailored to the cut and thrust of the hustings, loudly opposing the 'foul calumnies' against Keir Hardie being put out by 'fakers . . . Tories, protectionists, dukes and gradgrinds'.

The new theology had developed apace since 1906 and had reached the point where it was indistinguishable from political advocacy. Large numbers of local lay pastors now supported Hardie, while others, like the miners, A. J. Cook and Noah Ablett, had progessed from the local pulpit to trade unionism and thence to study at the Central Labour College. Like such men, Hardie too had developed his religious beliefs in an increasingly political direction. But unlike them, he kept the explicit tie to religion. He did not speak often at religious occasions, but when he did, it sounded like a political meeting.[140]

> 'Christianity . . . which has its origin . . . in the teachings and the life of a Common Working Man, must necessarily appeal to all who are seeking today to make life more worthy of its high purpose than it has been in the past. I am afraid still, however, . . . that Adam Smith and the 'Wealth of Nations' is a more potent factor than the Sermon on the Mount and the Apostle Paul. So long as that continues, there must appear to be antagonism . . . between the Christian Church and the Labour Movement.'

Hardie went on to explain why,

> 'Those of us who for many years past have practically deserted the religious platform, have not done so because our faith in religion has grown less, but because the Church thought fit to specialise in what it most unfairly calls the spiritual side of Christianity. Thus it became necessary for some of us to concentrate upon the human side . . . It is not merely that (Christ) denounced the rich; he did so unsparingly. It was not merely that He blamed the learned for wrangling over words and dogmas, forgetting the spirit of the message they were supposed to deliver; but Christ in His Gospels denounced property in all its forms. He did not merely denounce those who were rich; Christ's Gospel teaches us that life is the only thing of value and that the possession

of property comes between a man and the development of his life.'

Hardie always had the same central message,

> 'Christianity on its social side can never be realised, if it is to be interpreted in the light of Christ's teachings, until there is full, free Communism ... The rich and comfortable classes have annexed Jesus and perverted His Gospel. And yet He belongs to us ... Make no mistake about this. The only way we can serve God is by serving mankind. There is no other way'.

Hardie ended by uniting the political and religious movements, to show those who argued that socialism was anti-Christian, that socialism and religion were not only close, they were one,

> 'The Labour movement in its very essence is essentially religious. The men and the women who are in it are not working for themselves; they know perfectly well that all they can do is but to create the beginning of a condition of things which will one day bring peace and happiness and freedom and a fuller life for those who are to come after us ... Christ's great work was to teach the oneness of the human race, to remove the causes which divided man from man, to make it impossible for the strong to oppress the weak or the rich to rob the poor.'

A typical political meeting of the time might have heard much the same. Thus during a meeting called to support local railway strikers,[141]

> 'Oh, men and women, in the name of the God whom ye profess to believe in, in the name of Jesus of Nazareth who died to save your souls, how long do you intend to submit to a system which is defacing God's image upon you, which is blurring and marring God's handiwork, which is destroying the lives of men, women and children? Do not you think that God ... intended you to be free ... ? And here you are in bondage! Come out from the House of bondage, fight for freedom, fight for manhood, fight for the coming day when in body, soul and spirit you will be free to live your own lives, and give glory to your Creator'.

Hardie's mediation of politics by religion could not have succeeded had his politics not been as indifferent to ideology as his religion was to theology. He wanted Christianity freed from 'lifeless theology',[142] for it was not divinely based on God but humanly based on Christ. In the same way he did not want his socialism based on dogma. By this he meant the 'neo-Marxism' of a Hyndman or a Daniel DeLeon, not the socialism of Karl Marx whose life and works he reviewed with reverence in 1910, admitting Marx to his hagiarchy, 'his memory . . . a consecrated treasure . . . in . . . the hearts . . . of millions of all lands'.[143] Hardie perceived Marx as a social Darwin, the first to make 'the evolutionary inevitability of socialism plain', as well as the first to preach the classless society in which Hardie so fervently believed. Hardie firmly believed as well that the ILP was the 'advanced wing' of the working class, as 'Marx intended the socialist section of the working class movement to be'.

It was only after the Russian Revolution that commentators began to separate Hardie from Marx. In 1921 Ramsay MacDonald claimed Hardie learned 'more socialism from Burns than from Marx'[144] (which at least one historian claimed was MacDonald talking of himself rather than of Hardie),[145] although Hardie claimed he learned it from both. Fyfe in 1935 declared Hardie was 'repelled by Marx' and 'not in sympathy with the Communist Manifesto'.[146] In fact, Hardie said specifically that the Communist Manifesto was 'The most fateful document in the history of the working class movement' and 'the birth certificate of the modern socialist movement'. In the 1970s the attempt at separation continued. McLean said Hardie's idealism and common sense 'made him an anti-marxist',[147] Morgan that 'whatever Hardie's socialism consisted of it cannot be termed Marxist'.[148] That is so; nor would many say his religion could be termed Christianity.

Marx was simply one influential writer among many who had shaped socialist thinking. In *From Serfdom to Socialism* this is how Hardie treated him; in his politics that is how he used him. Hardie's writing abounds with statements that support Marxism, and with many that do not. Consistency of ideology was not Hardie's aim. Glasier said later, 'I doubt if he ever read Marx', being someone 'guided by moral convictions rather than scientific analysis of economic or social phenomena'.[149] Hardie certainly fought shy of economic theory and he probably had not read much Marx, as he had probably not read most of the Bible. But he had read and heard explanations of Marx, as he had so often heard and read of Christianity. He had grasped the essence of Christ. So too, according to Max Beer, Hardie's German contemporary, who wrote a history of British socialism, had he 'grasped the essence of Marxism better than any other socialist'.[150] In practice rather than theory, however. Maxton, who remembered Hardie at work, said he may have disowned the class war as theory, but 'in practice his own activities show he was probably more Marxist than those who paid greater deference to Marxist theories'.[151]

But the tradition continues to try to park Hardie either on the Christian or the Marxist shelf, when his greatest asset was that he himself saw no necessity to choose. Morgan said he was able to 'translate socialist ethics into images of popular non-conformity'.[152] In fact it was the reverse. He translated religious images into labour and socialist politics: 'Jesus belonged to the working class'; he was a leader who fought for his class.[153] Hardie had developed his religion to the point where Christianity became the metaphor that carried his politics in a very sophisticated way, contradicting Pelling's view that Hardie was so naïve he could not 'distinguish politics from morality'.[154]

Though religion continued to be important, Hardie had turned from churchgoing, justifying himself on the grounds that 'many have left the church in order to be Christians'.[155] His political experience had given an additional reason to move on. Hardie's travels had brought him into contact with every sort of religious tradition. He had worked with Egyptian socialists who were Muslims; and Indian socialists who were Hindus. He was interested in all religions. In India, for example, he made many notes on the beliefs and customs of the religions and societies he met.

Yet Hardie has suffered from religious stereotyping, so often talked of as a typical chapel man, or a Scots Covenanter,[156] both in his lifetime and after, a categorization that does not reflect the ecumenical way in which he had developed in life. Glasier was one who recognized that 'he gave up all belief in the Christian Church as an exclusive means to salvation. As he could not accept a religious dogma that excluded from the communion of citizens or saints, Jews, freethinkers, Mohammedans, Buddhists or people of any . . . enlightenment, race or colour'. For this reason Hardie was much attracted to the B'hai philosophy which encompassed all religions.[157]

If Hardie suffered from stereotyping, so too did the socialist and labour movement, always labelled, then and now, as a by-product of nonconformity. Josiah Wedgwood, for example, said that everyone in the Labour alliance in 1906 'from extreme right to extreme left had been brought up in chapel society'.[158] Many had, it was true, especially those who sat in Parliament; but many had not. Many Fabians and members of the South Place Ethical Society were agnostics or atheists. As were most social democrats. Eleanor Marx thought any mix of socialism and Christianity 'ludicrous' and entirely 'English'.[159] Hyndman thought religion 'useless';[160] so too did trade unionists like Harry Quelch.

Nor were those who were believers by any means limited to traditional Methodist or Baptist backgrounds, and those who were had discovered that the main nonconformist churches were often hostile to the working-class movement and, as William Cobbett wrote far earlier, 'the bitterest foes of freedom'.[161] The rise of labour and the coming of socialism caused a split in nonconformity, not a consolidation of it. Hardie had discovered this in the 1880s.

Twenty years later so did the young preacher A. J. Cook whose Baptist Church told him he must choose between his religion and his socialism. He resigned from the chapel and walked out, followed loyally by his mother, the chapel's longtime organist.[162]

But many socialists were not in this mould in the first place. A very large number were Jews, especially in the big towns. Grayson and Ramsay MacDonald were Unitarians; T. D. Benson was a Sweden-borgian; and Annie Besant turned from agnosticism to become a theosophist,[163] worshipping in the hall Lutyens later built in Tavistock Square for all who 'accept . . . a universal society based on brotherhood' where 'Parsees, Hindus, RCs, Protestants, 7th Day Adventists, Spiritualists, agnostics and deists' were all equally welcome. Other active socialists were Christian Scientists or New Ethnologists; or, like Isabella Ford, Quakers. A far larger number than is usually recognized were Church of England, including Edmund Stonelake, Hardie's Merthyr colleague,[164] and George Lansbury, who did regular battle in his early days against nonconformists in east London, and later campaigned for C of E clergy to be able to stand for parliament.[165] Lansbury belonged to the Church Socialist League, along with G. K. Chesterton, Frances Warwick and Conrad Noel, a group so radical that 'very few had any faith in the Labour Party'. Lastly, and possibly most significant of all, were the growing number of socialists and Labour activists who were Roman Catholics, whether lapsed or practising, including trade unionists like Pete Curran and James O'Grady, Hardie's great friend, David Lowe, and suffrage socialists like Theresa Billington. There was even a group of Christian anarchists.[166]

Not only were socialists spread among the religions, so too were they spread among causes. Practically all members of the ILP opposed vaccination, for example; Lansbury was anti-smoking; Shaw a vegetarian; Katharine Glasier active in the anti-vivisection movement.[167] Many, like Hardie and Ellen Wilkinson, had para-religious beliefs, like faith in reincarnation.[168] The Glasiers as well as the Hardies practised spiritualism, to communicate with those who had died. There were socialists who believed in dreams and in exchanging them. The suffragette, Annie Kenney, who sang inspirational hymns in the Clarion choir, claimed she had seen God and that he looked like Tolstoy.[169] Hardie, as Glasier discovered,[170] made a 'strange admission of belief in palmistry and horoscopes'. This worried Glasier, who wrote, 'I have ridiculed him but he smiles good naturedly and refuses to say' how serious his belief is. Later Glasier came to hear of further Hardie superstitions: a belief in omens, sun signs, lucky days and psychic manifestations.[171] Not that this last was unusual for socialists. Both Edward Pease and Frank Padmore of the Fabian Society were psychic researchers (who once made Shaw spend a night in a haunted house in Clapham for an experiment).[172]

Although Hardie got on best with those who had had a religious upbringing like Frank Smith, George Lansbury and the Glasiers (who used to give a joint lecture on 'The Religion of Socialism'),[173] he never discussed religion with colleagues. Many in the Labour movement – like Fenner Brockway – never knew at the time they knew Hardie that he had any interest in religion at all.[174] Some biographers too thought he was not particularly religious;[175] while contemporaries like Snowden, who thought him 'the most religious man I had ever known',[176] acknowledged that in day-to-day life he 'never talked of religion'.

As Hardie got older, increasingly he translated religious ceremony into secular activity – in a search for more appropriate observances for socialism. The ILP, for example, invented new marriage rites; and had Baby Naming Ceremonies,[177] replacing baptism. At one, Hardie and Sylvia pinned on to the baby a suffragette badge Sylvia had designed, to welcome it into the community.

At the end of his life, had anyone asked Hardie what his religion was, he would have said socialism, not Christianity. In the House of Commons he once asked the Home Secretary why it was that a prisoner who had put socialism down as his religion was not permitted 'a chaplain of the same persuasion' as every other prisoner was allowed for his professed religion.[178] The Home Secretary did not know how to treat this, but it was plain that Hardie was quite serious.

Hardie believed that people had a duty to the community – to look after others as well as themselves; and that the community had a reverse duty to its members to make sure all of them had the necessities of life. The old religious imperatives which had made people found orders and give away goods were reshaped by twentieth century political action, when sin became social as well as personal. Real poverty was as damning as poverty of the spirit. Hardie preached that 'any system of production . . . which sanctions exploitation of the weak . . . is sinful'.[179] Although Hardie used religion as metaphor, he kept the distinction clear. 'Believe, says the preacher. Believe and Act, says the Socialist'.[180]

The 'divine discontent' that Hardie and countless others spread at this time was pushing society over an important line with its message that God could not bring remedies. Only people themselves could – by combining in social activity. The transfer to social action as the test of God's kingdom had been made. Whatever a person's politics or religion, it was hard to see how either religion or politics could be the same again.

11
PARLIAMENTARY VERSUS
EXTRA-PARLIAMENTARY

During 1910 Hardie's relationship with Sylvia was at its closest point. In 1909 she had been much taken up with caring for her brother Harry. She had wanted him to continue his education but claims Emmeline Pankhurst would always answer, '"Keir Hardie never went to school" – how often she had said it!'[1] Emmeline Pankhurst sent him instead as a 'conscript' to one of the farms which Joseph Fels had started in Mayland in Essex – ostensibly to train as a gardener. Fels was now moving on from his flirtation with socialism, and what had been originally intended as brave new work-communes for the East Enders were now being run on market lines using 'volunteers' for 'training'. Harry was part of the cheap labour force and Sylvia believed he was over-worked and ill-treated.[2] He suffered repeated illnesses, when Sylvia would have him brought back to London.

To give Sylvia a rest, Hardie suggested she take a cottage in Cinder Hill in Kent, near Penshurst, where he knew the local shopkeeper, a man with a passion for neolithic flints. Hardie visited her regularly at the cottage during the summer of 1909 and the relationship deepened. Sylvia records that their discussion was mostly about the suffrage campaign, where forcible feeding of women hunger strikers in prisons had just begun. 'He told me that the thought of forcible feeding was making him ill.'[3] He tried to dissuade her from her intention of getting arrested herself, so that she too could take part in hunger striking. 'Of what use to make one more?' he asked.

In the middle of Sylvia's sojourn, Harry became ill again, this time seriously. She returned at once to help her sister Adela take care of him at a nursing home in Notting Hill Gate. His legs were paralysed, and the illness did not clear up. She was told the problem was a 'terrible and obscure disease' called 'infantile paralysis'.[4] Tragically, he died, and Sylvia reported her mother 'broken as I had never seen her'.[5] Out of the original Pankhurst family of seven, all the males were now dead. Only the women had survived.

Harry was buried as the general election was being held in January 1910. The result of the election showed no one need have worried for Hardie. His majority was the largest he ever enjoyed (although the Hardie camp was still very disappointed with the result).[6] His supporters celebrated the victory at a dance, where Hardie was asked to sing, this time choosing 'Annie Laurie'. Nationally, however, Labour stood still, while the Liberals lost heavily to the Conservatives. Labour, along with the Irish, now held the balance under a precarious Liberal government.

These events increased the impatience of MacDonald, waiting in the wings, the only other man, besides Hardie, who had the slightest chance of uniting socialists and trade unionists in Parliament. Hardie, who did not want the leadership himself, was still resisting MacDonald. He backed George Barnes at the Party Conference in Newport and in his chairman's address pointedly advocated Labour taking its own line in Parliament. He insisted, with recent experience in mind of 'the caricatured and vile misrepresentation of socialism' current in society, that anyone who wanted to stand under the Labour Party banner 'should be able to defend and expound socialism' when its enemies attacked it.[7] In the House he continued to advocate a right-to-work policy, but got little support from colleagues. He realized that the criticisms of the impossibilists had had substance. He was particularly bitter that a resolution to give a 'fighting lead' on the Lords veto issue and right-to-work legislation was 'attacked ... savagely' by MacDonald at Party meetings, and defeated by 17 to 11.[8] What 'jars me to the quick,' he wrote to another ILP member, 'is that it was our ILP men who sold the pass,' not the trade unionists.[9] He went so far as to say (although only privately) that resigning from the Labour Party altogether 'is still the feeling uppermost in my mind'.[10]

At the ILP Conference in April he urged Labour to risk bringing down the government if Liberals would not introduce a right-to-work law. Labour's job 'was to organize the working class into a great independent power to fight for the coming of socialism',[11] not to prop up the Liberals. Unfortunately, Barnes, who duly became leader, turned out to be even more inept and ineffective than Henderson. Glasier tried to assuage Hardie's anger, which he saw as threatening the Labour Party, while also keeping in touch with MacDonald, whom he admired for a business-like approach. Glasier confided to his Diary that he was fed up with 'this necessity of "petting" Hardie. I never have to do it with MacDonald.'[12]

After Harry's death Sylvia moved to rooms in 42 Linden Gardens, Notting Hill, near the nursing home where Harry had died. It was away from the centres of activity in which she and Hardie were involved and Hardie would occasionally come to visit, walking the whole distance through Hyde Park and Kensington Gardens. Sylvia claims they spent their time discussing 'the coming of socialism',[13] and there is no doubt that the political bond had tightened. But so too had the personal; and in time, the physical. Glasier noted with great interest that 'Hardie had been reading the letters of George Sand and [was] curiously interested in her abnormal sensuality'.[14] As Isabella Ford remarked, Hardie had been brought up in another world and was very repressed.[15] Sylvia was not. She bombarded Hardie with her emotions. The most explicit are the poems, all undated. One, headed only by the figure 2, was written from prison.[16]

> Last night when all was quiet you came here
> I felt you in the darkness by my side

At first sight it seems a straightforward erotic poem, telling of 'kisses on my mouth' and 'your dear length pressing upon me 'til my breath came short'. She sees 'myself at home again upon my couch/and you bending to take me in your arms'. However, she soon realizes Hardie is absent. Not only is he not in prison, he is not there at all. The poem asks, 'Will it ever be?', but ends in defeat, 'I saw myself released to find not you'.

Another poem begins with 'a shadow . . . twixt you and me', but ends with assurances that 'no shadow can come betwixt your heart and mine'.[17] The poetry may be banal but the feelings are clear: 'But for your love . . . it would all be grey.' Likewise, the admiration: 'Like a mountain is your character.'[18]

It is unlikely Sylvia would have been so deluded as to direct so much passion towards one who showed no feelings in return. We can assume Hardie responded. His letters to Sylvia become much more affectionate, addressing her as 'Little Sweetheart' and referring occasionally to kisses.[19] Whether they were lovers, and if so, when this side of their life began, must remain unknown. Romero believes it started in 1904;[20] Morgan suspects 'she may have been his mistress', but possibly not until now.[21] Either way, a full sexual relationship would not have been without difficulties. Romero suggests that since Sylvia would have refused to have an abortion – she did not believe in it – it was probable that Hardie practised *coitus interruptus*, a common method of birth control at the time.

It is also possible that the truth lies closer to the intense and passionate affairs Katharine Glasier had had before marriage, where she lived with the man as his 'spirit wife' in a highly emotional embrace that fell short of consummation. What is interesting about such speculation is not what we can deduce about Hardie's and Sylvia's sexual relations, because there is not the evidence to decide either way, but the extreme reluctance of biographers or historians to comment on the matter at all. Some of the writing has all the incredulity of children speculating about their grandparents. Reverence for Hardie as Labour father figure seems to prevent our seeing him as a man like any other; or perhaps a man like many another Victorian, attracted to sex with the innocent, the 'child' in all but years.

On the other hand, that Hardie did not hide his affection from visitors like Brockway, allowing Sylvia to remain upon his knee while they talked, suggests he did not perceive it as immoral, that he saw it, as Brockway did, as father/daughter affection.[22] Yet it was the same Hardie who had refused to stay with Robert Blatchford because he saw a girl sitting on a man's knee across the room. Either Hardie was applying double standards or his relationship with Sylvia never really compromised her.

During 1910, parliamentary life was uneasily poised, with Labour and the Irish holding the balance. The timid leadership of the Labour Party continued and the Liberal government was not pressed in any way. The situation was symbolized by the Labour Party's move to new seats on the government side below the gangway.[23] Behind the scenes[24] MacDonald was co-operating (and wining and dining) with Liberals at every turn and denying it publicly with every speech, as were Labour MPs, particularly trade union ones.[25] Hardie, however, commented, 'the Labour Party had ceased to count'.[26] He knew that rank and file feeling among socialists about the inertia at the top was running high, and in the summer the 'Green Manifesto' made its appearance, written by four disaffected members of the ILP,[27] calling for socialist unity and criticizing the Labour Party in Parliament for its refusal to oppose the government in any way. As it questioned the ILP's links with the Parliamentary Party, it received much press coverage, but was coldly reviewed by such ILP leaders as Glasier.[28] Although it contained criticism that Hardie was making privately – and the authors had contacted him about it – Hardie said nothing in public, no doubt preferring to make his own criticisms in his own way. Hardie did not tag along after others.

Despite a widespread wish for socialist unity – and the persistent requests of the International that Britain's socialists in the ILP, Labour Party, Fabians and SDF get together – suspicion and hostility among Left groups continued. Snowden saw the Labour Party as still torn between the 'possibilists' and the 'impossibilists'.[29] Now the argument was affecting the ILP. Hardie was particularly wary about Hyndman and Blatchford making common cause with disillusioned ILP members (still being stirred up by Grayson) threatening 'his' organization. In fact, what socialists outside the ILP and Labour Party had been organizing was only to be expected: a Socialist Representation Committee, which planned to launch a socialist party.

Hardie took what chances he could in 1910 to go abroad, where he felt far more appreciated. His deepest attachment – to his audiences – was weakening in Britain. The public was used to Hardie. A Unionist

backbencher wrote later that he had lost his power to fascinate.[30]
Abroad he found the honour he needed and he accepted all invitations,
however quirky. In May he was in Lille, as guest speaker for the
National Council of the Pleasant Sunday Afternoon. So many workers
turned up to hear him in the great union hall in Lille's centre, that he
had to repeat the speech to an overflow of 6,000 outside in the square.[31]
He wrote to Rose Davies, who was now a regular correspondent, that
it was all a 'great success'.[32] He gave his audience politics, religion
and mysticism: the general strike as a political force, like the 'power'
that exists beyond the natural world, at one with the Christianity of
Christ. French Catholic members of the CGT found him awesome
but incomprehensible.

In August the International's Bureau met in Brussels to prepare
for the International's meeting in Copenhagen in September. Hardie
wrote to Sylvia that they were working from 9 a.m. to 9 p.m. every day
and 'I am thoroughly enjoying the work'.[33] We are 'having the usual
trouble with the SDF', but we 'now have them in hand' and 'have
turned Hyndman off the Bureau', voted off by the British delegation
for his support for war preparations. Hardie told Sylvia, 'I shall postcard
you from place to place but dearie don't expect letters'. Hardie never
suspended his schedule for anyone – not even Sylvia. She had to be
fitted into his life like everyone else; and there is no doubt she felt
it keenly. In November he wrote, '. . . hope the gloom has passed'.[34]
He was going from Brussels to Antwerp to 'see the galleries'. Hardie
always took time out for art museums in any place he visited.

He was now sending as many postcards to Rose Davies as to
Sylvia and from many of the same places, and she would visit him
in London in the same way Sylvia did. She would usually stay at
the Hotel Bingham near Neville's Court,[35] sometimes arriving with
other Welsh socialists, sometimes on her own. They would eat (as
Hardie often did) at the Food Reform Restaurant in Furnival St[36] –
Hardie was now a firm vegetarian – and once they went to hear Harry
Lauder at the Palace Theatre.[37] Hardie had come to prefer vaudeville
and told Rose, 'I never go to the theatre any more'.[38] Most often,
however, they would go to the House of Commons. Rose was very
political. She and Hardie continually discussed the constituency and
the ILP. In Merthyr he often stayed with Rose and her husband,
but less often after 1910, when their first child was born. Once he
proposed to her how he and she and two other comrades might return
from a Merthyr meeting making a 'merry party of four: discreetly and
judiciously paired, crossing the mountain in delicious darkness'.[39] In
all his letters to Rose there is the same playful tone Hardie used with
women he really liked.

In September Hardie was the ILP delegate at the International
Socialist Congress in Copenhagen. The main resolution asked for

compulsory international arbitration in disputes, for ultimate disarmament, and the end of secret diplomacy, using the 'economical and
political crisis created by war in order to rouse the masses to hasten the
downfall of . . . the capitalist class.'[40] Hardic's amendment for a general
strike in the event of international war, supported by Edouard Vaillant,
an equally determined French anti-militarist had to be pushed against
the hidden opposition of German socialists, and met the same fate as
several resolutions from Karl Liebknecht at earlier SDP congresses.[41]
All Hardie could get in the end was an agreement 'to consider . . .
the general strike, especially in industries that supply war material, as
one of the methods of preventing war'.[42] The main bulk of German
socialists did not support him, believing that capitalism was developing
too quickly to make these tactics effective. Many of the majority who
voted for his amendment were sceptical. Hardie did not seem alarmed.
He wrote to Sylvia,[43] 'My speech was much applauded'.

Back in Britain another general election had been called as a result
of failure to resolve the deadlock between Commons and Lords, which
many socialists believed had developed because the House of Lords,
quiescent for decades, was now alarmed at the rise of Labour and the
threat of socialism, and had suddenly decided to assert itself. Hardie
spent his election time making his own 'independent' proposals, while
MacDonald saw to it that the Labour Party officially fought on a
platform of support for the Liberals' programme.

Hardie kept up his interest in suffrage matters, supporting where
he could, but militarism began to preoccupy him more. During
the autumn the ILP had been running an anti-militarist campaign.
In December it took the Albert Hall for a huge international
demonstration against the war that ILP socialists feared was coming
between European nations.[44] Jaurès came from France, Vandervelde
from Belgium, and Walter T. Mills from the USA. Hardie was in the
chair and Britain was represented by MacDonald. It was a big occasion
by any standard, especially with a general election in full swing. Yet
neither the subject nor the event received any real press coverage.
The growing fear about war went unheard. The election campaign
concerned itself almost entirely with the continuing political soap opera
of Lords versus people, boiling down, as far as voters went, according
to Stewart, to 'What was Mr Asquith going to give them?'[45]

Lillie and Nan came to London for the Albert Hall meeting, which
was also attended by several Lib-Lab MPs, Cunninghame Graham and
Max Beer.[46] Hardie spoke badly. George Bernard Shaw told Glasier
the speeches had been 'a deluge of cant'. Hardie brought Lillie and
Nan to the reception afterwards but left early to go to Wales, giving
Glasier the task of taking them to the Midlands the next day, where
they were due to say with the Bensons for two days, a visit Hardie had
arranged to give them a break. He still had them on his conscience.

Glasier confided to his sister, 'I was not gallant to them'. To Hardie's colleagues, Lillie and Nan were not easy going.

The second 1910 election was not as fraught as the first, though the anti-socialist campaign against Hardie had stirred up hostility. Declaring for Hardie was not always popular, especially for pastors of the more conservative churches. From the Railway Temperance Hotel in Cardiff he wrote to the Reverend John Hughes of the English Methodists in Abercynon, to say 'how deeply touched I am by the step you have taken at this election'.[47] He added, 'I hear that already you are being made to feel that the age of persecution is not yet over'.

Hardie told him that most ministers 'seem to have no desire other than to appear . . . respectable' for 'fear of offending the rich . . . the modern minister is not unlike the scribes and the pharisees whom Jesus denounced'. Nor was John Hughes unlike the Congregationalist Andrew Scott whom Hardie had defended long ago in Cumnock, when he took one of those significant first steps which changed his life's direction. Hardie tried to cheer Hughes by telling him his children 'are . . . I know feeling a new pride in their dear old father', and, as an afterthought, added 'your good wife . . . will stand by you'.

Elizabeth Hughes, whose life had been one long struggle to make ends meet, had no choice but to support her husband in his new battle against those in the congregation and community who opposed his support for Keir Hardie. She had been born the daughter of a well-to-do builder who had disapproved of her love for the poor theology student in the first place, when he was training at a Calvinistic Methodist College in Wales.[48] He was so poor he had to work in the pits during his holidays to earn money to keep himself. After they married, her life, according to her son, Emrys, was nothing but 'poverty and drudgery,' only 'sustained by two wisps of hair . . . kept in faded envelopes', curls from the heads of a boy and girl who had died when they were three and four.[49]

In 1898 the Hughes family had moved to Abercynon, a town at the bottom end of the Merthyr Boroughs constituency. The Reverend Hughes was a hard worker and suffered from pneumoconiosis, a condition he had contracted during his mining years.[50] Emrys recalled that life at home was nothing but 'cough, cough, cough'.[51]

The Reverend Hughes was also a scholar who had an implicit belief 'in the literal accuracy of the Bible'.[52] He hoped for recognition and in 1903 he had even sent a copy of a theological work to Queen Alexandra,[53] but over the years he had been disappointed in this. His children had become political and it was Hardie who helped him reconcile his religion with their socialism.

As Hardie's letter implies, he knew about the family's commitment because he had already made the acquaintance of all his children.

Roland, the oldest (always called Rowlie), had brought him home to tea earlier in the year. There he met Agnes, the family's only daughter, petite, pale, with large dark eyes, and longing to play her own role in life. She had been educated at home by her erudite father to a very high standard, but like so many other girls, plans for her future had stopped there. She balked at the idea of marriage as a career. Her parents did not want her to work. In her mid-twenties she was still at home, with no future of any kind, and energy to spend. Commitment to Keir Hardie and his cause offered her a start on life's work and she took it.

The last member of the family was Emrys, at sixteen the family rebel; he had already stopped going to his father's church on Sundays. He had met Hardie some years earlier when Hardie and Frank Smith had brought a lantern slide lecture to the Workmen's Hall in Mountain Ash, and Hardie had given a talk about his Empire tour.[54]

Hardie held his seat in the second election of 1910 and Labour held its numbers in Parliament. But there was no advance in Liberal numbers; and there was no alternative to MacDonald as leader of the Labour Party in Parliament. He took over in February 1911.

Hardie found compensation in the arrival of several new MPs who would strengthen the socialist contingent. The first was Tom Richardson, a miner from Whitehaven and a strong ILP supporter. Unlike Hardie who had left his family behind, Richardson's wife and daughters moved to London with him, and took lodgings round the corner from Neville's Court in High Holborn. By February Hardie wrote to Glasier that Richardson was already making his mark in Parliament.[55] But the new member who most cheered Hardie was George Lansbury. He had worked energetically for socialism for twenty years, almost all of it in the East End of London, almost all of it in local government, almost all of the time a member of the SDF. Lansbury was flamboyant in manner, ardent in intent. Hardie claimed he brought 'quite a new spirit into the party',[56] a party which Lansbury believed strongly should be explicitly socialist. He had already been elected on to the ILP's ruling committee (NAC), where during 1910 he had dutifully helped to persuade members not to accept Fred Jowett's proposal that the Labour Party in Parliament should vote on 'the merits' of each issue rather than give Liberal policy free passage.[57] He had also helped oppose the 'Green Manifesto'. When he got to the House, however, he found its criticism of Labour's inaction to be fairly accurate. He was astounded at the disaffected ranks and MacDonald's inert leadership, and he let it be known. In the *Labour Leader* in March he wrote that 'nothing will be accomplished . . . until fear of turning the government out of office has been overcome'.[58] In April Fenner Brockway, now working on the *Leader*, reported Lansbury saying, 'I am going to refuse to vote . . . from the Liberal standpoint' because my constituents 'sent me to face the question of poverty, poverty, poverty'.[59]

The 'new atmosphere' Hardie detected soon ran up against MacDonald's firm hand. As soon as he had become leader MacDonald immediately sent a memo to forty-two Labour MPs[60] to say something had to be done about the criticism from 'our members in the country' and the lack of loyalty and cohesion among MPs. Cleverly, he intimated the first was caused by the second, and ordered obedience to a Party line in public: 'Party meetings are the place to discuss differences.' This was a necessary public relations exercise. The problem, however, was that criticism was not arising because Labour MPs were saying different things, since they had always done so, but because the policy MacDonald wanted was not identifiably different from that of the Liberal government. In time, even the increasingly conservative Glasier complained to his Diary that MacDonald is just a 'progressive Liberal. All fight and lofty inspiration is lacking'.[61] As for Hardie, all 'he is ever thinking about is being displaced by MacDonald'.[62]

This was not quite so. Hardie may have been a prima donna, as Glasier observed, unhappy 'unless in the limelight',[63] but he never shirked his share of the work off stage. He still tramped the country as extra-parliamentary missionary for socialism. He complained about MacDonald's failure to encourage 'the revolutionary spirit of the working class' and about 'no young men of high purpose coming up in the movement'[64] (Grayson had been a bitter disappointment), and whenever he met one who seemed committed, he spared no effort to encourage him. In 1911 James Henderson, a young man he had heard speaking in Scotland, and found quite free of youth's 'besetting sin . . . pomposity', wrote asking how to become an agitator for socialism.

Hardie's advice throws light on his own approach to his 'life's work',[65] telling him first to understand 'Marxist socialism' (significantly, not to read Marx but rather a popular explanation of his ideas).[66] Second, to keep 'well in touch with current thought' – literary, religious and scientific. Hardie always did this himself. Sylvia testified to the interest he showed in subjects as far apart as Mendelian theory and *Hedda Gabler*.[67] The third was to do plenty of 'open air work' – speaking to people where they lived and worked. For this, always 'borrow your illustrations from current events' and 'deal with topics uppermost in the minds of your hearers, pointing out always the difference between what is proposed and what should be done'. You can show them at once 'how this leads to socialism'. His last word to a fellow Scot, 'When in doubt, stick close to Burns.'

At the same time Hardie knew that the old way – the 'open air' way – had a great rival. An increasingly literate population meant that newspapers and journals were taking over as the way people were made aware of political arguments. Since 1910, therefore, Hardie had been busy thinking about a socialist daily paper. It was a call that had waited a surprisingly long time, given the rise in anti-socialist propaganda after 1906. The Conservatives and Liberals countered socialism on every street corner through the *Chronicle, Telegraph, Mail, Express* and *Star*, but neither socialists nor Labour had a mass newspaper. The earlier successes were increasingly sectarian. *Justice* was in a tug of war with its own supporters and the *Clarion* had all but died, with Blatchford now writing for the *Daily Mail*, urging conscription.[68] There were radical papers like *Reynolds News*. But there was nothing in Britain like the large numbers of newspapers the German socialists could count on, and which much impressed Hardie whenever he went abroad.[69] Hardie believed the movement needed its own paper, if only to combat 'the newer rags of the Harmsworth type' that sound 'the depths of gutterdom'.[70]

Hardie had been spurred to do something about this when an 'unknown comrade' had sent him £1,000 to help start a socialist daily and a known one offered £5,000.[71] Among Hardie's papers is a letter from a woman called Miss Simu Seruya, a well-to-do Jewish socialist of Spanish descent, who worked at the Suffrage Shop at the Temple (and was possibly directed to Hardie by Sylvia Prankhurst). She too wrote to offer money to start a national socialist newspaper.[72] Hardie thanked her for her 'most generous offer' and said he would float the idea at once in the *Labour Leader*. Meanwhile, he asked if she 'would be able to help . . . with our new socialist weekly in my constituency' and suggests £50 for the *Merthyr Pioneer*.[73] She must have sent the money, for about this time the *Pioneer* started regular publication.[74]

Hardie's proposals for a national paper were ambitious but exclusive – basically, a *Labour Leader* writ large, run by the ILP with a regular Hardie input, a Hardie 'self-advertisement scheme' Glasier called it later,[75] but this was unfair. The scheme was democratic and realistic and Hardie had a serious point:[76]

> I want a daily paper that will be definitely socialist but which will give support to the Labour Party. By 'definitely socialist' I mean that its propaganda . . . [and] outlook, will be socialist and that socialism will dominate the whole tone and make of the paper.[77]

He wanted a counterweight to the anti-socialist 'outlook' of every other national newspaper. In 1906 he had told his Merthyr audience, 'your opinions are manufactured for you by the great organs of the daily press and these are bought and sold by the rich as it suits their purpose.'[78]

While Hardie's concern was for the perspective of the new paper (and keeping control of the money he was always able to attract), both the ILP and the Labour Party wanted a paper jointly run by the ILP and the Labour Party, so as to include trade union funding. Hardie, so firm a supporter of this wider alliance when it was a question of forming a political party, was completely opposed when it came to a national newspaper. Experience of the Labour Party had disillusioned him. If a paper followed the present policy of the official Labour Party, would it be any inspiration to the millions who needed it?

Hardie was overruled by both the Labour Party and the ILP. From then on he refused to have anything to do with the new paper and instead concentrated on the *Pioneer*, happy that he could once more address the world weekly with his own brand of aggressive but indeterminate socialism, or what Morgan calls his 'unofficial but constitutionally oriented militancy'.[79] He could also promote his protégés. Sylvia, for example, was given an occasional column, signing herself 'S'. Lansbury, who had a flair for publishing and was already bringing out a strike sheet called the *Daily Herald*, sided with Hardie. He began forming the idea of making the strike sheet into the kind of paper Hardie envisaged. Glasier, who had sided with MacDonald, soon had second thoughts, 'I noticed . . . MacDonald . . . used the word "democratic" rather than "labour" or "socialist" as describing the character of the paper. Why does MacDonald ALWAYS seem to try to shirk the word "Socialism"?'[80]

In Parliament in 1911, despite MacDonald's strictures, Hardie reverted to his Party of One. As Benson remarked, he was 'incapable of working with a party'.[81] On several other issues he was virtually alone. Parliament was to consider a proposal that MPs at last be paid; £400 a year was the amount suggested. Hardie voted against it. He also attacked it at the ILP Conference in Leicester in March 1911. Yet he was consistent, for he had always opposed it. It would mean careerists, not genuine socialists; in a later letter to Aggie Hughes in Abercynon, he told her not to worry about the ILP having no money to pay someone for some vital work, 'one volunteer is worth ten pressed men.'[82] The proposal roused in him the old fear of the corrupting effects of Parliament on working men, perhaps also unacknowledged fears of his own weakness as regards money. The ILP voted against him, and so did most Labour MPs in the PLP. At a time when the Osborne judgment was shutting off TUC funding and candidates were finding it impossible to raise money to fight elections, how could they do otherwise?

Although MacDonald continued temporizing politically, organizationally he was a much better leader of the Parliamentary Party than Barnes, Henderson, or Hardie, always *au fait* with what was happening at Westminster in both government and opposition, and attentive to all events in the political domain that could have a bearing on Labour's electoral success. He had by no means ruled out thoughts of a new alliance with the Liberals. Hardie, however, became increasingly critical of the Liberals' reforming legislation, which the PLP leadership was generally in favour of giving a clear passage. In 1911 it was the National Health and Unemployment Insurance Bill, which, like every other Liberal Act, was a poor substitute for measures Hardie had originally urged. Its provisions were limited to fewer than three million workmen, and only provided benefits for fifteen weeks. The most galling provision to Hardie was that workers were also expected to contribute, which he saw as a poll tax on the working class. He asked why the principle that was used for education, public health and old age pensions was not used here. In the committee stage of the Bill he criticized the inadequate level of compensation for workers, maternity benefits, and unmarried mothers' provision. On this last he also had to contend with the mixed morality of the women's movement. Suffragettes campaigned strongly against the Bill on the grounds that matters so domestic ought not to be legislated upon by men alone. On the other side was the Women's Mission to the Fallen, who supported the Bill but urged Hardie that 'in the interests of morality it is of vital importance that the maternity benefit of 30/- shall not be given when the child is illegitimate' (further proof of how public opinion still lay on a matter of such personal importance to both Hardie and MacDonald).[83] On the third reading, the Labour Party Whip required MPs to vote for the Bill. Hardie refused and abstained. Lansbury and Jowett and three others voted against it.[84] The rest of the Party voted for it. So much for MacDonald's first ruling that all Labour MPs take the same line.

As so often happened in Hardie's political life when he found himself drifting towards Liberalism (as he had been since 1908), it was events in the industrial field that re-radicalized him. For many years the labour movement outside Parliament had been quiescent. Harbinger of a new period of extra-parliamentary unrest was Hardie's old friend, Tom Mann, returning after eight years in New Zealand and Australia. It was the SDF, however, rather than the ILP, who marked the event by holding a welcome-back meeting on 23 May 1910. Hyndman took the chair and Ben Tillett told the audience about Mann's success in organizing unions in Australia. Harry Quelch, now editor of *Justice*, told him, 'we wanted someone to wake us up'.[85] Mann returned their compliments by joining the SDF rather than rejoining the ILP.

Mann's main activity during the rest of 1910 and into 1911, however, had nothing to do with either party. Instead he toured the country, trying to win converts to industrial unionism by speaking up and down the land, and by distributing a new journal called the *Industrial Syndicalist*, that sold for a penny. By these means he popularized the conclusions he had come to in New Zealand and Australia: 'Rely on

your own organization and your own methods. Resort to direct action'
to hasten the day 'when poverty will be banished for ever'. People
should 'work out their salvation with a minimum of parliamentary
action' because Parliament at heart is just another way 'to enable . . .
[the] ruling class to have more effective means of dominating and
subjecting the working class'.[86]

He told those who came to an SDF meeting in Blackburn[87]
that political action through elections had accomplished 'exceedingly
little' for the workers of Britain. Elections just took up their time,
and the result was that everyone 'had become so absorbed in
parliamentary work that they had given no attention to the industrial
side'. Everywhere he went he deplored the tame state of the unions,
signing agreements with employers for a mere pittance of a wage rise
instead of using their power as workers to organize politically. He saw
the main problem as being that unions were organized into trades
when they should be organized by industry: all workers in the mines
in one organization rather than a host of different unions according
to whether men were winders or face-workers. Mann set up shop at
the dock workers' headquarters in East London and invited British
workers to contact him: both sexes. Mann wanted women to join
trade unions equally.[88] His aim was gigantic: to force the reality of
a world workforce on his listeners.

Mann commanded respect for his knowledge of workers' organizations the world over. The word 'syndicalist' had come from France,
'a Latin version', Mann called it, of industrial unionism, the words
he always tried to use instead. Bill Haywood in the United States,
organizer of the Industrial Workers of the World (IWW), lent his
objectives to Mann's new venture: 'the merging of labour forces into
one gigantic organization' to 'unite the workers of all parts of the
world, no matter what race, creed or colour'.[89] In October, Mann
urged such an organization in Britain, 'unite' as Marx had urged
'so long ago'. Like Haywood, he too counselled, 'no contracts, no
agreements, no compacts' with employers.

Hardie had always respected Mann and believed union organization
and strikes were great teachers. Privately he would even have had to
agree that the parliamentary road – at least at present – was producing
very little that was of direct benefit to the majority of workers and
their families. But to cast aside all electoral activity, after having
staked his own career on trying to make it work, was not possible.
Nor was a system where workers and owners had no relationship,
as it blocked all development towards classlessness. At the same time,
Mann's words chimed with views Hardie himself had been putting
about the limitations of Parliament, 'If democracy has any meaning',
Hardie said, 'it must mean that the mass of the people in their own
strength, evolve solutions to their own problems.' They should not

depend on leaders, for 'unless the working class can evolve leaders from its own ranks, it is doomed'.[90]

Meanwhile, Mann's success was mixed. He found it difficult to wean British trade unionists away from their own unions. But he found it easy to stimulate interest in unions themselves, particularly among unskilled workers. The situation was ripe for it. Trade was booming but wages had stayed low and £1 was still the average wage, with 63 per cent of workers on the railways, for example, paid less.[91] Hardie had given figures to the Labour Party Conference in 1909, showing that since 1901 wages had gone down £1.3 million a year while incomes of those wealthy enough to pay income tax had gone up by £147 million.[92] Four years after Mann had arrived back in Britain union membership had nearly doubled to four million.[93]

Mann was a gifted orator whose impassioned speeches were delivered from all points of a platform, striding back and forth, firing his arguments to every section of an audience – the way a modern pop singer might perform. The young Harry Pollitt, who was taken along as a boy to hear him, whispered to his father, 'That's how I want to be!'[94] To have heard Hardie was moving; to have heard Mann, exhilarating.

'Syndicalism is now on the lips of all politicians,' said Glasier disapprovingly, 'the majority of whom do not know what it means.'[95] This was intended as a dart at Hardie who had half welcomed syndicalism as a sign of reviving activity in the working class, if only because a whole new generation of leaders seemed to spring into being, many in Hardie's own territory of South Wales. These were the leaders he had rhetorically asked for, the 'young men of high purpose', men such as Charles Stanton, one of Hardie's own local political organizers; and Noah Ablett, a checkweighman at Maerdy pit, who told a 1910 audience, 'The mission of the workers is not to go in for increased wages for themselves but to emancipate the whole of the working class.'[96] Behind these new leaders was a string of workers' education conferences and classes and new organizations like the Plebs League and the Central Labour College, formed by dissident Ruskin College students, teaching that political action began and ended with the workers' activity on their own behalf.

There was plenty of opportunity to see workers' own activity – and employers' intransigence, particularly over union recognition. The gap between wages and prices soon brought unrest everywhere: in the mines, the railways, the docks, iron foundries, shipping – with an average of ten million days a year lost by stoppages every year from 1910 to 1913.[97] Two Labour historians have recently called this unprecedented explosion after so many years of labour calm, the 'Big Bang'.[98] Snowden put it down to poor living conditions side by side 'with the spread of education, with the display of wealth and luxury of the rich'.[99]

At the end of 1910 a strike broke out at the Cambrian Combine in Tonypandy (the objective was pay parity with other colliers in respect of a new seam just opened in the Rhondda Valley – in fact, a minimum wage).[100] The stoppage was so swift, successful and prolonged, the government called in the police. Mann was quickly there to make sure that the men kept orderly and united, and did not return violence with violence. It was difficult, since he saw, and reported, that the police provoked the miners and their families.[101]

Hardie, who knew full well the abysmal standards of living that prevailed among miners, was soon there as well, as some of the mines were in the Aberdare area. He too saw 'men, women and children mauled by police'[102] and was outraged to read the press describing the miners and their families as 'hooligans' rather than workers (the word 'O'Hooligan', coined in the 1890s, being a denigratory reference to immigrant Irish workers). Hardie was able to show it was at the mine-owners' wish that the troops had come in and not, as the government claimed, because there was a threat to law and order.

It was very much the same situation Hardie had faced in 1887 in Scotland and it brought out the same fighting spirit. This time he went straight to Parliament and got the adjournment debate on 15 November,[103] reporting that he personally had seen the police 'bludgeon the people right and left', giving a graphic description of an old man whose barrow the police 'tipped into the canal and knocked him in after it'. Hardie faced Churchill to say the police at the colliery were 'guarding the owners' property' not the community's law and order. The government is 'taking sides with the employers and is sending these men into the colliery field to help intimidate . . . the strikers'.[104]

Churchill called Hardie a 'disgrace' for questioning police tactics, for attacking the use of the Hussars, and for suggesting the government's objective was to protect mine-owners and blacklegs. In some of his charges, however, Hardie had the backing of his fellow Merthyr Liberal MP.[105]

The emotion of the situation was much heightened because of two major colliery disasters that year, the first at Whitehaven in early summer, where 130 had died, and the second at the end of the year at the Hulton collieries in Lancashire.[106] Hardie threw himself into the political pulpit to draw the lessons from both, and to represent the grief of these communities. After rescue stopped in Whitehaven and the mine was bricked up, Hardie claimed the men were probably still alive.

Churchill called his statement 'disgraceful', but not only did Hardie not retract, he went on to say how the men could have survived if the owners had carried out the safety work for which the unions, and he himself, had been asking (by always providing an escape route around 'the bottleneck'). 'I hope Mr Churchill is not more concerned about shielding the mine-owner than he is about finding out the truth.'[107] It was from these occasions that Hardie developed his hatred and distrust of Winston Churchill as a man 'who cannot be trusted to go straight on any . . . subject'.[108]

The Cambrian colliery dispute dragged on throughout 1911, by which time the seamen were on strike, followed by the railway workers (for the first time), sparked by the railway companies' refusal to recognize the railway workers' union. In August 1911, one of the hottest summers ever recorded in Britain, troops were used again. At one point it was estimated that every available soldier in service was held ready for action. In the Commons Hardie called Churchill's statement that it was the local authorities rather than the government who asked for troops, 'the lie direct'.[109] A few days later on 22 August 1911, two workers were killed in Llanelli by troops. Another two were killed in Liverpool. A reporter from London who went to Liverpool where Tom Mann was in charge said, 'It was as near to a revolution as anything I had seen in England'.[110] Some months later, as strikes continued, the national conciliator gave gloomy warnings that the military could not hold the line and Austen Chamberlain commented, 'the whole machinery of national life is slowly stopping'.[111]

Hardie was touched by the suffering of strikers and their families and, as usual, wrote frantically to people he knew who had money. Simu Seruya, for example, was asked for 'an immediate £100' for the strikers at Tonypandy.[112] Hardie quickly brought out a pamphlet as well, *Killing No Murder*, surveying the duplicity of the Liberal government and explaining the people's grievance. He wrote that he had seen 'a degree of class solidarity . . . few believed possible' when the strike had started.

Hardie's stand caused MacDonald difficulty, because he was taking part in the conciliation activity being led by Lloyd George.[113] Very late in the day the government exerted the necessary pressure on railway-and mine-owners to settle. Transport unions got recognition and an inquiry into workers' grievances was promised. Instead of giving Lloyd George the credit for the settlement, which Lloyd George expected, Hardie attacked him bitterly for not having moved sooner. Lloyd George was infuriated; Hardie had made another powerful enemy. This time a Welshman – at a time when Welsh Nationalists were just beginning to question the idea of having a Scot like Hardie sitting for a Welsh seat.[114]

In time, Snowden began to worry that industrial action would harm Labour, as the public were increasingly inconvenienced.[115] Hardie saw the force of this argument[116] but he had also long believed that industrial action would strengthen the work to be done in Parliament: 'politicians never concede a reform because it is right but only because it is a danger to withhold it any longer.'[117]

As concession after concession was made to trade unions in 1911 and 1912, Mann saw this as proof that unions had no need of Parliament. Hardie's view had always been that 'the power of trade unions through the strike had been immense, but their power through the ballot box was immensely greater'.[118] To Mann and the syndicalists, and to many millions in the workforce, the ballot box had yet to prove itself. The work of consolidating unions had to go on.

By mid-1911 Hardie was beginning to take some of this argument on board. At the start of the railway strike he spoke at a huge open-air meeting in Merthyr Park, supporting the strikers and attacking the use of the military:

> I am getting not only an old man but an old politician . . . I can read the signs of the times . . . The old idea of separate unions has passed away. The colliers, the ironworkers, the steelworkers, the artisans, the railway men, the shop assistants, the school teachers, the gasworkers and the street cleaners have all got to stand together, not as members of different trades but as members of one class.[119]

Hardie had accommodated syndicalism in spirit but he was not prepared to concede elections, which he (like the suffragettes) always saw as opportunities for educating people and developing their political understanding. The issue was compounded when − at last − the British Socialist Party was formed officially at the end of 1911. They too planned to contest elections (despite the fact that they were split on almost every issue, syndicalism included). Mann's independent line had long before annoyed the SDF and after only a year of membership he had left, after which he made it clear he had no faith in political parties. Everything hinged on workers learning to take over the running of society themselves. Workers were warned of the developing 'servile state' (a phrase Hilaire Belloc had coined when the National Insurance Act was passed), including an education system designed to give capitalists more profit out of 'more intelligent labour'.[120] Mann argued that 'the politician of today' attaches so much importance to 'getting elected' that he neglects what used to be his main activity, 'the education of the worker himself'.[121]

Hardie would have had sympathy with this view as well as with Mann's assertion that 'when he gets to Parliament he simply gets swamped by his new environment', but Hardie stuck with the state and with Parliament not just because he believed 'the ballot is much more effective than the barricade',[122] but because he saw the political task of winning independence for Labour had not really been completed. He told his audience in Merthyr in 1911 that Liberals will give you insurance Bills and similar 'kinds of soothing syrups to keep you quiet, but in the end your Liberal Party, just like your Tory Party, is the party of the rich, and exists to protect the rich when Labour and Capital come into conflict . . . Make up your mind whom you will serve, Labour and Socialism, or Liberalism and Capitalism . . . The day for temporising is over'.[123] Although Hardie never expected the Labour Party to stay dominated by trade unions permanently,[124] their parliamentary connection had to be retained for the present. Finance always brought Hardie back to earth. There was no option but to try to mix 'the oil and water of socialism and radical trade unionism', as a contemporary commentator referred to the Labour Party,[125] even though Hardie used the same simile himself in a reverse direction when arguing to constituents in Merthyr that a Labour Party that was 'half Liberal, half Labour' would not succeed because 'you cannot mix oil and water'.[126]

On labour and socialist issues Hardie differed markedly from MacDonald, and the gap was widening, but on the international front, events were working to draw them closer, united in opposing the arms race and secret diplomacy. Hardie's proposal in 1910's International for the general strike against war had had MacDonald's support (even if not his confidence in its efficacy), as did Hardie's condemnation of Hyndman and Blatchford for the much disputed decision to make war preparation the cornerstone of the new British Socialist Party.[127] Foreign affairs was one sphere where the Liberal government had Conservative support, which left the field clear for Labour to carve out policy territory of its own against a background of increasing quarrels between capitalist countries over the world's resources.

In 1911 Hardie and MacDonald were again at one over the Moroccan crisis arising out of French and German rivalry in that area. The British government had indulged in brinkmanship on France's side, claiming it was a democratic issue, while German and British socialists tried to cool the temperature. Hardie drew the moral in a Commons debate in November. It was not about 'the promotion of the liberties of the peoples of those countries . . . It was about the protection of profits and dividends'.[128] But few shared Hardie's analysis or his fears about the build-up of military forces going on in Britain and the fact that the government was prepared to shoot its way out of both social and diplomatic crises. Again and again he highlighted the military nature of anti-strike operations. At home and abroad the same evil was at work. He was equally opposed to retaliatory military action by workers, or by the new 'brigades' of miners that younger socialists in Wales were advocating. Miners had real grievances, but settlement could only come when grievances were ended – by stepping up agitation if need be – but not through violence.

Hardie's fears internationally were shared by several radical Liberals inside Parliament, and others outside it who had also taken fright at the inevitability of endless conflict over world resources. One unlikely recruit was a journalist on the *Daily Mail*, Norman Angell, a diminutive bachelor, under five feet tall, who had become determined to wean the world away from the idea of territorial conquest as a means of gaining power and property. Angell saw the solution in conquest by trade. This was peaceful as well as more productive for the economy. He frankly recognized, as Marxists did, the reality of the trade war. Unlike them, however, he believed it need not necessarily lead to war provided nations with common interests developed collective security that replaced national armies. In 1908 Angell had published a book, *The Great Illusion*, setting out his views. It was an instant sensation and went into dozens of reprintings. Hardie read it and praised it in the House of Commons,[129] saying prophetically, 'You might sink the German fleets, you might even by a miracle destroy the German army, but the invasion of the German trader will continue,' since the 'successful trading nation is the nation without either army, navy or empire, which is not burdened by taxes.' Norman Angell got in touch at once.[130] His wish was to distribute his book to those not likely to be able to afford it, such as working people. Angell believed education was the key to peace.

Hardie invited him to the House and they agreed to have the book distributed to all ILP branches.[131] Hardie sent Angell addresses of unions, so they too could receive copies. The project was financed by Arnold Rowntree, who had committed the Quaker business community to Angell's ideas.[132] Angell, in thanking Hardie, said he was keeping an open mind on socialism, and implied he might be ready to join the Labour Party, possibly even the ILP. Hardie replied that 'it never occurred to me you were a socialist'.[133] Hardie's benevolent attitude to co-operating in foreign affairs with Liberals, or even progressive Conservatives, was in sharp contrast to his anger when a Lib-Lab MP had asked him to a meeting to discuss common ground on domestic issues like trade union legislation: 'I . . . ask you not to again take the unwarrantable liberty of inviting me to any future meeting of this kind.'[134] If the issue was peace, Hardie's usual political rules – even that of independence – did not apply.

Norman Angell also got in touch with MacDonald, but separately and without telling Hardie, an indication of the way the Establishment now viewed the respective roles of each leader. For MacDonald the invitation was to a lunch in Paris and later to a working weekend at a hotel in Le Touquet, where many influential Britons were assembled to meet their opposite numbers from Europe. Angell's book had already been published in France, Spain and Germany. Funds for this (and for the Le Touquet get-together) had come from Hardie's old enemy, Andrew Carnegie (whose foundation gave $36,000 for the purpose).[135] Although Angell's long-term plans for a new Europe did not materialize until two world wars had ravaged society, he caught the imagination of a wide range of opinion. His correspondence list numbered 2,500 contemporaries.[136]

In September 1911 Hardie attended the German Socialists' (SDP) own yearly conference as a fraternal delegate. Had he spent much time (which he did not) with rank and file German socialists, he might have heard them talking of the need to defend themselves and their country from external attack,[137] but such talk was rigorously excluded from the platforms by SDP leaders, and Bebel's address on this occasion was substantially the same as the one he had given to the International in 1907 in Stuttgart: that there would be no war. It lasted for one hour and fifty minutes.[138] Hardie marvelled at such a performance from a man of seventy with a well-known 'internal complaint'. Hardie, who was only fifty-four, wrote home, 'Bebel looks younger than I do.'[139]

German socialists were admired as by far the best organized and most disciplined of socialist parties in Europe. Hardie noticed too that they had many more women delegates than any party in Britain would have had;[140] and they organized massive peace demonstrations outside the conference the whole time. Delegates like Hardie read this as yet another sign of German socialists' more advanced understanding of the dangers of military solutions; in fact, it arose because the socialists who organized it were only too well aware of the militarism that pervaded Germany. Hardie shared with Bebel and Jaurès the mistaken conviction that the ordinary workers who never came to conferences or belonged to parties were as internationalist as those who did.[141] This detachment from the generality of working people's beliefs was yet another consequence of the change in Hardie's life that 'being at the top' – and in Parliament – had wrought. It was also a sign that he had been right about the need for some means of influencing opinion, for the capitalist press was raking out the seed beds for war, and building up support for war preparations, and there were few opposing voices, outside the political circles in which Hardie moved, giving any other view. Workers' organizations on domestic issues were proving increasingly successful in many countries, but neither inside nor outside Parliament was any action proving effective in the international field.

12

A QUESTION OF WOMEN

In late July 1911, Margaret MacDonald had shown her husband her badly swollen finger, where she wore her engagement and wedding rings. She joked, 'It is only protesting against its burdens!'[1] Margaret MacDonald had borne many such, including the loss earlier that year of her small son, David, from diphtheria. In April her best friend, Mary Middleton, wife of James Middleton, assistant secretary of the Labour Party, died. Yet Margaret MacDonald carried on working as hard as ever, as a member of the Home Office Committee appointed to investigate the management of Industrial Schools and as a working member of the Anglo-American Friendship Committee, just then entertaining Professor Dubois, a black American, who had written on the plight of American negroes.[2] Margaret MacDonald insisted on going to hear him despite her finger. Worn down in spirit and body, she was unable to resist the infection, which gradually developed into generalized blood poisoning. By August she was confined to bed. All during the late summer – as the railway strike dragged on – her life ebbed away. Doctors had no means to combat the developing septicaemia.

Margaret MacDonald hadn't an enemy, it was said. Glasier said her 'unselfishness and amazing capacity for helpful work made her one of the best LIKED women I have known'.[3] Fenner Brockway, looking back, said simply, 'I loved her'; everyone did.[4] She was devoted to the cause and to her large family and she overworked continually in an attempt to combine the two. One of the Christmas cards the Hardie family saved for years was a large photograph of the whole MacDonald family sitting upright in their hall on a wooden bench – as if ready for action. The children had bare feet. Margaret MacDonald was as renowned for her indifference to social niceties as her husband later became for his attraction to them. Towards the end when the doctors had given up hope for her, she did not express regrets to her husband about dying young – her own mother had died when she was born; she had only said, 'I am very sorry to leave you – you and the children – alone.'[5] When her children were brought to her one by one to say goodbye, she told each one, 'Never marry except for love.'[6] MacDonald had found in her and his children the secure family life he had missed as a child. His grief was genuine and intense; his oldest son remembers it as 'horrifying to see'.[7] The wound never healed, according to his biographer,[8] but in time the deep feelings were covered over, and his intellectuality returned to take command, led by what Glasier called his 'devious' mind. Many who knew them both believed that had Margaret MacDonald lived, Ramsay MacDonald would have had a very different political life.

In the middle of 1911 structural faults were discovered in No. 14 Neville's Court.[9] On 2 June, with Maggie Symons's help, Hardie moved across the courtyard and up the stairs to No. 10, a larger flat with a bedroom. No longer would he have to sleep, work and entertain all in one room.

Neville's Court had attracted its set of myths and Hardie likewise, as a self-sufficient working man who wrote all his own letters and did all his own housework and cooking (and no doubt he was far more proficient than most other MPs). But a closer look shows that he had considerable support. There was a char who came to clean regularly;[10] 'Mrs S', who oversaw the Court's management, undertook errands;[11] the faithful Frank Smith who acted the part of the nineteenth-century secretary and organized shopping;[12] Miss Shields, a secretary in the Labour 'pool', and several men who acted in lieu of Frank Smith from time to time, known only by their last names.[13] In Cumnock Hardie had now enlisted James Henderson, the young teacher in training he had earlier advised on public speaking, to help Nan answer mail. Some of these helpers would have been paid by honorarium and not by a wage. Hardie did not like paying for help and certainly used his commanding position in the labour movement to get as much as he could for love.

The most hard-worked of all was Maggie Symons. Over time Hardie loaded more and more on to her, firing instructions as he travelled round: 'Enquire from Pease if he knows how many parishes within the metropolitan area';[14] 'Open everything which isn't marked confidential . . . use your judgement about forwarding';[15] 'Send women's suffrage leaflets'; 'make summarized translations of the enclosed' into French;[16] arrange the personal cuttings 'for insertion in the S book';[17] 'Frank has failed to make any provision for natural man. If you are about could you supply the omission . . . you could cook on Mrs S's fire';[18] 'Come today . . . let me dictate for a couple of hours. I have an urgent piece of work';[19] 'offer Luton one of the free Fridays after Easter';[20] 'please send me a list of engagements booked for the whole year';[21] 'send a copy of the eight-hour Act';[22] 'go to British Museum to do research'; 'Open all letters and "winnow grain from chaff".'[23]

Hardie could be censorious. On one occasion he had dictated information about his childhood and found it later in the draft of a booklet Frank Smith was writing. 'These things are always confidential,' he wrote angrily, instructing the pages to be removed at once.[24] On another occasion it was, 'please NOTA BENE that I strongly object to rent being allowed to accumulate. I want it included in MONTHLY AC[count]'.[25] This revealed an additional task: Maggie kept his books and paid his bills. On a third it was a pile of unopened letters, 'Are you ill? This is the second time this has happened without my being told!'[26]

That Maggie endured far beyond what she should was partly her own fault. Hardie suspected that she was still depressed about her marriage. On Christmas Eve 1908 he had written to her from Cumnock that 'I was on the point more than once of speaking to you about your affairs'.[27] The diffident Maggie understood the diffident Hardie, and wrote in return later, 'You know you hate "talking things over"'.[28] Hardie always preferred to do it by pen, where he had no hesitation in advising, 'on the score of infidelity you have all along been entitled to a divorce. That, however, as you know, is not enough. Since cruelty also requires to be proved, a most unfair provision unknown by the way in the law of Scotland'.

He suggested she seek her freedom by taking an action for the restitution of conjugal rights to be followed in due course by divorce proceedings. Perhaps it occurred to him how humiliating this would be, and added, 'the sooner you get out of the tangle the better. You would find yourself in a more dignified position when the affair was over.' Sound and sensitive advice, including the financial rider, 'be careful of the lawyer', adding that such an action would only cost £25 in Scotland.

But Maggie did nothing about leaving any of the men in her life. Hardie continued to urge her towards divorce, saying that since her husband's heart was no longer hers, 'better his person should not be either'.[29] In 1909 he offered her the garden party tickets the King was again forced to send.[30] When she replied she was still too depressed, he wrote at once, 'you should regain your freedom now without delay. You are still young and there's no reason why the joys of loving and being loved should remain for ever sealed'.[31] In case this letter might be misunderstood (or possibly because he was urging a woman to divorce her husband) the watchful public man added, 'You will . . . regard what is written here as a confidence'.

While Maggie struggled in Hardie's office – and Hardie asked her to 'forgive and forget an occasional outburst of irritation' which should not mask the 'genuine regard' he had for her – and Lillie and Nan laboured in his home, Sylvia, quite another kind of woman, was getting on with her own work, dependent on Hardie emotionally, perhaps, but in no way dominated. She was taking every opportunity that came her way to keep herself prominent in the WSPU, for Sylvia's

Gordian knot was not her lover, it was her mother and sister. She was still tied to the WSPU, when other socialists had long since sighted the direction in which it was moving. In 1910 *Justice* declared flatly, it is 'anti-proletarian, anti-socialist and anti-democratic'.[32]

Both Emmeline and Christabel Pankhurst had turned down a commission to write a book about the suffrage movement, but Sylvia had accepted it. In 1911 it was published. Her celebrity increased. She was also asked to lecture in the USA, as her mother had done, and she accepted that offer too. Every inch of her journey across America in 1911 (and a similar tour she made the following year) was recorded for Hardie and sent in an endless stream of letters. In between thinking about 'my Darling's arms about me', Sylvia wrote about visits to Jane Addams at Hull House in Chicago and to Max Eastman in New York[33]. On the boat over she had another one of those encounters which punctuated her life and cause us to ask whether in some subconscious way she was – even at thirty years of age – still cultivating lack of sophistication as a trademark. The ship's doctor had taken a liking to her and she accepted his invitation to visit him alone. The inevitable had occurred. She wrote to Hardie, 'It was silly of me . . . to let him . . . take me to his cabin', saying she considered herself 'lucky . . . to escape', and adding tactlessly, in view of Hardie's own age, 'now I know how even a silly old buffer . . . may be quite a dangerous person.'[34] But her innocent act played successfully all over America. In New York she was called a 'slip of a girl';[35] in Kansas City a 'child face . . . hair gathered back with a total disregard for prevailing fashion'.[36] She tried to write daily to Hardie, just as she had written daily to Emmeline when she had first come to London in 1904,[37] and just as Hardie still wrote daily to Lochnorris.

Sylvia's prose far exceeds her poetry in originality and sharp observations. She wrote of Indian reservations, dinner parties in suburban Chicago, and a segregated black university in Tennessee.[38] In Milwaukee, a city with a newly elected socialist council, she was given a reception, and later wrote a shrewd and valuable account, detailed down to the wages of everyone involved, of this administration's attempt to set up socialism in one city, showing clearly the way the experiment was sabotaged by the press, state officials and liberal agrarian 'LaFollette' politicians.[39] Throughout both trips she tried to practise thought transference with Hardie, explaining that this was her way of trying to make herself 'less dependent' on his physical presence.

Hardie's letters in return were short and down to earth. In one of the longest[40] he wrote that when she is in his arms and he kisses her, it must be 'a transference of something' that could be 'effected without actual physical contact' but 'not the same satisfaction'. He relays the news: a 'big meeting' in Sheffield, opening a bazaar in Bradford, good weather. He hears Emmeline now has a motor. He likes to think of Sylvia in places in the USA where he has been.

After her return from her first visit, a Conciliation Bill (giving a very limited vote to women) was being supported by all suffrage groups. Privately, Sylvia opposed the Bill but publicly gave way to Emmeline and Christabel, who supported it.[41] She was still unable to break from their authority. Maggie was also one of those involved in a demonstration at this time. Emmeline Pethick-Lawrence gave her instructions in case their actions ended in arrest.[42] These included 'not to . . . wear jewellery, furs, nor to carry umbrellas'. If arrested, say nothing. If taken to prison, insist on 'wearing own clothes and keeping [own] hair pins, brush and combs' (Emmeline Pethick-Lawrence had found lice on prison combs during her first prison spell) '. . . insist upon having a window pane broken' or 'break it . . . explaining beforehand to the governor that this is . . . a precaution for health'. (To the 'new' woman fresh air was essential.) Lastly, 'exercise twice a day'. (The 'new' woman exercised regularly.)

These instructions were issued to Maggie on the day she was arrested, 21 November 1911. There was a press picture next day of Hardie in a fedora and gloves standing by the demonstration to support the women.[43] Maggie was fined five shillings or five days and like most suffragettes chose five days.[44] During those days she looked at the moon out of the prison window and wrote poetry:[45]

> Still the moon, the same moon
> on which have looked all other imprisoned eyes
> down the ages

Ironically, her faltering first efforts were recorded on her father's professional calling cards.[46] She did not even own her own notebook.

Maggie did not throw herself into suffrage campaigns as Sylvia did; she was too busy looking for some way to support herself independently. In the meantime, she was forced back to her family home, where some of her relatives disapproved of her suffrage activities. One wrote her, 'when women come down to window smashing . . . and even the refined daughters of . . . earls do not care what they look like . . . they do not deserve the vote . . . P.S. I asked your father not to discuss it with me.'[47] As anyone who lived through those days can testify, 'there was not a home which was not deeply split by the issue'.[48] The fact that Maggie's was one of them only added to her difficulties.

Sylvia's struggle was different. She had deliberately sent herself away on her travels. Loneliness was compounded by the troubles of the second tour. She was on circuit with Matthew Arnold's granddaughter, and they both hated their inefficient agent.[49] Sometimes she found

lectures cancelled when she arrived, 'They have had mother and so
don't want me'.[50] Most worrying, Hardie was not writing to her as
regularly as he had a year earlier. 'I am a bit down . . . I haven't
heard from you yet.'[51] A week later it was the same, 'It seems a long
time since I got a letter'.[52] She herself continued the regular letters
to him, pouring out her personal feelings about their relationship.
These see-sawed dramatically: 'I don't want anyone but you'; yet
acknowledging, 'I expect more from fate than I deserve'. A moment
later, 'I think fate ought to have given me a bigger share of what I
do want . . .' She suggests that they each give half an hour to talk to
each other every day by telepathy, but this ends with disappointment,
'It isn't substantial enough . . . I want you now, oh why can't we,
dear?' Finally, she got a short letter from Hardie. He had had a dream
in which he was worrying about her. In reply Sylvia tells him her own
revealing dream of coming up a steep staircase without any railing,
while a man 'in dirty white overalls' was behind her trying to catch
her ankles. To which she adds a significant detail, in the dream 'I was
a man too'.[53]

The rail and coal strikes were still continuing in 1912, when Ben Tillett
led the dock workers in their industrial action. It was bitterly fought
and ended in complete defeat, the workers starved into submission.
Mann and several colleagues,[54] having noted the connection between
the arming of Northern Ireland's Protestants and the use of troops to
attack strikers, published the letter of a Liverpool construction worker
who appealed to soldiers 'not to murder us as you did at . . . Belfast',
for one day 'you, like us, may be on strike'. They put it out in the
form of a leaflet called *Don't Shoot* and were arrested and jailed for
incitement to mutiny. Josiah Wedgwood said it was the first time
a government had tried to suppress the press since the unsuccessful
prosecution of Cobbett in 1831.[55]

Whichever way you looked, a more aggressive left was dominating
the world of agitation which Hardie had been used to calling his
own. With Emmeline Pankhurst being tried for conspiracy, even the
suffragettes were making more headlines than the Labour alliance led
by MacDonald.

The ILP too seemed sedate. In this year it joined with Fabians in
a campaign called a 'War on Poverty', operating more like a secular
version of the Salvation Army than a party of social revolution. Despite
the fact that Hardie urged revolution rather than reform at the ILP
spring conference, discussion among ILP delegates was less and less
(as it would once have been) about the ILP's own political activity
throughout the country, and more about what the policy of the
Labour Party in Parliament should be. The problem was not that the
conference reaffirmed the principle of letting parliamentary leaders

decide matters according to the exigencies of the moment – that was a tactical matter – but that the focus of the ILP was narrowing imperceptibly from social action at large to the activities of the men at Westminster.

The ILP Conference that year had compensating features for Hardie, however. It was held late, in June, because of the strikes; and it was held in Merthyr, Hardie's own patch. For once, the impecunious Hughes family would be able to attend. Hardie had got to know the family better in the last few years and had begun staying there whenever he was in that end of the valley. At the conference he introduced Lillie and Nan to Aggie, the Hughes's daughter, who brought to the conference a recent birthday gift, a small black leather album with blank gold-edged pages of different pastel colours.[56] Such albums were the fashion at the time. In them you were supposed to write a significant short thought and then sign your name. On the first page Aggie had pasted a picture of her father and her first entry was from Hardie, 'Votes for Women and Socialism for All'.

Later Nan and Lillie too were asked to write. They both chose negative quotes. Lillie, 'Man's inhumanity to man makes countless thousands mourn'; while Nan's was Robert Burns:

Mankind are unco weak
an little to be trusted
if Self the warring balance shake,
it's rarely right adjusted

Nan was now a regular companion to her father. In addition to going to conferences, she had also spent many months in London with Hardie during 1911 and 1912, helping in his work. So too another young woman who attended, Nancy Richardson, Tom's daughter. Nancy wrote to Aggie immediately after the conference to tell her she 'was the only real friend she made in Wales' and invited her to correspond. Her letter was entirely about her father.[57] She told Aggie that his election changed her life. She hero-worshipped him, 'I feel it is an honour to be able to spend time with him. But he is so busy as an MP' – like all the others. These men 'gave up home and all their relationships' to 'do their duty to their fellow men'. This is how the daughters of these early socialist MPs saw their fathers, deprived men. Nancy reported that her parents rarely met, but that when they did, father was always 'so excited'. Nancy ended by citing the one man above all who provided an example for others to live by in this respect, 'our champion, Keir Hardie'.

Unlike the ebullient Lansbury women, Lillie and Nan were weighed down by their duty to their 'champion'. Few ever noticed them. Later, few of Hardie's biographers gave them more than a passing line, and as far as Lillie went, these were the predictable words used for all Victorian wives of public men,[58] to note their 'selfless devotion to husband's duties' and their good housekeeping. Almost more inattentive are the fictitious re-creations of his life which some biographers have attempted, where Lillie is pictured as cheerful, smiling, busy and content, 'always . . . encouraging', ever surrounding Hardie with love and understanding, always 'in the opposite chair ready to respond to his mood . . . never supplemented in his love'.[59] Even to Sylvia's biographer, Lillie was merely 'the good and simple woman', and very probably happy.[60] But Lillie was far from simple; both she and Nan were highly complex, and neither was content. Hardie's emotions and attentions were seldom with them, yet theirs were expected to be with him – always.

Other politicians of the day realized the problem that dedication to the cause brought, even if only at the end of life. Thus Edmund Stonelake, Hardie's Merthyr contemporary:[61]

> I rushed to Council Meeting or Education Committee . . . Lighting or Health Committee, on an average of four nights a week, the remaining nights would find me at a Trade Union, Co-operative or Political committees . . . I left all the worry to the overworked harassed wife; the first call was to my public work.

She endured without protest what 'went on for twenty years,' as 'I pursued my politics . . . with such fanatical zeal that I became blind to my family obligations'. Stonelake had his punishment for 'unwittingly inflicting' such injustice on his wife and family: Rebecca Stonelake died before he could retire and spend the time together he had promised her.

The same fate had been Matilda Hyndman's. She died in 1913, after which Hyndman wrote that she had had her 'comfort and happiness . . . sacrificed by my foolishness and fanaticism'.[62] Will Thorne remembered he 'worked day and night' and that 'my wife often asked me whether I thought I would see the children before Sunday', to which he added, 'But I seldom did'.[63] The Glasiers thought they had solved the problem by fighting together. Katharine wrote to Ramsay MacDonald after Margaret MacDonald died, to say the Glasiers and MacDonalds had been alike, 'We both BELIEVED in real marriage', in 'men & women working shoulder to shoulder'.[64] Beatrice Webb had opted for working together as well, having rejected life with a public star, Joseph Chamberlain, because of the loss of 'freedom of thought' that subordinating life to his career meant.[65] For while he was courting her, she had asked him if it was true what she had heard, that in his household only one view on any subject was allowed – and that was his own. He had replied very quietly, 'That is so.'[66] Some who chose the star anyway found out it was not as they had hoped. Throughout politics at the time – in all parties – were examples of political men who admitted placing ambition before the health and happiness of their wives. Curzon, Cromer and Asquith were examples. Margot Asquith claimed she was never alone with her husband, a fact that generated such negative emotions in her that it made her ill. 'The more I control [the] showing of it, the ILLER I feel,' she shrewdly commented.[67]

Lillie was controlling and getting iller; her notorious glumness a silent protest at the life she led, or perhaps at the life she was never able to lead. Whereas Lansbury had strong views on the subject of his wife, Bessie, and the 'loneliness' she had to bear, saying, 'she should have the opportunity of thinking and doing too ... a much fuller kind of existence than has been possible',[68] Hardie appeared to have had few insights about the problem of Lillie's undeveloped life. When conscience overcame him, his resort was to yet another small gift. He spent money.

Nan's life was, if anything, worse. In an era when younger women could now more easily choose to be 'fighting' women, and some decided not to wait for marriage as their only career, her only offers were either helping mother or helping father. Hardie used Nan whenever he needed her. When in 1912 Maggie could no longer manage the pasting up of all the press cuttings, Hardie assured her Nan would be glad to take over the work, 'Nan feels elated today at all the nice things which people have been saying to her about her father'.[69] The problem was that no one was saying nice things to Nan about Nan.

At the start of 1912 Hardie had written to Maggie Symons that 'I am growing moody and broody for lack of interesting work, or for that matter, of enough work of any kind'.[70] It was an interesting comment on his growing isolation and detachment from the Labour Party, as well as on the Labour Party's own inactivity. In the same letter, however, he said he looked forward to being re-elected to the chair of the ILP in the spring, having ended his self-imposed boycott over putting himself forward. In the event he was not elected, which only gave him less to do. In Parliament he was out of sympathy with Labour's lie-low tactics. For the remainder of 1912 his politics became increasingly individualistic. One group of workers who benefited were the ironworkers in the Dowlais works in his own constituency. Dowlais had notoriously anti-union owners: Guest, Keen and Nettlefold. Dowlais wages were poor by comparison with iron-workers elsewhere and workers mounted a campaign over its parity, a matter Hardie constantly raised in Parliament, where he argued that firms on government contracts (as GKN was) were supposed to meet a national minimum. Finally, he forced the government to make GKN pay the going rate. GKN's response was a lockout that led to a prolonged and bitter dispute. The government's response was to send the new king and queen, King George V and Queen Mary, on a visit to Merthyr in June 1912; whereupon Hardie at once wrote an open 'letter' to the royal couple, which he published in the *Pioneer*.[71] It suggested the King was merely 'a political agent' whose task it was to 'out me from the parliamentary seat because I am a socialist and a republican', and because he was defending the ironworkers. Hardie repeated their case to the King: seven days a week working for twelve hours a day with pay of but fourteen to fifteen shillings, living in 'horrible hovels' which would not be seen by their majesties who will only go along a route specially beautified for the occasion. There is money to put up bunting for royalty but none to create a park in Merthyr where children might play. A typical piece of Hardie agitation, which resulted in the Dowlais workers being reinstated before the royal visit took place.

Hardie had scored a victory of sorts, but impertinent petitions to royalty were dated weapons in industrial warfare. The forward initiative in Wales was passing to such groups as the Unofficial Reform Committee in Tonypandy, where A. J. Cook and others were more openly committed to class struggle. It was the year of the publication of *The Miners' Next Step* by Noah Ablett of Maerdy and Will Mainwaring of Clydach Vale, arguing for a single mining union. New agitators were telling workers to take matters into their own hands and to argue their case themselves, while old agitators like Hardie were saying, come to us with your grievances, we will use our influence in Westminster to put things right. Although the difference was great, the establishment treated them as one and the same.

Neither Hardie nor the new agitators worked to agree an approach that would unite both their positions, another outcome of the failure to continue discussion on the ways the socialist project could be advanced in a bourgeois democracy.

The most immediate labour trouble in 1912 had been in Hardie's own office. Writing to Maggie from Cumnock on Twelfth Night, he told her he was badly in debt. Glasier suggests he had speculated and lost;[72] Benson that he had misused money given to start the Labour daily for his own purposes. To save money, Hardie wished to cut Maggie's hours or wages or both. He told her he thought of doing his own secretarial work but 'shrank . . . from the thought of being entirely without your presence'. So he made a new proposal.[73] He introduced it with the usual assurances of how much he appreciated her 'devotion and zeal'. He did not regard her as 'paid help' but 'one of the family'. Unfortunately, this was just the problem. She had no professional status and was expected to work as a family member would. Yet he knew this was impossible. So he resolved the dilemma by saying that George

Lansbury also wanted a secretary: 'five days in the week you come to me in the morning and go to him in the afternoon. The wage to be thirty shillings a week, with Saturday off.'

This was the last straw for Maggie Symons. On 14 January she replied.[74] It was a new Maggie writing – and on a relatively new instrument as well, for the letter was typed. In addition to all her other skills, she had mastered this important new technology which had finally been imported to Neville's Court some time during the previous year (MacDonald had had all his letters typed from 1905).

Maggie made it plain that she could not 'possibly face taking on your work and Mr Lansbury's as well'. Far from there being too little work in the office, she reminded him that in the summer she had asked him if he would take on a second secretary 'as soon as members were paid by the state' because:

> there was more work than I could comfortably do and I have never been able to bring myself during the last three years to leave off on a Thursday night and not turn up until Monday morning for the simple reason that I could not have faced Monday with the accumulation of work there would have been. That is why I have never done the journalism I meant to have done.

She knew that he would try to keep the work down but she also knew that 'when the session is in full swing . . . I simply cannot stand it'. Maggie still wanted to earn her own independent living by writing, but had to admit, 'Perhaps I have no real talent for writing.' Having thus confessed, she stated with new resolve, 'I have never had the chance to find that out.' In this spirit, Maggie set out her own financial dilemma: rent paid by her father, her only income from a room she rented out furnished. She said how frugally she lived, 'I do not seem to have spent much money on myself – certainly not on clothes. I want therefore to earn at least £2 a week and be independent of father.'

But this was not all Maggie had to say: she said she owed him an explanation for her refusal to do as he asked. It lay in her changed attitude to him. When Travers left her, the work she did for Hardie helped to 'save the situation for me' at the time of her deepest depression. She then confesses she had formed a special attachment to Hardie, 'at one time [I] thought of you in a still more unearthly way than I do now. I certainly deified you [and] got an exaggerated notion of my use to you.' Recently, however, she had found a new friend, Charles Vase, with whom she 'talked things over'. Although she had had 'some knock down blows . . . I have never after entered that awful slough of unhappiness and misery again'.

Vase did not approve of her relationship with Hardie. This 'icono-clast . . . showed me my deity in a very human aspect'. But bringing

down Hardie caused her the same sort of anguish as losing her
husband:

> Oh, what a horrid time I had of it, until bit by bit I picked up
> the fragments of my idol and set them . . . together again, and they
> grew into something better perhaps than a deity – into a great,
> human being, capable of developing and growing and learning by
> experience which, after all, mere gods cannot do. And so, there
> you are, Mr Human Being.

Hardie replied[75] – also on a typewriter. He said it was a new one
he had on approval and found it tricky. He told Maggie he 'always
suspected something of what you now tell me and am glad to have
such an insight into a woman's soul'. In view of what she said, he told
her to forget the fifteen shillings and stay with the present salary of
twenty-five shillings. So Maggie carried on, while a slow fuse burned.
Nothing had changed.

After a year she gave Hardie notice. She had decided to go out
to Egypt to 'help' her father again. Hardie replied that although this
'upsets me', 'something of this kind was bound to happen and only
a woman's sense of devotion could have postponed it so long'.[76]

Maggie was sailing from one dependency to another. As a linguist
or in some managerial capacity she would have flourished, had such
openings been available to women to earn a living. The suffrage
movement helped her to redirect some of her anger, but its narrow
focus on the vote alone prevented many women during this time
from working for changes in the many other spheres of their lives
that demanded attention, not least their economic and domestic
dependency. In many ways suffrage work only made matters worse
for Maggie. It gave her an illusion of acting to free herself without
giving her the means. Like so many of the women in Keir Hardie's
life, it looked like she would never escape to her own.

Hardie's last letter, enclosing £10, showed he suffered too by the
break, 'the future is . . . a blank. You have run the show so much for
the last . . . years that I know little if anything about the office and its
manifold complications.'[77] His own bereft condition is highlighted by
the fact that his letter is written from Metcalfe's Hydro at Richmond
Hill, where he was taking water treatment for his deteriorating body.

During the same year he had also watched the new Labour Party
newspaper, the *Daily Citizen*, proceed on its way to launching,
racked by internal rows over the high salary paid to its journalists
and its choice of a *Daily Mail* staffer, Frank Dilnot, as editor – not
to mention nepotism, for according to Glasier, 'Henderson shoved in
his son as Dilnot's private secretary.'[78] When it was finally launched on
8 October 1912, Glasier said he opened it with trembling, crying, 'No,

it will not do!'[79] Lansbury's strike bulletin, the new *Herald*, reviewed it too, 'It simply could not be true . . . too poor to be believed.'[80] Those who sat on the *Citizen*'s board tried to improve it but the arguments continued – not about its socialist approach, since this never materialized, but over issues like whether it should include racing tips. By a split vote it was decided to introduce a betting and racing column. This had little effect on circulation. Hardie complained of it constantly. To Rose Davies he wrote that it reported him unfairly (by not mentioning that his speech was cheered to the echo), 'That is because I am not on the Board.'[81] Lansbury believed the problem was that no one on the *Citizen* was allowed any real freedom – just as no one had it on the other national papers that pandered to 'Kipling's men'. He thought his *Herald* succeeded because 'I still firmly hold the view that it is always better to allow people to say what they think than pay them to say what you think.'[82]

Hardie poured his writing into the *Merthyr Pioneer*, managed by Merthyr and Aberdare ILP and Trades Councils. At least he again had a regular column in which to air his views, however isolated he was from the Labour Party mainstream, surrounded by a 'band of workers devoted to him'; Hardie's view of himself was recalled later by the trade unionist, Mary MacArthur, 'He told me he had very few cronies.'[83] Glasier, on the other hand, saw this trait as a strength. 'No man I have ever known had so deeply in him the capacity to stand alone, to fight alone, to win alone and to bear defeat alone.'[84]

But even Hardie needed support, and he found it (or so he assumed) in the International. Its congress was held in November 1912 in Basle. Twenty-three countries sent delegates, representing what Hardie later called the 'disinherited of all lands . . . the mob, the proletariat, the oppressed', those, he added optimistically, who 'have now no country'.[85] He remained convinced international working-class solidarity could cancel national rivalry. Prevention of war dominated proceedings. A choir sang in the Cathedral to which they all adjourned; peace was sanctified.

During a break from proceedings Hardie went into the city with one of the UK delegation, the Reverend James Wallace of Glasgow. Wallace spoke good German and French and had agreed to help Hardie in his search for the mandatory 'keepsake' for Lillie. Their mission was a small jeweller's shop, where Hardie worried the shop-owner might try to cheat him. In the event she was charming and helpful, and the item reasonable in price. James Wallace noted as he and Hardie walked the streets of Basle that while others were admiring the architecture or watching the people, Hardie was 'interested in all the different kinds of dogs, large or small, that crossed our paths'.[86] Each one he followed with fascination. In some ways their world was more real to him, and always had been. He was devoted to his several dogs

– there was always at least one at Cumnock. It was not sentimental. He identified with animals. They were his cronies. A press profile noted he was often seen to stop in London's streets and talk to the horses.[87] When a Dogs' Bill was debated in the House, giving power to put down stray dogs,[88] he objected on behalf of 'persons of a kind disposition who allowed stray dogs to sleep on their premises'. In 1913 he sufficiently befriended a parrot in a pub that its owner let it out to stand on his shoulder,[89] an event Hardie considered a mark of honour shown by the bird to himself. When visiting Eugene Debs in prison, Hardie had once spent half an hour trying to free a trapped insect from inside a bottle.[90] Debs had been much impressed. Cunninghame Graham also, 'He attracted children . . . and, I should guess, dogs'.[91]

At the Basle International, which Stewart later wrote 'wound up the old generation',[92] the British delegation was the only one to object to postponing the next meeting until August 1914. As they dispersed, Hardie could not dispel the foreboding he felt. When he returned he wrote that a 'European war will almost certainly lead to European revolution, the end of which no man can foresee'.[93]

While Sylvia was away on her second lecture tour, the WSPU's violence escalated under Christabel's command. After one particularly large-scale series of attacks on property, the WSPU offices were raided by the police. Emmeline and the Pethick-Lawrences were arrested. Refusing to pay the fines or the damages, they were jailed. There they refused to eat and were force-fed repeatedly. Just as repeatedly Hardie and George Lansbury protested in Parliament at this barbarism. From this time onwards suffragettes' activities were also stalked by Special Branch. To escape jail, Christabel fled to Paris and took the false name of Amy Richards.[94] When Sylvia returned from the USA she did not seek out Hardie, but instead disguised herself as a nurse to evade the police and went to Paris to obtain permission to take on the WSPU in Britain. But Christabel dismissed her, saying she had no use for her 'services'.[95] Sylvia would eventually be forced to choose between the path her mother and sister were taking towards an ever escalating politics of the vote, leaving behind any democratic or socialist dimension (and herself as well), or a path of her own that somehow combined socialism and suffrage. She probably also realized that her relationship with Hardie – in the way she wanted it – was never to be. He was not going to leave Lillie; he was not going to give her more time. Like Maggie, she had suffered for years in thrall to the hero, but unlike Maggie, when the time came, she acted decisively.

She moved, literally and figuratively. She left Linden Gardens for Bow Road in the East End, moving from genteel suburb to an area of overcrowded working-class back-to-back streets. There she began organizing her own independent East End branch of the WSPU, committing herself finally to universal suffrage. Initially Sylvia was viewed as a distinct oddity by East End women, whose main concern was to exist from day to day and for many of whom the vote was too intangible to have much meaning. But she renewed her friendship with the Lansbury family, who were thoroughly committed. Lansbury had only recently been ejected from the House of Commons for failing to apologize to Asquith for criticism over the suffrage issue, and Sylvia later called him 'by the far the most popular man in the House of Commons' as far as suffragettes went.[96] To a certain extent she turned her political affections to Lansbury, who helped her organize demonstrations in Victoria Park, where she always featured herself as the main speaker.

In fact, though nominally running a branch of the WSPU, Sylvia had decided to found her own movement. Instead of remaining a lieutenant, she gathered her own lieutenants. Possibly it was their arrival in her life that helped her change course. At some point she had begun sharing her Linden Gardens flat with Norah Smyth, an older, educated suffragette, who had independent means. In one of her letters to Hardie, Sylvia had said sadly, 'I can't afford to pay £65 a year for my studio . . . what shall I do, love?'[97] What she did was to allow Norah Smyth to pay.[98] Norah, who dressed 'as much like a man as possible',[99] seemed to give Sylvia courage as well as cash. At the same time another, younger woman appeared on the scene, Zelie Emerson, a short, dark, American woman from Jackson, Michigan, whose father, a wealthy industrialist, had died, like Sylvia's, early in her life. Zelie had attended the University of Michigan, had become a suffrage supporter, and possibly had heard – or met – Sylvia when she lectured in America. In 1912 she came to London to commit herself to Sylvia's cause; and her funds came with her. Zelie took a flat in the East End and Sylvia moved in. Norah acted as Sylvia's deputy and treasurer. It was her money that paid for the hiring of halls and parks and the holding of suffrage meetings. Zelie's money paid for the newspaper Sylvia founded, which she called *The Woman's Dreadnought*. Each issue ran to thousands of copies, and was given out as a freesheet in front of London stations and at demonstrations.[100]

All three women spent an increasing amount of time together. It is impossible to know what the personal relationships were – there is not the evidence – but it is well known that the suffragette movement attracted a number of lesbians, and that a few 'came out' (to each other, if not to the wider world) during this period. Among the majority, however, such feelings were far more likely to have been repressed. One who wrote later about Sylvia at this time was Ethel Smyth, the feminist musician, whose own feelings for Emmeline Pankhurst are easily discerned between the lines of their voluminous correspondence.[101] Smyth knew about Keir Hardie and Sylvia, which suggests Sylvia's relationship was common knowledge, but dismissed the attachment as transient hero worship: if it weren't Hardie on a pedestal, it 'will be someone else'.[102] Her references suggest Hardie's influence on Sylvia was thought to be more political than personal.

On sexual issues, Sylvia's views were very 'advanced',[103] shorthand for outside accepted moral codes. We know that a few years later Sylvia committed herself and her circle to free love. When Marie Stopes's book on sexual relationships was published, Sylvia wrote, 'We are for free sexual union contracted and terminated at will. We are for free love because love is free and no one can bind it. We believe that loveless unions should be terminated.' To which she added in her notebook, 'Polyandry . . . is legitimate'.[104] Whether these were her views five years earlier, and whether they extended to lesbian love, is impossible to say, but it is very probable that Sylvia was the moral adventurer that Hardie, in fact, was not. She was more wide awake to social interaction generally and tackled Hardie several times on his views that under socialism all relationships would be perfect. Sylvia found most family conversation limited; and having just returned from a visit to distant relatives whose life she found stultifyingly empty, she wrote to Hardie, 'Even socialism couldn't bridge . . . that ocean'.[105] Sylvia lived with Zelie for two years. Jill Craigie[106] considers the relationship romantic – at least on Zelie's part, and there is certainly later evidence to support this.[107] At the very least Zelie was a strong admirer and passionate friend.

During these years the relationship between Sylvia and Hardie gradually changed. Despite Sylvia's loving letters to him during her absences in the USA, and later, when she was travelling in Scandinavia, the old relationship was not resumed in its intense form. Sylvia had moved on. Romero believes Hardie did not meet her needs for involvement[108] in the way her new life in the East End did. It is likely too that Hardie made no objection. They were both performers who loved centre stage. Other observers at the time, like Fenner Brockway, believed Hardie was tiring of Sylvia's – and all the Pankhursts' – excessive public martyrdom,[109] and that Sylvia's obsession for him was by now something of a burden.

He may have been glad as well to be released from the obligation to support the WSPU line come what may. A weary, ageing and overcommitted Hardie might have found Sylvia just another woman making him feel he was not giving her the time she wanted. Later Sylvia recalled that Hardie was now in what she called 'his advancing years',[110] and showing it. He had given up his 'red tie and his warm brown homespun for sober greys'.[111] She heard from her mother that MacDonald told women not to take any notice of Hardie, he is 'only an old grandfather'.[112] He often seemed to be preoccupied. Rose Davies was also complaining (through Maggie Symons) that Hardie was neglecting her. Hardie replied sharply that 'it's a mutual sin',[113] pointing out that Rose had moved house to Aberdare without telling him, and Ed, her husband, had resigned as secretary of the local ILP, also without telling him.

Sitting at Hardie's feet was not a career; and in time the spirited Rose and the determined Sylvia moved on to their own careers. Sylvia seems to have decided that sitting at Christabel's feet was not a career either. She conducted her own escalating suffrage protests without regard to her mother or sister, but at the same time she also began to expand her own WSPU in the direction of working-class interests, identifying more and more with the women of the East End, their problems, and their poverty. As her involvement with Hardie slowly lessened, her regard for him remained, and almost as a token of it, imperceptibly her socialist commitment increased.

Sylvia was taking her life forward, instinctively protecting herself from the fate of a life's work dedicated to supporting the great man – the fate of most of the rest of the women in his life. These now included Agnes Hughes, who began taking Sylvia's earlier place as a young admirer who posed no problems, and to whom he could show the world. Unlike Sylvia, however, who approached Hardie without acknowledging his family, Aggie chose to enter Hardie's life and affections by winning over Lillie and Nan. At Christmas in 1912 Lillie Hardie received a book signed 'Agnes Hughes' sent from Merthyr. Her reply to 'Miss Hughes' was to tell her that Hardie was speaking in Glasgow that day, that the Hardies only celebrated New Year never Christmas, and that it was her holiday custom to send out shortbread to all their friends.[114] In a few days Aggie received her shortbread. She had been accepted.

In August 1912 the Hardies had gone to the island of Arran with Nan. Nan had had another 'bad turn' that had lasted all spring and the visit was to restore her to health. The family was fond of Arran, as one of Hardie's brothers lived there. Hardie enjoyed the stay and sent a Burnsian souvenir to a friend:[115]

> A happy home, a loving wife
> an ILP fu' healthy
> I wadna' swap my lot in life
> wi' any o' the wealthy

His good mood would have been because he was off once again to the USA, to spend two months touring for the socialist cause during yet another presidential election campaign of Eugene Debs.

Hardie was not alone on the voyage but was accompanied by a handsome thirty-three-year-old woman (described in the New York papers ten days later as 'a suffragette'). Her name was Marian

Dalrymple Stoddart – always called May – the fourth child of five
daughters and a son born to a Cumnock tailor, John Stoddart, and
his wife, Jean.[116] Unlike Nan, the five Stoddart sisters, all of whom
had gone to the same school in Cumnock as Nan and her brothers,
were working women. One was an artist, another worked at the post
office as a skilled Morse Code operator. A third was a photographer's
assistant. Four were unmarried as yet and two (who never married)
were excellent amateur actresses. May herself had trained as a nurse
in Dundee, and her affections had long been placed with her childhood
sweetheart, Jamie Hardie – or 'Jim' as he had signed himself two years
earlier when he wrote to Rose Davies, thanking her for having put
him up during the election in January 1910.[117] Jamie also told Rose
that he was 'packing my "bundle" to go "crossing the pond"' to the
United States in February 1910, where he had been offered a job in
Philadelphia. He sent Rose his photograph 'as a memento' of his stay
with her and told her she would be welcome in the USA any time,
which suggests he meant to stay. Those who knew Jamie later in
life say he was always carefully attired and hated to dirty his hands
– inconvenient for a working engineer.[118] Perhaps Jamie disliked the
life he had been offered and aspired to another? The main friction
showed itself between Jamie and Lillie, but sometimes a couple who
are themselves locked in dispute, as Lillie and Hardie were, shift their
hostilities on to a child and make him 'the problem'. In his gambling
Jamie had what he had previously lacked, attention from his father. But
it was not the kind he wanted. He showed his feelings by leaving; and
his mettle by succeeding in his new life.

By 1912 he had a carpet-cleaning (and later an engineering) business
at 228 Third Avenue in Brooklyn.[119] He was now in a position to
support a wife, and Keir Hardie was accompanying May to New
York to be married. There were no wedding photographs of Jamie
and May, only separate formal photographs showing two handsome,
serious and carefully dressed people in their Sunday best. Hardie was
there to share the day. The only record is the postcard Hardie sent
to Aggie Hughes, 'My son James married last Thursday', 29 August
1912.[120]

For the next eight weeks Hardie's American tour was the usual
strenuous cavalcade. He was handed from city to city, and addressed
forty-four meetings, including four in Canada. He wrote to Rose
Davies that he had been to a mining camp in Colorado, and had
had an enthusiastic reception in Minneapolis.[121] There were other
enthusiastic receptions in the large American industrial centres in
the Mid-west where Eugene Debs worked and lived: Indianapolis,
Pittsburgh, Cincinnati and Chicago.[122] Everywhere Scotland was
re-created by working men who had emigrated, and he danced

foursome reels and Irish jigs, and sang – yet again – 'Robin Tamson's Smiddy' and the 'Battle of Stirling'.[123]

His staple speech was on suffrage and socialism. His wife and daughter, he would tell audiences, would cast a wiser vote than some of the idlers who stand about polling stations on polling day – not a particularly democratic argument.[124] Stretching a point a bit, he told them that the UK had forty-one socialist MPs and '2,000' socialist 'municipal officers'; and he foresaw socialism imminent in the USA too, 'taking the place of the populist and greenback movements'. He talked of 'trusts as a menace to competition' and was notably low key about strikes, which can only ever 'be a temporary weapon'.[125]

In Chicago there was the largest rally of the campaign. There he chose to speak about the state – perhaps to defend it against the new left, for Tom Mann in particular saw the state as 'the final rampart' the working class had to scale, with Parliament as its most visible institution, 'dominated by plutocrats'. Mann was not an anarchist: 'I am not opposed to parliamentary action . . . I am for using it' when it can do something 'no other institution can do', but nothing good will come of it 'unless it has been the direct outcome of effort first put forth outside Parliament'.[126]

Hardie also believed Parliament would not work unless outside action came first, but he saw the state as an enabler, not a barrier. He did not share the view of Karl Marx, who saw the state as the direct descendant of rule by monarchs and their armies, the clergy and their bureaucracy, which the nascent middle class had 'to elaborate' as a means of its own emancipation from feudalism, having imperialism as its ultimate form.[127] Engels was no more enthusiastic. Writing with particular virulence against a suggestion from French Liberals that 'state aid' be used to help solve social ills, he said, 'The state is only a transitional institution', useful to the proletariat only to hold down adversaries during revolutionary struggle. After which it had to be replaced by *Gemeinwesen*: in English, possibly 'community rule', in French 'commune'.[128]

Hardie's view was that the state could enable this community rule. Like others in the Labour Party he saw it as a co-operative venture undertaken to secure for members 'the conditions of a good life'. If he disagreed with scientific socialists, he also disagreed with Liberals who saw no community, only competing individuals (and who always had a story of a worker who became an owner, as Maxton later wrote)[129] – with the state reserved for 'emergency use'. He disagreed too with the anarchists who believed the state 'stifles . . . liberty of thought . . . controls credit [and] compels honest labour to be dependent on idle . . . capital'.[130] Hardie believed that through the vote the state could be commandeered for the workers' benefit and expressed this view with characteristic directness in Chicago, 'The state is simply a good old donkey that goes the way its driver wants it to go.'[131]

The neutrality of the state marked Hardie off from both scientific socialists and syndicalists. To Hardie parliamentary action was primary, to Mann 'secondary'.[132] Australia had had the eight-hour day for years but there had been no legislation to get it. It had been won by strong labour organization, Mann proclaimed. Legislation for workers, on the contrary, according to the newest unionists, meant regulation by 'tyrannical' state legislation around compulsory arbitration and wage control. Eventually it meant workers' subjugation, even if the state was run by workers.

Hardie never saw this danger. He had made the long political pilgrimage from Liberal distrust of the state to socialist trust in it. He had an almost mystical vision of how a socialist state would be born (expressed a year later at the German Social Democrats' Congress), like some chrysalis, 'growing up ... within the [existing] state ... based not on force but on economic equality and personal liberty'.[133]

But already the means to achieve this were being blocked off in Britain. Despite popular socialist and co-operative movements which had thrived on self-help, and on local democracy and entrepreneurial activity in the preceding years, and despite a strong demand for local government to be given the wherewithal to act on its own in most matters of social welfare, and to engage with the local community in carrying out change, agitation for change was becoming more and more focused on Parliament and the statute book. Labour's victories were soon to be characterized by its enemies as support for positive 'state interference' which placed 'on the state burdens and obligations' which Liberals believed were either an infringement of the liberties of the subject or obligations that should be 'borne by the individual'.[134] Eventually, a reaction would come.

The possible dangers of statute-book socialism were not apparent to Hardie, who equated success with the state's taking full responsibility through changes in the law, and failure with token or absent legislation. The 'non constitutionalists' – like Mann – foresaw the problems state socialism would eventually bring, whether of the Right or Left, as well as the problems democratic Labour Parties would run into with inaction and a solidifying bureaucracy. On welfare issues Labour had secured important concessions from capitalism, which had been won by the Liberal government in the years since 1906. But Hardie never saw that such a genesis held dangers for the development of socialism in mediating between state and individual. Perhaps one fight is enough for one generation. Hardie's, as he put it, was to rout the 'Charity Organization school of thought' that 'imagined that the poor must be taught self-reliance and that to help them' to the basic necessities of life 'was to encourage them to be thriftless'.[135]

If syndicalists saw something Hardie did not appreciate, so too did the SDF in their stand against German militarism. There was something about the illiberal way the state operated in Germany, outlawing its socialists and trade unionists, which even its own Socialist Party, the most advanced in Europe, could not resist, and from time to time seemed to be joining, that should have caused alarm. A dangerous mix of old Prussian militarism and a new hatred of liberalism already foreshadowed fascism.

Hardie saw none of this. He believed that workers, once they had elected workers to run the state or an industry, would found a different world – just as women believed that once women could elect representatives to Parliament, social ills would pass away. Ending war through female suffrage was one of the main reasons Hardie so passionately continued to support votes for women, even when so many of those he had supported had now turned against him.

Back in Britain in late 1912 Hardie found he had lost his pre-eminent position as the champion of the women's vote. George Lansbury had decided he would force the pace by resigning his parliamentary seat and re-fighting it at once on the single issue of votes for women. He had every confidence he would be re-elected and could thus claim a popular mandate for legislation on the issue that continued to dominate political life.

As soon as he resigned, he went to Boulogne to meet Christabel,[136] while Emmeline and her supporters moved into the East End constituency of Bow and Bromley to start campaigning. The Labour Party Executive voted not to support him, whereupon Hardie resigned from it in disagreement.[137] Lansbury had always been more advanced on women's issues than other socialist men. His language was the least sexist, he believed in equal work, he encouraged his boys to campaign for women's suffrage (for which they were soon to be imprisoned) and his girls to have their own careers.

The campaign generated much enthusiasm but not enough support. The problem was that the 'rich, well placed' women who came in, many anti-socialist, alienated too many of Lansbury's natural supporters, one of whom wrote to him to say, 'they are using you as a tool'.[138] His most recent biographer believes Lansbury's campaign failed to build a bridge between women and the socialist movement.[139] It also alarmed the establishment that other MPs might be tempted to resign and seek re-election on specific issues as a way of using the parliamentary system for extra-parliamentary activity, to force support for causes, including industrial disputes. A strong challenge was mounted against him, and Lansbury lost by some 700 votes. Almost at once Emmeline and Christabel dropped him. It was the last moment when either had any contact with either Labour or socialism.

Sylvia (who had been pushed aside during the campaign and was in any case never a suffragette leader as her mother and sister were) thought Lansbury had been naïve, but his defeat did not deter her.[140] If anything, she began organizing even more ardently among working-class women and marching them ever more conspiciously to Parliament on deputations. Joseph Fels provided funding for some of these events.[141] Sylvia used the money to feed the women and set up free nurseries to care for their children while mothers were demonstrating, thus making a start on what would become the main contribution she would make to the area. Meanwhile, Emmeline and Christabel 'declared war on the Labour Party because' it declined to adopt the policy of voting against every government measure until women's demands had been conceded.[142] As a result, Labour and socialist speakers were heckled and their meetings broken up, Hardie's included. Women 'not only shouted him down, they had actually assaulted him', Stewart recalls.[143] This was despite the fact that Hardie was one of the leaders in the fight in Parliament against the Cat and Mouse Act (which let women out of prison when starvation became a danger to them, only to rearrest them when they had recovered), having started with only a handful of MPs supporting him, and ending up with over fifty.[144] Hardie was philosophical about the hostility to him, but Sylvia said, 'It made me sad'.[145]

Hardie was always anxious to champion women, and not only on suffrage issues. He had protested in Parliament when a self-confessed rapist was acquitted on the direction of the judge that the girl in the case had been the 'inciting party'.[146] During 1913 one of the issues he chose to pursue was the discovery of a brothel in a wealthy flat in Piccadilly patronized by establishment figures.[147] Hardie was approached by one of the jurors hearing the case, who had been outraged that pressure on the court to drop the prosecution (because a prince, a duke and several Sandhurst cadets were among its customers) had been accepted, and the case had been dismissed without being heard.

Hardie decided to raise the failure to prosecute in Parliament, where the law protected him, and McKenna, the Home Secretary, was forced to reply. Although Hardie claimed the details were 'too revolting' to mention, he let slip 'a whip, a cane, and a birch and a considerable quantity of correspondence and literature' in a flat that 'was decked with 16 dozen arum lilies [and] hot-scented baths . . . all reminiscent of oriental orgies'.

The subject was a difficult one for Hardie, who more than once listed precariously to the moral majority side, angry with those who would 'lure our maidens from the paths of virtue' and hoping the trial would 'strike terror into the heart of every roué in London'. He righted himself only when he touched the class issue, 'Are we to stand by' while 'rich men are allowed to debauch young girls . . . and then set them adrift to swell the ranks' of professional prostitutes? Hardie called on 'Labour organizations' to demand Queenie Gerald be put on trial for procuring and her customers summoned to testify. He attacked the cover-up and Scotland Yard's pretended powerlessness to find any of the guilty men. 'Suppose this had been a charge against a number of strike leaders, or militant suffragettes, does anyone doubt that ... Scotland Yard would somehow ... have discovered the identity of those involved?' Much of Hardie's moral outrage seemed more appropriate to the occupants of pulpits, but at the end, the essential Hardie showed through, '350,000 fallen women in Britain – all of them somebody's lassies!'

The press refused to print details of Hardie's speech; the Liberal papers spiked the whole story. Later Hardie's behaviour was called 'persecutory'. In some respects it was, but what was his target? The woman, the rich who had escaped any retribution, the police and government who covered up, or proclivities of his own which he feared? It was an odd exercise, coinciding with an even odder one by Christabel Pankhurst at much the same time.

Still living in Paris, with a poodle called Fay, and cultivating French political journalists, Christabel published a pamphlet entitled, *The Great Scourge – and How to End it*.[148] This claimed that 80 per cent of men had gonorrhoea,[149] and that only female suffrage would end all venereal disease. 'Votes for Women and Chastity for Men' became her new (and hardly realistic) rallying call.

Protests over the failure to concede the vote reached new heights after Emily Wilding Davison, a friend of Christabel's, threw herself under the King's horse at the Derby on 4 June 1913. The funeral was a suffragette state occasion. Though Hardie had earlier taken up Davison's case in Parliament,[150] he still continued to be attacked by suffragettes in Britain. Abroad, it was a different matter. In the same month he was invited to attend the pan-European Women's Suffrage Alliance rally in Budapest, not as a delegate, but as an honoured guest – in recognition of his work for women. Nan and Lillie in Scotland, Aggie Hughes and Rose Davies in Wales, Maggie Symons in Egypt, and May Hardie in the United States all received postcards to say how much he was enjoying himself in Europe.

In Britain Hardie was still undertaking his marathon tours. In the *Pioneer* he set out his record for the season:[151] seventy-five parliamentary questions and 11,000 miles in the UK alone to undertake speaking engagements. As Hughes later wrote, Hardie found it 'impossible to refuse' any invitation to speak. Everyone who knew him still spoke of his overworking. 'He could not spare himself.'[152]

On the last Friday in July he went to Euston station to take the train north to Keswick for an ILP summer school being held jointly with the Fabians, celebrating the new pan-socialism in progress. Will Anderson was taking the same train, and discovered Hardie slumped in his seat, nearly comatose.[153] He put him in a taxi and sent him back to Neville's Court. Stewart explains it only as another 'breakdown' caused by overwork, one of the 'very frequent attacks of this kind, known only to the friends with whom he happened to be staying'.[154] As usual, there was no recuperation, and two days later he arrived at the summer school. There he spoke on repression in South Africa, a subject he had repeatedly raised in the House that session. According to Glasier,[155] he was in fine form and after dinner sang in the drawing room, accompanied by young Jeannie Glasier, now aged sixteen. Afterwards there were the usual reels and jigs that the ILP loved. Glasier reported that Sidney Webb watched the merriment stony-faced, as if it were some primitive 'Indian orgy'.[156]

Lillie and Nan were also at the summer school and later Lillie and Hardie stayed on near Keswick. Hardie reported to Robert Williams that Lillie was 'as frisky as a young colt'.[157] Not so Nan. Earlier, in June, she and Lillie had gone together to Arran. Hardie wrote to both Rose Davies and Maggie Symons that this early holiday had been taken because 'Agnes had a very bad turn which has lasted since Easter'.[158] Nan's new depression began at the ILP Conference (exactly as it had the year before). The success of the holiday can be judged by Hardie's single comment, 'It appears to have rained every day.'[159]

In early 1913 Elizabeth Hughes died. Lillie Hardie wrote on black-banded paper to Aggie to offer condolences on her mother's death. Indelicately, she asked at once, 'did she die suddenly or have a long illness?',[160] revealing her own perpetual preoccupation with health. Although it was part of politeness to begin and end letters with revelation of one's own ailments and inquiry after others, with Lillie health matters substituted for communication itself.

In fact, Mrs Hughes had died of pneumonia.[161] When she had gone, Aggie's job – without thinking – was to take her place, to become the housekeeper and 'mother' to her father and brothers. Rowlie was already a schoolteacher, and Emrys was planning to enter teacher training at Leeds College in a few months. Lillie Hardie's view of this was revealing, 'I have no doubt you dread your brother going to college'. She advised Aggie to accept her fate, seeing men off from home and being left behind 'is just what mothers and sisters have to do'. Aggie should realize that Emrys 'is young and must push on'.[162] How little of the suffragette spirit had invaded Lillie's and Nan's world.

A few months after her mother's death Hardie wrote to Aggie and said he was going 'by motor' through the constituency and wondered if she could 'be spared household duties' to come with him? 'A run in the open air' would do her good and he would be glad of her company. He justified it tactfully, 'You must be brave to help comfort your dear father.'[163] On one of these visits someone took a photograph in the Hughes's garden. The Revd John Hughes and Hardie are seated on chairs, Hardie where Aggie's mother would have been. Behind them are Rowlie and Aggie, she with her hands on Hardie's shoulders – as she would have had them on her mother's. In another snapshot of a large public meeting where Hardie and Aggie and Emrys are standing, Aggie emphasizes their closeness by leaning towards Hardie, a surrogate wife or daughter. Aggie's need for a close relationship now her mother was gone kindled a pure passion for Keir Hardie. Hardie enjoyed it, and gently encouraged her.

Within a week of the motor ride Hardie asked her to Cumnock, ostensibly to cure her of her many ailments (of which neuralgia and anorexia were already being discussed in letters to Lochnorris).[164] The visit was all arranged and letters were flying, when, suddenly, Auguste Bebel died. It was the kind of death Hardie had always wanted,[165] 'at 73 the sudden, peaceful end is best.'[166] Without a moment to let anyone know – except Aggie to whom he promised, 'I shall write you from Switzerland telling you when to be ready'[167] – Hardie left for Basle and a sad reunion with comrades. Apart from the SDP Conference in Germany at Jena, to which Hardie paid his now usual visit, the funeral was the only international gathering of the year for socialists. The requiem observances were fully used to agitate against war. Looking back, many who were there must have felt it was more than a single comrade who was being laid to rest.

Hardie did not come straight home as promised but stole the chance to indulge his favourite pastime: sightseeing. He went off to Interlaken, from where he wrote to May in America to tell her bad weather obscured the view.[168] All correspondence to America was usually between Hardie and May. Very rarely did he write to Jamie (though he sent regards to him by his childhood name of Jiddie) and very rarely did Lillie write either. This summer was one occasion when she did. She wrote to her daughter-in-law to say she was worried about her health.[169] Hardie was equally worried and wrote to Robert Williams in Cairo about May's 'serious attack of fever' which had left her 'convalescent in the country' for months. 'She does not come of strong stock and that . . . gives me an uncomfortable feeling at the prolonged nature of her illness.'[170] The unspoken fear was always a disease like TB, although the reference to weak stock was to her sister who had just died in childbirth – and her baby with her.

Aggie's visit to Cumnock was an instant success. Hardie wrote to the Reverend Hughes from Lochnorris two days after her arrival to say that 'your Aggie . . . and my Aggie . . . and Lillie . . . all took to each other at once'.[171] Thanks 'to Mrs Hardie's plain, homely fare, excellently cooked',[172] he would soon be 'advertising Cumnock as a Health resort'.[173] Aggie wrote her father and brothers just before leaving to say that instead of taking the train straight home as planned, she would be staying the night in London with Hardie (who assured the Revd John Hughes that the Richardson girls would be chaperones).[174]

While Aggie was at Lochnorris, Sylvia was in prison again. She had thrown a stone through an undertaker's window during a demonstration in Bow, and her friend Zelie, a few minutes later, threw one through the Liberal Club window.[175] They were put in separate cells and not allowed to meet. They each refused food and were forcibly fed. Sylvia wrote that 'she closed her eyes and set her teeth' and then 'a man's hands' forced his way into her mouth with 'a steel instrument' puncturing her gums. She followed this 'symbolic rape' by starting a sleep strike.[176]

After her release, her mother visited her, apprehensive in case her visit coincided with one from Hardie. Christabel's paper had continued to attack him bitterly. Emmeline must have had mixed feelings about rounding on the man who had tried to be such a friend to the women's cause. She also probably now knew of Sylvia's close relationship with him,[177] though everyone else was still convinced it was Emmeline who orchestrated Hardie. Fenner Brockway recalled that Emmeline was 'logical, clear, decisive, dominant', while Sylvia, though 'softer, charming, sweet and loving . . . hadn't the dominant will of Emmeline'.[178] How little many knew the real Sylvia. When Emmeline asked Sylvia about Hardie, Sylvia replied that she need not worry, 'He will not come again.'[179]

When Aggie Hughes had returned to Wales she showered Lochnorris with cheeses and hankies in thanks for the 'Cumnock Cure'.[180] Lillie and Nan stepped up their separate correspondences with her, as both enjoyed having a trusted friend with whom to share news and problems. Aggie heard them all, most expressed in medical metaphor. Nan's 'illness' dominated the scene. It had no name, the indefinable illness of herself just turned thirty.

That autumn Nan decided to act. The cure she had decided on, encouraged by Lillie, was to go to Glasgow once a week and have her teeth removed one by one. After the first pulling in October, she was 'feeling much better'.[181] Her plan was to keep going until all the teeth were out. Pulling bad teeth was sometimes recommended at the time as a cure for chronic illness, often said to come from infected teeth. Nan, however, had nothing wrong with her teeth.

Despite Hardie's commitment to the Cumnock holiday for Aggie, he nevertheless left for Dublin in the middle of it. No holiday was ever complete for Hardie without some emergency political crisis calling him off. In this case it was the transport workers' strike in Dublin being run by Jim Larkin. Their strike for union recognition had begun on 31 August and after that workers had been forbidden to meet. Earlier in the summer in parliament Hardie had been defending the workers in South Africa who were trying to organize in unions but found their efforts hampered by the government in much the same way. In the United States he had heard about the brutal repression and shooting of strikers (and the law's support for employers who hired private 'armies'). Hardie could see there were concerted attempts everywhere to destroy organized labour as it was beginning to show its strength. In Ireland he also saw that nationalism and class–consciousness were beginning to travel hand in hand, not only in the south but in the north. From Dublin he went straight to Belfast, encouraging workers there to support the strikers in Dublin.[182] He repeatedly cited as the real obstacle to their efforts, Britain's Tories, who were fomenting Ulster Protestant rebellion against the Home Rule Bill with the tacit support of Dublin Castle.[183] During the year following, this incitement increased under cover of the war clouds forming in Europe, when men like Edward Carson and F. E. Smith were helping to arm the Ulster Volunteers to resist the united Ireland that the elected House of Commons had decided should now be able to rule itself. Hardie did not see it in any way as a religious issue but as a rebellion of the political Right protecting landed interests against the growing strength of working people.[184] Prophetically, during this Irish visit in 1913, he warned about the destructive potential of the Tories' actions for the future of Ireland.

In this same month Sylvia and Norah Smyth were on a convalescence tour of Scandinavia, where Sylvia was giving lectures on her own forcible feeding. Unlike the women in Cumnock, she turned even the most harrowing personal event to positive advantage. Journalists were charmed by her 'youth . . . eloquence . . . [and the] deepness of her conviction'.[185] Hardie went through his address book for names of suffrage supporters she could visit. When he sent a list, with notes of introduction, he confessed, 'I cannot say if it is suffrage or socialist'.[186] He had so large a list of foreign colleagues that he had lost track of who was involved in what. In the event the names turned out to be socialist and Sylvia visited them all in turn, including the leader of the Swedish socialists, Hjalmar Branting.

Just before Christmas there was another mining accident in Hardie's constituency. He raced to the pithead at Senghenydd to be with the rescuers and went down with them into the shaft to do what he could for the trapped men. He wrote to Aggie saying there was still hope.[187] But there wasn't. A few days later the national press pictured little children marching in to their fathers' funerals alongside a photograph of Hardie sadly coming up from underground, carrying a miner's lamp.[188]

By 20 December he was back in Cumnock and wrote to Aggie again with considerable happiness, 'I have a whole fortnight at home'.[189] Earlier in the month he had thanked her for the present she had delivered to him in Merthyr, especially 'the trouble you took to deliver it. When it is bringing comfort and perhaps sleep, to me in the weary and sleepless vigils of the night I shall think of you.'[190] He was sorry she had not stayed for the social after the meeting in the ILP rooms, where there were songs and jokes with Barnes and Snowden. Earlier in the autumn, Hardie and Glasier and Councillor David Williams (of Swansea) did a meeting together, and on the way home their car lost a wheel. They sought refuge in a pub, which stayed open to accommodate them. While waiting, Glasier wrote, 'We made merry. Hardie and Williams with two small glasses of Benedictine and I with several whiskeys.' Later they all sang 'Oh Lord Thou Art' at the top of their voices.[191]

Although the smear campaigns against Hardie had always claimed he was a drunkard, this is one of the only bits of evidence that his teetotalism in life was ever breached. Had he been asked, he would almost certainly have said it was medicinal – to steady himself after the car accident.

Over the festive season – when Duncan came home to Lochnorris and Emrys to Abercynon – everyone wrote to everyone, and exchanged the customary chocolates and cheeses. Hardie urged Aggie to write to him at Neville's Court, marking it 'personal. It will then be forwarded to me unopened'.[192] Lillie began writing to Emrys, and she sent her shortbread off in time for Hogmanay.[193] It was the last truly happy holiday any one of them ever had.

Once back in England from Scandinavia Sylvia began breaking the provisions of the Cat and Mouse Act by speaking in public. She adopted many forms of disguise to escape rearrest: posing as a prostitute, and (stuffed with a pillow) as a pregnant woman; and when surrounded by police at the Lansburys', from where she was due to leave for a public meeting, Daisy Lansbury left the house wearing Sylvia's clothes and was arrested instead,[194] Sylvia escaping out the back. At other times she was not so lucky. From the summer of 1913 to the summer of 1914 she went to jail nine times.

But the women's vote was not her only cause. She, like Hardie, was concerned at the transport strike in Dublin. With some of her local women she took part in demonstrations and spoke on the platform of the big strike rally in November at the Albert Hall, alongside Lansbury, whose *Herald* (still going strong) ran a headline, 'Industrial Rebels and Suffrage Rebels March Nearer Together'.[195] This precipitated her final break with her mother and sister, for such activity breached two of Christabel's cardinal rules: that no WSPU women should take part in any political campaigns other than suffrage ones, and none should speak on platforms with men – ever. Although Christabel claimed to welcome women of all classes to her campaign, it was also known she did not like Sylvia's heavy reliance on working-class suffragettes, 'the weakest and least intelligent of the sex'.[196] Sylvia spread her share of malice too – leaking information that the WSPU was losing members and funds (since the Pethick-Lawrences had been driven out). She refused to come to heel, whereupon Emmeline intervened and wrote to her that she was 'unreasonable, always have been and I fear always will be. I suppose you were made so.'[197]

Sylvia ignored them. The more she was able to step away from competition with Christabel for Emmeline's regard, as well as from her dependence on Hardie, the freer she became. She hardened herself to coming second in both areas. By Christmas even the *New York Times* had heard of the break-up of the Pankhursts.[198]

Sylvia and Hardie kept in touch but they were not as before. She saw less of the man, but her life began to be lived in the image of his socialism and pacifism. Hardie had given her more than himself, he had helped her towards a cause to call her own – that would carry forward Richard Pankhurst's own beliefs. Unlike her mother and sister, she found a way to unite women's suffrage and socialism, however idiosyncratically, and to stay afloat politically. When the women's vote was finally won, it was Emmeline and Christabel who were left to wander. Their greatest moment had passed. Sylvia, by contrast, was ready to start on a significant new phase of her life.

All the women who passed through Hardie's life were profoundly affected by his political beliefs. His divine discontent entered into them as it did to countless others. Those who were able to pass on to their own lives made use of this strength for themselves. Those who could not pass on had a different end.

PART THREE
PAYING THE PRICE
1914–1992

THE LAST CAUSE

Many who supported the cause of women became worried by the whole direction of suffragette campaigning after 1912. Hardie was one of them. Writing to Robert Williams in 1913 after Emmeline Pankhurst had been sentenced to three years in prison, he said she had 'made a grave error of judgement' in the way she chose to fight the women's case.[1] He would never have said this publicly.

Women were more willing to express their unease, particularly those dissatisfied with a campaign so narrowly focused on the vote alone. They wanted to debate all the other areas where women suffered inequality. In the years after 1906 some radical and socialist women had begun calling themselves feminists, and by 1912 several were breaking away from the WSPU. Mary Gawthorpe and Dora Marsden, for example, left at the end of 1911 to found *The Freewoman, a Feminist Review*, criticizing both the half-hearted suffragists and the 'slogan-parroting' suffragettes, 'feminism is the issue, political enfranchisement a branch issue . . . militant or otherwise'.[2]

The alliance between women and socialism which Hardie had done so much to build up had also broken down, and younger politicized men were moving away. Fenner Brockway remembered his own disillusionment at the suffragettes' 'departing from their identity with the working class'.[3] Brockway believed the domination of the suffrage issue was preventing discussion of the equally urgent matter of military build-up. The young men of his generation were facing a threat that women did not have to face: conscription. During the summer and autumn of 1913 the ILP ran a campaign to try to break through on the issue of war danger. It culminated in a huge international demonstration in the Kingsway Hall in London in December: Emile Vandervelde, Anatole France, Herman Molkebuhr and Jean Jaurès from Europe; MacDonald spoke for Britain. Fenner Brockway remembered the enthusiasm for Jaurès in particular. Although he spoke in French, his gestures were so explicit everyone understood him. At one point, placing his hand near to the floor, he lifted it higher and higher, to escalating cheering, as 'we all knew he was talking about the rise of the working class' stage by stage.[4]

Nan and Lillie had been there to hear him and Hardie wrote to

Aggie that very night, 'the conference was magnificent. The ILP has set out on a new lease of conquering strength. I am overjoyed!'[5]

As international tension grew, Hardie became less and less concerned about old feuds. At Jena in September he had talked about a 'United States of Europe'[6] and back in Britain, despite his longstanding differences with the Socialist Party and disinclination towards the Fabians, he began to see the case for lowering walls as well. His old personal enemies like Hyndman and Blatchford had lost influence; and Glasier reported he became positively 'enthusiastic' about unity with the Socialist Party, so that all candidates could stand at elections in future as 'Labour and Socialist'[7] (a proposition the Labour Party Conference had defeated yet again in 1910).[8]

The Bureau of the International had been pressing Britain's Fabians, ILP, Socialist Party and Labour Party to settle differences and unite, but a meeting in July 1913 between the four groups had proved abortive yet again.[9] By the December meeting of the ILP's executive, however, Hardie appeared to have been converted. Glasier reported angrily to his Diary[10] that on the crucial issue of unity Hardie voted in favour of affiliating the various socialist groups as one. Glasier felt it was a betrayal, and MacDonald also; both remained implacably opposed to any socialist co-operation.

During the early months of 1914, Hardie followed up his commitment by touring the country sharing platforms with Shaw, Sydney Webb and Hyndman, stimulating support for the sinking of differences that had kept British socialists apart. MacDonald continued his resistance as well as his clandestine discussions with Lloyd George's emissaries, not just about possible pacts, but perhaps even involving MacDonald in taking office.[11] Previously ready to turn a blind eye, Hardie found his patience for this bargaining with Liberals had run out. Publicly he joined with Jowett and others who were complaining about Labour's failure to run candidates against Liberals at by-elections. Hardie was all the more infuriated since the Liberals had for more than a year been mounting a virulent campaign in South Wales – first against socialism, and secondly against himself, having decided to end the cosy arrangements whereby Hardie and a radical Liberal shared the two-member seat at Merthyr. They had selected a second Liberal to fight him hard for the next general election.

Determined to halt MacDonald's secret bargaining, Hardie selected Fenner Brockway as a reliable confidant. Hardie had great faith in the young Brockway, whom he had personally converted to socialism, and had helped to obtain the editorship of the *Labour Leader* in 1912. He told him, 'Laddie, we must stop this plan'.[12] Hardie did not believe it was worth raising at the Labour Party Conference; it had to be raised at the ILP at Easter (an indication of where he saw power to lie).

By 1914 twin-hearted Labour was very visible: a rank and file of socialists and social activists centred on the ILP, who, together with the new Trades Councils, were the organizers in most local areas, and a Parliamentary Labour Party backed by the bulk of trade union leaders, as anxious to tame their own rank and file as MacDonald was to tame his. Anxious too not to risk themselves abroad. The Dublin transport strike had ended ignominiously, partly due to the failure of British union leaders to lend solidarity or financial support to James Larkin's efforts. Snowden for Labour was already preaching against the new industrial action, saying strikes harmed Labour's electoral prospects and workers should leave social improvement to parliamentary representatives.[13] Hardie would certainly have supported reliance on parliamentary representatives, but to him the strike was still the 'one experience ... which ultimately filters into the consciousness of the working class and propels the political will'.[14] He had warmly supported Larkin and had backed every strike in Britain since 1910. Not because he preferred strikes – he would have far preferred parliamentary action – but because he believed the grievances which had driven workers to take their action were real.

As in 1887 and 1898, it was industrial action, and the chance to harness it constitutionally, that again rescued him politically from sailing too close to political compromise with Liberals himself, or, on the other side, too close to syndicalism (and earlier, anarchism). That the 'public' found strikes upsetting was an argument Hardie recognized long before Snowden became publicly fearful about their effects.[15] But Parliament had to see that grievances were dealt with, not discourage the legal and peaceful means of airing them.

By 1914 Hardie was writing to Aggie Hughes twice a month, and very interested to learn that her brother, Emrys, was promoting war resistance at his training college in Leeds. When Aggie reported that fellow students refused to join his protest against conscription, Hardie poured scorn on these 'blacklegging classmates ... they are just common garden dirty scabs'.[16] Aggie asked to come to London to see Hardie and he told her he had a weekend free in mid-February, 'needless to say, I shall be glad to see you there come when you may'.[17] In the event, Nan and Lillie came instead. Nan had to see doctors. The report on her was 'hopeful' – whatever that meant.[18]

During the winter of 1914 Aggie was busy with a local campaign she was masterminding for a safer station approach in Abercynon and the construction of two more stops for miners between the pithead and the village. This involved a new contract between the colliery owner and the railway companies. She collected evidence for Hardie to present to the Ministry and got Rowlie to draw maps. Hardie complimented her on her tactics: 'No mere man would have thought of it.'[19] He added: 'You are a warrior.'[20] So was Hardie. To fight this case he had to 'block' a private railway Bill in the Commons. In March he was able to tell Aggie that by negotiating with government Whips and the railway company, he had managed to get an additional halt at Tyntetown as well as better coaches for the miners and compensation for any accidents on the railway.[21] The new station approach was to go ahead too, the cost shared by the district council and railway company. Such improvements in people's conditions, however limited, were a large part of what Parliament was about as far as Hardie was concerned, and were typical of many small improvements he negotiated during his years as an MP. He was not, as MacDonald had tried to characterize him, just a 'tub thumper'.[22] He also wanted to produce practical results.

Near the end of March Hardie asked Aggie anxiously, 'You didn't mention Bradford. Surely you are coming?'[23] Hardie assured Aggie 'it will be the event of a lifetime'.[24] Bradford was hosting celebrations for the ILP's twenty-first birthday at the yearly Easter Conference Plans for it had been in hand for well over a year. There were guests from abroad and a whole round of cultural events, including massed choirs and brass bands and a new 'Song of Liberty' (in which Hardie had taken a great interest) commissioned from Granville and Mrs Bantock. In April Hardie wrote to Rose Davies that he was 'very disappointed' that she was not coming;[25] 'I had been looking forward to seeing you with your sparkling eyes'. In the event, both Rose and Aggie missed the occasion, which also featured a grand reception given by Hardie and Lillie at the Central Baths, where the fiddler, Casey, played, Dick Wallhead's daughter recited, and everyone did the tango to the tune of 'On the Mississippi'.[26]

1914 was also the fiftieth anniversary of Marx's founding of the First International. One of its members, the elderly Camelinat, treasurer of the Paris Commune, who had been making the rounds of socialist party events in Europe for decades, was dutifully honoured again. Most of the socialist parties in Europe sent delegates and Camille Huysmans represented the Second International. More important, for the first time the Socialist Party in Britain sent two fraternal delegates. Also present were two younger hopefuls, who stood – unsuccessfully – for election to the NAC that year, Clement Attlee and Herbert Morrison. Blatchford was the only notable who refused, having pulled completely away from radical activities, and among those not invited who came anyway was a brigade of suffragettes. When Hardie rose to take the chair, they began their heckling. Stewart, looking back, spoke of their 'increasingly outrageous law-lessness'[27] which had contaminated politics. But he did not say so at the time.

MacDonald was given a great cheer when he entered the conference but was later challenged during the debates – through the motion duly introduced by Fenner Brockway – about his plans for an alliance with the Liberals. He denied there had ever been such discussions. However when he had left Snowden confirmed there had, but that MacDonald had asked they should not be minuted.[28] A vote condemning any Liberal link was resoundingly carried. MacDonald was less upset than he would have been earlier. In recent years he had attended ILP conferences only fleetingly. Beatrice Webb (whom Sylvia called that 'carefully reared indoor nineteenth century product')[29] had noticed this and shrewdly concluded that MacDonald was 'preparing for his exit from the ILP', whose delegates, she guessed, were disheartened because Labour MPs had 'utterly failed to impress the House of Commons'.[30] MacDonald, by contrast, had impressed it – he had presence and his debating skills commanded respect – and it was there he concentrated. Hardie concentrated on the Independent Labour Party in the country, whose supporters did not see Hardie as Beatrice Webb did, all 'used up'.[31] On the contrary, no one could challenge Hardie's ascendancy with thousands of ordinary voters – or with socialists the world over – as this 1914 ILP anniversary occasion confirmed. Flanked by such old friends as Bob Smillie, he dominated the day. The old feuds over Grayson were forgotten. When he rose to give his farewell address and reply to Henderson's vote of thanks, he was greeted ecstatically.

A year earlier when he had finally been re-elected to the chair, he had said, 'Nature never intended me to be a leader. I am far happier in the rank and file.' He repeated again in 1914, 'Nature never intended me to occupy an official position. I have my own work to do.'[32]

His theme was how far the Party had come since it was founded. He chose to attack the 'cruel, heartless dogmas' of individualism which had prevented municipal housing, a right to work and a minimum wage – as well as the trade union leaders who 'believed in these dogmas' as much as any Liberal statesman. He contrasted their views with the 'growing altruism of trade unionism' in the rank and file. He also spoke of women, and asked, 'Who is there who even dimly' understands 'the powers that lie latent in the patient drudging woman?'[33] Next to him sat Lillie, perhaps the prototype of such a woman in the minds of the audience, for when he looked back on his first Parliament and wondered how he had ever managed – in particular, how Mrs Hardie had 'kept my house going, kept my children decently and respectably clothed and fed on an income that did not ever exceed 25 shillings a week', to his immense surprise, he was suddenly interrupted by a roar of applause from the hall. The conference rose up as one for Lillie. In his report to Rose Davies about the conference she had missed,[34] he said how pleased he had been by its 'higher tone', especially the 'references to my wife'. He had long since ceased to feel for Lillie, but was genuinely cheered to find others could. When the applause subsided, he went on in an unrehearsed aside:

> You do well to honour her. Never, even in those days, did she offer one word of reproof. Many a bitter tear she shed, but one of the proud boasts of my life is to be able to say that if she has suffered much in health and in spirit, never has she reproached me for what I have done for the cause I love.

To Hardie and his audience this was an accolade, confirming the supportive role of one of life's supporters. To Lillie it might well have confirmed it was the cause he loved, not Lillie.

Hardie ended by saying, 'While I have anything to give, it shall be given ungrudgingly to the child of my life – the ILP.'

His true heir was a political movement.[35] His words could not have been clearer to his children. For Duncan and Jamie there was additional confirmation of their place in his answers to those who began asking him during 1914, what would happen if his sons were conscripted? Hardie always answered that he would rather see his sons 'put up against a wall and shot than join the military and fight'.[36] To the world this was Hardie's integrity; to any son of his it suggested their lives were less important than his political principles.

Yet other men's sons regarded him as the perfect father. During the weekend, for example, he left the conference to see Emrys at his training college in Leeds. There he was taken to meet the principal and fellow students, exactly as if he had been Emrys's father. Later in this same year a young Scotsman wrote to tell him that I have 'more love . . . for you than I have for my own father'.[37] The young man felt entirely at ease pouring out his personal tragedy: 'Hardie, I have lost my Bonnie Lassie. I buried her August 19th . . . and my little boy is with my father . . . I could not bear another parting.' The young man was emigrating to South Africa alone; he concluded he had 'too much emotion for a Scot'. Hardie's own emotions were touched by the child he left behind. Hardie loved children and had long believed in them as the mystic test of socialism,[38] 'some day the history of this movement of ours will be written, not merely in a book but in life', for 'the comrades who are toiling . . . will be forgotten . . . but their work will live . . . in the children that are to be.'

The last event of the Bradford conference was in St George's Hall, where a large group of children had been assembled to sing for Hardie. It was an occasion which moved Fenner Brockway to tears,[39] to see the old man and the very young people, and to hear Hardie's words, which would not have been out of place a hundred years later: defend 'the loveliness of the unspoiled world', love animals, love flowers, eliminate poverty and work for peace. His own generation had failed, Hardie told the children, but 'if these were my last words,' I would say, 'Lads and lassies, live for a better day.'

That particular day had been lived for Hardie: Liberal pacts routed, suffragettes subdued, the ILP's dominance as the conscience of Labour affirmed; and Hardie and Lillie presented with a large and handsome dinner gong (that stood in the Lochnorris hallway for the next forty years). Hardie told Rose Davies that 'I have never felt the same elation of spirit'.[40] It was truly his apotheosis. Glasier's comment was more sanguine. The event had been all heart and no head.[41]

The conference may have been a success for Hardie – perhaps even for Lillie – but not for Nan. She immediately went into a decline, as she had this same time the two previous years. Doctors were consulted in London before she returned to Cumnock, from where she reported to Aggie,[42] 'the Dr I saw in London gave me every hope that I would come all right but it would take a long time. I intend beginning treatment tomorrow.'

What this was, Nan does not say. Nor yet what the diagnosis was. Nan assumed this was related to 'the serious illness I had twelve years ago'. At the same time she had to confess that she had no physical symptoms and that 'I generally look well'. This contradictory state of affairs is inexplicable. As Nan admitted, 'I have been under many a Dr but with little result'. None of them had suggested Nan's illness could be psychological.

Hardie was not feeling well either.[43] He wrote to Aggie at the end of May that he was going to the Richmond Hydro again,[44] but claimed to be more worried about Aggie's health than his own. She 'looked pale and thin the other day and that won't do'.[45] She must come to Cumnock in the summer, as the 'warm-hearted folk there make it the best health resort I know'. Lillie and Nan wrote Aggie a joint letter to reinforce the invitation to Lochnorris, or failing that, for her to join them in Keswick. 'You know you will be welcome . . . so don't stand on ceremony.'[46]

In June Sylvia asked Hardie[47] to march with her East End women to No. 10 Downing Street, but Hardie told her he was unable to come. When Asquith refused to meet the women, Sylvia, who was hunger-striking and weak, had herself carried to Parliament, and laid next to 'the little square door to the left, near to Cromwell's statue' to stay without food until the Prime Minister relented – 'a mad scheme' Lansbury later commented.[48] Crowds gathered and the press made much of the martyrdom.[49] Eventually Asquith agreed to meet some of the women, but not Sylvia. At that point Hardie came out and persuaded her to leave and helped lift her into a cab and sent her off. On another occasion she came to see him and threw a stone at a painting inside the House of Commons, shattering the glass cover.

Hardie had to step in to prevent her from being arrested. On several occasions in the past he had asked questions on her behalf in Parliament, only to find himself confounded. One time he was told her statements were a 'tissue of falsehoods';[50] on another, where he had complained that a weakened Sylvia had been denied help to get home from prison, the Home Office minister replied she was 'not too weak to hold a press conference'.[51]

Sylvia was becoming tiring and Hardie escaped whenever possible to do what he really loved, his 'open air' work. At the end of June he went to Thatcham for a meeting on the green. A reporter came from the *Newbury Weekly News*[52] – as he wrote, expecting to hear 'a red revolutionist, an utterly impossible extremist' because that was 'the view . . . fostered by the daily press'. Instead, he found a man few 'could reconcile' with the press picture that always preceded him: a man of 'good humoured geniality, his absolute honesty of purpose and earnest sincerity' visible to all. Hardie's speech was about the lives of people in Thatcham, which surprised the reporter even more. The third surprise – again typical – was that Hardie stayed on the green answering questions and encouraging discussion for as long as his listeners wanted to go on talking.

Aggie had still not replied to the invitation to Cumnock. Towards the end of June Hardie wrote with another option, 'I shall be free and in London for the weekend following next . . . and I would be very pleased indeed to see you.' Aggie chose to meet Hardie in London rather than to go again to Lochnorris. Hardie said, 'Bring a sackful of sunshine![53] Aggie seemed sunny, young, optimistic, and – despite polite concerns for her pallor – healthy. Hardie, Nan and Lillie all wanted to be with her, and each one continued to correspond with her separately, a web constantly being woven between the four of them. In early July Hardie, Lillie and Nan went to Derwent for a short holiday. Three reports of it were sent to Aggie. According to Hardie, 'enjoying ourselves';[54] according to Lillie, getting no benefit at all, though 'Mr Hardie better',[55] while Nan was having trouble with her teeth again and very unhappy.[56] According to Nan, Lillie still 'sleepless'[57] – the first mention of Lillie's problem in this respect.

July 1914 was not a month when anyone believed the worst was about to befall. Sylvia crashed a garden party given by the Bishop of London. Other suffragettes were hacking paintings in art galleries and starting fires in houses. As late as the 25th Hardie was devoting his *Leader* column to attacking the King, a man 'destitute of even ordinary ability',[58] as a mediator in the Ulster aggravation, making him a 'tool' of the Tories who were backing Ulster Protestants.

As the month wore on, however, the international situation worsened, and increasingly took Hardie's attention. He had been corresponding with Edouard Vaillant in Paris about their plans for an international general strike. Hardie still believed the international working class was strong enough to impose 'international peace by the threat of social war'.[59] When the Balkan crisis escalated at the end of July, and Austria invaded Serbia, the International Socialist Bureau called an emergency meeting in Brussels at the Maison du Peuple for 29 and 30 July. Hardie, Glasier and Dan Irving (Katharine Glasier's spirit-lover of long ago) were elected by the ILP, LP and SP respectively, to attend. Hardie wrote to Aggie, asking her to postpone her trip by a week.[60]

To the International came Victor Adler from Austria, Jean Jaurès from France, and Haase from Germany; Emile Vandervelde from Belgium presided. The debate went on for two days, although Hardie only stayed for the first. Glasier assumed he left early because he was disappointed to find delegates debating imperialism rather than talking of the planned general strike and 'huffed at lack of attention to him'.[61] But he left early because he had assured Aggie he would be back by Friday for their planned weekend.[62] The only decision he heard taken in Brussels was to call a full congress in Paris on 9 August and this satisfied him. Before he left he joined the 7,000 demonstrating in the Cirque, chanting endlessly, 'Guerre à la guerre'. He was not present to endorse the resolution on the Thursday that included opposition to an unfamiliar phrase, 'a world war'.[63]

On the Friday he returned to London and attended the British section of the International. It agreed to meet again on 5 August, and Hardie, along with Henderson and Hyndman, meanwhile undertook on its behalf to call a large public demonstration for Sunday 2 August in Trafalgar Square.[64] Its object was to alert the still-slumbering millions to the danger of drifting into war, a possibility few imagined likely even at this date. Telegrams went out all over the country to urge socialists and trade unionists to hold their own local meetings to show the strength of feeling against war.[65]

Meanwhile, another influential group, made up of some thirty or forty radical Liberals, was equally active. In the House for some while Arthur Ponsonby, Charles Trevelyan and Philip Morrell had continually queried rocketing arms expenditure and devious diplomacy. Outside, men like Norman Angell were trying to get together as many influential people as possible to declare for neutrality in any conflict. On 1 August Angell helped organize a Neutrality Committee,[66] to try to prepare people for the shock waves that would hit Britain from the events taking place in Europe.

On 1 August Hardie had a letter printed in the *Daily Citizen*, pleading for 'an international strike against war'. All the 'social reforms of the

Capitalist classes are clearly designed to act as an opiate upon the workers', he wrote, but 'organized labour' can 'render war practically impossible'.[67]

The day before, he had returned to Neville's Court to spend the long-planned weekend with Aggie. Aggie kept a letter dating from that last weekend in July in the summer of 1914.[68] It is addressed to 'Dad and Em', whom she tells that on Friday the 31st, she and Hardie first 'went to the Fleet Street Picture Palace'. Afterwards, they had 'supper at the Savoy'.

Writing later about this same weekend, Stewart talked of 'the terrible strain' on Hardie of those last few days in July, and the 'wonder . . . that he was able to pass through it, and . . . did not break down'.[69] But this was in retrospect. At the time no one knew what was in store; there was still time to drown the future by taking supper at the Savoy with a young admirer; still time to issue a proclamation calling on workers to 'stand together . . . for peace . . . showing your power', the words Hardie used to call people to Sunday's rally.[70]

The first bad news came late on Friday night. Aggie's letter told of arriving back from supper with Hardie and finding the press 'awaiting him at the Court'.[71] They were there to tell him that Jean Jaurès, due to preside at the 9 August meeting of the International, had been assassinated earlier in the day in Paris, the work, it was said, of a madman.

Aggie's letter continued the next morning, 'I am now going across to the Court to get his breakfast . . . He must be terribly upset about the assassination. We are going perhaps to the Gaiety tonight'. Hardie and Aggie spent the day alone at Neville's Court, Aggie playing daughter, playing wife. For whatever reason – because of how this account might read, or perhaps because the shock of world events made such personal events too trivial – she thought better about sending her letter home. It remained unmailed, retained by her until her death.

On Sunday 2 August throughout Britain the ILP held demonstrations and meetings. Aggie and Hardie walked to Trafalgar Square where a huge crowd assembled. The platform was studded with speakers from every shade of socialist and Labour opinion, dropping for the day their normal antagonisms: George Lansbury,[72] Will Thorne of the General Labourers' Union, Mary MacArthur of the Women Workers, Margaret Bondfield of the Shop Assistants, Ben Tillett of the Dock Workers, Marion Phillips of the Women's Labour League, Herbert Burrows of the British Socialist Party, Mrs Despard and Cunninghame Graham.[73] Arthur Henderson spoke for the Labour Party, and Hardie for the ILP, to a 'storm of cheering'. He had to wait minutes for it to subside, and more minutes for the singing of the 'Internationale', before he could begin. 'You have no quarrel with Germany,' he told the crowd, calling on the long-assimilated words of Carlyle, 'German workmen have no quarrel with their French comrades ... We are told international treaties compel us [but] who made those? The People had no voice in them ... the only class which could prevent ... war ... was the working class.'[74] Again, Hardie set out the plan for a general strike if anyone dared declare war.

Ramsay MacDonald spent the weekend conferring with Liberals, including a vacillating Lloyd George.[75] On Monday 3 August Norman Angell sent Hardie a telegram to ask 'that you should speak tonight to a big mass meeting ... at Canning Town'.[76] Hardie could not go; the House was debating the crisis. Aggie, who stayed on in London, went with him to hear MacDonald speak about the importance of remaining neutral, since Britain had no quarrel with any of these nations currently in hostilities. Hardie did not speak until the end of the debate; he talked about the hardship and privation of war and how hard these would be on those already poor. Why, he asked, were the workers not consulted about such decisions that affected them so vitally?

As he spoke, however, a cold, cold wind began blowing at his back. It was the sound of the National Anthem being sung – softly. The voices were led by Will Crooks and Labour MPs from his own side. Aggie was at the House to hear it and she was there the next day too, when war was formally declared.[77]

'Britain declares war against Germany. Stupefied; cannot believe it.'[78] If the well-informed Glasier was caught out, the general population were unable to comprehend the news for days. 'In Brussels,' said Glasier, 'no one, not even the German representatives, appeared apprehensive of an actual rupture between the Great Powers ... until diplomacy had been tried.' Too late everyone discovered that diplomacy had never been an option.

The British section of the International met on 5 August and although the Labour Party had declared against the war on 2 August, when Cunninghame Graham and Glasier and a Socialist Party member tried to get a debate, the meeting was adjourned over their heads without one.[79] Within days the majority of German socialists voted for war credits by 78 to 14, with only Karl Liebknecht and his small band holding out. Belgian socialists supported the war when Belgium was invaded; French socialists supported their government, which wanted to fight Germany. Only a few days of press propaganda about the national threat, defending 'small nations' and protecting democracy, and within days British public opinion was also fully mobilized. The Labour Party leaned along with it. A War Emergency Workers' National Committee, representing the whole labour movement, was set up. Its job was to look after civilian life: health, education, food, homes and children. It must have made many wonder why such issues were not addressed with this urgency in peacetime.

Against this background on 6 August Keir Hardie took the train to Merthyr to meet with his constituents. The meeting, long arranged, was at Aberdare in the local market hall, a 'huge and dreary building'.[80] It was to be chaired by Charles Stanton, the local miners' agent and Hardie's organizer. The first ominous sign was that Stanton did not turn up and sent word he would not be coming. Edmund Stonelake, Miners' Federation president, took the chair instead. Stonelake took Hardie aside briefly before the meeting and wrote later that he would never forget the 'look of surprise and astonishment [that] came on to his face when I told him the feeling was intensely in favour of war'.[81] Not until this moment did it even enter Hardie's head that the working class would not stand together on this issue.

Stonelake and Hardie and Richardson filed on to the platform in silence. Neither they, nor Emrys Hughes, sitting in front, were aware at first of the unusual nature of the audience massed at the back, but 'as soon as Hardie rose, pandemonium broke out, a bell began ringing, and there was shouting which culminated in the singing of the National Anthem'.[82] Hardie attempted to say 'no one wanted a war but the Tory press'[83] but got no further. The place was packed with well-organized 'patriots', largely Liberals and Conservatives, determined to prevent him being heard. He tried again to speak about the real enemies being the Kaiser and the Czar, not the German working people, but the words were drowned by 'Rule Britannia'. Hardie tried to say that he was opposing the war in the interests of 'civilization and the class to which he belonged' which would have to bear the worst of it,[84] but the anger of Hardie supporters shouting for quiet only added to the noise.

After half an hour Hardie sat down and Tom Richardson tried. He too was drowned out. Then Evan Parker, Hardie's colleague who hired motorcars and always drove him around the constituency, moved towards the opposition. He 'pushed and shoved his way through the crowd until he reached the man with the Union Jack and tore it from him'.[85] It was plain to Hardie that reasoned debate was useless and that his energies would be better put to preventing his own supporters from further fighting, as the newspapers next day conceded would have been likely had Hardie not stopped the meeting. But jingoistic crowds jostled and pursued him all the same. As he left the hall, Emrys Hughes recalled, he had to be protected by a human circle of supporters, as 'shots rang out'.[86]

Some of the press the next day said Hardie was driven off at high speed, but Emrys, who stayed with him, wrote: 'we walked up the street followed by a howling mob. He looked neither left nor right, his head erect, grey haired, grey bearded chieftain, one of the grandest men that had ever braved the rabble.'[87] At last they reached the house in Elm Grove of the local schoolmaster, Matt Lewis, where Hardie was spending the night. The hostile crowds came up to the door, jeering

and singing and shouting, 'Turn the German out!'[88] Only when Mrs
Matt Lewis, holding her baby in her arms, stepped out to face them,
did they finally disperse.[89]

Inside, after smoking a pipe by the fire, and saying nothing for
a long time, Hardie said to the company waiting with him that
now he 'understood as well as any man what Christ had suffered
at Gethsemane'.[90] This seemed all the more apt when, next day,
the police came to escort him to the station. The *Western Mail* on
sale in the town had headlines, 'Mr Hardie Hooted'. The next day
it featured Charles Stanton on why he had not attended the meeting:
not because he was afraid of being hooted himself, he assured readers,
but because 'in times of distress I stand by my country'.[91] He declared
that 'although a socialist' he was also 'a Britisher'.

Labour in Merthyr – like Labour in Parliament – was split. Many
went the way of war, others stayed loyal to Hardie. Stewart later gave
the roll call: 'Dai Davies, Llewellyn Francis, John Barr, Evan Parker,
Matt Lewis, Stonelake, Morris, the Hughes family, all the stalwarts
who had fought and won with him, were now ready to fight and lose
with him.'[92]

Hardie stopped off in Abercynon on his way back to London, and
saw Aggie. Ten days later, when he had returned to Cumnock, he
wrote to her that he had 'seen the tear in your eye' as he said he had
not wanted her to accompany him to the station, which she usually
did. It was not because he did not want her with him but because
what people hurl at 'me sometimes vexes my friends'. He asked her
to write to him in London and mark the letter 'private'.[93]

Earlier, on his return to London, there had been the usual basket
of fruit from her, and another debate in the House on the war. The
government was solid in support and had suffered only a few minor
resignations in protest. One was Lord Morley, the elderly Liberal
statesman now aged eighty. The other, to everyone's surprise, was
John Burns. He had spent nine years sitting in Liberal cabinets, where
he had been in charge of the poor laws and had 'left the system as
he had found it – still detested by the poor, wastefully run . . . giving
doles to palliate the destitution with whose cause it had no concern'.[94]
Suddenly, his earlier radicalism had resurfaced.

Perhaps he had been influenced by Hardie's speech, on 10 August,
on how the Stock Exchange got a Relief Bill passed at once, while
there was nothing for the poor who would be held to ransom by food
speculators. As for the war itself, Hardie said, 'A few years hence we
shall look back in wonder and amazement at the flimsy reasons which
induced the government to take part in it'.[95]

He expressed his anger that all the demonstrations of the working
class had made no difference, 'We simply do not count.'[96] He did not
wish to see that the real problem was that so many in the working class

had decided against peace and neutrality. On 6 August the editor of Labour's *Daily Citizen* asked its board for permission to rejoice at the success of British arms.[97] On 7 August the Parliamentary Labour Party allowed war credits to pass through the Commons unopposed. On 29 August the Labour Party Executive agreed to help the government recruit.[98] On 3 September the TUC supported the war and virtually capitulated to conscription. By October the Party had decided that Prussianism was to blame and had to be crushed.

When the war had started Hardie wrote in the *Leader*[99] that 'The ILP at least will stand firm and Keep the Red Flag flying'. Officially it did. So did most of its leading members, such as Tom Richardson and Jowett, and later Snowden (who was in New Zealand at the time) and most startling to many, Ramsay MacDonald, who resigned the Labour leadership within a week, and was replaced by Arthur Henderson. What we know of the later MacDonald suggests he would have been instinctively a nationalist. One historian called it 'the most surprising action of his life'.[100]

But it was only surprising because MacDonald had kept his liaisons with Liberals so much a secret. His close personal, now almost daily, contacts with radicals and neutralists who were opposing the war meant he was honour bound to do so as well.[101] MacDonald had a future to win, and temporary social dishonour was a risk he was prepared to take. The war would not last for ever and after it people would want a new start. Meanwhile the Labour Party – which was at war with itself – would be compromised by having worked with the government. It was better to be free and working for the future. On 10 August MacDonald had dinner with Philip Morrell and Norman Angell and other Liberals.[102] They all took the long view, as MacDonald later confirmed in writing to Henderson (when the Party tried to persuade him to withdraw his resignation): he was going to 'attempt to take up a distinctive position which will in due course be the rallying centre for those who will wish that this war should not have been fought in vain'.[103] MacDonald always had a strategy and in this case a support group, which shortly announced itself in November as the Union of Democratic Control. Its purpose was to end the war honourably and bring all future diplomacy under parliamentary control.

But it was unpleasant having to gamble. Hardie was abused in print and in public as never before, in Cardiff and Merthyr editorials and in the national press;[104] by Tories and Liberals in the House, including Merthyr's Edgar Jones; by former colleagues like H. G. Wells; but most wounding of all, by fellow Labour Party members, together with the bulk of the trade union leadership. MacDonald began to get something of the same treatment. He did not like it, and it seared into MacDonald's soul a determination never to be ostracized again – to move always towards the centre. For not only were MacDonald and Hardie attacked in the press in 1914, but also in the street, when recognized. And not just by words. They soon began taking precautions. For several years MacDonald made an arrangement with a Liberal MP who lived near him in Hampstead,[105] who agreed to wait for him at night and go home with him. On one occasion in 1916 he appeared at the MP's home in the middle of the night, asking for temporary asylum, so fearful was he of an assault if he went to his own house.[106] Sylvia wrote that Hardie was 'hooted and hustled' constantly, including outside Neville's Court.[107] At one point Hardie too appealed for protection; he asked Glasier to go with him on a train from Merthyr to London so that he need not travel alone.[108]

It was not only the men who suffered. A Welsh miner who opposed the war recalled decades later the ostracization of his family, the suffering 'and indignity of being called traitors and cowards'.[109] Lillie wrote to Aggie about 'the awful business'[110] of the war, which had compounded troubles for her, Nan and Duncan. No one needed to ask what their views were. Every word Hardie said was taken to be theirs: 'I am afraid we are in the black books with our friends,' she confided, 'owing to our unpatriotism. But we shall survive their taunts and jeers'.[111] They survived by hardly ever going outside.

Hardie had been shaken by the night in Aberdare and tried very hard during September to get himself on to the local Relief Committee in Merthyr. Writing to Aggie in October, he told her he planned to go to one of its meetings.[112] But neither this Committee nor those in Mountain Ash or Aberdare asked him, despite the fact that he wrote to the mayors of all three to offer his services. He had had replies, 'but no invitation'.[113] He was worried how it would look to constituents because 'Of course the people cannot know these things'.

On the final weekend of July Sylvia had been at her cottage in Penshurst with Norah Smyth,[114] planning the next stage of suffrage activity. But suddenly there was no more suffrage movement. On 7 August 1914, an amnesty was granted to all suffragettes in jail; they were released with the expectation that they would shelve their campaigns and work for the war effort, as most promptly did.

When Sylvia got back to London, she sought Hardie out. He reinforced her resolve to oppose the war. She later claimed she found him 'already a broken man',[115] but this was in retrospect, as were most reports on Hardie's reaction to the war quoted in almost all biographies and recollections. Ramsay MacDonald spoke of seeing Hardie sitting on the terrace of the House, broken and staring blankly.[116] Fenner Brockway saw him, 'though only 58 . . . an old, old man, crumpled in body and broken in spirit'.[117] To Stewart it was Aberdare that gave him 'the fatal wound'.[118] Beatrice Webb concluded too that the war 'finished him'.[119]

Most such comments, however, were written long after 1914 –
Sylvia's in 1932 – and many referred to meetings in 1915. All support
the myth that Hardie's life shut down at the start of the war and
nothing significant happened to him after. Yet Hardie retained his
fighting spirit totally intact. If anything, the war spurred him to new
activity. For amidst the detraction were messages of strong support
from war opponents as far away as India and Turkey, and as near as
Stepney, where Clement Attlee sent congratulations on his stand on
behalf of local trade unionists.[120]

There was still the ILP to support, to stiffen its political war
resistance. On 11 August Hardie at last handed over to the NAC
the Kippen bequest – after years of negotiations that had absorbed
hours of his and his family's time.[121] The NAC congratulated Hardie
on obtaining the money, while it congratulated MacDonald on his stand
in Parliament.[122] There were ILP conferences in both Glasgow and
Edinburgh in mid-August. In the event Hardie found even the ILP was
too timid and reported to Aggie that their spirit was 'not so determined
in denunciation of the war as I would have liked'.[123] At a special NAC
meeting the vote for an immediate truce was only carried by 6 to 5.[124]
He took no holiday that year and in early September went on a speaking
tour to Leeds, Liverpool, Manchester, Eccles, Ipswich and Swansea,[125]
determined to rally opinion against the fighting. He had written a strong
Labour Leader article attacking the specious arguments of the new Labour
Party leadership that the war was really 'socialist' because it was against
the Kaiser who was an enemy of the German working man.[126] Hardie
pointed out that the UK was now allied to the Czar, even less a friend
of any working man. But he had by now accepted that the war could
not be ended tomorrow and he urged all work be bent to bring the 'war
to a close much more speedily than the military element contemplates at
present'.[127] He also urged a strong stand against conscription. Stewart,
his contemporary, reports that Hardie 'spoke with vigour and clearness'
at all his meetings, and with 'his mental powers . . . unimpaired'.[128] He
continued his constituency visits and his weekly columns in the *Pioneer*.
Thousands, if not millions, of working-class people had every reason to
expect Hardie would still be there when the war ended.

But Hardie felt wounded. He asked TU leaders why they were
touting for recruits to an army that had shot two railwaymen at Llanelli
in 1911.[129] He wrote to the Revd John Hughes immediately after the
Aberdare meeting[130] (to tell him he hoped to show Aggie 'attention'
that day or the next), deploring the 'organized hooliganism' at Aberdare
but adding frankly that 'the defection of so many of our people is what
chills to the marrow'. By far the greatest wound was the defection of the
Labour Party, and the rupturing of friendship with such men as George
Barnes.[131] The National Executive and the Parliamentary Labour Party
both took positions which Stewart said Hardie found 'mortifying and

painful',[132] and he frequently expressed his disgust at official Labour pronouncements on the war: the Party was now nothing but 'a War Office annexe'.[133]

This was not a sudden disillusionment, however. The last time Hardie had probably felt at one with the Party was during his chairmanship in 1910 when he had spoken so definitely of the need to link the Party to socialism now that all the unions had joined. But after 1911, when MacDonald had assumed command, he had been slowly losing faith. According to Snowden, Hardie had never had any idea 'of forming a Labour Party' when he had created his alliance in 1900.[134] After MacDonald became leader, he could not escape the fact that it was a party like other parties. As Reid commented, Hardie had become 'a prisoner of the Labour alliance he helped to create'.[135]

His faith began to ebb. G. D. H. Cole put this down to the Party's drift into identification with the Liberals.[136] Beatrice Webb shrewdly commented that since 1912 Hardie had been turning against the Labour Party 'because it became clear to his sincere but limited mind that Labour leaders in Parliament were no different from aristocrats' and were not going to bring in 'revolutionary programmes'.[137] Glasier believed that when the Labour Party was unpopular and weak Hardie 'fought . . . night and day . . . but when all began to speak well' of it, 'his ardour . . . began to cool'.[138] When Labour supported the war, it cooled still further. By 3 August 1914, Hardie made the precariousness of his link to the Party manifest when he spoke against the war in the House: 'I do not speak for the Party with which I am connected for the present moment . . . but for myself personally'; nor was he alone. One South Wales miner who shared Hardie's views remembered years after, the Labour Party in 1914 'was a disaster'.[139]

As well as moving away from the Labour Party, Hardie 'bitterly complained' of its paper, the *Daily Citizen*, which he denounced as nothing but a 'Jingo rag',[140] one he became 'ashamed to open', and stopped reading entirely. To Shaw he wrote, 'the paper is making rapidly for the void'[141] with a 'reactionary cad' in the chair. Hardie was right; the war killed the *Citizen*, which stopped publishing in 1915. Lansbury's *Herald*, on the other hand, kept going, even improving, but was still not good enough for Hardie. He believed it too could have been stronger against the war.[142] Attitudes to the war – both for and against – were extremely complex. Each side housed endless conflicting sub-sides.

Everywhere Hardie looked for signs of opposition to the war. He found some comfort in the writings of Brailsford[143] and in the speeches of radical Liberals, though he opposed MacDonald's attempts to link the ILP campaigns with the new Union of Democratic Control.[144] Shaw's pamphlet, *Common Sense and the War*, however, delighted him. In best Shavian fashion, it both supported and opposed the war (Sylvia called it the 'naughtiest agglomeration of contradictions the great jester had ever perpetuated').[145] But Hardie, desperate for support in the public arena, saw only the anti-war side, and wrote to Shaw that 'my heart grows towards you with almost feelings of devotion'.[146] In a postscript he added: 'Only a Celt could have done it.' Shaw never replied, a fact he later deeply regretted.[147]

Hardie's Party of One soon adapted itself to the war and began to fight on behalf of those he had always championed. He denounced firms making money out of the war by supplying shoddy goods.[148] He took up the cause of the poor who got no help from the new Relief Act (since their poverty was not due to the war); he protested against recruiting agents coming to local football matches.[149] At the end of October a big meeting was planned for Merthyr at the skating rink. It was to be the test of how much support he really had. He wrote to Aggie to say he hoped she and all her family were coming[150] and that afterwards he could stay with them in Abercynon for the night, 'if I may pay proper devotion to Morpheous [*sic*] on Sunday morning'. On the day 3,000 turned up; both Hardie and MacDonald spoke to a cheering audience. There was no opposition. Later another meeting at Aberdare gave Hardie a vote of confidence.[151] After the MacDonald meeting he wrote to Aggie that 'the demonstration was a glorious success'.[152] Yet the national press did not report these meetings,[153] the first signs of censorship.

Hardie, worried about this blackout, was determined to keep 'the lamp of freedom and free speech burning'.[154] But he was also sensitive to criticism in Merthyr. One particular charge he took pains to refute was that he was preventing young men from enlisting. On 8 November in the *Pioneer* he denied it and said he would offer any assistance to those who wanted to volunteer. He even apologized for not attending a local recruitment meeting[155] and was reported by the *Western Mail*[156] as distancing himself from opposition to war; later he said there need not have been a war, but now we must see it through;[157] just as earlier he had said, 'The lads who have gone forth . . . must not be disheartened by any discordant note at home'.[158]

These accommodations disheartened younger socialists like Fenner Brockway who felt very let down.[159] They believed Hardie should have tried to discourage everyone from enlisting and given no quarter to those supporting the war, though part of Hardie's attitude was sheer compassion for the tragedies that the war was already bringing. One day he saw a rich Tory MP in the House, one of the worst jingoists. Hardie knew that his only son had just been killed at the Front. All he wanted to do, Hardie told Glasier, was 'to go up to him and put my arms around his neck'.[160]

Wherever he went, militarism seemed to ring triumphant. Workers were bayoneting dummies in the streets, a sight that always upset him.[161] Officers swaggered everywhere. Raw recruits tramped the lanes singing patriotic songs. Killing was everyone's objective. He kept up his spirits by trying to remain optimistic. In November he wrote to Emrys Hughes that 'a saner spirit is beginning to obtain . . . certainly more doubt the wisdom of our having gone into the war'.[162] On thinking over why the working class agreed to do so so readily, Hardie had concluded, 'The press is largely to blame' – the same conclusion he had come to about the Boer War.[163]

Emrys Hughes had been in Cardiff when war was declared, passing time with local friends before going back to college. They went to the Empire Music Hall for diversion, where the programme was suddenly interrupted by a girl singing jingoistic songs; and 'then the cinema screen was lowered and after a few topical films came photos of the king, Mr Asquith and Sir Edward Grey', followed by 'God Save the King'. Emrys walked out, 'I felt sick and disgusted and wanted to be alone. There was no doubt about it, the war was going to be intensely popular.'[164]

A few days later he was walking in the mountains and looked down at his own little Welsh town, while a party of soldiers marched through it recruiting. 'I thought that in the Westphalian villages the same appeal was being made, and that the miners there would leave their homes among the hillsides . . . to fight for liberty in exactly the same spirit.'[165]

When he got back to college half of it had already been turned into a hospital for the wounded. In what had been the lab he found the bed of a young man with a shrapnel wound, 'realistic, unromantic, utterly unlike the heroic stories . . . filling the newspapers'.[166] The soldier was emphatic, he was not going back to the war. Emrys was equally emphatic, he would refuse to go at all, though he 'dreaded the thought of standing aloof from what appeared to be popular'.[167]

Hardie met Emrys several times to advise him on his future. Lillie started writing Emrys directly, encouraging him in his conscientious objection, as well as in his studies. It was almost as if Hardie and Lillie had taken Emrys over as their own son, to stand in for the absent Jamie, even for the present Duncan. Emrys exemplified all the attitudes and opinions they expected in a 'son'. He was a man for the last great cause.

Meanwhile, in the United States Jamie and May were expecting their first child. Hardie would have known, since up to the war he had kept in touch with them – and so had Nan and Duncan.[168] May Hardie retained an affection for the father-in-law who had charged her with the task of seeing that Jamie made something of his life. Hardie occasionally heard from Jamie, whom he always called by his childhood name of Jiddie. 'I had your nice long letter and will write in a day or so',[169] said a Hardie postcard in early 1914. Whether Hardie ever got around to his own long letter is doubtful, as 'we are in the thick of a great contest'. Jamie might well have asked, when was his father not in the middle of a great contest?

During the autumn of 1914 Aggie continued to correspond with all the Hardies in Cumnock. Hardie protested ardently that there is only one question that 'worries me at present' and that is Aggie's own health,[170] but it was Nan (still having her teeth removed) and Lillie (still sleepless) who had the health worries.[171] Aggie kept sending gifts to all of them: Keats, 'candies', fruit. Nan and Lillie tried to discourage the habit, but eventually Nan said, 'I suppose it is no use telling you to stop sending gifts. You never will.'[172] Hardie's tactic was to tease Aggie about her stream of presents, including a pair of gloves which he assured her he would lose. 'I am ashamed to think of what I have lost in the way of gloves during the past few years. A real bearskin pair from Canada and a pair of doeskin from Williams . . . I carry an old pair in my pocket . . . that cost me 9 pence nine years ago and they stick to me.'[173]

Hardie still had to deal with a large correspondence beyond that from the constituency. In November Grayson's wife, Ruth, wrote to plead for money, saying Grayson was ill and they were about to be evicted.[174] A pleasanter surprise was a letter from Maggie Symons in Alexandria at the end of October.[175] The war had given her a chance at last to earn her own living. Owing to the departure of staff on the largest English daily, the *Gazette*, Maggie was taken on as copy editor and journalist, writing up political news. She was thriving; and still full of admiration for 'Mr Human Being'; resisting this popular war, she wrote, 'requires more courage than to face gunpowder'.

The holiday season eventually arrived. Emrys came home to Abercynon; Duncan to Cumnock, with Hardie close behind. The day after Hardie arrived he informed Aggie about a curious event, 'my arm quite failed me in the train yesterday . . . after many hours of close writing'.[176] Lillie soon confirmed that Hardie had 'strained' his arm and could not move it.[177] She too put it down to too much writing, and even the doctor says 'the nerves and muscles of his arm are strained – probably due to too much writing.' Nan had to do all his writing for him, and under doctor's instructions, 'Mother has to foment and rub . . . It may take months to mend'.[178] None of them appears to have realized that Hardie had had a serious stroke.

Hardie's illness was not allowed to dent the domestic routine, Lillie writing Aggie that as always, 'I'm sending my shortbread'.[179] Hardie tried to keep up his own spirits by dictating an article on the fraternization between German and British troops in the trenches over Christmas, magnifying this small candle of hope.[180] After it went out, the slaughter went on, compounding the sad news that Lillie and

Hardie had received some time during the last half of 1914 themselves. In the United States, May had been rushed to hospital for her baby's premature arrival. It was to be their first grandchild. It turned out to be twin boys. Both died at birth.[181]

After Hogmanay Hardie insisted on setting out once more to campaign against the war. He and Lillie went to stay in Hamilton with Lillie's sister in order to attend an ILP Conference in Glasgow.[182] The 'pacifist minority',[183] as Sylvia called those who opposed the war, were already campaigning for a negotiated peace. The conference was for delegates only, but during proceedings four strangers were spotted in the hall. They turned out to be police in plain clothes, who left when challenged. That the ILP was under surveillance by its own government in its own country depressed Hardie deeply,[184] as did a government giving way to military rule and a press to orchestration of uncritical war support, triumphalist recruitment campaigns and untruthful attempts to popularize the Czar as an enlightened ruler.[185]

By contrast, everything German was denigrated. The day war broke out, a German living a few doors from the Hughes family in Mountain Ash Road was arrested and spirited away. Everyone concluded he was one of Germany's 'master spies' – long planted in the area to disrupt coal production – and that he would be executed in the Tower of London; in fact, he was a hairdresser, detained and later deported.[186] Another German who suffered was Max Beer (UK correspondent of the SDP's *Vorwärts*) who was stranded in London. The Labour Party dropped him but the ILP helped out with financial support until he too could get home.

The next night Hardie spoke at a public meeting in Hamilton, where he explained his reasons for opposing the war. At all public meetings he had to face awkward questions on Germans, and, increasingly, on his attitude to young men who had volunteered. To many in his audience, Hardie was seen to be comforting the enemy by his attacks upon the government. Others who came were torn between patriotism and socialism. But after hearing him, none doubted either his sincerity or the strength of his case; and although he was sometimes heckled, he was also cheered. Lillie – on the platform that night – was anxious to get him back to Cumnock as soon as possible,[187] so that he could continue his recuperation. He had planned to go to London to the ILP's January NAC meeting on the 8th and 9th and then to Merthyr. But all his January engagements were cancelled by Wright, the new London secretary Hardie had hired after Maggie left. (Hardie told Maggie that in his black silk topper and formal clothes he made Neville's Court look 'almost respectable – I am still here'.)[188] These cancellations soon set rumours flying about Hardie's 'paralysis'.[189] Wright also wrote to Aggie apologizing for Hardie's non-appearance; on the same day Hardie wrote her himself to say he was sorry he had had to break last week's date.[190] 'I shall make up for that in the future.' Hardie would still not admit he was ill.

By mid-month Hardie was able to go out for his daily walk, always his barometer of healthy functioning.[191] With Nan's help he wrote for the 6 February *Pioneer*, pursuing the theme of who was benefiting financially from the war. Countries always go to war 'on a fiction'. Talk about protecting little nations was an excuse: wars were for profit-mongers. 'The most popular man amongst bank managers and money lenders just now is Mr Lloyd George.'[192]

Although both Nan and Lillie begged Hardie not to try to attend the opening session of Parliament,[193] he insisted on leaving for it on 1 February 1915. In London he attempted to pursue his usual routine. He spoke at the City of London ILP's annual dinner, and on St Valentine's Day chaired the International Bureau in the Fabian offices. MacDonald, Sidney Webb, Hyndman and Henderson all took part, joined by Vandervelde and two other Belgians who had managed to get across the Channel, as well as by the Russian, Maxim Litvinov, who was living in London. There was an argument about whether Russian Bolsheviks were entitled to attend and Litvinov left.[194] The meeting agreed to convene a socialist conference in London a month later. The date itself was just about all they could agree on. Several sections, for example, disagreed with MacDonald's plan to limit the conference to socialists from allied countries. Hostilities between pacifist and non-pacifist socialists continued (they even split *Clarion* cycling clubs).[195] After the meeting Glasier noted that Hardie's speaking voice had been curiously slurred.[196] On the 15th his old friend and enemy and now friend again, John Burns, came to call at Neville's Court.[197] He said he found Hardie obsessed with the war and 'living a lonely life' – not that Burns's life was any the less so. He was an over-bearing husband, and his only child, a son, had always sided with the mother in the family household. In retaliation Burns had always called the boy a weakling.[198] Perhaps to prove otherwise, perhaps to rebel against his pacifist father, the boy had now enlisted. It was not the only family with this kind of problem. Two of Bob Smillie's sons enlisted, while a third became a conscientious objector. Duncan was holding to his father's line. Jamie, even if he was not, was still in the USA, where there was no war. Emrys had one more term in college and Hardie assumed he would seek to exempt himself as a teacher, as Matt Lewis had done.

Although reports from Glasier and Burns put Hardie down as failing badly on 15 February, on the same day he wrote to Aggie to say he was now feeling much better.[199] He may have been trying to scotch rumours, for Hardie was always furious when the press highlighted any bout of poor health. In one card to Aggie over an incident the year before[200] he said he would like to 'horsewhip' the journalists who gave such frights to his friends. On another occasion he sent Sylvia a telegram to say to take no notice of the report that he was ill. She got the message while speaking at Poplar Town Hall and went to Neville's Court at once, only to find him looking very poorly.[201]

During Christmas Sylvia and Norah Smyth had gone to Paris to see Emmeline. Sylvia found that with the war a 'thousand leagues had intervened' between herself and her mother.[202] Emmeline Pankhurst had abandoned suffrage, socialism and pacifism, and was as enthusiastic for the war as any jingoist. There was no talk of votes for women any more and Sylvia returned quickly, to throw herself back into work at her East London Suffrage Federation, with its headquarters at 400 Old Ford Road. Sylvia and her supporters – like Hardie – had tried to take part in the approved rescue efforts, such as the local relief committee set up by the mayor of Poplar; and when the much larger Women's National Committee was set up by the Labour Party and the TUC, she also offered her services. But Sylvia was refused membership on the grounds that only those 'affiliated to the Labour Party' could do relief work.[203] Sylvia found that the Labour Party had become part of the establishment – as necessary now to the government as the women's movement. Slowly, she withdrew from both. As with the break with her mother and sister, 'it was a sorrow to me . . . yet also a liberation'.[204] Her biographer claims she made a leap from 'suffragette to feminist' at this point,[205] but in fact she had made a much wider one: she had liberated her energy for general social activism. 'I believe in the Golden Age,' Sylvia once said.[206] Hers had arrived.

Her suffrage office was 'daily thronged with women and children, penniless, starving, ill from privation, and rent unpaid, the landlord threatening eviction'.[207] She mounted her own campaign on rents, wages, food shortages and living conditions of working people in the immediate area. She enlarged the *Dreadnought*'s remit to campaign for equal wages for women and for female recruitment to trade unions. 'Ours is a district where many homes are maintained either partially or wholly by women's earnings.'[208] She bombarded the government and the Cabinet, MPs and officials, not only for immediate relief but for decent long-term legislation on housing, schools and work programmes for East Londoners.[209]

What characterized the liberated Sylvia was that next to the barracking speeches and petitions to great men – activities she had always indulged in – she now placed a long list of practical achievements on behalf of those around her.

Beginning by badgering for second-hand clothes from better-off London women, particularly clothes for babies, and receiving a large supply, she began a distribution centre at No. 400. This went so well that she began collecting and distributing food. Within a month, taking advantage of the expertise in tailoring in the East End, she had opened a garment factory in the back, to make (rather than continue to beg for) clothes for those who needed cost-price wear. She trained women to machine-make clothes and 'decided to make our wage for women over 19 . . . £1 a week, the wage for an unskilled man labourer'.[210] The trained women went on to get excellent jobs when government factories started to make uniforms. She started a co-operative boot factory in yet another room. Finally, she opened a toy factory, recruiting the elderly Walter Crane to help illustrate children's books and design puzzles. Dolls became a speciality, since most UK dolls had come from Germany and the supply was now cut off. Imaginatively, her workshop specialized in Japanese and black dolls as well as standard Anglo-Saxon faces. During November and December Selfridges had agreed to take what she could produce and every week Sylvia rushed her dolls over to Oxford Street by taxi.

To care for the children of her workers, her group bought an old pub, The Gunmaker's Arms, at 438 Old Ford Road, and renamed it 'The Mother's Arms'. There she started a creche, which Bessie Lansbury came in to run. Upstairs there was eventually a Montessori Nursery School for older children (where Fenner Brockway's first child, Audrey, was later a pupil). Everyone in both buildings had to eat, so this led to the hiring of cooks and the establishment of a cost-price restaurant at the 'Arms'. In time she opened it to the neighbourhood and issued 'free tickets for dinner and supper . . . to nursing and expectant mothers . . . soldiers disabled . . . [and] . . . old age pensioners . . . existing on their 5/ a week'. She also added a campaign to raise the pension to eight shillings a week and organized a successful rent strike.[211]

Some of these ventures covered their own costs, a few made a profit for a while, others were helped by funding from Norah Smyth (who kept all the books) – and possibly also from Fels. But the organizer was Sylvia, an achievement she did not seek to hide. She wrote up her activity in the *Daily Herald* and journalists began to visit. The *Christian Commonwealth* conveniently played upon the theme of destitute East Enders with only Sylvia to rely on, comparing their lot to that of affluent West Enders whom the war had scarcely touched.[212] West End women began sending even larger contributions.

As always Sylvia used Hardie when she needed help.[213] For a woman with six children and a disabled husband, he got a temporary rent reduction of 17s.6d. a week. He helped to win better wages for Kent brushmakers who contributed to Sylvia's emporium. Early in 1915 Sylvia consulted him earnestly about the restaurant cook, Mrs Richmond, who favoured a 'large use of dried beans' and 'potatoes with skins ON', claiming these had real food value. Sylvia complained to Hardie that her regulars thought they were being insulted by inferior food. 'Shall I permit this "expert" to improve people against their will?'

'I think so,' he replied.

When she persisted with her doubts, Hardie interrupted wearily, 'Have we fallen so low that we must discuss potato skins?' Like everyone else, she found Hardie becoming strangely irritable.

During February and March Hardie kept up his questions in the House. Why were men on final leave not allowed free rail passes to visit their families?[214] Why couldn't a mother with two sons at war get two war allowances?[215] How could a 'poor man' accused of a crime defend himself under the new rules permitting trials to be moved outside the areas where they had occurred?[216]

He spoke in Parliament when a new bylaw was introduced to allow children under twelve to leave school and work on farms, objecting to 'education committees . . . robbing the child of the education which the law had provided for it'.[217] He objected to farmers getting the 'cheap labour . . . of children for their farms', while local authorities 'wink both eyes' at children as young as ten being used. He also attacked the argument that for children who were not 'intellectually bright' schooling was 'an unnecessary waste of money'. Again, as he always did in all debates about education, he insisted that education must be seen 'from the point of view . . . of the working classes'.

He told the House that if they wanted farm labour, let them use women's labour and pay them the going rate for it. Much farm work was suitable for women. His own mother, he said proudly, had worked on a farm while bringing him up.

Apart from a mention of those 'who have more power of physical exertion than I possess at the present moment', he made no reference to his bodily ills, and his attack was as vigorous as it had been on the first day he stood up to speak in the House twenty-two years earlier.

Lord Morley passed Hardie in the corridor of the House just after this speech, 'You have not been well? I expect it is the war.' Hardie said he had 'to nod a vague assent'.[218] But it was not the war, nor even his long history of small strokes which Hardie had been having for years – Pasteur, for example, had over fifty during his most productive years. It was the one stroke he had had in December and the redoubled pace of work that the war had induced. In the preceding months several exhaustive collapses at the House had brought several medical Members to attend to him;[219] most told him he would not live long if he went on at his present pace.[220] In March Hardie went to see Thomas Horder, a specialist in Harley Street;[221] and then back to Scotland to sign himself in to his favourite Wemyss Bay Hydro.[222] He told no one. Friends like Glasier, when he missed committee meetings, said that people fear Hardie 'is fading out from the scene'.[223] There was even a report in the *Boston Evening Transcript* that he had died – complete with obituary.[224]

The Wemyss sojourn appears to have revived him. He was back at

Lochnorris on 22 March, making fun in the *Pioneer* of the American obituary,[225] and two days later full of indignation in the *Leader* on behalf of:

> the worker who takes all the risks to life of . . . raising minerals . . . who tills the soil . . . who builds the mill and factory and sweats therein . . . and when a set of selfish and incompetent statesmen have plunged nations into shedding each other's blood, it is the worker who is called upon to line the trenches.[226]

Again he insisted that people should begin thinking about peace, for 'When the war is only a . . . blood-stained nightmare . . . surely there will be a mighty agitation for complete enfranchisement of democracy.'

Democracy was the theme to which Hardie had now returned. On 6 February in the *Pioneer* he had written that 'the blind patriotism of the masses and their lack of the faintest interest in what really concerns themselves, makes them an easy prey to . . . financiers plotting and scheming to make war.'[227] A few months later George Bernard Shaw also put all the blame on the working class, not fit for the vote since it slavishly followed its betters' views on what to do and did not think for itself.[228] Hardie took a more optimistic view of human potential:[229]

> Labour Parties and Socialist Parties at home and abroad have proved broken reeds . . . the revolutionary spirit has long been dead in democracy. There are signs of its resurrection . . . if the leaders of the working class will say frankly that Liberals and Unionists are equally props of finance . . . equally concerned in keeping the worker in subjection, then indeed a change will come. DEMOCRACY will raise itself up from its present helpless dependence and become a real power in control in the affairs of nations.

At the end of March Hardie went to Merthyr. He met Aggie briefly, and he had a meeting with Emrys, who had given notice that he would be working every spare moment in the campaign against conscription but would refuse to plead religion or morality – or teacher exemption – for himself. He would claim 'opposition to the war as a socialist and anti-militarist'. Hardie wrote to Aggie later that his truculent views were worrying not so much because of the danger – although a soldier who had refused to fight had already been executed – but 'I regret them for the sake of the Movement'. It meant Emrys would not be available for ILP work. Hardie concluded wearily, 'but it will be best for him'.[230] He returned to London, where Aggie sent him a box of food, and he told her, 'I felt so well that I could eat [it all] uncooked'.[231] The next day he went to Norwich for the Easter weekend ILP Conference.

For the first time in years Lillie and Nan did not go with Hardie.[232] The city was completely blacked out at night (after Zeppelin raids on the east coast) and so crammed with military personnel and patriotic fervour that the city fathers decided free speech was unwise. Permission for the ILP Conference to use the halls it had booked was suddenly withdrawn. Luckily, both the Primitive Methodists and Unitarians offered alternative venues.

At the NAC Hardie protested at Vandervelde's article in *Justice* attacking German socialists who opposed the war.[233] At the conference he spoke on a resolution to the government protesting that Britain's Russian 'allies' had just jailed dozens of trade unionists and socialist MPs.[234] This cruel and backward tyranny was always defended by conservatives; this was one last proof of the disreputable nature of the alliance the British government had committed Britons to die for. Although fellow delegates thought Hardie was poorly,[235] he wrote to Aggie from the conference that 'The spirit animating the Congress is splendid' and there was 'not a discordant word'[236] – not, that is, until the public meeting on Saturday night, when Hardie delivered an attack on Lloyd George that sparked a short national exchange of fireworks.

This was over references Lloyd George, Minister of Munitions, had made about workers' laziness and drinking habits in the same breath as urging forward manufacturing output. Hardie rose to the defence of men 'who are working eighty-four hours a week . . . being libelled, maligned and insulted'.[237] As for drinking (the habit he had spent so many of his earlier years attacking) Hardie insisted 'the strain of the seven days a week incapacitates a much greater proportion of men than does the drink habit'.[238] He added, 'one would have thought the rich classes would grovel on their knees before the working classes who are doing so much to pile up their wealth', pointing out that the boilermakers had already said that they could get all the war work done if the shipbuilders would reduce their contracts by only 10 per cent. But 'shipbuilders will not do that because ships were being sold at two and three times their value before the war'.

Lloyd George was stung into immediate, fulminating reply, which every paper carried, denouncing Hardie as 'reckless' and 'mischievous'. But no paper carried more than a token few of Hardie's words. Instead they noted, 'bitterness possesses the soul of the Labour leader'.[239]

Hardie returned to London, where Glasier had lunch with him and complained that Hardie kept falling asleep.[240] Glasier himself was far from well, suffering bad stomach pains which had been diagnosed tentatively as an ulcer. A week later Hardie put down a parliamentary question about a higher old age pension in view of the miserable present level of five shillings and rocketing wartime prices.[241] But Hardie was not getting any better. Frank Smith took over his mail and wrote to Aggie to send on 'any bad cases';[242] he would take them up on Hardie's behalf with the War Office. (Aggie had already begun to help those who were resisting the war.) Frank told her Hardie 'is, I think, a LITTLE better and with the return of the bright days, will I hope recover his old form'. Hardie's weekly *Pioneer* article came out two days later and on the 21st April he was back in Merthyr,[243] writing to Aggie ahead of time to say he hoped to see her as he passed through the station. He had not taken any of the good advice to rest. His pace of life and travel was as it had always been. Perhaps he was unable any longer to stop.

Nan had taken to her bed in March[244] – the fourth year running that her 'trouble' had struck her down at exactly this time of year. She told Aggie she was 'very weak and depressed and feeling like running away from everything'.[245] She felt trapped and said that if only Aggie lived nearer, 'I might have imposed on you but the distance makes that impossible. I hope I will buck up . . . soon'.[246] Hardie had just checked in at the Wemyss Hydro, and was enjoying its attentions, she reported resentfully. Duncan had come home too. 'The Dr signed him off for a fortnight so he will have another week at home. That is the benefit of being a man, you see . . . A woman gets no such privilege.' Aggie sent chocolates and a book of poetry, but they were both waved aside. Nan said she was 'not picking up . . . I seem to be dragging some enormous weight all the time'. After a few more months it was to be, 'I felt I would go mad getting up everyday with my work staring me in the face'.[247]

Gone was the Nan who had written to Aggie a few years earlier to tell her to stay bright 'for the sake of your father and . . . Rowlie';[248] and to insist that, 'Your housework will keep you busy and in trying to make others happy you will yourself be happy.' The central maxim by which these women were taught to live had not stood up. Now there was only the last great cause of war resistance to keep them going.

14
BREAKING TIES

On 19 May 1915, when casualties were running at 2,500 a day,[1] the Labour Party met to consider whether it should join in a coalition government, the ultimate incorporation. There was a bitter argument. Finally, Henderson agreed to serve in the Cabinet.[2] From Lossiemouth MacDonald wrote to his radical Liberal colleague, Charles Trevelyan, that it was a 'heartbreaking' decision.[3] Trevelyan was already predicting it was the end of the Liberals.[4] To Hardie the decision would have been even more heartbreaking. Towards the end of April he had signed himself into a hydro in Caterham just outside London, where he had spent a brief period the year before, when the press had pictured him and Lillie on the lawn in deckchairs. The Labour Party was well aware of Hardie's disillusionment and Jim Middleton wrote expressing the hope they could all 'let bygones be by gones' and 'keep the Party intact when the war ends'.[5]

Lillie and Nan were not alarmed to hear he had gone to Caterham and assumed he would soon be better.[6] They were planning to go away 'somewhere to brace me up',[7] Nan told Aggie. Aggie's news in return was positive. She had decided to start teaching. She had all the qualifications required, since she was familiar with Latin and Greek and most of the English classics (her fluent letters strongly contrasted with Nan's and Lillie's difficult and quaintly punctuated lines). Aggie had decided to take in young students to coach them for the matriculation examination. Her goal was to earn her own living. Nan commented, 'I quite understand your feeling of wanting to be out on your own. I think most stay at home girls have that experience. I know I did.'[8] To Nan, it was a past struggle. 'It resolves itself into a question of duty to yourself or your parents and I think everyone can best judge the issue for themselves.'

The core of Nan's depression is revealed: she had been elected to lose her life in order to care for her parents. Possibly she was frightened of the world as well and needed her burden as an excuse not to have to face it. Through the Hardie family eyes, the world was not friendly. Many of her letters mention refusal to leave home, even to going outside at all. She was invited to visit the Richardsons in London but she had an excuse for that: the journey would be too much for her. She couldn't visit Aggie either. 'I seldom go away and leave mother.'[9] Mother and daughter shielded each other. But Nan was also aware of the ultimate danger for herself. 'The one thing I always feel is that HOME cannot always be and what is to become of me then?'

Many daughters in nan's generation and earlier shared her dilemma of imprisonment in an old duty: the absolute obligation of daughters to care for parents.[10] Beatrice Webb was left at home after all her sisters had married, and wrote, 'The position of the unmarried daughter at home is an unhappy event even for a strong woman.'[11] Vera Brittain resented it too.[12] Many young women became ill as a result. One observer of the period saw women 'trapped in a social situation which prohibited the use of their talents', who would 'protest through invalidism'.[13] Elizabeth Barrett Browning was an earlier dramatic example.

For Nan the future was black; the present blacker. Even joyous events like the local christening of her friend Meg Dalziel's nephew were denied. 'We don't go to church now . . . so I won't see it.'[14] The town is too hostile, as they had reported earlier. Among those in Cumnock who were supporting the war were Jamie's wife's family, the Stoddarts. May's brother-in-law had joined up and was to spend three years at the Front.[15] This caused tension between the families. Mostly, however, the cause of Nan's misery was obscure. 'Life is simply not worth living while this . . . depression lasts.'[16]

Towards the end of May, after the Labour Party's decision to join the coalition, Hardie made his own dramatic decision. He would no longer attend Parliament and would return to Scotland. Frank Smith was put in charge of winding up his life in London. He wrote out a letter Hardie dictated to be sent to Sylvia, asking her to meet him at Neville's Court the following week. Hardie said he intended to 'sell a lot of the stuff that is there'.[17] He wanted to return the portrait she had done of him, though he would like to keep another of her paintings, which 'I have so closely associated with you that I would not like to part with it'. But most important, he wanted to return her letters, especially those written from America, 'They are well worth preserving'. He knew some of them were compromising, so he added, 'you could use your discretion as to which are most worthy of being kept and published and which should be destroyed . . . I must leave the matter entirely in your hands. I have not now the capacity for dealing with such a matter.' The word 'now' was added in his own hand.

When Sylvia arrived she found his voice 'low and muffled'.[18] He returned her letters and both paintings (forgetting he had said he wanted to keep one). In return he asked her whether she would not like to pick out something of his to take away as a 'keepsake'. She replied hastily, 'I don't want to be given anything' – a reaction her biographer calls thoughtless.[19] As a result, there was silence. 'We were tonguetied as never before,' she recalled.[20] Frank Smith came in and made small talk. Sylvia took the meeting to be Hardie's way of 'announcing the final close of his working life' and his return to his family; but Frank Smith was sure he would soon get well and return to political activity.[21] While they talked, 'Keir . . . seemed to loom over us like some great tragic ruin'.[22] When she left she was near tears, and Hardie said, 'You have been very brave.' It was typical of their relationship that he was comforting her when she had come to comfort him.

After sorting his affairs at Neville's Court Hardie returned to the Caterham hydro on 7 June and sent for Lillie and Nan. By now they were in the middle of their holiday at Leadhills, which was proving of very little benefit to either,[23] and were planning to move somewhere else instead. They did not wish to come to London, but by 10 June they had given way. Nan reported, 'Father is over-joyed.'[24] When they arrived, doctors told them Hardie had had a complete 'nervous breakdown' and that 'it will be at least six months' before they can expect any improvement.[25] Nan confided that he is physically well enough, the problem is that 'his brain refuses to go on'.[26] It is the first inkling that the problem is Hardie's mental condition.

Neither Nan nor Lillie took the news in at first, being preoccupied with their own ills. Lillie was still sleepless; Nan said she herself was now down to 8 stone 6 pounds and envying Aggie her 'plumpness'.[27] She also had 'dreadful headaches'[28] but added with satisfaction, 'I am to be examined and then my treatment will begin.' Nan and Lillie were not going to allow Hardie to be the only invalid.

Nan's spirits picked up with the attention. Surrey was beautiful and wooded, she wrote to Aggie, 'and the staff exceedingly nice'.[29] What's more, the establishment was strictly 'no fish, flesh nor fowl'.[30] Nan was glad, for she and her parents had been 'more or less . . . vegetarian . . . for years'. The Richardsons called to pay their respects and wanted her to visit them but Nan refused; Hardie was much too difficult, 'moody and irritable . . . but we have to put up with those things'. She asked if Emrys had got his job.

Emrys had applied for posts under the London Education Committee with three other newly trained teachers. At the interview there were a few perfunctory questions on infant class management[31] but the only thing the Board was really interested in was why these teachers had not enlisted. Recruiting campaigns were at fever pitch. The other applicants said it was family circumstances that prevented it. Emrys simply said, 'I don't agree with the war.'

The chairman 'raised his eyebrows in astonishment'. 'With this war?' he asked.

'Yes,' I answered.

He shrugged his shoulders.

The others got jobs, Emrys did not.[32] He decided to return to Wales.

By the third week in June Nan was warming to her role as rival patient. 'I got examined last Thursday. The doctor says I really ought to be in bed . . . He says my heart is very weak and heaps of other depressing things.' She would like to stay for treatment but if 'father goes home I must go too as mother could never manage by herself.' Lillie had had another bad night,[33] her 'sleeplessness' now a serious concern.[34] Nan was unable to understand Lillie's real problem, much less her father's. 'Some days he is quite stupid, other times . . . better'.[35] By July she was trying to find excuses: 'he is much worse mentally, I expect the heat is to blame'.

A month had gone by and it was plain no dramatic change was to be expected. The family decided to return to Scotland, stopping en route with the Bensons near Manchester and the Richardsons near Newcastle.[36] Frank Smith, who was keeping up Hardie's correspondence, went with them for the first week. Hardie broached the subject of finances with Benson, the ILP treasurer. He was obsessed with providing for Nan and Lillie should anything happen to him. When the war had started he had gone to lawyers about new wills for himself, Lillie and Nan (who was persuaded to change her own will in favour of her parents rather than her two brothers),[37] and about insuring Lochnorris now that the loan to Birkmyre had finally been paid off. He was alarmed to hear that the sum he had insured it for – £1,000 – was twice what the property was worth. In July he was now worried that he would not leave enough for Lillie and Nan. He sought assurance that the Kippen legacy would also be theirs.[38]

Back in Cumnock Nan found chocolates from Aggie and news that her students had passed their exams, 'Fancy your three children doing so well.'[39] At first all seemed to go well. Lillie has 'slept better the two nights we have been home', Nan reports. Hardie too. In fact, 'everybody says how much better he looks since we came home'.[40] But the problem was in his behaviour. Soon deterioration set in. Her parents were fighting all the time, Nan reported. 'He wants to sleep with her'; she refuses. Thereupon, 'he is angry with her'.[41] He also had 'strange notions' about the people around them.[42] 'His worst tendency is to fly to a doctor – in former days his pet aversion. He has just been to tell the Dr about a dream he had last night', as if it was something that had really happened. 'It is a dreadful calamity for us all.'[43]

Nan had to bear the main burden of caring for Hardie, who was still physically active. It was her job, she reported, to 'walk father'; she told Aggie how she hated his 'awful . . . temper'.[44] One day she let him go out alone but 'we discovered afterwards it wasn't safe'.[45] Nan hoped very much that Aggie could come to

Cumnock, which she knew would please her father. He would be 'OK with you'.[46]

> I shall be glad when you come to relieve me, especially when you take over the morning walk . . . Yesterday morning his temper was awful. I got very cross and spoke sharply to him and he has been meek as a lamb since. If we give in to him in everything we will spoil him.[47]

Nan talked of her father as if he were a toddler, 'he is quite childish and needs a lot of attention'.[48] Behind all these reports was the anger of the carer against the dependant who was sapping her life, and no understanding at all of the nature of mental illness. Hardie's behaviour was seen entirely in terms of character fault. In August Nan asked the doctor whether Hardie's disease had reached its 'climax', as she and Lillie still saw it having the profile of a febrile illness. The doctor said all that could be done was to give him good care and good nourishment. They had done this and he only seemed to get worse, 'very cross with mother', who had now been forced to sleep with him. Nan was upset by this, having said that if only Lillie could sleep on her own, 'she would have a chance . . . she needs a room by herself'.[49] But Hardie had insisted. 'We are kept at high tension all the time and the strain is terrible.'

Again, they press Aggie to join them, and to come with them to Arran, where they planned to take a house in September, 'to relieve us . . . it is going to take us both to keep things going on'.[50] Hardie now has 'visions' and keeps trying to get up and leave.[51]

Unknown to his family, Hardie was aware that his mind was going. Just before he left Caterham he managed to send a postcard to Sylvia, spelling her name 'Slyphia'.[52] He told her he was leaving in a week, but 'with no more mind control than when I came'. Later Sylvia asked Frank Smith, 'What did he mean?'

'He had delusions.'

'What sort of delusions?'

'. . . with Lloyd George riding in a motor car,' Smith answered, 'with a gesture of misery.'[53]

In her own life Sylvia now struggled to retain his presence. In August she had a dream of her own that summed up her feelings, if not their whole relationship:[54] 'I woke early on a Sunday morning with a dream of him fondling some little puppy, as he often did', and how the dog was 'appealing for sympathy and warmth' and 'snuggling up to him'.

Sylvia's response was to go at once to Bethnal Green market and buy a small mongrel puppy, which she intended to send to Hardie. Frank Smith tactfully talked her out of it. Had they but known, Hardie had suddenly taken against animals and developed a 'pure hatred' of the family's existing dog, Dai, which had had to be sent to friends.[55] Deprived of Hardie, Sylvia tried once more to reach her own mother. Sylvia was well aware of the treatment of Hardie in the press. Papers

like *John Bull* were calling him a 'traitor' and 'a coward', and her sister's
Suffragette had printed a cartoon of the Kaiser giving him gold. Sylvia
asked her mother to stop this persecution of Hardie: 'He's dying.'[56]
Emmeline never answered her daughter.

There were other partings. Zelie Emerson now found Sylvia remote
and not interested in re-establishing their old tie. She sadly acknowledged the end of their affair in a poem:

> Time was when all my being was thrown wide
> All veils were drawn aside
> That you might enter anywhere at will
> Now all is hushed and still . . .
> the shutting of a door.[57]

Sylvia was in no mood to respond. So, taking with her a lock of
Sylvia's hair, Zelie left for the USA for good. Sylvia's last suffrage
ties were cut.

In Cumnock it was coming up to Hardie's fifty-ninth birthday. Lillie
reported many visitors, including Hardie's sister and his two brothers
and some of their children. The same letter said Mr Hardie was 'a little
better' but 'I am not sleeping any better'. Aggie asked her what gift to
send Hardie. Lillie advised 'a tin of Macdonald's Cut Golden Bar' and
added, 'Don't get any other, as he won't smoke it.'[58] Hardie was still
smoking, still going out walking, and still trying to work. In a shaky hand
he wrote to James Henderson, now a school teacher, who was acting as
his local secretary, asking him to call, presumably to dictate.[59] Nan sent
Aggie train times and exact instructions about which connections to get
in order to reach Cumnock.[60] She added, 'I hope father is all right with
you as he has all sorts of notions about people just now.'[61] This seems
to have stopped Aggie, who did not want to find Hardie turning against
her. She never arrived and the Hardies, including Duncan, went off to
Arran without her.

Very few others outside the family were kept informed about Hardie's
condition. Only one person in the constituency heard anything and that
was Harry Morris, the trusted friend and agent from Dowlais whom
Hardie had come to rely upon particularly in recent years, and with
whom he corresponded regularly about the constituency and the ILP.[62]
On 12 September Nan wrote to Morris to say Hardie had suddenly taken
a 'turn for the worse' on Arran and that they had all returned.[63] At the
same time she wrote Aggie that a 'nerve specialist' from Glasgow had
been called in and insisted Hardie stay in Glasgow to be near him. The
family moved in with George Hardie at The Firs in Clarkston.[64] Once
there, however, Nan reported 'father took a dislike to the man and
wouldn't have him, so we had to stop that'. Nan was dispirited. 'He
has gone down rapidly this last month.'

Another specialist had to be consulted. He told Nan and Lillie that

Hardie had had a 'slight shock' in Arran (presumably another stroke).[65] It had coincided with the publication in *John Bull* of a scurrilous article by the anti-socialist gossip monger, Horatio Bottomley, exposing Ramsay MacDonald's 'illegitimate birth' as the son 'of a Scotch servant girl', and generally pouring scorn and abuse on MacDonald and Hardie for their refusal to support their country.[66] Lillie and Nan were very anxious that no news of Hardie's illness should leak out (and, possibly also, news of his own illegitimacy, the final ignominy). Nan pleaded with Aggie, 'Don't say anything to ANYONE. No newspaper fuss.'[67]

Not that Hardie was aware any more of these events. 'Mother and I were the only ones he seemed to know.' Nan seemed at last to understand, 'Best he goes now . . . if he's not right mentally.' Possibly she and Lillie were relieved when the new doctor had Hardie removed to a hospital on 22 September when chest complications added to his troubles.

Meanwhile, for Hardie's colleagues, his 'old donkey' of the state was being pushed by the new coalition government in an ever more repressive and authoritarian direction. In August 1915 police raided the ILP offices in London and the *Labour Leader* office in Manchester. Summonses for publishing seditious material were issued, and Fenner Brockway, as editor, was formally charged. Glasier insisted on being there as chairman of the board,[68] though he was suffering badly from his stomach pains. He wrote that Brockway 'made a capital witness . . . straight, tall, intelligent and obviously in earnest'. The state's case was conducted by William Cobbett, son of the Chartist, who had prosecuted Hardie and Emmeline for holding meetings in Boggart Hole Clough twenty years earlier. The result was that all ILP pamphlets and copies of the *Leader* were confiscated and publishing of any more prohibited except as the government allowed.

The Second International too was struggling to survive. It was split by the hostility of the French and Belgian sections to the German, and by support for the war from some constituent groups, including the British Labour Party, while others – like the ILP – continued to oppose it. In Britain the ILP was also one of the few groups that remained consistently interested in international action involving all the war participants rather than just the Allies. In September 1915, Italian socialists convened an anti-war conference, unofficially, at Zimmerwald near Berne. For the first time Hardie could not attend an international peace event. Instead, the ILP elected Glasier and Jowett as their representatives. Lord Robert Cecil denied them passports.[69] The Foreign Office had discovered passports as a form of government control of political activity. (Until this time British citizens could travel anywhere.) Among those who did get to Zimmerwald was Lenin. From then on his influence on the International increased, while that of socialists like Hardie waned.

In the Glasgow hospital where Hardie had been taken, Nan and Lillie kept their vigil by his bedside. His condition – diagnosed as pneumonia – did not improve, but on Saturday afternoon, 25 September, George Hardie wrote to Frank Smith to say Hardie was sleeping peacefully. The 'White Herald' was not expected just yet.

Aggie was in Wales anxiously awaiting news, along with Emrys, who was in his first term of teaching at Trehafod Primary School, five miles from the Hughes's home.[70] He was not happy there, in part because his heart was in war resistance. On 9 September the *Labour Leader* had printed the manifesto of the newly formed No-Conscription Fellowship, a movement suggested by Fenner Brockway's wife, Lilla, to bring together young men who opposed the war and military service.[71] Branches were rapidly formed and Emrys became secretary of the one in the Aberdare area, which met in the front room of the Hughes's house at 33 Mountain Ash Road, Abercynon.[72] In the Fellowship for the first time he met local 'kindred spirits'[73] who supported the cause. Previously he had felt himself isolated, with only Hardie for support.

Nan and Lillie maintained their vigil sitting by Hardie's bed in Glasgow. They were the only people he recognized and the only two he would allow to attend to him.[74] When he had come into the world it was women who had cared for him; going out, he demanded the same. On the fourth day, Sunday 26 September, Nan left the hospital to send Aggie a telegram. It said simply, 'Father died suddenly noon today.'[75]

On that afternoon Sylvia was one of a group of speakers, along with Hyndman, Charlotte Despard, Emmeline Pethick-Lawrence and Will Anderson, at a meeting in Trafalgar Square against conscription. She saw newsboys beginning to circulate in the crowds, carrying big placards. At first she could not make out what they were shouting or what the writing said. Eventually, 'the placards carried up by the boys caught my eye': 'Death of Keir Hardie.'[76]

'Is it true?' she asked Will Anderson.

'It must be,' he answered gently, and then practically, 'I'll draft a resolution. He was our man.'

Sylvia, who had already made her speech, collapsed dramatically and had to be helped to the side of the plinth. 'I was not faint,' she later wrote, 'but stunned and stricken . . . I felt as they who had lost their dearest in the war.' That night she recalled 'regrets . . . for words unsaid . . . hours unlived' and how inside her at that time 'rose the great rebellion against the cruelties of our life and its denials . . . its foolish, vain denials'.[77] Whether the denials refer to the consummation of their love or simply to more time together remains unknown. Frank Smith wrote to Sylvia that evening to say, 'I don't think anyone . . . knew, understood or loved him better than you and I.'[78]

Glasier was at home with Katharine in Liscard, where the family now lived.[79] The next morning, when the papers were brought, the headlines were of war victories at the Battle of Loos. On a back page was the news of Hardie's death. *The Times*'s mention was short and curt and, like most of the nationals, characteristically unable to rise above the politics of the day: Hardie had created a 'cleavage' between himself and 'patriotic fellow labourites'. He was 'the most extreme of British politicians . . . one of those men who spent their lives expressing the views of a minority' and 'advocating unpopular causes'. He was Scots as well; and dour. The *Mirror* was little better: Hardie 'was one of the best hated men of his time'.[80]

Glasier wrote in his Diary that he and Katharine had 'a strange feeling of fright . . . and wept together', just as Glasier had written to Hardie fifteen years earlier, 'the thought of you being ill has frightened me . . . we plead with you to rest . . . you are very precious to us'.[81] He was glad Hardie was 'not doomed to live years as a half imbecile'. Glasier was aware of doom himself. He had now lost two stone. MacDonald had witnessed one of his collapses[82] and had written to Katharine that the doctor had told him privately, 'Bruce ought to have an operation'. Everyone guessed the trouble was cancer, including Glasier, who had already decided he would not have an operation.

Hardie's funeral was in Glasgow on Wednesday 29 September 1915. The ILP paid for it. Glasier recalled that 'the cortège must have stretched nearly a quarter of a mile' on the way to the cemetery in Maryhill, where Hardie's parents had been cremated only thirteen years earlier. Harry Morris and three ILP members from Merthyr came for it. One was Rose Davies's husband, Ed.[83] The group did not include Emrys Hughes, who did not have enough money for the fare.[84] The custom of men only at funerals, strong also in Scotland, was not observed by the Hardies. Lillie attended in deepest black, supported by George Hardie and Duncan. Nan walked alongside. All Hardie's siblings were present. In the newspaper coverage Jamie's absence was explained by his living in the USA.

Large crowds lined the route and 'oftentimes one noticed old workmen standing reverently bare-headed, and occasionally men in khaki at attention' – the 'builders of cathedrals', as Hardie had once called them all.[85] On the way other processions joined and at the cemetery itself a further huge crowd had assembled. There was a wreath from Sylvia – of laurel, tied with the purple, green and white colours of the suffragettes but with the added red of her own East London Federation of Suffragettes, the ELFS.[86]

Outside the chapel, unable to get inside because of the crowd, was Cunninghame Graham.[87] He believed funerals showed 'the Scottish people at its best' because 'the deep underlying tenderness peeps through the hardness of the rind'. He watched the mourners; 'all of them had heard him speak a hundred times'. He saw that 'women tramped too' to honour Hardie's stand for women. It was a cold windy day, 'with water in the air'. Cunninghame Graham could not see much in the mist, so he fell 'to musing on the man . . . as he was thirty years ago, outlined against a quarry in some mining village . . . about him seemed to stand a shadowy band . . . all young and ardent . . . gone down to oblivion . . . those who live before their time . . . Had he too lived in vain?'

Inside the chapel were many well-known socialists.[88] Hardie's brothers had asked Glasier to speak. However, he deferred to Jowett, who in fact, to Glasier's dismay, said nothing about Hardie the socialist, labour leader or promoter of peace. The vicar, A. M. Forson, who had organized the petition for Hardie in the 1906 election, only talked of Hardie's early days in the Evangelical Union. Already Hardie was being reclaimed by the establishment as merely a colourful local figure – as Beatrice Webb wrote later, that 'picturesque prophet of the Labour Movement'.[89] It was 'ghastly', Glasier wrote to Katharine, 'Hardie might have been a grocer.'[90]

The service was ending when Glasier realized that 'They had nothing to say about HIM . . . the great Keir Hardie lying there'. Glasier suddenly got up and gave an impromptu address about Hardie the socialist, a 'few confused words . . . about his having been the greatest agitator of his day'. As he spoke, the coffin was already sliding away.

The next day Nan, Duncan and George came to the station to see the visitors off – most on their way to memorial meetings in other areas.[91] Glasier recorded that 'Poor Nan wept bitterly, saying her life now has gone'. The next day Nan wrote to Aggie[92] that it was not her father she missed so much as 'his daily letter'. This is what had always kept her and Lillie in touch with life; its absence signified their abandonment and the fact that 'He is not with us'. Then she added forlornly, as if it had only just occurred to her, 'But then he never was.'

For the following month there were memorial services all over the country, including one on 3 October 1915, in St Andrew's Hall, Glasgow. MacDonald gave the address there and at the one in London, which Sylvia attended. She remembered 'the hoarse, deep roar of applause which greeted' him and how 'Men sprang to their feet and cheered him . . . the target on whom the attack of the conscriptionists and the Jingos mainly centred' now that Hardie was dead.[93] Sylvia was busy editing a special edition of her Dreadnought, given over to tributes to Hardie. George Bernard Shaw contributed one. Overcome with remorse that he had failed to answer Hardie's last letter, he eulogized Hardie as 'the true patriot' whose 'soul goes marching on', taking up the theme of Hardie's separation from the Labour Party in his latter years. Mischievously, he spoke of the 'generous feeling of relief' now that 'Keir Hardie's body lies mouldering in the grave', for his absence meant MPs would be free again 'to lie at will'. With the war and the defection of his comrades, Shaw 'really could not see what Hardie could do but die'.[94]

Sylvia's contribution was straightforward and passionate, unlike the maudlin reminiscences she later composed. She called Hardie the 'greatest human being of our time', almost the very words that Maggie Symons had used to describe him three years earlier when she confessed she had stopped worshipping and started valuing him. Sylvia got straight to Hardie's essence. She noted, 'he was the most uncompetitive of human beings'.[95] He 'had loved humanity as others love their immediate families' – a shrewd summary of his life's emotional commitment (and an explanation of his family's negative feelings).[96] In this *Dreadnought* memorial issue – indeed in all she ever wrote or said about Hardie – there was not one single mention of Lillie or any of his children. Sylvia blacked them out completely from the beginning to the end and beyond.

The ILP was not able to ignore Nan and Lillie. A week later the ILP Council met to deal with their financial situation,[97] already painfully evident to Nan and Lillie themselves. Nan confessed to Aggie, 'We are struggling on as best we can. As the weeks slip by our want is more and more apparent. It is too terrible and sometimes I wonder if anything is real in life save sorrow and heartache.'[98]

Duncan's position was worrying them too. Glasgow Corporation was requiring all employees to enlist in the reserve. Nan wrote, 'Duncan of course won't at any cost so he may find himself not wanted'.[99] Nan joked, Aggie might have to take them as 'unpaying guests' because 'I can't exist on air altogether'. She even claimed she had considered going out to work and had looked into teaching. But she reported that under 'Scotch [sic] law no one can teach unless a formal training has been obtained'. Instead of deciding to take that training, she said (almost with relief): 'That puts teaching out of the question for me.' It was more and more evident that Nan was completely unable to take on anything outside the home. Her unacknowledged anger against her position continued to disappear inwards and immobilised her with depression.

The question of whether to raise money by selling Hardie's things in Neville's Court also came up. Lillie favoured it but Nan – and especially Duncan – did not.[100] Then there was the will.[101] Hardie had left everything to Lillie and Nan, but Hardie's assets were minimal: a few shares in the Pioneer Press, a single payment due of back parliamentary salary, and some stock in the Ayr Building Society. What was not there was provision from the ILP out of the Kippen bequest which Lillie had always regarded as rightfully hers.[102] It was she who first met the Kippens and persuaded them to donate the money. Lillie was convinced Hardie had been promised the Kippen money by Benson just before he died, although it turned out that Benson had probably only said it because he knew that if Lillie and Nan needed money the ILP would raise it somehow. At its meeting such a plan – a public subscription – was therefore agreed.[103]

However, when it was put to Lillie, her pride was offended. She did not wish to be the object of public charity. The ILP then reconsidered the matter and decided that in addition to the fund, it would divert to Lillie the income from £500-worth of stock in the City of Montreal at 4.5 per cent, originally bought with Kippen money, and after she died, to Nan for life, only reverting to the ILP at Nan's death. Lillie refused that offer as well. On 2 December she wrote to both Benson and Francis Johnson, the ILP's secretary, to say she would not accept 'any money in trust' because 'such a proposal would be against the wishes of my husband'.[104] No one in the ILP knew what to do, and the matter was shelved. Nan and Lillie struggled on.

One Friday afternoon, after another long week teaching fifty children, Emrys gave in his resignation.[105] He wanted to force the issue of his military service rather than wait to be hunted. Tribunals had been set up by local authorities, ostensibly to review exemptions, in fact to hasten recruitment under Lord Derby's national campaign.[106] Emrys went to the tribunal at Mountain Ash with twenty others – in a closed court – before a panel of local publicans and colliery officials.[107] Most of the others based their appeal for exemption on religious, domestic, employment or health grounds. Emrys waived all these and simply submitted a statement that the 'war . . . [was] detrimental to the welfare of people and the future progress of the race'. He was asked only one question: 'What would you do if someone assaulted your sister?' He explained again that he was not a pacifist but a socialist and anti-militarist. He was denied exemption. The death of Hardie was a 'big gap in all our lives . . . a great personal loss',[108] he wrote. But he believed that by his stand he was carrying Hardie's cause forward.

Nan and Lillie had no such means to fight their loss, 'We may be lonely . . . but Aggie that will be nothing new to us.'[109] In particular Nan saw that her mother's life 'has been one big sacrifice'. Although both Nan and Aggie were as anxious over the fate of Emrys and Duncan as Lillie and the Revd John Hughes, Nan was still able to say later, 'I think in such a crisis the Fathers and Mothers are most hurt'.[110] To Nan and Aggie, as guardians of their guardians, parents had to be protected first.

A week after Hardie died Aggie went to Cumnock to be with Nan and Lillie. Nan was hardly enthusiastic, 'If you feel you must come then I suppose it is no good trying to put you off'.[111] When she had gone back two weeks later, Nan wrote, 'We are still very much like children, you see . . . it would be easy for us to sit down and cry all the time but that would be the last thing Father would have us do. At times the feelings of desolation and loneliness are unbearable.'[112] To which had to be added the acute disappointment of subsequent events in Merthyr.

At Hardie's funeral the ILP had held a hurried meeting about retaining the Merthyr seat.[113] The electoral truce between the parties meant that whoever secured the nomination for Labour became the MP. Bob Smillie was rejected, and a stopgap candidate, president of the local Miners' Federation, James Winstone, was chosen. He was both for and against the war and Nan rightly characterized him as 'a poor will-o-the-wisp going whither the wind blew'.[114] He was promptly opposed by Charles Stanton, now a virulent war-supporter, who put himself forward as independent labour with Liberal and nationalist backing. On the ballot paper he put his party label as 'Britisher'. He won the election easily, hailed by the *Daily Express* as a true fighter for 'country and empire'.[115] Press, Liberals and right-wing union leaders regarded Stanton's victory as a decisive break with the revolutionary and pacifist Labour tradition in South Wales, and the remaking of Labour in the image of nationalism, imperialism and Labour realism.[116] Nan felt totally betrayed:

> I was speechless when I heard the election result. When I recovered I felt I wanted to have a good cry and now I grudge terribly the time Father spent in the constituency when he might have been . . . home. Even last winter when we begged him to stay at home for health reasons he said he must not disappoint the boys.[117]

All these 'boys' had let them down. 'I hope Stanton will be put out next time.'

Sylvia was equally outraged, especially to hear that Flora Drummond, the longtime WSPU lieutenant of Christabel's, had gone to Merthyr to work on Stanton's election team. Sylvia remembered her sitting on the hearthrug beside Keir Hardie's chair in Neville's Court, always running to him whenever 'trouble threatened'.[118] Hardie had asked questions for her in Parliament when she was in jail.[119] Flora had even named her first son Keir — as had many other women. Now she was working against him (and later went on to found an empire loyalist organization dedicated to the destruction of socialism). In November Christabel turned her *Suffragette* into a new journal called *Britannia*. She and Emmeline had thrown themselves into the British government's official recruiting campaigns, touring the country under government auspices, encouraging women to encourage men to enlist. They also campaigned against conscientious objectors and a negotiated peace.[120]

Sylvia had already added anti-war campaigning to her list of activities. On one occasion George Bernard Shaw came to speak. She wrote later that he equivocated so badly about the war that 'she was ashamed to chair' his remarks. Typically, she wrote to tell him so afterwards. He replied with characteristic aplomb, 'How can you expect to convert crowds to peace when you cannot even convert your mother and Christabel?'[121]

In Wales Aggie was now ill. She called it influenza. Nan wrote, 'I have been thinking of you lately through all my own worry and business . . . I feel you have been with us this sad time'.[122] Only Duncan's occasional visits home and the prospect of a New Year visit to Auntie Maggie (Lillie's sister) brought any sunshine. Lochnorris had become more prison than retreat: 'it will be better for us to be away from here at New Year.'

To help turn her mind from gloom, Aggie sent Nan a copy of Keats for Christmas. It only called out further gloom:

> I never did enjoy Christmas or New Year. Somehow there always was an indefinable DREAD of something which I could not shake off. I think I know now what the dread was. We have missed father very much and yet I cannot but feel he is in a happier place away from this carnage . . . I wonder . . . how we could expect that big heart of his to go on beating.[123]

Lillie wrote to confirm that she too dreaded Christmas and wished it were over.[124] Both women were convinced life had ended for them, signified by Lillie's pitiful announcement that this year 'I am not sending out any shortbread. That will be stopped now'.

At the end of 1915 the Hardie shrines of Merthyr and Lochnorris received two visitations. Both were designed to tie off the past. The first was from Glasier, sent to Lochnorris as the ILP's messenger, to persuade Lillie to relinquish her fight for the Kippen bequest and accept the financial package the NAC was offering.

'Agnes met me at the station,' Glasier recorded in his Diary,[125] 'and we talked about her father all the way home.' At Lochnorris they 'talked of the old days, Agnes often melting into tears'. Lillie was more composed, despite the fact that she had now developed phlebitis in her leg and lay on a couch to receive Glasier.

The visit lasted four hours and only towards the end did they finally get to the issue of money. Glasier had to explain that the ILP 'did not approve of . . . handing over large sums of money to individuals'. However, it did believe it had a duty to see that the families of those who gave their lives to it were 'maintained in comfort'. He tactfully explained that the ILP offer was a way of honouring Hardie by not permitting his widow and daughter to live with money difficulties. It is what Hardie would have wanted, said Glasier – indeed, what he believed the state should have provided for everyone. Glasier looked at it from their view. He believed Benson, the ILP Treasurer, had spoken to them as the ILP Treasurer, loath to part with any money. Lillie said they would think about it overnight. Meanwhile, Duncan was consulted.

Duncan seems to have been decisive, for the next day Glasier met Nan in Glasgow, this time with Duncan present. Nan and Lillie agreed to the plan, though Glasier, who had assured them the appeal could be worded as they wished, had to alter the appeal's wording several times (Frank Smith conveying the last-minute changes Lillie wanted). Glasier conceded them all; he also sweetened the deal by taking it upon himself to offer a 'little standby' of £100 from the ILP coffers in addition. What it cost Lillie in mauled pride to read about the appeal's progress during the next year can only be guessed. Yet within two years it raised £2,815 which would be invested to provide income.[126] Nan and Lillie would not live high, but slowly they realized they would not be in the poverty they feared. In fact, it was the first time either had ever enjoyed any real financial security.

Once money matters were out of the way, Glasier, Nan and Lillie talked openly of long-forbidden subjects. For example, 'for the first time I learnt that Mrs Hardie was always desirous . . . of removing to London but Hardie always dissuaded her'.[127] Glasier in turn told Lillie about a short autobiographical manuscript Katharine had discovered in the *Leader* office after Hardie had died, part of an article he was preparing for some American journal but had never sent. It revealed that he had been illegitimate, that David Hardie was not his real father. This was not news to Lillie, for Hardie had already told her, and she had told Nan (though not, Glasier understood, Duncan and Jamie). Lillie even knew his father's name was William Aitken. The three discussed how odd it was that knowing the truth Hardie had nevertheless tried to link himself publicly to Andrew Hardie the weaver who had been executed in Stirling in 1820 – to which Nan had said simply, 'my father . . . had some queer notions.'

The second pilgrimage was a sentimental journey taken by Norah Symth and Sylvia to Merthyr, accompanied by Jim, the mongrel dog Sylvia had bought for (and named after) Hardie but never sent. All three stayed with Harry Morris of the Dowlais Male Voice Choir, and watched children trim 'the ILP tree' and heard them singing the poem on liberty Hardie had written and set to the music of an old Welsh hymn, 'Land of our fathers'.[128]

Nearby in Abercynon Aggie was still ill. There is no record of the two women meeting, although Aggie always kept a postcard portrait of Sylvia because she was associated with Hardie. Wherever Sylvia went people wanted to talk about Hardie. At an ILP Conference in 1916 she met Katharine Glasier, accompanied by her daughter, Jeannie, who was now Margaret Bondfield's secretary. Sylvia observed acidly that Katharine would 'have been secretary to no one', and said of

Jeannie, 'I could not discern in the girl's pretty . . . face . . . a hint
of her mother's rebellious emotions'.[129] Sylvia was even more critical
of Malcolm, the oldest Glasier son, who came up to his mother's side
during their conversation – tall, blond and handsome but with 'blue
eyes cold'. Sylvia was shocked to find him in a 'brass buttoned naval
uniform', going to war. But Sylvia was wrong about Malcolm, though
she never discovered it. His 'naval' coat was from the merchant navy,
to which he had run away at the age of thirteen, falsifying his age to
join, because he had not been able to stand the taunting of classmates
at school about his parents' pacifism.[130]

Later Sylvia and Katharine sat down together. 'Katharine babbled
on in her incoherent fashion', reported Sylvia later, no mean babbler
herself, annoyed that Katharine talked so intimately of her 'Keir' and
how she 'obeyed him more than' Bruce. Suddenly, Katharine told her,
'Hardie wasn't his name you know. Hardie was only his stepfather.'[131]
This took Sylvia completely by surprise. When told about the fragment
of autobiography, 'I begged that I might see it and presently it was
sent'.[132] Katharine also told her of once meeting Hardie's mother Mary
and the 'dear old lady' telling her that her liaison with 'Hardie's father'
had been 'a love match'. Katharine had taken it to mean David Hardie
but now wondered if it was not the original father she had meant.
According to Lillie (who had been entrusted with a confidence that
had been kept from Sylvia), such public talk was unlikely. The subject
of Hardie's illegitimacy, she said, was never discussed in any Hardie
home.[133]

Sylvia's encounters with Hardie's past were not yet over. At about this
same time, when she was speaking at Glasgow, a woman approached her
after the meeting and said she was Hardie's sister, Agnes.[134] Sylvia saw a
look of Hardie 'in her tender face', the only one of the Hardie siblings
she thought resembled him. Later Agnes wrote to tell Sylvia, 'my heart
went out to you for the sake of one I knew who thought the world of
you'. Later still Sylvia went to stay with Agnes, whose married name was
Aiton, at her Cambuslang home, learning 'things of him which brought
both sorrow and wonder to my heart'. Uncharacteristically, Sylvia did
not confide them to the reader. By this time she was undoing the ties
of that part of her life. She only wrote that having heard of Hardie's
origins made her think of so many novels, but 'not one . . . so strange
. . . as the true romance of life'.

15

THE BATTLE OF THE
WAR RESISTERS

By the beginning of 1916 the early rush of volunteers for the fighting had begun to wane. Conscription was going to be required. The No Conscription Fellowship prompted Emrys Hughes to write an open letter to the Aberdare *Leader* to say that as the war 'will settle nothing' and conscription would endanger 'working class movements and individual liberty', a group of young men was preparing to refuse to serve. In these matters 'individual judgement is supreme'.[1] Emrys made many new contacts at anti-conscription meetings. In February he travelled to one in Cardiff with Noah Ablett and A. J. Cook.[2] They strengthened his resolve. In March, when his call-up came, he ignored it, 'daily waiting to be arrested'.[3]

During the war the ILP continued to meet once a year. Not so the Labour Party. It was called together for many special conferences, all important to the government. One was held in January 1916 to consider conscription. Asquith had words with Labour and trade union leaders and promised, falsely as it turned out, that the new Bill the government wanted to introduce would restrict conscription to unmarried men and be lenient with conscientious objectors. The Labour Party leadership was sympathetic but the conference voted against. Asquith continued to work on Labour MPs. By the time the House came to vote, only forty-one MPs were against it, thirty of them Liberals. Hardie's band was dwindling fast.

Nan saw in the *Pioneer* that Emrys's earlier appeal had failed and wrote her support to Aggie, calling the new Act's conscientious clause 'a farce'.[4] Duncan had also appealed but had not yet heard. 'It looks to me as if the jails will be pretty crowded ere it is all over.' Nan and Lillie were completely committed to the cause of war resistance, and their one positive activity was keeping up with it. They also kept up with Harry Morris who came from Merthyr to visit them in January.[5] Nan told Aggie, 'I was glad to have news of all the folks as we never hear from any of them.' More important, Morris said, 'there has been a STRIKE on the Clyde. WE had heard never a word!' Nor did they know about the Clyde Workers' Committee, organized by Willie Gallagher and others, to protect workers from war profiteering. Activity was continuing despite an agreement by the union officials to suspend all strikes during the war. In his last long article in the *Labour Leader* Hardie had spoken of 'the new spirit at work on the Clyde'.[6] Nan asked around and told Aggie that since January she had found out that there had been several more strikes on the Clyde. The news brought a little temporary cheer to Lochnorris, where escaping was still the main objective. In the early months of 1916 Nan and Lillie visited Lillie's sister; and Hardie's brother; Lillie's doctor sent her away to the seaside; Nan's dentist continued to require her to visit Glasgow, to have her remaining teeth pulled one by one.[7] But nothing helped. Lillie stayed sleepless; Nan's dental plate broke (leaving her without teeth for some time), and neither of them could get any answer out of Aggie. Only in March did they discover it was because she was still ill, having been almost continuously in bed since a month after Hardie's death. Over all three in addition hung conscription and the fate of Rowlie, Emrys and Duncan.

By April they heard that despite his continual coughing, Rowlie had 'been taken',[8] while, despite his 'unsympathetic boss',[9] Duncan had received exemption so long as he stayed at the same job at the Glasgow Corporation.[10] Only Emrys was still free. In early April he went to London for a No Conscription Conference at the Friends Meeting Hall in Devonshire House.[11] The Quakers had already established themselves as the backbone of war resistance and had set up a Women's and a Men's Service Committee – and now a Visitation of Prisoners Committee, to help men 'taken' against their will. Along with the Union of Democratic Control, whose recent meeting had just been broken up by a *Daily Express* campaign giving out its time and address and urging jingoists to attack it,[12] the Friends also held meetings. On 8 April the *Express* again invited pro-war mobs to show what they felt about the NCF meeting, but Friends House had organized security better. Emrys reported that although the crowd howled outside, the meeting carried on inside, led by Clifford Allen, a middle-class intellectual and passionate pacifist – with Snowden as a supporting speaker.

Eventually it was Emrys's turn. One day, as he went to catch a train to a Fellowship meeting and was passing through the barrier at Abercynon station, the ticket collector turned to two men standing nearby and said, 'There he is.'[13] Emrys never returned home. He was taken to the local jail and next day brought straight to court, presided over by Lord Aberdare and a trade union official, to be tried for failing to report for service. Aggie and the Revd John Hughes were in the courtroom when Emrys was led away to be forcibly inducted into the army. As he disappeared with his armed escort, a supporter at the back shouted, 'Keep the Red Flag flying!'[14] Over a year earlier

Lenin had urged workers everywhere to 'turn the imperialist war into a civil war'.[15] Emrys went off as if he were answering this call.

Sylvia had been active in peace work as a member of the British section of the Women's International League of Peace and Freedom. In 1915 it had held a meeting in The Hague with women from many nations, including the United States. In 1916, when she tried to go again, she found herself another victim of the new law requiring passports to travel. She was refused one. Undaunted, she stepped up her local work, changing the *Woman's Dreadnought* into the *Workers' Dreadnought*, and her Suffragette Federation (ELFS) into the Workers' Suffrage Federation (WSF), uniting gender and class for social action. She (or Norah Smyth) paid someone to look after the five children of a local woman, Charlotte Drake, so that Charlotte could take over the day-to-day organization of the activities at one of the sites.[16] Sylvia's style was to hand over management to local people, virtually all women. She may have been ignored by officials in the ministries,[17] but her determination to encourage local people to run the enterprises designed for their benefit won support and kept the services in step with reality. She did not join in the new umbrella organization of suffrage societies, nor did she take part in the work of any war emergency committees. She worked singlehandedly – a new Party of One. As Gwyn Williams described it, she made her area of the East End 'her own revolutionary kingdom'.[18]

At this time her hero was Ramsay MacDonald, now able to enjoy all he had once envied Hardie for: being widely recognized as leader of the Labour Party while holding no official position. In this same spring of 1916 he visited Glasier in Hampstead. Glasier, still suffering with stomach cancer, was in London staying with his sister.[19] MacDonald confided in him that he was sure the war was nearing an end and he intended to take up the issue of peace. He was in touch with Huysmans (whom Beatrice Webb so much admired) who had been in London in March, unknown to the public, trying to arrange a meeting of the International. It was still impossible, however, to get French and German socialists to agree to meet. MacDonald also told Glasier he now planned to return to the Commons – he had not been near it for over a year. Within a short time he was back speaking and suggesting that a basis for peace could be reached if Germany promised to leave Belgium. Glasier confided to his Diary that MacDonald's 'rehabilitation' with the establishment had begun.

Emrys was taken to Cardiff barracks to be inducted into the army.[20] A prolonged war of nerves took place as he was given a uniform and told to take a medical examination. He would not comply with any requests nor answer any questions. He simply said that he did not recognize military authority. He refused to put on military uniform. Repeatedly he put his rifle on the ground when it was given to him

to shoulder. Eventually he was reported for refusal to obey orders
and sentenced to the barracks' prison. It was full of soldiers who had
jumped troop trains or gone brawling, and in one case, a lad brought
back from France to stand trial for bigamy. Emrys had feared they
might assault him for being a resister but he found out quickly that
though they hated Germans, they hated the British military more.
'Soldiers,' he deduced early on in the war, 'were the most unpatriotic
people in the world.'[21]

That particular weekend the barracks were more restive than
normal, as many recruits were Irish and the Easter Rising was
going on. Information was hard to obtain, as all army prisoners
were kept in solitary confinement for twenty-three hours a day and
forbidden to talk during the hour in the exercise yard. Only snatches
of information, whispered in passing, told Emrys about events in the
Dublin Post Office. Of course, he was not permitted to write home.
Lillie wrote to Aggie when she heard, 'It is a terrible time to be
living in . . . the suspence [sic] must be killing'.[22] 'If only my sleep
would come,' she added.

As soon as Emrys was arrested, Aggie recovered from her illness
and went into action to support him – and all other war resisters.
She made contact with the Society of Friends who enrolled her as a
worker. When Emrys was court martialled a few weeks later, she was
in the barracks' courtroom as an observer. In the witness box Emrys
opposed conscription as a teacher, a socialist and an anti-militarist. He
told the court, 'My attitude was the same as that of Karl Liebknecht
. . . in prison in Germany', an allusion lost upon the colonels trying
his case.[23] Karl Liebknecht, one of the anti-war German socialists,
had just marched to a May Day meeting in Berlin in his military
uniform and published a manifesto that proclaimed: 'Our enemy is
not the English, French nor Russian people but the great German
landed proprietors [and] the German capitalists.'[24]

His example had inspired Emrys, who had composed his own
tribunal defence speech with care. Reporters were present, for
outcomes of tribunals were widely reported, in order to advertise the
stiff sentences handed out and thus deter future intending conscientious
objectors. The recruiting sergeant, who had failed to get Emrys to
hold the rifle gave perjured evidence that Emrys had threatened
him. The prosecuting officer told the court that 'revolutions are
more easily promoted than controlled'.[25] Emrys was found guilty –
as was customary – and the prosecuting officer asked for the heaviest
possible sentence. It was read out – again, as customary (in order
to increase the shame) – before the whole Welsh Regiment on the
parade ground a day later: two years' hard labour.

The next phase of the struggle, for all war resisters, was to obtain
permission to serve the sentence in an ordinary prison rather than

a military barracks. It was not merely symbolic of having defied the military, military detention was harder. It added vindictiveness to punishment. Hardened sergeants were meaner than the most sadistic prison officer.[26] Emrys was sent to a detention barracks in Devizes in early June. Again he refused to put on military uniform and was promptly wrestled to the ground and forcibly dragged into it, and locked up alone. He immediately removed the uniform and sat naked looking at the three planks on a trestle that formed the bed. The next morning he was dragged roughly from the cell and again forcibly dressed. Within minutes he had removed the uniform. This time the corporal struck him across the face. He was forcibly redressed and his arms restrained by guards on both sides. Relays of them marched him up and down a drill yard in the hot sun hour after hour, while sergeants called out, 'left right, left right, quick march, on the double'. Emrys refused to march in step, 'determined at all costs not to have anything at all to do with any kind of drill'.[27] At every point in the regime of punishment he found a way to defy orders. At every point he was abused and punched for doing so. He recorded his experiences day by day on scraps of paper he later copied into a notebook called 'A Journal of a Coward'.[28]

The conscientious objectors' movement captured the allegiance of only a small group nationally, though to those inside it, it seemed to be the heart of the war. The NCF, said Fenner Brockway, 'became very strong . . . 12,000 men who had decided they would not serve . . . 6,000 of them went to prison'.[29] Other estimates put it as high as 16,000, with 34 sentenced to death (most reprieved and sentenced to ten years), and 74 dying in custody.[30] A researcher in 1916 found the majority were Quakers, Congregationalists or Atheists (among whom Emrys would have numbered himself), but almost all Christian denominations, as well as Jews, were represented.[31] Though varied in belief, as a group they stood out in prison, since most were high-minded and many were educated. Half the objectors in Emrys's first prison were school teachers like himself, self-improving, helpful to other inmates, eventually winning respect among detained and detainers alike. This made them influential in any civilian punitive establishment. But it was not so in a military prison, where refusers were despised by the military hierarchy as malingerers and cowards. It was only as the war got bloodier that their defiance began to be understood, and their courage appreciated in civil prisons. But never among the military.

Attitudes within the Labour ranks were as varied as elsewhere, though politicians like MacDonald were finding an anti-war position was ever less crippling, especially as some end to the war had to come. Those who supported the war and were preaching hatred of Germans, hatred of Ireland and opposition to the Easter uprising – including socialists like Blatchford and Hyndman – were losing support among working people involved in Labour and socialist politics. Many had been stunned by the *Clarion*'s pro-conscription position. Brockway later said, 'It was a terrible shock to us . . . the *Clarion* was almost our bible.'[32] In 1916 the bible's readership had dwindled to nothing and Blatchford was working on the *Weekly Dispatch* owned by Lord Northcliffe. Jingoist he may have become but he still retained his old spirit. When he received a private note from the paper's editor, hinting at national power shifts, 'Will you please note that Lloyd George is our man now,' he replied characteristically,[33] 'Will you please note that Robert Blatchford is his own man'.

Freedom of speech was being systematically curbed, however. Prosecutions were launched against the ILP, *Forward* and the Society of Friends for refusing to submit their publications to the government censor.[34] James Maxton was jailed; so were radical Liberals like Edmund Dene Morel. Bertrand Russell, a young academic, said he 'went all over the place, making speeches . . . and helping conscientious objectors'.[35] He recalled one meeting in a church being attacked by women (spurred by Emmeline and Christabel's patriotic journalism) where war-resisting women had the 'clothes torn off their backs' as they left the service. Russell too was tried and convicted of sedition for writing an article thought to encourage 'bad feelings' towards the USA. He lost his university fellowship, but in jail he was given first division status and allowed books and visits. Upper-class objectors did not endure what Emrys did, although Emrys – because he was educated – was better treated than ill-educated or friendless objectors, who were threatened with death sentences, enduring leg irons and bread and water regimes, and used for medical experiments.[36]

'How much easier for them to go with the crowd but for conscience's sake,' Nan wrote Aggie,[37] who had stepped up her work for the Friends. Nan and Duncan began attending war resisters' meetings in Ayr and Glasgow. Lillie cheered from home, declaring, 'The military are a stupid lot of asses' for not believing the 'ample proof' Emrys had given of 'sincere' objection.[38]

War-resister women treated news of the men's imprisonment as other women treated the departure of brothers and sons and fathers for the trenches, borrowing the language and the emotion from the war they opposed. 'Aggie, we at home will never know what the suffering means but we can be justly proud of our brave boys of the ILP and the NCF whom nothing can daunt.'[39] Even the idioms were identical: 'Emrys is a fearless soldier,' declared Lillie,[40] while Nan praised the ILP boys for 'sticking to their guns'.[41]

By May 1916, the Friends Service Committee reported that 'there are already conscientious objectors in military custody in forty barracks and camps in different parts of the country'.[42] Their Prisoners

Committee aimed to see them all. In June the Revd John Hughes had a letter from a Quaker chaplain who had seen Emrys in the Devizes barracks for fifteen minutes. He reported him in 'splendid health' and enjoying the Wesleyan service as 'the happiest halfhour of the week'.[43] Privately, Emrys, like many a son of the manse, was allergic to religion. His respect for his Quaker visitor was because he had come to mediate in the bitter dispute that had developed because Emrys refused to do any work at all in the barracks, believing it aided the war effort. The Quaker chaplain wrote that a 'compromise has been arrived at after a good deal of controversy'. Emrys had agreed to work in the laundry of a nearby civilian hospital.

Aggie, who had now taken over as organizer of the No Conscription Fellowship in Aberdare, set herself to get Emrys transferred to ordinary prison. She already had support from George Lansbury, who told her she should be proud of Emrys's stand.[44] She went to London, where she contacted NCF workers and the MP, Llewellyn Williams, who went to the War Office on Emrys's behalf[45] and told Aggie he hoped to hear 'the end of the abominable treatment . . . your brother and other brave men who are suffering for conscience sake are having to endure'.[46] She also went to see Robert Williams (home from Egypt), who duly got in touch with Snowden.[47] Williams was steadfast in his commitment to Hardie's young friends, 'My only feeling is of sorrow that so little can be done for those dear fellows who are under the iron heel.'

In Scotland Nan was full of admiration for the new Aggie, 'You are very brave, Aggie, to go all the way to London on your own.'[48] But she knew 'how much you were built up on Emrys' and how 'his suffering reflects on you'. Work for conscientious objectors – as with the war effort – by its very nature reinforced the dynamic of women supporting men in a situation of male heroics.

Aggie next offered her services to counter the 'cat and mouse' practice of the military authorities, who would release men who had completed sentences but instantly rearrest them to go before a new tribunal. The original motive had been to wear down objectors and present them with an easy opportunity to join the military and avoid return to prison. Within a year they had realized that the objectors could not be worn down. They were not malingerers but men of principle. The authorities then began work on an Alternative Service plan for non-military war service, administered by the Home Office, where objectors could undertake war tasks in military camps or assist medically. Ramsay MacDonald was approached to see if he would head a volunteer ambulance corps in France, for example, as a way of incorporating this important resister into the war effort.

MacDonald thought about it seriously and took advice but eventually refused.[49]

The Friends' assistance to war resisters, explaining what was involved and what their rights were, all depended on knowing where resisters were being held and when they appeared before tribunals. The military prevented this by giving no notice of tribunals to prisoners or anyone else. All that could be done was to watch barracks and see who was being 'released' and 'rearrested', or moved to another prison for a new tribunal. Frequent moving of objectors was another tactic tried to break resistance.

Aggie became one of the Friends' regular messengers, charged by Isaac Goss, the Friends' national co-ordinator, with 'watching and visiting men in military and civil custody', with the specific brief of 'getting information'.[50] She was made the local representative in the south-west of England and Wales – with instructions that 'All the men should be met and you should . . . find out when it is expected they will be released'. For this she was to get in touch with 'local sympathetic people who would be prepared, if it is necessary, to watch detention barracks and prisons with a view of obtaining precise information'. He told her that the authorities were now taking some men to Wormwood Scrubs to a Central Tribunal where the new Alternative Service was being offered. The Friends were trying to find out who was accepting the offer and who was refusing. This was an added task. Goss asked Aggie to 'wire me instantly if men are sent back to their unit'.

Aggie took to her work with vigour and soon found ways of getting the required information. She visited Emrys at the end of June at Devizes by saying to the military authorities that she had come to persuade him to join the army. When she saw him she managed to slip him chocolates and give him news about the objectors' movement and the agitation that was continuing outside. In mid-July Emrys heard that he was to be court martialled again. This was supposed to give him a chance to change his mind. By now, however, the authorities were beginning to realize this was unlikely. When he got to the court, improvised in the barracks depot of the Wiltshire Regiment, Aggie was already there. While waiting to be tried he was allowed to read a newspaper. It told of the Battle of Jutland.[51] What he really wanted were labour or socialist publications. Aggie had thought of this too. During a brief moment outside the courtroom she slipped him some *Labour Leaders* and *Heralds*. He hid them up his trousers, tucked into his boots.

Eventually Aggie's lobbying paid off. Emrys was sent to Shepton Mallet civil prison at the end of July. On the way he had a chance to talk to the other conscientious objectors who had been with him in the barracks – brought in the same day – whom he had never been allowed to meet. It was military policy to keep objectors inside any single establishment isolated from one another. Some objectors had not been transferred and were forced to remain behind in the barracks. They had not had MPs inquiring about them at the Home Office. One of them was a young man from the south-west of England named Hedley Dennis.

In Shepton Mallet Emrys and his colleagues were marched down the main street from the railway, where they were hissed and booed at by passing residents – as well as by troops on the way to the Front. Part of the policy of breaking a resister's nerve was that everywhere he went everyone should know and be free to react. Emrys was not disappointed when the door slammed behind him in his first civil prison cell. After the shouting and tramping and abuse of the detention barracks, an ordinary prison 'was as silent as the grave'.[52] To his delight too he was able to shed his khaki, 'I preferred the broad arrow ten thousand times.'[53] Dinners were better too: 8 oz. of potatoes and 6 oz. of bread, on some days beans and on Thursdays 4 oz. of boiled meat. There were even fifteen minutes a week in the bath. But Emrys soon realized that what he had previously been told, 'that Elizabeth Fry and John Howard and some other philanthropists had . . . humanized the prisons',[54] was not true. The regime was hard, oppressive, endlessly monotonous. All day, every day, he sewed mailbags, alone in a single cell. Meals were shoved through the door hatch. Only chapel was a break. It was Church of England, a service Emrys had never heard before and found a 'meaningless ritual'.[55] Nevertheless, it had a chaplain who lent him *The Pilgrim's Progress*. Leaving aside its religion, Emrys found 'a work . . . quite up to date' and 'although John Bunyan had written it in Bedford prison in 1660 and I was reading it in a Somerset prison in 1916 it was still a vivid commentary on events which I had lived through and understood.'[56] One day the chaplain told him Roger Casement was to be hanged the next day and that George Bernard Shaw had made a last-minute appeal. 'It aroused all my hatred of the forces that controlled the government and public opinion.'

He was now allowed books from the library, brought to his cell. He got a book about shorthand and taught himself this skill. He found a German Bible and began teaching himself German. He worked day after day at self-improvement. This impressed the authorities and the other prisoners, including a forger in the cell next door. For prisoners soon developed ways of passing messages and having 'conversations'. In time he discovered that there were other conscientious objectors and occasionally, by means of brief whispers when they passed in the exercise yard, he 'talked' to them. But it was slow going.

Nan spent the usual week at the ILP summer school at Keswick. It failed to lift her spirits and by August, perhaps spurred on by Aggie's new independent life, she too took matters into her own hands. She went alone to London and checked herself into the Caterham clinic. Lillie, who wrote to tell Aggie that Nancy Richardson was getting married, claimed that Nan was spending her time lying around at Caterham 'on holiday'.[57] Being attended to personally lifted her spirits. Perhaps being away from Lillie and Lochnorris did too. Lillie asked her to see Frank Smith about Hardie's effects, still stored at Neville's Court. No decision had been taken. In the event Lillie decided to sell some, keep some, and give some away. She told Nan to tell Frank Smith to send one of the high-backed chairs down to Aggie's father. She wanted it made clear to the Revd John Hughes, 'It is a gift . . . from me.' The Hughes family were becoming increasingly important to Lillie, who was distressed to hear that Rowlie's cough was now so bad the army had discharged him.[58] Rowlie's first act on discharge was to break off with the girl he had planned to marry. As was her way, Lillie asked point blank, 'What happened with her?' Only later did it become clear that Rowlie had released the girl because he now believed himself to be dying. Why else would the army have set him free?

Lillie also included an update on her own illness, 'I was having a little natural sleep and of course doing without the Dr's bottle 'til I got quite exhausted'.[59] It is the first we have heard of the 'doctor's bottle'. Nan too was poorly. Back from Caterham, she seemed no better. Once again the remedy was yet another change of venue. She told Aggie that they were going to a new 'watering place' in September.

During this same summer of 1916 Bruce Glasier's stomach cancer continued to give him pain. He began seeing Lady Victoria Murray, daughter of the Earl of Dunmore, who had set up 'practice' in a room in Manchester as a Christian Science healer.[60] Almost instantly he had begun to feel better. Katharine was 'joyful', convinced he would be cured.

Katharine herself was hard at work as editor of the *Labour Leader*, another example of a 'male' job handed over to a woman owing to the war – in this case, when Fenner Brockway resigned to take over as secretary of the No Conscription Fellowship. Its previous secretary, Clifford Allen, was arrested as an army deserter.[61] Brockway assumed from the first that he would return to the editor's job when the war was over and that Katharine Glasier would willingly step down when he did.[62] Meanwhile, he too waited to be arrested.

During the summer Emrys was moved from sunny Shepton Mallet to gloomy Cardiff prison. After some months he was taken to Wormwood Scrubs to go before the Central Tribunal. Only on the day before did he learn that the purpose of the visit to London was to screen prisoners for the option of Alternative Service, which meant going to a camp in Weston-super-Mare. The government wanted to boost the numbers accepting such service (classed as helping the war) to reduce the growing numbers classed as war resisters.

In the courtroom in London an older officer asked him, 'Socialist, are you? Then why don't you obey the commands of the State?'

'I don't believe that Lord Derby and Lloyd George are acting in the interests of the State.'[63]

After Emrys returned to Cardiff he had three days to think it over, but concluded the new service was still under the domain of the military and accepting it meant that the issue of resistance to the war would die away.[64] In the event he was one of the few not offered it. Emrys was seen as a hard case: a man with political objections to this one war. These were 'ungenuine' reasons; he had to stay in prison.

When he had returned to Cardiff and was walking, handcuffed, off the train, he suddenly saw a pale and coughing Rowlie, who had travelled all the way from Abercynon in order to march a few steps alongside his younger brother on the way from the railway station to the prison doors. The brothers were forbidden to speak. Those trying to break conscientious objectors believed it important to deprive them of all support; those working on their behalf believed it was important for prisoners to know someone was watching out for them, even if they were never allowed to communicate. Every time a prisoner was moved, for whatever reason, someone should be visibly there. That was what the Friends' support group Aggie was working for organized.

Aggie continued to visit prisoners at Shepton Mallet and the barracks at Devizes, and sent information back to a solicitor acting for the Friends.[65] She liked the work, and the prisoners came to depend on her, especially nineteen-year-old Hedley Dennis, still in the barracks.

Hedley Dennis was a mild and unaggressive young man from a family that had radical atheist leanings. His mother claimed to be a communist and always wore a red hat.[66] Hedley had reacted against the family's atheism, and at the age of twelve, standing by the front wall of his house, had experienced a religious conversion. His religion had led him to object to the war, and inside the military barracks he had had to experience very rough treatment, and no little persecution, being assaulted and on other occasions dragged by his hair around his cell. Sergeant-majors thought he was using religion to avoid his stint at the Front. Aggie heard about the treatment[67] and contacted Snowden to try to get Hedley and others to civil prisons. She sent the letter via Frank Smith, who told her he was 'glad to hear that Emrys at least was in the "civil"', for 'prison is better than the camp of the savages'.[68] The resourceful Aggie did not find much difficulty in gaining admittance to the camp of the savages. She gained access to see Hedley Dennis by posing as his younger sister. Being very small, she had discovered that if she let her hair down and put on a gymslip, she was believable to middle-aged prison officers as a child. Yet Aggie was now in her early thirties.

Snowden worked actively on the conscientious objector cause, making the 'tribunal' system his special target. In 1916 he wrote about the illegality of tribunals and the 'kidnap' of men for service once they had attended.[69] He told too of their class bias: how in Market Bosworth a resister was convicted while all the men of the local hunt were exempted from service 'in the national interest'. Tribunals, he concluded, as Emrys had already realized, were arbitrary courts under no rule of law whatsoever, each 'a law unto itself'. Another book circulating in objector circles was *The Majesty of Conscience* by F. B. Meyer.[70] Meyer was not a pacifist, but the father of an only son killed at Vimy Ridge. He had scanned history for all those – from Socrates to Wesley – who had stuck by their conscience. They were the real leaders of civilization. Such writing boosted the small band who held out in their isolated cells.

Both Nan and Aggie began to breathe the new air of equality circulating among women supporting the war effort who wanted to play a bigger part. Nan wrote, 'It may be women will be conscripts ere long and then we will prove of what we are made.'[71] She planned to play her part by resisting any war service. She would resist, she said, even if she were recruited for 'munition purposes only' because making arms 'is all part of the war and I hate it with all my being'.[72] Although war resistance had given her a new spirit, it failed to conquer her daily battle with depression. Nan wrote to Aggie from Girvan, the latest resort being tried for her health,[73] 'I have been thinking about you often' and even 'had a great fancy to give you a surprise visit this month', but, she adds sadly, 'it did not come off'. 'I hope to feel better when we are home. God knows I've been miserable enough here.'

It was the old pattern: at home Aggie and Lillie feel trapped, and look forward to a move. When they change venues nothing else has changed and they concentrate on getting home again – still blaming circumstances for their inner distress.[74] 'Nan does not do with the sea,' said Lillie.

They always looked forward to news of Emrys and Nan approved wholeheartedly of his decision to turn down Alternative Service, 'I don't see any use accepting alternative service AFTER having served a term of imprisonment. But each one knows best what he wants to do.'[75] Fenner Brockway maintained, there was 'an extraordinary tolerance and friendliness between those who were absolutists and those who took Alternative Service'. This was one of the 'noble achievements of the No Conscription Movement, its tolerance.'[76] However, others, like Tom Williams, a miner in South Wales, were less mellow: 'I could wish they were all absolutist.'[77] In fact, most probably were.[78]

Brockway himself was finally arrested at the end of 1916 and later he too refused Alternative Service. His first imprisonment was in the Tower of London, which amused him very much at the time.[79] Brockway did not find his imprisonment an ordeal. 'Pshaw! It wasn't really very hard,' he said years later.[80] 'As a conscientious objector I had an easy time because all my friends, all my circle were sympathetic. The case of a conscientious objector who was alone in a village, even in a church, without sympathy, for them it was so much harder.' Lillie and Nan knew that well enough.

Resistance was not hard for Sylvia either, surrounded by her enterprises and her organization. The latter sent a delegate to a conference on national service (Sylvia called it 'national slavery')[81] and recalled that 'our Mrs Walker ... was struck several times on the head by "patriotic ladies" sitting near her'. But East Enders were able to stand up to this. Sylvia's efforts that summer were put to setting up an information office to deal with 'landlords' illegal action ... illegal action by employers and insurance companies ... mistakes made by national insurance officials ... difficulties with education authorities ... care committees ... poor law guardians ... and old age pensions'.[82] In short, a prototype Citizens Advice Bureau. She corresponded with every government department, fortified by now with new legal expertise. For another addition to her workforce was a law firm who donated services for nothing, and she had already started a health care service as well, having found two doctors to give their services free.[83] There was practically no public service that would one day be run by the community to which Sylvia was not already giving a prefigurative life.

By contrast Nan had little to do. During the summer she sent Aggie a snap of herself in the garden reaching up to a fruit tree. She could have been a lady of leisure. Duncan had taken the photograph, perhaps with the camera Hardie had once owned but found so difficult to operate.[84] The news from Lochnorris was all domestic. A cat had died; a dog had defected. It was now the first anniversary of Hardie's death. Nan wrote, 'the dark days are upon us again and we feel strangely sad and lonely.'[85] But the anniversary seems to have activated Lillie. In a postscript to Nan's letter, out of the blue she announced:

> We expect to sell Lochnorris and remove into the suburbs of Glasgow where Duncan would be with us. It will be a turn up but I don't think I will be very sorry to leave Cumnock. They have never been nice to us. Due, of course, to the stand my husband took in politics.[86]

The latest local insult was that the Town Council had turned down a request to put up a statue to Hardie. 'Mean enough ... surely,' said Lillie.

By now Aggie was trying to get Emrys released from gaol altogether. Snowden put down a question in the House but wrote privately that Emrys 'is difficult to deal with. I understand he will not accept Alternative Service'.[87] More than that, he was making a political stand. The authorities drew tight lines around such men. They feared their effect on others – not so much any more because they would increase war resistance but because their influence would lead to the questioning of authority.

Emrys knew full well how much disaffection there was among ordinary soldiers. War-resisting prisoners continued to pour in to the prison system. As one of them, Emrys was given the lowest-status work in prison – cleaning and looking after the stores. He had hardened himself to concentrate on his self-education and was now reading Carlyle. But as January 1917 approached, the weather got colder, and solitary confinement was beginning to tell. Alone perpetually, and losing weight, he wrote in his Diary, 'I thought . . . I would ultimately go mad'.[88]

In the Labour movement at large, revulsion against the slaughter was also beginning to tell. Apart from its jingoist wing, Labour was now devoting itself to the serious business of how people were surviving at home. Its national War Relief Committee examined housing and health and education and general living conditions. Sidney Webb was planning the new human services that Sylvia was already pioneering. All were looking ahead. Before he had been 'taken', Brockway planned a pamphlet warning about the future when colonial rule would be replaced by economic imperialism, and the USA and Britain would build factories in Africa and Asia and try to 'hold workers down' there.[89] Brockway was determined not to succumb to hatred of other races, while men like Glasier were determined not to succumb to hatred of Germans.

In 1916 Glasier was at the House of Commons and by chance ran into Cunninghame Graham. When the war started Cunninghame Graham had offered himself for service, but only so long as it did not involve killing and he did not have to wear a uniform. The government had sent him to South America to train and bring back horses for the cavalry at the front. On the way back the boat went aground off south-west England and Cunninghame Graham personally led every horse to safety across the surf and on to a deserted beach.

Bruce Glasier regarded Cunninghame Graham as pro-war. 'I was frigid,' he wrote in his Diary after they had said 'hello'.[90] Cunninghame Graham asked Glasier if he had seen the Arts and Crafts Exhibition, which Cunninghame Graham had reviewed. Glasier replied, 'I asked him why he had made the Exhibition the excuse for an attack on German art?' He was taken aback and did not answer. Glasier pressed further, particularly about William Morris: 'why did you use his name to sneer at Germany?' Cunninghame Graham stayed silent but Glasier continued, 'Why further . . . the blind hatred of the British public against Germany?' After several more requests for an answer, Cunninghame Graham, ever the gallant, said perhaps he had made a mistake but 'We must not allow a thirty-year friendship to be broken by this stupid war.'

Yet friendships were broken. And skulls. South Wales was one of the most divided areas. In Cardiff on 11 November 1916 a peace group had booked the Cory Hall for a meeting, with James Winstone, Ramsay MacDonald and J. H. Thomas, leader of the railwaymen, all speaking. At the same time a counter-demonstration was organized to disrupt it, led by Charles Stanton, Merthyr's new MP and Hardie's successor, together with the leader of the Seamen's Union – both as fanatically in favour of the war as those inside the hall were against it.[91] Men who would have shared the same platform only two years before were re-enacting the war itself.

The pro-war marchers broke into the meeting and fighting started, becoming fiercer as the invaders climbed on the platform. J. H. Thomas had his watch and chain ripped away. The spectacle of the labour movement at each other's throats got wide coverage and there were demands by Stanton and others to have subsequent peace meetings banned. The government eventually took Stanton aside[92] and hinted that he should take the opposite line: ignore all anti-war demonstrations and see that local newspapers did as well. Coverage always promoted disaffection. The First World War was teaching the authorities some valuable lessons in how to blank out dissent.

But Labour was not as divided as it might seem. The overlap of opinion within factions on various war-related issues was enormous. As time went on, and casulaties mounted, the jingoist wing lost its glamour. The principled conscientious objectors in their dungeons gained a grudging respect. Public opinion in turn became used to Labour ministers – like Henderson and Barnes – being in government (where their main job was advising the War Cabinet on labour issues). The working class got used to Labour MPs fighting for working-class rights in matters like war pensions and food provision.

MacDonald's gifts were suited to the shifting situation and to the clandestine and difficult diplomacy that was now required to sound out a possible set of agreements that might unite all these elements – despite the fact that tension still continued between the main body of Labour, solidly nationalist, and the internationalist peace wing, each regarding the other as traitors to the socialist cause. Labour might still have fallen apart at the end of 1916 had not the Liberal Party done so first. Lloyd George suddenly manoeuvred Asquith out of office and took over as prime minister. Though the Liberal Party appeared as united after this coup as it had been before, it never really recovered;

while Labour, though it appeared divided, was slowly knitting itself together.

On the last night of 1916, fifty-two years to the day after the eight-year-old Hardie had had to return without his job to the family's fireless and foodless room in Glasgow, where the baby Duncan later died and the new baby had been born, May Hardie in the United States, only just recovered from her long illness, was rushed to a hospital in Massachusetts. Her second pregnancy was again ending in an unexpected premature delivery. To compound the problem, this time she had to have a Caesarean – a rare operation at that time. It was successful and the baby was a strong girl. Jamie and May called her Jean Stoddart Keir Hardie.

At the end of 1916 Lillie wrote to Aggie, 'I am sorry to say I am still sleepless'. This time she confided that 'I am at present attending a Lady Doctor in Glasgow who hopes to be able to help me.'[93] Lillie was now fifty-seven and still unaware of what her real problem was. It was not for lack of attempts to inform herself. The Hardie library was well stocked with medical information. *Papers on Health* by the Congregationalist, Professor E. B. Kirk,[94] was the staple reference work, running to many volumes, each conveniently organized for quick reference to standard complaints. The text was both moral and medical. Under 'Paralysis' Professor Kirk recommended fomentations to the limbs, the remedy Lillie had applied for all Hardie's strokes. Under infant feeding the text cautioned mothers not to give narcotics to babies to help them sleep – a common and dangerous practice. Under 'Alcohol' it spoke of the 'terrible danger . . . to young ladies' whose 'mothers dose them with it in secret' to give them social courage in the husband stakes. But it was the sections on 'Nerves' and 'Sleeplessness', Lillie's long-standing complaints, that were particularly well thumbed. When sleep eluded, soaping the head was recommended. When that failed the stronger remedy was 'chloral', easily available at any chemist's and a favourite with Victorian women.

After Hardie died Nan and Lillie acquired their own medical books. Some were not fireside health homilies but professional books, the kind used only by medical students or pharmacists.[95] The passages on narcotics were thoroughly underlined and annotated, in particular all the drugs that would 'induce sleep, relieve pain and calm excitement': 'nitrous Oxide gas', alcohol chlorodyne, 'sulphonal', belladonna, opium, morphine, cannabis indica and cocaina. There were also several lines under 'hypodermic injection is an invaluable means of administration when a rapid effect is desired'. Left unmarked was the warning that such drugs may be used for temporary relief but that after time their habit is a real 'disease', and that 'the effect of the use of opium chloral . . . to gain soothing sleep is DREADFUL', for when deprived after continuous use we have seen patients perfectly MAD with agony'.

Lillie's letters to Aggie over the previous years make it painfully obvious that she was by now addicted, probably to opium chloral – her 'doctor's bottle'. Even when she had other illnesses – like painful phlebitis – it was always the 'sleeplessness' that loomed largest. Nan tried to explain the problem away. First, it had been the war; the next year, 'her reaction' to the strain of Hardie's long illness.[96] Now, to his death.

Lillie had a better understanding of the problem in that she knew she was dependent and was trying to fight it.[97] She saw her problem as being unable to get 'natural sleep' without dosing up. Many Victorian women had faced the same problem after abusing such readily available medication. Jane Carlyle, the wife of Hardie's early hero, was one. She wrote that she longed 'for sleep, sleep, unfathomable sleep, as the only conceivable heaven';[98] continually increasing her drug doses until the remedy suddenly stopped her heart for good one day when she was sixty-six.

Lillie knew the dangers and tried to go without her bottle, these occasions recorded as painful and anxious. She always returned. Possibly she moved on up the scale to other drugs and other ways of using them.[99] Whether Lillie's new woman doctor in Glasgow recognized the nature of the illness, or if she did, was trying to treat it, is unknown. Today's practitioners find it difficult enough. In 1917 there would have been the additional pretence to accommodate: Mrs Hardie was a woman with a sleeping problem, not a woman with a drug problem. Like many another woman of her time her problem was hidden and she probably had to cope alone.

At the start of 1917 the Labour Party agreed to join in Lloyd George's new coalition, and yet another special Party Conference was held.[100] The vote on this move was by no means unanimous and the disagreements within the Party proliferated. MacDonald had chosen wisely in staying out of it. His stature within the ranks of Labour was reviving, for although he was anti-war, he still managed to be pro-Allies and pro-nation – in short, to be pro-war too. Sylvia called it his constant compromising, but in other circles it was looking increasingly like growing statesmanship.

Aggie was now addressed as 'Dear Friend' (no longer Miss Hughes) by Friends headquarters, who sent her reports on what had happened to those she helped. One young man,[101] she would be glad to know, 'made a good statement . . . he has been doing good work among the soldiers and the escort were most sympathetic . . . and impressed with the stand he is making.' Emrys's Diary also shows a softening among warders and military escorts to the conscientious objectors at the start of 1917. (He was now allowed monthly visits from his family.) Their own brand of bravery, especially in a civil prison filled with hard-case criminals, won respect. Even in military circles it could be seen that these men were the opposite of the caricatured weak-kneed coward commonly depicted as evading service. If anything, most were more thoroughly disciplined and resolute than most soldiers. In February 1917[102] Aggie's album shows a rash of signatures next to anti-militarist verses and a statement, 'The People will survive'. She had even managed to smuggle her album into the prisons she visited.

Emrys's first prison sentence 'ended' on 1 March 1917, St David's Day. This meant he was handed back to the military authorities. 'To go back to this after being in prison all winter,' Emrys wrote, I thought it 'the most atrocious treatment that was ever meted out to anyone.'[103] He was also forced back into uniform. As he was marched out of prison by the military escort, Aggie was waiting at the corner with John Hughes. The corporal let them walk by Emrys's side and even talk as they went, another sign of softening. Emrys learned from Aggie that he was going to Rhyl to the Welsh Regiment's detention barracks. As they walked, Aggie slipped him fruit and chocolate and a bundle of *Pioneers* and *Leaders*. A few days later Emrys wrote to his father,[104] 'Dear Dad, I shall be court martialled tomorrow and have written out a short statement which I shall send to the *Pioneer*.'

At his third court martial Emrys said that the war:

> came as a result of the commercial rivalry between the Triple Entente and the Triple Alliance and that the British government is as responsible as the German Kaiser and that all pleas that we are defending small nations . . . are but superficial excuses for a policy of imperial ambition and commercial aggrandisement which can only bring misery to this generation.

The statement ended: 'By refusing to obey military orders I am rendering the greatest possible service to the people of the world.'

He was sentenced to two more years and sent to Caernarvon civil prison, housed within the walls of the castle. He had a light and airy cell overlooking the sea. Although the regime was difficult, there was a far better library than at Cardiff prison. He began reading Bergson and Omar Khayyám. Through the clandestine network which he mastered in each prison, he 'met' other conscientious objectors from the north, including two millworkers, as well as J. H. Hudson, another ILP member. The chaplain, who had prisoners put on bread and water if they smiled during his sermon, had lost his only son at the Front, and preached emotional sermons about having 'seen' his son in a trance, under the influence of a recently published best-seller recounting 'communion' between war dead and their loved ones.[105] Emrys found him an old 'sentimental Jingo believing everything that the *Daily Mail* said', but he had not the heart to oppose him. Besides, the services at the prison had excellent Welsh singing – with women prisoners brought in to join the male prison choir and hidden behind a partition. 'One . . . had a glorious contralto voice. I was never able to see what she was like.'[106]

In the library Emrys found a new book by Norman Angell, which gave him encouragement. Angell, at the outbreak of war, had gone to the United States to write for the *New Republic*. He continued to spread his doctrine of conquest by trade rather than military adventure. Such were the contradictions within capitalism that the war had thrown up that when Angell returned to Britain, the Lloyd George government considered his message so dangerous to the nation that the globe-trotting Angell was denied a passport to travel. This enraged him, and he joined the Labour Party's tiny radical liberal fringe. 'I think I shall always be glad I was a member of a Party all of which at present could be got into a taxi cab,' he claimed.[107]

It was well into March 1917, when exercising in the yard, that Emrys heard from another prisoner, as they passed each other going in opposite directions, 'There has been a revolution in Russia and the Czar's abdicated.'[108] On the next turn around the yard he asked for more news but there was none. He thought of it all the next week. Was it even true, he wondered? It seemed so unlikely.

After ten days a new war resister was brought in to the prison; he had managed to smuggle in a copy of Lansbury's *Herald*, now going strong as a socialist newspaper. Whenever a newspaper was smuggled in, the practice was to pass it from cell to cell one day at a time. Emrys did not know when he would get to see it. After a few impatient days, 'One of our COs handing out the clean clothing handed me the paper in a handkerchief. I waited 'til dinner time and spread it out, crouching in the corner with my back to the door and the peephole.' To his joy:

> the paper had a long verbatim account of a huge demonstration held at the Albert Hall to celebrate the success of the revolution with a full report of speeches by Smillie, Lansbury . . . There was no doubt about it, the Russian Revolution had come . . . the prophecies of the tortured souls in Siberia had come true . . . the old order was dead, a new society was being born . . . the end of the war was in sight.[109]

Lansbury later wrote about that same Albert Hall meeting: 'When . . . the organ pealed out the "Internationale", the audience rose and sang as at a revival meeting – atheists, Christians, deists, and Jews, Moslems and Hindus . . . tears coursing down the cheeks of strong men.'[110]

In his solitary cell Emrys wrote in his prison Diary that when he had finished reading: 'It was the moment of a lifetime ... I buried my head in my hands and sobbed.'[111]

16

THE PARTING OF SOCIALISTS

When news of the Kerensky revolution came in March 1917, Glasier wrote, 'It takes the breath away. The most powerful aristocracy in the world's history overthrown in a day.'[1]

He got in touch at once with Bolshevik members of the Socialist Party to try to stop the war.[2] In April he was elected top of the poll at the ILP Conference, where it was decided to send delegates to Petrograd to counteract the presence of the official Labour Party delegation sent to urge Kerensky to continue the war. The conference also asked for the Second International to meet; and later, to mark the Glasier's silver wedding, the ILP gave Katharine a watch and Glasier a couch,[3] his battle with stomach cancer now widely known. MacDonald, as pleased as anyone else with the new Kerensky government, believed it marked the moment when he could begin to re-emerge as a Kerensky himself and throw off the Labour Party's existing yoke which had turned it into 'a mere echo of the old governing classes' opinions'.[4] These were the words he spoke to a great convention that was called by a spontaneously formed group representing all Britain's socialists and organized jointly by the secretaries of the ILP and the Socialist Party.[5] It took place in early June at the Leeds Coliseum and Lansbury called it 'the most representative of socialists, progressives, Labour men and women and pacifists ever held'.[6] Meeting at one of those moments when the unity of the Left was a genuine possibility, it welcomed the revolution in Russia and pledged itself to civil liberties and a peace without indemnities. Hardie's friend, Robert Smillie, now President of the Miners' Federation, was in the chair. Snowden spoke and Tom Mann, in the balcony, supporting a motion by Will Anderson, called for the establishment in Britain of the workers' and soldiers' councils being set up in Russia and known as 'soviets'.[7] In fact, some were already being tried in Britain, including in mining villages around Merthyr.[8] To MacDonald, in the middle of delicate tightrope walking his way back to leadership, attendance at the convention was one of many events he had to negotiate. To a wide range of socialists, however, it heralded the way to a more genuine democracy. Never had there been so much agreement on fundamental issues: no intervention against the new Czar-less Russia and no allied troops to bolster Russia's armies in an attempt to keep the war going against Germany. However, the convention neglected to set up a permanent secretariat to continue the initiative. When the day ended, each delegate passed back to his or her own socialist group. The moment had passed.

Hyndman had not joined in. In 1916 he had been forced out of the Socialist Party and, taking *Justice* with him, set up his own National Socialist Party. It supported the war. After the Kerensky overthrow, he told a friend 'there is a general feeling that . . . I ought to go to Petrograd or Moscow'. But he decided against, commenting in passing, 'the slav is very tawdry'.[9] In any case, 'We may have a revolution here . . . and then I ought to be present.' Little Englander to the last, he still clung to his dream of being summoned to run Britain.

Blatchford still clung to Empire. He had been an ardent war supporter and the press barons had kept him working overtime in an effort to win working class opinion for it. Now he was required to work even harder against what was called a 'premature peace'.[10] His articles were put together in a book called *General Von Sneak*, which stoked up hatred of Germany and no longer touted the Merrie England of roses and fenland, but 'the England of Bombay and Hong Kong . . . Quebec . . . and Suez and Shanghai'.[11] Large sections of the working class and many trade unionists supported imperialist Britain, and the government had already chosen two of the most popular Labour converts – Will Thorne and James O'Grady – as the delegation that visited Russia.

Thorne returned from his mission just as the Leeds convention ended, with its promise to 'begin to do for this country what the Russian Revolution has accomplished in Russia'.[12] This statement and the unusually wide coalition of forces gathered in Leeds seemed very threatening to the Czar's cousin, George V. As Thorne alighted in London from his boat train, he was summoned to Buckingham Palace, and took a taxi straight there. Later he wrote, 'the King seemed greatly disturbed by the famous Leeds Conference'.[13]

Thorne was not disturbed. On the contrary, he was flattered and 'very pleased' that the King was receiving him in so 'homely' a manner. He told his host not to worry, 'there would be no revolution in Britain'. The official Labour Party had not backed the Leeds initiative.

The government then sent Emmeline Pankhurst to Russia, to urge the women of Russia to urge their men to continue to fight. She and Christabel had criticized Sylvia and Adela for their war resistance[14] and now Sylvia rebuked her mother for her further war mission. Sylvia had supported the Leeds convention, having originally greeted the overthrow of the Czar with unbridled joy. But Kerensky's havering made her change her mind. She soon concluded he was reformist, and would change nothing. On 2 June the *Dreadnought* stated prophetically, 'Kerensky too . . . will go', for he has 'failed to realize the greatness of the movement he would lead'.[15]

MacDonald too wanted to go to Russia, as the emissary the ILP had voted should gainsay the government's war messengers. After scrupulous vetting by a Foreign Minister, Robert Cecil, and dinner with Lloyd George, MacDonald was finally granted a passport – only to find that an ultra-right official of the Seamen's Union named Edward Tupper, an ally of Stanton in South Wales, long known for heavy drinking and rampant racism,[16] had persuaded the crew of the liner upon which MacDonald was booked to refuse to carry him as a passenger.[17] As it turned out, Tupper was aggrieved that his pro-war intervention had been rejected by the Leeds convention.[18] The old conservative union presence, which had depressed Hardie so often, was still very powerful, and increasing its hold on the Labour Party. MacDonald's Diary sadly recorded the Party's 'stupidity', 'vanity' and 'delusions' during this period.[19]

Though America had finally entered the war in April, Glasier concluded that it was the 'Russian triumph' that marked 'the beginning of a big popular tide against the war' in Britain.[20] Peace meetings hotted up. On 9 June Glasier spoke in Manchester, joined by Bertrand Russell. During the meeting soldiers entered the hall to ask for the military status of all present. They were chased away with derision by the audience, and retired, a sign of the weakening of the official war position in the face of new hopes for an end to the fighting.

Aggie's intervention for Hedley Dennis had also been successful and he had at last been transferred to a civil prison. Dartmoor had the largest collection of conscientious objectors of any prison in the country. Many were in the ILP and later some 200 ILP members, Dartmoor 'graduates' of 1917, collected for a reunion photograph.[21] Conscientious objectors in some prisons were now allowed to wear their own clothes. Hedley Dennis, relieved at last at being away from military cruelty, became very close to Aggie, his rescuing angel, the one person he could count on to look out for him, his insurance that the brutal treatment he had had before would not be repeated. She was also something else he wished to be: well educated. From this time onwards Aggie became indispensable to Hedley Dennis.

Emrys Hughes, still in Caernarvon prison, was now able to receive letters once a month and to talk to other resisters during exercise hour. It seemed like a tremendous concession after years of solitary confinement. In July Emrys's latest sentence was commuted from two years to twelve months, and he was made the prison librarian. He ordered books from the Society of Friends, not a group immediately congenial to Emrys, the sceptic. But he wrote in his Diary, 'I had learned to respect the Friends. They stood by us so staunchly'.[22]

In the summer of 1917 the coalition government's continuing misuse of the new passport system as a form of political control unexpectedly reunited the Labour Party. Henderson, still Labour Party leader, had remained in the coalition government. Lloyd George decided to send him too to Russia, to boost the war. Henderson was willing but he wanted to stop off en route at an important conference in Stockholm that Camille Huysmans was organizing to revive the Second International in the wake of peace moves and the changed situation in Russia. Lloyd George calculated that the right-wing Henderson, not a socialist anyway, would not press the matter if he was prevented. Lloyd George used the power of refusing a passport to keep Henderson waiting. At last Henderson rebelled. He took the issue of this prevarication to two special Labour Party Conferences and they agreed to back him. He resigned from the coalition in November 1918, and the Labour Party was once more in opposition.

Inside the Party the pro-war and anti-war groups continued to burn, however. It was strenuous new peace initiatives by MacDonald that acted as a coolant – even on the ILP. For the Labour Party had stolen a march on the government and the Allies by publishing the Labour Party's War Aims (first hinted at in the resolution passed at the International meeting on 14 February 1915, over which Hardie had himself presided). These Aims had been reaffirmed at yet one more special Labour Party Conference in December 1917, and contained the essence of what Lloyd George and Woodrow Wilson (in his Fourteen Points) would shortly advocate: an honourable peace, support for democracy, foreign policy under democratic control, an end to conscription, abolition of profit from arms trading, and a league of nations. Defeated countries would not be carved up and every country could decide its own destiny.

The Aims had nothing particularly socialist in them, but they united Labour's socialists and non-socialists and even the war resisters and most of those who had supported the war.

In October 1917 the Russian story continued, with Bolsheviks taking over from Mensheviks. This event which so polarized the world later was not immediately seen as a great change. Many of those in the labour and socialist movements were unsure what the differences were between the various socialist groups in Russia and how to fit them all into the old possibilist and impossibilist framework. How could the Revolutionary Socialists be the possibilists, for example, and the 'majority' socialists the impossibilists? More interest was centred on whether the new group would continue with the war or try to settle.

One person not in two minds about new events in Russia was Sylvia. In July she had called for the armies in Russia to lay down arms (for which the *Dreadnought* was raided by the Special Branch). Both Sylvia and Adela supported the Bolsheviks, whose movement Adela characterized as continuing 'our father's work'.[23] Sylvia might have seen it as protecting Hardie's work – even without his permission. After one of her last visits to see him, she remembered standing at a bus stop and reflecting on his faith in socialists who would one day capture a parliamentary majority, 'I saw them at last make entry into the citadel, only to find it empty, the power gone – removed to an international government wherein the dead-weight of backward peoples would strangle all progress for generations to come', aided by international cartels and trans-national capitalist organizations.[24] In the October Revolution she saw the possibility of developments which might prevent this disappointment.

She immediately began printing Bolshevik decrees in the *Dread-nought*, starting with No. 212 giving the local soviet councils power to take over 'vacant premises suitable for dwelling purposes . . . for citizens in need of dwellings';[25] followed by No. 230 authorizing state banks to pay 'industrial commercial enterprises' so that they can pay workers; and directing that unemployment funds be managed jointly by the unions and local social services.[26] She saw these as the sort of initiatives she would like to see started by councils in cities like London.

Within months she had renamed her organization yet again. It became The Workers' Socialist Federation for Revolution and International Socialism. The *Dreadnought* was also rerouted to become 'an organ of International Socialism with a Bolshevik policy'. A subtitle read, 'Revolutionary News a Speciality – 2d. a week'. This much was certainly true. In few other journals in Britain could such detailed reporting of current events in Russia be found. Special Branch stepped up its interest in her work.[27] Meanwhile the popular press denounced the second Russian Revolution as heartily as it had the first.

By now a few conscientious objectors were starting to be released. Emrys was not one of them. His sentence ended on 9 January 1918 and he was transferred once again back to the military in Redcar. There he found the military authorities were trying new inducement tactics with conscientious objectors. They claimed they were not 'ready' for his case and said he could stay at liberty until further notice, eating and sleeping in a recuperation centre the Army ran on the seafront. It was a measure of the reputation for integrity that objectors had now acquired that the authorities could be perfectly certain Emrys would not abscond. They hoped the taste of freedom would undermine his determination to return to prison. But Emrys was not to be bought at this late stage, and at once sought out the local nonconformists as his best chance of locating Redcar's war resistance. He guessed correctly. His first port of call, the Wesleyan minister, was a member of the Fellowship of Reconciliation (formed by Christians in Cambridge at the start of the war to promote a lasting peace). He ran a social centre for war dissidents. Every day Emrys, the non-believer, mixed with his sympathetic parishioners and on Sundays felt obliged to attend his lengthy service. The old connection between religion and politics was still holding – even non-believers had to pay their respects.

When Emrys was at last taken back into custody he found himself in a crowded barracks housed in an old stable. So great were the numbers of resisters that now had to be accommodated, they were all in one room.

'You're a bloody conchy?' said one, as he answered the inevitable question. What came next was a dramatic indication of how much had changed since Emrys had marched through Shepton Mallet less than two years earlier, hissed by every passing soldier. These had had experience of the fighting, and the memory was unbearable. His questioner replied, 'Well, here's good luck to you, I wish to God I had had the sense that you've got.'[28]

He and all of these soldiers were awaiting trial for the single offence of 'deserting a draft on the way to France'. Every soldier present hated the military and talked all night of the ruses they and friends had worked to get out of serving. Many were from the Welsh valleys and a few Emrys knew by sight.

In short, at Redcar he found a completely demoralized army – entirely different in spirit from two years earlier. Later, even the farce of forcing Emrys to get into uniform and shoulder a rifle had degenerated into set ritual. He was handed the rifle and handed it back and was taken straight to the guard room. All the soldiers there were handcuffed, on their way back to the Front. A few days later a heavily escorted train came to take them to their ship. Their escort had fixed bayonets. 'They went sullenly, resentfully, reluctantly, and I watched them as, packs on backs, they marched away down the road. I wondered if they would ever come back.'

Emrys was re-sentenced to a civil prison at Northallerton, where he undertook a regime for his health and fitness, determined not to sink into despondency again. A local Quaker visited him regularly and pressed for better treatment. As a result, prisoners now had their cell doors left open during the day while they sewed their mailbags. Next door was an objector who had been a millworker and shared his socialist views. Together – in whispers, as they sewed – they discussed the new world that would be built.

★   ★   ★

In late February 1918 there was a conference of socialists in London, limited to those from Allied countries. No Russians were present, neither Mensheviks nor Bolsheviks, as all had been denied entry by the British government. What was to become the cold war many decades distant had already begun. From this time onwards conservatives in capitalist countries had only one enemy: Russian communism. Their response was automatic and unrehearsed – in corporation and newspaper boardroom, military or government corridor.

For liberals the problem was more complex. Although they did not support Bolshevism they were alarmed at the way it was portrayed. Sylvia printed not only articles supporting the workers' government but the thoughts of journalists such as Philips Price of the *Manchester Guardian* and Dr Hagberg Wright,[29] observers who believed the simplistic reaction was always dangerous. Wright, for example, had written criticizing Russia in the *Contemporary Review*. Nevertheless he denounced the popular press image of Bolsheviks as 'mere scum' and Trotsky and Lenin as 'mob leaders and hooligans', when 'they were serious, cultivated men' embarking 'on a reasoned experiment'.

The Labour Party did not have a single view on events in Russia. Some trade unionists opposed. Will Thorne and Ben Tillett were now populist nationalists, their faction denouncing foreigners and intellectuals, 'long-haired men and short-haired women';[30] others were cautious, most of the ILP enthusiastic. But it was not the ILP that was making the running any more; it was the Labour Party. In 1918 the Labour Party began a programme of reorganization, preparing to become a mass party – a process that continued until 1924. It bypassed ILP branches, then numbering 672,[31] to form entirely new local Labour Parties. Anyone joining these could have direct membership of the Labour Party, it was no longer necessary first to be a member of one of the federated bodies like the ILP or the TUC. The TUC, however, was not bypassed. Union funds were just as crucial in 1918 as in 1900; even more so was trade union agreement, as the war had incorporated the unions into the national structure. Government had depended upon them to keep production going and to decide which men fought and which stayed behind as 'essential';[32] now they would be needed to control the peacetime workforce in the same way. The new Labour Party gave them a majority voice in determining Labour policy. In February 1918 the Party Conference endorsed the new organization – in effect a victory for the TUC over the ILP.[33] In June Sidney Webb's *Labour and the New Social Order* was published, and the Fabians took up residence in the revamped Party's ideological heartland as the Labour leadership's natural choice for policy making.

The ILP was left to organize local enthusiasm, unaware that their vision of a transformed society was being replaced by a socialism that was symbolic rather than real, tailored to what Pelling called the 'undogmatic labourism'[34] of the unions and to MacDonald's flexible methods of power broking. As might be expected, it would develop a policy centred on parliamentary activity and government action: top-down nationalization of basic industries and financial reform from the Treasury, not locally managed change, as Hardie had once wanted to see. Agitation and education, which Hardie had believed the first line of political action, had much less priority. Local political interest was redirected to electoral activity. Most ILP members were not yet aware that the ILP had been outmanoeuvred, because most were delighted with the immediate prospects for peace, with the new Clause 4 that they believed would safeguard socialism, and by the prospect that for the first time it seemed remotely possible that Labour might triumph at Westminster.

In late 1918 the armistice was signed and the fighting ended. Immediately, there was another khaki general election – called by Lloyd George to capitalize on his popularity as a war leader. Earlier in the year the new Suffrage Act had been passed, finally permitting women to vote if they were over thirty and qualified under the law of property, or if they had university degrees. Sylvia found the Act a travesty of universal suffrage, and said that 'the mirage of a society regenerated by enfranchised women' was gone.[35] At the general election there were seventeen women candidates. One was Christabel, standing for the Women's Party, her own invention, with Emmeline as her campaign manager. Sylvia was asked to stand for Hallam in Sheffield by the Socialist Labour Party, and refused on the grounds that a new political system with continual voting was required to replace voting every few years to decide which members of the ruling class should 'represent' and repress the people in Parliament.[36]

The Labour Party fielded 388 candidates against the 78 when Hardie had won his last election in 1910. Glasier was sure it would do really well. On 11 December he called at Labour Party headquarters in London to compare notes with Jim Middleton, still the Party Secretary. 'He thinks we will win 130 seats. I think about 150'; that was not counting candidates like Cunninghame Graham who had decided to return to politics.[37] Cunninghame Graham believed that without Hardie the Labour Party had simply replicated the faults of the older parties, and even with Hardie had got totally 'tame' after 1906. He compromised by calling himself an 'Independent Liberal' while urging all voters to vote for Tom Johnson, his Labour opponent. The results were declared on 28 December. Glasier noted the outcome in his Diary with one word: 'calamity'. Not only had fewer than sixty Labour candidates won, but every leading figure, including MacDonald, Lansbury, Snowden and Henderson, had been defeated. So had Cunninghame Graham, and even Asquith.

It was calamity for the women as well. The only woman elected was Constance Gore Booth (who had become Countess Markievicz, having married a Polish exile), a campaigner for women's equality who had ironically been spared death due to the sexist laws of Ireland. Only men who had taken part in the Easter Rising – as she also had – were hanged. She had been imprisoned in 1916, when her sister, Eva, visited her to tell her that Connolly had been executed. Constance received the news with tears running down her face, and the words, 'Well, Ireland was free for a week.'[38] As a protest at the repression of Irish freedom, she refused to take her seat at Westminster. The new Parliament had no women Members.

Emmeline was devastated by Christabel's failure. Nan, Aggie and Lillie were devastated by the re-election of Charles Stanton from Merthyr, who had stood again as a 'Britisher' and gained a huge majority over the Labour candidate, the ILP member, the Reverend T. E. Nicholas. Nicholas was widely reckoned to have lost long before polling day, when, during a public meeting, a Britisher asked him, 'Would you shake hands with a German?' and he answered, 'Yes, why not?'[39] The ghost of Hardie's Aberdare meeting still lingered.

Although the war was well over, conscientious objectors like Emrys still had to serve on in prison. The military had plans to bring them to heel yet. Emrys had more or less stopped eating and was losing weight. The prison doctor put him on a 'hospital diet' and he was allowed milk and puddings. As he recovered, he began to organize conscientious objectors inside Northallerton jail. This culminated in a strike against the meaningless work they and all the other prisoners were given to do. Emrys was transferred to Wakefield jail, where he was told he could organize as he liked among the conscientious objectors provided they all agreed to a new 'scheme of work' the government had devised. They were told, accept this 'scheme' and within weeks they would be released from both prison and the army. Emrys realized the government was now blackmailing resisters by withholding release until they could be presented as having agreed, at last, to an 'alternative' which could be presented as accepting some form of military service. At a mass meeting in the prison, every resister present voted to refuse the new plan and serve on. Emrys's last words in his prison journal were that he would hold out to the end for unconditional release – no matter how long it took.[40]

In December 1918 a group of workers and returning soldiers in Berlin – organized by socialists who had opposed the war – supported a strike calling for workers' justice in post-war Germany. Rosa Luxemburg and Karl Liebknecht, its leaders, were hoping to reconstruct a new socialist party out of the old, which they believed had degenerated with incorporation as part of the government that pursued the Kaiser's war. This same government now called out the troops to break the strike and there was widespread resistance. Glasier noted the 'great fighting' in his Diary but was unable to come to terms with the now visible split among German socialists: 'utterly sick of all this socialist blood shedding . . . socialists have recourse to all the means of force and repression . . . we have denounced as . . . instruments of kingship and capitalism.'[41]

Glasier's stomach pains had returned and he had lost faith in Christian Science healing as well. In Britain prices had gone up steeply and there had been several strikes, which upset him. Earlier, as strikes continued in the war, he had written, 'Trade Unionism is as selfish as Capitalism'.[42] Even when Rosa Luxemburg and Karl Liebknecht, the two who had heroically stood out against the war, as Glasier himself had, were murdered by government troops, all Glasier could manage was, 'I never really liked Liebknecht'.[43]

Sylvia, by contrast, at once composed an elaborate poem to the dead pair,[44]

Oh Rosa in your winter you have passed . . .
Great Karl . . . heroic heart that vaulted onward.

Her first thought was to get to Germany and make contact with those who were carrying on the fight for revolutionary socialism. She was denied a passport. Instead of protesting, this time she disguised herself and slipped abroad without one. The journey first took her to Italy (possibly arranged by Silvio Corio, the Italian printer and journalist who was now in charge of the *Dreadnought*). From Italy Sylvia went across the Alps to Switzerland, a journey she made on foot, with a single local guide, to evade border checks, and finally – illegally – on foot into Germany. It was a formidable physical accomplishment.

She brought back a notebook containing a full account – as told by Clara Zetkin and her colleagues – of the oppositional socialists' movement in Germany during the war and just after.[45] Many who had joined it were women. These groups had formed a coalition at the Gotha Conference in 1917, and now concluded that the fighting in January 1919 (Sylvia described it as 'advanced socialists' against 'non-class-conscious workers')[46] had been premature. 'At best Berlin would struggle alone and be a new Paris commune.' They concluded a new approach was needed to ensure democratic workers' government would replace a bourgeois Parliament.[47] What was wanted was 'a working, not a parliamentary body', as Marx had characterized the system 'where executive and legislative functions were exercised together'.[48] During the visit Sylvia met several Russian Bolsheviks. She told them about her organization and publications, and when she returned home she was £500 the richer.[49]

Passports were freely available for all those who wanted to attend the Second International called in Berne in February 1919. It only barely struggled into being, and anxious though British Labour leaders had been to attend, even they had to concede it was a shadow, with half its possible members absent. Lansbury, who was there as an observer,[50] saw the main problem as a conflict between the right-wing German socialists and absent Bolsheviks. The dilemma for socialists was now acute. Their tradition had been for all socialists in one International. But the differences between the various parties within and between each country was so wide that a Third International was being set up, powered by the Russians, bidding for many of the same parties as the Second. Many rank and file socialists in Britain were anxious to join it. Others, including MacDonald, who aspired to government in Britain, had no intention of joining; instead he pinned his hopes on yet persuading the majority of socialist parties, particularly those in the European Vienna Union, to join in reviving the Second International. Lenin was scornful of events in Berne and called it 'the yellow international'.[51] On May Day 1919, the first meeting of the Third International, he said the Second was 'obsolete . . . because its objective was to educate the masses within the confines of bourgeois democracy [where] freedom was really freedom for the rich'.

Sylvia declared her own allegiance at once to the Third International and gave over her publication to anyone who wanted to discuss events in Russia, including G. D. H. Cole, Tom Mann and Harry Pollitt.[52] She hired a black American journalist, Claude McKay, recommended by Max Eastman (who called her that 'picturesque and passionate' political figure).[53] She even had a 'correspondent' sending her news from Moscow. Her socialism remained unimpressed by ideology or pragmatism; it just held to no participation in parliamentary activity, no link with the Labour Party. Sylvia was detached from political reality, not accountable to any electorate; in fact, not accountable to anyone other than the members of her small federation, who continued to support her because of her practical efforts on behalf of local people – and her capacity to attract funding.

By April 1919, Sylvia was helping in the organization of a general strike across Europe to prevent governments from intervening to put down the new Russian government. It was a development of Hardie's idea of an international general strike, but called itself a 'demonstration strike'. She was already distributing pamphlets sent from the USA in support of it,[54] designed to be given out to any troops asked to go to Russia:

> Why should we give our lives to fight working men like ourselves who have never done us or our country any harm and with whom we have no quarrel? . . .
> Refuse to go.
> If you do go, refuse to shoot.

British Security did not act against her but continued to keep her under surveillance.[55] It also had its eye on Lansbury, noting he was potentially more influential, but concluding that while he may have talked revolution, in practice he is 'afraid to descend from the fence' and opt for it.[56] Lansbury was busy running the still successful *Herald* which had survived the war very much intact.

In June, continental socialists, particularly those in Italy, still persevering with the idea of a 'demonstration strike', sent a delegation to a Labour Party Conference to get support for it. They were coldly received by Henderson, who said only that each country should do what it thought best. In the event the Italians struck alone and for some while workers were in charge of several towns in Italy, showing they were capable of running them. The action had its effect. Labour leaders in Britain took a firm line against trying to crush the Russian revolution by force, as many in Britain were already urging.

By this time Sylvia was denouncing the Versailles Treaty just signed (as well as the League of Nations which she regarded as a rich nations' club) and was writing in *Communist International*, the journal of the Third International, that 'we in this country are actually in the revolution', the problem was that 'the eyes of most of us are still shut to the fact'.[57] Lenin did not agree. The real revolution would be a long time coming, 'To abolish the distinction between manual and brain workers is a very long process.'[58]

Sylvia had no taste for anything that was 'a very long process'. In July she wrote to Lenin personally and asked him whether it was not best to 'concentrate your forces upon revolutionary action; and have nothing to do with the parliamentary machine'. Lenin's reply skipped the niceties: '. . . to renounce participation in the parliamentary elections is a mistake on the part of the revolutionary workers of Britain'.[59] This was not the reply she wanted. Yet there was a certain logic in Sylvia's question – that if Parliament was so useless, why should she take part in it? If it was already known that Snowden and Henderson would betray socialism (as Lenin was saying), why join the party they were leading? As she wrote, go straight for the revolution 'without stopping or turning'.[60]

In August 1919, Glasier began taking morphia for his pain, the first medical attention he had agreed to receive. Emrys was now back living in Abercynon, having finally been released from prison, his conscientious objector status fully recognized. He had never bowed to a war that by now almost everyone had turned against. He did not find it hard to get work, and was already teaching in a school in the Rhondda.

Hedley Dennis was also released. He did not go back to his family home in Devon but chose to live near Emrys and Aggie. He found a job as a chemist's assistant at Penrhiweiber. Fenner Brockway came back from imprisonment and took up residence in Hardie's old flat at Neville's Court. He also expected he would be able to take over the editorship of the *Labour Leader*, but Katharine Glasier saw no reason why she should step down. More to the point, Snowden, who oversaw the paper, was anxious to keep the *Leader* moderate and keep Brockway out. Brockway, puzzled and offended, said, 'I didn't know why I was being kept out'.[61] Katharine certainly did not become Snowden's lackey. She took a strong line on Russia and refused to print two of Snowden's anti-Bolshevik articles, explaining why to readers.[62]

But the rivalries between socialist groups, the ascendancy of the Labour Party and the imminence of a Communist Party, began to squeeze the ILP. Emile Burns, Secretary of the ILP's Information Bureau, wrote to tell Katharine he was leaving: 'I want to identify with that section of the socialist movement which definitely sides with Russia.'[63] By 1920 1,000 members had slipped away to follow him. Older members like Emmeline Pethick-Lawrence turned to the new Labour Party and anti-revolutionary centrism. Younger socialists wanted to turn the ILP in a revolutionary direction and John MacLean, a Scottish teacher, wrote in Aggie's autograph album in 1919: 'We shall this year kill capitalism!'[64] Trade unionists continued to divide between those who opposed socialism and those who supported it, while social-ists divided between those who opposed Russia (like Hyndman who called it a 'pseudo-marxist tsardom')[65] and those, like Lansbury, who supported it. Lansbury was particularly taken with workers' councils, which he saw as complementary to bourgeois democracy, as 'alternative loci [sic] of power in a parliamentary system'.[66] Like Hardie he was something of an old William Morris communist, who believed, like Morris, that socialism should be run by a 'unit of administration small enough for every citizen to feel himself responsible for its details'.[67]

At the end of 1919 Lansbury went to Russia himself, which he found 'hemmed in . . . by foes without and foes within', blockaded by the USA, UK and France, and harassed at home by anarchists.[68] Lansbury thought the Russian councils very like the LCC 'except that they dealt with everything, which we left most essentials to private enterprise', a difference upon which he did not comment further.[69] Although he noted that Lenin made no apologies for curtailing free speech in order to establish the new state, he said meeting him was 'simply the great event of my life'.[70]

In London Labour did well in the local elections, and Lansbury was elected leader in Poplar, which he tried to run more effectively in terms of providing for local needs. For this he needed money from the richer areas of London. When this was denied, he decided to refuse his rates precepts to the London County Council until there was equalization of funding between the poorer and richer boroughs. He was promptly imprisoned for contempt, but since he had already informed every

householder in Poplar what he was doing and why, he got massive
support. A crowd gathered outside the jail and sang the 'Red Flag'.
Inside Lansbury demanded his own release.[71] Herbert Morrison came
in to mediate but Lansbury rejected Morrison's compromise solution
to leave it to government.[72] In October 1919 the government gave
way and opened a fund into which all boroughs paid for London-wide
relief. He had won a significant victory.

In 1919, May Hardie came back to Scotland without her husband,
Jamie, the first time she had visited her family since she and Hardie
had sailed to America in 1912. In Cumnock the war had widened the
gap between May's family, the Stoddarts, and Lillie, Nan and Duncan,
but it was not so wide that it prevented May from visiting Lochnorris
to introduce Lillie to her only grandchild, two-year-old Jean.

In Britain, 1920 was a year of decision for the Left. Some wanted
to join the Labour Party, some did not. Others wanted to set up a
Communist Party that would affiliate to the Labour Party; others to
set up a Communist Party that would be independent, still others to
stick with one or other of the smaller socialist parties already formed.[73]
Even if some decided to form a separate Communist Party, would it
participate in elections or not? All the old questions that the 1880s
had thrown up were still there.

In theory the Labour Party's declaration in 1918 that it was a socialist
party should have solved the problem. There was no reason why any
of the proliferating socialist parties and groups should not have come
under the umbrella. But events in Russia had made this difficult, for
they had raised the possibility of another form of socialist government
and another kind of socialist party. Negotiations had begun in May 1919
about a 'united convention' for socialists outside the Labour Party but
it was deferred until those interested had attended the Second Congress
of the Third International held in Moscow in July 1920. Minimal
agreement seemed possible on the workers' council system and for
the Third International (rather than the Two-and-a-half International,
as the new Second International came to be called).

Right up to the end of May 1920 Glasier worked on the two books
he was still writing. One was on William Morris and the other was
The Meaning of Socialism. When he had completed them, he died.
The *Manchester Guardian* summed him up as a friend of Hardie's –
neither politician nor writer, but 'evangelist'.[74] The word seemed
very odd in the new disciplined political era of parties, programmes,
and ideological demarcation disputes; his socialism – as a set of moral
imperatives – even odder.

In the middle of June Sylvia suddenly jumped the gun and decided
she would single-handedly found the Communist Party in Britain.

She renamed her own East End organization The Communist Party
– British Section of the Third International (CPBSTI). Lenin wired
the British Socialist Party (much more in line with communists of the
Russian Revolution) that 'the tactics of comrade Sylvia Pankhurst of
the WSF are wrong'.[75] Sylvia sent word to Lenin that she was coming
to Moscow to debate with him during the International. Meanwhile
she prepared her group for the coming crisis by setting up a 'Dances
and Social Committee' and ordering all 'branches' to buy a typewriter.
To raise funds she held a social at the Old Ford Road headquarters
and a 'Garden Party' in Woodford, Essex, where she now lived.[76]

When the British government refused her a passport for Moscow,
she slipped out of the country through Harwich, where communist
crewmen on a Norwegian freighter took her aboard as a stowaway.
She was passed from ship to ship, including small fishing vessels which
ran aground twice, before landing in Murmansk.[77] When she finally
reached Moscow, Lenin had already handed out his pamphlet, *Left
Wing Communism; an Infantile Disorder*,[78] designed to discourage the
Spartacists in Germany and Sylvia's band in the UK. In it Willie
Gallacher, the Scottish shop steward, who had travelled part of the
way to Moscow with her, was criticized for supporting her.

Lenin urged British socialists to unite 'their four parties . . . into a
single Communist Party on the basis of the principles of the Third
International and of obligatory participation in Parliament'.[79] He also
sanctioned participation in the Labour Party, as it had the support of
the majority of workers. Change could take time, but 'a revolution
is impossible without a change in the views of the majority of the
working class'. He wrote pointedly, with Sylvia in mind, that 'change
[is] brought about by . . . political experience . . . never by propaganda
alone'.[80] Sylvia argued in the open (7th) session of the Congress that she
was indeed basing her tactics on her own experience. The suffragette
movement had taught her 'how important it is to be extreme'.[81]

Even when they met, Lenin was unable to cajole her to go
along with plans for a single communist party in Britain. Nevertheless, he arranged for her to visit factories and women's centres,
where she was eager to join in discussions. Alexandra Kollentai,
who saw the revolution as 'the destroyer of dominant values . . .
the herald of new values' (and who became Commissar for Public Welfare until Lenin dismissed her), recalled this period as 'rich
in magnificent illusions . . . ardent initiatives to . . . organise the
world anew'.[82] She was one of several women who argued for
the complete liberation of the working woman and the 'creation
of a new sexual morality'. Lenin did not approve. He told Clara
Zetkin later that year, 'I couldn't believe it . . . we are struggling
against counter-revolution all over the world . . . and meanwhile
our women are talking about sexuality and marital issues.'[83] These

discussions probably influenced Sylvia far more than those on the floor of the Congress.[84]

Back in Britain the other Communist Party was duly born on the last weekend in July 1920, exactly seven years on from the outbreak of the war.[85] The largest group came from the British Socialist Party but there were several branches from the Herald League and from the ILP,[86] as well as the City of London Labour Party. Proceedings began with a minute's silence in honour of Jean Jaurès's assassination. The chair, Arthur McManus, a Clyde shop steward, warned against those calling themselves communists who were not there – a clear reference to Sylvia. He hoped there was no one present who, 'when there was a question of a thing being done, if the process . . . was likely to soil the coat or skirt' of the doer, would cite 'the non-conformist conscience' as the reason why it had to be dropped.[87] If this was also a reference to Sylvia, who boycotted the proceedings, it was wide of the mark. She had no non-conformist conscience; she was just unable to work with anyone else. As Claude McKay observed, she was a 'one woman show'.[88] Shaw called her someone everyone made 'a spoiled child of',[89] including Keir Hardie. Although Sylvia talked perpetually of revolution, Lenin spotted that she did not have 'the serious tactics of a revolutionary class'.[90] She lacked discipline: personal, organizational, intellectual. Lillian Hellman wrote many years later, 'rebels seldom make good revolutionaries'.[91] Sylvia was a rebel, and one working overtime at that. Shaw, looking on at the time, wrote to her to recommend a period of 'total abstinence from *Weltverbesserungswahn*' – single-handed solving of the world's ills.[92]

In August 1920, when it looked as though the British government was about to attack the workers' government in Russia, the revived Labour Party Rose to the occasion. Henderson sent telegrams to all the new Labour parties and Trades Councils urging them to hold demonstrations on Sunday 8 August to protest at any war with Russia. On no other occasion would any Labour Party leader ever act this way again – the tactic that China's later leader, Mao, called 'bombard the headquarters'. Labour also called a national conference to confirm its stand, which a contemporary account said was 'the most harmonious' conference Labour ever held.[93]

The Hughes family stood by the Labour Party and the ILP. Emrys became chairman of the Welsh ILP and Aggie was on the local ILP Committee in Cardiff.[94] In both 1919 and 1920 – around ILP Conference time – her autograph album was crowded with signatures; and on 25 June 1920, Britain's first Communist MP, the Battersea GP born in India, Shapurji Saklatvala, wrote, 'Let us get on with true pure socialism and stop talking of consequences'. Emrys stopped teaching altogether in 1920. Even if he had not wanted to take up political work, he had come to hate the strict disciplinarian attitudes teachers were forced to display at that time and which the ILP soon turned against, calling the 'education of the masses a drudgery to both pupil and teacher', designed for 'a man to be kept subordinate'. The working class 'do not want ladders ... and patronage' but 'culture, independence, and power'; not to know things but 'to know how to think of things', because 'it is much easier to mislead people who read but cannot think than people who think but cannot read'.[95] Rowlie, the older Hughes son, who had wanted to be a teacher, correctly guessed he had contracted tuberculosis, and died within a year of the war's end.[96] Aggie lived on at the house in Mountain Ash Road and looked after her father and Emrys. She continued to see Hedley Dennis and began to tutor him. He had decided he wanted to become a chemist.[97]

Lillie and Nan, despite their plans, never made the move out of Lochnorris and back to Glasgow to be with Duncan. Duncan in his own way was as frightened of life – and society's hostility – as Nan, and sought the same sort of sanctuary. He continued to stay often at Lochnorris. He continued to be frequently ill; he spent his holidays golfing and fishing in Scotland, from where he occasionally sent postcards to May and Jamie Hardie in America.[98] After the war, he got engaged. He and his fiancée are photographed formally but separately in two oval portraits mounted within the same frame that survive in the Cumnock library. For a while it looked as though it might be a happy ending for the young man who had written a poetic fragment in Aggie's album in 1913:

naebody cares for me/ I care for naebody.

But it was not to be. During the summer of 1920 there was a fire at the engineering section of the Glasgow Corporation, where Duncan had worked since he was sixteen. He was hideously burned. Brought back to Lochnorris, Lillie and Nan tended him, but the burns were too extensive for him to survive. He had escaped death in the trenches only to find it at the workplace where he had dutifully remained to fulfil his father's commitment to conscientious objection.

By the end of 1920 Sylvia had managed to alienate all political factions and parties on the Left. By refusing to share power, or take responsibility, she ruled herself out of the very arena in which she wanted to work. But she had instinctively spotted the flaws of both the communist and labourist roads and held out for something better – what Gwyn Williams later called 'a lost tradition of European Communism'.[99]

Many of those on this third road had been women: Eleanor Marx, Rosa Luxemburg and even then, Clara Zetkin and Alexandra Kollentai Kollentai had posed the problem in 1921 as a choice between a 'bureaucratic state system or the wide practical self-activity of the working masses'.[100] Luxemburg's criticism of the two paths into which socialism had now split (and support for a third it might yet choose) had been written even earlier, in 1904, in a pamphlet later reproduced by the ILP.[101] On the one side there was Western European parliamentarianism, 'opportunistic' and a refuge for 'ambitious . . . political upstarts'. On the other, Lenin's disturbing 'ultra-centralism', where 'his thought is patterned upon the control of party activity and not upon its promotion, upon narrowing not unfolding, upon hemming in and not the drawing together of the movement'.

If there was a third way, Sylvia gave up looking for it and turned her attention back to the problems of the East End. Towards the end of 1920 she became worried by disorder in the docks, particularly attacks on the non-white community there. Her *Dreadnought* printed a piece from a young British sailor, serving on a warship, calling 'Parliament . . . an institution of the capitalist state for doping the workers' and urging an uprising as the way to deal with the problems that were being blamed on race. As the writer showed considerable knowledge of naval matters, Sylvia's office was raided. But just as police were coming up the stairs, Sylvia flushed the identifying letter down the toilet. Refusing to name him, she was arrested for sedition.[102] The *Daily Sketch* commented that in the old days she had a 'misleadingly weak face . . . pretty in the pussycat manner' but today she was a 'dangerous character'.[103]

Sylvia did not accept the verdict brought against her and appealed to the Recorder and Aldermen of the City of London. Her appeal was heard in the Guildhall in January 1921.[104] She defended herself and spoke of the growing racism in the East End, whipped up by the press in the 'connection of white women with yellow men'. Racism could only be cured by uniting people on the basis of their economic interest. She told the court that her father had brought her up as a socialist and a communist and she then began to read from one of the books he had read to her. When she was stopped on the grounds that the material was seditious, she told them it was *News from Nowhere* by William Morris. She next tried reading Marx and was stopped, whereupon she said, 'You cannot stamp out views of this kind by sending me to prison.' When the hearing was at an end, she declared, 'It is wrong that people like you should be comfortable and well fed while around you . . . people are starving.' The courtroom applauded loudly. But for her truculence, her sentence would probably have been light. Having spoken as she did, she got six months – in the lowest division. Back she went to the thieves and prostitutes. Shaw sent a telegram: 'I am furious with you for getting into prison quite unnecessarily.'[105]

While she was in jail her Workers' Federation disintegrated. The only ones who stood by her were Norah Smyth and Silvio Corio, the Italian anarchist writer. Sylvia had never learned the discipline of collectivity. She was happier – a bit like Hardie – in a Party of One.

Lansbury, like many another colleague of Hardie's, was unhappy to discover that the emergence of two disciplined and competing socialist groups – each beset by rules, ideological tests and conflicting international allegiances, meant he could not go to canvass in a by-election for an old friend of his, who happened to have joined the Communist Party, while he himself had remained in the Labour Party. In the old days Keir Hardie had come to speak for him when he was in the SDF and Hardie was in the ILP, and no one thought this was an issue so great that all else had to bow before it. Now they did, and unity was forbidden on both sides.[106] As socialism got stronger, and drew ever more adherents, inevitably different interpretations competed ever more seriously. Battles between socialists were going to be just as telling as the battle between socialism and capitalism – if not more so.

17

LABOUR'S RISE AND FALL

In 1921 George Lansbury concluded that despite the war, society had not really changed. The wartime spectacle of the aristocracy opening up their houses to the wounded workers and the rich washing up for the poor had vanished. The old class divisions snapped back into place. Unemployment rose. The miners lost a particularly long strike culminating on 15 April, known as 'Black Friday', when it was clear the railway workers and dockers were not going to lend their support as had been agreed under the Triple Alliance. The plans for 'one big union' fell to the ground. The dreary round of recession and recovery and recession returned.

Tom Mann, still travelling the world preaching direct action, visited Russia and praised the workings of the workers' councils, so superior to 'a centralized government bureaucracy giving instructions and commands'.[1] Hyndman continued to preach that the end of capitalism was nigh until he died in November 1921, and was buried in a coffin draped in the Red Flag. Tom Johnston, a Scottish member of the ILP, was brought in to take over the editorship of the *Labour Leader*. Katharine Glasier was dismissed as quickly as she had been called in. The shock of losing her work – and losing Bruce the year before – caught up with her. She suffered a nervous breakdown. Her depression was severe but short-lived, recovery brought about by her decision to return once more to evangelizing. Speaking on the same platforms she had toured forty years earlier, she found she still retained her capacity to raise the eyes of an audience. One of the many who heard her and was brought to socialism as a result was a young Ellen Wilkinson. She had tried ILP meetings earlier but found them just 'old men talking'.[2] With Katharine there was that vision which Keir Hardie had claimed was the first essential of successful political work. Wilkinson joined the ILP. She had started life as a teacher but (like Emrys Hughes) had found the constant canings and the heavy hand on innovative work hateful. She decided to go into politics.

Emrys hated teaching for just the same reasons and decided to try political journalism; he started to send pieces to the *Manchester Guardian*.[3] Another Scottish journalist, William Stewart, who had worked on the *Labour Leader* with Hardie, had been given the task of writing Hardie's official biography, and published it in 1921. Frank Smith thought it was 'a mistake to combine the history of the movement' with the history of Hardie.[4] But Nan and Lillie liked the account, including an introduction which MacDonald later added. One of MacDonald's sentences, however, seemed rather superfluous to those who knew Hardie, 'The drawing rooms of the rich never allured him into a sycophantic servitude.'[5]

This was MacDonald writing about his own weakness rather than Hardie's strength, for by this time MacDonald was already seeking solace with the socially prominent as well as working his way back into the heart of the Labour Party and perfecting his 'ambiguous' diplomacy. In particular, he was trying to drive a wedge between the ILP and the Third International by continuous efforts to revive the Second.[6] He was also preparing for a revived Labour Party at home.[7] He did not have long to wait. In 1922 the Conservatives at last pulled out of the wartime coalition government and a general election was held. MacDonald won his way back to Parliament; and despite a Conservative government, the real electoral triumph was Labour's. It won 142 seats. Even more gratifying to Hardie would have been the knowledge that the two sets of Liberals between them only had 117.[8]

The pro-war and anti-war split inside Labour was also healing; it was time to bury the war. This was reflected in the overturning of Britisher candidate Stanton's 18,000 majority in Merthyr by a Labour miner, George Hall, with a 5,000 majority. Nan's wish had finally come true: Stanton had been sent off the field. As a bonus, even their firebrand friend James Maxton was elected – and Lansbury too eventually got back. But the most exciting outcome for the Hardies was that George, Hardie's favourite brother, had won the Springburn division of Glasgow.

MacDonald was elected leader of the Party and the ILP got a new leader, Clifford Allen, the London intellectual who had served three years in jail for conscientious objection. He chaired the meeting in St Andrew's Hall called to commemorate the eighth anniversary of Hardie's death – a large event, accompanied by massed socialist choirs.[9] Anniversary meetings for Hardie were still taking place regularly in the ILP, where Hardie was still revered – though Labour Party members had to defend his memory against charges that his tradition was injurious to the new-look Labour Party.[10] Allen, perhaps conscious of this, was anxious to move the ILP forward. He wanted it to become a policy-making body. He set up a new headquarters in London and relaunched the *Leader* as the *New Leader* in 1922 under H. N. Brailsford. He urged a new alliance between the ILP and the Labour Party at the top – to compensate for the ILP's loss of power at the grassroots after the reorganization of the Labour Party.

Lillie and Nan kept up with all the changes, and with Emrys. On May Day in 1923 Lillie wrote Emrys to compliment him on his report of the ILP Conference written for the *New Leader*.[11] She had also liked David Lowe's article in the same issue, but thought it a pity that Snowden had dropped out of the ILP. She ventured her view that it was because 'he will never forgive the ILP for criticising his wife's doings'. Renewed criticism of Ethel Snowden's circulation in fashionable circles – a failing Glasier pointed out in 1910 – had coincided with her husband's sharp rightward turn and both were being criticized publicly in the ILP.

In government circles the old argument of free trade and protection was back again too, absorbing all interest. In December 1923 Baldwin called an election to test government protection policy. Emrys decided to stand and was adopted at Bosworth in Leicestershire. He lost; but Labour won even more seats than the year before and now had 191. The Conservatives had lost their majority with only 259 seats, while the Liberals had 159. Labour was asked to form a government. Only eight years after Hardie's death what Hardie had never dared to hope for became possible but in circumstances he had always dreaded, dependence on Liberals. The dependency did not unduly disturb MacDonald, who nevertheless found it hard to believe he was to live at No. 10 Downing Street, 'I laugh at myself as panjandrum & wonder if it is a stage play'.[12] His daughter, Ishbel, acted as his hostess. He noted that 'the little maid is sedate as a judge and reminds me every day of her mother'.[13]

MacDonald went into office at the height of his popularity with the Party and with the ILP. He was one of the regular contributors to *Forward*, and if anything, more popular in Scotland than in England. But, as always, he was dealing from a second pack, and soon became more influenced by liberals like Norman Angell. Angell was in touch continually with Arnold Rowntree about making a Liberal-Labour government 'one of the possibilities of the next Parliament'.[14] Angell's immediate advice to MacDonald on Labour was to 'hold . . . [its] social programme in abeyance and concentrate on . . . Liberal foreign policy'.[15] This is more or less what MacDonald did. MacDonald took over foreign policy himself and adroitly settled several old arguments hanging over from the war – but in the process cutting ties with the old pacifism and internationalism of the ILP.[16] Behind the scenes Angell made sure he continued this way by privately writing the speeches of those who were criticizing MacDonald.[17]

There was no great outcry from the bulk of the Labour Party when the government began, even when MacDonald failed to include Lansbury in his Cabinet. As the year wore on, however, the ILP's old suspicions of the Liberal Party, and its capacity to deflect Labour, were renewed. Internationally, the ILP also grew suspicious of the League of Nations as an alliance of capitalist states.[18] Lansbury continued to assert that a Labour government 'must mean diverting wealth from the wealthy . . . to the poor' and those who pretend that Labour can operate 'without making the rich poorer should find another Party'.[19] Socialists took heart in the only area of government policy that seemed remotely progressive, the housing programme under the ILP's energetic John Wheatley. The surcharges that had been levied on Poplar – and Lansbury – were lifted.[20] Several new 'garden cities' were begun. Good housing became a legitimate demand of working people – as Hardie had always insisted it should be.

During April Aggie got 'Robert Smillie and his lass Anne'[21] to write in her album at the ILP Conference. Katharine was also there, and spoke passionately for more social improvements. One of the delegates who heard her was Oswald Mosley, who was so impressed by her oratory he insisted on meeting her.[22]

Lillie followed all these events with interest, but she did not leave Lochnorris. Nan, whose work in the world was to care for Lillie, stayed close by her side. Mother and daughter were pictured during this time in their garden under the trees, Lillie presiding at the tea table, Nan in the hammock reading. Over the scene hovered, 'I never leave Mother', the words Nan had written so many times to Aggie. Occasionally Nan and Lillie would visit the Bensons at

Disley, the only ILP members who kept up with them.[23] Lillie was still trying to sell Lochnorris, but, she told Emrys, 'so far without success'.[24] It was always an unrealistic option, for Lillie's health had continued to deteriorate. She spent more and more time in nursing homes, finding it very tiresome 'to be so much in the Doctor's hands'.

But Lillie had good news too. May Hardie wrote from the USA to say she was bringing Jean, now eight years old, for another visit. As Jean later wrote about her mother, 'May was ambivalent about the USA . . . when she was here Scotland was wonderful and when she was in Scotland America was the place to be.'[25] In 1924 the place to be was going to be Cumnock.

Even more gratifying was the news that Emrys Hughes was given a job on *Forward*, the successful socialist journal published from Civic Street in Glasgow. He left Wales and came to live in Scotland and began working closely with Hardie's brothers, David and George, who helped on *Forward* as they had once helped on the *Labour Leader*. Lillie had never lost her commitment to the motherless Emrys (now more intense since Duncan's death and her complete estrangement from Jamie). He began visiting Lochnorris. Nan found he was no longer the younger brother of her friend, Aggie, but a political journalist out in the world. She saw him completely anew. Emrys discovered Nan was no longer merely Hardie's daughter but a woman in her own right. Their perception of each other began to shift rapidly; and no doubt Lillie's hopes rose.

In July of 1924 the Scottish Council of the ILP held a conference at Cumnock, and the *New Leader* covered a visit by James Maxton and Bob Smillie to Lillie at Lochnorris to present her with a token of the ILP's esteem. The reporter spoke of Lillie 'frail and worn, her hair white, a shining contrast with her black dress', and Nan beside her, a woman in whose 'bearing so much of Hardie's uprightness is suggested'.[26] The taking of tea was set out in detail, Lillie pouring with the greatest of difficulty and handing round the cups with the 'exquisite courtesy' of one who counted good housekeeping her greatest merit. A short word of tribute was paid to her and Nan responded: 'We have a Labour government but my father's work is not done. It will not be done so long as a child is born in hunger'. According to the reporter, Bob Smillie was 'openly wiping tears from his eyes', as dignified, containing her misery to the end, Lillie reaffirmed her faith in Hardie's cause and became a heroine at this last hour, when bad health – and long addiction – had brought her to nothing. Possibly it was her rapidly deteriorating condition that made Nan and Emrys bring forward their marriage to make sure she saw it. It took place on 8 August 1924.[27] Emrys was just thirty and Nan nearly forty. Shortly after it, May and little Jean arrived in Scotland. But Lillie never saw her granddaughter again. Lillie died the day they arrived in Cumnock.

In October another general election was forced on Labour by the loss of Liberal support. The ostensible reason was whether or not the government should have prosecuted a newspaper editor, who was also a Communist. Behind this was Liberal and Tory hostility to socialism and the determination to tar the increasingly moderate MacDonald with the Bolshevik brush. The security forces worked overtime to plant forged evidence in the form of a false letter from the Russian Bolshevik, Zinoviev, suggesting it was Russia who was giving orders behind the scenes to Labour in Britain, when in practice it had really been men like Norman Angell. Huge Labour demonstrations congregated in the streets in favour of the editor and Labour's vote rose at the election. Unfortunately, the Tories' vote did too. By the end of November Baldwin was back.

May and Jean Hardie returned to the USA, determined to come back again. There was never any question of Jamie coming with them. He and Lillie had remained estranged to the end. As Jean wrote later, 'He lost all interest in the family and I am sure the feeling was reciprocated.'[28] The mutual wall of disowning was worse after 1924. 'When he was left out of his father's will and subsequently his mother's, he became very bitter . . . being the oldest son did not help any.' In her will Lillie had forgotten her granddaughter as well as her son. She left everything to Nan. This included Lochnorris, into which Emrys Hughes now moved.

In Abercynon Aggie kept up her tutoring of children for 'the scholarship' and of Hedley Dennis for his chemist's course. Hedley was no longer the young boy he had been when Aggie had first met him. He was a serious young man who depended on Aggie for support and she in turn came to depend on him. They decided on marriage, perhaps spurred by the example of Nan and Emrys, who had not let the barrier of age deter them. With Hedley and Aggie the difference was even greater: Hedley was twenty-eight and Aggie forty-one. When Hedley told his family of his plans, they refused to accept Aggie; his mother in particular thought the age gap obscene. He was forced to choose between Aggie and his family, and he chose Aggie. They were married in 1925 and he moved into the house on Mountain Ash Road with her and the Revd John Hughes. Hedley Dennis's mother broke off all communication with her son and they never spoke again in her lifetime.[29]

During 1924 Sylvia finally realized the extent of her own political isolation. She stopped publishing the Dreadnought, abandoned the

East End and moved permanently to Woodford Wells in Essex, where she called her house 'Red Cottage'. Silvio Corio moved in with her. In Italy he had for a brief while been a printer, then a correspondent for *Avanti*, but he did not like being pinned down, and moved about Europe, moody and mercurial, keeping aloof from organized politics. He had come to Britain originally as a supporter of the exiled Italian anarchist, Enrico Malatesta, whom Sylvia's parents had also supported.

Corio was a man of wide cultural curiosity who had briefly converted into (and out of) Islam after he had come to London.[30] He had lived with several women, Italian and English, and already had several children. He did not believe in marriage and neither did Sylvia. She was not even sure she believed in sex, calling it 'one of the great mysteries; there is nothing in it and there is all in it'.[31] When Corio moved in he was bald and short and aged fifty-one. Sylvia was forty-four and soon to chop her hair off at the ears in advanced 1920s fashion. They got on well. He undertook home improvements and helped in her publications, while she tried to earn money by writing articles.

Through Corio Sylvia took an interest in the problems of anarchists in Russia, which further tempered her love affair with Bolshevism. One group of 'socialists and anarchists', as they styled themselves, who had staged a protest at the end of 1923 against the government and had been removed by the GPU to a concentration camp in Solovietz, wrote asking for her help.[32] She did all she could, but the British government was hardly likely to sympathize with socialists imprisoned by socialists.

In 1926 Lansbury went to Russia again, where he found out that before Lenin had died, he had paid back the money that Joseph Fels had lent him in 1907[33] Now Stalin and Trotsky were feuding. Lansbury was sure this would never have happened had Lenin lived on. In 1926 the Labour Party was also feuding. It had had time to think about its first spell of government and concluded it had missed many opportunities. The ILP in particular believed the Party needed some iron in its soul. James Maxton was voted into the leadership and Clifford Allen's new-look ILP, a shadow Fabian Society, slipped into history, though ILP members continued to write policy papers. One pamphlet said, 'in the midst of capitalism we are in socialism',[34] the view that Hardie had taken: socialism will win its way into our lives almost without our knowing it.

Nevertheless, progress in raising working-class living standards seemed very slow. Lansbury kept up his campaign for fundamental but peaceful change, and backed the one great weapon of the working class, 'the power of standing still and doing nothing'.[35] In 1926 there was widespread support from all sections of the Left for the miners who had decided to strike, and for other workers backing them in a General Strike. During the strike two ILP members, Maxton and Arthur Cook, now general secretary of the Miners, published a joint manifesto denouncing all form of class collaboration. The establishment threw everything into defeating the workers. In the House of Commons George Hardie said it was evident that the government 'were going to risk smashing British industry and commerce in an effort to smash the Miners' Federation'.[36] The strike was lost. The Labour Party and trade unions turned to the right, but the ILP did not. It consolidated the work of its 'commissions' covering all areas of policy, which advocated public ownership of land, banks, electricity and transport, a minimum wage for all industries, family allowances, and enormous expansion of education. Later George Hardie published a short pamphlet on energy,[37] urging the same community control of the mining industry Hardie had urged thirty years earlier. MacDonald ignored this work and some in the ILP concluded that MacDonald was more anxious to defeat the Left than to transform society. MacDonald stopped coming to ILP conferences. The ILP continued to canvass at Labour Party conferences for 'socialism in our time'. Labour conferences, now dominated by the unions, defeated the ILP line year after year.[38]

These internal arguments were distressing for old ILP members like Katharine Glasier, Emrys and Nan Hughes, and Aggie and Hedley Dennis. Given their commitment to MacDonald as a colleague who had stood by Hardie for peace, and Clifford Allen likewise, they were very reluctant to turn on either without good reason. As if to underline their continuing commitment, on 17 December 1927 Aggie got MacDonald to sign her autograph album. She and Hedley Dennis had just returned from a visit to Nan and Emrys. They found that Lochnorris had modernized itself, one of the first houses in Cumnock to have a modern bathroom, and now a telephone. A photograph of Agnes and Hedley was taken there, flanking their dog, Turk, who was treated very much as their child. Aggie still wore the gymslip dresses of a young girl. Nan was busily engaged in writing a book on her father and asked the ILP for all his papers to be returned.[39] She also wrote to George Bernard Shaw for permission to quote from his articles and letters.[40] Shaw agreed, writing respectfully back to her as Mrs Hardie Hughes (a name no one else ever used). She and Emrys went on country holidays 'to do a bit of tramping',[41] taking part in the passion the Left developed for hiking and rambling. Emrys attended ILP conferences regularly and Nan went with him, once insisting on going as a delegate simply to obtain the pooled fare;[42] money still obsessed her. Money had also soured Lillie's last days. She had felt 'insulted' that the ILP had only sent £5 to Nan as a wedding gift, and Nan had sent the money back.[43] Yet until the end of her life the ILP continued to pay Nan a quarterly income under the old agreement Glasier had negotiated.

Sylvia left no one in any doubt what her new cause was to be. In 1927 she told her friends she was pregnant. Silvio's role as future father was not acknowledged and even when pressed she would not name him. This was her baby, not theirs. Emmeline Pethick-Lawrence paid for her to go to a nursing home when labour began in December. Because of her age she expected a difficult birth; and had one. The baby, a boy, she called Richard Keir Pethick Pankhurst. Although later she wrote that she suffered from the incursion of the press over the birth, it was she who chose to contact the *News of the World* in April 1928 to give an interview about her 'eugenic baby',[44] claiming that 'my union . . . is entirely free' and that it was 'the tendency of the future', predicting (quite correctly once again) that 'posterity . . . will see nothing remarkable in our decision' to live together and have children without marriage and without the woman losing her own name.[45] Not unexpectedly, the paper turned her social experiment into 'Sylvia Pankhurst's Amazing Confession'.

Emmeline Pankhurst was living in London, preparing to stand as a Conservative at Whitechapel in the next general election.[46] The news of Sylvia's baby – and the publicity it received – was said to have shocked her mortally. Sylvia became 'that scarlet woman', according to one of Emmeline's adopted daughters.[47] When Sylvia called at her house with baby Richard, Emmeline refused to see either of them. Christabel pleaded with Sylvia to let baby Richard's father be named,[48] but Sylvia stuck to her convictions. When Emmeline died on 14 June, the last time the sisters met was at their mother's funeral.

Ill-will against Sylvia from many former suffragettes continued for years, some believing it was her behaviour that had caused her mother's death. A few months after Emmeline's death, a universal suffrage Act passed all its readings and became law. Sylvia hardly noticed. She had just joined Fenner Brockway's League Against Imperialism;[49] and had begun campaigning on maternal health,[50] producing pamphlets demanding welfare centres, maternity grants, action to combat puerperal fever for mothers and action to combat measles, whooping cough and diphtheria for babies.

During this same year, 1928, Katharine Glasier was sixty-one. Her oldest son Malcolm now worked for a shipping company in Liverpool; Jeannie had married and gone to Australia. Glen, the youngest, was on a scholarship in his last term at a Quaker boarding school in Saffron Walden, the family prodigy, having already received offers of further scholarships to Balliol College in Oxford and Trinity College in Cambridge. He was even good at games. While playing a routine match on the school playing field, a single ball struck him directly on the heart and killed him instantly. Katharine coped with the tragedy quite differently from Lillie, who had shut Duncan's death in. She shared her grief and accepted support; she retained her optimism and kept busy in the world, campaigning for that new society she still believed possible. She kept on selling Bruce's pamphlets.

In Hartford, Connecticut, young Jean Hardie, now aged twelve, was also athletic and growing up quickly. In 1929 May Hardie decided she would go back to work as a nurse at Hartford City Hospital and that Hardie's only grandchild would go back to Scotland to be educated. She was sent to live in Cumnock with her Stoddart aunts and attended Cumnock Academy, where, during one hockey game she was hit by another player's stick and had to retire. The local paper had a small item about her injury, which was read by Keir Hardie, her father's first cousin, George's son, later a physical education instructor at Troon Academy.[51] Through him Jean established a connection with the wider Hardie family.

Such a connection was difficult to establish otherwise. Jean did not remember her grandmother, Lillie, but was sure she 'felt lonely at times having my grandfather away so much defending other people's causes while she was at home coping with three children and the household'.[52] She recalled the information that had persisted locally that 'when he was battle worn he always came home to the nest and I am sure she was there to comfort him'. But the Stoddarts were not close to the Hardies, 'My maternal aunt had great respect for Keir Hardie the man but not for his politics.' In Cumnock, therefore, her relationship with Emrys and Nan was formal and limited to the 'duty call' she paid to them 'every second Sunday'.[53] A duty too was Jean's weekly visit to the Presbyterian church 'more or less under duress', and to the Band of Hope.

In 1928 Lansbury published his autobiography, *My Life*. He paid tribute to Hardie and Glasier, William Morris and Margaret MacMillan, 'men and women [who] had no intention of creating a party organ- isation controlled from the top, but were true democrats'. Lansbury hated the tight new authoritarian Labour Party that was 'steam rolling' individual opinion.[54] It was his way of expressing his disappointment that MacDonald had left him out of his Cabinet in 1924. He contrasted Hardie's attitude to Parliament with theirs: they were only interested in occupying ministerial office, while Hardie had wanted to capture Parliament 'not to perpetuate it . . . [but] solely . . . for transforming it into a machine for social reconstruction and revolution'. The Labour Party had 'retreated' from this objective. Lansbury's popularity in the Party grew. Behind the scenes MacDonald too had turned cynical about the Labour Party, but in a different direction. When a long-time radical Liberal decided to resign his seat in order to stand again as Labour, MacDonald tried to dissuade him, saying, 'This is a rough-jawed lot, stay where you are.'[55]

Everyone seemed to be growing more conservative. Sylvia sketched out a novel[56] whose heroine was a well-to-do woman who worked in the East End to relieve poverty, going from 'mild labourism . . . step by step' to contact with revolutionary activity. She meets an 'old revolutionary' who attracts her and discovers 'they are in love'. Her friend, Lady Laura, marries a young revolutionary but finds 'he is selfish and neglectful' and she commits suicide. The group disperses and the heroine 'immerses herself in domesticity and . . . returns to the quiet work of reform'. It was Sylvia's way of closing her revolutionary chapter.

In May 1929 there was another general election. Labour improved its position yet again. Still short of a majority, it was large enough to form another government, backed by elected Members who now included Frank Smith, Fenner Brockway and Norman Angell, and soon after, Hardie's other political brother, David, already a member of Rutherglen Town Council. The effervescent Katharine called it 'the harvest of a lifetime!'[57] and came to London for a reunion in the House of Commons with her friends Margaret Bondfield, James Maxton and Lady Cynthia Mosley. She was overjoyed to find the ILP had 147 members and one of 'its own' in No. 10 Downing Street.

This time MacDonald included George Lansbury in his Cabinet. Everything seemed set for Labour to make a difference at last. But in October the Wall Street Stock Exchange crashed and an unending series of financial crises beset the Labour government. The Left urged radical expansionist measures. George Hardie urged nationalization of the mines. The ILP wanted Labour to fight on 'the people vs the banks'.[58] MacDonald and his Cabinet dithered. They had no strategy for capitalism in crisis, and the banks took over. MacDonald's Diary for 9 March 1930 recorded 'cabinet hopelessly divided on home emergency policy'.[59]

MacDonald began taking refuge in his friendships with women like Lady Londonderry, and concerning himself with the world of patronage. When Jim Middleton refused an honour MacDonald had offered him, MacDonald told him that 'Men whose names would surprise you, clamour for . . . a title.'[60] He assured Middleton that he, MacDonald, was not among them; he was sticking to his principles and had 'refused everything offered to me'. Turning down a knight-hood had become synonymous with socialism in MacDonald's mind.

By the summer of 1930 a report forecast a huge budget deficit and the banks called for cuts in public spending. Resistance to this built up in the socialist and labour movements during the next year. Eventually the banks demanded a 10 per cent cut in unemployment benefits and the trade unionists in the Cabinet rebelled, including even the conservative Henderson. MacDonald insisted; but the socialist movement, the labour movement and Labour MPs backed Henderson.

MacDonald interpreted each one of their decisions to resist cuts as deserting the socialist cause.[61]

Everyone was to blame except himself. Younger men were not sufficiently socialist; as for older men, 'Stiff necks may bring us down', while trade unionists were 'pompous and self important (of the type reduced by an inferiority complex)'.[62] As the crisis deepened, he began calling draconian measures against the working-class 'equality of sacrifice'.[63] He recorded that 'the socialist movement is going to rack and ruin'; some even said that if nothing can be done about the crisis it is better to go.[64]

MacDonald had no intention of going. In order to stay, he crossed the House to sit and work with the Conservatives in a new 'national' government, which he claimed the King had 'implored' him to form.[65] He received national praise from every side of the Establishment. It was the balm he craved. Ten years earlier he had commented on the public odium Hardie had had to endure and that he was himself then experiencing. 'Nothing,' MacDonald wrote at the time, 'can ever make a man go through it a second time' except his convictions.[66] Hardie chose to go through it a second time; MacDonald did not.

The labour movement and socialists were stunned by MacDonald's act. Although he only made a formality of what Labour governments since have occasionally done informally, all shades of labour and socialist opinion read it as total betrayal. Yet MacDonald continued to claim he was working for the cause he had always supported. There was an immediate general election and Labour was all but wiped away, as voters panicked and plumped for the 'national' option. The majority of ILP members, including both Hardie's brothers, were defeated; and MacDonald phoned a defeated former colleague, and said, 'The Labour Party will have to wait for new leaders and another day, to come back.'[67] George Lansbury, one of the ILP members who remained, became the new Party leader; Clem Attlee, who also survived, deputy.

At the end of 1931 Katharine Glasier recorded that MacDonald kept trying to stay in touch, still trying to justify his decision. She commented, 'I don't know whether to weep or RAGE as at an insult . . . what delusions still hold him about what he has done and is doing – poor, poor man.'[68]

In 1931 Sylvia was bothered by headaches and decided to have all her teeth removed.[69] Her updated version of The Suffragette Movement was finished,[70] and soon provoked further quarrels among suffragettes. Mrs Fawcett's biographer, Ray Strachey, wrote in the Women's Leader that Sylvia's account of the suffrage movement showed an 'undisguised animus against Mrs Pankhurst and Christabel' as well as against the

Labour Party – and much self-fixation:[71] 'Miss Pankhurst . . . appears to believe that nothing but her own activities in the East End was of any political significance.'

But suffragettes who had supported her mother and Christabel showed an equally undisguised animus towards Sylvia. When the London statue to Emmeline Pankhurst next to the Houses of Parliament had been unveiled on 7 March 1930, the empire loyalist Flora Drummond was in charge of the ceremonies. A telegram was read out from Christabel, then in the USA. Sylvia's message was not read out and she herself, in the audience with young Richard, was not acknowledged. It was this event that prompted her to undertake yet a third commission, a book on her mother's life,[72] her last chance to reclaim her mother for herself.

The Labour Party faced recriminations set in train by electoral massacre and MacDonald's continuing to preside over a conservative national government. ILP members took against the Labour Party for not having been strong enough when in government. They debated whether they should continue to take the Labour Whip in Parliament. At a special conference in 1932 the matter was resolved by disaffiliating.

When the ILP split with Labour, Katharine left the ILP. She spent the 1930s on good causes, including raising funds for Margaret MacMillan's training college. She avoided active political life. So did Christabel Pankhurst, who turned her back on the women's cause and became a 'born again' Christian, spending the decade touring North America as a Second Adventist. Ben Tillett, having had two brief stints as an MP, left politics in 1931 and also joined a religious sect, the Moral Rearmament Group. Bob Smillie had already stopped being politically active, having been shattered earlier by the loss of the General Strike; while John Burns, upon losing his only child from the effects of war wounds (and his wife immediately after), became an almost complete political recluse for the rest of his days.[73] It was very hard for those brought up in Hardie's years to keep going.

Aggie and Hedley, who now lived alone in Abercynon – the Revd John Hughes having died – found the split more difficult. It is unlikely they broke from Labour in any formal way but their activity in the 1930s turned more and more towards religion and peace work. In 1936 they became Quakers and members of the South Wales Monthly Meeting.[74] Aggie kept up her coaching, which was their main income, while Hedley continued to commute for years to Cardiff Technical College, known to neighbours as a 'perpetual student'.[75] Most of Hardie's former colleagues in Wales stayed in the Labour Party as well, continuing the tradition of agitation he had started. Rose Davies, Hardie's special friend from Aberdare, was elected to the Glamorgan

County Council in 1925; stood unsuccessfully for Parliament in 1929, and in 1934 received an MBE for her political work.[76] She was well on her way to becoming one of the most significant leaders in local government. In the 1930s the depression affected every community in Wales. In 1935 Merthyr activists organized the largest demonstration of the unemployed ever seen in Britain up to that time. Worklessness continued as the perpetual curse of capitalism.

During the early 1930s Sylvia and Silvio were bringing up Richard in the suburban West Dene house where they now lived. Silvio was a dedicated anti-Fascist and had been active in exiled resistance to Mussolini from the middle of the 1920s. Sylvia soon organized a committee to defend the widow of Giacomo Mateotti, a socialist murdered on Mussolini's orders. She asked Shaw to join it and when he refused she accused him of being unaware of 'the corporate state . . . soviet and fascist' that threatened them all. Few listened to her and in a BBC programme Shaw compared her to Joan of Arc[77] – who wasn't listened to either.

In 1933 Sylvia wrote to Lansbury about the 'reactionary class dictatorship against the socialists' which was Hitler's new regime,[78] as well as about 'the terror against the Jews'. She urged Lansbury, 'we are not awake to it as the Jews are'. She called attention to the North-West Frontier and British massacres in India. Later she wrote of the problem of Palestine and Jewish settlers in the Middle East and their quarrel over territory: 'The two . . . must learn to live together,' she insisted.[79] Earlier, in The Truth about the Oil Wars[80] she had tried to alert readers to the wars oil would some day cause in the Middle East if international action were not started to control oil in the world interest. By 1935 Sylvia had become alarmed at the prospects of war in the air and put up a monument (which still stands) beside the road in Woodford, which she called 'an anti-Aerial Bombing Memorial'. She opened it with a fanfare but again few were interested, since few believed civilians would ever be bombed from the air.[81] She wrote to Norman Angell in 1936, 'as I see it, all Fascisms are one in their menace to society, that of Italy, of Germany, of Austria, of Japan, and in this country . . . Mosley.'[82] Angell agreed. He too had become alarmed at the 'British government's encouragement . . . to fascist policy in . . . Spain and elsewhere'.[83] Angell had come to the conclusion that the issue of capitalism vs communism was irrelevant. The real issue was 'how a modern state fulfils its economic functions without sacrificing the individual . . . How can we have peace without sacrificing freedom?'

Sylvia relayed her views to officials, but every office in Whitehall, and most MPs, had learned to take no notice of what she wrote. The Foreign Office even had a separate file called 'How to answer Letters from Miss Sylvia Pankhurst'.[84] It never occurred to any of

them that she might be right about Jews under Hitler, the oil, the
aerial bombings, Palestine, and Fascism in Europe and Japan.

Jean Hardie worked in a hospital after finishing at Cumnock Academy.
She had decided to follow her mother's footsteps and, after a visit to
America, returned to start her general training in the Glasgow Royal
Infirmary. In the USA Jamie had been working as a travelling salesman
for Sinclair Oil since the 1920s. He won awards for salesmanship
(as, later, Jean did for nursing). The family moved from Brooklyn
to Long Island to Pennsylvania, finally coming to rest in Hartford,
Connecticut. His daughter described Hardie's only surviving son at
the time as medium height and handsome, 'straight as a ramrod . . .
immaculate in his attire'.[85] He was a man who 'hated to get his hands
dirty' which may be why he moved from engineering to selling. He
was still out of contact with Cumnock and Jean was the uncertain
go-between between him and Lochnorris.

Cunninghame Graham spent his last years with the woman companion whom he had rescued on a runaway horse in 1916 in Hyde
Park, Ann Dummett. They visited South America often. He did not
join the Labour Party, which he thought was 'as much taken up with
office seeking as the Whigs and Tories',[86] and was led by 'piss-pot
socialists . . . disillusioned baronets, surrounded by . . . bourgeois social
climbers'. Even if Labour had won, Cunninghame Graham believed it
would merely mean we 'all sit . . . at little tables, drinking table water
approved by the County Council and reading expurgated bibles'.[87]
Instead he became the president of a new national party for Scotland,
and wrote that he looked forward to the 'pleasure of knowing taxes
were wasted in Edinburgh instead of from London'.[88] He refused to
speak into a microphone, but continued to believe that 'Gold . . . has
closed the mouths of three parts of mankind'.

Early in 1936, as an old man, he decided to return to Argentina for
one more visit, dying shortly after arrival. Argentina gave him a huge
state funeral led entirely by animals, including many riderless horses.

Like many a Hardie friend he was a man the world laughed
at during his life but honoured afterwards. He fought for reforms
that eventually won support, such as protection of native peoples
and vanishing animals – just as Sylvia had been thought absurd for
taking up the issue of pollution in lakes and rivers during her travels
abroad, and even tackling the subject of sewage disposal, protesting
at cities dumping sewage in lakes and rivers.[89] She believed sewage
should be treated and 'converted into useful products for farming and
other purposes'.

In 1934 Lansbury became ill and retired, and Attlee defeated Herbert
Morrison for the Labour leadership. MacDonald stayed in office until
1935 and another general election (where Labour again did badly), after

which he too retired, dying on a cruise at the age of seventy-one. The Labour Party and the Communist Party continued in opposition and the ILP in the mid-1930s regarded itself as a 'bridge' between them, while perpetually debating reaffiliation to the former.[90]

In Cumnock Nan decided to enter politics on her own account. In 1933, she stood successfully for Cumnock Council (where her father had failed to get elected in 1886) and within two years was the town's Provost. Her main project was to provide good public housing and her principal battle was with Lord Bute, who owned most of the land on which the council would need to build. After prolonged struggle the council won the right to purchase compulsorily and by 1939 the town had three-quarters of its population in new council dwellings. After this Nan and Emrys worked equally successfully for the provision of a new park and a large swimming pool. Her municipal socialism – showing 'what socialists could do in small towns',[91] as *Forward* put it – won the hearts of the Cumnock population to such a degree that she was never challenged for any council seat she chose to contest.

George Hardie was re-elected as an MP in 1935 but died in 1937. Hardie's sister-in-law, another Agnes, carried on the family's parliamentary tradition. Elected for the seat in 1937, she sat until 1945.[92]

In 1935 Sylvia's Italian orientation (through Silvio Corio) and anti-fascist commitment brought her the last great cause of her life, and her most successful father-figure. That year colony-greedy Italy invaded the Christian country of Abyssinia. Its Emperor, Haile Selassie, who had joined the League of Nations, fled with his entourage, intending to appeal to the International Court in Switzerland. Sylvia espoused his cause from the first day. When the Emperor arrived at Waterloo station in 1936 to seek asylum, Sylvia was one of those waiting. She went with him when he travelled to Switzerland to put his case. And, of course, she started a newspaper for his cause, the *New Times and Ethiopia News*.

Many found it difficult to accept Sylvia's commitment to an undemocratic hereditary emperor. Fenner Brockway did not. To him it was an outcome of anti-fascist concern. It was also a colonial issue, self-determination for African countries. Brockway, now editing the *New Leader*, supported her efforts at the time, along with black African leaders like the young Jomo Kenyatta (and later Tom Mboya) of Kenya.[93] Lastly, it was an issue of race. Sylvia had become aware of racism – unlike many socialists and members of the labour movement, where racism was endemic and denigration of black, Indian, and Chinese workers routine, particularly in the trade unions.[94] Anti-Semitism was equally widespread. Hyndman had called the Boer War a 'Jews' war' run by the 'Jewish international'.[95] Will Thorne in his memoirs wrote gratuitously of 'the way Jews used to swindle and cheat people by selling shoddy goods' in the East End.[96] Even Hardie in the 1880s had abused 'filthy foreigners' who were emigrating into Scotland, some fleeing progroms[97] (because they were undercutting local workers), though as soon as he began meeting foreigners his view changed. His middle life was relatively free of the prejudice of many of his contemporaries, while after his visits to India and South Africa, political equality for all races and religions became a positive belief. But Sylvia went much further. She campaigned against racism in all its forms, and she fought anti-semitism. Brockway recalled, 'she was one of the first to stand for racial equality and against discrimination of the blacks, not only black Africans but brown Indians. She deserves deep recognition as one of the pioneers of that struggle.'[98]

In Abercynon Aggie and Hedley Dennis continued their quiet life, devoting themselves to a succession of dogs. Visitors to the house were not encouraged.[99] They were assumed to be extremely poor. Eventually, Aggie's eyesight began to fail. At this point, to help her, Hedley switched from training to be a chemist to training to be an optician. Outside the home, they continued to be involved in peace work. In 1938 Aggie's album records the signatures of Swedish, German, Finnish, Chinese and Indian delegates at an international peace conference. On another occasion George Lansbury – now committing himself exclusively to peace campaigning (to the extent of visiting Hitler personally to plead for a change of policy) – wrote, 'Love gives life; hatred brings death . . . never give way to despair.'[100]

Towards the end of the decade, younger socialists and many members of the labour movement switched their concern from anti-imperialism to the anti-fascist struggle. More immediately, to the Spanish Civil War, where a new split developed over an old issue between socialists who wanted direct action and those who favoured the more circuitous parliamentary route. Brockway was one of those who went to Spain and experienced the split, recalling:

> The ILP had a difference with the communists about the resistance. In Catalonia and Barcelona there was the most wholehearted work-ers' revolution that I have ever seen. The workers just took control of everything and the ILP supported that workers' revolution. At the same time outside . . . in Madrid the struggle against Franco wasn't a revolution but . . . for the control of the right to elect at the polls . . . and so quite rightly the communists on the International Brigade supported that demand, while we in the ILP were supporting the demand for the workers' revolution in Barcelona. And the result was some conflict between us.[101]

In short, the Communists put down the Workers' Party which the ILP Brigade, including George Orwell, had gone to support. Direct action had lost again. So too in this case did constitutional action, for the Communists were defeated by the Franco fascists.

Nan and Emrys, now married ten years, spent their holidays trav-elling. Emrys, now fluent in Russian as well as German, had started translating Burns into Russian. In every photograph taken at the time, hiking up glaciers with European socialists or crossing Russia (where Emrys had amassed tidy sums for royalties on his translations of Burns), Nan looked like the mother of the young and energetic Emrys. She had gone grey very quickly. Emrys was now the editor of *Forward*, a journal that still prospered and which he regarded as his 'bairn'. George Bernard Shaw told Emrys it was 'the first Labour [*sic*] weekly that was really worth a workman's penny', and that not until it appeared did the 'Labour movement enter into real journalism'.[102]

As the end of the decade approached, so did the prospect of another war. Leon Trotsky, another contributor to *Forward* (who told Emrys, 'we agree on some questions, but disagree on many others'), assured Emrys from exile in Mexico that 'war is not the end' even if comes. Out of it 'will come a great demand for peace and fundamental change.'[103] In 1939 Willie Gallacher, the Scots Communist, took issue with Trotsky, and Emrys allowed the columns of *Forward* to contain their debate. Trotsky[104] wrote that Gallacher didn't 'deserve an answer', recalling Lenin's 'Infantile Sickness of the Left' and concluding that for those still supporting Stalin, there should be a 'Senile Sickness of the Right'. He sent a plea for Professor Plentyeff, a victim of the Moscow trials,[105] scoffing at the long list of his supposed crimes, including 'sexual delinquency' and 'sadism'. He told Emrys that Stalin was contemptuous of public opinion, did not read the foreign press, listened only to agents who reported his 'victories', and people did not dare reveal the truth to him. He is a thirsty man 'constrained to drink salt water'. Trotsky also made a recording and sent it to Emrys, congratulating him on being the only English-language socialist paper prepared to print the truth about Russia.[106]

Nan had revived Lillie's practice of sending Lochnorris produce to friends, and she even started baking shortbread.[107] Shaw's wife reported, 'GBS likes it and eats (for him!) quite a lot of it'.[108] In return Shaw had dispatched a brief history of British socialism, somewhat wide of the facts. He dated the 'socialist movement' as having been started in 1881 by the Fabians with the object 'of getting Labour into Parliament as an independent party',[109] but Labour men could not do so without trade union money. Shaw held the view that when the unions entered the scene Labour was pushed to the right. 'Even when they consented as a matter of form to be classed politically with the socialists, it meant no more than their religious description as Christians.' Shaw foresaw the day when the 'Old School Ties' would be ousted by the 'proletariat'. This would make 'trade unions into branches of the Civil Service. Now no Civil Servant can ever be so despotic as a trade union secretary under Capitalism'.

In August 1939 Nan was at last able to unveil a public memorial
to her father. The memorial, standing on the High Street between
old and new Cumnock, was a bust in bronze by Benno Schotz, an
Estonian sculptor who had sought political asylum in Scotland.[110]
Fenner Brockway, James Maxton and William Stewart all attended.
A choir was there to sing 'Banner of Freedom', Hardie's poem set to
the music of a Welsh hymn. At last, after twenty years of struggling,
the town agreed to acknowledge its most famous resident. Perhaps the
Labour Party's cause was not yet dead.

18
DEATHS AND SURVIVAL

The Second World War posed a problem to many of those who had
stood out against the First. Emrys's opposition to the First had been
political rather than religious. A war against facism was also a justifiable
political object, even though war was still to be opposed. For Nan it
was equally difficult, especially as she was still Provost when the war
started and faced with decisions like requests for the billeting of troops
in the town.[1] In fact, as a contemporary reported, 'She never approved
of our country's participation in the war',[2] and solved the problem
by resigning as Provost and becoming president of the Red Cross in
Cumnock – with the job of looking after the welfare of any 'lad or
lass serving in any branch of the forces'.

As 1939 approached Katharine Glasier found the prospect of war
very troubling. She had rejoiced at Chamberlain's return from Munich
but soon realized the piece of paper he waved was chimeric. She
compromised by supporting the war when it came but resolutely
refusing to hate Germans.[3] In Abercynon Aggie and Hedley Dennis
continued as strong pacifists, declining in any way to help the war
effort. They were well known in their neighbourhood for refusing
even to accept gas masks with which all civilians were issued.[4] It was
their statement of continuing faith.

Aggie and Hedley Dennis met no hostility for their view, however.
It was accepted as part of their eccentricity. A young neighbour recalled
them walking in the area at the time, a devoted couple, Aggie leaning
on Hedley, with her failing eyesight, always a dog by their side. Said
the neighbour, 'As a child I regarded them as very strange – they were
certainly unique in Abercynon' – not just their behaviour but the fact

that they were Quakers, pacifists, and vegetarians, 'but I never heard anyone speak of them with disrespect'.[5]

Aggie continued to coach her pupils. One of her own essays, on Charles Lamb, is preserved from this time and showed there were no signs of fading intellect. Yet when June Bond, Hedley's niece, visited Aggie and Hedley from time to time as a child, she found Aggie hard to get on with. Aggie told June's mother once that she did not like children, nor women who had had them. 'It made women unclean.'[6] The whole house was a Hardie shrine, with pictures and busts of him stationed around it. June Bond always assumed both of them knew Hardie, not realizing until later that it was only Aggie who had ever known him and that it was Aggie's relationship with Hardie that this devoted couple were living their life honouring.

Behind the placid outer life Aggie was deep into troubled contact with the spirit world. She had kept in touch with Frank Smith, who kept up his own contacts with spiritism after his 1931 election defeat in Nuneaton and his world travels. He claimed to be in regular communication with Hardie and told Aggie that Hardie had said that 'democracy has been a failure without God',[7] a reflection, perhaps, of Frank Smith's own continuing beliefs. Smith and Aggie regularly met, and at the end of the 1930s they began to share the services of a London medium, Abdul Latif. On the 24th of September 1940, Aggie met Frank Smith just before he died. He told her he expected to be reunited with Hardie at that time.[8] After his death Aggie continued to meet Latif; she continued to communicate with spirits in an attempt to reach Hardie herself, and she kept a Diary of all her encounters with the spirit world. Hedley Dennis, at first in sympathy with the practice, gradually became upset by it because Aggie herself seemed increasingly troubled by her 'encounters'.[9]

During the was Sylvia and Silvio continued to publish the *New Times and Ethiopia News* and to view world events through Ethiopian eyes, while sheltering with Richard in their garden bunker from the air raids which materialized exactly as Sylvia had feared. When, finally, military progress was made against the Italians in Africa, Haile Selassie returned to Africa. Meanwhile, his substantial funds in the Ethopian Bank in London continued to support Sylvia's work.

Emrys continued to publish *Forward* during the war and Shaw continued to send contributions. One was a review of Labour's great leaders. He started with Cunninghame Graham, 'a thoroughbred aristocrat' who refused office and 'damned the House's hypocrisy to its face and shook its dust from his feet'. As for MacDonald, 'having begun as the most intransigent of socialists out of Parliament, in it became such a complete do-nothing bunk merchant that he was made prime minister', while 'Bradlaugh was hated and dreaded . . . then subsided as a quiet anti-socialist . . . Maxton is still wasting his life there, making no legislative difference by his presence'. Only Keir Hardie 'kept the faith', but died of the 'futility' of Parliament.[10] Blatchford, who lived on until he was ninety, dying only in 1943, disagreed. One of his final outbursts was against Hardie, whom he had never learned to like: he had 'neither brains nor guts' and 'Ramsay MacDonald . . . wiped his boots on Hardie's whiskers'.[11] Over twenty-five years after his death Hardie was still prompting passion.

When war broke out, Hardie's granddaughter, Jean Hardie, insisted on staying to complete her training at the Glasgow Royal Infirmary, afterwards moving to the Simpson Memorial Hospital in Edinburgh to do midwifery. Still putting off her return to the USA, even when America had entered the war, she moved to London in 1941 to work at the Brook Hospital, Woolwich, where she trained for two further years in infectious diseases. Only when that was complete did she make the dangerous journey back, travelling in a shipping convoy escorted by the Navy across the Atlantic in 1943. Back in the USA, she moved in with her parents, Jamie and May, in Hartford. Jamie had returned to engineering and worked for a submarine suppliers.

Later, Jean described the routine kept by Keir Hardie's son on days when he was at home. Up early, made his own breakfast, and always went for a long walk, as his father had always done. He would stop by at the library for books, three and four at a time, as his father often did. He always spent an hour or two in the garden, again as his father would have done. After dinner he retired to a couch to listen to opera – unlike his father – and was in bed by 9 p.m. The estranged Jamie was entirely apolitical. 'He did greatly admire his father and what he stood for', said his daughter, but he did not support his cause – or any other cause.[12] He stuck to his hobby, which was refinishing furniture and, like his father, he was completely competent in housework. Like his mother he was a proud cook, well known for his jams. Jean commented, 'he was not ambitious for himself', as if what he had accomplished was not an achievement in itself. He had survived.

During the war and just after, Emrys wrote regularly to his sister Aggie in Abercynon. Increasingly, the letters revolved around one topic: Nan and her health. The war had started it on a downward path again. Now there was no pretence that she had a physical ailment. It was recognized as mental illness. On occasions her depression and associated distress transmuted into behaviour that made it impossible for Emrys to take care of her at Lochnorris. During these times she would enter a mental institution. When she came out, Emrys would be cheerful, telling Aggie, 'Now that she's better . . . we are off to . . .'[13] But increasingly it was downhill, though not discussed locally. According to Cumnock residents who looked back on that time, mental illness was still an embarrassment. There was a generally held view in that nonconformist society, put by a young Cumnock resident as late as the late 1980s: 'You should be able to prevent yourself from being mentally ill.'[14]

The long war finally ended, with fascism defeated, and a general election was held in 1945. Everyone looked forward to rebuilding society. Labour scored its greatest victory ever, and Clement Attlee, a long-time ILP member, became prime minister. The ever ebullient Katharine Glasier summed it up as 'all sunshine and roses!'[15] In Morgan's view, the Labour government of 1945 was the 'posthumous climax' to Hardie's politics.[16]

In Wales Aggie continued to 'communicate' with Hardie – according to Hedley Dennis,[17] now locking herself in her room at night to do so. According to Aggie's Diary,[18] in 1946 Hardie appeared to her about 9.45 p.m. after a political meeting for George Hall, the MP for Merthyr. Aggie recorded, 'I told him I thought he looked sad.' Hardie's message to her was to doubt Labour's victory at the polls because 'the only real success is that which is built upon the teachings of Christ – the Sermon on the Mount'. Again, this reflected what Aggie probably thought herself.

In the beginning these spirit encounters were only to carry out the benign practice Hardie had himself urged on both Sylvia and Lillie, and no doubt on Aggie as well: to set a time of day to communicate with him. But now it was getting thoroughly out of hand. Hedley Dennis was not permitted in her room when Aggie was communicating with spirits. Sometimes in his own room he would hear her calling out distressed, or telling the spirits to go away. Sometimes she would cry out that the spirits were holding her down. Sometimes they came when she had no clothes on. Hedley later told his niece, June Bond, that he began calling it 'playing with the Devil'.[19]

Aggie's visits to Abdul Latif in London only seemed to make matters worse. In time Latif began taking an interest in her physical ailments as well. His unwholesome and unprofessional approach only added to her distress. For her vanishing eyesight, for example, his prescription was to have Aggie massage his own eye with her tongue.[20] It was passages like these that drove the Bonds in the end to burn Aggie's private Diary. Only Kenneth Morgan, Hardie's earlier biographer, ever saw it. His note at the side of the few passages he chose to record was revealing: 'Mrs D often communicated with Hardie during Second World War (Mrs Hardie and Nan Hardie jealous of her relationship with Hardie. Unhappy home background?)'[21] Morgan had picked up the unhealthy competition between the women in Hardie's life.

Aggie was able to carry on normally at all other times. She and Hedley

still attended Quaker meetings and Labour Party events. Emrys's letters
to Aggie and Hedley made it clear this was not the case with Nan.
Emrys, though suffering illness himself, continued to cope as best he
could. In 1946 he took a decision which may have made matters
worse. He was approached by local miners when there was a sudden
by-election in the local parliamentary seat of Ayrshire South. That a
man from Merthyr would stand for Keir Hardie's home area seemed
an elegant balance to the past, where a man from Ayrshire had stood
for the valleys of South Wales where Emrys had been born. And that
man Hardie's own son-in-law, living in Hardie's own house. When
he decided to enter Parliament – and all the familiar political life closed
in on her – it must have intensified Nan's anxiety and depression to an
unbearable degree. Emrys described her harrowing descent in detail to
Aggie. Aggie kept the letters. It was June Bond who burned them.[22]

Shaw was sorry that Emrys was leaving journalism. He sent him
a postcard during the campaign: 'Worst news of the week. Another
first-rate journalist lured to the gabble-shop and lost. I am praying
daily for your defeat.'[23] Unfortunately for Shaw – and Nan – he was
successful. Within a year Nan was dead.[24] Many years later, when Emrys
died, *The Times* wrote that Nan's death had 'clouded his judgement'
because after she had gone, he found himself 'increasingly at loggerheads
with the official party leaders'.[25] Keir Hardie might not have thought
Emrys's judgement clouded. Like Hardie he was a Party of One. Like
Hardie too he used Parliament for a life of ceaseless international travel
and campaigning for the cause of peace. Like Hardie, he did not allow
the politics of the day to limit his map of the world. Among his papers
are stunning photographs taken in 1946 of the Allied bomb damage in
East Germany, for the moment the war was over, he had made contact
with friends in Europe. The fact that he had friends in Eastern Europe
as well as Western Europe accounts for *The Times*'s opinion that his
view was 'clouded'. The Cold War, begun so long ago, was reaching
its height.

Post-war politics of the Left began to rearrange itself. Most of the leading ILP figures now rejoined the Labour Party, as a Labour government
began grappling with the problems of once again rebuilding civil society
after a war. There was optimism about making real social change.

Labour's major victory had confounded Shaw, who had predicted
firmly to Emrys that the 'Old School Ties' would reassert themselves.[26]
As the war was ending, Shaw switched to an attack on Communists
in Britain – for being so ineffective. Willie Gallacher (the only
communist MP) merely 'drivels . . . commonplaces of 1861'. As for
Piratin, someone should remind him of Robert Owen's rule, 'Never
argue; repeat your assertions'.[27]

Such advice would have been helpful for Sylvia at this time. On several occasions she contradicted those who were reviving the story of the suffragettes' struggle. She sent thirty pages of critical commentary to Teresa Billington Grieg, who was writing her own account;[28] she argued with Roger Fulford over his book, *Votes For Women;*[29] and when invited on to the film-set of *Fame is the Spur*,[30] where Emmeline Pethick-Lawrence had been hired as the official consultant for suffragette sequences, she found fault with everything. Finally the director, Roy Boulting, lost patience, and called, 'Get that woman out of here!'[31]

As soon as she had returned from Britain, Jean Hardie had started work as a nurse in Mount Sinai Hospital in Hartford, Connecticut.[32] She was put on night duty and liked it enough to stay on through the rest of the war, after which she became night supervisor. In 1948 she was joined at the hospital by Jorge Lizaso Scott, a doctor trained in Havana, from a distinguished family. He had left Batista's Cuba in 1946 to emigrate to the USA and was completing his residency at Mount Sinai. Fate assigned him to night duty, where Jean assisted him with his English and shared a quiet lunch at midnight every night. In 1950 they were married.

In 1949 Emrys remarried – to Martha Cleland, daughter of a Glasgow headmaster. Mattie, as she was always called, was medically trained, but gave up work when she came to Cumnock (except for a continuing interest in herbal cures). It was a marriage which her family opposed, possibly for political reasons.[33] Photographs show her as a slim, dark-eyed woman with straight black hair, who defied her family and moved in to Lochnorris, joining Emrys in his new life in Westminster and on his continuing trips abroad. Emrys visited the USA on several occasions and looked up Jean Hardie. Only she and he maintained the link. Jamie continued estranged.

Katharine Glasier had continued to electrify her audiences even into her eighties. Then one day she fell ill – her only real illness in life. Her oldest son, Malcolm, was at her bedside when she died, quickly, at age eighty-three, the same year in which Shaw died, who had proposed to her three-quarters of a century earlier. She had recently seen her daughter, Jeannie, who had come home to visit from Australia with her children. Jean broke the news to her mother that she did not intend to live the same way her parents had. 'You and Daddy put the Movement first,' she told Katharine with some feeling. Katharine listened to the criticism and reported: 'Jeannie and I talk it out. The bairnie tells me she and Webbie are determined to put their bairns first and to slave for their advancement, come what may.'[34] Jeannie had gone straight from her parents' cause to her children's. Perhaps in passing she had also articulated what the Hardie children – and many another who grew up in a family highly involved in public life or great causes – felt but never consciously realized.[35]

In 1952 Jorge and Jean were living in Providence, Rhode Island, and expecting their first child. Jamie and May looked forward to becoming grandparents. Just before the baby was due Jamie had a cerebral haemorrhage. May insisted on nursing him at home. On 22 February 1953, in Providence, Jean and Jorge had a girl, Dolores May. The next day, Jamie Hardie, some hundred miles away, died. His ashes were buried in Springfield, Massachusetts; he never saw his only grand child. [36] In Cumnock some time later a new tombstone was put up in the Cumnock cemetery and all the Hardie family's ashes were gathered in and buried together: Hardie and Lillie, the baby, Sarah, and Duncan and Nan. It is beautifully maintained and doubles as a monument to the family in Cumnock, showing them the respect they achieved in death but often missed in life. Only Jamie's ashes and name are missing. Yet only Jamie had in the end achieved a contented life.

After Jamie died May went to live with Jean, Jorge and baby Dolores May. It was the time of the Korean War and Jorge enlisted as a doctor in the medical corps. They all moved to Fort Bragg, North Carolina. A few months later in Britain, Richard Keir Pethick Pankhurst, Sylvia's son, was called up for National Service for the same war. He and Sylvia together went to court to give notice of his refusal to serve and to ask for recognition that he was a conscientious objector. Sylvia testified as well, making clear she opposed war. Richard testified that he opposed fighting against the Mau Mau in Kenya, a British colonial war also in train. He lost his appeal but in contrast to the prison sentences given to resisters in the First World War, he was merely fined.[37] By now a Ph.D., Richard spent his time helping Sylvia in her research, as well as lecturing to adults at Toynbee Hall at night, and by day working for the Institute of Economic and Social Research.[38] Together they had visited Ethiopia in 1951, when he began a book on its history. When Silvio died of a heart attack in his eightieth year in their home one lunchtime, only Richard attended his father's funeral, as Sylvia was recovering from a small heart attack of her own. Mother and son lived on in the house which had always had Sylvia's portrait of Keir Hardie hanging prominently.

In time the grateful and wealthy emperor invited Sylvia and Richard to settle permanently in Ethiopia. Richard was to lecture at the new university, while Sylvia would continue her good works, living in a villa Haile Selassie provided. Of course she found time to edit a journal for English readers in Ethiopia, which was said to be 'too Ethiopian . . . even for Ethiopians'.[39]

The regime was medieval and brutal and the court one of the most antiquated and detached from reality in the world, where 'dogs were allowed to pee on guests' shoes', each dog accompanied by an attendant who would follow it throughout the day and wipe up after it.[40] Sylvia never lived long enough to see Haile Selassie become what Stuart Hall called the 'symbol of long neglected African identity' to a whole generation of Afro-Caribbean and American blacks,[41] some of whom worshipped him as a god; but she much enjoyed his absolute power. As she went about Addis Ababa, chauffeur-driven in a royal car, her foibles were honourable: she picked up ailing children in the slums and took them for world-class treatment in the new hospital.[42] Here, as one of the élite in a society too élite even for the British officials, who had no way to stop her, she could do as she wished. Her saving grace was that all she did was for others. She remained her father's daughter although at the same time − the McCarthy witch hunts were on − she denied ever having been a communist.[43] One autumn day in 1960[44] when she was seventy-eight, she never woke from her midday nap. Her adopted country gave Sylvia, the lifelong atheist, a Christian state funeral in its Trinity Cathedral, and later a huge monument in front of it.

In 1955 Jorge Scott left the army. The family, with toddler Dolores, and grandmother May, moved to Warwick, Rhode Island. There Jorge started a general practice with Jean acting as his nurse. In 1957 there was one more trip to Cumnock for her mother, May, who had never been able to say goodbye to Scotland. She came to look after her sister, Lil, and became ill herself. Jean and Dolores had to come to Cumnock to bring her back by air and ambulance to the family home in Rhode Island, and there they nursed her until she died in 1959, at the age of eighty.[45] Dolores May remembered 'Grannie' as 'a wonderfully kind person'.[46]

After the war Agnes and Hedley Dennis were back in active membership of the Labour Party and Hedley became secretary of the Abercynon Ward, a post he retained for the next thirty years. Aggie attended ward meetings through the 1950s, when the Labour Party lost office and became an Opposition again. On 13 February 1956 she reported on a meeting at which Nye Bevan − Labour's shadow Foreign Secretary − had spoken. She had been disappointed that he had not dealt with the issue of Cyprus, where young, inexperienced servicemen were being sent to the conflict in that area. She wanted them sent home at once. The ward passed a resolution to this effect and forwarded it to the district Labour Party.[47] Eventually it would reach Rose Davies, now chair of the Glamorgan County Council, who had been given a CBE in 1952.

In 1959 Aggie was still responding to letters asking her for help with problems,[48] although Trevor Stonelake, who knew her at the end of her life, said she was 'a woman who kept herself very much to herself'[49] and others commented cryptically on 'memories not safe for publication'.[50] When she died in the mid-1960s, the plaque put up recording her age at the Glyntaff crematorium as being only twelve years older than her husband was assumed by many neighbours to be a falsification.[51] Like Nan, Aggie had aged quickly. No one who had not known them earlier – except possibly those who went through the experience of conscientious objection during wartime – could understand why the two younger men had chosen to marry the two older women who had fought for them outside. And no one who had not known Keir Hardie understood why both had kept their homes as Hardie shrines.

With Aggie's help Hedley had at last qualified as an optician, a practice he carried on at the Mountain Ash address after she died. Later he became chairman of the Abercynon Old People's Welfare Association. He kept to his religion and was well known as one 'ready to preach the Gospel at any church of any established denomination without any payment of any kind'.[52] He kept up with Emrys and Mattie in Cumnock and regularly visited them. There are photographs of him sitting in the garden at Lochnorris well into the 1960s; he may even have been there when Jean, Jorge and Dolores came for a short visit of their own in 1964, when Dolores was eleven.

Emrys stayed an individualist Member of the House of Commons, a wry wit and a promoter of peace, who stood out against his Party's policy on nuclear weapons and its increasingly hard line in the Cold War. He marched on all CND marches. He had become an ever more eminent Burns scholar and accomplished linguist, according to Michael Foot, enjoying good relations with editors and writers in many countries, including the principal translator of Shakespeare into Russian, Samuel Marshak, in Russia.[53] In the 1960s he wrote three political biographies.[54] He always wore a dark-blue duffel coat, or donkey jacket, over his suit, the oriflamme of his own generation. A neighbour said later, 'He was in great shape . . . not smoking or drinking and swimming every day at Cumnock pool.'[55] The same neighbour spoke of being invited in to Lochnorris where Emrys 'showed me the bell used by the first chairman of the Labour Party to order meetings' (in fact it was the bell from the first meeting of the ILP). He also showed me 'a beautiful carved sideboard from the Woodworkers of New Zealand',[56] the gift sent to Lillie in 1908. Lochnorris was becoming more of a shrine every day. It must have been a problem for Mattie Hughes.

Labour became the government again in 1964. While Harold Wilson, the new prime minister, called for the white heat of a technological revolution, Emrys spoke to his electors only of using the 'new discoveries of science . . . to reduce working hours' and to see to 'new industries . . . new schools . . . every family with a home at a reasonable rent, more hospitals, more facilities for leisure'.[57] Not so very different from the demands Hardie made. Not so different, either, his continued attendance at peace conferences, including a large peace conference in Nagasaki in 1968 to commemorate victims of the atom bomb.[58]

Emrys had never learned to drive a car and needed lifts everywhere he went, and never acknowledged what Hardie had always called 'motors'. In 1969 he was knocked down by one. 'It was the only time I ever saw him despairing,' said Michael Foot, who visited him in hospital.[59] He had good reason to despair; he would never leave. He died on 18 October 1969.

Hardie had left all his money and Lochnorris to Lillie; Lillie had left it all to Nan; Nan had changed her earlier will and left it all to Emrys; and Emrys had had no time to leave it to anyone but Mattie. Mattie, who had no real connection with socialism or the Hardie family, now had all the papers, the books, the letters, the presentation items, the memorabilia, and all the personal effects of all the Hardies. Sadly too, Mattie seemed also to have acquired the need to disconnect from reality. Slowly, she became less and less sane. How long she had been moving in this direction is not known. Local people only began to notice it after Emrys died.[60] Increasingly, she signed herself into the local mental hospital at Ailsa. As others had before her, she felt the need to escape from Lochnorris.

In 1975 the ILP wound itself up as a political party. It became a socialist publishing house and ginger group within the Labour Party, and revived the *Labour Leader* as its journal. Income from past bequests, including that from the Kippen sisters, still came in.

In 1967 Jean Hardie Scott had fallen downstairs and broken her arm. 'Recuperating was so much fun I decided that I didn't want to go back to the office.'[61] Instead, Jorge Scott gave up home practice and went to work at the Rhode Island Medical Center. Later he became its director. In 1971 Dolores May finished high school in Rhode Island and began studying at Sweetbriar College in Virginia, where her main subjects were anthropology and sociology. Her third year of the course, in 1974, was spent in the Netherlands, from where she paid a month's visit to Cumnock, where there were still Stoddarts. In 1975 she got her BA.

It was not until 1973 that June Bond began visiting her uncle Hedley Dennis again at the house in Abercynon. There she discovered that Hedley kept the house as a shrine to Aggie and her devotion to Keir Hardie. All the memorabilia were still in place.[62] There was lavender everywhere, just as Aggie had put it out before she died. Aggie's room was untouched from the day she had died. In it was a cake half eaten, now fossilized. In the hall were her two small gloves on the table, as if she was about to go out or had just come in. Sometimes Hedley would sit in his living room, facing a vacant chair, where he would enjoy 'talks' with Aggie, just as Katharine Glasier had enjoyed talks with Bruce, and, very likely, Sylvia with Hardie. This was not the degraded spiritism Aggie had practised; this was a belief in the presence of the spirit after death.

In 1977 Dolores May started in Boston College Graduate School of Social Work, after having spent two years in outreach work for a local anti-poverty agency in Rhode Island. Her MSW in Social Work came in 1979, in community organization and social planning. At the Graduate School she met Max Arias, a native of the Lower East Side of Manhattan – from a family with a part Puerto Rican background. He went to Aviation High School and graduated as a mechanic, after which he attended the State University of New York in Binghamton for his BA in psychology and political science. He was already a fluent Spanish speaker by the time he met Dolores on the MSW course. After both had qualified, they married and went as volunteers to the south-west of the United States, working for a domestic equivalent of the Peace Corps. It seemed an entirely appropriate life for Hardie's only great-grandchild.

Mattie Hughes stayed on in Lochnorris, the inheritor of the Hardie legend and worldly goods. This fact saddened the James Hardie family, his real inheritors. Jean Hardie Scott journeyed to Scotland and visited Lochnorris to try to speak to Mattie about the house and its contents. She was even contemplating buying it or helping to turn it into a local museum. But every time she came to Cumnock, 'Mattie signed herself into a mental home'.[63] On one trip Jean managed to meet Mattie and asked if she could have one of her grandfather's inkwells, as she collected them. Mattie refused, telling Jean her family 'had had enough already'. Considering the fact that Jamie was cut out of the wills of both parents and of his sister and brother-in-law, it was a completely irrational answer. Very possibly it referred back to the long distant past, which Mattie would only have known about through hearsay, when the Hardie family had paid off Jamie's debts and financed him to leave for America. It was clear that bitterness from that past still lived on – what Jean Hardie Scott referred to charitably as 'the dark side of the family'.

Whatever the explanation, Mattie, like Nan before her, became increasingly deranged. Local people remembered her strange ways and talked of her disappearing and reappearing, without warning, from the institution at Ailsa. The local Cumnock community, knowing she was disposing of Hardie possessions, embarked on a fruitless search for someone to take on Lochnorris and finance it as a Hardie museum. Approaches were made to the Labour Party and the National Trust, but none would take up the offer. The town could not afford it and neither could the District Council. Mattie never told any of them about Jean's visit and her offer to buy the house. In turn, when Lochnorris finally went up for auction, Jean was not told. It was sold in 1983, with the community managing to salvage only a few of the Hardie effects – now displayed at the small Baird museum in Cumnock town centre. Immediately after the sale Mattie Hughes died in Ailsa.[64]

Hedley Dennis kept up his optician's practice and his ward secretary-ship in the local Labour Party – where he entered meticulous minutes in a large ledger. In 1978 ill health forced him to stop practising. It was only with the greatest difficulty that June Bond and her husband could persuade her uncle to come to live with them in Manchester and leave the Abercynon home. He finally agreed. In Manchester he was regularly visited by local Quakers.[65]

Hedley Dennis should have been at peace but he was not. It was his turn to be beset by spirits that would not let him rest. The same spirits that had visited Aggie (of which he so disapproved) returned. June Bond told of the distress it caused them all as 'Night after night after night . . . he would get out of bed and wander around'. Later June and Robert would hear him shouting, 'Help, Help' from inside his room. June and Robert did not like to interfere but finally they could stand it no longer, and one morning asked why he cried out so. He explained about Aggie and her spirits. They said they would pray for him. Miraculously, this cleared his soul and 'he never had that trouble again . . . he turned from someone fearful . . . to someone who was saying, "Oh, what a lovely day!"'[66]

At this time Robert Bond experienced the same kind of conversion as Hedley Dennis (and so many others in the Hardie story had had, including Hardie himself). He left his business and began training for the ministry in the Church of England.

When he received a Rectoral Benefice Vicarate at Cwmbran, and caring for their uncle became too exacting, Hedley was moved to Mount Pleasant Hospital in Chepstow. However, Hedley Dennis's trials were not over. Being in an institution unhinged him. The hospital routine forced his mind back to the military prison that he had experienced as a conscientious objector. What June Bond called this 'lovely mild gentle man' suddenly became convinced he was being held prisoner, and turned aggressive, on one occasion hiding behind the door with a knife to strike whoever might enter, so convinced was he that the military were about to abuse him all over again for his resistance to war. He had been 'very badly treated' and regularly brutalized, and he told June Bond once that had he not been released from the barracks when he had (when Aggie had had him moved to civil prison) he would have been killed.[67] These memories took him over. Constantly he would ask when he was to be released and how far was the railway station. June and Robert Bond would take him to the door and say he was free to go. They would open it and repeat the words. Gradually, their patience helped him to return to some sort of reality.

Before Hedley's move to Chepstow, when there were long periods of lucidity, June Bond would tend to him. She found him very resistant to having his bedclothes changed or taking a bedbath. One day she cajoled him by reminding him that he was after all a married man and need not be so reticent. At this he turned to her and said simply, 'But I have never had sexual intercourse.'[68] June Bond was surprised, remembering the closeness of Aggie and Hedley as a couple, to realize that perhaps the marriage had never fully been. It could have been yet another sacrifice that Keir Hardie – unknowingly – had exacted.[69] The small box on top of the closet, containing the letters of Aggie's relationship with the Hardies, was still the Ark of the Covenant to Hedley Dennis.[70] It contained their common commitment to Hardie, to the socialism of the ILP, to war resistance, and, possibly also, it now seemed, to Aggie's own love for Hardie, which together Agnes and Hedley Dennis had preserved inviolate for nearly forty years.

Dolores May Arias, Jean's daughter, and the last descendant of the original Keir Hardie family, returned with Max to the Boston area in 1984, the same year that Hedley Dennis died.[71] Jorge Scott retired in 1986 – after which he and Jean travelled to Russia and China, or stayed home and gardened and cooked and baked, all good Hardie pursuits. Jean also began tap-dancing; and, together with a group of contemporaries – all over sixty – formed a dance troupe called The Happy Hoofers. It performed at hospitals and churches and in nine years raised $8,000 for every kind of good cause.

Dolores May took a job as an in-patient social worker at Boston City Hospital, the large public hospital serving Boston's inner city. 'My area of special interest is gerontology and my assignment is in an adult medical ward.'[72] Max Arias worked on inner city programmes to help people of all ages come off drink and drugs. Both he and Dolores May and Jean and Jorge Scott carried on the Hardie family teetotalism. Dolores May and Max attended the First Unitarian Universalist Church in Jamaica Plains, dedicated 'to the service of humanity'[73] – a bright and socially active church with endless echoes of the Evangelical Union Church that Keir Hardie had loved in his early days. Its Lord's Prayer begins, 'Our Father and Mother in Heaven, Hallowed be thy Name'.

Their work was difficult and demanding and both often dreamed of Scotland, and regularly visited it, and thought sometimes they would like to return and settle there. Meanwhile, they did what they must in the inner area of a large city. More than 130 years after her great-grandfather was born – in a different country and a different political culture – Dolores May remained a true descendant, battling in difficult terrain. As did so many who passed through Hardie's life, and countless numbers more who carry on his causes. It is impossible to predict where his legacy lies. As William Morris foretold in *A Dream of John Ball*, the hedgerow priest and agitator whom Hardie so much resembled:

While I pondered on all these things, and how men fight and lost the battle, and the thing that they fought for comes about in spite of their defeat, and when it comes turns out not to be what they meant and so other men have to fight for what they meant under another name.[74]

CONCLUSION

Keir Hardie was a legendary figure while he lived. Even today we still speculate about where his tradition is, whether he would be a Labour Party member still, or expelled long ago, agitating on Third World issues perhaps, or returned to religion. Part III shows why all such speculation is fruitless, for we saw how those who held nearly identical opinions at the time of Hardie's death developed in every kind of political direction in the decades afterwards.

The question of whether his life holds any lessons for those determined on social justice today can only be answered, if at all, in terms of the principles he held, and the way in which he worked.

He was strongly self-reliant. Working people could not count on anyone but themselves. Though he shed the political beliefs that went with doctrinaire individualism – which he afterwards denounced, along with its charity imperative – he always accepted personal responsibility to self and community. What he added – and progressively refined as he matured politically – was an equally strong belief in the community's responsibility towards individuals. People were owed the means of life, not just any life, but a full life.

This became his socialism. He expressed it as a world where industry was ordered for 'use instead of for profit'[1] and where 'the land and industrial capital' were 'held as common property to be administered by the community in the interests of the whole of its members'.[2]

How the common wealth was administered, and by what forms of democratic accountability control was exercised, were details he was often content to leave to others, though he always favoured strong local oversight and parliaments for Scotland, Wales and Ireland.

Hardie had little interest in political or economic theory. Yet he was a teacher, and when he delivered an economic homily, it often made more sense to more people than loftier formulations. When severe unemployment and starvation wages were afflicting Britain in 1903, he noted the capitalists' remedy was to lower wages, which only increased suffering, for 'the more wages were reduced the less there is to spend and the less there is to spend the less there is for commodities and the greater the number of people out of employment'. The remedy is to 'organise industry in such a manner as to increase the spending power of the community and thereby increase the amount of work to be performed'.[3]

Hardie always coupled such advice with a list of the jobs that needed tackling in the community, such as house-building, foreshore reclamation or setting up creches. It grew longer each year. If the great theorists and economists of both Left and Right have better answers to the problems and needs Hardie saw at the start of this century (many of which we still see at the end of it), they have yet to reveal them. Academics laugh at Hardie at their peril. Hardie would not have cared if they did. If he never warmed to theoreticians, he positively hated dogmatists, including 'neo-marxists'[4] as well as religious sectarians, individualist Liberals and high Tories.

What Hardie stood or fell by were certain principles, and many were in place early in his life. The first was the democratic. His oldest political memory was campaigning on the republican issue and he never lost his commitment to the absolute necessity of conducting society without the burden of privilege and hereditary rule. From this he drew his early conviction that he was as good as any man. Later, when working with groups denied their rights, he advised them to accept the same about themselves, and behave accordingly. Out of this principle grew Hardie's adult and women's suffrage commitments, as well as his support for Indian self-government. More widely, it also underlay his conviction that all human religions – and cultures – have equal value.

Yet Hardie rarely used the word 'equality'. When he did, it was usually to pose its political paradox, 'Socialism implies the inherent equality of all human beings. It does not assume they are all alike, only that all are equal',[5] a response he shared with William Morris's old-fashioned communism, 'variety of life is as much the aim of true communism as equality of condition'.[6]

Many of Hardie's deepest commitments were contradictory. He was not an insurrectionist, but he continually urged the 'overthrow' of the capitalist system. He wanted local control but favoured a strong, legislating state. He stood 'for realising socialism by working with and through working class organisations, especially the trade unions',[7] but he also made clear that in all political alliances 'what I contend for is breadth'.[8] More centrally, his commitment to the entire human community was always pitted against an exclusive commitment to the working class, which had priority in all he said and did.

It was Marx who helped him reconcile what for Hardie were moral rather than philosophical questions – by providing a dialectical process that projected society's development. Hardie saw the working class forging its way through to an outcome of classlessness, the highest stage of social development. Like Marx too, he too saw nations disappearing and society moving to a point when history 'becomes world history'.[9]

He was a loyal Scot with a global perspective that grew steadily more important.

Because Hardie had personally experienced the poverty that we associate today with much of the Third World, he was closer than we are now to those special men and women living in that world's hunger, homelessness and oppression, unable to lead their own lives because the urgency of improving the common weal has chosen them, as it chose Hardie, to speak and act for their communities.

In these struggles many will be adopting what Hardie called 'the fundamental principle' of organization in a piece he wrote for the Ayrshire mining community as early as 1882: combination.[10] He told those 'atoms of human society' that the only way to make their dispossessed voices heard was to forge themselves into 'one grand moral, social, mental and political federated brotherhood'. Long before his socialism developed, Hardie was preparing its foundations in collective industrial and social action. Spelling out too the goals its action was meant to achieve, the first of which was 'to secure the right to live by the fruits of honest labour'. Hardie did not see unemployment as a systemic statistic. To him it was a denial of a human right to each individual. Low wages were nearly as great a denial because they applied to so many more people, most of whom wanted to work, provided the job gave them enough to keep themselves and their families.

Later, when he became a socialist, Hardie was outraged that there should be so large a group in society 'which owns no property and is always in poverty.'[11] Although he accepted any small improvements (some would say too many and much too small) he never argued for second–class development. The poor deserved the same standard of living their 'betters' already had; as well as the same education and work opportunities. Socialism meant everyone should own, manage, be commensurably rewarded; not tied to rent, overseen, and living as wage slaves. Like Lenin he believed socialism's long-term definition was the disappearance of distinctions based on mental and manual work.[12] In 1882 this objective was embryonic, merely to 'demand a better share of the wealth created'. Later, as a socialist, not only wealth, but 'work . . . should be equitably distributed'.[13]

But what were the wealth and work for? Not for possessions as ends in themselves, but rather that people should 'exercise all the faculties of body and mind' to the full. This 1882 formulation later flowered into socialist demands for health and education. And, incidentally, answered the question still asked, what is education for, if not to obtain a high standard of life? Hardie saw it quite the other way around: a high standard of living was necessary in order to support education and good health for everyone. For socialism's goal is never primarily material gain, it is human development. Without education people would win possessions but remain enslaved. As early as 1882 he saw that it was well-being, culture, knowledge and learning that would 'liberate'.

At the same time, he came to see that 'combination' alone was inadequate because collective self-interest alone, however liberating, was not a worthy cause for a life. Socialism added that essential new dimension: the goal of the general welfare, others' development as well as our own. There was no protection in any other political system and Hardie was always stern with those who refused to take part in a trade union's life, cleaving instead to 'ignorance, cowardice and grovelling serfdom'. In 1882 he spelled out why, in setting out the last of the reasons he gave for combining, the need 'to secure protection from violence'.

This was the violence of the coal-master to the miner, but also of miners – and family members – to each other, as well as the violence of the state and its military, as he was to see so often later, rushed in to protect owners' interests in any dispute. Ultimately, it was the state's military violence senselessly turned against other nations in wars of commercial greed and imperial aggrandisement.

Hardie was one of the first to enter freedom from violence to the catalogue of working-class demands. His later war resistance grew from this conviction. So too his preference for constitutional routes, for he opposed the armed uprising as a path to social change. A revolution, yes – Hardie often claimed to be a revolutionary – but not a violent one. He believed in a revolution that would come anyway, if struggle went on wisely, well and long enough. Socialism would overtake society so slowly we might not even be aware of it. This mystic expectation, a product of a religious cast of mind (and the 'noble but cloudy' socialism of the ILP),[14] was where Hardie most parted company with Marxists.

In practice, however, Hardie always worked in a highly class-conscious way. He may have disowned violence but he never disowned strength. In 1882 he was already saying, 'How can justice be got when there is no strength?' Nor, later, unless there is the capacity to make the union bureaucrat sweat, the well-to-do uncomfortable, the pious ashamed, and the mighty fearful? Agitating for immediate change – by awakening people to their inherent rights and urging them to organize together to claim them (as well as working on that altruism he believed lurked in the heart of the capitalist) was what he considered to be his life's work.

Agitation to Hardie was the highest form of political action, almost a principle in itself. Nothing would ever be done or given because people 'asked', or even demanded; only when it was a danger to withhold it any longer. How those with power are apprised of that danger is a task for each generation. Hardie's own view was that the constitutional path would only work if agitation was constant and the law permitted freedom to act.

When the law hobbled working people, or prevented free speaking by any group, struggle against unjust laws had priority and became an added burden which he was ready to shoulder. Much of his life in Parliament was spent trying to reverse or replace laws designed to stem the rising tide of independent Labour. That is why Parliament remained important, and why Labour independence remained important, despite the fact that personally, as Glasier observed, Parliament 'was a prison for him'.[15] Hardie made it more so by continually confusing 'social reforms' with the 'passage to socialism',[16] and parliamentary activity with the people's own. But he defended himself by saying the Parliament he had in mind was one where the old vested interests of capital would have disappeared. That is why those who constantly challenge these interests, as he did, will be 'scorned and hated and feared . . . by the wealthy and the privileged and their servitors in the press'.[17] That you can agitate as Hardie knew was necessary, and remain acceptable to those with real economic and political power, however popular with others, he knew to be impossible.

The antagonism he met accounts for his uncooperative nature and tendency to work alone. Yet he also went in harness with those he would rather have avoided; as well as with those outside his own group – with women of every political view, to secure the female franchise, with radical Liberals in resisting imperialist wars, with SDF-Marxists in fighting unemployment. On certain issues it was important to cross the line of class, on others, imperative to stay behind it. He insisted on being allowed to determine this for himself, not without misjudgements on several occasions. Yet he successfully avoided a narrow class-based politics while remaining the voice of the working class for a generation.

Sometimes it was only the working class who really understood. When he said that under socialism 'the rivers would run pure and clear as they did of yore and the wood would again cover the mountain-side',[18] even when he made clear that market capitalism's rapacious greed was the cause of the many environmental problems being left to future generations,[19] few really understood except workers who were daily experiencing the ill effects. The wealthier classes could still escape pollution or find undefiled nature. Socialists were the first modern ecologists.

Some of his causes even the working class did not understand, he was so far ahead of his time. Food reform and vegetarian living, advanced for political reasons, were ignored. Animal rights were laughed at, often by those being treated little better than animals themselves. For all his impatience, Hardie understood why agitation was slow work, and that 'everything has to grow', even socialism.[20]

What gave Hardie his strength as an agitator was his ethical perspective. Capitalism was epitomized by the 'selfish greed of each for himself',[21] while socialism was an 'instinct' in each of us, 'that highest impulse to share'. The ring of religion was always heard. 'Faith without works is dead' and capitalism 'in the end is bound to work its own overthrow', equivalent messages he found in all major world religions. Hardie believed each such religion (however subsequently commandeered by the state or by power-seekers) had started with the plight of the common people, and was a political movement; just as he believed scientific socialism was an ethical commandment.

As he grew older and left the organized church behind, he refined his ethics on the anvil of social consciousness until they were as near universal as he could make them. His flexible, humanitarian, but essentially cultural socialism, long thought to be so outdated, today assumes a new importance in a world where millions of people's politics are still confined to expression through their religion.

Hardie showed the way individual world religions could be transcended to reach a common political ethic, and the way common history could become its repository. For 'the same political life force' was in 'every just struggle' of the past,[21] sweeping 'in the true line of apostolic succession' from the Old Testament prophets through the 'pure communism' of the early Christian Church to the more familiar modern martyrs and revolutions. Every culture told the same story.

Hardie operated simultaneously in the lowest and highest spheres of politics. His main arena was the common people, whom he valued far above the rest; and popular support for socialism his major concern. If Hardie failed in the middle sphere of ideological debate, grasp of economic theory and parliamentary leadership, as he did, he more than made up for it at the higher end by his capacity to project that 'transforming vision',[22] so central a part of socialist success in the past. He and his contemporaries, but especially Hardie, were able to change the way a whole generation thought about what was possible, putting before people an alternative social vision that gave their work tremendous power, a power that is all but lost to today's politics of the Left.

Few tap it today, for it cannot be conjured artificially or used to fuel electoralism. It is a perception that informs year after year, in tract or in song, campaign by campaign, struggle by struggle, worked on by the named and nameless alike, and undertaken relentlessly for its own sake. It has to be its own reward, as early socialists always understood. One such, Helena Born, asked why she had given up her life to work for socialism, said simply, 'Social effort is (somewhat as love is) its own fulfilment, irrespective of success.'[23]

Most efforts for social justice tend to end in failure and always have done. Hardie met failure again and again. Yet for the sake of the successes that come when least anticipated or long after, he willingly spent a lifetime making the case for transformational social change, feeding the springs of that ever renewable activity of common people sharing a will to the common good.

When he was looking for a quotation to end his major piece of writing on socialism, *From Serfdom to Socialism*, he did not choose Mill or Marx or Morris, but a poem from George Eliot.[24]

He found a woman's poetry characterized the social effort he believed would always continue and always be the most valuable human activity.

No good is certain but the steadfast mind,
The undivided will to seek the good.
'Tis that compels the elements, and wrings
A human music from indifferent air . . .
We feed the high tradition of the world.

Keir Hardie surpassed all his contemporaries in carrying forward 'that high tradition of the world' which alone transforms society and advances social justice. Despite all its failure and failings, his life was successful.

NOTES

KH – Keir Hardie; ESP – Sylvia Pankhurst; JHS – Jean Hardie Scott;
NH – Nan Hardie; EM – Eleanor Marx; JRM – Ramsay MacDonald;
MS – Maggie Symons; RD – Rose Davies; AH – Agnes Hughes; LH
– Lillie Hardie; GBS – George Bernard Shaw; NA – Norman Angell;
CB – Caroline Benn

Acknowledgements

1. Hedley Dennis made his bequest of papers and artifacts in 1979, some five years before he died. According to a local historian who had visited Dennis (A. M. O'Brien, March 2 1985), 'It is clear that they were his most cherished possession'. Tony Benn was not known to Dennis personally, but was chosen, according to the witness to Dennis's will, (W. S. Bowden, 5 March 1985), because he 'exemplified the Labour Party'. William Wood, a Quaker colleague, wrote that Dennis also felt Benn's 'voice was the only voice which spoke with sanity and truth, particularly at the time of the Falklands War' (William Wood, 3 March 1985).

   The bequest consisted of correspondence from Keir Hardie and other members of the Hardie family, material relating to conscientious objection and work with Quaker organizations during World War I, newspapers (*Merthyr Pioneer, Labour Leader, Forward, Cumnock News*, and *Christian Commonwealth*), several busts of Keir Hardie, a collection of photographs of Hardie and Hughes family members, a chair (from Neville's Court), and an Indian walking stick believed to have come from Mahatma Gandhi but probably from S. K. Gokhale, his predecessor.

Introduction

1. Emrys Hughes, *Keir Hardie*, George Allen and Unwin, 1956, p. 8.
2. Kenneth O. Morgan, *Keir Hardie*, Radical and Socialist, Weidenfeld and Nicolson, 1975, paperback edition, 1984, p. 276.
3. See, for example, 'Jas Keir Hardie', Self Help Press, c. 1908; and W. T. Stead, 'James Keir Hardie', in series, 'Coming Men on Coming Questions', January, 1905.
4. See A. W. Humphrey, *A History of Labour Representation*, Constable and Co, 1912, and *The Book of the Labour Party*, Vols I, II, III, ed. H. Tracey, 1925.
5. See Emrys Hughes, *Keir Hardie*, 1956, p. 7.

6. See, for example, Henry
   Macnicol, 'Keir Hardie – the
   Man They Could Not Buy', a
   playscript (foreword by John
   Boyd) Westminster Productions,
   Grosvenor Books, 1984.
   The play was put on at the
   Westminster Theatre, sponsored
   by the Moral Rearmament
   Movement.
7. See, for example, John
   Cockburn, The Hungry Heart,
   a romantic biography of Keir
   Hardie, Jarrolds, London, 1956.
8. Sun, June 1 1987.
9. Emmanuel Shinwell, interviewed
   in 'A Generation Lost', in
   series Scotland's Story, Scotland
   Before World War I, Channel
   4, transmitted 12 December
   1987; preserved in National Film
   Archive.
10. Don Simpson, Introduction, to
    KH chapter from Garth Lane,
    Brave Men Chose, 1961, reprinted
    by Waterfront and Industrial
    Pioneer, London, 1979.
11. For example, Sylvia Ayling,
    Lecture, 1 July 1992, West Ham
    Town Hall. Sylvia's American
    biographer, Patricia Romero,
    Sylvia Pankhurst, Portrait of a
    Radical, Yale University Press,
    1987, is an exception.
12. Yvonne Kapp, Eleanor Marx,
    A biography in two volumes,
    Virago Press, Vol I, Family
    Life, 1972; Vol II, The Crowded
    Years, 1976.
13. Robert E. Dowse, ed., The
    Labour Ideal, six essays by
    socialists, Harvester Press,
    1974 (in series 'Society and the
    Victorians', ed., John Spiers),
    Introduction to Vol I, which
    includes Hardie's From Serfdom to
    Socialism, p. ix.
14. See Morgan, Keir Hardie,
    Chapter X.
15. Fred Reid, Keir Hardie: The
    Making of a Socialist, Croom
    Helm, 1978; 'Keir Hardie's
    Conversion to Socialism', Briggs,
    A. and Saville, J., eds., Essays in
    Labour History, Macmillan, 1971.

16. See, for example, Ian Taylor,
    'Keir Hardie – Marching at the
    Pace of the Slowest', Socialist
    Worker, March 8 1986.
17. G. B. Shaw, 'The Lessons
    of Burns and Lloyd George',
    article submitted to Forward, 25
    January 1943, National Library
    of Scotland, Dep 176, Box
    1, ff. 1–3.

Chapter 1 – Bitter Beginning

1. Fred Reid, 'The Early Life
   and Political Development of
   James Keir Hardie, 1856–1892',
   Ph.D. thesis, p. 348, (referred
   to hereafter as Thesis). Dr Reid
   commissioned a genealogical
   search of the family by the Scots
   Ancestry Research Society,
   included as Appendix I.
2. J. Bruce Glasier, James Keir
   Hardie, A Memorial, p. 9
   reprinted 1919, as Keir Hardie,
   the Man and his Message (referred
   to hereafter as Memorial).
3. See, The Essentials of Lenin,
   II, p. 474, quoting Karl Marx.
   Lenin, On Britain, Foreign
   Languages Publishing House,
   Moscow, p. 395.
4. Francis Johnson, Keir Hardie's
   Socialism, 1922. The rising was
   against George II and led to the
   Battle of Culloden.
5. Glasier, Diary, 28 December
   1915, University of Liverpool
   Archives; Elspeth King, The
   Strike of the Glasgow Weavers.
6. Reid, Thesis. p. 348
7. The spelling today is
   Legbrannock (though the village
   has been largely demolished)
   and another house stands on
   the site in what was once
   Woodhall Row. KH also spelled
   it 'Ligbrannock' in Ardrossan and
   Saltcoats Herald, 10 June 1882.
8. Keir Hardie's description is
   among the papers of KH's
   son-in-law, Emrys Hughes,

part of material collected for his biography of KH. It is written in Hughes's hand, quoting, he says, from an account KH wrote in adult life. Possibly it is one of the accounts cited p. 357 or p. 286. National Library of Scotland, Hughes Papers, Dep 176, Box 25, File 6. The first page of 18 numbered sheets is missing. See also Chapter 14, note 132.

9. Allan A. Durward, 'The Truth about James Kerr Alias James Keir Hardie and the ILP', MS, Nuffield College, Oxford, 1948. A.A. Durward was a member of the Aberdeen Socialist Society from 1888. From 1891 to 1896 Socialists in Aberdeen were organized by H. H. Champion in rivalry with Hardie for leadership of the SLP/ILP in Scotland. This helps to explain the animus that pervades the MS, which is of interest mainly to show the type of gossip that was circulating about Hardie in Scotland at the end of his life and afterwards.

10. The note about William Aitken (sometimes spelled Aitkin) was added to the side of Hardie's birth certificate, after the court found paternity proved on 14 October 1856.

11. Report of Katharine Glasier's meeting with Mary, told in S. Pankhurst, *The Homefront*, p. 237.

12. Durward op. cit.

13. Fred Reid, *Keir Hardie – The Making of a Socialist*, Chapters 1 and 2.

14. Emrys Hughes, *Keir Hardie*, p. 15.

15. *Ardrossan and Saltcoats Herald*, 3 June 1882.

16. Sylvia Pankhurst, 'Notes for an Obituary', Pankhurst Collection, file 9, folder 9c, International Institute of Social History (IISH), Amsterdam; S. Pankhurst, *The Suffragette Movement*, p. 177.

17. S. Pankhurst, 'Notes for an Obituary'.

18. Ibid.

19. He was the son of David Hardie, then dead, and Elizabeth Hill. Reid, Thesis, Appendix II, p. 351.

20. Ibid., pp. 346–7.

21. 1861 and 1871. Reid, Thesis, Appendix I.

22. G. B. Clark, quoted Iain McLean, *Keir Hardie*, p. 164.

23. Agnes (1862), Duncan (probably 1865–6; he is the only child not included in the genealogy, Reid, Thesis, Appendix I), and Alexander (1864).

24. For example, W. T. Stead, 'Jas Keir Hardie, MP', in the series, 'Coming Men on Coming Questions', January 1905, and Frank Smith, quoted in *James Keir Hardie*, Self-Help Press, n.d., c. 1908.

25. Letter to KH signed 'Affectionate Teacher' (the signature is hard to read, the library has interpreted it as A. P. Bosdet), dated 10 August 1867, National Library of Scotland, Dep 176, Box 1, File 1.

26. Reid, Thesis, p. 12. One of KH's favourite shops, where he loved the window displays, was run by Thomas Lipton. See also David Lowe, *From Pit to Parliament, The Story of the Early Life of James Keir Hardie*, p. 11.

27. The Education Act making it compulsory was not passed until 1870 in England and Wales, in 1872 in Scotland.

28. Jas K Hardie, Diary (Fragment) January through April 1884, Museum of Labour History, Manchester.

29. Lowe, *Pit to Parliament*, p. 10.

30. Reid, *Keir Hardie*, p. 14.

31. Lowe, *Pit to Parliament*, p. 16.

32. *Merthyr Pioneer*, 26 December 1914.

33. 'Christmas Message', *Labour Leader*, 1897.

34. *Labour Leader*, 1906, 50th birthday message quoted in *Keir Hardie, Writings and Speeches*, ed. Emrys Hughes, pp. 124–5; also W. Stewart, *Keir Hardie*, p. 245.

35. At some point Agnes Paterson had married a quarry labourer. She died in 1873 at the age of sixty-three. Reid, Thesis, Appendix I.

36. Quoted in Fyfe, *Keir Hardie, pp.* 7 and 17, also in *Ardrossan and Saltcoats Herald.*

37. *Ardrossan and Saltcoats Herald,* 13 May 1882. KH states here he was only nine years old, but elsewhere he says he was ten, and if all his other dates are correct, he would have been ten.

38. Stewart, p. 6; and Lowe, p. 19.

39. According to G. B. Clark, quoted in McLean, p. 164.

40. *James Keir Hardie, the Father of the British Labour Party,* Cumnock and Doon Valley Tourist Association brochure, undated, but about 1985.

41. Hughes, *Keir Hardie,* p. 23; Stewart assumes it must have had, p. 6.

42. Hughes, *Keir Hardie,* p. 23.

43. Stewart says that they were not forbidden, p. 6, but Hughes is probably more accurate, p. 23.

44. Stewart, p. 6.

45. Glasier, *Memorial,* p. 10.

46. *Labour Leader,* 3 July 1908.

47. See, McLean, p. 164.

48. Reid, Thesis, Appendix I. The last, Elizabeth, was born in 1876, when Hardie was 20.

49. Ibid.

50. ESP, 'Notes', file 9, folder 9c, IISH, Amsterdam.

51. Letter, 10 August 1867, National Library of Scotland, Dep 176, Box 1, File 1.

52. Hughes, *Keir Hardie,* p. 17.

53. Reid, *Keir Hardie,* p. 20.

54. *Labour Leader,* 15 August 1906.

55. *Ardrossan and Saltcoats Herald,* 13 May 1882.

56. *Labour Leader,* 15 August 1906.

57. *Ardrossan and Saltcoats Herald,* 3 June 1882.

58. Stewart, p. 7.

59. *Ardrossan and Saltcoats Herald,* 23 December 1882; also Sylvia Pankhurst, 'Notes', file 9, folder 9c, IISH, Amsterdam.

60. *Labour Leader,* 24 August and 3 December 1906.

61. *Ardrossan and Saltcoats Herald,* 13 May 1882.

62. Tom Mann, *Memoirs,* p. 3.

63. *Labour Leader,* February 1893, quoted in Reid, *Keir Hardie,* p. 17.

64. Ibid.

65. *Ardrossan and Saltcoats Herald,* 23 December 1882.

66. ESP, 'Notes', file 9, folder 9c, IISH, Amsterdam.

67. *Labour Leader,* 26 March 1898, quoted also in Hughes, *Writings,* p. 3.

68. *Labour Leader,* 22 January 1909, and Hughes, *Writings,* p. 139.

69. Quoted in Hughes, *Keir Hardie,* p. 19.

70. Ibid.

71. *Ardrossan and Saltcoats Herald,* 3 June 1882.

72. Stewart, p. 7.

73. ESP, 'Notes', file 9, folder 9c, IISH, Amsterdam.

74. Mann, *Memoirs,* p. 7.

75. Hughes, *Keir Hardie,* pp. 23–4; Reid, *Keir Hardie,* p. 39.

76. E. P. Thompson, *The Making of the English Working Class,* Penguin, 1980, Part 1, Chapter 16.

77. Keir Hardie, 'The Labour Party and the Books that helped to make it', *Review of Reviews,* 1906.

78. KH to James Henderson, 17 October 1911, Cumnock Library.

79. *Labour Leader,* 22 June 1909.

80. Sylvia Pankhurst, *The Suffragette Movement,* pp. 175–6.

81. W. T. Stead, 'Jas Keir Hardie, MP', in the series, 'Coming Men on Coming Questions', January 1905.

82. Ibid., also Philip Snowden, *Autobiography,* Vol I, p. 315.

83. Lowe, *Pit to Parliament,* p. 20.

84. Snowden, Vol I, p. 304. From KH's own account (*Ardrossan and Saltcoats Herald,* 13 May 1882), it would seem Lowe is correct.

85. Snowden, Vol I, p. 315.

86. Hughes says he read Carlyle at sixteen, while Stewart claims he was twenty-six. The former is correct. See *Keir Hardie, Review of Reviews*, June 1906.
87. *Review of Reviews*, June 1906.
88. Ibid.
89. Elspeth King, *Scotland Sober and Free – The Temperance Movement, 1829–1979*, p. 5.
90. *Ardrossan and Saltcoats Herald*, 2 November 1883.
91. Hughes, *Keir Hardie*, p. 16.
92. Morgan,*Keir Hardie*, p. 4, assumes he did not know until adulthood, while Reid, *Keir Hardie*, p. 185, suggests he always knew. There is no direct evidence either way.
93. King, *Scotland, Sober and Free*, p. 16.
94. Ibid.
95. Ibid., p. 23.
96. KH, Diary, 13 March 1884.
97. Ibid., 7 February 1884.
98. Ibid., 13 February 1884.
99. Stewart, p. 13.
100. KH, Diary, 4 March 1884.
101. Ibid.
102. Ibid.
103. Hughes, *Keir Hardie*, p. 27.
104. This is her occupation given on the marriage banns when published for the third time, 1 August, Hamilton, Parish of Cadzow, preserved in the Hardie-Hughes papers, Cumnock and Doon Valley Library. The document is dated 1880 (though 1879 is always given subsequently)
105. Lowe, *Pit to Parliament*, p. 35.
106. Pankhurst, 'Notes', file 9, folder 9c, IISH, Amsterdam.
107. See R. Page Arnot, *History of the Scottish Miners*, 1955.
108. H. Tracey, ed., *The Book of the Labour Party*, Vol I, p. 32.
109. *Ardrossan and Saltcoats Herald*, 29 April 1882. Reid, Thesis, p. 20.
110. Stewart, p. 8.
111. Stewart, pp. 11–12.
112. Stewart, p. 12.
113. *Review of Reviews*, 1906. Hughes, *Writings*, pp. 140–2, 'Labour and Christianity,' Speech at Browning Hall, 5 May 1910.
114. David Strauss, *Life of Jesus*, 1835, translated by George Eliot.
115. *Review of Reviews*, 1906; and Hughes, *Writings*, p. 138; Ernest Renan, *La Vie de Jésus*, 1863, was translated into English in a cheap popular edition, Mathieson and Co., 1875.
116. *Review of Reviews*, 1906.
117. A. P. Bosdet, Letter, 10 August 1867, National Library of Scotland.
118. Stewart, p. 365.
119. *Labour Leader*, 25 June 1898. Lowe, *Pit to Parliament*, p. 142.
120. Keir Hardie, Overtoun Series, 1899; Hughes, *writings*, pp. 85–93.
121. Reid, *Keir Hardie*, p. 44; and Morgan, *Keir Hardie*, p. 193.
122. Quoted in Snowden, Vol I, p. 317.
123. Snowden, p. 317.
124. J. C. Kenworthy, *Weekly Times and Echo*, USA, quoted in Lowe, p. 63.
125. Durward.
126. There are differences between Reid, Thesis, p. 26; Morgan, p. 8; KH, Diary fragment, Museum of Labour History; Hughes, *Keir Hardie*, p. 24; and Stewart, p. 8.
127. KH, Diary Fragment, Museum of Labour History.
128. Reported in *West Ham Daily Herald*, 22 July 1893
129. Laurence Thompson, *Robert Blatchford, Portrait of an Englishman*, pp. 69–71.
130. McLean, p. 164.
131. E. King, *The People's Palace*, p. 25.
132. T. Honeyman, *Good Templary in Scotland*, p. 49f, quoted in Reid, Thesis, p. 114. See also William Adamson, *The Life of the Reverend James Morison* 1898, and Morgan, p. 8.
133. Bede, *A History of the English Church and People*, Penguin Classics, 1968, pp. 58–66; also J. H. Blunt, *Dictionary of Sects*,

*Heresies, Ecclesiastical Parties
and Schools of Religious Thought*,
Rivingtons, 1874.
134. Hughes, *Keir Hardie*, p. 24.
135. *Labour Leader*, 26 August 1906.
136. Hughes, *Keir Hardie*, p. 23.
137. Reid, *Keir Hardie*, p. 39.
138. ESP's observation, quoted in
P. Romero, *Sylvia Pankhurst,
Portrait of a Radical*, p. 32.
139. Lowe, *Pit to Parliament*, p. 19.
140. Reid, *Keir Hardie*, p. 39, quoting
a speech of KH's reported in the
Chicago Chronicle, 1895.
141. Hughes, *Keir Hardie*, p. 24.
142. *West Ham Daily Herald*, 22
July 1893

Chapter 2 – Climbing the Liberal Ladder

1. Stewart, p. 8.
2. Evidence to the Royal
Commission on Labour, Report
of the Royal Commission
on Labour, 1892, Minutes
of Evidence xxxvi, QQ
12891, 13021.
3. Correspondence on miners'
behalf, in KH's Letter Book,
where he kept carbon copies
of all letters he wrote from
1879–81, National Library of
Scotland, Dep 176, Vol 8.
4. Hughes, *Keir Hardie*, p. 27.
5. Ibid., p. 26, probably to
Corresponding Secretary.
6. Stewart, pp. 8–9.
7. Hughes, *Keir Hardie*, p. 193. It is
from the poem *Asolande*.
8. KH, Diary, 13 February 1884.
9. Edmund Stonelake, *Autobiography
of Edmund Stonelake*, p. 27.
10. Reid, *Keir Hardie*, p. 24.
11. Hughes, *Keir Hardie*, p. 27,
Hardie Diary Fragment, 1884.
But see note 104, ch. 1.
12. *Glasgow Weekly Mail*, 7
September 1879
13. Reid, Thesis, p. 41.
14. Ibid., p. 43.
15. Reid, 'Keir Hardie's Conversion
to Socialism', in *Essays in Labour*

History, eds A. Briggs and J.
Saville, p. 27.
16. Reid, Thesis, p. 44.
17. Ibid., quoted in *Glasgow Weekly
Mail*, 20 December 1879.
18. Ibid., p. 46 quoted in *Hamilton
Advertiser*, 3 January 1880.
19. Ibid., p. 47 quoted in *Glasgow
Weekly Mail*, 10 January 1880.
20. Reported in *Ardrossan and
Saltcoats Herald*, 19 August 1880.
Reports *North British Daily Mail*,
10, 14 August 1880, quoted in
Reid, Thesis, pp. 51–2.
21. Francis Johnson, *Keir Hardie's
Socialism*.
22. Smillie, *My Life For Labour*, 1924,
p. 4. Hardie thought the 'general
strike' a success (KH to A.
MacDonald, 11 November 1880,
Dep 176, Vol 8, National Library
of Scotland).
23. Reid, Thesis, pp. 52–3.
24. Hughes, *Keir Hardie*, p. 28.
25. Reid, Thesis, p. 55.
26. MacDonald's letter is dated
8 November 1880, and is
reproduced point by point in
KH's reply, dated 11 November
1880, KH disputing each point.
KH's Letter Book, National
Library of Scotland, Dep
176, Vol. 8.
27. Hughes's handwritten note in
his Notes for KH's biography
commenting on the MacDonald
correspondence; marked 'unused'
in the margin, National Library
of Scotland, Dep 176, Box
25, File 6.
28. In KH's later articles for the
Ardrossan and Saltcoats Herald he
mentions MacDonald several
times, pointedly referring to
his wealth and to plans for
a memorial statue, which
encountered many difficulties.
See, for example, 10 June 1882.
29. KH to *National Labour Tribune*,
31 November 1880, Dep 176,
Vol 8. In later reports (26 April
1881, for example) KH greatly
exaggerates the success of the
Ayrshire Miners' Union.
30. Correspondence with E.

Chapman, 1880–1, Dep 176, Vol 8, especially KH to EC, 4 July, 5 August and 31 November 1881.

31. KH to Alexander Begg, 12 November 1880, Dep 176, Vol 8.

32. Rules of the Ayrshire Miners' Association, Kilmarnock, 1881, Scottish Record Office, FS 7/3, quoted in Reid, Thesis, pp. 55–6.

33. Ibid.

34. Hughes, *Keir Hardie*, p. 28.

35. Ibid.

36. Ibid.; KH, Correspondence, Dep 176, Vol 8. *passim*.

37. Reports, 8 January, 27 August and 3 December 1881, quoted in Reid, Thesis, pp. 57–8.

38. Morgan, *Keir Hardie*, p. 12.

39. Stewart, p. 10.

40. KH, Diary, Introduction, January 1884. The *Cumnock News* editions for the early 1880s were all destroyed by fire; only the columns as they appear in the *Ardrossan and Saltcoats Herald* survive.

41. *Ardrossan and Saltcoats Herald*, 13 May 1882.

42. For example, *Androssan and Saltcoats Herald*, 5 January 1883.

43. *Ardrossan and Saltcoats Herald*, 31 March 1884.

44. Ibid., 5 January 1883; 19 January 1883.

45. Ibid., 20 May 1882.

46. KH, Diary, 8 February 1884.

47. *Paisley Daily Express*, 25 July 1883.

48. Stewart, p. 20.

49. *Ardrossan and Saltcoats Herald*, 10 December 1881.

50. Ibid., 22 July 1882.

51. Dep 176, Vol 8; Reid, *Keir Hardie*, p. 58; John Strawhorn, *New History of Cumnock*, p. 153.

52. Stewart, p. 20.

53. *Ardrossan and Saltcoats Herald*, 30 December 1882.

54. *Ardrossan and Saltcoats Herald*, 27 May 1882.

55. Ibid., 14 June 1883.

56. Ibid., 20 February 1885; Reid, *Keir Hardie*, p. 76.

57. *Ardrossan and Saltcoats Herald*, 9 March, 26 March 1883.

58. Ibid., 10 December 1881.

59. *Ardrossan and Saltcoats Herald*, 30 September 1884.

60. Strawhorn, pp. 153–4; Reid, *Keir Hardie*, p. 70. His hat and coat are also mentioned in H. Escott, *History of Scottish Congregationalism*, Glasgow, 1960, p. 328; KH reported in *West Ham Herald*, 22 July 1893.

61. Mann, *Memoirs*, p. 3.

62. Ibid., p. 14.

63. Ibid., p. 25.

64. Chushichi Tsuzuki, *H.M. Hyndman and British Socialism*, p. 33.

65. Ibid., p. 34.

66. Quoted in ibid., pp. 34–5.

67. Engels to Bebel, 20 August 1883. Quoted in Yvonne Kapp, *Eleanor Marx*, Vol I, p. 210, Vol II, p. 44; see also Vol I, p. 210.

68. Raymond Unwin, 'Reminiscences', *ILP News*, January 1902.

69. Engels to Laura Lafargue, 4 May 1891. Quoted in Kapp, Vol II, p. 475.

70. Quoted in Ibid.

71. Hyndman to Liebknecht, 31 August 1897. Quoted in Ibid., p. 56.

72. Ibid., p. 44.

73. Engels to Laura Lafargue, 22 August 1894. Quoted in Ibid., p. 656.

74. Morris to James Joynes, 25 December 1884. Quoted Ibid., p. 60

75. Mann, p. 32.

76. James Neil, 'Memories of an Ayrshire Agitator', *Forward*, 4 July 1914. Neil was himself converted by another miner, James Patrick.

77. Mann, p. 33; p. 63.

78. EM to Laura Lafargue, 21 July 1884. Quoted Kapp, Vol II, p. 57.

79. Fabian Society, Tract No. 70, 1896.

80. Mann, p. 17.

81. 'The Labour Party and the

Books that Helped to Make it', *Review of Reviews*, 1906, pp. 570–1. Lowe, Pit to Parliament, says KH spent the two days with him in 1884, p. 20.

82. Hughes, *Keir Hardie*, p. 145. The Communist Manifesto was not generally available in English until 1887.

83. *Ardrossan and Saltcoats Herald*, 14 October 1882.

84. KH, Diary, 6 and 13 February 1884.

85. Ibid., Introduction.

86. Reid, Thesis, p. 157.

87. KH, Diary, 7 February 1884.

88. Ibid.

89. Ibid., 21 February 1884.

90. Ibid., 12 March 1884.

91. Ibid., 15 February 1884.

92. Ibid., 1 January 1884.

93. Ibid., 11 March 1884.

94. Ibid.

95. Ibid., 13 February 1884.

96. Ibid., 18 February 1884.

97. Ibid.

98. Ibid., 20 February 1884.

99. Ibid., 17 March 1884.

100. Ibid., 14 March 1884.

101. Ibid., 23 March 1884.

102. Ibid., 29 March 1884.

103. Ibid., 7 April 1884.

104. Ibid., 11 April 1884.

105. Ibid., 3 March 1884.

106. Pelling, p. 129.

107. Ibid.

108. Beatrice Webb, *My Apprenticeship*, Longman's Green, 1926, p. 140.

Chapter 3 – Conversion

1. ESP, 'Notes for Obituary' of KH, file 9, folder 9c, IISH, Amsterdam.

2. Morgan, *Keir Hardie*, Chapter 10, and *passim*.

3. Morgan, *Keir Hardie*, pp. 89–92, pp. 202–4; Fyfe, *Keir Hardie*, pp. 70–1; McLean, *Keir Hardie*, p. 172.

4. Reid, *The Making of a Socialist*, pp. 181–4.

5. Hughes, *Keir Hardie*, p. 24.

6. McLean, *Keir Hardie*, p. 52; Fenner Brockway, *Towards Tomorrow*, p. 21.

7. G.D.H. Cole, *Keir Hardie, A Biographical Sketch*, p. 3; Lowe, *Pit to Parliament*, p. 22.

8. Francis Johnson, *Keir Hardie's Socialism*.

9. Kapp, *Eleanor Marx*, Vol II, pp. 314, 633; Engels to Sorge, 2 July 1889, quoted Kapp, p. 314. It would appear from this letter that the term 'Marxist' did not begin to be used until 1889, when it was given to those attending the Second International by those attending the rival congress.

10. Hughes, *Keir Hardie*, p. 29.

11. Small, a friend of John Glasse, (socialist minister of Greyfriars Church), Edinburgh, held regular discussions on socialism at his home. According to a note his daughter left in the flyleaf of an ILP Jubilee souvenir programme, KH was also an attender (B. Small Collection, Acc 3359, National Library of Scotland). There is evidence, however, that KH and Small did not get on. See, for example, KH to CG, 15 February 1888, National Library of Scotland, Dep 176, Vol 8.

12. *Cumnock News*, 1 October 1915. These were rooms the Liberal Party made available for meetings in Cumnock.

13. Morgan, *Keir Hardie*, p. 14. If he did read *Justice* it was not regularly. See KH to Engels, 24 May 1889, Letter 2159, Marx/ Engels Collection, IISH, Amsterdam. He admired and read Morris, see Hughes, *Keir Hardie*, p. 29. KH might also have read socialist journals through James Patrick, a fellow miner, who had already heard John Burns and Henry Hyndman in London. See *Memories of an*

Ayrshire Agitator, edited by John Roe, *Forward*, 4, 11 and 18 July 1914.

14. Hughes, *Keir Hardie*, p. 29.
15. Keir Hardie, *Young Men in a Hurry*, 1897.
16. *Ardrossan and Saltcoats Herald*, 12 September 1884.
17. Ibid., 20 November 1885.
18. Records of the Auchinleck School Board. He is first recorded in the minutes on 26 March 1885, and last on 20 October 1887. Strawhorn, *History of Cumnock*, p. 110, Minute Books, Auchinleck Parish School Board.
19. Pelling, *Origins*, pp. 40, 146, quoting Barry's letter to the *Workman's Times*, 3 September 1892, where he makes the admission.
20. 4 December 1885.
21. Pelling, p. 41.
22. David Marquand, *Ramsay MacDonald*, p. 5.
23. Samson Bryher (ed.), *An Account of the Labour and Socialist Movement in Bristol*, Part I, pp. 30–2.
24. KH, Diary, 8 April 1884.
25. *Ardrossan and Saltcoats Herald*, 26 March 1886.
26. Victoria to Gladstone, dated 11 February 1886, in *The Letters of Queen Victoria*, quoted Tsuzuki, p. 174.
27. Marx to Jenny Marx, 11 April 1881, quoted Kapp, Vol I, pp. 209–10.
28. Tsuzuki, p. 80.
29. In 1884, quoted in McLean, p. 32.
30. Strawhorn, p. 110, Minutes, Cumnock Town Council, November 1886.
31. Auchinleck School Board, Minutes, 26 March, 14 May and 13 August 1885.
32. *Ardrossan and Saltcoats Herald*, 26 September 1884.
33. Ibid., 19 November 1886.
34. Rules of the Ayrshire Miners' Union and Guild of Comrade Colliers, October 1886, Scottish Record Office, FS 7/18; quoted in Reid, Thesis, pp. 153–4.
35. Ibid., K. H. Preamble.
36. Report of a speech to Derbyshire ILP, *Derbyshire Times*, 11 September 1897. In the report the *Cumnock News* is misreported as the *Cambrian News*.
37. Hughes, *Keir Hardie*, p. 30.
38. Stewart, p. 36.
39. First issue of *The Miner*, January 1887.
40. Reid, Thesis, p. 166.
41. Stewart, p. 31.
42. *Miner*, January 1888.
43. M. MacArthur, R. MacDonald, R. Smillie, *Memoir of Keir Hardie*.
44. On 27 November 1886.
45. *Ardrossan and Saltcoat Herald*, 3 December 1886.
46. Ibid., 21 January 1887.
47. Quoted in Stewart, p. 34.
48. *The Miner*, February 1887.
49. *Commonweal*, 26 February 1887.
50. *Ardrossan and Saltcoats Herald*, 25 February 1887.
51. *The Miner*, February 1887; Reid, Thesis, p. 172; Hughes, *Writings*, p. 5.
52. Laurence Thompson, *The Enthusiasts*, p. 19. The farmer's name had been John Bruce but the mother adopted the name Glasier and the boy became known as Bruce Glasier in the same way as KH was known as Keir Hardie. See Thompson, p. 21.
53. The words of James Leatham, quoted by Thompson, *The Enthusiasts*, p. 41.
54. Kapp, Vol II, pp. 38–9, for a description of these observances.
55. James Leatham, quoted in Thompson, *The Enthusiasts*, p. 41.
56. Glasier, *Memorial*, p. 57.
57. Ibid., p. 58.
58. Ibid., p. 14.
59. Ibid., p. 54.
60. Thompson, *The Enthusiasts*, p. 14. Glasier, *Memorial*, p. 114.
61. Glasier, *William Morris and the Early Days of the Socialist Movement*, 1921, p. 32.

62. See *Ardrossan and Saltcoats Herald*, 26 January 1883 for KH's comments on this subject.
63. Glasier, *Memorial*, p. 20.
64. Andrew Lang, the antiquarian, makes the assertion in A. F. Tschiffely, *Don Roberto, The Life of R. B. Cunninghame Graham*, p. 4.
65. Tschiffely, p. 24.
66. Ibid., p. 265. *Santa Teresa; Her Life and Times*, given the Vatican's *permissio superiorum*.
67. Ibid., p. 24.
68. Books on CG since 1970 include: Cedric Watts, *Cunninghame Graham, A Critical Biography, Cup* 1979; *Selected Writings*, ed. Cedric Watts, Associated University Presses, 1981; *The North American Sketches*, ed. John Walker, Scottish Academic Press, Edinburgh, 1886; *The South American Sketches*, ed. John Walker, University of Oklahoma Press, 1978; *The Best of Cunninghame Graham*, ed. Paul Harris, Edinburgh, 1979.
69. He was not elected in this year but rather at the next election in 1886.
70. Morgan, *Keir Hardie*, p. 21. Fyfe also dismissed him, *Keir Hardie*, pp. 76–7, as did Glasier, *Memorial*, p. 28.
71. McLean, 1975, p. 88.
72. Hughes, *Keir Hardie*, p. 33.
73. Ibid., p. 35.
74. Reid, 'Keir Hardie's Conversion to Socialism' in *Essays in Labour History*, eds. A. Briggs and J. Saville, p. 45.
75. Kapp, Vol II, p. 487.
76. Pelling, p. 105.
77. Maiden speech to the House of Commons, 1886, quoted, Hughes, *Keir Hardie*, p. 34.
78. Report of speech during 1886 election campaign, *North British Daily Mail*, 29 June 1886, quoted in Reid, Thesis, p. 201.
79. Engels to F. D. Nieuwenhuis, 23 February 1888
80. Tschiffely, p. 207.
81. Quoted in *Ardrossan and Saltcoats Herald*, 25 February 1887.
82. Tschiffely, p. 212.
83. Ibid., p. 195.
84. *The Miner*, May 1887.
85. Ibid.
86. Ibid.
87. Ibid., July 1887; Reid, Thesis, p. 208.
88. *The Miner*, July 1887.
89. Ibid., January 1888; Reid, Thesis, p. 179.
90. Reid, *Keir Hardie*, p. 98.
91. Tschiffely, p. 207.
92. Ibid., p. 204.
93. Ibid., p. 195.
94. Ibid., p. 205.
95. *Commonweal*, 22 October 1887; Reid, Thesis, p. 223. Among others who had proposed a Labour Party was Michael Davitt (*Leaves from a Prison Diary*, 1885).
96. *The Miner*, April 1887.
97. This was generally reckoned to be in early 1887 (Morgan, *Keir Hardie*, p. 18), although Smillie recalls it as 1886 (MacArthur, MacDonald and Smillie, *Memoir*).
98. *Glasgow Herald*, 11 February 1887, reported in Reid, Thesis, p. 193.
99. *Ardrossan and Saltcoat Herald*, 25 February 1887.
100. Ibid., 1 July 1887.
101. Parliamentary Debates (Commons), 17 August 1887, 3rd series, Vol CCCXIX, cols. 900ff.
102. *Ardrossan and Saltcoats Herald*, 18 February 1887.
103. Hughes, *Keir Hardie*, pp. 35–6.
104. *The Miner*, July 1887; *Ardrossan and Saltcoats Herald*, 10 September 1887.
105. *Ardrossan and Saltcoats Herald*, 3 December 1886. KH had criticized Broadhurst for promoting temperance when it was well known he drank.
106. TUC Report, TUC Congress, 1887, p. 29.
107. Glasier, *Memorial*, p. 16.
108. TUC Report, p. 31; the Biblical reference was to the last chapter of the book of Jonah.
109. *North British Daily Mail*,

24 September 1887; Reid, Thesis, p. 219.

110. NH, Biographical Note, Hughes, *Writings*, p. ix.

111. Quoted in Stewart, p. 49.

112. KH to James Young, c. 1888, National Library of Scotland, Acc 8125. James Young was a contributor to *The Miner* and later became manager of the Co-operative Baking Society.

113. Lowe, *Pit to Parliament*, p. 26. She spoke in French for the benefit of a French trade union delegation visiting the TUC.

114. Charles Brown, Typographical Association, quoted in Morgan, *Keir Hardie*, p. 38.

115. Lowe, *Pit to Parliament*, p. 31. TUC Congress, Liverpool, 1890.

116. Pelling, *Origins*, p. 62.

117. Smillie, *My Life for Labour*, p. 74.

118. 17 September 1887.

119. Recollected by J. Neil, 'Memoirs of an Ayrshire Agitator', *Forward*, 4 July 1914.

120. *The Miner*, July 1887.

121. Ibid.

122. *Ardrossan and Saltcoats Herald*, 14 May 1887.

123. *The Miner*, July 1887.

124. Mann, p. 44.

125. Ibid.

126. *Ardrossan and Saltcoats Herald*, 24 May 1887.

127. Mann, pp. 40–1.

128. Recalled in *Labour Leader*, 'Between Ourselves', 24 December 1898.

129. CG had a high opinion of EM and her work. See *The Labour Elector*, 27 July 1888, quoted in Kapp, Vol II, p. 316. Morgan, *Keir Hardie*, p. 16, believes the introduction to Engels came from William Small.

130. Letter EM to Wilhelm Liebknecht, quoted Kapp, Vol II, p. 306.

131. Ibid.

132. 29 October 1887.

133. The ban was illegally imposed by government in advance of the legislation required, which was

not passed until March 1888; see Kapp, Vol II, p. 222.

134. 16 November 1887, quoted in Kapp, Vol II, p. 229–30.

135. Letter to William Morris, 22 November 1887, quoted ibid., Vol II, p. 231.

136. EM to Laura Lafargue, 16 November 1887, Vol II, p. 229.

137. Aymer Vallance, *The Life and Work of William Morris*, p. 362; *Commonweal*, 19 November 1887.

138. The Law and Liberty League, which held its first meeting on 18 November 1887.

139. Reid, *Keir Hardie*, Chapters 4 and 5.

140. Quoted in Stewart, p. 29.

141. Ibid., p. 28.

142. At Dudston, 28 May 1887.

143. *Ardrossan and Saltcoats Herald*, 10 June 1887; Reid, Thesis, p. 196.

144. Stewart, p. 34.

145. JHS to CB, 28 June 1989.

146. KH to James Young, 29 July, 1887, National Library of Scotland, Dep 176, Vol 8.

147. There is an account of her death, given by KH to ESP, in 'Notes,' file 9, folder 9 (9b), IISH, Amsterdam.

148. Stewart, p. 29.

149. Ibid.

150. All but one member of the Hardie family are buried in a common grave in Cumnock cemetery. There is a common single headstone. Sarah's dates are 1884–7.

151. Quoted in Jalland, *Women, Marriage and Politics, 1860–1914*, p. 182.

152. KH, Diary, 15 March 1884.

153. ESP, 'Notes', file 9, folder 9, IISH, Amsterdam.

154. Quoted in Stewart, p. 54.

155. Tschiffely, p. 210.

156. GBS, Introductory Source Note, *Three Plays for Puritans*, 1900, quoted Ibid., p. 262; Hughes, *Keir Hardie*, p. 35.

157. Source Note, 1900, quoted Tschiffely, p. 263.

158. Quoted in Hughes, *Keir
      Hardie*, p. 34.

Chapter 4 – National and International Stage

1.   William Morris, in *Commonweal*,
     25 June 1887.
2.   *Ardrossan and Saltcoats Herald*,
     13 May, 2 September and 11
     November 1887.
3.   Reid, 'Keir Hardie's Conversion
     to Socialism', p. 19; and Reid,
     Keir Hardie, p. 110.
4.   Reid, Thesis, p. 223.
5.   *Commonweal*, 22 October 1884,
     article by J. H. Mahon.
6.   *The Miner*, January 1888.
7.   *Ardrossan and Saltcoats Herald*, 18
     February 1887.
8.   Reported in the *Scottish Leader*, 3
     September 1887.
9.   KH to Baillie Burt, Chair of the
     Mid-Lanark Liberal Association,
     15 March 1888, National Library
     of Scotland, Dep 176, Vol 8.
10. NH, Introduction, to Hughes,
     Writings, p. x. The candidate
     was J. Wynford Phillips, later
     Viscount St Davids.
11. KH pencil notes on Mid-Lanark
     by-election, undated, Museum
     of Labour History, Manchester.
12. C. A. V. Conybeare, MP.
13. Pencil notes on Mid-Lanark
     by-election. This visit from
     George Trevelyn seems to have
     been in addition to the visit
     made later by F. A. Schnadhorst,
     secretary of the National Liberal
     Federation, but it could be that
     KH confused them when he
     wrote about the incident later
     in the *Labour Leader*, 12 March
     1914. In that account the visits
     were merged into one.
14. John Ferguson, Letter, *Glasgow
     Observer*, 21 April 1888, quoted
     in Reid, Thesis, p. 237.
15. Ibid.
16. In his Election Address,
     reproduced in *The Miner*, April

1888, KH claimed, 'I have
all my life belonged' to the
Liberal Party.
17. Hughes, *Keir Hardie*, p. 45.
18. Ibid.
19. Ibid., p. 44.
20. Mann, *Memoirs*, p. 39.
21. Minute Book of Scottish Home
     Rule Association, quoted in
     Morgan, *Keir Hardie*, p. 27.
22. Pelling, *Origins*, p. 67.
23. Champion to KH, 14 March
     1888, Letter 88/2, Francis
     Johnson Correspondence, LSE.
24. Ibid., 6 April 1888, Letter
     88/39.
25. Ibid., 14 March 1888.
26. KH to CG, 15 February 1888,
     National Library of Scotland,
     Dep 176. Vol 8. In a letter on
     March 15, KH told CG the
     election would cost £600, but
     that if 'the mining and Irish vote
     can be secured, the seat is ours'.
27. E. Harford to KH, 13 April
     1888, Letter 88/47, Francis
     Johnson Correspondence.
     Harford was treasurer of the
     'Labour Party' section of the
     Association.
28. F. Threlfall to KH, 19 April
     1888, Letter 88/61, Francis
     Johnson Correspondence.
     See also Threlfall, 24 April,
     Letter 88/75.
29. C. A. V. Conybeare, MP, to
     CG 20 April 1888, Letter 88/64,
     Francis Johnson Correspondence.
     Not being satisfied, Conybeare
     pulled out of KH's campaign.
     CG remained loyal and said later
     he didn't care 'a farthing' where
     Champion got his money, *North
     British Daily Mail*, 22 June 1888.
30. Kapp, *Eleanor Marx*, Vol II,
     p. 221. KH reviewed *Out of
     Work*, in the *Ardrossan and
     Saltcoats Herald*, 13 July 1888, and
     Engels earlier had sent Harkness
     comment on *A City Girl* in
     1887. (Their correspondence
     is in the Institute of Leninism-
     Marxism, Moscow.) According
     to Beatrice Webb a year later
     (Diary, written as Beatrice

Potter, 13 November 1889, quoted in Reid, *Keir Hardie* p. 126, n.36), Harkness claimed she had sent nothing.

31. Letter to the *North British Daily Mail*, 28 June 1888.

32. KH to Champion, 24 March 1888, National Library of Scotland, Dep 176, Vol 8. KH said he had exaggerated the campaign cost to £800 for their 'consumption'.

33. KH, quoted in the *Glasgow Herald*, 16 April 1888, reprinted in Morgan, *Keir Hardie*, p. 33.

34. Hughes, *Keir Hardie*, p. 46. The voting figures were Liberals 3,847, Conservatives 2,917 and KH 617.

35. KH's lawyer was T. McNaught. See McNaught to Schnadhorst, 21 April 1888, and McNaught to KH, 25 April 1888, Francis Johnson Correspondence. A settlement was eventually reached, as the case never came to court.

36. KH's remarks quoted in Humphrey, *History of Labour Representation*, 1912, p. 122.

37. MacArthur, MacDonald, Smillie, *Memoir*.

38. Hughes, *Keir Hardie*, p. 47.

39. Ibid.

40. *The Voice of Labour*, being the Report of the first annual Labour Electrol Congress, 1888.

41. Hughes, *Keir Hardie*, p. 48.

42. *The Miner*, September 1888.

43. Morgan, *Keir Hardie*, p. 34.

44. Stewart, *Keir Hardie*, p. 48. The dates were 6–10 November 1888.

45. Mann, p. 51.

46. Klugman, *The History of the Communist Party*, Vol I, p. 18.

47. *The Miner*, December 1888; Stewart, p. 50.

48. *The Miner*, December 1887; and *Ardrossan and Saltcoats Herald*, 18 November 1887.

49. See his evidence to the Select Committee on Emigration and Immigration, 1889, quoted

in Reid, *Keir Hardie*, p. 126, footnote 59.

50. Report in *The Miner*, November 1888.

51. Ibid.

52. Ibid.

53. Ibid.

54. ESP, file 9, folder 9b, IISH Amsterdam.

55. Kapp, *Eleanor Marx*, Vol II, p. 248; *Justice*, 21 February 1891.

56. Kapp, Vol II, pp. 456–7.

57. Romero, p. 8.

58. Quoted in Mitchell, *The Fighting Pankhursts*, p. 24.

59. Romero, p. 9.

60. S. Pankhurst, *The Suffragette Movement*, p. 7.

61. Ibid., p. 47. Jacob was the brother of John Bright.

62. Quoted in Jalland, *Women, Marriage and Politics*, p. 215.

63. Organized by Mrs Humphrey Ward and published in *Nineteenth Century*, in 1889.

64. Jalland, p. 214.

65. Kapp, Vol II, p. 293.

66. Ibid., p. 325.

67. Will Thorne, *My Life's Battles*, p. 67.

68. Kapp, Vol II, p. 318.

69. Bryher, *Labour and Socialist Movement in Bristol*, p. 192.

70. E. J. Hobsbawm, *Labour's Turning Point*, Lawrence and Wishart, 1948.

71. EM to her sister, Laura, June 1889, quoted in Kapp, Vol II, p. 306.

72. Ibid., p. 303.

73. Ibid., p. 306, letter to Laura Lafargue.

74. KH to Engels, L2158, 21 May 1889, Marx-Engels Papers, IISH, Amsterdam.

75. Ibid., L2160, 19 June 1889, loc. cit.

76. Engels to Guesde, K 557, 11 June 1887, loc. cit.

77. KH to Engels, L2159, 24 May 1889, loc. cit.

78. Ibid., L2158, 21 May 1889, loc. cit.

79. Ibid., L2160, 19 June 1889, loc. cit.

80. EM to Laura Lafargue, 11 April 1889, quoted in Kapp, Vol II, p. 304.
81. Ibid., p. 306.
82. Glasier, *Memorial*, p. 24.
83. John Burns, 'The Paris International Congress', *Labour Elector*, 3 August 1889, quoted in Kapp, Vol II, p. 313.
84. Ibid.
85. Ibid., p. 315.
86. His contribution is reported in Lowe, *Souvenirs of Scottish Labour*, p. 44; see also Lowe, *Pit to Parliament*, p. 27.
87. KH to Engels, 31 May 1889, Letter L2158, Marx-Engels Correspondence, IISH, Amsterdam.
88. KH to Engels, L2158, loc. cit.
89. *Ardrossan and Saltcoats Herald*, 24 June 1887.
90. *The Miner*, February 1889.
91. Lowe, *Pit to Parliament*, p. 27; Lowe, *Souvenirs of Scottish Labour*.
92. Mann, p. 61.
93. Ibid.
94. Stewart, p. 66.
95. Statement of Accounts from 14 August to 16 November 1889, Dockers' Union Council, 1889, quoted in Kapp, Vol II, p. 332.
96. Tillett, *Memoirs and Reflections*, p. 135, quoted Kapp, Vol II, p. 331.
97. Thorne, p. 86.
98. *Labour Elector*, 7 September 1889, quoted in Kapp, Vol II, p. 328.
99. Letter to Laura Lafargue, 27 August 1889, quoted in Kapp, Vol II, p. 334.
100. John Burns, 'The Great Strike', *New Review*, October 1889, p. 420, quoted Kapp, Vol II p. 331.
101. Ibid.
102. Chairman of the Concilation Committee of the London Chamber of Commerce, S. B. Boulton, quoted in Kapp, Vol II, p. 329. See also note 62, p. 417.
103. Mann, pp. 64–5.
104. Report of the 22nd Annual TUC Congress.
105. The vote was 88 to 63.

106. KH quoted the letter (from workers in Clerkenwell Green) in the *Ardrossan and Saltcoats Herald*, 16 September 1887.
107. Quoted in Thompson, *The Enthusiasts*, p. 69.
108. B. Tillett, *Brief History of the Dockers' Union*, quoted in Mann, p. 66.
109. EM, 'Report from Great Britain and Ireland', Brussels Congress of Second International, 1891, quoted in Kapp, Vol II, p. 486.
110. KH to Randolph Churchill, 18 December 1889, National Library of Scotland, Dep 176, Box 1, File 1. The letter was the collective decision of Hardie and his socialist colleagues, James Neil, James Patrick and Alexander Barrowman. See 'Memories of an Ayrshire Agitator', *Forward*, 18 July 1914.
111. Strawhorn, *New History of Cumnock*, p. 110.
112. KH to James Young, 21 January 1889, Acc 8125.
113. Report of TUC Congress, 1889; see also Morgan, *Keir Hardie*, p. 38–9; and Reid, *Making of a Socialist*, p. 121.
114. *Glasgow Herald*, 3 February 1890; Reid, Thesis, pp. 182–3. Some Scottish Socialists, like A. A. Durward (*The Truth About James Kerr* op. cit.) criticized Hardie for deserting, saying he 'left the Scottish Labour Party to fight and die in Scotland without him.'
115. Morgan, *Keir Hardie*, p. 36.
116. Lowe, *Pit to Parliament*, p. 33.
117. J. Neil, *'Memories of an Ayrshire Agitator'*, *Forward*, 1914.
118. On 11 May 1890. Kapp. Vol II, p. 381. On 6 July 1890. Ibid., pp. 288–9.
119. Ibid., p. 367.
120. Ibid., p. 516. The club was later taken over by anarchists.
121. House of Commons, 25 January 1890, quoted in Tschiffley, p. 257.
122. November 28, Kapp, Vol II, pp. 423–6.

123. Source Note, 1900, quoted in Tschiffley, p. 335.
124. Described in *People's Press*, 19 July 1890, Kapp Vol II, p. 389.
125. Kapp, Vol II, p. 393.
126. Morgan, *Keir Hardie*, p. 45. For subsequent visits see *East and West Ham Gazette*, 12 April 1890. See also *Stratford Express*, 19 April 1890. For a discussion of West Ham's political, social and industrial history, and the forces at work when Hardie arrived, see John Marriott, *London Over the Border: A Study of West Ham during Rapid Growth*, 1840–1910, unpublished Ph.D., Cambridge University, 1984.
127. A. McBriar, *Fabian Socialism and English Politics*, p. 245n.
128. J. E. Williams, *The Derbyshire Miners*, p. 308.
129. *Ardrossan and Saltcoats Herald*, 13 July 1890.
130. Letter, *People's Press*, 6 September 1890, quoted Kapp, Vol II, p. 394 (written on 31 August).
131. *Labour Leader*, May 1898, quoted also in Hughes, *Writings*, pp. 79–81.
132. KH to Engels, Letter 2159, 24 May 1889, IISH, Amsterdam.
133. Ibid.
134. Royal Commission on Labour, Parliamentary Proceedings, 1892, xxxvi, p. 12891, Q12584, Q12891, Q13019–21.
135. *Labour Leader*, April 1889.
136. KH to Burns, May 1891, British Museum ADD MSS 46288, quoted in Pelling, *Origins*, pp. 104–5.
137. CG to Burns, 22 October 1891, quoted in Pelling, p. 106.
138. Eleanor to Laura Lafargue, 25 May 1889, Kapp, Vol II, pp. 305–6.
139. *The Miner*, May 1887.
140. Lowe, *Pit to Parliament*, pp. 32–3. Presentation Dinner Programme and Account Book, Ayrshire Building Society, Box 2(5) National Library of Scotland.
141. Ibid., *Pit to Parliament* p. 32.
142. NH, Foreword, Hughes, *Writings, Speeches*, p. x.
143. Kapp, Vol II, p. 270.
144. Lowe, *Pit to Parliament*, p. 34.
145. Ibid., Hughes p. 203; *Keir Hardie*, p. 86; Reid, *Keir Hardie*, p. 151.
146. A history of the original Lochnorris was sent to KH by a local journalist, A. B. Todd, National Library of Scotland, Dep 176.
147. Morgan, *Keir Hardie*, p. 57.
148. Hughes, *Keir Hardie*, p. 29.
149. Glasier, Diary, 24 September 1903, Glasier Papers, Liverpool University.
150. Lowe, *Pit to Parliament*, p. 96.
151. Reid, Thesis, p. 278.
152. Mann, pp. 73–4.
153. Kapp, Vol II, 535, p. 151.
154. Hughes, *Keir Hardie*, p. 87.
155. Ibid., p. 79.
156. Quoted in ibid., p. 50.
157. Lowe, *Souvenirs*, p. 84.
158. Lowe, *Pit to Parliament*, p. 160.
159. Reid, *Keir Hardie*, pp. 151–3.
160. Kapp, Vol II, p. 550.
161. Laurence Thompson, *Robert Blatchford*, p. 57. Edward Hulton was later succeeded by a son of the same name.
162. Ibid., p. 55.
163. Thompson, *The Enthusiasts*, p. 96. A column was about 600–700 words.
164. Edmund Stonelake, *The Autobiography of Edmund Stonelake*, p. 119.
165. Thompson, *Blatchford*, p. 64.
166. Ibid., quoting from *The Dream of John Ball*.
167. Thompson, *Blatchford*, pp. 69–71.
168. Ibid. The story was told to Thompson by Katharine Glasier, who had heard it from Blatchford.
169. Hughes, *Keir Hardie*, p. 185.
170. Quoted McLean, *Keir Hardie*, p. 162.
171. Quoted Lowe, *Pit to Parliament*, p. 114.
172. Quoted in Hughes, *Keir Hardie*, p. 184.

173. Thompson, *Blatchford*, p. 165.
174. Quoted in Humphrey, *A History of Labour Representation*, p. 125.
175. Thompson, *Blatchford*, p. 63.
176. Ibid., pp. 74–5.
177. *Borough of West Ham and Stratford Express*, 27 January 1892.
178. It was published from 1890 to 1894.
179. *Workman's Times*, 27 March 1891, quoted in Humphrey, p. 98.
180. Stewart, p. 69.
181. Joseph Leicester, a former MP.
182. Quoted in *West Ham Herald*, 25 June 1892.
183. Keir Hardie, *Young Men in a Hurry*, ILP, 1897.
184. Kapp, Vol II, p. 339.
185. Reid, Thesis, p. 320. See also Marriott, *London Over the Border: A Study of West Ham*, 1984.
186. At a meeting of trade unions and temperance associations, 14 February 1892, quoted in Reid, Thesis, p. 325.
187. *West Ham Herald*, 22 February 1892; quoted in Reid, Thesis, p. 299.
188. Lowe, *Pit to Parliament*, p. 28.
189. Reid, Thesis, p. 234.
190. Pelling, *Origins*, p. 106; *West Ham Herald*, 25 June 1892, quoted in Reid, Thesis, p. 325.
191. Engels to Laura Lafargue, 22 September 1885, in Kapp. Vol II p. 71.
192. Lansbury, *My Life*, p. 84.
193. National Liberal Federation Annual Conference, 4 December 1889; incident reported 7 December in *Pall Mall Gazette*.
194. Called *Coming Times*, 1889–91.
195. Lansbury, p. 137.
196. Ibid., pp. 71–2, 75–6.
197. *Labour Leader*, 17 December 1898.
198. Stewart, p. 70.
199. Election Address reproduced in Hughes, *Writings*, p. 20.
200. Quoted in Lowe, *Pit to Parliament*, p. 34.
201. Election Address, 1892.
202. *Labour Leader*, February 1889; Reid, Thesis, p. 314.
203. Morgan, *Keir Hardie* p. 48.
204. Election Address, 1892, see note 199.
205. *Poverty and the State* appeared in 1886, written by a Unitarian minister. It argued for co-operative development of the land and KH was much influenced by it. Morgan, *Keir Hardie* p. 48.
206. Royal Commission on Labour, Parliamentary Reports, 1892, Vol xxxvi, QQ13019–21.
207. Quoted in *Derbyshire Times*, 3 May 1891.
208. Reid, *Keir Hardie*, p. 182.
209. Election Address, 1892.
210. CG, quoted in Hughes, *Keir Hardie* p. 54.
211. Election Address, 1892.
212. Quoted in Hughes, *Keir Hardie*, p. 54.
213. Stewart, p. 70.
214. Report of a speech in Canning Town, *Workman's Times*, 31 October 1891.
215. Speech given to open air meeting at Becton Road, reported in *Stratford Express*, 25 June 1892.
216. *Ardrossan and Saltcoats Herald*, 13 July 1888.
217. Ibid.
218. Reported by CG, quoted in Hughes, *Keir Hardie*, p. 54.
219. Humphrey, p. 126; *West Ham Herald*, 9 July 1892.
220. *Daily Chronicle*, quoted in Humphrey, p. 128; Marx and Engels, *Selected Works*, Vol III, p. 452.

Chapter 5 – Domestic Divisions

1. *West Ham Herald*, 9 July 1892.
2. Morgan, *Keir Hardie*, p. 53.
3. Ibid., p. 52., See also Engels to Sorge, 10 November 1894, IISH, Amsterdam; and to Eleanor Marx, 9 July 1895, quoted Kapp, p. 595. By 1895 profound distrust had set in.

4. *Workman's Times*, 25 August 1892.
5. Ibid., 16 August 1892; Reid, *Keir Hardie*, p. 137.
6. *West Ham and Stratford Express*, 20 August 1892.
7. 20 August 1892, quoted in Reid, *Keir Hardie*, p. 138.
8. KH to Thomas Cape, 14 June 1914, Rowe MSS, University of Wales, Swansea. Cape, a member of the public, had written to *Reynold's News*, 10 June 1914 (Rowe MSS), for a copy of the issue where KH had been defended over the West Ham funding (Horatio Bottomley, a journalist, having raised it again in 1911). Since the issue was out of print by 1914, KH replied to Cape instead.
9. Humphrey, *A History of Labour Representation*, p. 127.
10. Quoted in Kapp, Vol II, p. 543.
11. Lowe, *Pit to Parliament*, p. 64.
12. Humphrey, pp. 127–9. McLean, *Keir Hardie*, p. 41.
13. Katharine Glasier, quoted in Thompson, *The Enthusiasts*, p. 74.
14. McLean, p. 40.
15. 6 August 1892.
16. Glasier, *Memorial*, p. 20.
17. Stead, 'Jas Keir Hardie, MP', 1905.
18. *Daily Chronicle*, 27 September 1915.
19. Hughes, *Keir Hardie*, p. 56.
20. Morgan, *Keir Hardie*, p. 54.
21. The radical MP Joseph Cowen was an earlier exception; he wore a large soft hat. See Nigel Todd, *The Militant Democracy, Joseph Cowen and Victorian Radicalism*, 1991.
22. Snowden, *Autobiography*, Vol I, p. 185.
23. *Daily Telegraph*, 7 August 1892.
24. George Lambert, MP, quoted in Morgan, *Keir Hardie*, p. 54.
25. NH, Introduction, Hughes, *Writings*, p. x.
26. CG, quoted in Stewart, p. 55.
27. Ibid.

28. *West Bromwich Labour Tribune*, May 1887.
29. Stirling Robertson, to KH, 8 March 1892, Letter 92/10, Francis Johnson Collection, LSE.
30. Raymond Unwin, *ILP News*, January 1902.
31. Fyfe, p. 39.
32. Glasier, *Memorial*, pp. 74–5.
33. Snowden, Vol I, p. 316.
34. James Mavor, reported in Thompson, *The Enthusiasts*, p. 54.
35. Pankhurst Collection, Amsterdam, file 9, folder 9. Hardie's suits were made in Cumnock by Hugh Lorimer.
36. Snowden, Vol I, p. 316
37. Ibid., p. 317.
38. Interview with CB, 25 November 1987.
39. Glasier, *Memorial*, p. 71.
40. Mavor, quoted in Thompson, *The Enthusiasts*, p. 55.
41. Quoted in Stewart, *Keir Hardie*, p. 54.
42. F. Rogers, *Labour, Life and Literature*, p. 195.
43. On 18 August 1892.
44. Pelling, *Origins*, p. 101.
45. E. I. Champness, *Frank Smith – Pioneer and Modern Mystic*, p. 21.
46. Humphrey, p. 120. Pelling, *Origins*, p. 112.
47. Pelling, *Origins*, p. 111.
48. Humphrey, pp. 130–1.
49. Labour Electoral Association's list of those admissable, generally only working-class men. Humphrey, p. 97.
50. Ibid., p. 132; Pelling, p. 112 (whose comments were highly sexist).
51. Details of Katharine's life are from Thompson, *The Enthusiasts*.
52. Ibid., p. 70.
53. Ibid.
54. Ibid., p. 73, Quotes Letter from Enid Stacey to 'Our Fabian Circle', 1891.
55. Ibid., GBS to Sidney Webb, c. 1891.
56. Ibid., p. 74.
57. Pelling, *Origins*, p. 114.

58. Hughes, *Keir Hardie*, pp. 65–6,
    Pelling, pp. 113–120. Among
    those present were Pete Curran,
    Fred Jowett, Joseph Burgess,
    Russell Smart, Shaw Maxwell
    and John Lister.
59. Pelling, p. 116.
60. Ibid., p. 118. Bob Smillie
    proposed the new party be called
    the Socialist Labour Party.
61. *The Miner*, April 1887.
62. Pelling, p. 107. Tillett had
    2,749 votes, only 700 less than
    the Liberal.
63. Humphrey, p. 131; Broadhurst,
    *From the Stonemasons' Bench to the
    Treasury Bench, passim.*
64. Humphrey, p. 131.
65. Humphrey, p. 106, quoting from
    J. G. Mackail, *Life of William
    Morris*, London 1907.
66. Fyfe, *Keir Hardie*, p. 69.
67. Pelling, pp. 118–19.
68. Morgan, *Keir Hardie*, p. 63.
69. 'The Fabians and the ILP',
    Tracey, *The Book of the Labour
    Party*, Vol I, p. 90.
70. Pelling, p. 118–19.
71. Humphrey, p. 118.
72. Engels to Sorge, 18 January 1893,
    quoted Pelling, p. 123.
73. Reported in *Workman's Times*,
    25 March 1893.
74. *Labour Leader*, 24 December
    1898.
75. Keir Hardie, 'Introduction' to
    H. Russell Smart, *The ILP, its
    Programme and Policy*, 1893.
76. Pelling, p. 111.
77. Stewart, p. 79.
78. Hughes, *Writings*, p. 162.
79. Thompson, *The Enthusiasts*,
    p. 75.
80. Margaret Cole, *Makers of the
    Labour Movement*, Longman's,
    1948, p. 214.
81. McLean, p. 50.
82. *Justice*, 21 January 1893.
83. Reported in *Workman's Times*,
    11 February 1893.
84. Report of debate, 7 February
    1893; Hughes, *Writings*, p. 25.
85. Hughes, *Writings*, p. 60.
86. *Labour Leader*, April 1889.
87. Letters written to KH in 1892,

88. W. Johnson to KH, 15
    November 1893, Letter 93/136,
    loc. cit.
89. A. C. Dilke to KH, 26 June
    1893, Letter 93/89, loc. cit.
90. Parliamentary Debates
    (Commons), 27 June 1893, 4th
    series, Vol XIV.
91. Ibid., 3 July 1893, 4th series,
    Vol XIV.
92. Ibid., 30 June, 4th series, Vol
    XIV, line 545.
93. Ibid., 3 July, 1893, 4th series,
    Vol XIV.
94. Hughes, *Writings*, pp. 162–3.
95. Stewart, pp. 72–3; Hughes,
    Writings, p. 163.
96. This story was told by KH in
    the *Labour Leader*, February
    1914; also in *Merthyr Pioneer*,
    February 1914.
97. Stewart, p. 73.
98. Pelling, *Origins*, p. 123.
99. *Labour Leader*, 17 December
    1898.
100. Thompson, *The Enthusiasts*,
     p. 73.
101. Edward Carpenter founded
     Millthorpe in 1886. He
     had abandoned his career at
     Cambridge and, together
     with fellow homosexuals, ran
     workshops and horticultural
     experiments in co-operation
     with the Sheffield Socialist
     Society. Bellamy and Saville,
     eds., *Dictionary of Labour
     Biography.*
102. Champness, p. 41.
103. Quoted in Morgan, *Keir Hardie*,
     p. 219; JRM was writing to
     Glasier in 1908.
104. See Romero, p. 33.
105. These events (in 1893) were
     retold by KH in the *Labour
     Leader*, February 1914, and
     reprinted in *Writings*, pp. 165–6.
106. *Writings*, p. 78.
107. Ibid., Introduction,
     p. xi.
108. Ibid., p.xi.
109. Ibid.
110. KH to Lowe, 20 April

preserved in the Francis Johnson
Correspondence, LSE.

1899, quoted in Lowe, *Pit to Parliament*, p. 74.

111. H. Hyndman to Richard Ely, 28 September 1894, quoted in Tsuzuki, *Hyndman*, p. 100.

112. Ibid., p. 93; letter 25 September 1894.

113. Mann, p. 72, reply to George Shipton.

114. 5 October 1893, Mann, p. 73.

115. Pelling, *Origins*, p. 192.

116. Labour Leader, 17 February 1900, quoted *Speeches*, p. 101; address on Labour and Christianity, 5 May 1910, quoted *Speeches*, p. 141.

117. Pelling, pp. 132–6, October 1891; see also *Labour Leader*.

118. *British Weekly*, 5 November 1891, quoted Pelling, p. 134.

119. *Labour Leader*, 27 April 1895.

120. Ibid., 23 November 1895, quoted Reid, *Keir Hardie*, p. 139.

121. The incident is described in Lowe, *Pit to Parliament*, pp. 71–3.

122. Quoted in Bryher, Part II, p. 73.

123. Morgan, KH, p. 9.

124. Quoted by Lowe, *Pit to Parliament*, p. 104.

125. Pankhurst Papers, file 9, folder 9c, IISH, Amsterdam.

126. National Library of Scotland, postcard dated 8 June 1905.

127. *Ardrossan and Saltcoats Herald*, 13 July 1888; Reid, Thesis, p. 305.

128. Lowe, *Pit to Parliament*, p. 26; the date was 1889.

129. The letters are in the National Library of Scotland, Acc 4494. The sequence of letters has to be deduced, as only one letter is dated, the formal one to Miss Hines, 5 June. The others have no dates and were all out of their envelopes. These have postmarks from 3 to 26 June, but many envelopes are missing.

130. Lowe, *Pit to Parliament*, p. 45.

131. Ibid., p. 83.

132. Ibid., pp. 49–50.

133. McLean, pp. 162–3; also Reid, *Keir Hardie*, p. 170, and Lansbury, p. 91.

134. Lansbury, p. 91.

135. Morgan, *Keir Hardie*, pp. 57–8.

136. Quoted in Thompson, *The Enthusiasts*, p. 81.

137. NH, Introduction, Hughes, ed., *Writings*, p. x.

138. Ibid.

139. Lowe, *Pit to Parliament*, p. 38.

140. From an anonymous article in *Seedtime*, July 1894, identified by MacDonald's biographer as 'almost certainly' by JRM; Marquand, *Ramsay MacDonald*, p. 807.

141. Marquand, pp. 34–5.

142. Letter printed in Elton, *The Life of Ramsay MacDonald*, pp. 68–9, quoted in Marquand, p. 36.

143. Marquand, p. 45.

144. Ibid., p. 46.

145. Ibid., p. 45, quoted from *Margaret Ethel MacDonald*.

146. Quoted in Jalland, *Women, Marriage and Politics*, p. 69.

147. MacDonald, *Margaret Ethel MacDonald, A Memoir*, privately printed 1911, p. 50, quoted Marquand, pp. 23–4.

148. Stewart, p. 14.

149. Ibid., p. 177.

150. KH to unnamed correspondent, 4 December 1896, Murray Collection, Amsterdam, quoted in Reid, *Keir Hardie*, p. 53.

151. Lowe, *Pit to Parliament*, p. 55.

152. Ibid., pp. 118, 198, during the 1896 Barnsley by-election.

153. Ibid., p. 160.

154. Ibid., p. 76.

155. Ibid., p. 65.

156. Ibid., p. 55.

157. Comments on CG by Pelling, *Origins*, p. 105.

158. Champness, p. 35.

159. Tillett, *Dictionary of Labour Biography*, Vol X. p. 179.

160. Lowe, *Pit to Parliament*, p. 38; Hughes, *Keir Hardie* pp. 67–8.

161. Glasier, Diary, 7 October 1896.

162. Lowe, p. 125.

163. Ibid., pp. 63–4.

164. Ibid., p. 104. The year was 1896.

165. KH, speech notes, preserved in the Museum of Labour History, Manchester. They relate to a speech in Portsmouth,

where he made emigration and immigration his starting themes. See also KH to James Henderson, 17 October 1911.

166. The Glasgow office moved to Nile Street at the end of the decade.

167. Lowe, p. 38.

168. Hughes, *Writings*, p. 166.

169. Reid, *Keir Hardie*, p. 140.

170. Lowe, *Pit to Parliament*, p. 155.

171. Lowe, p. 164.

172. Ibid., p. 94.

173. Glasier, *Memorial*, p. 12.

174. ESP draft obituary, file 9, folder 9, ESP, IISH, Amsterdam.

175. Lowe, pp. 93–4.

176. Glasier, Diary, 17 October 1896.

177. Lowe, p. 38.

178. Ibid., p. 89, in 1895.

179. Champion had tried to organize a rival version of the ILP in Scotland, which failed. (Pelling, *Origins*, p. 194–50 and 165.) The struggle is retold from Champion's point of view in Baron Corvo's *Hadrian VII*, where the KH character is an assassin.

180. Lowe, p. 76.

181. Hughes, *Writings*, p. 167

182. Lowe, *Pit to Parliament*, pp. 84–6.

183. Ibid., p. 35.

184. Ibid., p. 85.

185. David Mitchell, *Queen Christabel*, p. 23.

186. Lowe, *Pit to Parliament*, p. 85.

187. Report of the Twenty-Seventh Trade Union Congress, Norwich, September 1894, *Book of the Labour Party*, Vol I, p. 99.

188. Stewart, p. 102.

189. Lowe, p. 110.

190. *Labour Leader*, 3 November 1894, quoted in Hughes, *Writings*, p. 37.

191. *Labour Leader*, 20 December 1894, quoted in ibid., pp. 38–9.

192. *Nineteenth Century*, September 1894.

193. A. J. P. Taylor, *The Trouble Makers*, p. 92.

194. 17 November 1893 (reprinted R. Page Arnot, *The Miners*, p. 149).

195. 29 April 1895, quoted in Hughes, *Writings*, p. 45.

196. Parliamentary Debates, 14 July 1893, Fourth Series, Vol XIV, line 1580.

197. *West Ham Herald*, quoted in Stewart, pp. 93–4.

198. *Labour Leader*, 19 June 1897.

199. Parliamentary Debates, 28 June 1894, Fourth Series, Vol XXVI, lines 462–3, quoted in Hughes, *Writings*, pp. 33–6.

200. David Brooks, ed., *The Destruction of Lord Rosebery*, E. Hamilton's Diary, p. 152.

201. Ibid.

202. Hughes, *Writings*, pp. 106–7; Hughes, *Keir Hardie*, p. 110.

203. Lowe, *Pit to Parliament*, p. 64.

204. *Labour Leader*, 30 June 1894.

205. Quoted Hughes, *Keir Hardie*, p. 184.

206. Hughes, *Writings*, p. 63; also *Labour Leader*, 3 July 1908, reporting KH saying that a change to a president will not 'solve any of the great social, economic, and industrial problems'. First, we must end the economic system, 'then deal with the form of government'.

207. Hughes, *Writings*, p. 35.

208. Reid, *Keir Hardie*, p. 221.

209. Joseph Arch retired midway through the parliament.

210. Coates and Topham, *The Making of the Transport and General Workers Union, passim*.

211. Morgan, *Keir Hardie*, p. 75.

212. Pelling, *Origins*, p. 82.

213. Stewart, p. 88.

214. Quoted in Kapp, Vol II, pp. 549–50.

215. 'What the ILP is driving at', 1884, quoted in Mann, p. 101.

216. Ibid., p. 101.

217. Engels to Laura Lafargue, 30 September 1892, in Kapp, Vol II p. 551.

218. Ibid., Vol II, p. 547, note 1.

219. Hughes, *Writings*, p. 40.

220. Ibid., p. 41.

221. Ibid., p. 43.

222. Quoted in Lowe, *Pit to Parliament*, p. 81.

223. Ibid., p. 79.
224. Ibid., p. 80.
225. Stewart, p. 109.
226. Ibid., p. 83.
227. Lowe, p. 137.
228. *Labour Leader*, 28 May 1908.
229. Lowe, p. 26.
230. Stewart, p. 55, quoting CG.
231. Ibid., p. 282.
232. Ibid., p. 55, quotes CG.
233. 3 January 1894, Letter 94/4, JRM to KH, Francis Johnson Correspondence, LSE.
234. Reid, *Keir Hardie*, Chapter 7.

Chapter 6 – Defeat and Depression

1. JRM in Southampton, Richard Pankhurst in Gorton, Manchester, and Mann in Colne Valley. There was also Tillett in Bradford and Curran in Barrow.
2. *Workman's Times*, quoted in Humphrey, p. 135.
3. Tschiffely, p. 279.
4. Quoted in Hughes, *Writings*, p. 48.
5. *Labour Leader*, 15 July 1895, *Speeches*, p. 47. Some Liberals thought it was Liberal policy on the local option that defeated KH. See Brooks, p. 102.
6. Quoted in Hughes, *Writings*, p. 48.
7. Figures were Bancs 4,750 and KH 3,975.
8. An address given after the election, quoted in Humphrey, p. 136.
9. Pelling, *Origins*, p. 179.
10. Tracey, Vol I, p. 90.
11. Engels to Laura Lafargue, 23 July 1895, quoted in Kapp, Vol II, p. 596.
12. Engels to EM, 9 July 1895, quoted in ibid., p. 595.
13. Engels to Sorge, 10 November 1894, IISH, Amsterdam.
14. Snowden, Vol I, p. 69.
15. Quoted in Morgan, *Keir Hardie*, p. 81.
16. Hughes, *Keir Hardie*, p. 76.
17. Ibid., p. 70.
18. Ibid.
19. Snowden, Vol I, p. 316.
20. JRM to Herbert Samuel, 16 August 1895, quoted in Marquand, p. 60, from Viscount Samuel, *Memoirs*, p. 27.
21. Quoted in Humphrey, p. 103.
22. 10 August 1895, *South Western World*, quoted Humphrey, p. 137.
23. Frank Smith, *Labour Leader*, 30 September 1915.
24. 27 July 1895, also quoted in Hughes, *Writings*, p. 49.
25. Stewart, p. 101.
26. *Labour Leader*, 27 July 1895. Ibid., 3 August 1895. Also quoted in Hughes, *Writings*, p. 50.
27. *Labour Leader*, 27 July 1895.
28. Stewart, p. 115.
29. Kapp, Vol II, p. 135.
30. Ibid., p. 137.
31. Stewart, p. 116.
32. Lowe, *Pit to Parliament*, p. 86.
33. Stewart, p. 118.
34. Ibid.
35. Retained in the National Library of Scotland, Dep 176, Box 2, File 9; in the Cumnock Library, and by granddaughter and great-granddaughter, JHS and Dolores May Arias.
36. *Labour Leader*, 25 September 1908, 'America Revisited'.
37. Ibid.
38. Stewart, p. 121.
39. *New York World*, 1895; quoted in Stewart, p. 120.
40. Hughes, *Writings*, pp. 167–8. originally in *Labour Leader*, 1914. W. R. Scott was the pastor.
41. Hughes, *Writings*, pp. 167–8.
42. The story is told in Stewart, pp. 122–3, but quotations are from KH's fuller written account in the Museum of Labour History, Manchester.
43. Ibid.
44. Quoted in Stewart, p. 56.
45. Ibid., p. 126; 21 December 1895.
46. Kapp, Vol II, p. 525.
47. Stewart, p. 128.

48. Adam Birkmyre to KH, 6 January 1896, National Library of Scotland, Dep 176, Box 1, File 1.

49. Glasier, Diary, 14 November 1896.

50. Ibid., 24 October 1896.

51. Ibid., 4 November 1896.

52. Morgan, *Keir Hardie*, pp. 91–2.

53. Lowe, *Pit to Parliament*, pp. 115–16; J. E. Williams, *Derbyshire Miners*, p. 494.

54. Lowe, p. 117; Morgan, p. 90.

55. *Derbyshire Times*, 9 October 1897.

56. KH to Lowe, 4 November 1897, quoted Lowe, p. 117.

57. *Labour Leader*, 9 May 1896; see also Morgan, p. 87.

58. Lowe, p. 114.

59. Glasier, Diary, 4 January 1896.

60. Ibid., 3 January 1896.

61. John Burns to Lowe, Letter 97/124, no date, Francis Johnson Collection, LSE,

62. Glasier, Diary, 17 October 1896.

63. EM to Van der Goes, 25 January 1896, quoted in Kapp, Vol II, pp. 651–2.

64. Ibid.

65. Ibid., Vol II, Chapter 3.

66. EM to Van der Goes, 25 January 1896, in Kapp, Vol II, pp. 651–2.

67. For example, letter to Laura Lafargue, quoted in Kapp, Vol II, p. 653.

68. K. Kautsky to V. Adler, 12 November 1896, from Adler, V., *Briefwechsel*, Vienna, 1954, p. 221.

69. Kapp, Vol II, p. 651.

70. Engels, 1893, Speech to Second International, Kapp, Vol II, pp. 549–50.

71. W. Liebknecht to KH, 27 May 1896, Letter 96/49, Francis Johnson Collection, LSE.

72. Quoted in Stewart, p. 129.

73. Marquand, p. 60. JRM's satirical piece was called 'Whi i am Anarkist'.

74. Reported in the *Westminster Gazette*, 1 August 1896.

75. Mann, p. 65.

76. Glasier, quoted in E. P. Thompson, *William Morris: Romantic to Revolutionary*, p. 746.

77. Ibid.

78. *Justice*, 23 May 1896.

79. Glasier, Diary, 20 August 1898.

80. Lowe, *Pit to Parliament*, p. 178.

81. Glasier, Diary, 30 July 1898.

82. L. Thompson, *Blatchford*, p. 165.

83. Glasier, Diary, 18 April 1897.

84. KH to Lowe, 21 September 1898.

85. Glasier, Diary, 5 and 6 March 1897.

86. Ibid., 12 April 1898.

87. Ibid., 13 December 1897.

88. Morgan, *Keir Hardie*, p. 88.

89. *Reynolds News*, 4 September 1897.

90. Thomas Johnston, MP, 'James Keir Hardie, The Founder of the Labour Party', in Tracey, Vol III, pp. 109–11.

91. Lowe, *Pit to Parliament*, p. 14.

92. Ibid., p. 149.

93. *Bradford Observer*, 24 October 1896.

94. Pelling, *Origins*, p. 162.

95. Frances, Countess of Warwick, *Life's Ebb and Flow*, 1929, pp. 90–2.

96. Lowe, p. 95. The *Labour Leader* issues carrying the stories were in January 1896.

97. Keir Hardie, 'Lord Overtoun', No. 3, White Slave Series, 1899.

98. Kapp, Vol II, p. 41.

99. Like those made by residents of the Welsh village living near the Rechem Toxic Waste Site (*Open Space*, June 1991, BBC).

100. Mr Oatts, quoted on the cover of Keir Hardie, 'More About Overtoun', 1899.

101. Keir Hardie, *Lord Overtoun*, op. cit.

102. G. Mitchell to KH, 27 July 1894, Letter 94/166, Francis Johnson Correspondence, LSE.

103. The second two were 'More about Overtoun' and 'The Overtoun Horrors', both 1899.

104. Lowe, *Pit to Parliament*, pp. 163–4.

105. For example, Cowcaddens, Glasgow, incident, where

police banned public speaking, 13 July 1893, Parliamentary Debates (Commons), Vol XIV, Line, 1459; and 28 June 1894, Pollokshaws incident, Parliamentary Debates (Commons), Vol XXVI, Line 457.

106. Glasier, Diary, 3 July 1896.
107. Romero, p. 17.
108. Mrs Stanton Blatch, *Unshackled*, p. 30, quoted in Mitchell, *Queen Christabel*, p. 328n.
109. S. Pankhurst, *The Suffragette Movement*, pp. 98–9.
110. Mrs Cobden-Sanderson, quoted in Romero, p. 49.
111. Romero, p. 16.
112. Ibid., p. 31.
113. MacArthur, MacDonald, and Smillie, *Memoir*, p. 6.
114. *Labour Leader*, 10 December 1898.
115. Lowe, *Pit to Parliament*, p. 144; Glasier, Diary, 10 June 1898.
116. Glasier, Diary, *passim*, July 1898.
117. Quoted in Humphrey, p. 13. Annie Besant's essay was included in the collected Fabian essays published in 1889.
118. Humphrey, p. 139.
119. Keir Hardie, *Young Men in a Hurry*, ILP pamphlet, 1897.
120. ASE, Stamford Street, Blackfriars, London, Kapp, Vol II, p. 673.
121. Ibid.
122. Letter to Kautsky, 1 January 1898, quoted in Kapp, Vol II, p. 675.
123. *Labour Leader*, 29 January 1898.
124. *South West Ham Worker*, September 1897, The 'toy' was a new yacht.
125. Stonelake, *Autobiography*, p. 151.
126. *Labour Leader*, 9 July 1898.
127. Ibid., 9 June 1898.
128. Ibid., 25 June 1898, also quoted in Hughes, *Writings*, p. 82.
129. Lowe, *Pit to Parliament*, p. 145.
130. Stewart, p. 146.
131. KH to Lowe, 21 June 1898, quoted in Lowe, p. 142.
132. Taylor, *Trouble Makers*, pp. 92, 105.

133. Lowe, pp. 133–4. Milanese workers rioted when they were forbidden to meet to discuss the famine occuring in the south of Italy. They were shot by the military.
134. Mary MacPherson translated articles; her husband, Duncan MacPherson, working in Paris, acted as the *Leader*'s correspondent; Lowe, *Pit to Parliament*, p. 154.
135. Lowe, pp. 157–8.
136. Letter column, *Labour Leader*, 26 November 1898.
137. For example, KH to Lowe, 27 February 1897 and 17 October 1898, relating to articles and information on Belgian, French and Italian events; *Labour Leader*, 7 January 1899 for discussion by KH of events in Cuba and the Sudan. Hardie's 'Black Diamonds' column in the *Ardrossan and Saltcoats Herald* from 1882–7, contained regular reporting on mining matters from the USA, New Zealand, France, Chile, China, and the Middle East.
138. Revd James Wallace, quoted in Stewart, p. 341.
139. Lowe, *Pit to Parliament*, pp. 168–9.
140. Letters 99/13, 18, 20, 22, 28, 38 and 129, Francis Johnson Correspondence, LSE.
141. KH to John Trevor, 23 April 1895, Letter 95/78, loc. cit.
142. John Trevor to KH, 29 April, loc. cit.
143. Glasier, Diary, 17 May 1896.
144. Ibid., 18 April 1897.
145. Ibid., 30 August 1897.
146. Ibid., 11 September 1897.
147. Ibid., 19 September 1897.
148. Ibid., 30 August 1897.
149. Ibid., 19 September 1897.
150. Ibid.
151. Stewart, p. 140.
152. Mann, p. 121.
153. *Labour Leader*, Christmas 1897, reprinted in Hughes, *Writings*, p. 73.
154. KH to Lowe, 8 December

1897, Lowe, *Pit to Parliament*, p. 120.

155. Ibid., 22 December 1897; Lowe's comments, p. 123.
156. Quoted in Lowe, *Pit to Parliament*, p. 69.
157. Mann, p. 102; Lowe, pp. 107–8.
158. These three deaths are recorded in Lowe, pp. 178, 199, 200–1.
159. KH to Lowe, 16 April 1899, quoted Lowe, p. 172.
160. Ibid., pp. 108–9.
161. Ibid., p. 51.
162. Ibid., pp. 137–9; Hughes, *Writings*, p. 81.
163. *Labour Leader*, 28 May 1898, quoted in Hughes, *Writings*, pp. 79–81.
164. Ibid. This was a reference to Lord Rosebery's speech.
165. Lowe, *Pit to Parliament*, p. 147. Her contribution was recorded in the ILP correspondence, where she had signed herself 'Daughter of Wales' (Francis Johnson Correspondence).
166. Romero, p. 20.
167. Letter to Lowe, 6 July 1898, quoted in Lowe, p. 147.
168. Letter of 7 April 1898, quoted in ibid., p. 131.
169. Kapp, Vol II, p. 677.
170. Kapp, Vol II, p. 720; see also *Labour Leader*, 21 July 1898, quoted in Kapp, Vol II, pp. 718–21 and footnote, p. 680.
171. KH to Lowe, 7 April 1889, Lowe, p. 131.
172. Hélène Demuth, who is buried in the Marx family grave.
173. Jean Longuet, see Kapp, Vol II, p. 697.
174. Lowe, *Pit to Parliament*, p. 147.
175. KH to Glasier, 28 December 1899.
176. Glasier, Diary, 16 February 1899.
177. October 1896, quoted in Lowe, p. 110.
178. 12 July 1898, ibid., p. 148.
179. Ibid., p. 110.
180. Ibid., p. 156. He did not see them on this occasion either, as both were ill.
181. Ibid., p. 156.
182. Ibid., p. 96.

183. Katharine Glasier, quoted in 'Keir Hardie, The Man and his Message', c. 1919.
184. KH to Lowe, 30 January 1898, Lowe, p. 127.
185. KH to Lowe, 6 April 1899, ibid., pp. 170–1.
186. Quoted in Kapp, Vol II, p. 663.
187. Lowe, *Pit to Parliament*, p. 171.
188. Thompson, *Blatchford*, p. 141.
189. KH to Lowe, 15 June 1900, quoted in Lowe, p. 183.
190. KH to Lowe, 6 May 1899, quoted in ibid., p. 175.
191. Ibid., p. 160.
192. KH to Lowe, 21 November 1896, quoted in ibid., p. 110.
193. Ibid., p. 36. KH was speaking in Durham in 1902, accepting a presentation of silver candlesticks, and looking back on his life to date.
194. *Labour Leader*, 15 August 1906; Hughes, *Writings*, pp. 124–5.
195. Lowe, *Pit to Parliament*, p. 132. KH was closing the 1898 ILP Conference.
196. *Labour Leader*, 15 August 1906; Hughes, *Writings*, p. 125.

Chapter 7 – Political Return, Bodily Retreat.

1. Lyons v Wilkins, 1899, limited picketing, for example. Pelling, *Origins*, p. 200.
2. In Oldham, July, 1899, J. Mawdsley was the candidate.
3. Paul Adelman, *Rise of the Labour Party*, p. 28.
4. Stewart, pp. 161–2.
5. 26–8 April 1899, Dundee.
6. Miss W. H. Irwin, Secretary of the Scottish TUC, to JRM, 4 May 1899, quoted in Morgan, *Keir Hardie*, p. 99.
7. Quoted in McLean, p. 78.
8. Pelling, p. 205; Snowden, Vol II, p. 88; Tracey, Vol I, p. 93; Morgan, *Keir Hardie*, p. 100 and Marquand, pp. 66–7.
9. Pelling, p. 205.

10. Ibid., p. 206.
11. Ibid.
12. Ibid., p. 207.
13. There were 116 trade unions represented, Marquand, p. 67; Hughes, *Keir Hardie*, p. 100.
14. Pelling, p. 207; *Labour Leader*, 13 January 1900.
15. Hughes, *Keir Hardie*, p. 100.
16. Quoted in Humphrey, p. 145.
17. McBriar, p. 309.
18. Hyndman, *Further Reminiscences*, p. 268; quoted in Tsuzuki, p. 106.
19. KH to Lowe, 17 December 1900, quoted in Lowe, *Pit to Parliament*, p. 188.
20. Hughes, *Keir Hardie*, p. 100.
21. Report of the Conference, Labour Representation Committee, 3 Lincoln's Inn Fields, London; quoted in Humphrey, p. 146.
22. Pelling, *Origins*, p. 209.
23. Letter to Lord Elton, quoted in Hughes, *Keir Hardie*, p. 102.
24. Pelling, p. 209.
25. *Justice*, 3 and 10 March 1900.
26. McLean, p. 88; Snowden later verified that no one at this time expected the LRC to become a political party, *Autobiography*, Vol I, p. 93.
27. *Labour Leader*, 22 February 1896; Hughes, *Writings*, pp. 52–3; and Pelling, p. 201.
28. Quoted Lowe, *Pit to Parliament*, p. 79.
29. Humphrey, p. 144.
30. Lowe, *Pit to Parliment*, pp. 57–8.
31. Ibid., p. 38.
32. Marquand, pp. 61–4; JRM was not successful.
33. *A Short History of the British Working Class Movement, 1789–1927*, Vol III, p. 23.
34. Marquand, p. 51.
35. Ibid., p. 49.
36. Ibid., p. 52.
37. Lowe, *Pit to Parliament*, p. 153.
38. Writing in *Ethical World*, 30 December 1899, quoted Marquand, p. 67.
39. JRM, *The Socialist Movement*, London, 1911.
40. Reprinted in *Labour Leader*, 6 January 1900, reprinted in Hughes, *Writings*, p. 100.
41. Ibid.
42. Thompson, *The Enthusiasts*, p. 116.
43. Quoted ibid., p. 115.
44. Marquand, p. 66.
45. *Justice*, 20 July 1901, quoted in Tsuzuki, p. 129.
46. Ibid.
47. Tracey, Vol I, p. 91.
48. Lowe, *Pit to Parliament*, pp. 181–2.
49. Thompson, *The Enthusiasts*, p. 116.
50. Lowe, October 1899, p. 181.
51. Bryher, p. 81.
52. Lowe, p. 181.
53. *Labour Leader*, 14 October 1899; quoted in Hughes, *Writings*, p. 96.
54. Lowe, p. 180.
55. *Labour Leader*, Christmas 1899, quoted in Hughes, *Writings*, p. 99.
56. Hughes, *Keir Hardie*, p. 109.
57. Stewart, pp. 166–7.
58. Lowe, p. 103.
59. Ibid., pp. 175–6.
60. Quoted in Hughes, *Keir Hardie*, p. 104.
61. Morgan, *Keir Hardie*, p. 277.
62. Glasier, Diary, 16 April 1900.
63. KH to David Lowe, 2 May 1900, Lowe, p. 182.
64. Ibid., 2 May.
65. Stewart, p. 177. Glasier reported Hardie having 'domestic troubles'. Thompson, *Blatchford*, p. 139.
66. Thorne, *My Life's Battles*, pp. 203–4.
67. Lowe, p. 184.
68. Letter to Lowe, 17 July 1901, Lowe, *Pit to Parliament*, p. 202.
69. Thompson, *The Enthusiasts*, p. 120.
70. KH to Glasier, 21 July 1900, University of Liverpool.
71. Marquand, p. 73.
72. 'Labour and Politics', LRC, Leaflet No. 1, quoted in Humphrey, p. 151, footnote 2.
73. Stewart, p. 176.

74. Ibid., pp. 173–4.
75. Lowe, p. 173.
76. Adelman, p. 27. Half this sum was the returning officer's fee.
77. Recollections of Lance Rogers, South Wales miner, recorded 4 April 1975, in Interview, Hywell Francis, Swansea University.
78. 22 September 1900.
79. Morgan, *Keir Hardie*, p. 112.
80. Stonelake, *Autobiography*, p. 161.
81. See Gwyn Williams, *The Merthyr Rising*; Glanmore Williams, Merthyr Politics.
82. Aberdare Trades Council, *Jubilee Souvenir History*, ed. Stonelake, 1950, p. 9.
83. Lowe, p. 108.
84. Stonelake, *Autobiography*, p. 114.
85. Ibid.
86. The story of Arnott Reid, told originally in the *Labour Leader*, retold in McLean, pp. 83–4.
87. Glasier, Diary, 25 September 1900.
88. Morgan, *Keir Hardie*, pp. 183–4.
89. Hanbury, Tomlinson 8,067 and KH 4, 834.
90. Lowe, *Pit to Parliament*, p. 187.
91. Glasier, Diary, 3 October 1900;
92. Stewart, pp. 176–7; Lowe, p. 186.
93. Hughes, *Keir Hardie*, p. 106.
94. Lowe, p. 187.
95. Glasier, Diary, 28 October 1900.
96. Ibid.
97. Lowe, p. 188.
98. Ibid., p. 186.
99. Ibid., p. 191, 24 January 1901.
100. Ibid., pp. 186–7.
101. *Labour Leader*, February 1914; Hughes, *Writings*, p. 167.
102. Stewart, pp. 180–1.
103. Hughes, *Keir Hardie*, p. 87.
104. Lowe, p. 136.
105. Georgina Battiscombe, *Mrs Gladstone*, p. 180. This was also common in the labour movement. Robert Blatchford's daughter, Winnie, gave up a journalist's career to care for her father; Daisy Lansbury was her father's secretary for many years. See L. Thompson, *Robert Blatchford*; and Daisy Lansbury,

Dictionary of Labour Biography, Vol VII.
106. Hughes, *Keir Hardie*, p. 87.
107. Stewart, pp. 196–7.
108. McLean, p. 105, suggests it was a combined appendicitis and pleurisy but this is unlikely. It is a reference to a lung complication she sustained during the illness.
109. KH to MS, 26 December 1902, National Library of Scotland, Dep 176, Box 25, File 6.
110. Lowe, p. 167.
111. Stewart, p. 195.
112. Lowe, p. 201.
113. Ibid., p. 200.
114. Stewart, p. 197, *Labour Leader*, 2 February 1902
115. KH letter to Glasier, 26 December 1901.
116. Hughes, *Keir Hardie*, p. 87.
117. EM to Olive Schreiner, 16 June 1884, reporting what Marx said. Kapp, Vol I, p. 229.
118. Glasier, Diary, 24 September 1903; KH to Glasier, 22 October 1903.
119. Ibid.
120. David Hardie, *Dictionary of Labour Biography*, eds. Bellamy and Saville, Vol VII. KH had even given up smoking for a year in the late 1880s in the hope of influencing his siblings (Pankhurst Collection, file 9, folder 9, IISH, Amsterdam), 'Our Leaders: Jas Keir Hardie' by TMD, *Miner*, March 1887.
121. Glasier, Diary, 15 June 1901.
122. Ibid., 18 June 1901.
123. Lowe, *Pit to Parliament*, p. 202.
124. T. Johnston, 'The Founder of the Labour Party' in Tracey, Vol III, p. 104.
125. Glasier, Diary, 26 August 1901.
126. Stewart, pp. 192–3; Tracey Vol I. p. 114, Glasier, Diary, 26 August 1901. The NAC first decided this at its October 27–29 meeting, 1900, at Manchester. It was 1903 before the LRC was able to consider paying MPs' expenses. S. Pankhurst, *The Suffragette Movement*, p. 168.

127. Humphrey, p. 151.
128. Frank Smith wrote that Hardie considered his mother the 'one perfect woman in the world' (*Jas Keir Hardie*, Self-Help Press, c. 1908, p. 17).
129. Letter to Glasier, 23 January 1901.
130. 21 January 1901, quoted in Stewart, pp. 185–6.
131. Ibid., pp. 186–7.
132. Ibid., p. 186.
133. Quoted in Reid, *Keir Hardie*, p. 163.
134. Glasier, Diary, 11 November 1910.
135. Parliamentary Debates (Commons), 26 February 1901. Vol LXXXIX, Line 1276.
136. Ibid., the increase was from £553,000 to £620,000 a year.
137. Parliamentary Debates (Commons), 31 July 1901, Vol XCVIII, Line 733f. Lord Roberts was the Commander.
138. *Labour Leader*, February 1901, quoted in Stewart, pp. 111–12.
139. KH to Lowe, 14 February 1901, in Lowe, *Pit to Parliament*, p. 191.
140. *Woolwich Labour Journal*, October 1901.
141. Hughes, *Keir Hardie*, p. 112.
142. Seebohm Rowntree, *Poverty: A Study of Town Life*, 1900 (first of 3 reports on York; also 1936 and 1950.)
143. Parliamentary Debates (Commons), 18 February 1903, CXVIII new series No. 1, Vol I.
144. Ibid., 10 December 1902, CXVI series; 18 December 1902, CXVI; 5 May 1903.
145. *Morning Post*, 29 October 1900.
146. Parliamentary Debates, 23 April 1901, Volume XCII, Line 1175.
147. *Leeds Mercury*, quoted Stewart, pp. 188–9.
148. Parliamentary Debates, 23 April 1901, Volume XLII, Line 1175.
149. Glasier, Diary, 24 April 1901.
150. KH writing in September 1894, quoted in Lowe, p. 100.
151. Lowe, p. 87.
152. KH to Glasier, 23 August 1901, Glasier Papers.
153. *Labour Leader*, 21 February, 7 March, and 28 March 1903.
154. KH, open letter to Lloyd George, *Labour Leader*, 1903.
155. KH to JRM, April 1902, quoted Morgan, *Keir Hardie*, p. 129.
156. KH to JRM, 23 May 1902, Labour Party Archives.
157. Klugman, Vol I, p. 16.
158. EM to Laura Lafargue, 31 December 1884, quoted Kapp, Vol II, p. 61.
159. Tsuzuki, pp. 137–40.
160. Ibid., p. 143, Hyndman to Wilshire, 23 September 1902.
161. Ibid., p. 142.
162. George Haw was the author of the book on Crooks; Lowe the author of the book on KH; other titles include *From Colliery to Castle*; from *Smithy to Senate* (G. Hodgson's life of J. A. Annard, 1908), *Pitman to Privy Councillor* (T. Burt's biography, 1924), and *From Stonemason's Bench to the Treasury Bench* (Henry Broadhurst's autobiography, 1901).
163. KH to Glasier, 1 April 1903, Glasier Papers; Tracey, Vol I, p. 116.
164. Hughes, *Keir Hardie*, p. 128.
165. KH to Glasier, 28 July 1903, Glasier Papers.
166. Morgan, *Keir Hardie*, p. 135.
167. Hughes, *Keir Hardie*, p. 114.
168. KH to Glasier, 24 January 1902, Glasier Papers,
169. Marquand, pp. 70–1.
170. KH to Lowe, 15 February 1901, quoted in Lowe, *Pit to Parliament*, p. 189.
171. KH to Lowe, 24 February 1901, ibid., p. 191.
172. Ibid., p. 188.
173. *Labour Leader*, quoted in Hughes, *Keir Hardie*, p. 105.
174. Ibid.
175. Hughes, *Keir Hardie*, pp. 121–2. They had been married 33 years, socialists (according to KH) 25 years. The account is from Hughes; see also Stewart, p. 198.

176. Stewart, p. 199.
177. No longer there, it was bombed in the Second World War. It dated from the late fifteenth century.
178. Stewart, p. 199.
179. Fenner Brockway, *Inside the Left*, p. 16.
180. Sylvia Pankhurst Papers, file 9, folder 9, IISH, Amsterdam.
181. A note on a photograph of MS puts the date of first starting work as 11 May 1902, National Library of Scotland, Dep 176, Box 2, File 2.
182. W. T. Stead, when editor of *Pall Mall*, had offered equal pay in the 1880s.
183. KH to MS, 26 December 1902, National Library of Scotland, Dep 176, Box 25, File 1.
184. Morgan, *Keir Hardie*, p. 126.
185. McLean, p. 56.
186. Mary MacArthur's contribution in MacArthur, MacDonald and Smillie, *Memoir*.
187. KH to Lowe, 15 August 1901, quoted in *Pit to Parliament*, pp. 202–3.
188. Quoted in August 1906, by J. M. Knight, Interview with KH, *Millgate Monthly*.
189. Fyfe, p. 61.
190. Morgan, *Keir Hardie*, pp. 57, 126.
191. James Maxton, *Keir Hardie, Prophet and Pioneer*, p. 6.
192. Letter to Lowe, summer 1901, quoted in Lowe, pp. 203–4. (It was intended as a note in the *Labour Leader* and used later.)
193. Hughes, *Keir Hardie*, p. 116.
194. Lowe, pp. 46 and 105.
195. Morgan, *Keir Hardie*, p. 122.
196. Ibid., p. 95.
197. Lowe, p. 76.
198. Ibid., p. 203; quoted in Hughes, *Keir Hardie*, p. 118.
199. For example, over 250,000 were estimated to have been at the first and second May Days in London, according to EM, Kapp, Vol II, pp. 380 and 474; KH also spoke of large numbers at open-air meetings during all his election campaigns.
200. *Labour Leader*, 28 February 1903, quoted in Hughes, *Keir Hardie*, p. 114.
201. Glasier to JRM, 1 September 1908.
202. Stewart, p. 204.
203. Glasier, Diary, 14 October 1902.
204. Stewart, pp. 204–5. The deputy was M. Gerault Richard.
205. Ibid.; and Snowden, Vol I, p. 317.
206. Parliamentary Debates (Commons), Volume CXVI, 1902, Line 231.
207. Stewart, p. 208.
208. Merthyr *Pioneer*, 27 May 1910, quote in Hughes, *Speeches*, p. 144.
209. Quoted in Hughes, *Keir Hardie* p. 119.
210. KH to Lowe, *Pit to Parliament*, p. 67.
211. Ibid., pp. 67–8.
212. Glasier to sister Lizzie, 29 September 1903, Glasier Papers.
213. Ibid.
214. Glasier, Diary, 21 December 1903.
215. Ibid., 26 September 1903.
216. *Labour Leader*, January 1901; quoted in Stewart, p. 185.
217. KH to Glasier, 25 July 1903, Glasier Papers.
218. Glasier to sister Lizzie, 29 September 1903.
219. Stewart, p. 211.
220. Glasier, Diary, 21 December 1903.
221. Stewart, p. 212.
222. KH to Glasier, 22 October 1903.
223. KH to Glasier, 22 October 1903.
224. 23 October 1903.
225. Stewart, p. 213.
226. KH to Glasier, 22 October 1903.
227. Taken on 1 December 1903, Cumnock Library.
228. KH to MS, 29 December 1903, National Library of Scotland, Box 25, File 1.
229. Glasier, Diary, 27 December 1901.
230. Thompson, *The Enthusiasts*, p. 138.
231. KH to Glasier, 28 January 1904, Glasier Papers.

232. KH to MS, from Villa Viale, undated letter, Box 25, File 1.
233. Mowatt, 'Ramsay MacDonald and the Labour Party', p. 130.
234. Mowatt, ibid., p. 151.
235. KH to Glasier, 10 April 1904, Glasier Papers.
236. *Labour Leader*, 7 March 1903, quoted Humphrey, p. 155.
237. KH to MS, letter undated, May 1905, Box 25, File 1.

Chapter 8 – The Woman Question

1. *Labour Leader*, 21 June 1902.
2. KH to Glasier, 26 December 1901.
3. Marquand, p. 47.
4. 'Why I Joined the ILP', ed. J. Clayton, quoted Laybourn, p. 32.
5. Quoted in Stewart, p. 200.
6. KH to MS, 3 April 1903, National Library of Scotland, Box 25, File 6.
7. P. Romero, p. 23.
8. Ibid., pp. 17, 25, 44.
9. Ibid., p. 28.
10. Ibid.
11. S. Pankhurst, *The Suffragette Movement*, p. 173.
12. Ibid., p. 174.
13. Sylvia Pankhurst Papers, file 9, notes for her book, *The Home Front*, IISH, Amsterdam.
14. Lowe, *Pit to Parliament*, p. 78.
15. KH to MS, 1 October 1904, National Library of Scotland, Dep 1765, Box 25, File 6.
16. Ibid., 5, 24 October and 7 November 1904.
17. Ibid., 3 April 1903, Box 25, File 6.
18. Ibid., Christmas Day, 1904, Dep 176, Box 25, File 1.
19. Stewart, p. 217.
20. Pleckanoff and Professor Katayam were the delegates from Russia and Japan.
21. Glasier, *Memorial*, p. 24.
22. Naoroji was the Indian delegate; Stewart, p. 221.
23. Ibid.
24. Tsuzuki, p. 134.
25. Lowe, *Pit to Parliament*, p. 104.
26. *Labour Leader*, 16 September 1904.
27. Keir Hardie, 'The Great International', in ibid., 26 August 1905.
28. Ibid., 9 September 1904.
29. Ibid.
30. Ibid.
31. Ibid., 2 September 1904, 'An Indictment of the Class War'. There was also an additional piece in the September issue of *Nineteenth Century*, summarized in Stewart, pp. 221–4. See also profile of Cunninghame Graham, MP, *The Miner* April 1887.
32. *Labour Leader*, 9 September 1904.
33. Ibid., 30 September and 7 October 1904.
34. M. Beer, 'Marxism and the Class War', in ibid., 30 September, 7 October and 4 November 1904.
35. Marquand, p. 83.
36. *New Liberal Review*, September 1903.
37. *Socialism and Society*, 1905.
38. Ibid., p. 143; Marquand, pp. 88–93.
39. 16 September 1905.
40. R. H. Tawney, *The Radical Tradition*, p. 64.
41. Quoted in Tsuzuki, p. 150.
42. Hyndman to Wilshire, 7 January 1904, Wilshire Papers, quoted Tsuzuki, p. 149.
43. Glasier, Diary, 7 October 1904, Morgan, *Keir Hardie*, p. 141.
44. *Labour Leader*, October 1904.
45. Frances Warwick to KH, 1 August, 20 December 1904, 5, 18, and 26 January 1905, Francis Johnson Correspondence, LSE.
46. KH to Frances Warwick, 28 December 1904, Letter 04/67, loc. cit.
47. McBriar, pp. 299–300.
48. Tracey, Vol I, p. 155.
49. Parliamentary Debates (Commons), 4 July 1893, Volume XIV, Line 807.
50. Parliamentary Debates (Commons), 18 December

1902, Volume CXVI, Line 1628.

51. Influenced by writers like Thorold Rogers (who had also influenced H. V. Mills), KH believed pre-industrial workers were better off.

52. KH, *The Unemployed Problem*, 1904.

53. Lansbury, p. 79.

54. Minority Report CD 4499, 1909.

55. Fels had pioneered a scheme in Philadelphia based on one introduced by Michigan's Governor Pingree, using innercity land to grow potatoes. Mary Fels, *Joseph Fels, His Life and Work*.

56. At Laindon and Mayland in Essex and Hollesley Bay in Suffolk.

57. Fels, p. 65.

58. Lansbury, *My Life*, p. 100.

59. Keir Hardie, *John Bull, and the Unemployed*, ILP, 1905.

60. Parliamentary Debates (Commons), 18 April 1905, Volume CXLV, Lines 554 and 557.

61. Report of LRC Conference, 1903; Tracey, Vol I, pp. 120–5 and Humphrey, pp. 157–8.

62. Report of LRC Conference, January 1905.

63. Tracey, Vol, I, p. 119.

64. V. Oulianoff to JRM, 23 March 1905, Labour Party Archives.

65. J.D. Macrea, Labour Party Correspondence. Quoted Laybourn, pp. 62–3.

66. Ibid., p. 64, Calderdale Archives, c. 1906, signed 'Tom Halifax'.

67. Parliamentary Debates, 11 August 1905, Volume CLI, Line 1001.

68. S. Pankhurst, 'Myself When Young', writing in *Myself When Young*, Margot Asquith, p. 276.

69. F. Balgarnie, 'The Women's Suffrage Movement in the 19th Century', p. 39.

70. J. Schneer, *George Lansbury*, p. 74.

71. 15 November 1883, Freud to Martha Bernays, *Letters of Sigmund Freud, 1873–1939*, ed. Ernst L. Freud, Hogarth Press, London, 1961, p. 60.

72. Glasier, Diary, February 1904.

73. Ibid.

74. Elizabeth Glendower Evans, an American philanthropist, quoted in Thompson, *The Enthusiasts*, p. 160.

75. Her views are set out in Marquand, pp. 51 and 148–9.

76. Ibid., p. 148.

77. Ibid., p. 149.

78. Schneer, p. 74.

79. Speech reported in *Leicester Pioneer*, 8 June 1912, quoted in Marquand, p. 148.

80. Sylvia Pankhurst Papers, Notes for Obituary, file 9, folder 9, IISH Amsterdam.

81. S. Pankhurst, *The Suffragette Movement*, p. 178.

82. Quoted in Marquand, p. 51.

83. Quoted in ibid., p. 52.

84. 1 July 1890, quoted in Schneer, p. 84.

85. Lansbury, writing in *Votes for Women*, 25 April 1913.

86. Snowden, Vol I, p. 185. I am indebted to John Burns's greatniece, Mrs Bernice Stone, for information about his family.

87. S. Pankhurst, *The Suffragette Movement*, p. 178.

88. Ibid.

89. *Serfdom to Socialism*, January 1907.

90. Morgan, *Keir Hardie*, p. 163.

91. Keir Hardie, Preface, 'A Plea for Women's Suffrage', *The Citizenship of Women*.

92. *Social-Democrat*, April 1904, quoted Tsuzuki, p. 190.

93. Thompson, *Blatchford*, p. 183.

94. Hyndman to Wilshire, 27 May 1904, Wilshire Papers, quoted Tsuzuki, p. 190.

95. D. Montefiore, *The Position of Women in the Socialist Movement*, 1909, p. 3, quoted in Tsuzuki, p. 191.

96. Tsuzuki, p. 190.

97. D. Montefiore, *From a Victorian to a Modern*, 1927, pp. 72–82.

98. S. Pankhurst, *The*

Suffragette Movement, p. 178.

99. Ibid., p. 180.
100. Ibid., p. 183.
101. Ibid.
102. Ibid., p. 174.
103. Richard Pankhurst, *Sylvia Pankhurst*, p. 27.
104. S. Pankhurst, *The Suffragette Movement*, p. 177.
105. Ibid., p. 175.
106. Malcolm MacDonald, speaking at a memorial dinner for JRM, House of Commons, 22 March 1978; also Stewart, p. 311.
107. S. Pankhurst, *The Suffragette Movement*, p. 176.
108. G. Lewis, *Eva Gore-Booth and Esler Roper*, p. 115. Several postcards KH sent (10 August 1905, for example, National Library of Scotland, Dep 176, Box 21, File 1) featured a photograph of himself or showed the drawing of himself by Cosmo Rowe. Unfortunately, Rowe had great difficulty getting the payment due from the ILP (and KH), who commissioned the drawing, Letters 10/125, 10/616, 26/3, Francis Johnson Correspondence, LSE.
109. S. Pankhurst, *The Suffragette Movement*, p. 190.
110. Stewart, p. 232.
111. Printed in *Review of Reviews*, January 1905.
112. He asked for 30 shillings a week and a 48-hour week, Parliamentary Debates, 18 December 1902, Volume CXVI, Line 1628.
113. JRM speaking at a harvest festival in Leicester, reported in *Labour Leader*, 30 September 1904.
114. Open letter to Lloyd George, *Labour Leader*, 7 March 1903.
115. Stewart, p. 223, says 52.
116. 1905 Northampton Conference, proposed by Rochdale; Tsuzuki, p. 155.
117. Hyndman to KH, 11 July 1905, Museum of Labour History, Manchester.
118. Tsuzuki, pp. 157-8.
119. Ibid., pp. 159-60.
120. Ibid.
121. Lansbury, p. 112.
122. Snowden, Vol I, pp. 109-10.
123. Tschiffely, p. 279.
124. Ibid., p. 333. The late was January 1901.
125. Ibid., p. 269.
126. Ibid., p. 339.
127. Ibid., p. 342.
128. Speech at Bentley's Hall, Merthyr, 6 January 1906, printed as a handbill, 'Labour's Battle at the Merthyr Boroughs', *Labour Pioneer*, PY 3/8, Aberdare Library.
129. Morgan, *Keir Hardie (1967 edition)*, p. 33.
130. Pelling, *Origins*, p. 128.
131. *Merthyr Express* and *South Wales Daily News*.
132. Election speech, 10 January 1906, printed as a handbill, *Labour Pioneer*, PY 3/8, Aberdare Library.
133. Testimonial sheets, 1906 election, Aberdare Library.
134. *Labour Pioneer*, 6 January 1906.
135. Hughes, *Keir Hardie*, pp. 120-1.
136. *Labour Pioneer*, 6 January 1906.
137. *Labour Pioneer*, 10 January 1906.
138. Ibid.
139. The *Labour Pioneer*, January 1906, poster, Swansea University.
140. *Labour Leader*, 25 March 1915.
141. Speech at Bentley's Hall, 6 January 1906.
142. Thomas 13, 971, KH 10, 187, Radcliffe 7,776.
143. Stewart, p. 236.
144. Speech reprinted *Labour Pioneer*, 10 January 1906.
145. Thomas Kirkup, *A History of Socialism*, 1906, p. 333.
146. Wedgwood, p. 157.
147. Tracey, Vol I, p. 149.
148. Ibid., p. 152.
149. Ibid., p. 127.
150. Humphrey, p. 183.
151. Morgan, *Keir Hardie*, p. 155.
152. Hyndman to Wilshire, 31 March 1906, quoted in Tsuzuki, p. 162.
153. Humphrey, p. 166-7.
154. Sylvia Pankhurst, 'Notes' on

KH, Sylvia Pankhurst Papers, file 9, folder 9, IISH, Amsterdam.

155. Stonelake, p. 82.
156. Sylvia Pankhurst, file 9, folder 9, IISH, Amsterdam.
157. Snowden, Vol I, p. 125.
158. KH to CG, 5 December 1905, ILP 4, LSE.
159. Glasier to KH, 11 February 1906, Glasier Papers.
160. Pollard, 'The Foundation of the Cooperative Party', p. 191.
161. Labour Leader, 1906; Thompson, The Enthusiasts, p. 144.
162. MS to KH, 14 January 1911, National Library of Scotland, Dep 176. Box 25, File 1.
163. KH to Robert Williams, November 1906, Dep 176, Box 25, File 2.
164. KH to MS, 8 November 1906, Box 25, File 1.
165. Ibid.
166. Morgan, Keir Hardie, p. 141; Thompson, Blatchford, p. 179.
167. Thompson, Blatchford, p. 180.
168. Ibid., pp. 181-2.
169. Snowden, Vol I, p. 123.
170. Labour Leader, February 1906, quoted Hughes, Keir Hardie, p. 129.
171. Introduction, Hughes, Writings, pp. xi and xii.
172. Quoted in Humphrey, p. 164.
173. Fels, pp. 59-60.
174. S. Pankhurst, The Suffragette Movement, p. 201.
175. Snowden, Vol I, p. 124.
176. Report, Labour Party Conference, February 1906.
177. Signed by Bankes, Liberal agent for Westminster, 6 March 1906, reproduction, Tracey, Vol I, p. 128.
178. Snowden, Vol I, p. 134.
179. S. Pankhurst, The Suffragette Movement, p. 204.
180. S. Pankhurst, 'Myself When Young', p. 283.
181. Stewart, p. 242. The date was 25 April 1906.
182. S. Pankhurst, 'Myself When Young', p. 281.
183. Stewart, p. 246.

184. Thompson, The Enthusiasts, p. 139.
185. Labour Leader, 24 August 1906. Letter from R. Smillie.
186. Glasier, Diary, 27 August 1906.
187. Reported by Glasier, Diary, 21 July 1906.
188. In June 1906 she was awarded her degree; the prize was given by Victoria College, Manchester University.
189. S. Pankhurst, The Suffragette Movement, p. 221; a play, Votes for Women, written by Elizabeth Robins, was put on in 1907.
190. Quoted Romero, p. 49.
191. Ibid., p. 43.
192. Ibid., p. 44.
193. S. Pankhurst, The Suffragette Movement, p. 221-2.
194. Ibid., p. 217.

Chapter 9 – High Tide

1. Snowden; Vol I, p. 318.
2. Labour Leader, 15 August 1906.
3. Glasier, Memorial, pp. 71 and 52.
4. Labour Leader, 15 August 1906.
5. Snowden, Vol I, p. 317.
6. Stewart, p. 241.
7. Glasier, Memorial, p. 52.
8. JRM to Glasier, 21 July 1906, Glasier Papers.
9. Glasier, Diary note, 21 July 1906; quoted in Thompson, The Enthusiasts, p. 148.
10. Hughes, Keir Hardie, p. 133.
11. Parliamentary Debates (Commons), 12 December 1906, Volume CLXVII, Lines 439-442.
12. The Bill, introduced 2 March 1906, is discussed in S. Bryher, Part III, p. 5.
13. KH, Parliamentary Report to the Labour Party Conference, dated December 1906, presented to the Seventh Conference of the Labour Party, January 1907.
14. Hughes, Keir Hardie, pp. 136-7; Stewart, p. 244.
15. Stewart, p. 244.

16. Hughes, *Keir Hardie*, pp. 86 and 137.
17. Reported ibid., p. 204.
18. S. Pankhurst, *The Suffragette Movement*, pp. 230–1.
19. The bill was introduced on 7 November 1906. He asked suffrage questions on 25, 26 and 27 October.
20. Glasier, Diary, 30 November 1906.
21. Reported in ibid.
22. Ibid., 19 January 1907.
23. Reported in ibid.
24. 1906 meeting to support Bamford Slack Bill, described in S. Pankhurst, *The Suffragette Movement*, p. 182.
25. S. Pankhurst, *The Suffragette Movement*, p. 247, March 1907.
26. Letter addressed 'Dear Comrade', Acc 5234, National Library of Scotland, undated, but refers to Party Conference in Belfast.
27. Interview, CB, 25 November 1987.
28. Speech to the 1914 ILP Conference.
29. Morgan, *Keir Hardie*, p. 166.
30. S. Pankhurst, *The Suffragette Movement*, p. 238.
31. Ibid., p. 252. held the day after Parliament had convened, 13 February 1907.
32. Richard Pankhurst, *Sylvia Pankhurst*, p. 73.
33. S. Pankhurst, *The Suffragette Movement*, p. 255.
34. Report of the Labour Party Conference, 1907.
35. The voting in favour of leaving 'time and methods' to the PLP was 642,000 to 252,000; against mandatory socialism 835,000 to 98,000; against mandatory trade union membership 553,000 to 381,000; and in favour of universal rather than limited suffrage 605,000 to 268,000.
36. Report of the Labour Party Conference, 1907.
37. Glasier, Diary, 26 and 28 January 1907.
38. S. Pankhurst, *The Suffragette Movement*, p. 248.
39. Both letters in Sylvia Pankhurst Papers, file 9, folder 9b, IISH, Amsterdam; KH to ESP, 21 February 1907; second letter undated.
40. Romero, p. 37.
41. Sylvia Pankhurst Papers, file 9, folder 9a, IISH, Amsterdam.
42. Hugh Dalton, *Call Back Yesterday*, quoted Hughes, *Keir Hardie*, p. 139.
43. S. Pankhurst, *The Suffragette Movement*, p. 254.
44. Hughes, *Keir Hardie*, p. 174.
45. Glasier, *Memorial*, p. 4.
46. S. Pankhurst, *The Suffragette Movement*, p. 249.
47. Glasier, Diary, 21 July 1906.
48. Stewart, p. 226.
49. S. Pankhurst, *The Suffragette Movement*, p. 245.
50. JRM to Glasier, 13 March 1907, Glasier Papers.
51. Ibid., 19 March 1907.
52. Stewart, pp. 249–51.
53. MacDonald, Preface, Stewart, *Keir Hardie*.
54. 188 to 180. Stewart, pp. 250–51.
55. KH to Glasier, 5 April 1907.
56. S. Pankhurst, *The Suffragette Movement*, p. 257.
57. JRM to Glasier, 3 May 1907. Glasier Papers.
58. Glasier, Diary, 2 November 1913.
59. JRM to Glasier, 3 May 1907, loc. cit.
60. *Labour Leader*, 15 August 1906.
61. Quoted from the *Labour Record* in S. Pankhurst, *The Suffragette Movement*, p. 248.
62. Parliamentary Debates (Commons), 20 February 1907, Volume CLXIX.
63. Quoted in S. Pankhurst, 'Myself When Young', p. 249.
64. Quoted in Stewart, p. 255.
65. Liverpool, 1905 had voted for state control, Belfast, 1907 had voted against.
66. See reports of J. O'Grady, MP, of the National Amalgamated Furnishing Trades Association

on this issue in the Association's 'Monthly Reports', 1906–7.

67. Romero, p. 50: S. Pankhurst, *The Suffragette Movement*, pp. 257–8.

68. Stewart, pp. 256–7.

69. Ibid., p. 257.

70. KH to Robert Williams, 28 June 1907, National Library of Scotland, Dep 176, Box 25, File 2.

71. Hughes, *Keir Hardie*, p. 141.

72. *Labour Leader*, quoted in Hughes, *Writings*, pp. 125–6.

73. KH to Glasier, 6 May 1907, Glasier Papers.

74. KH to Robert Williams in Alexandria, 27 June 1907, Dep 176, Box 25, File 2.

75. Hughes, *Keir Hardie*, p. 141.

76. Stewart, p. 257.

77. Hughes, *Keir Hardie*, p. 141.

78. KH to Glasier, 7 May 1907, Glasier Papers.

79. Jarrow Election Supplement, July 1907, Benn Archives.

80. Report from W. F. Black, subeditor, who heard him at an open-air meeting, quoted in Thompson, *The Enthusiasts*, p. 151.

81. KH to JRM, 11 July 1907, quoted in Morgan, *Keir Hardie*, p. 174.

82. Snowden, Vol I, p. 164.

83. Glasier, *Memorial*, p. 50.

84. Snowden, Vol I, pp. 125 and 314.

85. Morgan, *Keir Hardie*, p. 190.

86. Snowden, Vol I, p. 218.

87. KH deposited £100 and £600 in his Clydesdale bank account on 11 July 1907, (Dep 176, Box 1, File 2). The larger sum probably came from Fels. In each country individual groups paid for him. In Central India, for example, Mahayana Sabha 'met his expenses'. (Entry 4 November 1907, Minto Diary, MS 12609, National Library of Scotland.)

88. *Labour Leader*, 12 July 1907.

89. Stewart, p. 270.

90. Morgan, *Keir Hardie*, p. 160.

91. For example, KH, Parliamentary Debates (Commons), 20 July 1906, Volume CLXI, when the East India Revenue Accounts were debated.

92. Reports for 21, 19 and 26 October 1907. KH's progress through India was recorded by J. E. M. K. Gilbert, 4th Earl of Minto (MS 13690, ff. 17–23, National Library of Scotland).

93. Hughes, *Keir Hardie*, p. 150.

94. NH, Introduction, Hughes, *Writings*, p. xxi.

95. Minto Diary, 5 November 1907, loc. cit.

96. Stewart, p. 262.

97. Ibid., p. 263.

98. Sir Herbert Risley to Dunlop Smith, 17 October 1907, National Library of Scotland, MS 12757, f. 343, reporting his talk with KH.

99. KH to Glasier, 8 October 1907, Glasier Papers.

100. Edward VII to Lord Minto, 17 August 1909, quoted Morgan, *Keir Hardie*, p. 193.

101. Stewart, p. 267.

102. Ibid., p. 269.

103. Letter to LH from Secretary of Keir Hardie Reception Committee, Wellington, New Zealand, 21 August 1908, National Library of Scotland, Dep 176, Box 1, File 1.

104. Elspeth King, 'The Scottish Women's Suffrage Movement', 1978.

105. Ibid.

106. D. Montefiore, *From Victorian to Modern*, quoted Tsuzuki, p. 191.

107. *Labour Leader*, 30 August, 1907.

108. Romero, p. 50. ESP records the letter's arrival in *The Suffragette Movement*, pp. 271–2.

109. KH letter, undated, no heading, no signature, Sylvia Pankhurst Papers, file 9, folder 9c, IISH, Amsterdam.

110. S. Pankhurst. *The Suffragette Movement*, p. 272.

111. Snowden, Vol I, pp. 174–5.

112. Tracey, Vol I, p. 150.

113. 7 September 1907.

114. Snowden, Vol I, p. 151.

115. Frank Smith to Glasier, undated Letter 1907/94, Glasier Papers.
116. Glasier, 21 March 1908, Letter 1908/6, loc. cit.
117. JRM to Glasier, 31 May 1907, Letter 07/76, loc. cit.
118. Ibid.
119. Ibid., August 29 1908.
120. Ibid.
121. *Labour Leader*, 10 April 1908, quoted in Hughes, *Writings*, p. 133.

Chapter 10 – Action versus Ideology

1. 21 March 1908, Letter 1908/6, Glasier Papers.
2. 16 May 1908, loc. cit.
3. Ibid.
4. Glasier, Diary, 26 January 1907. Quoted in Thompson, *The Enthusiasts*, p. 149.
5. Brian Harrison, *Separate Spheres*, Croom Helm, 1978.
6. Thomas Hardy, Preface to 1895 edition, *The Hand of Ethelberta*.
7. Ibid., 1912 Preface.
8. KH to ESP, Sylvia Pankhurst Papers, file 9, folder 9, undated, IISH, Amsterdam.
9. Romero, p. 36.
10. S. Pankhurst, *The Suffragette Movement*, p. 177.
11. Romero, p. 49.
12. Both are in the National Portrait Gallery.
13. Fenner Brockway, Interview, 26 January 1984, Cumnock Library.
14. Fenner Brockway, Interview, 23 January, Sylvia Ayling, Sylvia Pankhurst Society,
15. I am indebted to Jill Craigie for this information.
16. Fenner Brockway, Interview with CB, 24 November 1987,
17. Hughes, *Keir Hardie*, p. 144.
18. KH to Glasier, 11 April 1908.
19. Ibid., 16 May 1908.
20. Quoted in Stewart, p. 174.
21. Ibid., p. 278.
22. Quoted in Hughes, *Keir Hardie*, p. 186.
23. Parliamentary Debates (Commons), July 1909, Volume VIII, Lines 678 and 720.
24. Glasier, Diary, 8 May 1910, also quoted in Thompson, *The Enthusiasts*, p. 145.
25. Speech, June 1908, reported *Labour Leader*, 3 July 1908.
26. A. J. P. Taylor, *The Trouble Makers*, p. 113.
27. Plans for the Federation were outlined to the editor of the *Madrid Herald* before he left, and reported in the *Labour Leader*, 28 August 1908.
28. Stewart, p. 287; see correspondence between March and June 1910, Letters 10/146, 148 and 82, Francis Johnson Correspondence, LSE.
29. Later when Fels was approached to support the ILP (rather than KH) he refused. See Fels to Benson, 22 June 1910, Letter 10/282, loc. cit.
30. Glasier to his sister, Elizabeth, 5 May 1908.
31. 21 September 1908, MacDonald Papers 5, Public Records Office Classification number, quoted Marquand, p. 109.
32. Stewart, p. 287.
33. Reported *Labour Leader*, 2 October 1908.
34. Hughes, *Keir Hardie*, p. 168; see also KH's articles in the *Socialist Review*, 1912.
35. National Amalgamated Furnishing Trades Association (NAFTA), Monthly Report, February 1909, Vol 8, no. 2, p. 12; Hughes, *Keir Hardie*, p. 172.
36. Cahm and Fisera, eds., *Socialism and Nationalism*, Vol II, p. 83.
37. Stewart, p. 288.
38. Cahm and Fisera, Vol II, pp. 84–91.
39. S. Pankhurst, *The Suffragette Movement*, p. 257.
40. Stewart, p. 224.
41. M. Beer, for example, London correspondent of *Vorwärts*,

quoted Stewart, p. 291; Beer later wrote *A History of British Socialism*, 1919.

42. Quoted in Lenin, *Lenin on Britain*, p. 111; Arnot, *The Miners*, p. 125; Tracey, Vol I, p. 119 (whose translation is used).

43. Glasier, Diary, 21 July 1906.

44. Vallance, *William Morris*, p. 311.

45. Keir Hardie, *Serfdom to Socialism*, p. ix. In fact, KH deferred to JRM as the Party's main thinker. See Labour Party Conference Report, Birmingham 1911, p. 62.

46. *Serfdom to Socialism.*

47. Ibid.

48. Morgan, *Keir Hardie*, p. 46.

49. Quoted in Stewart, p. 230.

50. *Labour Leader*, 9 September 1904. Quoted, *Writings*, p. 121.

51. Quoted in Thompson, *The Enthusiasts*, p. 145.

52. Upton Sinclair chronicled this change in the American press in *The Brass Check*, first published c. 1919, revised in dozens of reprintings through the early 1920s.

53. A.J. Balfour, Introduction, *The Case Against Socialism*.

54. 20 July 1907.

55. Balfour, p. 19.

56. Snowden, Vol. I, pp. 147 and 197.

57. Ibid., pp. 170–3.

58. These were recorded in Hanover, Germany in 1907 by Kaley Kalvert, a music hall artist. One, a parody on the song 'Smoke, smoke, smoke', attacked KH and Grayson. I am indebted to K. Malcolm of Flixton, Yorkshire, for a recording of these songs.

59. These included *The Case Against Socialism*, with an introduction by A. J. Balfour, 1909, and *A Critical Examination of Socialism*, by W. T. Mallock, John Murray, 1908; as well as Professor Flint, *The Case Against Socialism*; Onslow Yorke, *The Secret History of the International.*

60. *Rerum Novarum*, 1891, from Pope Leo XIII.

61. Balfour, p. 372.

62. Ethel Snowden argued this in her pamphlet, 'The Woman Socialist': Harry Quelch's views were given at a public meeting on 12 November 1907. Quoted in Balfour, pp. 386–8.

63. Balfour, p. 5.

64. Ibid., p. 33.

65. Ibid., p. 23.

66. Ibid., pp. 30, 392.

67. *The Morning Post*, 22 January 1908, reporting the Labour Party Conference in Hull.

68. Speech at Leeds, 9 December 1907, reported in Balfour, pp. 28–30.

69. Richard Bell, MP, *Trade Unions*, published by T. and E. C. Jack, undated, pp. 88–9.

70. Speaking in a Debate in the House of Commons, 29 March 1906, Parliamentary Debates, Volume CLIV.

71. *Labour Leader*, 26 August 1906.

72. KH to MS, undated, August 1908, National Library of Scotland, Dep 176, Box 25, File 1.

73. Ibid.

74. *Daily Express*, 28 October 1906.

75. Parliamentary Debates (Commons), 13 October 1908, Volume CLXIX, Line 172f.

76. J. Collings, MP, Parliamentary Debates, Volume CLXXII, 13 October 1908, Line 191.

77. Sir F. Banbury, MP, ibid.

78. MS, note, 8 December 1911, National Library of Scotland, Dep 176, Box 2, File 3.

79. *Daily Chronicle*, 14 October 1908.

80. Report of speech by Mr Greenwood, a Liberal, *Daily News*, 15 October 1908.

81. *The Country Gentleman*, 17 October 1908.

82. Parliamentary Debates (Commons), 8 December 1908, Volume CXCVIII, p. 259.

83. KH to Glasier, 27 December 1908, Glasier Papers.

84. Ibid.

85. JRM to Glasier, 26 October 1908.
86. Hughes, *Keir Hardie*, p. 173.
87. Parliamentary Debates, 17 February 1909, Fifth Series, Volume 1, Line 179.
88. Ibid.
89. Tsuzuki, p. 169.
90. *Labour Leader*, 23 October 1908.
91. B. Tillett, *Is the Parliamentary Party a Failure?* (Pamphlet), July 1909.
92. Ibid.
93. *Daily Graphic*, 26 July 1909; the film is preserved in the National Film Archive in London (incorrectly titled 'Land League Demonstration'). KH appears for about 10 seconds on platform 7.
94. Glasier, Diary, 18 July 1909.
95. Reported, *Sheffield Independent*, 17 July 1909. Hancock was a Nottinghamshire miner.
96. KH to Glasier, 27 December 1908.
97. Hughes, *Keir Hardie*, p. 173.
98. Facilitated through an Act of 1911 which permitted trade unionists to levy for voluntary Labour Party support.
99. Humphrey. p. 168. This was a quote from a fund-raising document signed by H. G. Wells on behalf of the independents.
100. Thompson, *The Enthusiasts*, p. 155.
101. Ibid., p. 157.
102. Ibid., p. 160.
103. Ibid., p. 156.
104. Parliamentary Debates (Commons), 15 October 1908, Volume CLXI, Lines 495f.
105. Thompson, *The Enthusiasts*, p. 154; K. Morgan, *Labour People*, p. 66.
106. Stewart, p. 290.
107. Dick Wallhead to JRM, 3 November 1907, MDP 5/18; and B. Riley to JRM, 25 January 1909, MDP 5/119, quoted Marquand, p. 112.
108. Stewart, p. 298.
109. Snowden, Vol I, p. 165.
110. *Labour Leader*, 24 September 1909; Stewart, pp. 301–2.
111. Romero, pp. 55–6.
112. Hughes, *Keir Hardie*, p. 172.
113. Lowe, *Pit to Parliament*, p. 48.
114. Glasier, Diary, 27 July 1909.
115. *Labour Leader*, November 1908, quoted in Hughes, *Keir Hardie*, p. 170.
116. Shaw to KH, 1 January 1910, National Library of Scotland, Dep 176, Box 1, File 3.
117. *Daily Mirror*, 8 January 1910.
118. Quoted in Hughes, *Keir Hardie*, p. 191.
119. Quoted and photographed, *Daily Mirror*, p. 1, 8 January 1910.
120. *Merthyr Pioneer*, 27 May 1910; Hughes, *Writings*, p. 143. The *Merthyr Pioneer* was the new journal KH had started in Merthyr.
121. Stewart, p. 305.
122. Hughes, *Writings; Labour Leader*, 27 May 1911, *Keir Hardie*, p. 204; also Leaflet D/VA 24/4a and D/DVA 24/15, Glamorgan Country Archives, Cardiff.
123. Snowden, Vol I, p. 207.
124. Nan Hardie, Introduction, Hughes, *Speeches*, p. xi.
125. Glasier, *Memorial*, p. 30.
126. MacDonald, Preface, Stewart, *Keir Hardie*, p. xxv.
127. JRM, in MacArthur, MacDonald and Smillie, *Memorial*.
128. Ibid.
129. For example, Morgan, *Keir Hardie*, p. 29.
130. KH to BG, 25 November 1909.
131. Stanfield MSS/12, 22 March 1909, Swansea University.
132. Correspondence, D/DVhj 23456, Glamorgan Country Archives.
133. Speech Dowwfais, 1911, quoted Hughes, *Writings*, p. 148.
134. KH to RD, D/Dxik 81.2, loc. cit.
135. James Hardie to RD, D/Dxik 30/3, loc. cit.
136. The leaflets are in D/DVAN 24115, loc. cit.
137. Election Address, quoted Stewart, p. 306. Also in MS in Aberdare Library.
138. *Labour Leader*, January 1910,

quoted in Hughes, *Keir Hardie*, p. 191.

139. Quoted, Preface, Hughes, *Writings*, p. xi.
140. Manifesto by Christian Ministers, PY 3/4/5, Aberdare Library.
141. 3 March 1912, 'What Think Ye of Christ?', Address to the Adult School Union, Dowlais.
142. Address to Congregational Union, Bradford, October 1892, reported in *The Labour Prophet*, November 1892.
143. *Labour Leader*, 18 September 1908, 10, 19, 26 August 1910. See also KH, *Karl Marx: The Man and His Message*, National Labour Press, Ltd., 1910. See also *My Confession of Faith in a Labour Alliance*, 1909.
144. Preface, Stewart, p. xxiii.
145. Mowatt, 'Ramsay MacDonald and the Labour Party', p. 136.
146. Fyfe, pp. 70 and 76; Cockburn, *Hungry Heart*, p. 135.
147. McLean, p. 172; see also p. 42.
148. Morgan, *Keir Hardie*, p. 204.
149. Glasier, *Memorial*, p. 62.
150. Paraphrased by Stewart, p. 292. See M. Beer, *A History of British Socialism*, 1919.
151. Maxton, *Keir Hardie, Prophet and Pioneer*.
152. Morgan, 'The Merthyr of Keir Hardie', in *Merthyr Politics*, p. 67.
153. Dowlais, Address to Adult School Union.
154. Pelling, *Origins*, p. 64.
155. Address on Labour and Christianity, 5 May 1910, National Library of Scotland, Dep 176, Box 25, File 6.
156. For example, JRM in MacArthur, MacDonald and Smillie, *Memoir*; Blatchford too called KH a covenanter.
157. Glasier, *Memorial*, pp. 67–9.
158. Wedgwood, *Memoirs of a Fighting Life*, p. 77.
159. Kapp, Vol II, p. 68.
160. Letter, 28 September 1894, to Richard T. Ely, in Tsuzuki, p. 101.
161. Quote from William Cobbett, *The Political Register*, 3 January 1824; R. F. Wearmouth, *Methodism and the Struggle of the Working Class*, 1954, p. 287.
162. Paul Davies, *A. J. Cook*, series 'Lives of the Left', Manchester University Press.
163. In 1914; Lansbury, p. 78.
164. Stonelake, *Autobiography*, pp. 30 and 151.
165. Lansbury, pp. 5, 113, 116.
166. Ibid., p. 117.
167. Glasier, Diary, 28 May 1900, Glasier Papers.
168. Snowden, Vol I, p. 317.
169. Mitchell, p. 59.
170. Glasier to sister Elizabeth, 23 October 1900, Glasier Papers.
171. Glasier, *Memorial*, p. 70.
172. M. Cole, *The Webbs and their Work*, 1949, p. 7.
173. Thompson, *The Enthusiasts*, p. 88, published by the ILP as an 1893 pamphlet.
174. Fenner Brockway, Interview with CB, 25 November 1987.
175. McLean, pp. 164–5.
176. Snowden, Vol I, p. 318.
177. S. Pankhurst, *The Suffragette Movement*, p. 245.
178. Parliamentary Debates (Commons), 1 May 1912, Volume XXXVII, Line 1864.
179. Lowe, *Pit to Parliament*, p. 75.
180. Keir Hardie, 'Can A Man be a Christian on a Pound a Week?', 1901.

Chapter 11 – Parliamentary versus Extra-Parliamentary

1. S. Pankhurst, *The Suffragette Movement*, p. 306.
2. Ibid., p. 274.
3. Ibid., p. 320.
4. Ibid.
5. Ibid., p. 324.
6. Letter from Jamie Hardie to RD, 4 February 1910, D/Dxik 30/2, Glamorgan Country Archives Cardiff.
7. Speech quoted in Stewart, p. 307.

8. Letter to Glasier and Benson, February 1911, quoted *The Enthusiasts*, p. 167.
9. KH to T. D. Benson, 22 February 1910, Glasier Papers.
10. Ibid.
11. Report of Conference, 1910, ILP.
12. Glasier, Diary, 28 February 1910.
13. S. Pankhurst, *The Suffragette Movement*, p. 176.
14. Glasier, Diary, 19 June 1910.
15. Quoted in S. Pankhurst, *The Suffragette Movement*, p. 174.
16. Sylvia Pankhurst Papers, Poem II, file 9a, IISH, Amsterdam.
17. Poem I, loc. cit.
18. Ibid.
19. KH to ESP, 1 August 1910, 10 March 1911, file 9c, loc. cit.
20. Romero, p. 37.
21. Morgan, *Labour People*, p. 30; Morgan, *Keir Hardie*, p. 165.
22. Fenner Brockway, *Towards Tomorrow*, p. 22.
23. Snowden, Vol I, pp. 210–11; he says it was lack of room on the opposition side.
24. Marquand, pp. 124–5.
25. James O'Grady, Monthly Report, February 1910, NAFTA, p. 8.
26. Snowden, Vol I, p. 215, letter from KH; *Labour Leader*, 11 March 1910.
27. Leonard Hall, C. T. Douthwaite, J. M. MacLachlan and J. H. Belcher were the authors. So called because its cover was green.
28. Thompson, *The Enthusiasts*, p. 169.
29. Snowden, Vol I, p. 217.
30. Earl Winterton, quoted Morgan, *Keir Hardie*, p. 233.
31. Stewart, p. 318.
32. KH to RD, 16 May 1910, D/Dxik Letter 30/5, Glamorgan County Archives.
33. KH to ESP, 1 August 1910, file 9, folder 9c, IISH Amsterdam.
34. Ibid., 26 November 1910, loc. cit.
35. Letters D/Dxik 30/30 and 22, Glamorgan County Archives.
36. KH to RD, undated, D/Dxik 30/15, loc. cit.
37. Ibid., D/Dxik 30/26, loc. cit.
38. Ibid., undated, D/Dxik 30. 16, loc. cit.
39. Ibid., D/Dxik 30/32 loc. cit.
40. Stewart, pp. 313–14.
41. At Bremen in 1904, for example.
42. Stewart, p. 315.
43. KH to ESP, 7 September 1910, file 9, folder 9c, IISH, Amsterdam.
44. Stewart, p. 322.
45. Ibid., p. 323.
46. Glasier to his sister, 12 December 1910, Letter 1910/12, Glasier Papers.
47. KH to the Revd John Hughes, 11 December 1910, Book II B 18, Benn Archives.
48. Hughes's notes on his family, National Library of Scotland, Box 25 (8). The description of the college is Emrys Hughes's.
49. Notes on the Hughes family, two pages pencil, 'Notes for a Biography', Cumnock Library, in envelope marked 'Unknown Photos'.
50. Ibid.
51. Hughes, Notes on his family, National Library of Scotland, Box 25 (8).
52. Ibid.
53. 1903, undated letter from Queen's Secretary, Buckingham Palace, Hedley Dennis Papers, Benn Archives.
54. Hughes, Notes for biography, Cumnock Library.
55. KH to Glasier, 13 February 1911. He had been elected in January 1910.
56. Ibid.
57. Schneer, p. 91.
58. *Labour Leader*, 24 March 1911.
59. Ibid., 21 April 1911.
60. Laybourn, ed., *Labour Party Reader*, p. 71, 7 February 1911.
61. Glasier, Diary, 1912, quoted Thompson, *The Enthusiasts*, p. 172.
62. Ibid.
63. Glasier, Diary, 28 February 1910.

64. Thompson, *The Enthusiasts*, p. 172.
65. KH to James Henderson, 17 October 1911, Cumnock Library.
66. Robert Hunter, *Socialism at Work* or John Spargo, *Socialism*, books that were popular at the time but long since out of print.
67. ESP Notes for KH's obituary, Pankhurst Collection, file 9, folder 9, IISH, Amsterdam.
68. Thompson, *Blatchford*, pp. 214–18.
69. Hughes, *Keir Hardie*, p. 194.
70. Ibid, pp. 128–9.
71. E. Whitely, working with National Labour Press, offered KH £5,000 (Morgan, *Keir Hardie*, p. 235) in January 1911; Hughes, *Keir Hardie*, p. 194.
72. KH to S. Seruya, 1 October 1910, National Library of Scotland, Acc 4461.
73. KH to S. Seruya, undated, 1910–11, loc. cit.
74. Morgan says the first issue was June 1911 (*Keir Hardie* p. 237); Hughes (*Writings*, p. 142) gives March 1910. The *Merthyr Pioneer*, had been published, at least as a one-off publication, since 1906. See MS PY3/3 in Aberdare Library.
75. Glasier, Diary, 14 August 1911.
76. KH's proposals, sent to NAC of ILP, 13 May 1911, National Library of Scotland, Acc 5121.
77. KH to Glasier, 17 May 1911.
78. Speech, Bentley's Hall, 6 January 1906, PY3/3, Aberdare Library.
79. Morgan, *Keir Hardie*, p. 237.
80. Glasier, Diary, June 1911, quoted Thompson, *The Enthusiasts*, p. 182.
81. Benson to JRM, 11 January 1911, 5/21 MacDonald Papers, quoted Marquand, p. 130.
82. KH to AH, 11 January 1911, Card 71 (ii), Benn Archives.
83. Letter to KH from secretary to the Woman's Mission to the Fallen, 16 June 1911, National Library of Scotland, Dep 176, Box 1, File 3.
84. Thorne, Jowett, O'Grady and Snowden.
85. Quoted in Brown, Introduction, *The Industrial Syndicalist*, p. 8.
86. Speaking in the debate on industrial unionism with Frank Rose, fellow member of the Amalgamated Society of Engineers, in Brown, pp. 209–261.
87. 26 July 1910.
88. Brown, p. 173.
89. Ibid., p. 127; the *Industrial Syndicalist*, Vol I, No. 4, October 1910, Mann reporting W. D. Haywood.
90. Quoted in Hughes, *Keir Hardie, Writings*.
91. Snowden, Vol I, p. 235, speaking of 1911.
92. Speech reported in 'Trade Organiser's Report', *NAFTA Journal*, February 1909, p. 13.
93. Brown, *The Industrial Syndicalist*, p. 14.
94. Harry Pollitt, *Serving My Time*, 1940, p. 130.
95. Thompson, *The Enthusiasts*, p. 172.
96. Speaking at the first Conference on Industrial Syndicalism, Coal Exchange, Manchester, 26 November 1910, quoted in Brown, pp. 179–80.
97. Pelling, 'The Labour Unrest – 1911 to 1914', in *Popular Politics and Society in Late Victorian Britain*, 1968, quoted Brown, p. 14.
98. K. Coates and T. Topham, *The Making of the Transport and General Workers' Union*, Vol I, Part 1, Chapter 10.
99. Ibid., quotes Philip Snowden, 1910, p. 337.
100. Ibid., p. 341.
101. Reported in *Industrial Syndicalist*, Vol I, No. 5, November 1910, 'Editorial notes', by Tom Mann.
102. *Labour Leader*, 18 November 1910.
103. Parliamentary Debate (Commons), 15 November 1910, Volume XX.
104. Ibid., 24 November 1910.

105. R. P. Arnot, *The Miners*, p. 66.
106. The Pretoria Pit disaster, December 1910. Stewart, p. 323.
107. Quoted in ibid., p. 310.
108. Hughes, *Keir Hardie*, p. 164.
109. 16 August 1911.
110. Philip Gibbs, *The Pageant of the Years, London*, 1946, quoted in Brown, p. 15.
111. Lord Askwith, *Industrial Problems and Disputes*, London, 1920, p. 150; Austen Chamberlain, writing on 12 March 1912, from his book *Politics From Inside, an Epistolary Chronicle, 1906–14*, London, 1936, pp. 434–44, quoted in Brown, p. 16.
112. KH to S. Seruya, 3 August 1911, National Library of Scotland, Acc 4461.
113. Marquand, p. 145.
114. Hughes, p. 148.
115. Snowden, Vol I, p. 238; See also Marquand, p. 144.
116. Speaking in Covington, Kentucky, USA, reported in *Cincinnati Enquirer*, 5 October 1912.
117. Quoted in *The Life Story of Mr James Keir Hardie MP*, Self-Help Press, c. 1908, p. 10.
118. Late 1901, speaking at Clifford's Inn, quoted by Stewart, p. 196.
119. Speaking in Merthyr Park, August 1911, quoted in Hughes, *Writings*, pp. 145–6. This view was reinforced in the *Merthyr Pioneer* of the same month (August 26).
120. 'How to Get Rid of the Capitalist System', an anti-state view given in the *NAFTA Journal*, Vol 7, no. 3, March 1908, p. 15. The union disagreed with the view.
121. Speaking in March 1911, reported in Brown, p. 323.
122. Keir Hardie, *From Serfdom to Socialism*, p. 28.
123. Merthyr Park, Speech, loc. cit.
124. Snowden, Vol I, p. 225.
125. Humphrey, p. 183.
126. Merthyr Park, Speech, loc. cit., quoted Hughes, *Writings*, p. 146.
127. Stewart, p. 316. Hyndman's views were opposed within the new Party, particularly by internationally minded members like Zelda Hahan.
128. Quoted in Stewart, p. 328. Parliamentary Debates (Commons), November 1911, Volume XXVI, Line 574.
129. Parliamentary Debates, 13 March 1911, Fifth Series, Volume XXII.
130. NA to KH, 17 March 1911, Angell Collection, Ball State University, Indiana, USA.
131. The meetings between KH and NA, starting on 6 April 1911, are recorded in KH to NA, 17 April 1911, Angell Collection, loc. cit.
132. Gavignan, 'Ralph Norman Angell Lane, An Analysis of His Political Career', Ph.D. thesis, Ball State University, unpublished, p. 16.
133. KH to HA, 17 April 1911, Angell Collection, loc. cit.
134. KH to Richard Bell, MP, 9 March 1903, quoted Morgan, *Keir Hardie*, p. 128, Angell Collection, loc. cit.
135. The Paris meeting was on 13 May 1911; the Le Touquet weekend followed. See Gavignan, *passim*, and NA to JRM, 30 July 1913, Angell Collection.
136. This correspondence (preserved in the Angell Collection) includes most major political figures of the period.
137. Jolyon Howorth, 'The Left in France and Germany, Internationalism and War; a Dialogue of the Deaf, 1900–1914', in *Socialism and Nationalism*, Cahm and Fišera, eds., Vol II, pp. 81–100.
138. Hughes, *Keir Hardie*, p. 195.
139. KH to AH, 1911.
140. Ibid., p. 196.
141. Howorth, in Cahm and Fišera, eds., pp. 81–100.

Chapter 12 – A Question of Women

1. Marquand, p. 131.
2. Ibid.
3. Quoted in Thompson, *The Enthusiasts*, pp. 172–3.
4. Fenner Brockway, Interview with CB, 25 November 1987.
5. Thompson, *The Enthusiasts*, p. 174. Glasier was one of the first to visit JRM after the death, and recorded his conversation in detail.
6. Ibid.
7. Quoted in Marquand, p. 134.
8. Ibid., p. 133.
9. Date on a photograph of MS at work in No. 14 with furniture covered, National Library of Scotland, Dep 176, Box 3, File 1.
10. In Richard Pankhurst, p. 50, it is weekly; in S. Pankhurst, *The Suffragette Movement*, p. 174, it is daily.
11. KH to MS, undated, Box 25, File 1.
12. Ibid.
13. KH to Robert Williams, 4 April 1913, loc. cit.
14. KH to MS, undated, loc. cit.
15. KM to MS, November 1907, loc. cit.
16. Ibid., from the House of Commons, undated, loc. cit.
17. Ibid., from Lochnorris, undated, loc. cit.
18. Ibid., undated, loc. cit.
19. Ibid., 14 November 1908, loc. cit.
20. Ibid., 18 January 1912, loc. cit.
21. Ibid., from Glasgow, September 9, no year but between 1903–5, loc. cit.
22. Ibid., 2 January 1912, loc. cit.
23. Ibid., 1906, undated, loc. cit.
24. Ibid., from Lochnorris, undated, loc. cit. These might have been the pages on his illegitimate birth found among his papers at his death, see p. 357.
25. Ibid., 24 December 1908, loc. cit.
26. Ibid., 10 November, 1909.
27. Ibid., 24 December 1900, loc. cit.
28. Ibid., 14 January 1912, loc. cit.
29. Ibid., undated, summer 1909, loc. cit.
30. Ibid.
31. Ibid., 26 July 1909, loc. cit.
32. *Justice*, 23 July 1910; *Social Democrat*, July 1910. ESP to KH, 26 February 1912, Pankhurst Collection, file 9, folder 9a, IISH, Amsterdam.
33. Romero, p. 57.
34. ESP to KH, 28 January 1912, loc. cit.
35. Quoted in Romero, p. 57.
36. Ibid.
37. S. Pankhurst. 'Myself When Young', p. 277. In some reminiscences she records she wrote once every other day, in others, every day.
38. Fisk University, Nashville.
39. ESP to KH, 5 February 1912, file 9, folder 9b, loc. cit. ESP, Report on Milwaukee, file 117A.
40. KH to ESP, 10 March 1911, file 9, folder 9c, loc. cit.
41. S. Pankhurst, *The Suffragette Movement*, pp. 388–9.
42. Mrs Pethick-Lawrence's 'Final Instructions', WSPU Notice, 21 November 1911, National Library of Scotland, Dep 176, Box 2, File 2.
43. *Daily Sketch*, 22 November 1911.
44. Reported in *Votes for Women*, 8 December 1911.
45. Poem, unheaded, 25, Box 2, File 2, loc. cit.
46. 'Robert Williams, Architect, 10 Clifford's Inn, EC', 25, Box 2, loc. cit.
47. Family letter to MS Dep 176, 25 (1), loc. cit.
48. Quoted from Margaret Stansgate, Interview, CB, 30 March 1989.
49. ESP to KH, 22 January 1912, file 9, folder 9a, loc. cit.
50. Ibid.
51. Ibid.
52. Ibid., 26 February 1912, file 9,

folder 9a. All following quotes from this letter.

53. Ibid.
54. The others were Guy Bowman and Fred Crowley, co-worker and printer of the pamphlet, 'Don't Shoot', 1912.
55. House of Commons, 25 March, 1912, Wedgwood, *Memoirs*, p. 82.
56. Album (given 1910) currently in possession of the June Bond family.
57. Nancy Richardson to AH, 4 June 1912, Benn Archives, Book II, B-24.
58. Jalland, p. 222.
59. Cockburn, pp. 91 and 101.
60. Romero, p. 33.
61. Stonelake, *Autobiography*, op. cit., p. 59.
62. Tsuzuki, p. 215.
63. Thorne, p. 82.
64. Katharine Glasier to JRM, 9 December 1912, MDP 3/21, MacDonald Papers, quoted Marquand, p. 134.
65. Beatrice Potter, Diary, Passfield Papers, 1884, 12 and 24 January and 22 April 1884, quoted Jalland, p. 221.
66. Margaret Stansgate, Interview. Beatrice Webb was her next-door neighbour in Millbank, SW1, for 20 years.
67. Margot Asquith to Edith Lyttleton, 1915, quoted Jalland, p. 226.
68. Lansbury to Marion Coats Hansen, Lansbury Collection, quoted Schneer, p. 125.
69. KH to MS, 17 January 1912, Box 25 (1), loc. cit.
70. Ibid., 6 January, 1912, loc. cit.
71. Open letter to King George V, *Merthyr Pioneer*, 11 June 1912.
72. Glasier, Diary, 3 and 5 January 1912.
73. KH to MS, 6 January 1912, loc. cit.
74. The letter is dated 14 January 1911, National Library of Scotland, Box 25 (1). But it is

clearly in answer to Hardie's of 6 January 1912. The date is inadvertently given as the previous year, as sometimes happens in early January.
75. KH to MS, 17 January 1912, Box 25 (1), loc. cit.
76. Ibid., 1 January 1913, loc. cit.
77. Ibid., 24 February 1913, loc. cit.
78. Thompson, *The Enthusiasts*, p. 183, early edition only.
79. Ibid., p. 185.
80. Ibid.; the *Herald* was launched on 15 April 1912.
81. KH to RD, 3 March 1914 (D/Dxik 30/22), Glamorgan County Archives.
82. Lansbury, p. 176.
83. Hughes, *Keir Hardie*, p. 191; MacArthur, MacDonald, Smillie, *Memoir*.
84. Glasier, *Memorial*, p. 65.
85. Quoted in Stewart, p. 341.
86. Ibid., p. 340f.
87. *Daily Mirror*, 18 May 1906.
88. Parliamentary Debates, 24 July 1906, Fourth Series, Volume CLXI, 10th column.
89. Glasier, quoted in Thompson, *The Enthusiasts*, p. 199; the incident occurred in South Wales, December 1913.
90. Morgan, *Keir Hardie*, p. 86; this was in 1895.
91. Quoted in Hughes, *Keir Hardie*, pp. 241–2.
92. Stewart, pp. 338–40.
93. Ibid., p. 341.
94. Romero, p. 62.
95. Ibid.
96. S. Pankhurst, *The Suffragette Movement*, p. 390.
97. ESP to KH, 22 January 1912, Pankhurst Collection, file 9, folder 9a, loc. cit.
98. Romero, pp. 41–72 *passim*. Norah's notepaper was headed with the Linden Gardens address for many years (see correspondence 9c (c), Pankhurst Collection).
99. Romero, p. 73.
100. Ibid., p. 74. In 1914 total sales

were only 100, but 20,000 were printed each run.

101. Some letters are quoted in Ethel Smyth's *Female Pipings in Eden*, 1933; copies of the full correspondence are in the possession of Jill Craigie, to whom I am indebted for permission to read them.

102. Ethel Smyth to Emmeline Pankhurst, letters dated 10 December 1913 and 16 January 1914, written from Helouan, Egypt. Copies in possession of Jill Craigie.

103. Romero, p. 73.

104. Notebook, dated 1918, quoted Romero, p. 118.

105. ESP to KH, 26 February 1913, Pankhurst Collection, file 9, folder 9a, loc. cit.

106. Jill Craigie, quoted in Romero, pp. 72 and 296, note 50.

107. Romero, poem, p. 108.

108. Ibid., p. 59.

109. Ibid., p. 79; see also Fenner Brockway, interview, 25 November 1987.

110. Pankhurst Papers, IISH, file 9, folder 9c.

111. Ibid.

112. S. Pankhurst, *The Suffragette Movement*, p. 399.

113. KH to RD, 23 January 1913, 30/10, Glamorgan County Archives.

114. LH to AH, December 30 1912, no. 36, Benn Archives.

115. Sent to Tom Mackley, Woolwich, signed 'Keir' and dated 'Arran August 15 1912', quoted Stewart, pp. 334–5.

116. I am indebted to Jean Keir Hardie Scott, May's daughter, for information about the Stoddart family.

117. Jamie Hardie to RD, 4 February 1910; D/Dxik 30/2, Glamorgan Archives.

118. JS to CB, 28 June 1989.

119. New York newspaper clipping, August 29 1912, Cumnock Library; also JS to CB, 4 May 1991.

120. KH to AH, 3 August 1912, No. 30, Benn Archives. Since the wedding was definitely on the 29th, and KH was not in the USA on the 3rd, we can assume the post mark 3 should read 30 or 31.

121. KH to RD, 23 September 1912, Letter 30/9, Glamorgan County Archives.

122. Stewart, p. 335.

123. Ibid., p. 337.

124. Speaking in Covington, Kentucky, reported in *Cincinnati Enquirer*, 4 October 1912.

125. Ibid.

126. E. J. B. Alien, *The Industrial Syndicalist*, November 1910, and Tom Mann, speaking in a debate with Frank Rose, J. R. Clynes in the Chair, 27 January 1911; reprinted in Brown, pp. 148, 221–2.

127. Karl Marx, 'The Civil War in France', *Selected Works*, Vol II, pp. 217–18.

128. Engels to Bebel, 18 March 1875, *Selected Works*, III, p. 452.

129. Maxton, p. 5.

130. From the format of *The Anarchist*, London, c. 1940.

131. Quoted in Stewart, p. 336.

132. Tom Mann in *Industrial Syndicalist*, April 1911, quoted in Brown, pp. 301–2.

133. Quoted in Stewart, p. 350.

134. 'Converting the Electors', Tracey, Vol I, p. 154.

135. Address at Dowlais Adult School Union, 'What Think ye of Christ?', 3 March 1912.

136. Lansbury, p. 121.

137. NEC Minutes, 13 and 14 November 1912, 6 December 1912. KH stood again and was elected in January 1913.

138. G. S. Jacobs to Lansbury, 27 November 1912, quoted Schneer, p. 110.

139. Schneer, pp. 105–18.

140. S. Pankhurst, 'Myself When Young', p. 304.

141. Romero, p. 66.

142. Stewart, p. 343.

143. Ibid., p. 343.

144. Ibid., p. 343.

145. S. Pankhurst, *The Suffragette Movement*, p. 302.

146. Parliamentary Debates (Commons), 1 March 1911, Volume XXII, Line 364.

147. *The Queenie Gerald Case: A Public Scandal*, 1913; all references are to this pamphlet, which reprints KH's parliamentary speeches.

148. 1913, London.

149. Romero, p. 99. It was not clear if this was 80% of all men, or just men in England. Nor was any source given for the figure.

150. Parliamentary Debates (Commons), 1 May 1912, Volume XXXVII, pp. 1864–2010.

151. 30 August 1913.

152. Hughes, p. 87.

153. Stewart, p. 346.

154. Ibid.

155. Thompson, *The Enthusiasts*, p. 198.

156. Ibid.

157. 14 August 1913, to Robert Williams, Box 25 (2), loc. cit.

158. 12 June 1913, Box 25 (1), loc. cit. Also KH to RD.

159. KH to MS, 12 June 1913, Dep 176, Box 21 (1), loc. cit.

160. LH to AH, 8 May 1913, No. 24, Benn Archives.

161. Emrys Hughes, Notes on his life, in pencil, Cumnock Library Archives.

162. LH to AH, 26 September 1913, No. 25, Benn Archives.

163. KH to AH, July 31 1913, No. 16, Benn Archives.

164. KH to AH, 7 August 1913, Letter 93, Benn Archives.

165. KH to Robert Williams, 14 August 1913, Box 25 (f1), loc. cit; Stewart, p. 348.

166. KH to Robert Williams, loc. cit.

167. KH to AH, 15 August 1913, No. 94, Benn Archives.

168. KH to May Hardie, 20 August 1913.

169. 7 August 1913, LH to May Hardie, in the possession of Jean Scott.

170. KH to R. Williams, 14 August 1913.

171. KH to the Revd John Hughes, 27 August 1913, No. 58, Benn Archives.

172. KH to the Revd John Hughes, undated card, September 1913, No. 8, loc. cit.

173. KH to the Revd John Hughes, September 20, 1913, No. 10, loc. cit.

174. Card No. 10, no date, 1913.

175. Romero, p. 78.

176. Ibid.

177. See Chapter 12, note 102.

178. Fenner Brockway, interview with CB, 25 November 1987.

179. Quoted Romero, p. 79.

180. KH to AH, undated, No. 8, Benn Archives.

181. NH to AH, 9 October 1913, No. 103, loc. cit.

182. Stewart, p. 349.

183. Ibid.

184. Ibid., pp. 348–9.

185. Report on 'Sylvia Pankhurst', National Association of Women's Suffrage Associations, Library of Congress. LC 69. Quoted Romero, p. 80.

186. KH to ESP 9 9c), n.d., Pankhurst Collection, IISH, Amsterdam.

187. KH to AH, 17 December 1913, No. 17/18, Benn Archives.

188. *Daily Mirror* 20 December 1913.

189. KH to AH, 20 December 1913, No. 55, loc. cit.

190. Ibid., 3 December 1913, No. 72, loc. cit.

191. Glasier, Diary, 4 December 1913.

192. KH to AH, 3 December 1913, No. 72, loc. cit.

193. LH to AH, 28 December 1913, No. 31, loc. cit.

194. Romero, p. 80.

195. Quoted Romero, p. 66.

196. Quoted in Ethel Smyth, p. 219.

197. Emmeline Pankhurst to ESP, Pankhurst Collection, IISH, Amsterdam.

198. Romero, p. 69.

Chapter 13 – The Last Cause

1. 4 April 1913, National Library of Scotland, Box 25, File 2.
2. *Feminist Review*, 23 November 1911. Among others who had expressed the same view was Cunninghame Graham ('The Real Equality of the Sexes', *The New Age*, 11 July 1908) who said changes were needed as well in social and economic spheres and in 'Religious (especially religious)' ones.
3. Fenner Brockway, J. Hamill, Interview, 26 January, 1984, Cumnock.
4. Ibid.
5. KH to AH, 17 December 1913, No. 99, Benn Archives.
6. The SDP Conference where he attended as a fraternal delegate, Stewart, p. 350.
7. Glasier, Diary, 13 December 1913.
8. Report of Labour Party Conference, Newport, February 9 1910. The vote was 492,000 to 441,000 against allowing candidates to adopt title of 'Socialist and Labour' candidate.
9. 18 July 1913, called by International Bureau of Second International, held in Fabian offices. See *The Enthusiasts*, p. 195.
10. Glasier, Diary, 13 December 1913.
11. Morgan, *Keir Hardie*, p. 250.
12. Hughes, *Keir Hardie*, p. 219.
13. 9 October 1913, *Labour Leader*.
14. *Labour Leader*, 23 October 1913.
15. *Cincinnati Enquirer*, 5 October 1912.
16. KH to AH, January 14 1914, BII, B 11 Benn Archives.
17. Ibid., 5 February 1914, No. 62, loc. cit.
18. Ibid., 28 February 1914.
19. Ibid., 24 March 1914, No. 63, loc. cit.
20. Ibid., undated, March 1914, BII, No. 15, loc. cit.
21. Ibid., 10 March 1914, No. 75, (enclosing minutes of the meetings and the new plans), loc. cit.
22. JRM to Glasier, 31 May 1907, Letter 1907/81.
23. KH to Agnes Hughes, BII, B 12, undated, loc. cit.
24. Ibid.
25. KH to RD, 7 April 1914, Glamorgan County Archives, Cardiff, D/Dxik 30/13.
26. Programme of Easter Saturday Evening Reception, 1914, Central Baths, Bradford, MSS/16, Len Williams Collection, University of Wales, Swansea.
27. Stewart, p. 353.
28. Fenner Brockway, *Inside the Left*, pp. 37–8.
29. Pankhurst, *The Home Front*, p. 380.
30. Beatrice Webb, Diary, ed. Margaret Cole, p. 23, quoted Adelman, p. 113.
31. Ibid.
32. Stewart, *Keir Hardie*, p. 342, Hughes, *Writings*, p. 170, spoken during closing address of the Bradford Conference, 1914.
33. Ibid., pp. 171–2; see also Hughes, *Keir Hardie*, p. 218.
34. KH to RD, Glamorgan County Archives, Letter D/Dxik/30/27.
35. At the 1907 Labour Conference he had used much the same phrase, the Labour Party was 'my own child'.
36. S. Pankhurst, *The Home Front*, p. 34. On another occasion it was, 'my own boy may be taken and I would rather see him in his grave than compelled to fight against other workers', Stewart, p. 368.
37. The signature is hard to read, but could be David Farrell, letter to KH, 6 October 1914, National Library of Scotland, Dep 176, Box 1, File 1.
38. Lowe, *Pit to Parliament*, p. 162.
39. Fenner Brockway, *Inside Left*, p. 39.
40. KH to RD, Glamorgan County Archives, D/Dxik/30/27.
41. Diary, April 1914; paraphrased

Thompson, *The Enthusiasts*, p. 200.

42. NH to AH, 28 April 1914, No. 103, Benn Archives.

43. KH to AH, 30 April 1914, No. 12, loc. cit.

44. Ibid., 22 May 1914, No. 10/12, loc. cit.

45. Ibid., May 5, 1914, No. 87, loc. cit.

46. NH to AH, postscript from LH 31 May 1914, No. 21, and Lillie to AH, 28 April 1914, No. 103, loc. cit.

47. S. Pankhurst, *The Suffragette Movement*, p. 566.

48. Lansbury, p. 126.

49. *World*, 25 June, 1914.

50. Parliamentary Debates (Commons), 1912, Volume XXXVII, Line 752.

51. Parliamentary Debates (Commons), 31 March 1913, Volume LI, Line 173.

52. 'A Force to be Reckoned With', reported *Newbury Weekly News*, 25 June 1914, Working Class Museum Library, Salford.

53. KH to AH, 7 July 1914, No. 90, Benn Archives.

54. Ibid., 14 July 1914, No. 17/18, loc. cit.

55. Lillie Hardie to AH, 15 July 1914, No. 50, loc. cit.

56. NH to AH, undated, No. 27, loc. cit.

57. Ibid.

58. *Labour Leader*, July 1914; Hughes, *Writings*, pp. 172–3.

59. KH, interviewed on war in August 1908, reported in *Labour Leader*, 28 August 1908.

60. KH to AH, 16 July 1914, No. 91, loc. cit.

61. Glasier, Diary, 29 July 1914.

62. KH to AH, 29 July, No. 13, loc. cit.

63. Thompson, *The Enthusiasts*, p. 202, quotes the resolution from Glasier's account in the *Labour Leader*. No record was kept of this meeting; Morgan pieces it together, *Keir Hardie*, p. 264.

64. Stewart, pp. 358–61.

65. Stewart, p. 358.

66. Cameron Hazelhurst, *Politicians at War*, p. 123.

67. *Daily Citizen*, 1 August 1914, quoted in Hughes, *Writings*, pp. 173–4.

68. AH to 'Dad and Em', undated, late July 1914, No. 57, loc. cit.

69. Stewart, p. 363.

70. Proclamation of the British Section of the International, signed by KH as Chairman, issued after the meeting on the 31 July 1914, for the rally on the 2 August, quoted Stewart, pp. 359–60.

71. AH to 'Dad and Em', No. 57, loc. cit.

72. According to Schneer, it was Lansbury who organized the demonstration (p. 134). According to the NAC of the ILP, their members organized it. See correspondence on this disputed point with Lansbury, Francis Johnson Correspondence, LSE, Letter 14/278, undated, August 1914.

73. Stewart, p. 361.

74. Speech to War Meeting, 2 August 1914, quoted in Hughes, *Keir Hardie*, pp. 226–7.

75. Marquand, p. 164; Lord Riddell's War diary, pp. 3–5, quoted Hazelhurst, p. 109 and footnote 4, quoting from H. A. Taylor's interview with MacDonald, Taylor MSS.

76. NA to KH from Kings Bench Walk, Temple, BII, B 17, Benn Archives.

77. Emrys Hughes, *Journal of a Coward*, p. 6.

78. Glasier, Diary, August 4.

79. Thompson, *The Enthusiasts*, p. 205.

80. Stewart, p. 364.

81. Stonelake, *Autobiography*, 1950, p. 157.

82. Hughes, *Journal of a Coward*, p. 7.

83. Hughes, *Keir Hardie*, p. 230, quoting report in the *Aberdare Leader*.

84. Report in *Western Mail*, 7

August, quoted in Stewart, p. 366.

85. Anthony Mor-O'Brien, 'Keir Hardie, C.B. Stanton, and the First World War', in *Lafur*, Vol 14, No. 3, 1986, p. 36.

86. Hughes, *Journal of a Coward*, pp. 7–8.

87. Ibid., p. 8.

88. Report in *Aberdare Leader*, quoted in Hughes, *Keir Hardie*, p. 230.

89. Stewart, p. 365,

90. Hughes, *Journal of a Coward*, p. 8.

91. C. B. Stanton, quoted in *Merthyr Express*, 8 August 1914, reported in Mor-O'Brien, p. 35.

92. Stewart, p. 366.

93. KH to AH, 17 August 1914, Letter 68, Benn Archives.

94. C. M. Lloyd, 'The Poor Laws', in Tracey, Vol III, p. 9.

95. Speaking in the House, 10 August 1914, quoted in Hughes, *Writings*, p. 176.

96. 'The Government's Crime', *Labour Leader*, 6 June 1914, also quoted ibid., p. 181.

97. Thompson, *The Enthusiasts*, p. 206.

98. Minutes of Labour Party National Executive, 29 August 1914.

99. 6 August 1914, *Labour Leader*, quoted Hughes, *Keir Hardie*, p. 232.

100. Mowatt, p. 140.

101. See Cameron Hazelhurst, p. 109–10; and David Marquand, pp. 171–4.

102. JRM, Diary, 23 September 1914, quoted in Marquand, p. 171. Also present were Trevelyan, E. D. Morel and Arthur Ponsonby.

103. 5/98 MacDonald Papers, 24 August 1914, quoted Marquand, p. 172.

104. Stewart, p. 367.

105. Daniel Holmes, MP, father of Margaret Stansgate; see Margaret Stansgate, Interview with CB, 30 March 1989.

106. Stansgate, Interview.

107. S. Pankhurst, *The Home Front*, p. 34.

108. Glasier, Diary, 26 October 1914.

109. Tom Williams, taped interview, 4 February 1982, South Wales Miners Library Archives, University of Wales, Swansea.

110. LH to AH, 13 September 1914, No. 42, Benn Archives.

111. Ibid., 13 September 1914, No. 42, loc. cit.

112. KH to AH, 7 October 1914, No. 89, loc. cit.

113. Ibid., undated, October 1914.

114. S. Pankhurst, note, file 64, folder 6, IISH, Amsterdam.

115. S. Pankhurst, *The Home Front*, p. 34.

116. Hughes, *Keir Hardie*, p. 232.

117. Ibid., p. 231.

118. Stewart, p. 336.

119. Beatrice Webb, unpublished Diary 32 and 53, Passfield Papers, LSE, quoted Romero, p. 109.

120. Letters 14/235, 237, 249 and from Attlee, 282, 2 September 1914, Francis Johnson Correspondence, LSE.

121. Francis Johnson Correspondence, LSE. Letters to and from solicitors Melville and Lindsay, continuous from 1912.

122. NAC minutes, LSE, 11 August 1914. This was a special NAC.

123. KH to AH, 26 August 1914, No. 69, Benn Archives.

124. NAC minutes, 31 August and 1 September, held at the House of Commons.

125. Stewart, p. 375.

126. 27 August 1914.

127. Ibid.

128. Stewart, op. cit., p. 373.

129. *Labour Leader*, 10 September 1914.

130. KH to Revd John Hughes, 8 August 1914, National Library of Scotland, Dep 176, 26 (1).

131. Stewart, p. 372.

132. Ibid.

133. Ibid.

134. Snowden, Vol I, p. 93.

135. Fred Reid, *Tribune*, 23 January 1970.

136. Cole, *Keir Hardie*, p. 31.

137. Webb, *Diary*, pp. 32 and 53,

Passfield papers, LSE, quoted
Romero, p. 109.

138. Glasier, *Memorial*, p. 66.
139. KH speaking in Parliament,
Parliamentary Debates
(Commons), 3 August 1914,
Volume LXV, Line 1839, quoted
in Hughes *Writings*, p. 177;
Tom Williams, Interview by
Hywel Francis, University of
Wales, Swansea, recorded 4
February 1982.
140. S. Pankhurst, *The Home
Front*, p. 68.
141. Quoted Stewart, op. cit., p. 377,
26 November 1914.
142. S. Pankhurst, *The Home
Front*, p. 60.
143. H. N. Brailsford, *The War of
Steel and Gold*, 1914.
144. NAC minutes, ILP, 16
October 1914.
145. S. Pankhurst, *The Home
Front*, p. 68.
146. Quoted Stewart, 26 November
1914, pp. 377–8.
147. G. B. Shaw, 'Keir Hardie the
Patriot', *Merthyr Pioneer*, 9
October 1915; *Dreadnought*, 16
October 1915.
148. *Merthyr Pioneer*, 24 October
1914.
149. Ibid., 28 November 1914.
150. KH to AH, 13 October 1914,
loc. cit.
151. Stewart, p. 375.
152. KH to AH, 26 October 1914,
loc. cit.
153. Hughes, *Keir Hardie*, p. 235.
154. *Labour Leader*, September
1914.
155. *Merthyr Pioneer*, 8 November
1914.
156. *Western Mail*, 27 September
1914.
157. *Merthyr Pioneer*, 9 December
1914.
158. Ibid., 15 August 1914,
159. Fenner Brockway, *Towards
Tomorrow*, 1977, p. 41.
160. Glasier, *Memorial* p. 66;
also S. Pankhurst, *The Home
Front*, p. 145.
161. Stewart, pp. 378–9.
162. KH to Hughes, 20 November

1914, card, National Library of
Scotland, Dep 176.
163. Ibid.
164. Hughes, *Journal of a Coward*, p. 4.
165. Ibid., pp. 9–10.
166. Ibid., p. 12.
167. Ibid., pp. 14–15.
168. Cards and letters, mostly from
KH to May Hardie, in the
possession of JHS and Dolores
May Arias.
169. KH to Jamie Hardie, February
1914, Cumnock Papers.
170. KH to AH, 11 November 1914.
171. LH to AH, 19 November 1914,
No. 35, Benn Archives.
172. Nan Hardie to Agnes Hughes,
14 March 1915, No. 110,
loc. cit.
173. KH to Agnes Hughes, 11
November 1914, No. 92,
loc. cit.
174. Ruth Grayson to KH, Letter
14/423, 29 November 1914,
Francis Johnson Correspondence,
LSE. Ruth Grayson died in
childbirth in 1917.
175. MS to KH, 28 October 1914,
Francis Johnson Correspondence,
LSE.
176. KH to AH, 18 December 1914,
No. B 20 II, Benn Archives.
177. Postscript to NH to AH, 21
December 1914, No. 101,
loc. cit.
178. Ibid.
179. Ibid., LH's postscript.
180. *Merthyr Pioneer*, 9 January 1915.
181. JHS to CB, 28 June 1989.
182. 29 December 1914, No. 37,
Benn Archives.
183. S. Pankhurst, *The Home
Front*, p. 33.
184. Stewart, pp. 380–1. KH
also insisted the press leave,
Manchester Guardian, 3
January 1915.
185. Russian supplement to *The
Times*, 26 April 1915, a later
example.
186. Mor-O'Brien, 'Conchie: Emrys
Hughes and the First World
War', p. 329.
187. Stewart, p. 382.
188. KH to Robert Williams and

MS, 14 August 1913, Dep 176, loc. cit.

189. Due to an announcement from the ILP when KH did not attend the NAC on 8 and 9 January. Neither LH or NH ever knew about the announcement. The NAC had intended to give KH a special gift for having secured the Kippen Bequest for the ILP (NAC minutes, LSE).

190. Wright to AH, 24 January 1915, and KH to AH, 24 January 1915, No. 71 (iii), Benn Archives.

191. LH to AH, 18 January 1915, No. 28, loc. cit.

192. *Merthyr Pioneer*, 6 February 1915.

193. NH to AH, 2 December 1915, No. 12, loc. cit.

194. Morgan, *Keir Hardie*, p. 268.

195. Richard Stone, *John Woolliscroft*, p. 26.

196. Glasier, Diary, 22 February 1915.

197. Burns, Diary, 15 February 1915, quoted Morgan, *Keir Hardie*, p. 267.

198. I am indebted to Mrs Bernice Stone for information about her great uncle, John Burns.

199. KH to AH, 15 February 1915, No. 14, loc. cit.

200. Ibid., 22 May 1914, No. 10/12, loc. cit.

201. S. Pankhurst, *The Home Front*, p. 34.

202. Ibid., p. 124.

203. Executive minutes, War Emergency National Women's Committee, 11 September 1914, Passfield Papers, LSE.

204. S. Pankhurst, 'Myself When Young', pp. 308–9.

205. Romero, p. 97.

206. S. Pankhurst, 'Myself When Young', p. 312.

207. Quoted Romero, p. 95.

208. Sylvia Pankhurst, notes on early days of the war, file 62, IISH Amsterdam.

209. Romero, p. 95.

210. Sylvia Pankhurst, notes, file 62, folder 2, loc. cit.

211. Ibid.

212. *Christian Commonwealth*, 28 October 1914; see later *Sunday Herald*, 16 May 1915.

213. S. Pankhurst, *The Home Front*, pp. 45, 93, 353.

214. Parliamentary Debates (Commons), 24 February 1915, Volume LXX, Line 271.

215. Parliamentary Debates (Commons), 8 March 1915, Volume LXX, Line 1151.

216. Parliamentary Debates (Commons), Defence of the Realm Bill, 8 March 1915, Volume LXX, Lines 744, 746.

217. Parliamentary Debates (Commons), 25 February 1915, Volume LXX, Lines 402, 565.

218. On 27 February 1915, see Stewart, p. 384.

219. On one occasion it was Christopher Addison (*The Suffragette Movement*, p. 34); on another (August 1914) Dr Metcalfe, a Tory MP (Hughes, *Keir Hardie*, p. 233).

220. Hughes, *Keir Hardie*, p. 233.

221. Appointment card, Dr Thomas Horder, (afterwards physician to King George VI), National Library of Scotland, Dep 176, Box 25, File 2.

222. NH to AH, 12 March 1915, No. 110, Benn Archives.

223. Glasier, Diary, 11 March 1915.

224. Reported in *Merthyr Pioneer*, 25 March 1915.

225. NH to AH, March 22, 1915, No. 92, Benn Archives; *Merthyr Pioneer*, 25 March 1915.

226. *Labour Leader*, 27 March 1915, quoted in Hughes, *Writings*, pp. 182–5.

227. Ibid.

228. G. B. Shaw, 'Keir Hardie the Patriot', *Merthyr Pioneer*, 9 October 1915; and *Dreadnought*, 16 October 1915

229. *Labour Leader*, 27 March 1915.

230. KH to AH, 5 April 1915, No. 10, Benn Archives.

231. Ibid., 1 April 1915, No. 12, loc. cit.

232. NH to AH, 22 March 1915, No. 92, loc. cit.

233. NAC minutes, ILP, 2, 2–3 April 1915, LSE.
234. Report of Annual Conference ILP, 1915.
235. S. Pankhurst, *The Home Front*, p. 225; Fenner Brockway, *Socialism over Sixty Years*, p. 133.
236. KH to AH, 5 April 1915, No. 10, loc. cit.
237. Quoted in Stewart, p. 388.
238. KH letter to the press, 12 April 1915, National Library of Scotland, Box 25, File 2.
239. Edinburgh *Evening News*, 9 April 1915.
240. Glasier, Diary, 15 April 1915.
241. Parliamentary Debates (Commons), 27 April 1915, Volume LXXI, Line 595.
242. Frank Smith to AH, 15 April 1915, No. 83, Benn Archives.
243. KH to AH, 17 April 1915, No. 70, loc. cit.
244. NH to AH, 12 March 1915, No. 110, loc. cit.
245. Ibid., 22 March 1915, No. 92, loc. cit.
246. Ibid., 12 March 1915, No. 110, loc. cit.
247. Ibid., 2 December 1915, No. 12, loc. cit.
248. Ibid., 16 October 1913, Nos 12, 13, loc. cit.

Chapter 14 – Breaking Ties

1. Ponsonby to Trevelyan, 22 May 1915, quoted in C. Hazelhurst, *Politicians at War*, p. 289.
2. As President of the Board of Education.
3. JRM to Trevelyan, 28 May 1915, quoted Hazelhurst, p. 287.
4. Trevelyan to his wife, 21 May 1915, quoted Hazelhurst, p. 287.
5. Jim Middleton to KH, 28 April 1915, Francis Johnson Correspondence, LSE.
6. LH to AH, undated, No. 33, Benn Archives.
7. NH to AH, 3 May 1915, No. 111, loc. cit.
8. Ibid.
9. Ibid., 28 April 1914, No. 103, loc. cit.
10. See Frances Power Cobbe, *The Duties of Women*, 1881; also see Jalland, p. 258.
11. B. Webb Diary, 19 December 1885, quoted Jalland, p. 257.
12. Vera Brittain, *Testament of Youth*, 1978, pp. 420–2, 536. Some were sent on long sea voyages like Edith Durham (later a travel writer) and the Duke of Atholl's daughter, Alice; Jalland, pp. 276–9.
13. Jalland, p. 273.
14. NH to AH, 3 May 1915, No. 111, Benn Archives.
15. George Connell, married to Agnes, youngest of the Stoddarts, JHS to CB, 28 June 1989.
16. NH to AH, 3 May 1915, No. 111, loc. cit.
17. KH to ESP, 27 May 1915, dictated to Frank Smith, file 9, folder 9c, IISH, Amsterdam.
18. An account of the meeting is in the notes for ESP's book, *The Home Front*, notebook, file 66, IISH, Amsterdam; the book itself, *The Home Front*, p. 227, also has an account.
19. Romero, pp. 109–10.
20. S. Pankhurst, *The Home Front*, p. 227.
21. Ibid., p. 228.
22. Ibid., p. 227.
23. NH to AH, 8 June 1915, No. 103; No. 33, undated, loc. cit.
24. NH to AH, 8 June 1915, No. 103.
25. Ibid., 17 June 1915, No. 56.
26. Ibid.
27. Ibid., 24 June 1915, No. 18.
28. Ibid., 17 June 1915, No. 56.
29. Ibid.
30. Ibid., 24 June 1915, No. 18.
31. Hughes, *Journal of a Coward*, pp. 18–19.
32. NH to AH, 24 June 1915, No. 18.
33. Ibid.
34. Ibid., 9 July 1915, Nos. 17, 18.
35. Ibid. 24 June 1915, No. 18.
36. Ibid., 5 July 1915, No. 64; Stewart, p. 391.

37. Correspondence with John
    Hood, solicitor to KH, Port
    of Glasgow, 7 and 31 October
    1914, National Library of
    Scotland, Dep 176, Box 1,
    File 2. NH had originally
    left everything to Jamie and
    Duncan even if she died before
    her parents. There are several
    additional codicils to KH's will
    during 1914–15 (unsigned),
    disposing of papers and books.
    For details of the will as proved,
    see Morgan, *Keir Hardie*, p. 272.
38. Glasier, Diary, 28 December
    1915, NAC minutes.
39. NH to AH, 11 July 1915, No.
    113, Benn Archives.
40. Ibid.
41. Ibid., 18 July 1915.
42. Ibid., 13 August 1915, No. 100.
43. Ibid., 11 July 1915, No. 113.
44. Ibid., 9 July 1915, Nos. 17/18.
45. Ibid., 18 July 1915, No. 67.
46. Ibid., 18 July, No. 67.
47. Ibid., 9 July 1915, Nos. 17/18.
48. Ibid., 18 July 1915, No. 67.
49. Ibid.
50. Ibid., 11 July 1915, No. 113.
51. Ibid., 18 July 1915, No. 67.
52. KH to ESP, 28 June 1914,
    Pankhurst Collection, IISH,
    Amsterdam.
53. S. Pankhurst, *The Home
    Front*, p. 232.
54. Ibid., p. 229.
55. NH to AH, 18 July 1915,
    No. 67.
56. S. Pankhurst, *The Home
    Front*, p. 228.
57. Zelie Emerson, undated poem,
    quoted Romero, p. 108.
58. LH to AH, 8 August 1915,
    No. 29.
59. KH to James Henderson, no date
    (July/August 1915), Cumnock
    Library.
60. NH to AH, 12 August 1915,
    No. 96.
61. Ibid., 13 August 1915, No. 100.
62. The correspondence between
    KH and Harry Morris, who
    was his agent, covers 1912
    to 1915, in Francis Johnson
    Correspondence, LSE.
63. NH to Harry Morris, 12
    September 1915.
64. NH to AH, undated, September
    1915, No. 44.
65. Ibid.
66. *John Bull*, 4 September 1915.
67. NH to AH, September 1915,
    No. 44.
68. Thompson, *The Enthusiasts*,
    p. 211.
69. Ibid., p. 212.
70. Mor-O'Brien, 'Conchie', p. 332.
71. Fenner Brockway, Interview
    with CB, 25 November 1987;
    also 'Conchie', p. 332.
72. Hughes, *Journal of a Coward*,
    p. 22.
73. Ibid., p. 20.
74. NH to AH, undated, September
    1915, No. 44, Benn Archives.
75. Ibid., telegram, 26 September
    1915, Benn Archives.
76. ESP, file 65, Notes for *The Home
    Front*, IISH Amsterdam; see also
    The Home Front, p. 230.
77. S. Pankhurst, *The Home Front*,
    pp. 230–1.
78. Frank Smith to ESP, 26
    September 1915, folder 9c,
    loc. cit.
79. Across the Mersey from
    Liverpool, where the Glasiers
    had moved from Chapel-en-le-
    Frith in 1910. Thompson, *The
    Enthusiasts*, p. 221.
80. *Mirror* and *Times* 27
    September 1915; Hughes, *Keir
    Hardie*, p. 239.
81. Glasier, Diary, 27 September
    1915; Glasier to KH, 12 July
    1901, Hardie Papers, Cumnock.
82. *The Enthusiasts*, p. 220.
83. Edward Davies to RD,
    Glamorgan County Archives,
    No. 30/14. The others were
    Edmund Stonelake and
    Matt Lewis.
84. Hughes, Diary fragment,
    National Library of Scotland.
85. Glasier, *Memorial*, p. 41.
86. Reported in *Dreadnought*, 2
    October 1915.
87. Quoted in Hughes, *Keir
    Hardie*, p. 241.
88. Bob Smillie and Sandy Haddow

from Scotland, JRM, T. D. Benson, W. C. Anderson, and Fred Jowett. See Stewart, p. 392.

89. Beatrice Webb, *Diary*, quoted Romero, p. 109.

90. Glasier to Katharine Glasier, 29 September 1915, loc. cit.

91. Glasier, Diary, 30 September 1915.

92. NH to AH, 1 October 1915, No. 74, Benn Archives.

93. S. Pankhurst, *The Home Front*, p. 233.

94. G. B. Shaw, 'Keir Hardie the Patriot', in *Dreadnought*, 16 October 1915; also printed in *Merthyr Pioneer*, 9 October 1915.

95. S. Pankhurst, 'Keir Hardie as I Knew Him', *Labour Leader*, 5 October 1915.

96. S. Pankhurst, *Dreadnought*, 2 October 1915.

97. NAC minutes, 22 October 1915, ILP 2, LSE.

98. NH to AH, 10 November 1915, No. 112, Benn Archives.

99. Ibid., 2 December 1915, No. 12.

100. Ibid., 10 November 1915, No. 112.

101. Morgan, *Keir Hardie*, p. 271–2. It amounted to £426, made up of shares in the *Merthyr Pioneer*, back Parliamentary salary and £387 in an Ayrshire building society, part of which Morgan says the Trustees claimed.

102. Hughes, *Writings*, p. 164. During the period when distant relatives had contested the Kippen Bequest, witnesses had come forward to confirm LH's part in obtaining the money (as well as the Kippens' intention to leave KH half, the other half going to the Irish cause).

103. NAC minutes, 21 and 22 October 1915, ILP 2, LSE.

104. LH to Benson, 2 December 1915; LH to Francis Johnson, 2 December 1915, Francis Johnson Correspondence, LSE.

105. Hughes, *Journal of a Coward*, p. 26.

106. Mor-O'Brien, 'Conchie', pp. 333–4.

107. Hughes, *Journal of a Coward*, pp. 23–4.

108. Hughes, 'Pulpits and Prisons', National Library of Scotland, typescript in Dep 176, Box 8, File 2.

109. NH to AH, 1 October 1915, No. 74, Benn Archives.

110. Ibid., 14 April 1916, No. 51.

111. Ibid., 1 October 1915, No. 74.

112. Ibid., 21 October 1915, Nos. 65, 66.

113. Thompson, *The Enthusiasts*, p. 216.

114. NH to AH, 2 December 1915, No. 12.

115. Quoted Morgan, *Keir Hardie*, p. 274.

116. Ibid; Mor-O'Brien, 'Keir Hardie'.

117. NH to AH, 2 December 1915, No. 12, Benn Archives.

118. S. Pankhurst, *The Home Front*, p. 228.

119. Parliamentary Debates (Commons), 11 June 1914, Volume LXIII, Line 539.

120. Mitchell, *Queen Christabel*, p. 150.

121. S. Pankhurst, *The Home Front*, p. 239.

122. NH to AH, 26 December 1915, Benn Archives.

123. Ibid.

124. LH and NH to AH, undated, December 1915, No. 30, Benn Archives.

125. Glasier, Diary, 28 December 1915.

126. Morgan, *Keir Hardie*, p. 272.

127. Glasier, Diary, 28 December 1915; Thompson, *The Enthusiasts*, p. 217

128. S. Pankhurst, *The Home Front*, p. 274.

129. Ibid., p. 237.

130. Thompson, *The Enthusiasts*, p. 235.

131. ESP, Notes on KH's life, file 66, IISH, Amsterdam; *The Home Front*, pp. 237–8, where the encounter is retold in shortened form.

132. ESP, Notes, file 66, p. 67, IISH; *The Home Front*, p. 238; the

words read, 'presently, it was lent to me'. Possibly it is the same fragment Hughes copied out but never used, See Chapter 1, note 8.

133. Glasier, Diary, 28 December 1915. It was nevertheless gossiped about locally within a few years. See A. A. Durward, op. cit.

134. ESP Notes, file 66, also *The Home Front*, where the encounter is retold in shortened form.

Chapter 15 – The Battle of the War Resisters

1. *Aberdare Leader*, 15 January 1916, quoted in Mor-O'Brien, 'Conchie', p. 336.

2. Hughes, 'Pulpits and Prisons', pp. 85–6, National Library of Scotland; also quoted in Mor-O'Brien, 'Conchie', p. 337.

3. Hughes, *Journal of a Coward*, p. 26.

4. NH to AH, 17 March 1916, No. 97, Benn Archives. Duncan appealed on 16 February.

5. Ibid., 2 February 1916, No. 115.

6. *Labour Leader*, 25 March 1915.

7. NH to AH, 8 June 1916, No. 104, and 2 February 1916, No. 115.

8. Ibid., 14 April 1916, No. 51.

9. Ibid., 17 March 1916, No. 97.

10. Ibid., 14 April 1916, No. 51.

11. 8 and 9 April 1916, Hughes, *Journal of a Coward*, pp. 25–6.

12. E. D. Morel, 'The Attack upon Freedom of Speech', c. 1916.

13. Hughes, *Journal of a Coward*, p. 27.

14. Ibid., p. 31.

15. Lenin, *Farewell to Swiss Workers*, 8 April 1917, quoting a slogan first used in November 1914.

16. Romero, p. 117.

17. Ibid., p. 115.

18. Professor Gwyn Williams, 'Sylvia Pankhurst', series, *Cracking Up*, Teliesyn Ltd, transmitted December 1989.

19. The visit was on 23 May 1916, recalled in Thompson, *The Enthusiasts*, pp. 213–4.

20. Hughes, *Journal of a Coward*, pp. 40–6.

21. Ibid., p. 44.

22. LH to AH, undated, 1916, No. 46, Benn Archives.

23. Hughes, *Journal of a Coward*, p. 52.

24. The May Day Manifesto, 1916.

25. Hughes, *Journal of a Coward*, p. 53.

26. For accounts of military 'punishments' of conscientious objectors, including torture, see John Taylor Caldwell, *Come Dungeons Dark*, 1988. The book is an account of the war resistance of Guy Aldred.

27. Hughes, *Journal of a Coward*, p. 70.

28. The 'journal' was kept from August 1914 until 1919. Later, it was written out in full in a notebook, now in the National Library of Scotland. A shortened version was made in another notebook, now in the possession of Dr Paul Bond. All quotations in this book, unless specified otherwise, are from the shortened version.

29. Fenner Brockway, Interview with CB, 25 November 1987.

30. Figures given in '*Socially Unacceptable*' – *Conscientious Objection in World War I*, transmitted 23 September 1987, Channel 4.

31. F. B. Meyer, 'The Majesty of Conscience', 1916. Meyer contacted 317 jailed COs and found 122 were Quakers, 37 Congregationalists, 36 atheists, 20 Church of England, 15 Baptists, 15 Unitarians, 12 Jews, 7 Roman Catholics, 6 Presbyterians, 5 Spiritualists and 6 Theosophists.

32. Fenner Brockway, Interview, 25 November 1987.

33. Thompson, p. 225.

34. Snowden, Vol I, pp. 422–8, contains an account.

35. Speaking in 'Face to Face', first

shown, 1959, BBC 1, re-shown
13 November 1988.

36. Testimony given by Norman
Proctor in '*Socially Unacceptable*';
see also Caldwell, *Dungeons
Dark*, for detailed account of
torture and ill-treatment of
working-class objectors; and
Huw Reid, 'The Furniture
Makers, A History of Trade
Unionism in the Furniture
Trade, 1868–1992', p. 76.

37. NH to AH, 14 April 1916, No.
51, Benn Archives.

38. LH to AH, 21 August 1916,
No. 26.

39. NH to AH, 14 April 1916, No
51.

40. LH to AH, 21 August 1916,
No. 26.

41. NH to AH, 17 October 1916,
No. 114.

42. Friends Service Committee
notes, 1916.

43. 24 June 1916, unsigned letter
from Quaker, Benn Archives.

44. Lansbury to AH, 5 April 1916,
Book II B 14, Benn Archives.

45. NH to AH, 16 June 1916,
Book II.

46. Llewellyn Williams to
AH, 16 June 1916, Book
II. B13.

47. Robert Williams to AH, 21 June
1916, No. 65.

48. NH to AH, 16 June 1916,
No. 52.

49. Reported by Glasier, Diary,
2 December 1914, see also
Marquand, pp. 187–8.

50. Isaac Goss to AH, 23 August
1916, Book II, B 10.

51. Hughes, *Journal of a Coward*,
p. 81.

52. Ibid., p. 87.

53. Ibid., p. 88.

54. Ibid., p. 100.

55. Ibid., p. 93.

56. Ibid., p. 102.

57. LH to AH, August 21 1916,
No. 26; the chair was eventually
bequeathed to the Benn family.

58. LH to AH, 17 August 1916,
No. 46.

59. Ibid.

60. Thompson, *The Enthusiasts*,
p. 221.

61. Ibid., p. 224.

62. Fenner Brockway, Interview
with CB, 25 November 1987.

63. Hughes, *Journal of a Coward*,
pp. 114–15.

64. Ibid., pp. 117–18.

65. Isaac Goss to AH, 4 September
1916, Book II B8, Benn
Archives.

66. June and Robert Bond,
Interview with CB, 14
December 1987.

67. Isaac Goss to AH, 16 October
1916, Book II B 916.

68. Frank Smith to AH, 16
September 1916, No. 91 (ii) 1
from Clifford's Inn.

69. Snowden, 'British Prussianism',
ILP pamphlet, 1916.

70. F. B. Meyer, 'The Majesty of
Conscience'.

71. NH to AH, 17 October 1916,
No. 114, Benn Archives.

72. Ibid.

73. NH to AH, 28 September 1916,
No. 107.

74. LH to AH, undated, September
1916, No. 12.

75. NH to AH, 17 October 1916,
No. 114.

76. Fenner Brockway, Interview
with CB, 25 November 1987.

77. Tom Williams, Interview, 4
February 1982, University of
Wales, Swansea.

78. The Friends Survey of Quakers
published in 1922 found that
33% had enlisted and 40% been
given Conscientious Objector
status. Only 17% applied for
Alternative Service, Wartime
Statistics YMPROC 22
Committee, loc. cit.

79. Fenner Brockway, Interview,
1987. In all he served time in
seven prisons.

80. Ibid.

81. ESP, Pankhurst Collection, 288,
file 63, IISH, Amsterdam. The
meeting was on March 17.

82. Ibid.

83. Charles Barker, of Kenneth,
Brown and Barker, was the

lawyer; Dr Richmond and Dr Amy Shephard, the doctors; Romero, p. 115.

84. KH to MS, 5 August 1909, National Library of Scotland, Box 3, File 1. Although KH possessed his camera for six years, not a single photograph he ever took has been identified.

85. LH and NH to AH, 17 October 1916, No. 114, Benn Archives.

86. Ibid.

87. Snowden to AH, 12 October 1916, Book II B 17, Benn Archives.

88. Hughes, *Journal of a Coward*, p. 145.

89. Fenner Brockway, 'How to End War', undated, ILP pamphlet, published after the war, c. 1920.

90. The exchange is printed in Thompson, *The Enthusiasts*, p. 209. It is taken from Glasier, Diary, 1 November 1916.

91. Mor-O'Brien, 'Keir Hardie', p. 38.

92. Ibid., p. 40.

93. LH to AH, 17 October 1916, No. 114, Benn Archives.

94. Published by Congregational House, Scotland, 1899, Hardie Collection, Baird Museum, Cumnock.

95. For example, *Materia Medica*, B. J. Mitchell, Bruce and Walter Dilling, Cassell, 1917, loc. cit.

96. NH to AH, 2 December 1915, No. 12, Benn Archives.

97. Ibid., 17 August 1916, No. 46.

98. Thea Holme, *The Carlyles at Home*, p. 52; Jalland, p. 274, analyses of Victorian drug use by women to escape a restricted life

99. The family also possessed catalogues of scientific and medical equipment, including syringes and burners. When outdated, they were used to paste up press cuttings, see Large Volumes section of National Library of Scotland, Dep 176, for example, Vol 3, 1917, war cuttings pasted in *Scientific Apparatus for Pure Chemicals*,
Thompson, Skinner and Hamilton, 1914.

100. Manchester, January 1917.

101. Robert Thompson to AH, 14 February 1917, CO Information Bureau, 6 John St, Adelphi, WC, Book II B 23, Benn Archives.

102. 13 and 14 February 1917, entries come from Charles Pett, Stanley King Beer, Edward Pearce, Reg Rogers, W. Hodkinson.

103. Hughes, *Journal of a Coward*, p. 146.

104. Hughes to the Revd John Hughes, 5 March 1917, Book II B 28, Benn Archives.

105. Sir Oliver Lodge, 'Raymond'; Hughes, *Journal of a Coward*, p. 178.

106. Hughes, *Journal of a Coward*, p. 180.

107. NA to Dennis Robertson, 25 September 1914, loc. cit.

108. Hughes, *Journal of a Coward*, p. 173.

109. Ibid., p. 174.

110. Lansbury, pp. 186–7.

111. Hughes, *Journal of a Coward*, p. 175.

Chapter 16 – The Parting of Socialists.

1. Diary, 16 March 1917.

2. Ivan Maisky and G. Chicherin; Bolshevik leaders living in London. Thompson, *The Enthusiasts*, p. 225.

3. NAC made presentation in June 1917, Thompson, *The Enthusiasts*, pp. 226–7.

4. Quoted in Marquand, p. 200.

5. The invitations were signed by Albert Inkpin and Francis Johnson.

6. Lansbury, p. 188.

7. Thompson, *The Enthusiasts*, p. 225.

8. Glanmore Williams, ed., *Merthyr Politics*, p. 79.

9. Hyndman to C. E. Russell, 13 May 1917, quoted in Tsuzuki, p. 236.

10. Blatchford, *General Von Sneak*, p. 169.
11. Ibid., p. 175.
12. Invitation letter for the convention, 23 May 1917, Pankhurst Collection, file 247, IISH, Amsterdam.
13. Will Thorne, p. 195.
14. Romero, p. 107.
15. *Dreadnought*, 2 June 1917, quoted in Romero, p. 121.
16. Coates and Topham, Vol I, Part II, p. 541 *passim*.
17. Marquand, pp. 214–15.
18. Ibid., p. 214, Diary, 13 June 1917.
19. Ibid., p. 212, quotes from JRM's Diary, 9 May.
20. Diary, June 1917, quoted Thompson, *The Enthusiasts*, p. 225.
21. Titled 'Dartmoor Prison Branch. 1 September 1917'. Photograph in possession of ILP Publications, Leeds.
22. Hughes, *Journal of a Coward*, p. 201.
23. Adela Pankhurst to ESP, 23 November 1917, IISH, Amsterdam.
24. Pankhurst, *The Home Front*, p. 152.
25. Decree printed in *Dreadnought*, 31 October 1917, file 247, IISH, Amsterdam.
26. Decrees printed in *Dreadnought*, 19 November 1917, file 247, IISH, Amsterdam.
27. Romero, p. 131.
28. Hughes, *Journal of a Coward*, p. 231f.
29. Phillips, Price, 'Rulers of England are Strangling the Russian Revolution', Pankhurst Collection pamphlet, 1918, file 252. Hagberg Wright, 'Bolshevik Ideals and their Failure', *Contemporary Review*, November 1918, File 247. IISH.
30. Jack Jones, speaking at a rally with Will Thorne in East London, reported *Stratford Express*, 1 June 1918, quoted in John Marriott, *The Culture of Labour*, p. 30.
31. Adelman, *The Rise of the Labour Party*, p. 50.
32. G. D. H. Cole, Vol III, p. 123.
33. Ross MacKibbon, *The Evolution of the Labour Party*, OUP, 1974, quoted Adelman, p. 51.
34. Pelling, quoted ibid., p. 54.
35. S. Pankhurst. *The Suffragette Movement*, p. 608, commenting on the introduction of the Bill, 7 December 1917.
36. S. Pankhurst, *Dreadnought*, 10 and 30 November 1918, quoted in Romero, p. 125.
37. Thompson, *The Enthusiasts*, p. 227; C. Watts, *Cunninghame Graham*, pp. 225, 243.
38. Quoted in Gifford Lewis, *Eva Gore-Booth and Ester Roper*, p. 139.
39. Stonelake, *Autobiography* p. 159.
40. The first Journal in the National Library of Scotland continues until his release, see p. 389–90.
41. Glasier, Diary, 9 January 1919.
42. Quoted Thompson, *The Enthusiasts*, p. 223. The date was 1916.
43. Glasier, Diary, 10 January 1919.
44. ESP, 'Rosa and Karl', Pankhurst Collection, file 62, folder 1, IISH, Amsterdam.
45. ESP 351, file 62, Committee of 33, IISH, Amsterdam. See also Linda Jones, 'The Red Twilight', MA Thesis, University of Warwick.
46. ESP, file 62 (351), Pankhurst Collection, IISH, Amsterdam.
47. Ibid.
48. Marx, 'The Civil War in France', in Marx and Engels, *Selected Works*, Lawrence and Wishart, 1968, p. 291.
49. Romero, p. 138.
50. Lansbury, pp. 216–18.
51. Lenin, *Lenin on Britain*, p. 408.
52. Romero, pp. 127–8.
53. Ibid., pp. 128–9.
54. ESP, Pankhurst Collection, file 65, IISH, Amsterdam. The pamphlets were from the Progress Mailing Company, New York (preserved in file 247) to

returning UK troops who might be sent to Russia.

55. Romero, p. 131.
56. Security Report quoted in Romero, pp. 131–2.
57. Sylvia Pankhurst, 'The New War', in *Communist International*, June 1919.
58. Lenin, speaking on May 27 1919, *The Essentials of Lenin*, Vol II, p. 492.
59. Lenin to ESP, 29 August 1919, in *Lenin on Britain*, p. 424.
60. 'Towards a Communist Party', 21 February 1920.
61. Fenner Brockway, Interview with CB, 25 November 1987.
62. Thompson, *The Enthusiasts*, p. 232.
63. Ibid., pp. 231–2.
64. AH, autograph album, in the possession of Bond family.
65. Hyndman, *Evolution of Revolution*, 1920, quoted in Tsuzuki, p. 239.
66. Lansbury, p. 287.
67. William Morris, 'Looking Backward', *Commonweal*, 22 June 1889.
68. Lansbury, p. 230.
69. Ibid., p. 248.
70. Ibid., p. 245.
71. Ibid., p. 156.
72. Schneer, p. 66.
73. Klugman, Vol I, pp. 13–30.
74. Quoted in Thompson, *The Enthusiasts*, p. 228. He died 4 June 1920.
75. Quoted in Romero, p. 141. ESP's party was created on 19 June 1920.
76. Ibid., p. 142.
77. Ibid., p. 143.
78. Written in April 1920, published June 1920.
79. Lenin, *Left Wing Communism, An Infantile Disorder*, p. 70.
80. Ibid., p. 67.
81. Quoted in Romero, p. 144.
82. *Kollontai, Autobiography of a Sexually Liberated Woman*, eds. Orbach and Cawbers, 1972, p. 78, quoted in Kathryn MacVarish, 'Alexandra Kollontai', unpublished

dissertation, April 1991, University of Keele, p. 9.
83. Angelika Bammer, *Woman and Revolution – Their Theories, Our Experiences*, p. 143, quoted in MacVarish, loc. cit.
84. Romero, p. 145.
85. On 31 July and 1 August 1920. See Klugman, Vol I, pp. 163–7 for CPGB official account.
86. The ILP branches were those from Barking and Glasgow.
87. Chairman's Address, 31 July 1920.
88. Claude McKay, *A Long Way From Home*, New York, 1969, p. 87.
89. GBS to Silvio Corio, 14 September 1921, quoted Romero, p. 54.
90. Lenin, *Left Wing Communism*, p. 69; also quoted Romero, p. 70.
91. Lillian Hellman, *An Unfinished Woman*, Bantam Books, New York, 1979, p. 101.
92. GBS to Corio, 14 September 1921, quoted Romero, p. 154.
93. Tracey, *Book of the Labour Party*, Vol I, p. 221.
94. Minni Pallister to AH, undated (1920s), B27, Benn Archives.
95. Hughes, *Journal of a Coward*, biographical notes, Cumnock Library; and 'Education: what it is and what it is not', ILP leaflet, No. 4, c. 1917.
96. Hughes, biographical notes, in pencil, Cumnock Library.
97. June and Robert Bond, Interview with Caroline Benn, 14 December 1987.
98. Cards in possession of JHS and Dolores May Arias.
99. Gwyn Williams, 'Sylvia Pankhurst', *Cracking Up*.
100. Alexandra Kollontai, 'The Workers' Opposition', pamphlet, 1921. Kollontai was dismissed from government shortly after.
101. Rosa Luxemburg, *Leninism or Marxism?*, *Die Neue Zeit*, Vol 22 (2), Stuttgart, 1904. ILP reproduction printed 3 times 1935–69.

102. Romero, pp. 148–9.
103. 20 October 1920.
104. 5 January 1920, Appeal of ESP
      against conviction for sedition,
      Guildhall, London, Pankhurst
      Collection, file 252, IISH,
      Amsterdam. All quotations
      following are from the verbatim
      transcript of the Appeal.
105. 15 January 1921, quoted
      Romero, p. 151.
106. Lansbury, p. 263.

Chapter 17 – Labour's Rise and Fall.

1.   Mann, p. 270.
2.   Ellen Wilkinson, 'Myself When
     Young', p. 421.
3.   Hughes, biographical fragments,
     pencil, Cumnock Library.
4.   Frank Smith to Francis Johnson,
     29 October 1921, Francis
     Johnson Correspondence, LSE.
5.   MacDonald, Introduction,
     Stewart, Keir Hardie, p. xx.
6.   Marquand, p. 257.
7.   Ibid., p. 263.
8.   Independent Liberals 60,
     National Liberals 57.
9.   30 September 1923.
10. Tracey, Book of the Labour Party,
     1925, passim.
11. LH to Hughes, 1 May 1923,
     National Library of Scotland,
     Dep 176, Box 26, File 1.
12. Marquand, p. 305.
13. Ibid., p. 304.
14. NA to Rowntree, 1924, Angell
     Papers, Ball State University,
     Indiana.
15. Ibid.
16. Henry R. Winkler, 'The
     Emergence of a Labour Foreign
     Policy in Great Britain 1918–29',
     Journal of Modern History, Vol
     28, 1956, quoted Adelman, p. 59
17. Gavignan, op. cit.
18. Adelman, p. 59.
19. 23 June 1922, Labour Monthly,
     quoted in Schneer, p. 155.
20. Lansbury, pp. 167–8.

21. AH autograph album, 21 April
     1924, in the possession of
     Bond family.
22. Thompson, The Enthusiasts,
     p. 237n.
23. LH to Francis Johnson, 21
     March and 17 July 1922, Francis
     Johnson Correspondence, LSE.
24. LH to Hughes, 1 May 1923,
     National Library of Scotland,
     Dep 176, Box 26, File 1.
25. JHS to CB, 28 June 1989.
26. New Leader, 11 July 1924.
27. 8 August 1924; date in wedding
     band, preserved Baird Museum,
     Cumnock.
28. JHS to CB, 28 June 1989.
29. June and Robert Bond,
     Interview with CB, 14
     December 1987. Hedley Dennis
     did renew ties with his father
     once his mother had died. He
     also kept up with his brother.
30. Romero, p. 161.
31. News interview, untitled, 14
     September 1930, The Times,
     quoted Romero, p. 195.
32. Letter to ESP from 'Socialists
     and Anarchists', in Solovietz
     Concentration Camp, 19
     December 1923, Pankhurst
     Collection, file 247, IISH,
     Amsterdam.
33. Lansbury, p. 246.
34. R. Neft, 'Chunks of Socialism',
     ILP, 1927.
35. 27 March 1920, Daily
     Herald.
36. Parliamentary Debates
     (Commons), 31 August 1926.
37. George Hardie, 'Coal and the
     Miner', c. 1929–30. George
     Hardie, a great coal expert,
     later invented smokeless coal
     (Morgan, p. 278).
38. Barry Winter, The ILP, A
     Brief History.
39. NH to Francis Johnson, 9 March
     1925, LSE.
40. 19 November 1927, Letter,
     GBS, National Library of
     Scotland, Dep 176, Box 1, File
     3. The book was a collection of
     KH's speeches. NH wrote the
     Foreword.

41. NH to Francis Johnson, 12 July 1925, LSE.
42. Ibid., 9 March 1925.
43. Ibid.
44. Romero, p. 170.
45. Ibid., quoting *News of the World*.
46. Ibid., p. 168.
47. Ibid. During the war Emmeline had formally adopted two girls, Ethel Smyth, p. 237.
48. Romero, p. 171.
49. Fenner Brockway, Interview, 23 January 1986, Sylvia Ayling, Sylvia Pankhurst Society.
50. Sylvia Pankhurst, file 75, IISH, Amsterdam, contains material relating to these campaigns.
51. He died young, leaving a widow but no children.
52. JHS to CB, 28 June 1989 and 4 May 1991.
53. JHS to CB, 1991.
54. Lansbury, p. 277.
55. Margaret Stansgate, recalling William Wedgwood Benn's joining the Labour Party, 1927, Interview, 30 March 1989.
56. ESP, 'Sketches for a Novel', file, 86, IISH, Amsterdam. The novel was never published.
57. Quoted Thompson, *The Enthusiasts*, p. 237.
58. Winter, p. 9.
59. JRM, Diary, 8 March 1930.
60. JRM to Jim Middleton, 25 May 1930, copy Benn Archives (gift of Lucy Middleton).
61. JRM, Diary, 8 August, 1 and 8 September 1931, quoted Marquand, pp. 609, 653 and 658.
62. JRM to Jim Middleton, 25 May 1931.
63. Diary, 21 August 1931.
64. Quoted Marquand, p. 609.
65. Ibid., p. 636.
66. MacArthur, MacDonald and Smillie, *Memoir*
67. David Hardie had only been elected in May 1931, for Rutherglen. Margaret Stansgate, Interview. The telephone call was to W. W. Benn.
68. Quoted in Thompson, *The Enthusiasts*, p. 239.
69. ESP, Notes, 1931, file 87, IISH, Amsterdam.
70. S. Pankhurst, *The Suffragette Movement*, 1931.
71. *Women's Leader*, 20 February 1931, quoted in Romero, p. 187.
72. Her *Life of Emmeline Pankhurst* was published in 1936.
73. Thompson, *The Enthusiasts*, p. 238; 'John Burns' and 'Bob Smillie', in Bellamy and Saville, op. cit. They both died in the early 1940s. Tillett had two short spells in Parliament but did not stand again after 1931.
74. South Wales Society of Friends, Records, 18 January 1936, Glamorgan County Archives, Cardiff. I am indebted to Hugh Gulliford for this information.
75. Jennie Cuthbert, 17 October 1987.
76. Information on Rose Davies kindly provided by Trevor Stonelake and Dilys Evans.
77. GBS, BBC, 6 June 1931, quoted Romero, p. 191.
78. ESP to Lansbury, 30 March 1933, ibid., p. 195.
79. *New Times and Ethiopia News*, 11 March 1939, ibid., p. 212.
80. Ibid., p. 193
81. Fenner Brockway, Interview, Sylvia Ayling.
82. ESP to NA, 23, March 1936, Angell Papers, Ball State University.
83. NA to ESP, 13 December 1938, loc. cit.
84. Romero, p. 243.
85. JHS to CB, 28 June 1989.
86. Tschiffley, p. 382.
87. Ibid., p. 260.
88. Cedric Watts, p. 255, Tschiffley, p. 398.
89. ESP, 1911, Sylvia Pankhurst Papers, file 117A, IISH, Amsterdam.
90. Fenner Brockway, Interview with CB.
91. 'Nan Hardie Hughes', *Dictionary of Labour Biography*, eds. Bellamy and Saville, Vol VII; obituary of NH in *Forward*, 29 October 1947.

92. Agnes was George's widow and took over his seat. See A. Hardie, Election Address, 1937, Labour Party Archives.

93. Romero, p. 213; Rita Pankhurst, 'Sylvia Pankhurst in Perspective', p. 254. ESP later published interviews with Mboya of the People's Convention Party in the *Ethiopia Observer*.

94. Coates and Topham, Vol I, Part II, *passim*.

95. *Justice*, August 1900. Hyndman faced a motion of censure for this statement within the SDF (Hyndman, *Further Reminiscences*, p. 165).

96. Thorne, p. 49.

97. Keir Hardie, *The Miner*, December 1887.

98. Fenner Brockway, Interview with CB.

99. Robert and June Bond, Interview with CB.

100. Autograph album, May 1938, in the possession of the Bond family.

101. Fenner Brockway, Interview.

102. Michael Foot, Interview, 26 January 1984, Cumnock Library; GBS to Hughes, 17 October 1939, National Library of Scotland, Dep 176, Box 1, File 3. Foot claimed Hughes wrote most of it 'by himself' under different names.

103. Leon Trotsky to Hughes, 3 April 1939, National Library of Scotland, Dep 176, Box 1, File 3.

104. Ibid., 14 December 1938 and 3 April 1939.

105. Ibid., 28 February 1939.

106. National Library of Scotland, Dep 176, Box 1.

107. Mrs G. B. Shaw to NH, 15 August 1941, thanks her for jellies, as does another letter in August 1941, written from Cliveden, the home of the Astors.

108. Ibid., 4 August 1940, DEP 176.

109. GBS to Hughes, 17 October 1939, Box 1, File 2.

110. Unveiled 19 August 1939, see Souvenir Programme, Unveiling, 19 August 1939, Cumnock Library; also interview Fenner Brockway, 1987. A copy of the Schotz bust of KH stands in an inner lobby of the House of Commons. Fenner Brockway (*Towards Tomorrow*, p. 252) claimed incorrectly that the Cumnock bust was the copy. In a nearby Members' Tea Room of the House of Commons is a portrait of KH. CG's portrait is painted into a mural by Solomon J. Solomon of Sir Walter Raleigh, on the stairs leading up from the same inner lobby, where CG is the courtier at the left.

Chapter 18 – Deaths and Survival

1. Letter from St Andrews House to NH, 23 May 1940, Cumnock Library.

2. *Cumnock Chronicle and District Advertiser*, 4 July 1947.

3. Thompson, *The Enthusiasts*, pp. 241–2.

4. Jennie Cuthbert to Tony Benn, 8 and 17 October 1987, neighbour of Hedley and Agnes Dennis, Abercynon.

5. Ibid.

6. June and Robert Bond, Interview with CB, 14 December 1987.

7. Reported in Morgan, *Keir Hardie*, p. 286.

8. Recorded in AH's Diary for that date, as seen by Morgan. I am indebted to him for making a copy of his notes available.

9. June and Robert Bond, Interview.

10. GBS to Hughes, 'The Lesson of Burns and Lloyd George', typed article, 25 January 1943, National Library of Scotland, Box 1, Files 1 and 3.

11. Thompson, *Blatchford*, p. 235.

12. JHS to CB, 28 June 1989.

13. June and Robert Bond, Interview.

14. Ella Kerr, Assistant Librarian, Cumnock, 16 February 1989, Interview with CB.

15. Quoted in Thompson, *The Enthusiasts*, p. 243.

16. Morgan, *Keir Hardie*, p. 287.

17. June and Robert Bond, Interview.

18. 26 July 1945, Diary entry, seen by Morgan, recorded in his notes and kindly made available to the author.

19. June and Robert Bond, Interview.

20. Ibid.

21. Morgan, notes on AH's Diary, kindly made available to author.

22. June and Robert Bond, Interview.

23. GBS to Hughes, 1946, National Library of Scotland.

24. 27 June 1947; Dictionary of Labour Biography, Vol VII, p. 124. The death certificate giving cause of death is missing from local records; possibly she died in an asylum.

25. *The Times*, obituary of Emrys Hughes, September 1969.

26. GBS to *Forward*, 4 June 1941, National Library of Scotland, Dep 176, Box 1, File 3.

27. GBS to Hughes, 22 March 1944, National Library of Scotland, Dep 176, Box 1, File 3.

28. Romero, p. 280.

29. Ibid., pp. 189–90.

30. Rita Pankhurst.

31. From an account of Sylvia's visit to the set by the actress Rosamund John Silkin, quoted Romero, p. 189.

32. JHS to CB, 28 June 1989.

33. The view of Assistant Librarian, Ella Kerr, Interview.

34. Thompson, *The Enthusiasts*, p. 236.

35. See, for example, the writings of the children of Ruth First and Joe Slovo, involved in the South Africa struggles of the late twentieth century.

36. JHS to CB.

37. *The Times*, 2 December 1952 and 21 May 1953, quoted Romero, p. 265.

38. Rita Pankhurst, 'Sylvia Pankhurst in Perspective'.

39. Romero, p. 280.

40. Commentary by the documentary film-maker, Richard Kapuschinski, *Arena*, BBC 2, 29 January 1988, when two of his films were shown, one on Haile Selassie, the other on the last Shah of Persia.

41. Stuart Hall, 'Out of Africa', *Redemption Song*, Barraclough Carey Production, BBC 2, West Indies, 4, July 1991.

42. Memory of chauffeur, Interview, Romero, p. 279.

43. Ibid., p. 282, although she might have meant she had never joined the second British Communist Party formed in August 1920.

44. Romero puts her death as November on p. 3, but September on p. 283; Barbara Castle, *Sylvia and Christabel*, p. 155, has it as the 27 September.

45. May Stoddart Hardie was born 11 July 1879 and died 8 December 1959.

46. Dolores May Arias to CB, 7 June 1989.

47. Abercynon Ward Labour Party, Minute Book, 13 February 1956.

48. Mrs P. White to AH from Maerdy Hospital, complaining that her daughter's mother-in-law had moved in with her daughter and could AH get her to leave. Dennis Papers, IIb 32, Benn Archives.

49. Trevor Stonelake to CB, April 1991.

50. Hugh Gulliford, Religious Society of Friends, Cardiff, Letter to CB, 23 March 1991.

51. Jennie Cuthbert, neighbour, 8 October 1987, Letter to CB.

52. Hedley Dennis obituary, W.

G. Bowden, *The Leader*, 27 December 1984.

53. Michael Foot, Interview, 26 January 1984, Cumnock Library.
54. One of prime minister Harold Macmillan (1962), another of prime minister Alec Douglas-Home (1964), and a third of Sidney Silverman, socialist MP, published posthumously, 1970.
55. John Forshaw to Tony Benn, 2 March 1985.
56. Forshaw to CB, 25 September 1987, Scottish Labour History Society. In an earlier letter, the bell was said to have been from the founding of the ILP (2 March 1985).
57. Printed Election Address, 'Letter from Lochnorris', 1 October 1964.
58. Hughes, biographical notes, Cumnock Library.
59. Michael Foot, Interview.
60. Forshaw, 2 March 1985; Interview, Ella Kerr.
61. JHS to CB, 28 June 1989.
62. June and Robert Bond, Interview.
63. JHS to CB, 28 June 1989.
64. In July 1893.
65. One of his visitors was W. W. Wood.
66. June and Robert Bond, Interview.
67. Ibid.
68. Ibid.
69. Ibid.
70. See Acknowledgements note, p. 435.
71. 16 November 1984, cremation attended by the South Wales Religious Society of Friends, Glamorgan County Archives.
72. Dolores May Arias, letter to CB about her work, 7 June 1989.
73. First Church, Unitarian Universalist Church, Jamaica Plain, Order of Worship, 12 May 1991.
74. William Morris, *The Dream of John Ball, The Collected Works of William Morris*, Longmans, Green, 1912, p. 231.

Conclusion

1. Hughes, *Keir Hardie*, pp. 48–50
2. Parliamentary Debates (Commons), 18 Feb 1903, Volume I, CXVIII, Line 251.
3. Ibid.
4. These were socialists like Henry Hyndman, or later, Daniel DeLeon, always distinguished by Hardie from other socialists and Marxists. See, for example, *Labour Leader*, 18 September 1908; 24 December 1898; 25 September 1904.
5. Quoted in Hughes, *Writings*.
6. *Commonweal*, 22 June 1889.
7. Keir Hardie, 'My Confession of Faith in the Labour Alliance', ILP, 1909.
8. Quoted in Hughes, *Keir Hardie*, p. 56.
9. Karl Marx, 'The Germany Ideology', quoted in *Selected Works*.
10. *Ardossan and Saltcoats Herald*, 15 July 1882.
11. KH, *From Serfdom to Socialism*.
12. V. I. Lenin, *Essentials*, p. 549.
13. Quoted in Hughes, *Writings*.
14. Robert Keith Middlemas, *The Clydesiders*, Hutchinson, 1965, p. 31.
15. Glasier, *Memorial*, p. 4.
16. Fred Reid, *Tribune*, 23 January 1970.
17. Glasier, *Memorial*.
18. KH, Parliamentary Debates, 23 April 1901. Many have confused Hardie's environmentalism with his nostalgia for the golden age of the common worker, which he placed in the late Middle Ages (under the influence of writers like Thorold Rogers), and failed to credit him with the environmental vision he had.
19. *Labour Leader*, 1906.
20. KH, *From Serfdom to Socialism*.
21. Quoted in Hughes, *Writings*, p. 46.
22. See, for example, Jonathan Schneer, *George Lansbury*, pp. 24–5. Schneer poses 'a revolutionary – or, at any rate, a

millenarian – tradition' that was opposed to the Labourist one. The phrase 'transforming vision' was also used earlier by Edward Thompson, 'The Peculiarities of the English', *Socialist Register*, 1965, p. 11; and Stephen Yeo, 'The Religion of Socialism', *History Workshop Journal*, 4, Autumn 1977, pp. 5–56.

23. Samson Bryher, 'Labour and the Socialist Movement in Bristol', 1929, p. 8. Helena Born and her friend Miriam Daniell were active in the 'new unionist' movement at the end of the 1880s, organizing women workers in Bristol. Great admirers of Walt Whitman, they later emigrated to the USA to continue their work.

24. George Eliot, 'The Spanish Gypsy', 1868. Hardie took several liberties with the poem but in the lines quoted here, his version matches Eliot's. (*See* George Eliot, *Selected Essays, Poems and other Writings*, A. S. Byatt and Nicholas Warren, eds., Penguin Classics, 1990.)

BIBLIOGRAPHY

Primary Sources — Manuscript, Print, Film and Tape

Aberdare Central Library, Aberdare
Election literature, 1906–10.
Ardrossan Library, Ardrossan
Ardrossan and Saltcoats Herald, 1882–7 (microfilm).
Baird Museum, Cumnock
Hardie Family library and artifacts.
Ball State University, Indiana, USA, Special Collections
Norman Angell Papers and Correspondence.
Benn Archives Collection, London
Selected Papers (Lucy Middleton).
Hedley Dennis/Agnes Hughes Papers.
Bond Family, Yorkshire
Agnes Hughes, Autograph Book, 1912–45.
Emrys Hughes, 'Journal of a Coward' (2), 1914–19.
British Library of Political and Economic Science, London School of Economics and Political Science, London
Independent Labour Party, National Administrative Council, Minutes, ILP2.
Francis Johnson Correspondence, ILP4.
Cumnock Library, Cumnock and Doon Valley District Council
Hardie-Hughes Papers, correspondence, photographs.
Interviews, Fenner Brockway and Michael Foot, 1984.
Glamorgan County Archives, Glamorgan Record Office, Cardiff
Rose Davies Papers.
Vaughan Collection.
Papers of Aberdare Socialist Society.
Labour Party, miscellaneous.
International Institute of Social History, Amsterdam (IISH)
Sylvia Pankhurst Papers.
Marx/Engels Papers.
Labour Museum of History, Manchester

Keir Hardie Diary, 1884.
Hardie–Hyndman Correspondence, 1905.
Hardie Speaking Notes, 1909,
Hardie Notes on Mid-Lanark Election, 1888.
Hardie Notes on American Visit, 1895.
Marx Memorial Library, London
Pamphlets, Independent Labour Party and others, 1894–1927.
National Amalgamated Furnishing Trades Association (courtesy, General Secretary, FTAT)
Monthly Reports, 1905–20.
National Library of Scotland, Edinburgh
Acc 4494 Hardie-Hines Correspondence.
Acc 3350 Small Papers.
Acc 4461 Hardie-Seruya Correspondence.
Acc 5234 Hardie-Women's Suffrage.
Acc 8125 Hardie-James Young Correspondence.
Acc 8895 Hardie-W. J. Joss Correspondence.
Acc 5121 Hardie-Labour Newspaper.
MS 12609 Earl of Minto Papers.
MS 12757 Sir Herbert Risley Papers.
Dep 176. Emrys Hughes-Nan Hardie Hughes Papers (deposited 1971 through 1983).
Sydney Jones Library, University of Liverpool
Correspondence and Diaries of J. Bruce Glasier and Katharine Conway Glasier, 1879–1976.
Jean Keir Hardie Scott and Dolores May Arias, USA
Correspondence (Keir Hardie, James and May Hardie) 1912–15.
Correspondence 1989–92.
Library of the Religious Society of Friends, London
Minutes of the Service Committee (1915–20), Visitation of Prisoners' Committee (1916–20), Wartime Statistics Committee (1917–22).
YM PROC 1916–19, 1920, 1922, 1923.
Nuffield College, Oxford
Durward, A. A., 'The Truth about James Kerr, Alias James Keir Hardie and the ILP', Aberdeen, 1948.
Keir Hardie Correspondence, Fabian Society, 1891–1912.
TUC Library
The Miner: a Journal for Underground Workers, 1887–9, Burns Collection.
Reports of TUC Congresses, 1887–94 (microfilm).
University College of Swansea, University of Wales, Department of Adult and Continuing Education, South Wales Miners Library
Rowe MSS.
Stanfield MSS.

Wilson MSS.
Len Williams MSS.
Taped Interviews, Lance Rogers, Griff Jones,
Norman Thomas, W. H. Gregory, P. J. Matthews and Tom Williams.

Official and other Records

Parliamentary Debates (Commons) 4th series, 1892–1895, Vols 7–35, 1900–1908, Vols 89–198; 5th series, 1909–1915, Vols 1–70.

Royal Commission on Labour, 1892, Minutes of Evidence, 1892, XVIII, XXXVI.

Select Committee on Distress from Want of Employment, Minutes and Evidence, 1895, VIII.

Reports of Independent Labour Party Conferences, 1893–1920.

Reports of Socialist International, 1889–1914.

Reports of Labour Representation Committee and Labour Party Conferences, 1900–15.

Selected Pamphlets

CONWAY, KATHARINE and GLASIER, J. BRUCE, 'The Religion of Socialism', ILP, 1893.
MANN, TOM, 'What the ILP is Driving At', ILP, 1894.
LUXEMBURG, ROSA, 'Leninism or Marxism?', *Die Neue Zeit*, Vol 22 (2), Stuttgart 1904, reprinted by ILP.
MACMILLAN MARGARET, Infant Mortality, ILP, 1905.
TILLETT, BEN, 'Is the Parliamentary Labour Party a Failure?', 1909.
BELCHER, J. H., DOUTHWAITE, C. T., HALL, L. and MCLACHLAN, J. M., 'Let Us Reform the Labour Party', The Green Manifesto, 1910.
'The Miners' Next Step', Unofficial Reform Committee, Tonypandy, 1912.
'Memories of an Ayrshire Agitator', John Roe, ed., *Forward*, July 4, 11, and 18, 1914.
FRIEDMAN, F. B., 'Capitalism, The Cause of Social Evils', ILP, 1914.
MOREL, E. D., 'The Attack upon Freedom', Union of Democratic Control, 1915.

BRAILSFORD, H. N., 'Belgium and the Scrap of Paper', 1915.

KNEESHAW, W. J., 'How Conscription Works', ILP, c. 1916.

MEYER, F. B., 'The Majesty of Conscience', 1916.

GLASIER, J. BRUCE, 'Militarism', ILP, 1915.

HUNTER, ERNEST, 'Conscription', ILP, March 1916.

——'Democracy and the War', ILP, 1917.

SNOWDEN, PHILIP, 'British Prussianism', ILP, 1916.

MACLEAN, JOHN, 'Condemned from the Dock', 1918.

LENIN, V. I., 'Lessons of the Russian Revolution', British Socialist Party, 1918.

ANDERSON, W. C., SHAW, G. B., WEBB, B, and S., BONDFIELD, M., LANSBURY, G., MACDONALD, R., 'The War Against Poverty', c. 1918.

'Education – What it is and What it is not', ILP, No. 4, undated, c. 1918.

BROCKWAY, FENNER, 'How to End War', ILP, c. 1920.

'Six Months of Labour Government', ILP, 1924.

PAUL, WILLIAM, ed., 'Keir Hardie Special', Communist Party, 1924.

HENDERSON, FRED, 'The ABC of Socialism', ILP, undated, c. 1925.

NEFT, R., 'Chunks of Socialism', ILP, 1927.

HARDIE, GEORGE D., 'Coal and the Miner', Reformers Bookstall, Glasgow, c. 1930.

Selected Periodicals and Newspapers

Benn Archives, London
British Library, Colindale
Labour Party Library, Walworth Road, London
Marx Memorial Library, London
National Library of Scotland, Edinburgh
Working Class Museum Library, Salford

Aberdare Leader	*Labour Elector*
Christian Commonwealth	*Labour Leader*
Clarion	*Labour Prophet*
Commonweal	*Merthyr Pioneer*
Cumnock News	*Socialist Review*
Derbyshire Times	*South West Ham Worker*
Forward	*West Ham and Stratford Express*
Freewoman 1911–1912	*Woman's Dreadnought*
ILP News	*Worker's Dreadnought*
Industrial syndicalist	*Workman's Times*
Justice	

And others as given in Notes.

Film, Tape and Video

Demonstration for People's Budget, Hyde Park, 25 July 1909, National Film Archive, British Film Institute.

A *Generation Lost* series, 'Scotland's Story, Scotland before World War I', Independent Television, Scotland, transmitted 12 December 1987.

Pioneers of Socialism, The Development of the Labour Party from Keir Hardie to 1930, 'Keir Hardie to 1906', Channel 4, Skyline Production, with Scottish Labour History Society, transmitted 14 February 1987.

Gwyn Williams, *Sylvia Pankhurst*, 'Cracking Up', Channel 4, Teliesyn Ltd, Wales, transmitted December 1989.

'The Man Who Made the Labour Party', BBC TV Magazine, Schools' History File, transmitted 28 April 1986.

Interview, Fenner Brockway, with Sylvia Ayling, Sylvia Pankhurst Society, 23 January 1986.

Interview, Fenner Brockway, with Caroline Benn, 25 November 1987.

Taped reminiscences, Malcolm MacDonald, 22 March 1978.

Interview, June and Robert Bond, with Caroline Benn, 14 December 1987.

Interview, Margaret Stansgate, with Caroline Benn, 30 March 1989.

Conservative and Unionist Party, Anti-Socialist Songs, recorded by Kaley Kalvert, Gramophone and Typewriter Company (Hanover), c. 1907 (Collection of K. Malcolm).

Stuart Hall, series *Redemption Song*, Barraclough Carey Productions, 'Out of Africa', transmitted BBC 2, 4 July 1991.

Socially Unacceptable, Conscientious Objection in World War I, transmitted Channel 4, 23 September 1987.

Bertrand Russell, series *Face to Face*, BBC 1, 1959.

Keir Hardie Selected Writings

'The Christianity of Christ', in *Labour Prophet*, November 1892.
'The Independent Labour Party, its Programme and Policy', Russell Smart, H., introduction by Hardie, J. Keir, MP, ILP, 1893.

'Young Men in a Hurry', ILP, 1897.
'Lord Overtoun', White Slave Series, ILP, 1898.
'More about Overtoun', 1899.
'The Overtoun Horrors', 1899.
'Can a Man be a Christian on a Pound a Week?', 5th edition, ILP, 1901.
'Labour Politics: a Symposium', Hardie, J. Keir, Snowden, Philip, and Shakleton, David, ILP, 1903.
'The Unemployed Problem', ILP, 1904.
'The Unemployed Bill: What it does and does not do, but should be made to do', ILP, 1905.
'John Bull and the Unemployed', ILP, 1905.
'The Labour Party and the Books that helped to make it', in *Review of Reviews*, June 1906.
'A Plea For Women's Suffrage', Preface to 3rd edition, *The Citizenship of Women*, 1906.
From Serfdom to Socialism, George Allen, 1907.
'Socialism, the Hope of Wales', ILP, 1908.
India: Impressions and Suggestions, 1909.
'My Confession of Faith in the Labour Alliance', ILP, 1909.
'Socialism in America', in *Socialist Review*, April 1909.
'The British Labour Party', in *International Socialist Review*, May 1910.
'Socialism and Civilization', 1910.
'Labour and Liberalism in Wales', 1910.
'Labour and Christianity', 1910.
'The Common Good: An Essay in Municipal Government', 1910.
'Killing No Murder: The Railway Strike', ILP, 1911.
'Karl Marx: The Man and His Message', National Labour Press Ltd, 1911.
'The Red Dragon and the Red Flag', 1912.
'Radicals and Reform', 1912.
'America Revisited', in *Socialist Review*, December 1912.
Labour Woman, inaugural issue, May 1913, Introductory Message from Keir Hardie.
'The Queenie Gerald Case. A Public Scandal, An Exposure by J. Keir Hardie, MP', National Labour Press, 1913.

Select Bibliography

ADELMAN, PAUL, *The Rise of the Labour Party, 1880–1945*, Longman, 1972.
ANGELL, NORMAN, *The Great Illusion* (f.p. 1908), Heinemann, 1933.

ARNOT, R. PAGE, *The Miners, A History of the Miners' Federation of Great Britain from* 1910 *Onwards*, Allen & Unwin, 1954.
——*History of the Scottish Miners*, Allen & Unwin, 1955.
ASQUITH, MARGOT, ed., *Myself When Young*, Frederick Muller, 1938.
BALFOUR, RIGHT HON A. J., Introduction, *The Case Against Socialism*, George Allen and Sons, 1909.
BALGARNIE, FLORENCE, 'The Woman's Suffrage Movement in the 19th Century', in Villiers, ed., *The Case for Women's Suffrage*, T. Fisher Unwin, 1907.
BATTISCOMBE, GEORGINA, *Mrs Gladstone*, Constable, 1956.
BEER, MAX, *A History of British Socialism*, Allen & Unwin, 1948.
BELLAMY, JOYCE and SAVILLE, J., eds, *Dictionary of Labour Biography*, Vols I-VII, 1972–84.
BLATCHFORD, ROBERT, (Numquam), *Merrie England*, f.p. 1893, Journeyman Press, facsimile, 1976.
——*General Von Sneak*, Hodder & Stoughton, 1918.
BRIGGS, A. and SAVILLE, J., *Essays in Labour History*, Macmillan, 1971.
BROADHURST, HENRY, *From the Stonemason's Bench to the Treasury Bench*, Hutchinson, 1901.
BROCKWAY, FENNER, *Inside the Left*, Allen & Unwin, 1942.
    ——*Socialism Over Sixty Years*, 1946.
    ——*Towards Tomorrow, an Autobiography*, Hart Davis, 1977.
BROOKS, DAVID, *The Destruction of Lord Rosebery, Edward Hamilton's Diary*, Historians Press, 1986.
BROWN, GEOFF, Introduction to *The Industrial Syndicalist*, Spokesman Books, 1974.
    ——Introduction to *The Syndicalist* 1912–1914, facsimile reproduction, Spokesman Books, 1975.
BRYHER, SAMSON, *An Account of the Labour and Socialist Movement in Bristol*, Bristol Labour Weekly Publishers, 1929.
CAHM, ERIC, and FIŠERA, VLADIMIR CLAUDE, *Socialism and Nationalism*, 1848–1945, Vols I, II and III, Spokesman Books, 1980.
CALDWELL, JOHN TAYLOR, *Come Dungeons Dark*, Luath Press, Ayrshire, 1988.
CASTLE, BARBARA, *Sylvia and Christabel Pankhurst*, Penguin, 1987.
CHAMPNESS, E. I., *Frank Smith – Pioneer and Modern Mystic*, White Friars Press, 1943.
COATES, KEN and TOPHAM, TONY, *The Making of the Transport and General Workers' Union*, Vol I, Parts I and II, Blackwell, 1991.
COCKBURN, JOHN, *The Hungry Heart, A Romantic Biography of Keir Hardie*, Jarrolds, 1956.
COLE, G. D. H. *James Keir Hardie*, Fabian Society, 1941.
    ——*A Short History of the British Working Class Movement*, 1789–1927, Allen & Unwin, 1932.
COLE, MARGARET, *Makers of the Labour Movement*, Longman, 1948.

COLLINS, HENRY, 'The Marxism of the SDF', in Briggs and Saville, eds., *Essays in Labour History*, Macmillan, 1971.

DALTON, HUGH, *Call Back Yesterday, Memoirs*, 1887–1931, Muller, 1953.

DAVIES, EVAN, *Merthyr Iron and Merthyr Riots*, 1750–1860, Longman, 1987.

DAVIES, PAUL, *A. J. Cook*, Lives of the Left Series, Manchester University Press, 1987.

DAVITT, MICHAEL, *Leaves from a Prison Diary*, 2 vols, Chapman & Hall, 1885.

DOWSE, ROBERT E., ed., *The Labour Ideal*, six essays by socialists published in 1906–7 (Society and the Victorians Series, ed. John Spiers), Vol I, Harvester Press, 1974.

DUNLEAVY, J., 'The Irish Dimension of the British Labour Movement, 1886–1929', in *North West Labour History*, No. 15, 1990–91.

FELS, MARY, *Joseph Fels, His Life and Work*, Allen & Unwin, 1920.

FROW, EDMUND and FROW, RUTH, 'The General Strike in Salford in 1991', Working Class Movement Library, Salford, 1990.

FYFE, HAMILTON, *Keir Hardie*, 1935, reprinted in Great Lives Series, Duckworth, 1985.

GARDNER, A. G. *Prophets, Priests and Kings*, Wayfarers Library, 1917.

GAVIGNAN, PATRICK J., 'Ralph Norman Angell Lane: An Analysis of his Political Career', unpublished Ph.D., Ball State University, Indiana, USA, 1972.

GLASIER, J. BRUCE, *James Keir Hardie, A Memorial*, National Labour Press, ILP, incorporating GLASIER, J. BRUCE and GLASIER, KATHARINE, 'Keir Hardie – The Man and the Message', ILP, 1919.

HAFER, PAUL CARL, 'Two Paths to Peace: The Efforts of Norman Angell, 1914–1931', unpublished Ph.D., Education Department, Ball State University, Indiana, USA.

HARDIE, KEIR (see separate bibliography of Selected Writings).

HARDY, THOMAS, *The Hand of Ethelberta* (with 1895 and 1912 prefaces), Macmillan, 1972.

HARRISON, BRIAN, *Separate Spheres*, Croom Helm, 1978.

HARRISON, ROYDEN, 'The War Emergency Workers' National Committee, 1915–1920', in *Essays in Labour History*, Briggs and Saville, eds., Macmillan, 1971.

HARRISON, ROYDEN, et al., *Guide to British Labour Periodicals*, 1790–1970, Harvester Press, 1977.

HAZELHURST, CAMERON, *Politicians at War, July 1914-May 1915*, Cape, 1971.

HEALEY, EDNA, *Wives of Fame*, Sidgwick & Jackson, 1968.

HOLME, THEA, *The Carlyles at Home*, Oxford University Press, 1965.

HUGHES, EMRYS, ed., *Keir Hardie's Writings and Speeches*, from 1888 to 1915, Preface by Nan Hardie, Forward Publishing Company, Glasgow, 1928.

——*Keir Hardie: Some Memories*, London, 1940.

——*A Pictorial Biography of Keir Hardie MP*, Lincolns Prager, London, 1950.

——*Keir Hardie*, Allen & Unwin, 1956.

HUMPHREY, A. W., *A History of Labour Representation*, Constable, 1912.

IVESON, STAN and BROWN, ROGER, *Clarion House, a Monument to a Movement*, ILP, Lancashire Community Press, 1987.

ALLAND, PAT, *Women, Marriage, and Politics*, 1860–1914 Oxford University Press, 1988.

JOHNSON, FRANCIS, *Keir Hardie's Socialism*, ILP, 1922.

JOHNSON, THOMAS, MP, 'James Keir Hardie, The Founder of the Labour Party', in *The Book of the Labour Party*, Vol III, ed. Herbert Tracey, 1925.

JONES, LINDA, 'The Red Twilight, Sylvia Pankhurst and the Workers' Socialist Federation, 1918–1924', unpublished MA, Centre for Social History, University of Warwick, 1972.

KAPP, YVONNE, *Eleanor Marx*, Vol I, *Family Life*, 1972; Vol II, *The Crowded Years*, Virago, 1976.

——*The Act of Freedom, Birth of the New Unionism*, Lawrence & Wishart, 1989.

KENT, W., *John Burns, Labour's Lost Leader*, 1950.

KING, ELSPETH, *The Scottish Women's Suffrage Movement*, Peoples Palace, Glasgow, 1978.

——*Scotland Sober and Free, The Temperance Movement*, 1829–1979, Glasgow Museums and Art Galleries, 1979.

——*The People's Palace*, Richard Drew Publishers, Glasgow, 1985.

——*The Strike of the Glasgow Weavers*, 1787, Glasgow Museums and Art Galleries, 1987.

KIRKUP, THOMAS, *A History of Socialism*, A.&C. Black, 1906.

KLUGMANN, JAMES, *History of the Communist Party of Great Britain*, Vol I, 1968; Vol II, Lawrence & Wishart, 1969.

KNOX, WILLIAM, *James Maxton*, Lives of the Left Series, Manchester University Press, 1986.

LANSBURY, GEORGE, *My Life*, Constable, 1928.

LAYBOURN, *The Labour Party: A Reader in History*, Allan Sutton, 1988.

LEAN, GARTH, 'Keir Hardie, Father of the British Labour Movement', chapter reprinted from Lean, *Brave Men Choose*, 1961. Introduction, Don Simpson, Waterfront and Industrial Pioneer, Grosvenor Books, London, 1979.

LENIN, V. I., *The Essentials of Lenin*, Vols I and II, Lawrence & Wishart, 1947.

——*On Britain*, Foreign Language Publishing House, Moscow.

——'"Left Wing" Communism, An Infantile Disorder', Progress Publishers, 1950 (from Lenin, *Collected Works*, Vol 31, 5th edition, Progress Publishers, Moscow).

LEWIS, GIFFORD, *Eva Gore-Booth and Esther Roper*, Pandora, 1985.

LOWE, DAVID, *Souvenirs of Scottish Labour*, W. and R. Holmes, 1919.

——*From Pit to Parliament, The Story of the Early Life of James Keir Hardie*, Labour Publishing Company, 1923.

MACARTHUR, MARY, MACDONALD, J. RAMSAY and SMILLIE, ROBERT, *Memoir of James Keir Hardie*, c. 1915.

MCBRIAR, A. M., *Fabian Socialism and English Politics, 1884–1918*, Cambridge University Press, 1962.

MACDOUGAL, IAN, ed., *Essays in Scottish Labour History*, Donald, Edinburgh, 1978.

MCKERRELL, T., and BROWN, J., *Ayrshire Miners Rows*, Evidence Submitted to the Royal Commission on Housing (Scotland), 1913, Archaeological and Natural History Society, 1977.

MCKIBBIN, R. I., *The Evolution of the Labour Party, 1910–1924*, Oxford University Press, 1974.

MCLEAN, IAIN, *Keir Hardie*, Allen Lane/Penguin, 1975.

MACNICOL, HENRY, *Keir Hardie – The Man They Could Not Buy*, Playscript, Foreword by John Boyd, Westminster Productions, Grosvenor Books, Waterfront Press, 1984.

MACVARISH, KATHRYN, 'Alexandra Kollontai', unpublished MA, University of Keele, 1991.

MANN, TOM, *Memoirs*, f. p. MacGibbon & Kee, 1923, Preface by Ken Coates, Spokesman Books, 1967.

MARQUAND, DAVID, *Ramsay Macdonald*, Cape, 1977.

MARRIOTT, JOHN WESLEY, 'London Over the Border: A Study of West Ham During Rapid Growth, 1840–1910,' Unpublished Ph.D., University of Cambridge, 1984.

——*The Culture of London in the East End Between the Wars*, Edinburgh University Press, 1991.

MARX, KARL and ENGELS, FREDERICK, *Selected Works*, Progress Publishers, Vols I, II and III, Moscow, 1977.

——*Selected Works*, Lawrence & Wishart, 1968.

——*Correspondence, 1846–1895*, 1934.

MAXTON, JAMES, *Keir Hardie, Prophet and Pioneer*, Francis Johnson, London, 1939.

MILIBAND, RALPH, *Parliamentary Socialism*, a Study in the Politics of Labour, Allen & Unwin, 1961.

MITCHELL, DAVID, *The Fighting Pankhursts*, Cape, 1967.

——*Queen Christabel*, Macdonald & Evans, 1977.

MONTEFIORE, DORA, *The Position of Women in the Socialist Movement*, 1909.

——*From a Victorian to a Modern*, Archer, London, 1927.

MORGAN, KENNETH O., 'The Merthyr of Keir Hardie', in Williams, Glanmore, ed., *Merthyr Politics*, Cardiff, 1966.

——*Wales in British Politics 1868–1922*, Cardiff, 1970.

——*Keir Hardie, Radical and Socialist*, Weidenfeld & Nicolson, 1975, paperback, 1984.

——*Labour People*, Oxford University Press, 1987.

MOR-O'BRIEN, ANTHONY, 'Keir Hardie, C. B. Stanton, and the First World War', in *Llafur, the Journal of the Society for the Study of Welsh Labour History*, Vol 3, 1986.

—— 'Conchie: Emrys Hughes and the First World War', in the *Welsh Labour History Review*, Vol 13, No. 3 1987.

MORTON, A. L., ed., *Political Writings of William Morris*, Lawrence & Wishart, 1984.

MOWATT, C. L., 'Ramsay MacDonald and the Labour Party', in Briggs and Saville, eds., *Essays in Labour History*, Macmillan, 1971.

PANKHURST, RICHARD, *Sylvia Pankhurst* – Artist and Crusader, Paddington Press, 1979.

PANKHURST, RITA, 'Sylvia Pankhurst in Perspective', in *Women's Studies International Forum*, No. 3, pp. 245–62, Pergamon, 1988.

PANKHURST, SYLVIA, *The Suffragette Movement*, Longman, 1931.

——*The Home Front, a Mirror to Life in England During the World War*, Hutchinson, 1932.

——'Myself When Young', in *Myself When Young*, ed. Margot Asquith, Frederick Muller, 1938.

PELLING, HENRY, *The Origins of the Labour Party 1880–1900*, Clarendon Press, Oxford, 1965.

POLLARD, SIDNEY, 'The Foundation of the Cooperative Party', in Briggs and Saville, eds., *Essays in Labour History*, Macmillan, 1971.

REID, FRED, 'The Early Life and Political Development of James Keir Hardie, 1856–1892', unpublished Ph.D., Oxford University, 1968.

——'Keir Hardie's Conversion to Socialism', in Briggs and Saville, eds., *Essays in Labour History*, Macmillan, 1971.

——'Keir Hardie's Biographers', in the *Bulletin of the Society for the Study of Labour History*, No. 16, 1968.

——*Keir Hardie, The Making of a Socialist*, Croom Helm, 1978.

REID, HEW, *The Furniture Makers, A History of Trade Unionism in the Furniture Trade, 1868–1972*, Malthouse Press, Oxford, 1986.

RENAN, J. E., *Life of Jesus Christ*, translated by A. D. Howell Smith, 1935.

ROGERS, FREDERICK, *Labour, Life and Literature, Memories of Sixty Years*, Smith, Elder and Co., 1913.

ROMERO, PATRICIA W., *Sylvia Pankhurst, Portrait of a Radical*, Yale University Press, 1987.

SAVILLE, JOHN, *The Labour Movement*, Faber & Faber, 1988.

SCHNEER, JONATHAN, *George Lansbury*, Lives of the Left Series, Manchester University Press, 1990.

Self Help Press, No. 3, *The Life Story of Mr James Keir Hardie, MP*, Self Help Press, London, c. 1908.

SMILLIE, R., *My Life for Labour*, Mills and Boon, 1924.

SMYTH, ETHEL, *Female Pipings in Eden*, Peter Davies, 1934.

SNOWDEN, PHILIP, *An Autobiography*, Vols I and II, Ivor Nicholson and Watson, 1934.

STEAD, W. T., 'Jas Keir Hardie MP', in 'Coming Men on Coming Questions', January 1905.

STEWART, WILLIAM, *J. Keir Hardie, A Biography*, with foreword by J. Ramsay MacDonald, ILP, 1925.

STONE, RICHARD G., *John Woolliscroft, Socialist, Internationalist and Trade Unionist*, Derbyshire County Council, 1987.

STONELAKE, EDMUND, *Aberdare Trades and Labour Council, 1900 to 1950*, Aberdare, 1950.

—— *The Autobiography of Edmund Stonelake*, ed., A. Mor-O'Brien, Mid-Glamorgan Education Committee, 1981.

STRAWHORN, JOHN, *New History of Cumnock*, Cumnock Town Council, 1966.

TAWNEY, R. H., *The Radical Tradition*, Pelican, 1964.

TAYLOR, A. J. P., *The Trouble Makers*, Hamish Hamilton, 1959.

THOMPSON, E. P., *William Morris, Romantic to Revolutionary*, Merlin Press, 1977.

THOMPSON, LAURENCE, *Robert Blatchford, Portrait of an Englishman*, Gollancz, 1951.

—— *The Enthusiasts, A Biography of John and Katharine Bruce Glasier*, Gollancz, 1971.

THORNE, WILL, *My Life's Battles*, f.p. 1925, Introduction by John Saville, Lawrence & Wishart, 1989.

TILLETT, BEN, *Memories and Reflections*, John Long, 1931.

TODD, NIGEL, *The Militant Democracy, Joseph Cowen and Victorian Radicalism*, Berwick Press, Tyne and Wear, 1991.

TRACEY, HERBERT, ed., *The Book of the Labour Party*, Vols I, II and III, Caxton, 1925.

TSCHIFFELY, A. F., *Don Roberto, Being the Account of the Life and Works of R. B. Cunninghame Graham*, Heinemann, 1937.

TSUZUKI, CHUSHICHI, *H. M. Hyndman and British Socialism*, Oxford University Press, 1961.

VALLANCE, AYLMER, *The Life and Work of William Morris*, f.p. George Bell, 1897, facsimile edition, Studio Editions, 1986.

VAN THAL, HERBERT, ed., *The Prime Ministers, From Lord John Russell to Edward Heath*, Vol II, Allen & Unwin, 1975.

VILLIERS, BROUGHAM, ed., *The Case for Women's Suffrage*, Introduction by Keir Hardie, T. Fisher Unwin, 1907.

WALLHEAD, R. C., *The Keir Hardie Calendar*, National Labour Press, c. 1916.

WARWICK, FRANCES, *Life's Ebb and Flow*, 1929.

WATTS, CEDRIC, *Cunninghame Graham, A Critical Biography*, Cambridge University Press, 1979.

WEBB, BEATRICE, *The Diaries of Beatrice Webb*, ed. Margaret Cole, 1952.

WEDGWOOD, JOSIAH, *Memoirs of a Fighting Life*, Hutchinson, 1940.

WILKINSON, ELLEN, 'Myself When Young', in *Myself When Young*, ed. Margot Asquith, Frederick Muller, 1938.

WILLIAMS, GLANMORE, ed., *Merthyr Politics, The Making of a Working Class Tradition*, University of Wales, Cardiff, 1966.

WILLIAMS, GWYN A., *The Merthyr Rising*, Croom Helm, 1978.

WILLIAMS, J. E., *The Derbyshire Miners, A Study in Industrial and Social History*, Allen & Unwin, 1962.

WINTER, BARRY, *The ILP – A Brief History*, ILP, 1982.

And others as given in Notes.

INDEX